GREAT BRI IRELAND

TOURIST and MOTORING ATLAS / ATLAS ROUTIER et TOURISTIQUE / STRASSEN- und REISEATLAS
TOERISTISCHE WEGENATLAS / ATLANTE STRADALE e TURISTICO / ATLAS DE CARRETERAS y TURÍSTICO

Contents
Sommaire / Inhaltsübersicht / Inhoud / Sommario / Sumario

Inside front cover: key to map pages

Intérieur de couverture : tableau d'assemblage / Umschlaginnenseite: Übersicht / Binnenzijde van het omslag: overzichtskaart
Copertina interna: quadro d'insieme / Portada interior: mapa índice

II - III

Channel Tunnel - Tunnel sous la Manche

Folkestone Terminal - Terminal de Calais (F)

Shipping Services

Liaisons maritimes / Schiffsverbindungen / Scheepvaartverbindingen / Collegamenti marittimi / Líneas marítimas

IV - XXI

Main road map

Grands axes routiers / Durchgangsstraßen / Grote verbindingswegen / Grandi arterie stradali / Carreteras principales
1 inch = 15.8 miles - 1:1 000 000 - 1 cm = 10 km

1 - 119

Key **1**

Légende / Zeichenerklärung / Verklaring van de tekens / Legenda / Signos convencionales

Great Britain & Ireland **2 - 119**

Grande-Bretagne & Irlande / Großbritannien & Irland / Groot-Brittannië & Ierland
Gran Bretagna & Irlanda / Gran Bretaña & Irlanda
1 inch = 4.75 miles - 1: 300 000 - 1 cm = 3 km

120 - 147

Index Great Britain **120 - 138**

Index Grande-Bretagne / Register Großbritannien / Register Groot-Brittannië / Indice Gran Bretagna / Índice Gran Bretaña

Index Ireland **139 - 147**

Index Irlande / Register Irland / Register Ierland / Indice Irlanda / Índice Irlanda

148 - 192

Key **148 - 149**

Légende / Zeichenerklärung / Verklaring van de tekens / Legenda / Signos convencionales

Town plans Great Britain **150 - 188**

Plans de ville Grande-Bretagne / Stadtpläne Großbritannien / Stadsplattegronden Groot-Brittannië
Piante di città Gran Bretagna / Planos de ciudades Gran Bretaña

Town plans Ireland **189 - 193**

Plans de ville Irlande / Stadtpläne Irland / Stadsplattegronden Ierland / Piante di città Irlanda / Planos de ciudades Irlanda

Eochair / Allwedd / Comnarthai ar phleanna bailte / Symbolau ar gynlluniau'r trefi **194**

Back of the guide: distances

En fin de volume : distances / Am Ende des Buches: Entfernungen / Achter in het boek: afstanden
Alla fine del volume: distanze / Al final del volumen: distancias

Channel Tunnel
Tunnel sous la Manche

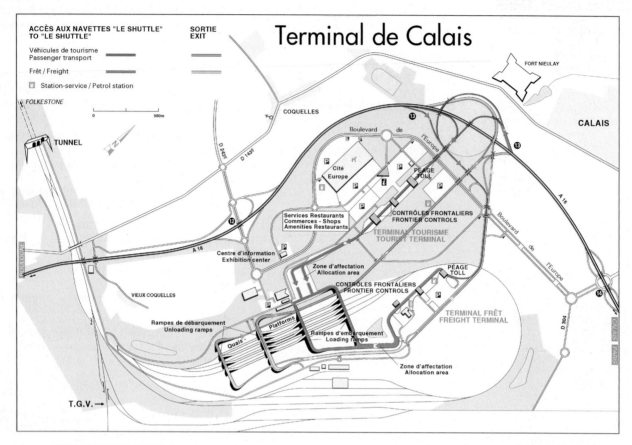

Terminal de Calais

ACCÈS AUX NAVETTES "LE SHUTTLE"
TO "LE SHUTTLE"

SORTIE
EXIT

Véhicules de tourisme
Passenger transport

Frêt / Freight

Station-service / Petrol station

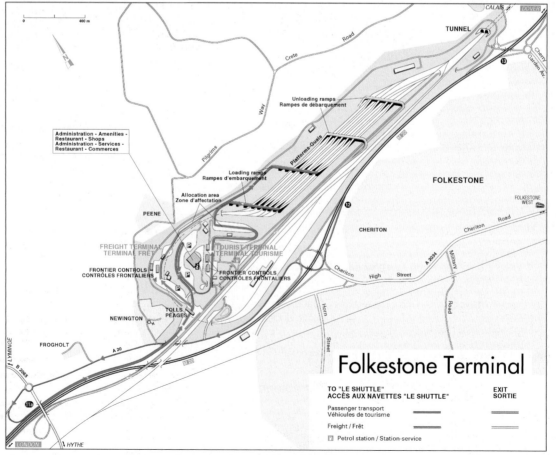

Folkestone Terminal

TO "LE SHUTTLE"
ACCÈS AUX NAVETTES "LE SHUTTLE"

EXIT
SORTIE

Passenger transport
Véhicules de tourisme

Freight / Frêt

Petrol station / Station-service

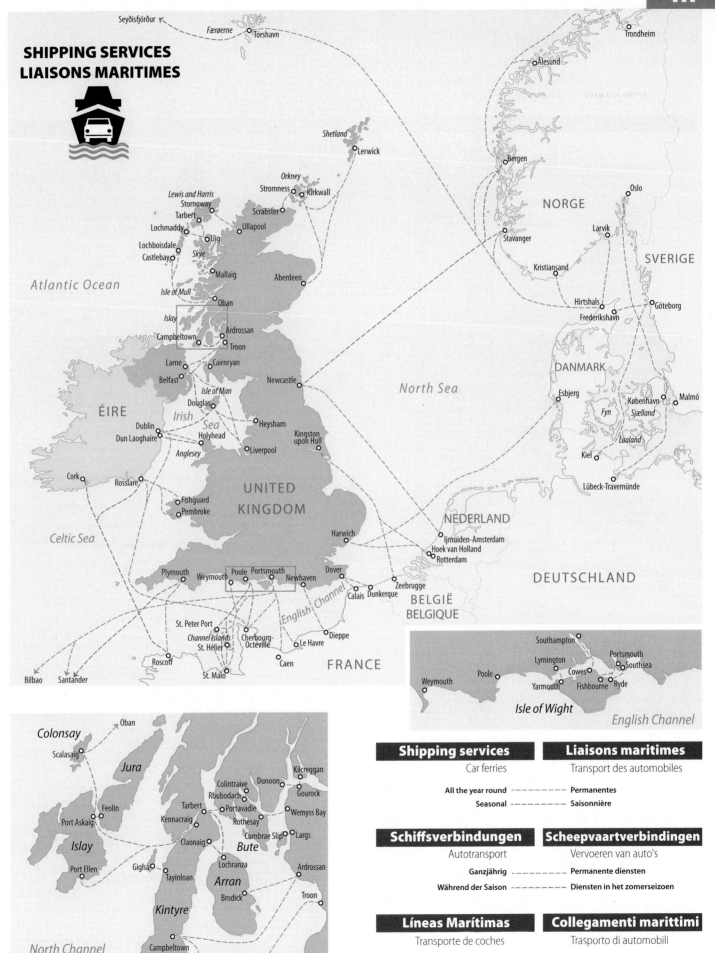

SHIPPING SERVICES
LIAISONS MARITIMES

Seyðisfjörður
Færøerne · Tórshavn
Trondheim
Ålesund
Shetland · Lerwick
Bergen
Orkney
Stromness · Kirkwall
Oslo
NORGE
Lewis and Harris
Stornoway
Scrabster
Larvik
Tarbert
Stavanger
Lochmaddy · Uig · Ullapool
SVERIGE
Lochboisdale
Kristiansand
Castlebay · Skye
Atlantic Ocean
Mallaig
Aberdeen
Hirtshals · Göteborg
Isle of Mull
Frederikshavn
Oban
Islay
DANMARK
Campbeltown · Ardrossan
Esbjerg · København · Malmö
Troon
Larne · Cairnryan
Fyn · Sjælland
Belfast
Newcastle
North Sea
Isle of Man
Kiel · Laaland
ÉIRE · Douglas
Irish
Dublin · Heysham
Sea
Lübeck-Travemünde
Dun Laoghaire · Holyhead
Kingston
upon Hull
Anglesey · Liverpool
NEDERLAND
Cork
Rosslare
UNITED
KINGDOM
Ijmuiden-Amsterdam
Fishguard
Hoek van Holland
Pembroke
Rotterdam
Celtic Sea
Harwich
DEUTSCHLAND
Plymouth · Weymouth · Poole · Portsmouth
Dover
Newhaven
Zeebrugge
English Channel
Calais · Dunkerque
BELGIË
BELGIQUE
St. Peter Port
Channel Islands · Cherbourg-
St. Hélier · Octeville · Le Havre · Dieppe
Roscoff
Caen
FRANCE
Bilbao · Santander · St. Malo

Isle of Wight

Southampton
Lymington · Portsmouth
Cowes · Southsea
Weymouth · Poole · Yarmouth · Fishbourne · Ryde
English Channel

Scotland inset

Colonsay · Oban
Scalasaig
Jura
Kilcreggan
Colintraive · Dunoon
Rhubodach · Gourock
Tarbert · Portavadie
Feolin · Wemyss Bay
Port Askaig · Kennacraig · Rothesay
Claonaig · Cumbrae Slip · Largs
Islay · Bute
Port Ellen · Gigha · Lochranza
Tayinloan · Arran
Kintyre · Brodick · Ardrossan
Troon
North Channel
Campbeltown
Ballycastle · Larne
(Northern Ireland) · (Northern Ireland)

Shipping services
Car ferries
All the year round ---------
Seasonal - - - - - -

Liaisons maritimes
Transport des automobiles
Permanentes
Saisonnière

Schiffsverbindungen
Autotransport
Ganzjährig ---------
Während der Saison - - - - - -

Scheepvaartverbindingen
Vervoeren van auto's
Permanente diensten
Diensten in het zomerseizoen

Líneas Marítimas
Transporte de coches
Todo el año ---------
De temporada - - - - - -

Collegamenti marittimi
Trasporto di automobili
Fissi
Stagionali

Main road map
Grands axes routiers / Durchgangsstraßen / Grote verbindingswegen
Grandi arterie stradali / Carreteras principales

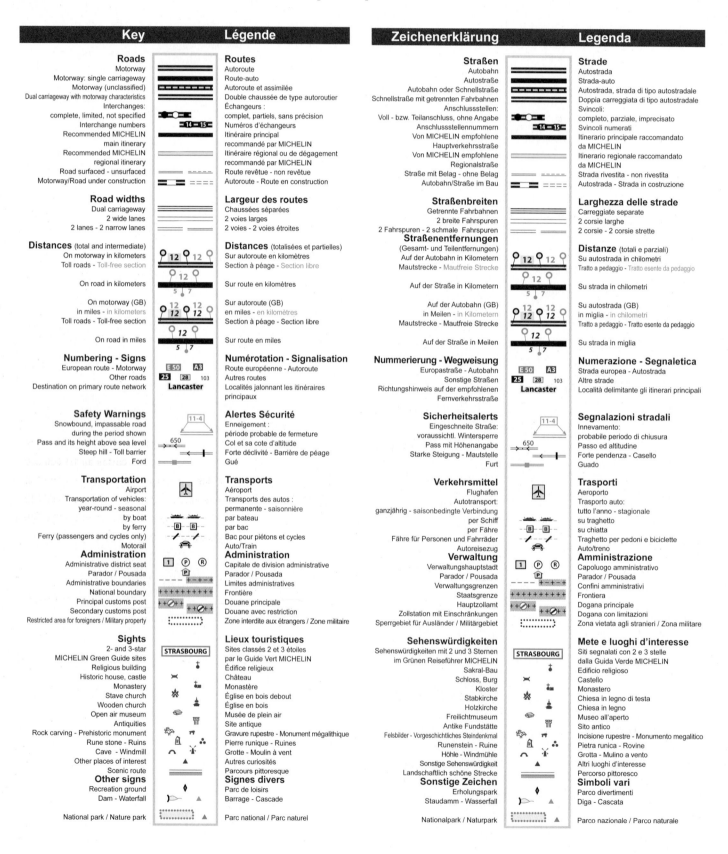

Key	Légende	Zeichenerklärung	Legenda

Roads / Routes / Straßen / Strade

Key	Légende	Zeichenerklärung	Legenda
Motorway	Autoroute	Autobahn	Autostrada
Motorway: single carriageway	Route-auto	Autostraße	Strada-auto
Motorway (unclassified)	Autoroute et assimilée	Autobahn oder Schnellstraße	Autostrada, strada di tipo autostradale
Dual carriageway with motorway characteristics	Double chaussée de type autoroutier	Schnellstraße mit getrennten Fahrbahnen	Doppia carreggiata di tipo autostradale
Interchanges:	Échangeurs :	Anschlussstellen:	Svincoli:
complete, limited, not specified	complet, partiels, sans précision	Voll - bzw. Teilanschluss, ohne Angabe	completo, parziale, imprecisato
Interchange numbers	Numéros d'échangeurs	Anschlussstellennummern	Svincoli numerati
Recommended MICHELIN main itinerary	Itinéraire principal recommandé par MICHELIN	Von MICHELIN empfohlene Hauptverkehrsstraße	Itinerario principale raccomandato da MICHELIN
Recommended MICHELIN regional itinerary	Itinéraire régional ou de dégagement recommandé par MICHELIN	Von MICHELIN empfohlene Regionalstraße	Itinerario regionale raccomandato da MICHELIN
Road surfaced - unsurfaced	Route revêtue - non revêtue	Straße mit Belag - ohne Belag	Strada rivestita - non rivestita
Motorway/Road under construction	Autoroute - Route en construction	Autobahn/Straße im Bau	Autostrada - Strada in costruzione

Road widths / Largeur des routes / Straßenbreiten / Larghezza delle strade

Key	Légende	Zeichenerklärung	Legenda
Dual carriageway	Chaussées séparées	Getrennte Fahrbahnen	Carreggiate separate
2 wide lanes	2 voies larges	2 breite Fahrspuren	2 corsie larghe
2 lanes - 2 narrow lanes	2 voies - 2 voies étroites	2 Fahrspuren - 2 schmale Fahrspuren	2 corsie - 2 corsie strette

Distances / Straßenentfernungen / Distanze

Key	Légende	Zeichenerklärung	Legenda
Distances (total and intermediate)	Distances (totalisées et partielles)	Straßenentfernungen (Gesamt- und Teilentfernungen)	Distanze (totali e parziali)
On motorway in kilometers	Sur autoroute en kilomètres	Auf der Autobahn in Kilometern	Su autostrada in chilometri
Toll roads - Toll-free section	Section à péage - Section libre	Mautstrecke - Mautfreie Strecke	Tratto a pedaggio - Tratto esente da pedaggio
On road in kilometers	Sur route en kilomètres	Auf der Straße in Kilometern	Su strada in chilometri
On motorway (GB) in miles - in kilometers	Sur autoroute (GB) en miles - en kilomètres	Auf der Autobahn (GB) in Meilen - in Kilometern	Su autostrada (GB) in miglia - in chilometri
Toll roads - Toll-free section	Section à péage - Section libre	Mautstrecke - Mautfreie Strecke	Tratto a pedaggio - Tratto esente da pedaggio
On road in miles	Sur route en miles	Auf der Straße in Meilen	Su strada in miglia

Numbering - Signs / Numérotation - Signalisation / Nummerierung - Wegweisung / Numerazione - Segnaletica

Key	Légende	Zeichenerklärung	Legenda
European route - Motorway	Route européenne - Autoroute	Europastraße - Autobahn	Strada europea - Autostrada
Other roads	Autres routes	Sonstige Straßen	Altre strade
Destination on primary route network	Localités jalonnant les itinéraires principaux	Richtungshinweis auf der empfohlenen Fernverkehrsstraße	Località delimitante gli itinerari principali

E 50 A3
25 28 103
Lancaster

Safety Warnings / Alertes Sécurité / Sicherheitsalerts / Segnalazioni stradali

Key	Légende	Zeichenerklärung	Legenda
Snowbound, impassable road during the period shown	Enneigement : période probable de fermeture	Eingeschneite Straße: voraussichtl. Wintersperre	Innevamento: probabile periodo di chiusura
Pass and its height above sea level	Col et sa cote d'altitude	Pass mit Höhenangabe	Passo ed altitudine
Steep hill - Toll barrier	Forte déclivité - Barrière de péage	Starke Steigung - Mautstelle	Forte pendenza - Casello
Ford	Gué	Furt	Guado

11-4
650

Transportation / Transports / Verkehrsmittel / Trasporti

Key	Légende	Zeichenerklärung	Legenda
Airport	Aéroport	Flughafen	Aeroporto
Transportation of vehicles: year-round - seasonal	Transports des autos : permanente - saisonnière	Autotransport: ganzjährig - saisonbedingte Verbindung	Trasporto auto: tutto l'anno - stagionale
by boat	par bateau	per Schiff	su traghetto
by ferry	par bac	per Fähre	su chiatta
Ferry (passengers and cycles only)	Bac pour piétons et cycles	Fähre für Personen und Fahrräder	Traghetto per pedoni e biciclette
Motorail	Auto/train	Autoreisezug	Auto/treno

Administration / Administration / Verwaltung / Amministrazione

Key	Légende	Zeichenerklärung	Legenda
Administrative district seat	Capitale de division administrative	Verwaltungshauptstadt	Capoluogo amministrativo
Parador / Pousada	Parador / Pousada	Parador / Pousada	Parador / Pousada
Administrative boundaries	Limites administratives	Verwaltungsgrenzen	Confini amministrativi
National boundary	Frontière	Staatsgrenze	Frontiera
Principal customs post	Douane principale	Hauptzollamt	Dogana principale
Secondary customs post	Douane avec restriction	Zollstation mit Einschränkungen	Dogana con limitazioni
Restricted area for foreigners / Military property	Zone interdite aux étrangers / Zone militaire	Sperrgebiet für Ausländer / Militärgebiet	Zona vietata agli stranieri / Zona militare

1 P R

Sights / Lieux touristiques / Sehenswürdigkeiten / Mete e luoghi d'interesse

Key	Légende	Zeichenerklärung	Legenda
2- and 3-star MICHELIN Green Guide sites	Sites classés 2 et 3 étoiles par le Guide Vert MICHELIN	Sehenswürdigkeiten mit 2 und 3 Sternen im Grünen Reiseführer MICHELIN	Siti segnalati con 2 e 3 stelle dalla Guida Verde MICHELIN
Religious building	Édifice religieux	Sakral-Bau	Edificio religioso
Historic house, castle	Château	Schloss, Burg	Castello
Monastery	Monastère	Kloster	Monastero
Stave church	Église en bois debout	Stabkirche	Chiesa in legno di testa
Wooden church	Église en bois	Holzkirche	Chiesa in legno
Open air museum	Musée de plein air	Freilichtmuseum	Museo all'aperto
Antiquities	Site antique	Antike Fundstätte	Sito antico
Rock carving - Prehistoric monument	Gravure rupestre - Monument mégalithique	Felsbilder - Vorgeschichtliches Steindenkmal	Incisione rupestre - Monumento megalitico
Rune stone - Ruins	Pierre runique - Ruines	Runenstein - Ruine	Pietra runica - Rovine
Cave - Windmill	Grotte - Moulin à vent	Höhle - Windmühle	Grotta - Mulino a vento
Other places of interest	Autres curiosités	Sonstige Sehenswürdigkeit	Altri luoghi d'interesse
Scenic route	Parcours pittoresque	Landschaftlich schöne Strecke	Percorso pittoresco

STRASBOURG

Other signs / Signes divers / Sonstige Zeichen / Simboli vari

Key	Légende	Zeichenerklärung	Legenda
Recreation ground	Parc de loisirs	Erholungspark	Parco divertimenti
Dam - Waterfall	Barrage - Cascade	Staudamm - Wasserfall	Diga - Cascata
National park / Nature park	Parc national / Parc naturel	Nationalpark / Naturpark	Parco nazionale / Parco naturale

Signos Convencionales | Verklaring van de tekens

Carreteras | Wegen

Autopista		Autosnelweg
Carretera		Autoweg
Autopista, Autovía		Autosnelweg of gelijksoortige weg
Autovía		Gescheiden rijbanen van het type autosnelweg
Accesos:		Aansluitingen: volledig, gedeeltelijk,
completo, parcial, sin precisar		zonder aanduiding
Números de los accesos		Afritnummers
Itinerario principal recomendado por MICHELIN		Hoofdweg
Itinerario regional recomendado por MICHELIN		Regionale weg
Carretera asfaltada - sin asfaltar		Verharde weg - onverharde weg
Autopista - Carretera en construcción		Autosnelweg - Weg in aanleg

Ancho de las carreteras | Breedte van de wegen

Calzadas separadas		Gescheiden rijbanen
Dos carriles anchos		2 brede rijstroken
Dos carriles - Dos carriles estrechos		2 rijstroken - 2 smalle rijstroken

Distancias (totales y parciales) | Afstanden (totaal en gedeeltelijk)

En autopista en kilómetros	12 12	Op autosnelwegen in kilometers
Tramo de peaje - Tramo libre		Gedeelte met tol - Tolvrij gedeelte
En carretera en kilómetros	12 / 5 7	Op andere wegen in kilometers
En autopista (GB) en millas - en kilómetros	12 12	Op autosnelwegen (GB) in mijlen - in kilometers
Tramo de peaje - Tramo libre		Gedeelte met tol - Tolvrij gedeelte
En carretera en millas	12 / 5 7	Op andere wegen in mijlen

Numeración - Señalización | Wegnummers - Bewegwijzering

Carretera europea - Autopista	E 50 A3	Europaweg - Autosnelweg
Otras carreteras	25 28 103	Andere wegen
Localidades situadas en los principales itinerarios	Lancaster	Plaatsen langs een hoofdweg met bewegwijzering

Alertas Seguridad | Veiligheidswaarschuwingen

Nevada:	11-4	Sneeuw:
Período probable de cierre		vermoedelijke sluitingsperiode
Puerto y su altitud	650	Bergpas en hoogte boven de zeespiegel
Pendiente Pronunciada - Barrera de peaje		Steile helling - Tol
Vado		Wad

Transportes | Vervoer

Aeropuerto		Luchthaven
Transporte de coches:		Vervoer van auto's:
todo el año - de temporada		het hele jaar - tijdens het seizoen
por barco	B - B	per boot
por barcaza		per veerpont
Barcaza para el paso de peatones y vehículos dos ruedas		Veerpont voor voetgangers en fietsers
Auto-tren		Autotrein

Administración | Administratie

Capital de división administrativa	1 P R P	Hoofdplaats van administratief gebied
Parador / Pousada		Parador / Pousada
Limites administrativos		Administratieve grenzen
Frontera	+++++++	Staatsgrens
Aduana principal	++⊘++	Hoofddouanekantoor
Aduana con restricciones	++⊘++	Douanekantoor met beperkte bevoegdheden
Zona prohibida a los extranjeros / Propiedad militar		Terrein verboden voor buitenlanders / Militair gebied

Curiosidades | Bezienswaardigheden

Lugares clasificados con 2 y 3 estrellas por la Guía Verde MICHELIN	STRASBOURG	Locaties met 2 en 3 sterren volgens de Groene Gids van MICHELIN
Edificio religioso	†	Kerkelijk gebouw
Castillo		Kasteel
Monasterio		Klooster
Iglesia de madera		Stavkirke (houten kerk)
Iglesia de madera		Houten kerk
Museo al aire libre		Openluchtmuseum
Zona de vestigios antiguos		Overblijfsel uit de Oudheid
Grabado rupestre - Monumento megalítico		Rotstekening - Megaliet
Piedra rúnica - Ruinas		Runensteen - Ruïne
Cueva - Molino de viento		Grot - Molen
Otras curiosidades	▲	Andere bezienswaardigheden
Recorrido pintoresco		Schilderachtig traject

Signos diversos | Diverse tekens

Zona recreativa	◆	Recreatiepark
Presa - Cascada	▲	Stuwdam - Waterval
Parque nacional / Parque natural	▲	Nationaal park / Natuurpark

0   10   20   30   40 miles
0 10 20 30 40 50 60 km

Republic of Ireland: All distances and speed limits are signed in kilometres.

République d'Irlande: Les distances et les limitations de vitesse sont exprimées en kilomètres.

Irland: Alle Entfernungsangaben und Geschwindigkeitsbegrenzungen in km.

Ierland: Alle afstanden en maximumsnelheden zijn uitsluitend in kilometers aangegeven.

Repubblica d'Irlanda: Distanze e limiti di velocità sono espressi soltanto in chilometri.

República de Irlanda: Distancias y límites de velocidad están expresados sólo en kilómetros.

Key to 1:1 000 000 map pages
Légende des cartes au 1/1 000 000
Zeichenerklärung der Karten 1:1 000 000
Verklaring van de tekens voor kaarten met schaal 1:1 000 000
Legenda carte scala 1:1 000 000
Signos convencionales de los mapas a escala 1:1 000 000

 = UNITARY AUTHORITIES

ENGLAND

UNITARY AUTHORITIES

1	Bath and North East Somerset
	Bedford
	Blackburn with Darwen
	Blackpool
	Bracknell Forest
	Brighton and Hove
7	Buckinghamshire
8	Cambridgeshire
9	Central Bedfordshire
10	Cheshire East
11	Cheshire West and Chester
	City of Bristol
13	Cornwall
14	Cumbria
	Derby
16	Derbyshire
17	Devon
18	Dorset
19	Durham
20	East Riding of Yorkshire
21	East Sussex
22	Essex
23	Gloucestershire
	Greater London
	Greater Manchester
26	Halton
27	Hampshire
	Hartlepool
29	Herefordshire
30	Hertfordshire
31	Kent
	Kingston-upon-Hull
33	Lancashire
	Leicester
35	Leicestershire
36	Lincolnshire
	Luton
38	Medway
39	Merseyside
	Middlesbrough
41	Milton Keynes
42	Norfolk
43	North East Lincolnshire
44	North Lincolnshire
45	North Somerset
46	North Yorkshire
47	Northamptonshire
48	Northumberland
49	Nottinghamshire
	Nottingham
51	Oxfordshire
	Peterborough
	Plymouth
	Portsmouth
	Reading
56	Redcar and Cleveland
57	Rutland
58	Shropshire
59	Somerset
60	South Gloucestershire
61	South Yorkshire
	Southend-on-Sea
63	Staffordshire
	Stockton-on-Tees
	Stoke-on-Trent
66	Suffolk
67	Surrey
	Swindon
69	Telford and Wrekin
70	Thurrock
	Torbay
72	Tyne and Wear
	Warrington
74	Warwickshire
75	West Berkshire
76	West Midlands
77	West Sussex
78	West Yorkshire
79	Wiltshire
	Windsor and Maidenhead
	Wokingham
82	Worcestershire
	York

SCOTLAND

UNITARY AUTHORITIES

1	Aberdeen City	17	Inverclyde
2	Aberdeenshire	18	Midlothian
3	Angus	19	Moray
4	Argyll and Bute	20	North Ayrshire
5	Clackmannanshire	21	North Lanarkshire
6	City of Edinburgh	22	Orkney Islands
7	City of Glasgow	23	Perth and Kinross
8	Dumfries and Galloway	24	Renfrewshire
9	Dundee City	25	Scottish Borders
10	East Ayrshire	26	Shetland Islands
11	East Dunbartonshire	27	South Ayrshire
12	East Lothian	28	South Lanarkshire
13	East Renfrewshire	29	Stirling
14	Falkirk	30	West Dunbartonshire
15	Fife	31	West Lothian
16	Highland	32	Western Isles

NORTHERN IRELAND

DISTRICT COUNCILS

1	Antrim	14	Down
2	Ards	15	Dungannon
3	Armagh	16	Fermanagh
4	Ballymena	17	Larne
5	Ballymoney	18	Limavady
6	Banbridge	19	Lisburn
7	Belfast	20	Magherafelt
8	Carrickfergus	21	Moyle
9	Castlereagh	22	Newry and Mourne
10	Coleraine	23	Newtownabbey
11	Cookstown	24	North Down
12	Craigavon	25	Omagh
13	Derry	26	Strabane

32
32 = **UNITARY AUTHORITIES**

WALES

UNITARY AUTHORITIES

1	Anglesey/Sir Fôn	12	Merthyr Tydfil/Merthyr Tudful
2	Blaenau Gwent	13	Monmouthshire/Sir Fynwy
3	Bridgend/Pen-y-bont ar Ogwr	14	Neath Port Talbot/Castell-nedd Phort Talbot
4	Caerphilly/Caerffili	15	Newport/Casnewydd
5	Cardiff/Caerdydd	16	Pembrokeshire/Sir Benfro
6	Carmarthenshire/Sir Gaerfyrddin	17	Powys
7	Ceredigion	18	Rhondda Cynon Taff/Rhondda Cynon Taf
8	Conwy	19	Swansea/Abertawe
9	Denbighshire/Sir Ddinbych	20	Torfaen/Tor-faen
10	Flintshire/Sir y Fflint	21	Vale of Glamorgan/Bro Morgannwg
11	Gwynedd	22	Wrexham/Wrecsam

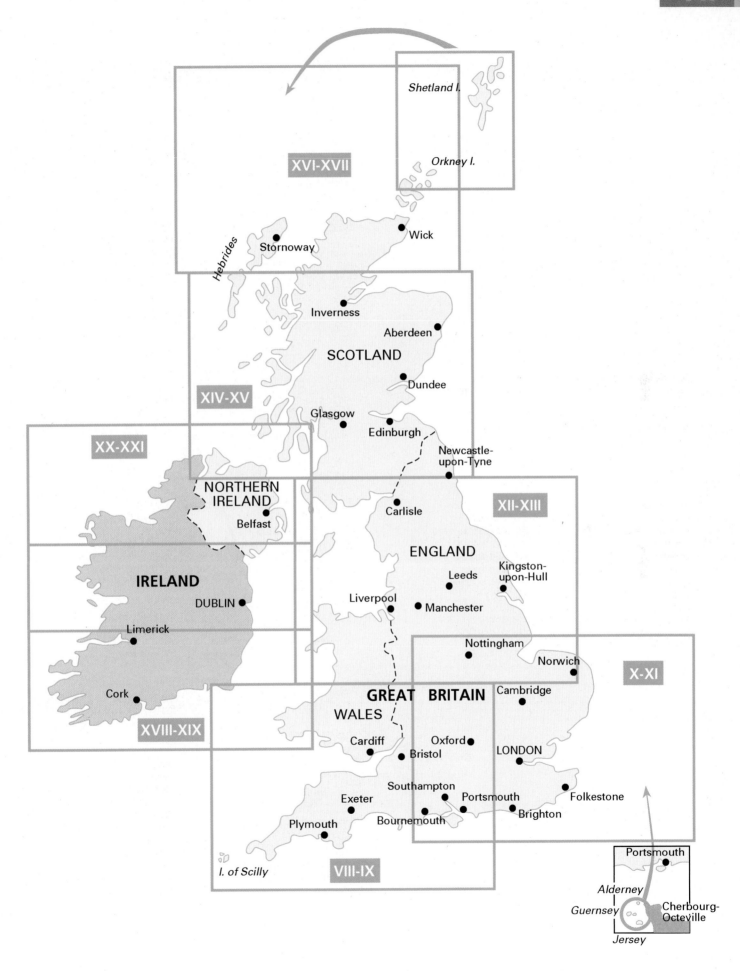

XVI-XVII

Shetland I.

Orkney I.

Hebrides

Stornoway

Wick

XIV-XV

Inverness

Aberdeen

SCOTLAND

Dundee

Glasgow

Edinburgh

Newcastle-upon-Tyne

XX-XXI

NORTHERN IRELAND

Belfast

Carlisle

XII-XIII

ENGLAND

Leeds

Kingston-upon-Hull

IRELAND

Liverpool

Manchester

DUBLIN

Limerick

Nottingham

Norwich

X-XI

Cork

Cambridge

XVIII-XIX

GREAT BRITAIN

WALES

Cardiff

Oxford

LONDON

Bristol

Southampton

Portsmouth

Folkestone

Exeter

Bournemouth

Brighton

Plymouth

I. of Scilly

VIII-IX

Portsmouth

Alderney

Guernsey

Cherbourg-Octeville

Jersey

St. George's Channel

e Harbour/
Ros Láir
Saltee Islands

St. George's Channel

Bristol Channel

Strumble Head
St. David's Head
St. David's
Haverfordwest/Hwlffordd
St. Bride's Bay
Milford Haven/
Aberdaugleddau
Neyland
PembrokeDock
Pembroke
St. Govan's Head

Pembrokeshire Coast National Park
Pembrokeshire Coast National Park

Newport
Fishguard/
Abergwaun
Cardigan
Newcastle Emlyn
Crymmych
Narberth
Whitland
St. Clears
Saundersfoot
Tenby/
Dinbych-y-pysgod
Pendine
Carmarthen Bay
Worms Head
Rhossili
Port-Eynon
The Mumbles

New Quay
Aberaeron
Aberporth
Synod Inn
Llandysul
Llanrhystud
Tregaron
Lampeter
Llanwrtyd Wells
Llandovery
Llangadog
Sennybridge
Brecon National

Carmarthen/
Caerfyrddin
Llandeilo
Black Mountain
Ammanford
Cross Hands
Kidwelly
Burry Port
Pontarddulais
Pontardawe
Hirwaun
Merthyr
Aberdare
Llanelli
SWANSEA/
ABERTAWE
Neath/
Castell Nedd
Port Talbot
Maesteg
Bridgend/
Pen-y-bont
Porthcawl
Elan Valley

Lundy

Ilfracombe
Combe Martin
Lynton
Lynmouth
Porlock
Croyde
Exmoor National
Simonsbath
Braunton
Northam
Barnstaple
South Molton
Tarr steps
Bideford
Great Torrington
Hartland Point
Clovelly
Cliffs of Morwenstow
Kilkhampton
Holsworthy
Hatherleigh
Winkleigh
Tiverton
Stratton
Bude
Crediton
Okehampton
High Willhays
Moretonhampstead
EXETER
Tintagel
Launceston
Lydford Gorge
Dartmoor National Park
Camelford
Bovey Tracey
Padstow
Tavistock
Princetown
Ashburton
Newton Abbot
Wadebridge
Callington
Buckfastleigh
Newquay
Bodmin
Liskeard
Buckland Abbey
Plympton
Fraddon
Lostwithiel
Saltash
Torpoint
Plymstock
Totnes
St. Austell
Fowey
West Looe
Torpoint
PLYMOUTH
Modbury
Dartmouth
Tregony
Polperro
Newton Ferrers
Truro
Mevagissey
Trelissick Garden
Camborne
Redruth
Penryn
Salcombe
St. Ives
Hayle
Penzance
St. Mawes
Falmouth
Kingsbridge
St. Just
Glendurgan Garden
Helston
Start Point
Sennen
St. Michael's Mount
St. Keverne
Land's End
Mount's Bay
Subtropical Gardens
St. Martin's
Tresco
Isles of Scilly
St. Mary's
Lizard
Lizard Point
Trewithen

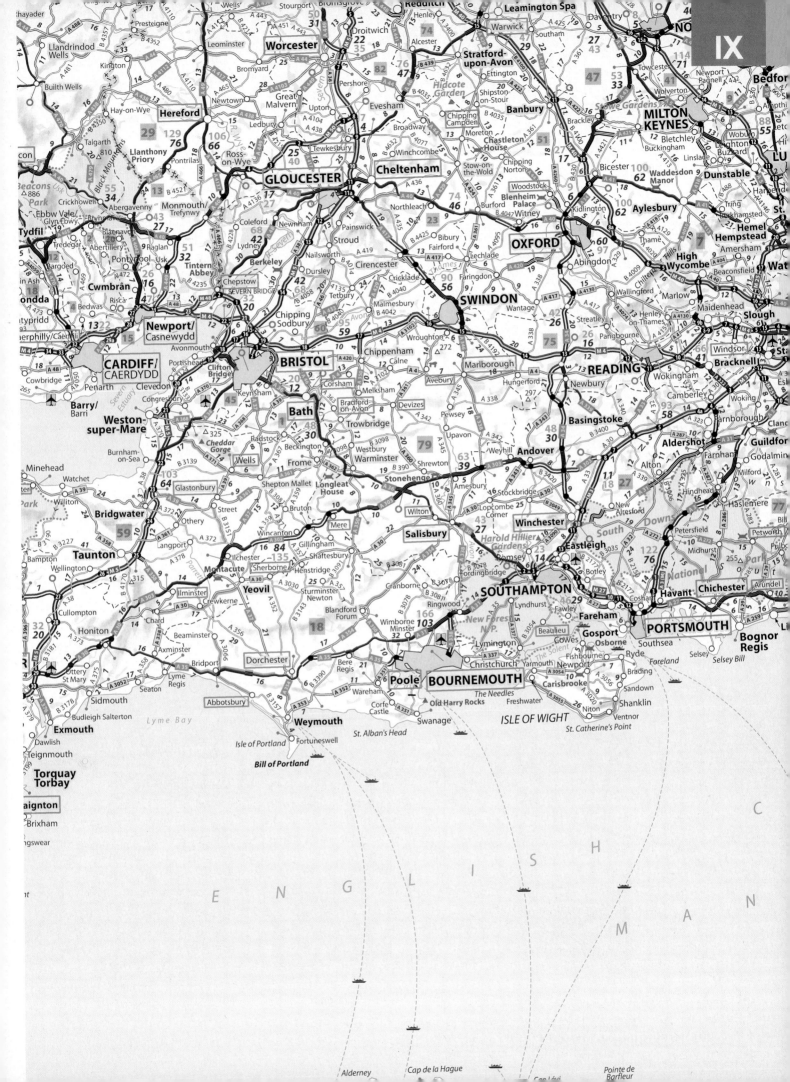

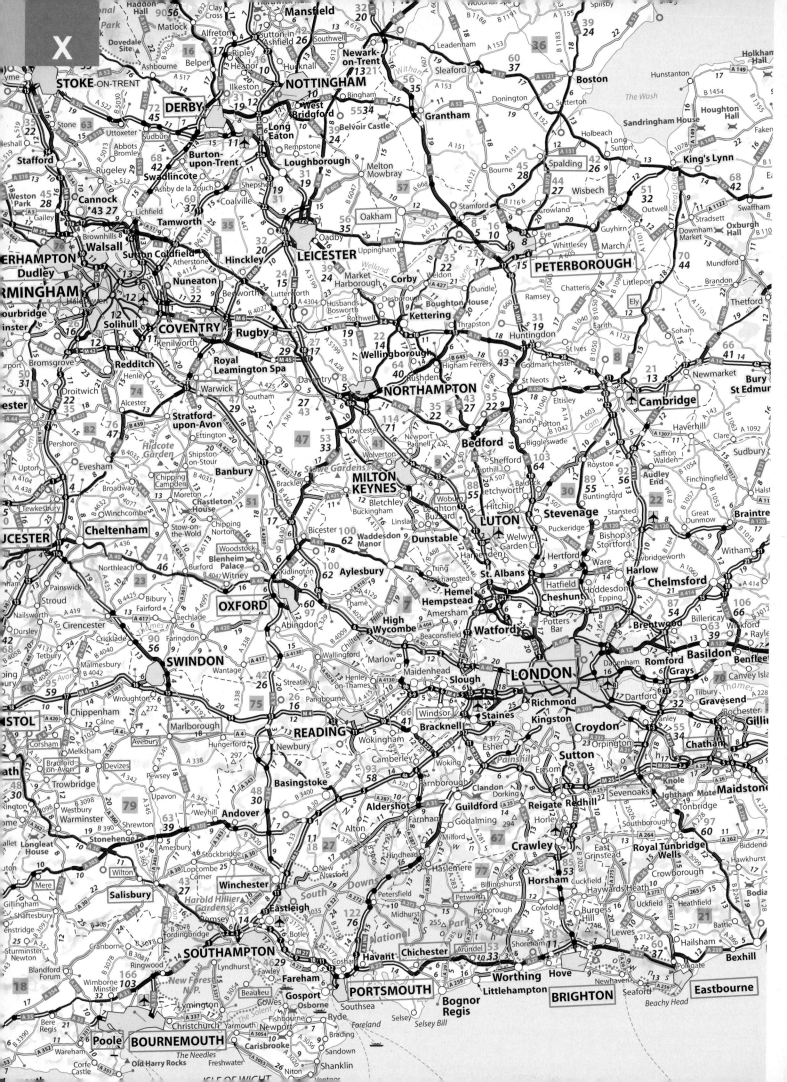

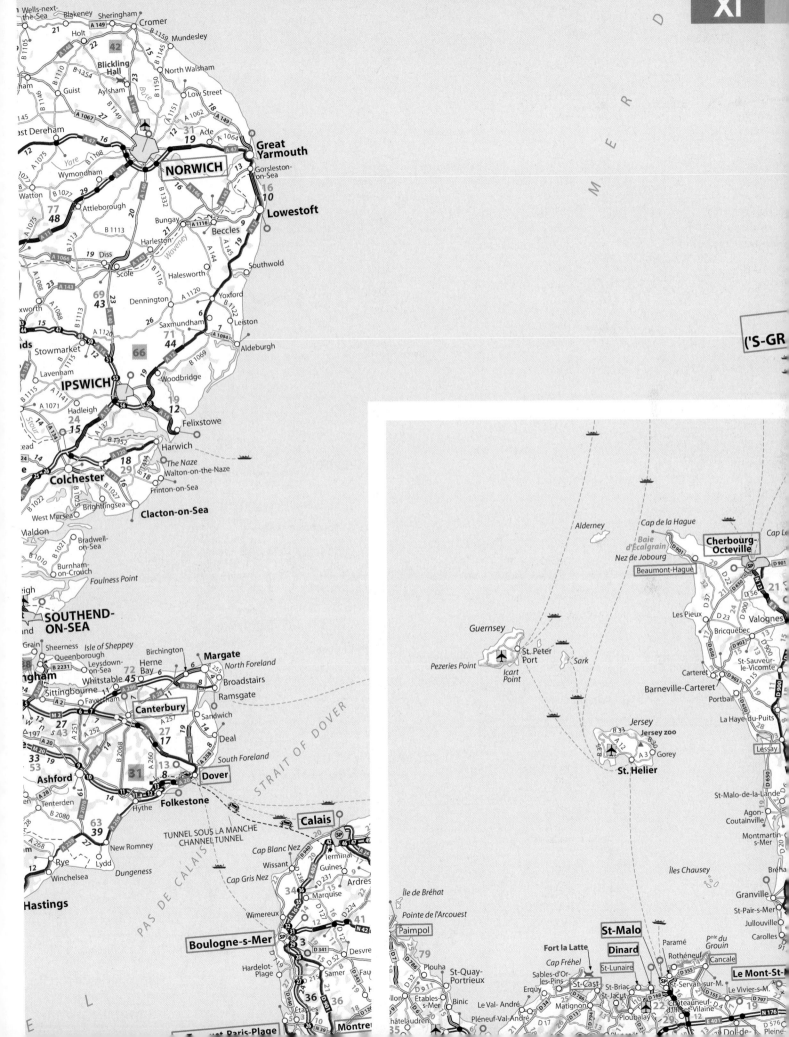

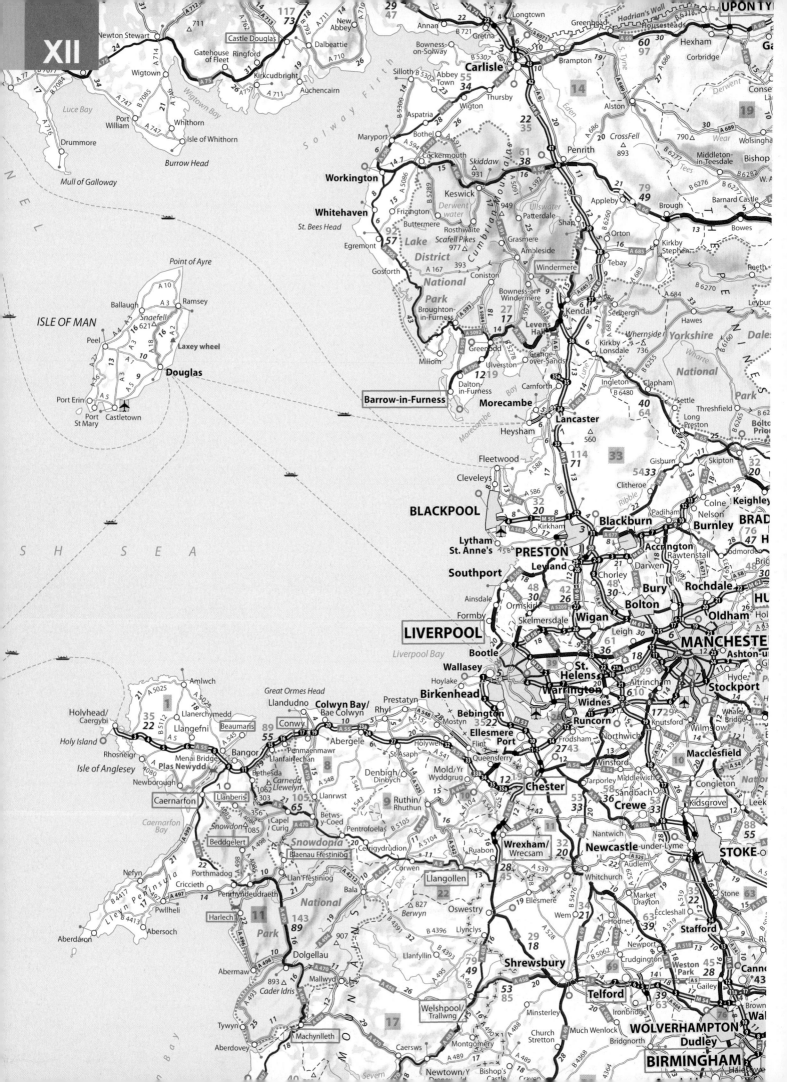

South Shields
Jarrow
SUNDERLAND
Gateshead
Washington
Seaham
Chester-le-Street
Houghton-le-Spring
Horden
Durham
Hartlepool
Peterlee
Sedgefield
Billingham
Redcar
Marske-by-the-Sea
Saltburn-by-the-Sea
Brotton
Stockton-on-Tees
Newton-Aycliffe
Darlington
Eaglescliffe
MIDDLESBROUGH
Guisborough
Loftus
Whitby
Richmond
Northallerton
Cleveland Hills
North York Moors National Park
Scarborough
Scalby
Filey
Bedale
Thirsk
Ripon
Rievaulx Abbey
Helmsley
Pickering
Flamborough Head
Pateley Bridge
Boroughbridge
Easingwold
Malton
Norton
Bridlington
Knaresborough
YORK
Wetwang
Driffield
Beeford
Harrogate
Wetherby
Tadcaster
Market Weighton
Leven
Hornsea
Otley
Bingley
Harewood
Selby
Barlby
Beverley
KINGSTON UPON HULL
Withernsea
LEEDS
Garforth
Howden
Goole
Hedon
Patrington
Kilnsea
BRADFORD
Castleford
Snaith
Barton-upon-Humber
Immingham Dock
Spurn Head
Halifax
Pontefract
Thorne
Scunthorpe
Immingham
Dewsbury
Wakefield
Crowle
Grimsby
Cleethorpes
HUDDERSFIELD
Barnsley
Doncaster
Bentley
Brigg
Caistor
Rotherham
Conisbrough
Epworth
Market Rasen
Louth
Mablethorpe
SHEFFIELD
Maltby
Bawtry
Gainsborough
Sutton-on-Sea
Ashton-under-Lyne
Stocksbridge
Worksop
Retford
Wragby
Alford
Dronfield
Staveley
Ollerton
Tuxford
Lincoln
Horncastle
Partney
Skegness
Chesterfield
Mansfield
Woodhall Spa
Spilsby
Bakewell
Hardwick Hall
Chatsworth House
Haddon Hall
Clay Cross
Southwell
Matlock
Alfreton
Sutton-in-Ashfield
Newark-on-Trent
Leadenham
Boston
Hunstanton
Holkham Hall
Wells-next-the-Sea
Blakeney
Holt
Ashbourne
Ripley
Heanor
Hucknall
Sleaford
Donington
Sutterton
Sandringham House
Houghton Hall
Fakenham
Belper
Ilkeston
NOTTINGHAM
Bingham
Grantham
Holbeach
Long Sutton
King's Lynn
East Dereham
DERBY
West Bridgford
Belvoir Castle
Spalding
Wisbech
Swaffham
Long Eaton
Rempstone
Bourne
Growland
Outwell
Downham Market
Oxburgh Hall
Watton
Uttoxeter
Burton-upon-Trent
Loughborough
Melton Mowbray
Stamford
Guyhirn
Mundford
Brandon
Swadlincote
Shepshed
Coalville
Oakham
Whittlesey
March
Thetford
Lichfield
Tamworth
Ashby de la Zouch
Uppingham
Eye
Peterborough
Littleport
Ely
Sutton Coldfield
Hinckley
LEICESTER
Oadby
Market Harborough
Corby
Weldon
Oundle
Chatteris
Ramsey
Nuneaton
Bedworth
Lutterworth
Husbands Bosworth
Rothwell
Boughton House
Kettering
Desborough
Diss

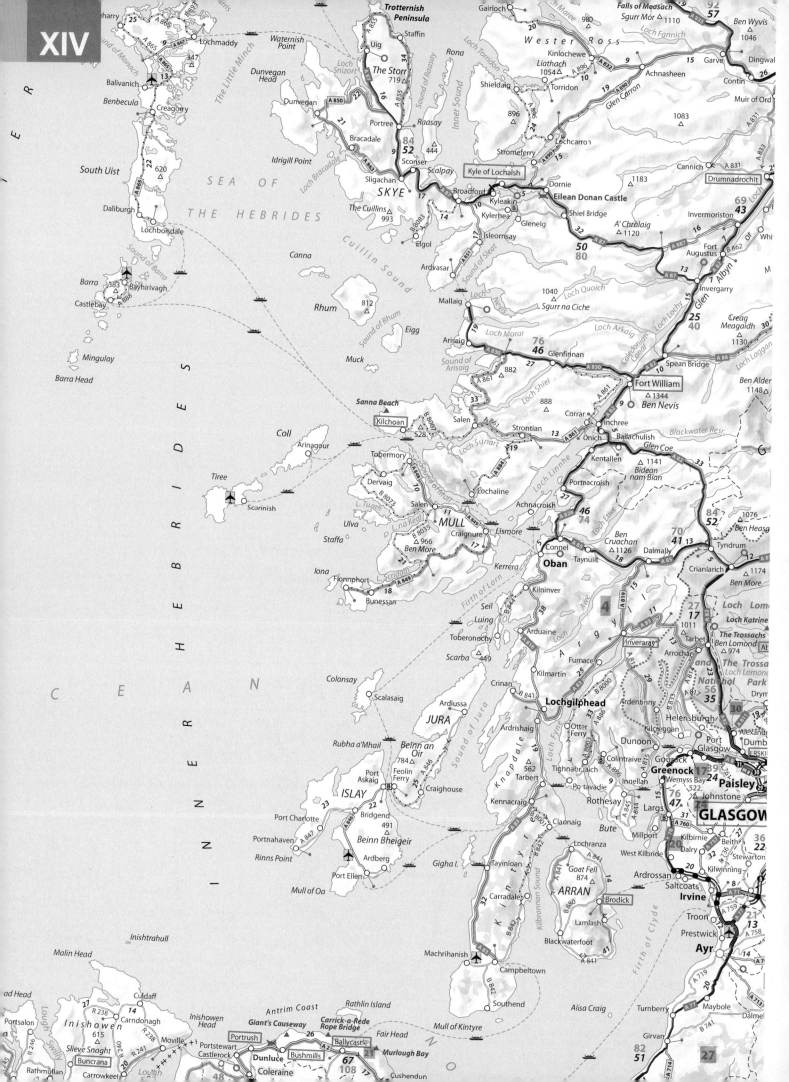

Alness Invergordon Lossiemouth Buckie Banff Macduff Fraserburgh Loch of Strathbeg Rattray Head 83 51

Cromarty Elgin Cullen Keith Fochabers Turriff New Deer Mintlaw Peterhead Buchan Ness

Black Isle Fortrose Nairn Forres Rothes Huntly Pitmedden Garden Ellon Cruden Bay

Inverness Tore Craigellachie Dufftown Rhynie Mossat Alford Oldmeldrum Newburgh 109 66

Findhorn Dava Grantown-on-Spey Tomintoul Craigievar Castle Inverurie Kintore 2

Carrbridge Glenmore Forest Park Dulnain Bridge 840 944 941 Crathes Castle ABERDEEN

Aviemore Cairn Gorm Cairngorm Mountains Colnabaichin 871 Craigievar Castle

Kingussie Ben Macdui 1309 Ballater Aboyne Banchory Stonehaven

Carn Ban Newtonmore Cairngorms National Park Braemar Balmoral Castle 89 55

Laggan 111 179 Devil's Elbow Glas Maol 1120 The Pleasance Laurencekirk Inverbervie

Dalwhinnie Pass of Drumochter 462 Beinn a' Ghlò 1155 Marykirk Montrose

Blair Castle Blair Atholl Brechin Forfar Glamis Castle Arbroath

Kinloch Rannoch Pitlochry Kirriemuir Alyth Glamis 19 12

Loch Rannoch Schiehallion 1083 Aberfeldy Dunkeld Blairgowrie Meigle Coupar Angus DUNDEE Carnoustie

Ben Lawers 1214 Loch Tay Killin Perth Newburgh Newport-on-Tay Tayport Buddon Ness Monifieth

Lochearnhead Ben Vorlich 985 Crieff Auchterarder Auchtermuchty Cupar St. Andrews Fife Ness

Callander 69 43 Ochil Hills Falkland Glenrothes Crail Anstruther Pittenweem St Monans

Doune Dunblane Dollar Kinross Leven Methil Buckhaven Firth of Forth

Stirling Alloa Dunfermline Lochgelly Kirkcaldy Burntisland North Berwick Dunbar

Falkirk Grangemouth Cowdenbeath Inverkeithing Aberlady East Linton Cockburnspath St Abb's Head

Kilsyth Kirkintilloch Linlithgow Bo'ness FORTH BRIDGE South Queensferry Prestonpans Haddington St Abb's Head National Nature Reserve

Cumbernauld Bathgate Livingston Leith Musselburgh Tranent Eyemouth

Clydebank Armadale Whitburn EDINBURGH Dalkeith Lauder Berwick-upon-Tweed

Airdrie Coatbridge Motherwell RosslynChapel Penicuik Duns Holy Island

Barrhead East Kilbride Hamilton Wishaw West Linton Peebles Galashiels Mellerstain Coldstream Bamburgh Castle

Kilmarnock Strathaven Lanark Biggar Innerleithen Melrose Abbey Dryburgh Kelso Belford

Galston Douglas Abington Selkirk Newtown St Boswells Jedburgh Woofer 100 63

Mauchline Muirkirk Elvanfoot Broad Law 840 Hawick The Cheviot 815 Alnwick Warkworth

Cumnock Sanquhar Moffat Carter Bar Northumberland National Park Rothbury Amble

New Cumnock Drumlanrig castle Thornhill Beattock Otterburn Ashington Newbiggin-by-the-Sea

Lochmaben Lockerbie Langholm 169 105 Morpeth Blyth

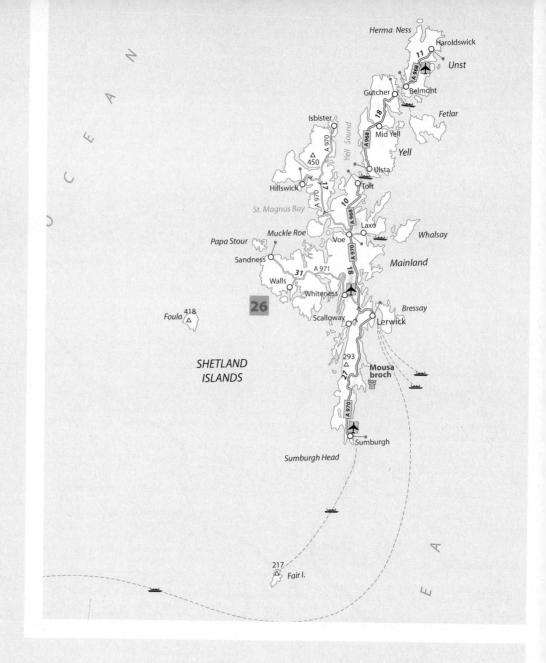

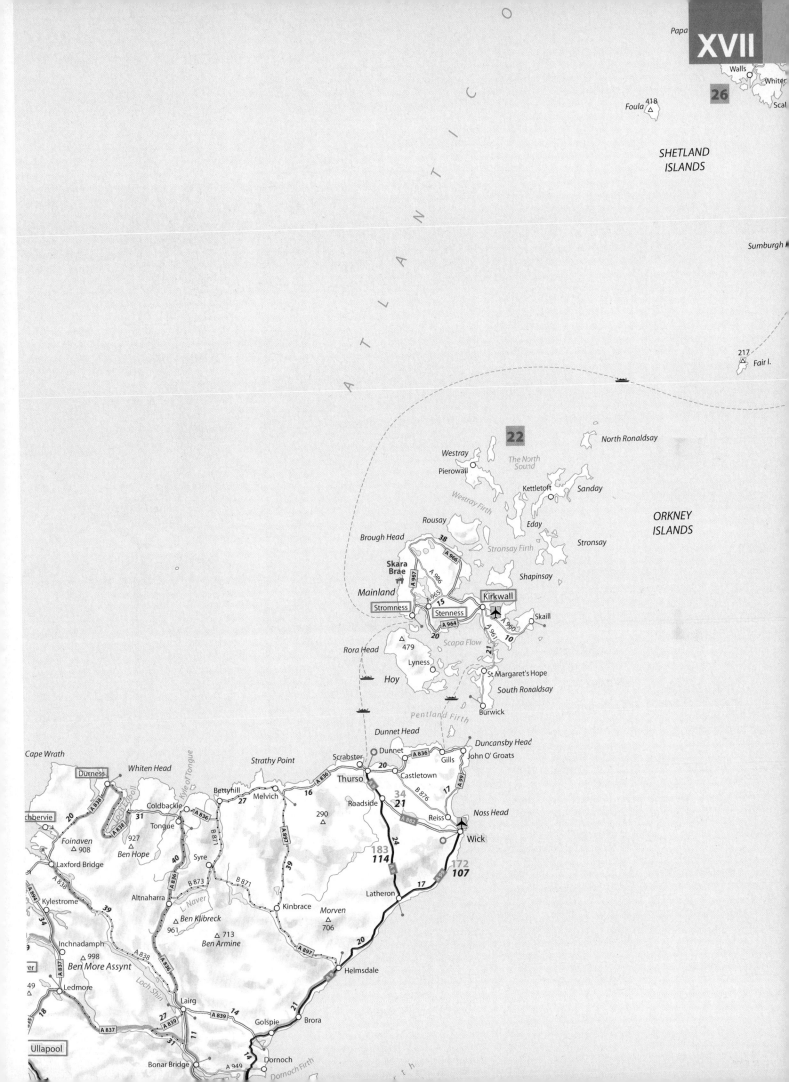

Papa

Walls

Whiter

Foula 418 △

Scal

SHETLAND
ISLANDS

Sumburgh

217 △ Fair I.

22

Westray

North Ronaldsay

Pierowall

The North
Sound

Kettletoft

Sanday

Rousay

Eday

ORKNEY
ISLANDS

Brough Head

Westray Firth

Stronsay Firth

Stronsay

38

A 966

Skara
Brae

A 986

Shapinsay

A 967

A 965

Kirkwall

Skaill

Mainland

15

A 960

Stromness

Stenness

10

A 964

20

A 961

Scapa Flow

A 961

Rora Head

479 △

21

Lyness

St Margaret's Hope

Hoy

South Ronaldsay

Pentland Firth

Burwick

Dunnet Head

Duncansby Head

Dunnet

John O' Groats

Cape Wrath

Strathy Point

Scrabster

A 836

Gills

Durness

Whiten Head

20

Castletown

A 99

Kyle of Tongue

Thurso

A 836

Bettyhill

16

34

B 876

17

Melvich

Roadside

21

Laxford
Durness

A 838

27

290 △

A 882

Reiss

Noss Head

hbervie

20

Coldbackie

A 836

31

Tongue

B 871

24

Wick

Foinaven
△ 908

927

Ben Hope

40

Syre

183

A 897

114

Laxford Bridge

A 838

B 873

B 871

39

172

A 894

Altnaharra

107

Kylestrome

39

L. Naver

Latheron

17

34

Kinbrace

Morven
△ 706

Inchnadamph

△ 998

Ben Klibreck
△ 961

Ben Armine
△ 713

20

Ben More Assynt

A 838

A 897

A 837

Ledmore

Loch Shin

Helmsdale

49 △

18

Lairg

14

21

Ullapool

A 837

27

11

A 839

Golspie

Brora

31

Bonar Bridge

A 949

14

Dornoch

Dornoch Firth

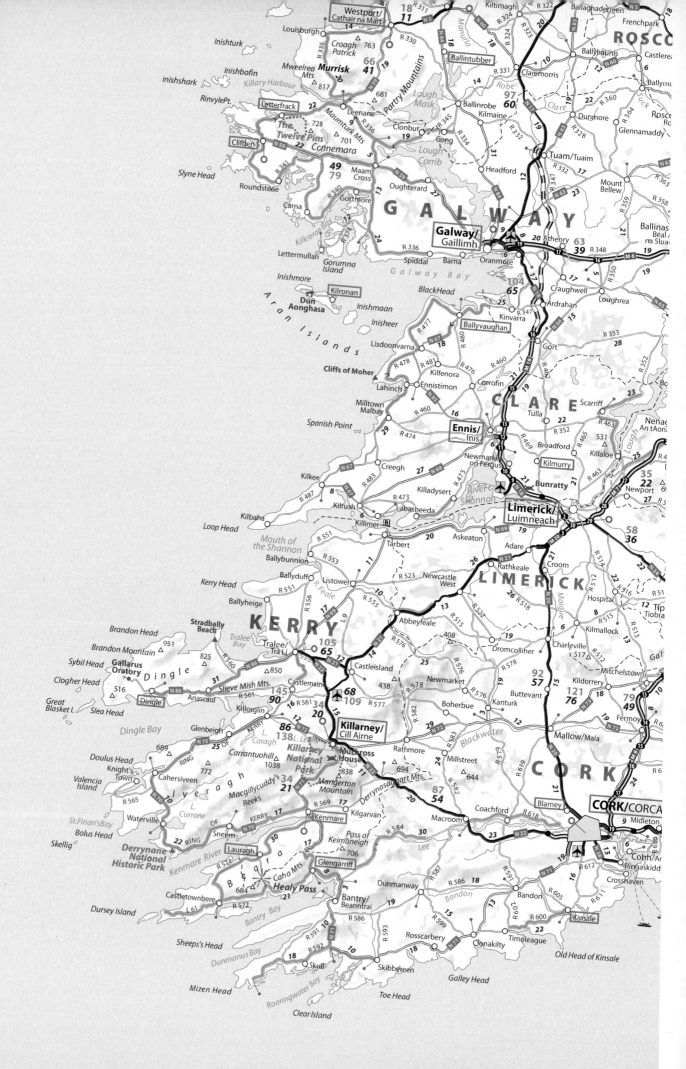

R 369 Elphin
R 368
Tulsk
COMMON
Strokestown
Shannon
Mohill
Ballyjamesduff
Bailieborough
R 165
Kingscourt
LOUTH
Castlebellingham
Dundalk Bay
N 33
Ardee
Clogherhead

LONGFORD
80 50
Longford/An Longfort 15
Granard
L. Sheelin
Virginia
R 194
Kells
Slane
Monasterboice Old Mellifont
Drogheda/Droichead Átha
R 166

N 5
Edgeworthstown
Derravaragh
Oldcastle
Navan/An Uaimh
Newgrange
Duleek
Balbriggan
Skerries

87 54
Lanesborough
Lough Ree
Ballymahon
Delvin
Athboy
Trim
Dunshaughlin
Ashbourne
Swords
Naul
Rush
Lusk

WEST MEATH
Mullingar/An Muileann gCearr
Ballymore
Kinnegad
Innfield
Kilcock
Maynooth
Lucan
MEATH
FINGAL
Malahide/Mullach Íde
Portmarnock
Howth/Binn Éadair

Athlone/Baile Átha Luain
21 13
Moate
Kilbeggan
Grand Canal
Castletown House
Clondalkin
DUBLIN/BAILE ÁTHA CLIATH
Dún Laoghaire
Dalkey

Clonmacnoise
Ferbane
Clara
Tullamore/Tulach Mhór
Edenderry
Newbridge/An Droichead Nua
Naas/An Nás
S DUBLIN
Kippure
Enniskerry
Bray/Bré
Greystones

Clonfert
Cloghan
OFFALY
Portarlington
Kildare
Poulaphouca Resr.
Powerscourt
Russborough House

Banagher
Kilcormac
Monasterevin
Kilcullen
Hollywood
WICKLOW
Glendalough
Laragh
Wicklow Mountains
Greystones

Portumna
Birr
Kinnitty
Slieve Bloom Mts.
Mountmellick
Emo Court
Portlaoise/Port Laoise
Athy
Baltinglass
Lugnaquillia Mountain
Laragh
Rathnew
Wicklow Head
Wicklow/Cill Mhantáin

Roscrea
Mountrath
LAOIS
Abbeyleix
Castledermot
Aughrim
Rathdrum
Rathnew

NORTH TIPPERARY
63 39
Moneygall
Rathdowney
Durrow
Carlow/Ceatharlach
Castlecomer
Tullow
Tinahely
Arklow/Antinbhear Mór

Templemore
89 55
Thurles/Durlas
Freshford
KILKENNY
Bagenalstown
Cárnew
Gorey
Courtown

Holycross
Urlingford
Kilkenny/Cill Chainnigh
Borris
Bunclody
Courtown

Cashel/Caiseal
Ballingarry
Killenaule
Callan
Thomastown
Graiguenamanagh
Blackstairs Mts
Kiltealy
Enniscorthy/Inis Córthaidh

SOUTH TIPPERARY
Fethard
Slievenamon
Jerpoint
New Ross
Blackwater

Cahir
Clonmel/Cluain Meala
Carrick-on-Suir
Wexford/Loch Garman

Clogheen
Knockmealdown Mts.
Comeragh Mts.
WATERFORD
Waterford/Port Láirge
Wellington Bridge
Arthurstown
Rosslare
Rosslare Harbour/Calafort Ros Láir

Lismore
Cappoquin
Tallow
Dungarvan
Dungarvan Harbour
Helvick Head
Tramore
Dunmore East
Bunmahon
Kilmore Quay
Carnsore Point
Saltee Islands

Youghal
Ardmore
Youghal Bay
Ballycotton
Hook Head
Waterford Harbour

ST. GEORGE'S CHANNEL
IRISH
Strumble Head
Pembrokeshire Coast National Park
St. David's Head
St. David's
Haverfordwest
St. Bride's Bay
Milford Haven
Aberdaugleddau
Pembroke

Ordnance Survey Ireland

Aran Island

Gweebarra

Rossan Point   Glencolumbkille
R 263   Killybegs
Bunglass Cliffs

Donegal B

Inishmurray   Bu
Bun D

Erris Head   Broad   65
Haven   40

Belmullet   Glenamoy   379△   Ballycastle   Killala   Easky   Slygo Bay   Rosses
R 314   31   12   R 314   R 297   Point
12   R 313   17   Strandhill
Inishkea   Bangor   20   Crossmolina   Inishcrone   Mountains   33   N 59
R 313   Oweniny   N 59   Ballina/   543   Ballysadare
12   720   19   Béal an Atha   △
BlacksodBay   R 316   20   R 294   SLIGO   18
670   Ballycro   10   The O   Tubbercurry   47   N 17   Ballymot
Keel   △   521   698   Nephin   R 310   Moy   29   R 294
Achill Island   R 319   17   804   Foxford   Charlestown   Gorteen   21
Mulrany   11   R 317   Pontoon   N 26   25   21   L Ga
Corraun   521   39,   25   Swinford   R 293
Clare Island   Newport   24   15   28   N 5
Clew Bay   11   Castlebar/   R 320   Ballaghaderreen   Car
Caisleán an   Kiltimagh   R 322
Westport/   18   Bharraigh   R 324   R 323   Frenchpark   18
Louisburgh   Cathair na Mart   11   11   R 311   18   18   ROSCO
14   N 84   Manulla   R 331   Ballyhaunis   Castlere
Inishturk   Croagh   763   R 330   Ballintubber   10   Ballymo
△   Patrick   66   19   Robe   12   N 60   6
Mweelrea   41   Claremorris   97   R 360   Rosc
Inishbofin   Mts   817   681   Ballinrobe   60   22   Ro
Inishshark   Killary Harbour   △   Lough   14   19   Dunmore   R 364
RinvylePt.   Letterfrack   22   Mask   Kilmaine   R 328   Glennamaddy
The   728   Maumturk Mts   Clonbur   R 345   19   R 332   Tuam/Tuaim
Twelve Pins   701   19   Cong   31   N 63   Mount
Clifden   N 59   22   Connemara   5   R 334   Headford   12   R 347   17   Bellew   R 363
49   Maam   Lough   23   R 350
Slyne Head   79   Cross   13   Corrib   R 341   79   Oughterard   27   N 63   Ballinas
Roundstone   R 340   Béal
Carna   Gortmore   GALWAY   9   na Slua
R 374   Galway/   Athenry   63
Lettermullan   Gaillimh   R 336   Spiddal   Barna   Oranmore   17   39   R 348   19
Gorumna   R 336   20   16   M 6
Island   Galway Bay   104   17   R 350   19
Inishmore   Kilronan   BlackHead   65   Craughwell   Loughrea   N 65
Dún   25   Ardrahan
Aonghasa   Inishmaan   R 347   Kinvarra   15
Inisheer   R 477   Ballyvaughan   R 353
Aran Islands   Lisdoonvarna   R 480   R 460   28
R 478   R 481   Gort

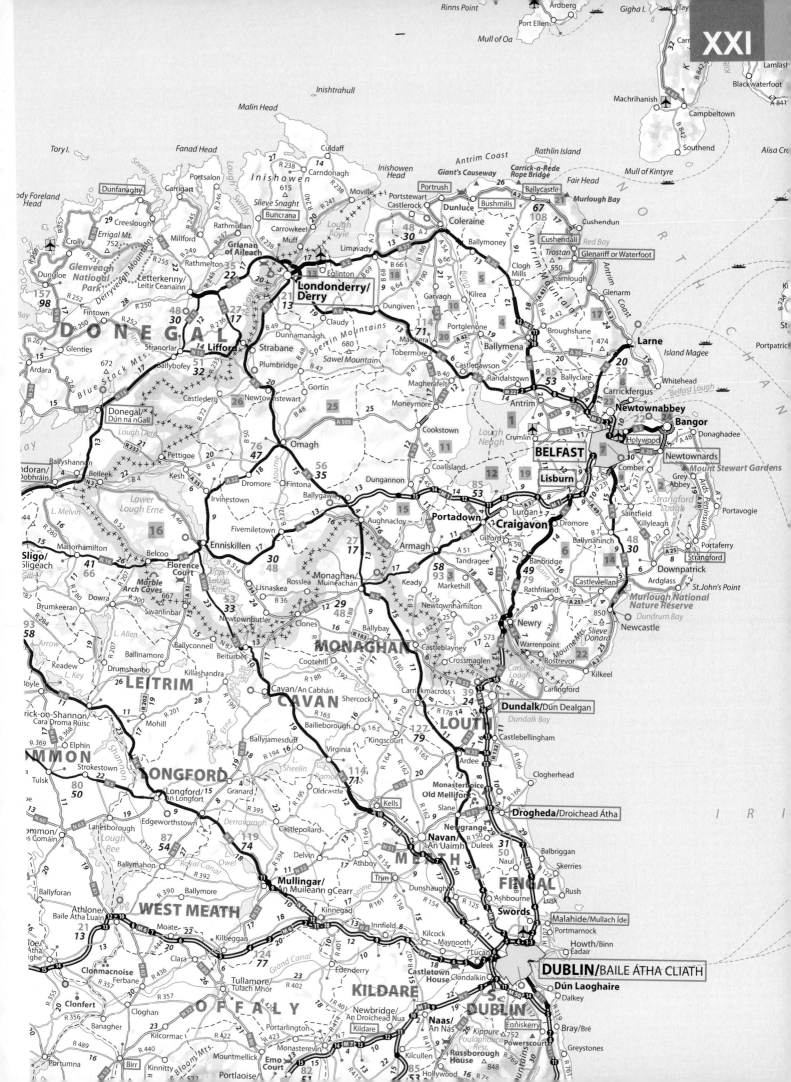

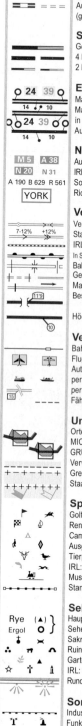

Roads

Motorway - Service areas
Dual carriageway with motorway characteristics

Interchanges: complete, limited
Interchange numbers
International and national road network
Interregional and less congested road
Road surfaced - unsurfaced
Footpath - Waymarked footpath / Bridle path
Motorway / Road under construction
(when available: with scheduled opening date)

Road widths

Dual carriageway
4 lanes - 2 wide lanes
2 lanes - 2 narrow lanes

Distances (total and intermediate)

Toll roads on motorway
Toll-free section on motorway
in miles - en kilometers
on road

Numbering - Signs

Motorway - GB: Primary route
IRL : National primary and secondary route
Other roads
Destination on primary route network

Obstacles

Roundabout - Pass and its height above sea level (meters)
Steep hill (ascent in direction of the arrow)
IRL: Difficult or dangerous section of road
In Scotland: narrow road with passing places
Level crossing: railway passing, under road, over road
Prohibited road - Road subject to restrictions
Toll barrier - One way road (on major and regional roads)
Height limit under 15'6'' IRL, 16'6'' GB

Load limit (under 16 t.)

Transportation

Railway - Passenger station
Airport - Airfield
Transportation of vehicles: (seasonal services in red)
by hovercraft - by boat
by ferry (load limit in tons)
Ferry (passengers and cycles only)

Accommodation - Administration

Town plan featured in:
THE MICHELIN GUIDE
THE GREEN GUIDE
Administrative boundaries
Scottish and Welsh borders
National boundary - Customs post

Sport & Recreation Facilities

Golf course - Horse racetrack
Racing circuit - Pleasure boat harbour
Caravan and camping sites
Waymarked footpath - Country park
Safari park, zoo - Bird sanctuary, refuge
IRL: Fishing - Greyhound track
Tourist train
Funicular, cable car, chairlift

Sights

Principal sights: see THE GREEN GUIDE
Towns or places of interest, Places to stay
Religious building - Historic house, castle
Ruins - Prehistoric monument - Cave
Garden, park - Other places of interest
IRL: Fort - Celtic cross - Round Tower
Panoramic view - Viewpoint - Scenic route

Other signs

Industrial cable way
Telecommunications tower or mast - Lighthouse
Power station - Quarry
Mine - Industrial activity
Refinery - Cliff
National forest park - National park

Routes

Autoroute - Aires de service
Double chaussée de type autoroutier

Échangeurs : complet, partiels
Numéros d'échangeurs
Route de liaison internationale ou nationale
Route de liaison interrégionale ou de dégagement
Route revêtue - non revêtue
Sentier - Sentier balisé/Allée cavalière
Autoroute - Route en construction
(le cas échéant : date de mise en service prévue)

Largeur des routes

Chaussées séparées
4 voies - 2 voies larges
2 voies - 2 voies étroites

Distances (totalisées et partielles)

Section à péage sur autoroute
Section libre sur autoroute
en miles - en kilomètres
sur route

Numérotation - Signalisation

Autoroute - GB : itinéraire principal (Primary route)
IRL : itinéraire principal (National primary et secondary route)
Autres routes
Localités jalonnant les itinéraires principaux

Obstacles

Rond-point - Col et sa cote d'altitude (en mètres)
Forte déclivité (flèches dans le sens de la montée)
IRL : Parcours difficile ou dangereux
En Écosse : route très étroite avec emplacements pour croisement
Passages de la route : à niveau, supérieur, inférieur
Route interdite - Route réglementée
Barrière de péage - Route à sens unique
Hauteur limitée au dessous de 15'6'' IRL, 16'6''GB

Limites de charge (au-dessous de 16 t.)

Transports

Voie ferrée - Gare
Aéroport - Aérodrome
Transport des autos: (liaison saisonnière en rouge)
par aéroglisseur - par bateau
par bac (charge maximum en tonnes)
Bac pour piétons et cycles

Hébergement - Administration

Localité possédant un plan dans :
LE GUIDE MICHELIN
LE GUIDE VERT
Limites administratives
Limite de l'Écosse et du Pays de Galles
Frontière - Douane

Sports - Loisirs

Golf - Hippodrome
Circuit automobile - Port de plaisance
Camping, caravaning
Sentier balisé - Base ou parc de loisirs
Parc animalier, zoo - Réserve d'oiseaux
IRL : Pêche - Cynodrome
Train touristique
Funiculaire, téléphérique, télésiège

Curiosités

Principales curiosités : voir LE GUIDE VERT
Localités ou sites intéressants, lieux de séjour
Édifice religieux - Château
Ruines - Monument mégalithique - Grotte
Jardin, parc - Autres curiosités
IRL : Fort - Croix celte - Tour ronde
Panorama - Point de vue - Parcours pittoresque

Signes divers

Transporteur industriel aérien
Tour ou pylône de télécommunications - Phare
Centrale électrique - Carrière
Mine - Industries
Raffinerie - Falaise
Parc forestier national - Parc national

Straßen

Autobahn - Tankstelle mit Raststätte
Schnellstraße mit getrennten Fahrbahnen

Anschlussstellen: Voll- bzw. Teilanschlussstellen
Anschlussstellennummern
Internationale bzw.nationale Hauptverkehrsstraße
Überregionale Verbindungsstraße oder Umleitungsstrecke
Straße mit Belag - ohne Belag
Pfad - Ausgeschilderter Weg / Reitpfad
Autobahn - Straße im Bau
(ggf. voraussichtliches Datum der Verkehrsfreigabe)

Straßenbreiten

Getrennte Fahrbahnen
4 Fahrspuren - 2 breite Fahrspuren
2 Fahrspuren - 1 Fahrspur

Entfernungen (Gesamt- und Teilentfernungen)

Mautstrecke auf der Autobahn
Mautfreie Strecke auf der Autobahn
in Meilen - in Kilometern
Auf der Straße

Nummerierung - Wegweisung

Autobahn - GB: Empfohlene Fernverkehrsstraße (Primary route)
IRL: Empfohlene Fernverkehrsstraße (National primary und secondary route)
Sonstige Straßen
Richtungshinweis auf der empfohlenen Fernverkehrsstraße

Verkehrshindernisse

Verkehrsinsel - Pass mit Höhenangabe (in Meter)
Starke Steigung (Steigung in Pfeilrichtung)
IRL: Schwierige oder gefährliche Strecke
In Schottland: sehr schmale Straße mit Ausweichstellen (passing places)
Bahnübergänge: schienengleich, Unterführung, Überführung
Gesperrte Straße - Straße mit Verkehrsbeschränkungen
Mautstelle - Einbahnstraße
Beschränkung der Durchfahrtshöhe bis 15'6'' IRL, 16'6' GB

Höchstbelastung (angegeben, wenn unter 16 t)

Verkehrsmittel

Bahnlinie - Bahnhof
Flughafen - Flugplatz
Autotransport: (rotes Zeichen: saisonbedingte Verbindung)
per Hovercraft - per Schiff
per Fähre (Höchstbelastung in t)
Fähre für Personen und Fahrräder

Unterkunft - Verwaltung

Orte mit Stadtplan im:
MICHELIN-FÜHRER
GRÜNEN REISEFÜHRER
Verwaltungshauptstadt
Grenze von Schottland und Wales
Staatsgrenze - Zoll

Sport - Freizeit

Golfplatz - Pferderennbahn
Rennstrecke - Yachthafen
Campingplatz
Ausgeschilderter Weg - Freizeitanlage
Tierpark, Zoo - Vogelschutzgebiet
IRL: Angeln - Windhundrennen
Museumseisenbahn
Standseilbahn, Seilbahn, Sessellift

Sehenswürdigkeiten

Hauptsehenswürdigkeiten: siehe GRÜNER REISEFÜHRER
Sehenswerte Orte, Ferienorte
Sakral-Bau - Schloss, Burg
Ruine - Vorgeschichtliches Steindenkmal - Höhle
Garten, Park - Sonstige Sehenswürdigkeit
IRL: Fort, Festung - Keltisches Kreuz - Rundturm
Rundblick - Aussichtspunkt - Landschaftlich schöne Strecke

Sonstige Zeichen

Industrieschwebebahn
Funk-, Sendeturm - Leuchtturm
Kraftwerk - Steinbruch
Bergwerk - Industrieanlagen
Raffinerie - Klippen
Waldschutzgebiet - Nationalpark

Verklaring van de tekens

Wegen
Autosnelweg - Serviceplaatsen
Gescheiden rijbanen van het type autosnelweg

Aansluitingen: volledig, gedeeltelijk
Afritnummers
Internationale of nationale verbindingsweg
Interregionale verbindingsweg
Verharde weg - Onverharde weg
Pad - Bewegwijzerd wandelpad / Ruiterpad
Autosnelweg in aanleg - weg in aanleg
(indien bekend: datum openstelling)

Breedte van de wegen
Gescheiden rijbanen
4 rijstroken - 2 brede rijstroken
2 rijstroken - 2 smalle rijstroken

Afstanden (totaal en gedeeltelijk)
Gedeelte met tol op autosnelwegen
Tolvrij gedeelte op autosnelwegen
in mijlen - in kilometers
op andere wegen

Wegnummers - Bewegwijzering
Autosnelweg - GB: Hoofdweg (Primary route)
IRL: Hoofdweg (National primary en secondary route)
Andere wegen
Plaatsen langs een autosnelweg of Primary route met bewegwijzering

Hindernissen
Rotonde - Bergpas en hoogte boven de zeespiegel (in meters)
Steile helling (pijlen in de richting van de helling)
IRL: Moeilijk of gevaarlijk traject
In Schotland: smalle weg met uitwijkplaatsen
Wegovergangen: gelijkvloers, overheen, onderdoor
Verboden weg - Beperkt opengestelde weg
Tol - Weg met eenrichtingsverkeer
Vrije hoogte indien lager dan 15' 6'' IRL, 16'6'' GB

Maximum draagvermogen (indien minder dan 16 t)

Vervoer
Spoorweg - Reizigersstation
Luchthaven - Vliegveld
Vervoer van auto's: (tijdens het seizoen: rood teken)
per hovercraft - per boot
per veerpont (maximum draagvermogen in t.)
Veerpont voor voetgangers en fietsers

Verblijf - Administratie
Plaats met een plattegrond in:
DE MICHELIN GIDS
DE GROENE GIDS
Administratieve grenzen
Grens van Schotland en Wales
Staatsgrens - Douanekantoor

Sport - Recreatie
Golfterrein - Renbaan
Autocircuit - Jachthaven
Kampeerterrein (tent, caravan)
Sentiero segnalato - Recreatiepark
Safaripark, dierentuin - Vogelreservaat
IRL: Vissen - Hondenrenbaan
Toeristentreintje
Kabelspoor, kabelbaan, stoeltjeslift

Bezienswaardigheden
Belangrijkste bezienswaardigheden: zie DE GROENE GIDS
Interessante steden of plaatsen, vakantieoorden
Kerkelijk gebouw - Kasteel
Ruïne - Megaliet - Grot
Tuin, park - Andere bezienswaardigheden
IRL: Fort - Keltisch kruis - Ronde toren
Panorama - Uitzichtpunt - Schilderachtig traject

Diverse tekens
Kabelvrachtvervoer
Telecommunicatietoren of -mast - Vuurtoren
Elektriciteitscentrale - Steengroeve
Mijn - Industrie
Raffinaderij - Klif
Staatsbos - Nationaal park

Strade
Autostrada - Aree di servizio
Doppia carreggiata di tipo autostradale

Svincoli: completo, parziale
Svincoli numerati
Strada di collegamento internazionale o nazionale
Strada di collegamento interregionale o di disimpegno
Strada rivestita - non rivestita
Sentiero - Sentiero segnalato / Pista per cavalli
Autostrada, strada in costruzione
(data di apertura prevista)

Larghezza delle strade
Carreggiate separate
4 corsie - 2 corsie larghe
2 corsie - 2 corsie strette

Distanze (totali e parziali)
Tratto a pedaggio su autostrada
Tratto esente da pedaggio su autostrada
in miglia - in chilometri
su strada

Numerazione - Segnaletica
Autostrada - GB: itinerario principale (Strada «Primary»)
IRL: itinerario principale (Strada «National primary» e «Secondary»)
Altre Strade
Località delimitante gli itinerari principali

Ostacoli
Rotonda - Passo ed altitudine (in metri)
Forte pendenza (salita nel senso della freccia)
IRL: Percorso difficile o pericoloso
In Scozia: Strada molto stretta con incrocio
Passaggi della strada: a livello, cavalcavia, sottopassaggio
Strada vietata - Strada a circolazione regolamentata
Casello - Strada a senso unico (su collegamenti principali e regionali)
Limite di altezza inferiore a 15'6'' IRL, 16'6''GB

Limite di portata (inferiore a 16 t.)

Trasporti
Ferrovia - Stazione viaggiatori
Aeroporto - Aerodromo
Trasporto auto: (stagionale in rosso)
su idrovolante - su traghetto
su chiatta (carico massimo in t.)
Traghetto per pedoni e biciclette

Risorse alberghiere - Amministrazione
Località con pianta nella:
GUIDA MICHELIN
GUIDA VERDE
Confini amministrativi
Confine di Scozia e Galles
Frontiera - Dogana

Sport - Divertimento
Golf - Ippodromo
Circuito Automobilistico - Porto turistico
Campeggi, caravaning
Sentiero segnalato - Area o parco per attività ricreative
Parco con animali, zoo - Riserva ornitologica
IRL: Pesca - Cinodromo
Trenino turistico
Funicolare, funivia, seggiovia

Mete e luoghi d'interesse
Principali luoghi d'interesse, vedere LA GUIDA VERDE
Località o siti interessanti, luoghi di soggiorno
Edificio religioso - Castello
Rovine - Monumento megalitico - Grotta
Giardino, parco - Altri luoghi d'interesse
IRL: Forte - Croce celtica - Torre rotonda
Panorama - Vista - Percorso pittoresco

Simboli vari
Teleferica industriale
Torre o pilone per telecomunicazioni - Faro
Centrale elettrica - Cava
Miniera - Industrie
Raffineria - Falesia
Parco forestale nazionale - Parco nazionale

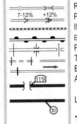

Signos convencionales

Carreteras
Autopista - Áreas de servicio
Autovía

Enlaces: completo, parciales
Números de los accesos
Carretera de comunicación internacional o nacional
Carretera de comunicación interregional o alternativo
Carretera asfaltada - sin asfaltar
Sendero - Sendero señalizado / Camino de caballos
Autopista, carretera en construcción
(en su caso: fecha prevista de entrada en servicio)

Ancho de las carreteras
Calzadas separadas
Cuatro carriles - Dos carriles anchos
Dos carriles - Dos carriles estrechos

Distancias (totales y parciales)
Tramo de peaje en autopista
Tramo libre en autopista
en millas - en kilómetros
en carretera

Numeración - Señalización
Autopista - GB: Vía principal (Primary route)
IRL: Vía principal (National primary et secondary route)
Otras carreteras
Localidad en itinerario principal

Obstáculos
Rotonda - Puerto y su altitud (en métros)
Pendiente Pronunciada (las flechas indican el sentido del ascenso)
IRL: Recorrido difícil o peligroso
En escocia: carretera muy estrecha con ensanchamientos para poder cruzarse
Pasos de la carretera: a nivel, superior, inferior
Tramo prohibido - Carretera restringida
Barrera de peaje - Carretera de sentido único
Altura limitada (15'6'' IRL, 16'6''GB)

Limite de carga (inferior a 16 t)

Transportes
Línea férrea - Estación de viajeros
Aeropuerto - Aeródromo
Transporte de coches: (Enlace de temporada: signo rojo)
por overcraft - por barco
por barcaza (carga máxima en toneladas)
Barcaza para el paso de peatones y vehículos dos ruedas

Alojamiento - Administración
Localidad con plano en:
LA GUÍA MICHELIN
LA GUÍA VERDE
Limites administrativos
Limites de Escocia y del País de Gales
Frontera - Puesto de aduanas

Deportes - Ocio
Golf - Hipódromo
Circuito de velocidad - Puerto deportivo
Camping, caravaning
Sendero señalizado - Parque de ocio
Reserva de animales, zoo - Reserva de pájaros
IRL: Pêche - Cynodrome
Tren turístico
Funicular, Teleférico, telesilla

Curiosidades
Principales curiosidades: ver LA GUÍA VERDE
Localidad o lugar interesante, lugar para quedarse
Edificio religioso - Castillo
Ruinas - Monumento megalítico - Cueva
Jardín, parque - Curiosidades diversas
IRL: Fortaleza - Cruz celta - Torre redonda
Vista panorámica - Vista parcial - Recorrido pintoresco

Signos diversos
Transportador industrial aéreo
Emisor de Radiodifusión - Faro
Central eléctrica - Cantera
Mina - Industrias
Refinería - Acantilado
Parque forestal nacional - Parque nacional

KEELE

24 39   14 10   24 39

M 5   A 38   N 20   N 31
A 190 B 629 R 561
YORK

7-12%   +12%

11'9

Rye (▲)
Ergol O

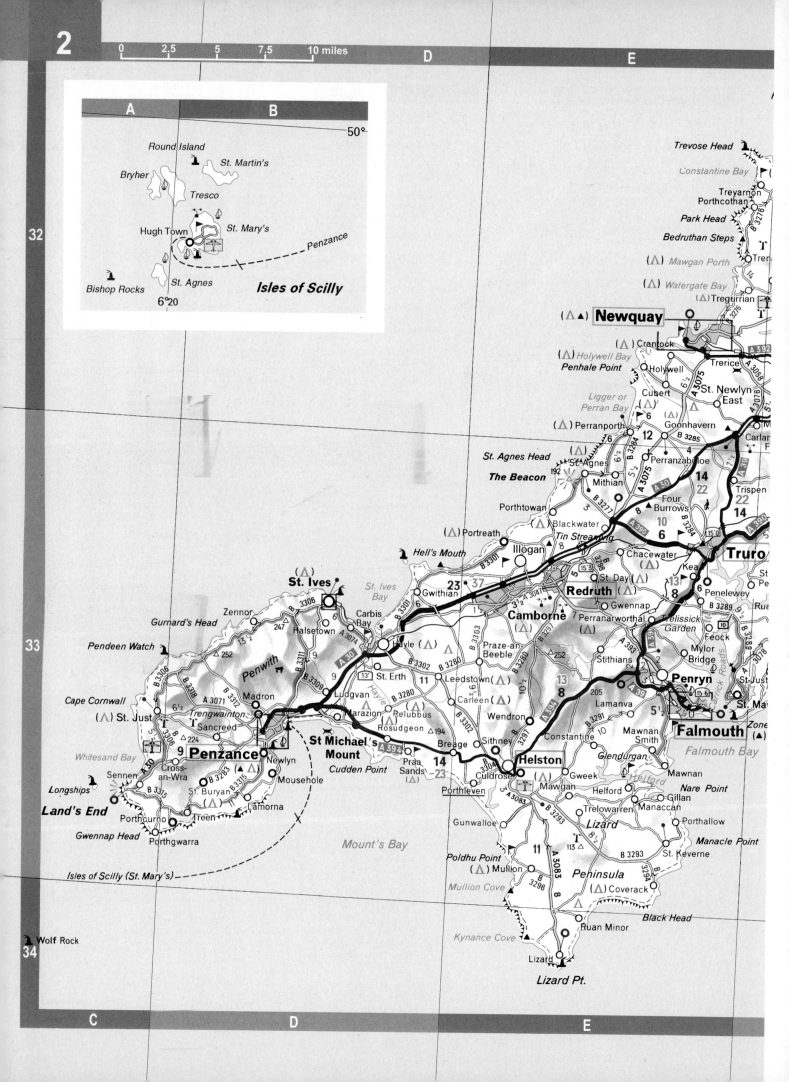

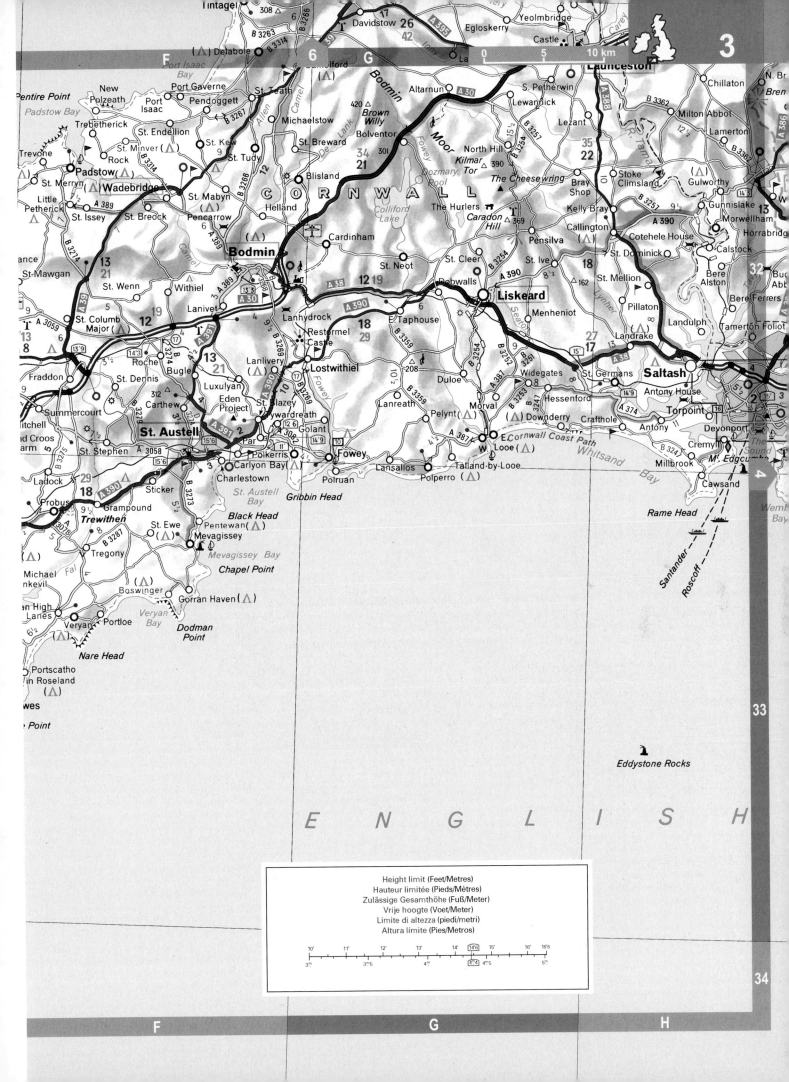

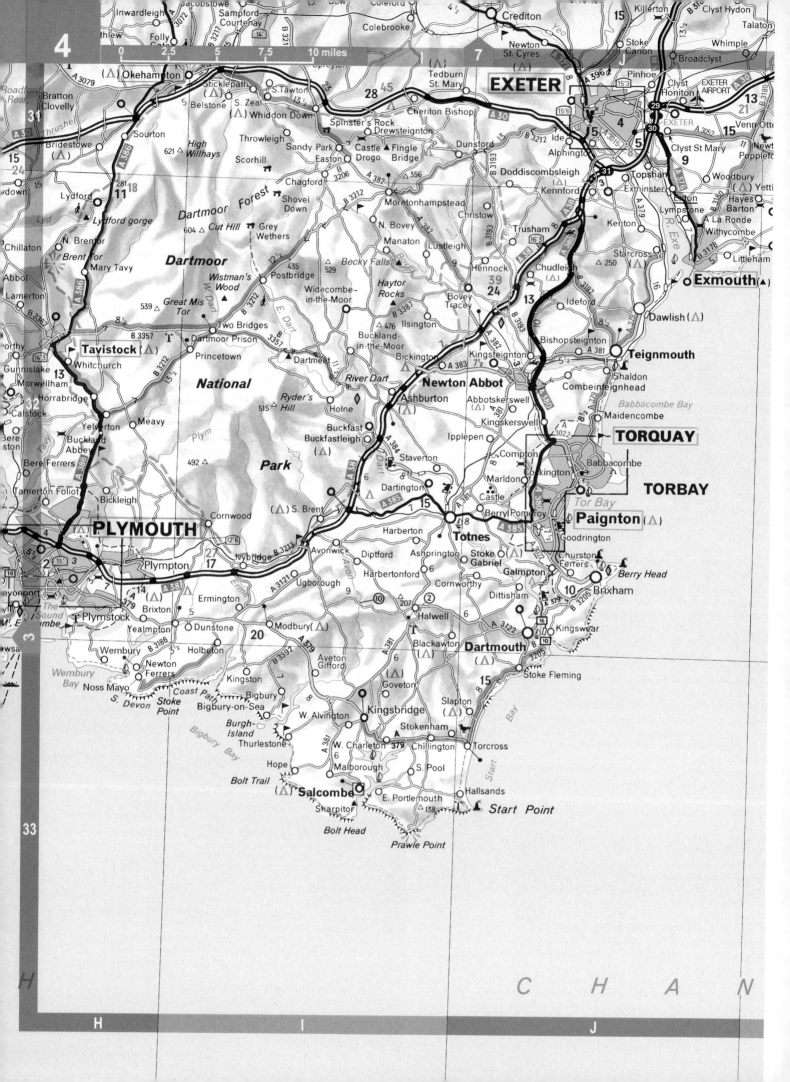

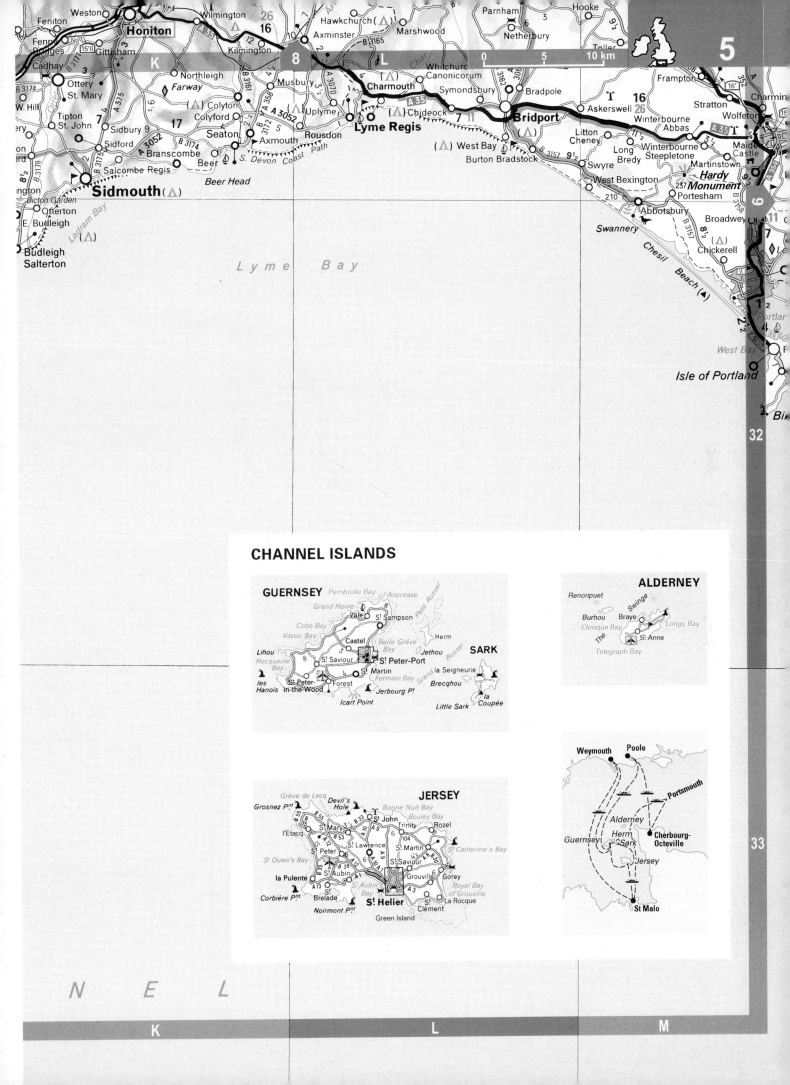

Weston · Wilmington · 26 · Parnham · Hooke
Feniton · Honiton · 16 · Hawkchurch (△) · Netherbury · Toller
Fenny · Gittisham · Axminster · Whitchurch · Frampton
Bridges · Kilmington · Char · Canonicorum · Charmin
Cadhay · Northleigh · Musbury · Charmouth · Symondsbury · Bradpole · 16
W. Hill · Ottery · Farway · Colyton · Chideock · Bridport · Askerswell · 26 · Stratton · Wolfeton
St. Mary · Colyford · Uplyme · Lyme Regis · Winterbourne · Maide
Tipton · Sidbury · Seaton · Rousdon · Litton · Abbas · Castle
St. John · Sidford · Axmouth · West Bay · Cheney · Winterbourne · Martinstown
Salcombe Regis · Branscombe · S. Devon Coast Path · Burton Bradstock · Long · Steepletone · Hardy
Beer · Swyre · Bredy · West Bexington · Monument
Sidmouth (△) · Beer Head · 210 · 257 · Portesham · Broadwey
Bicton Garden · Abbotsbury · Swannery · Chickerell
Otterton · Ladram Bay
E. Budleigh
Budleigh · (△)
Salterton

Lyme Bay

Chesil Beach (△) · West Bay · Isle of Portland · Bi

CHANNEL ISLANDS

GUERNSEY · Pembroke Bay · l'Ancresse
Grand Havre · Vale · Sampson
Cobo Bay · St. Sampson · Herm
Vazon Bay · Castel · Belle Grève · Bay · Jethou · **SARK**
Lihou · St. Saviour · St. Peter-Port · la Seigneurie
Rocquaine · St. Martin · Fermain Bay · Brecqhou
Bay · St. Peter- · Forest · Jerbourg Pt. · la Coupée
les · in-the-Wood · Icart Point · Little Sark
Hanois

ALDERNEY
Renonpuet · Swinge
Burhou · Braye · Longy Bay
Clonque Bay · The · St. Anne
Telegraph Bay

JERSEY
Grève de Lecq · Devil's · Bonne Nuit Bay
Grosnez Pnt · Hole · Bouley Bay
l'Etacq · St. Mary's · St. John · Rozel
· · Trinity
St. Peter · St. Lawrence · St. Martin · St. Catherine's Bay
St. Ouen's Bay · St. Saviour
la Pulente · St. Aubin · Grouville · Gorey
Corbière Pnt · St. · Aubin's · La Rocque · Royal Bay
Brelade · Bay · of Grouville
Noirmont Pnt · **St. Helier** · St. Clément
Green Island

Weymouth · Poole
Portsmouth
Alderney
Guernsey · Herm · Cherbourg-
· Sark · Octeville
Jersey
St Malo

K · L · M

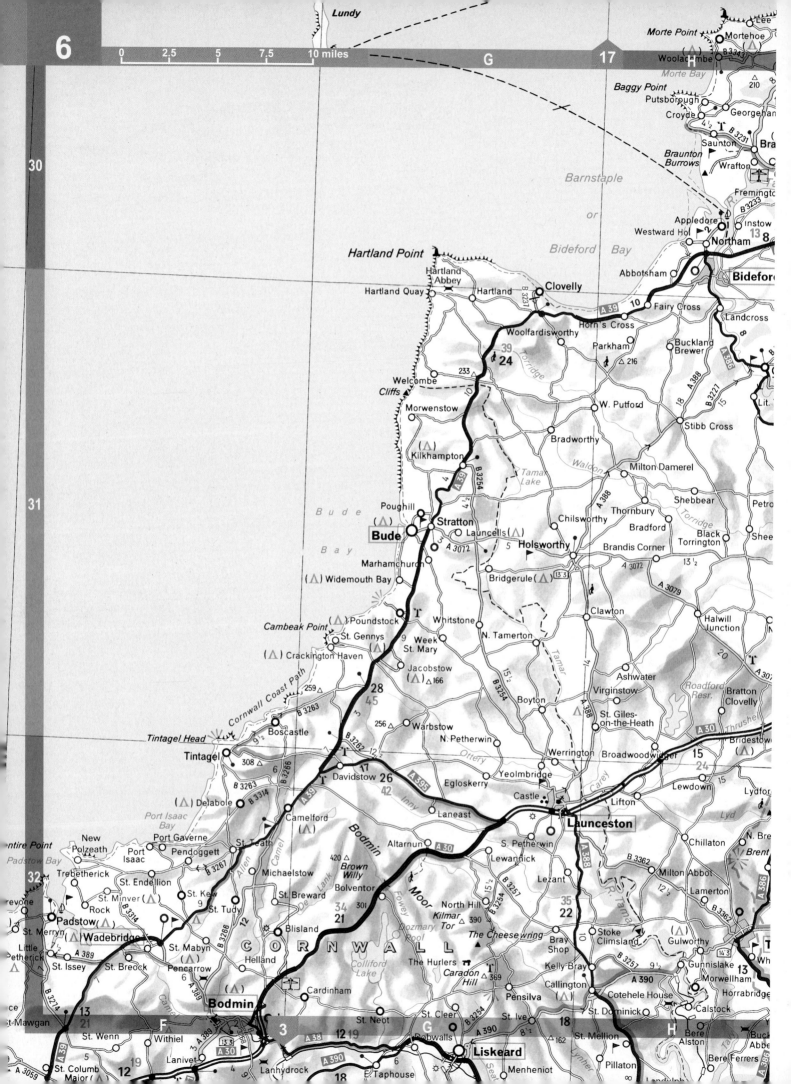

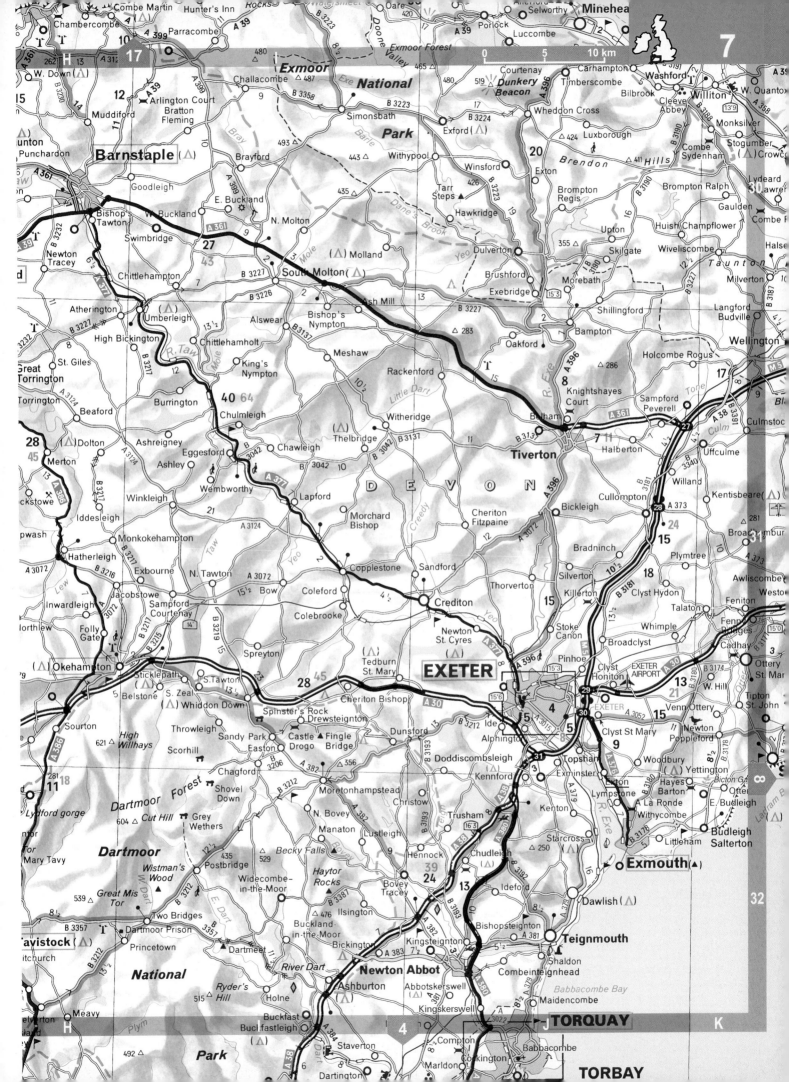

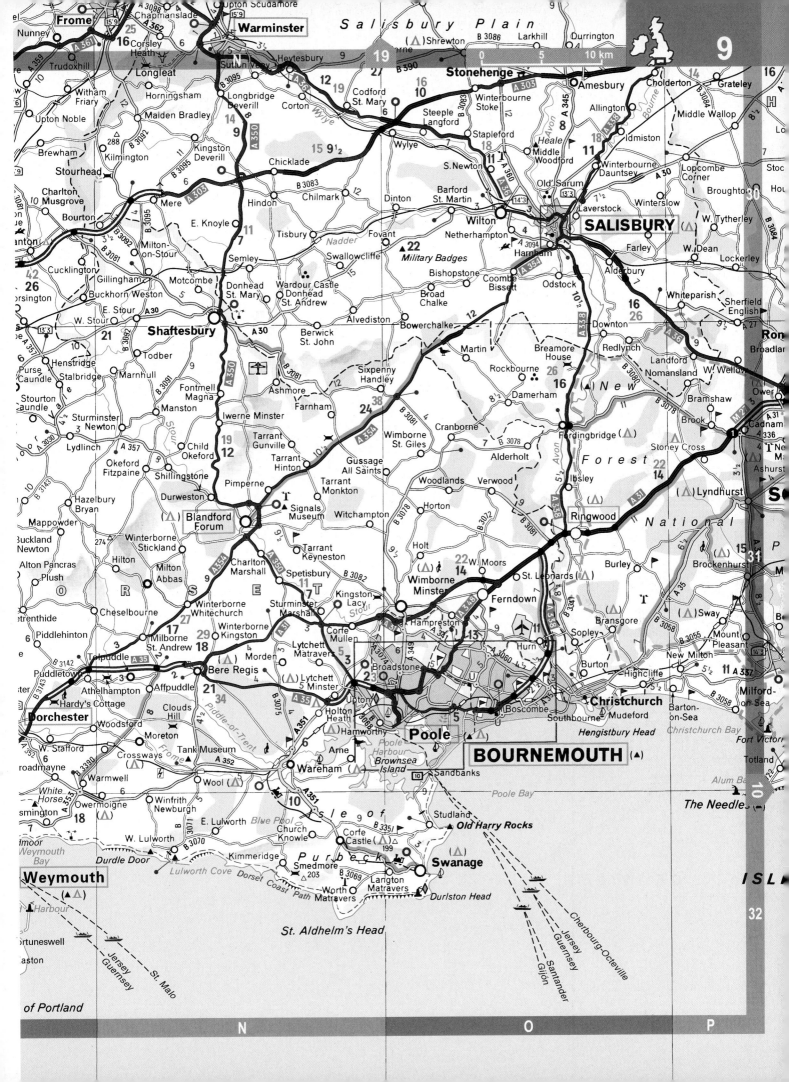

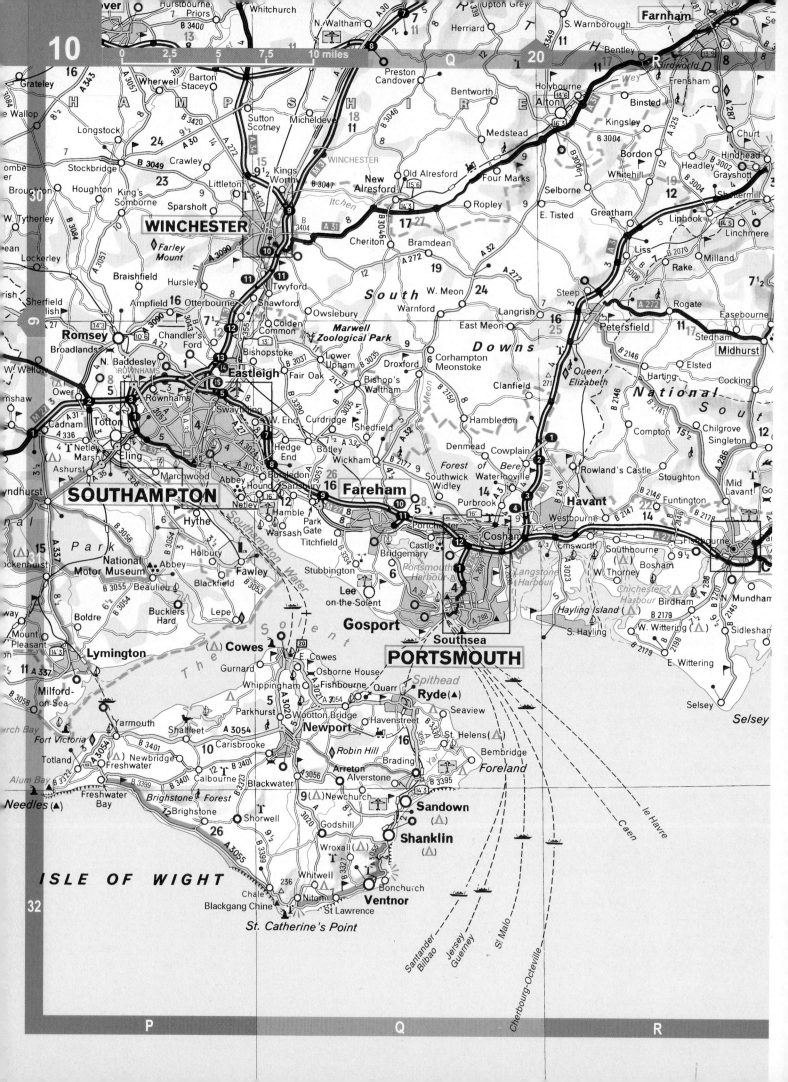

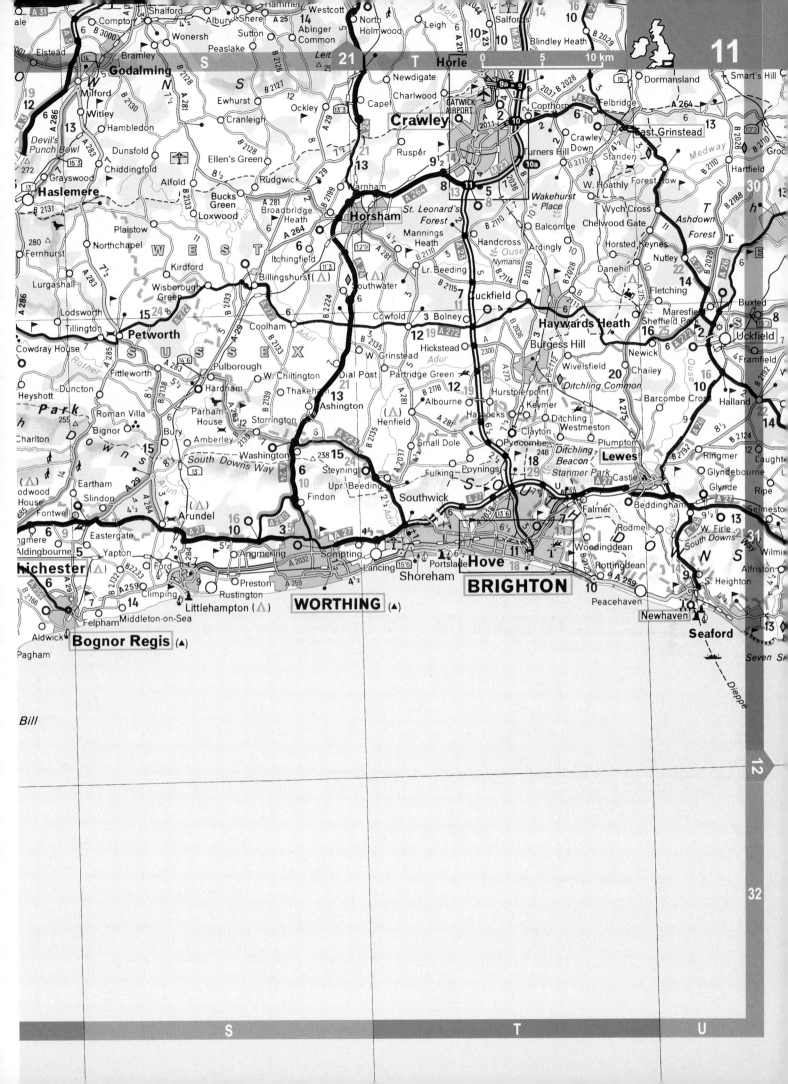

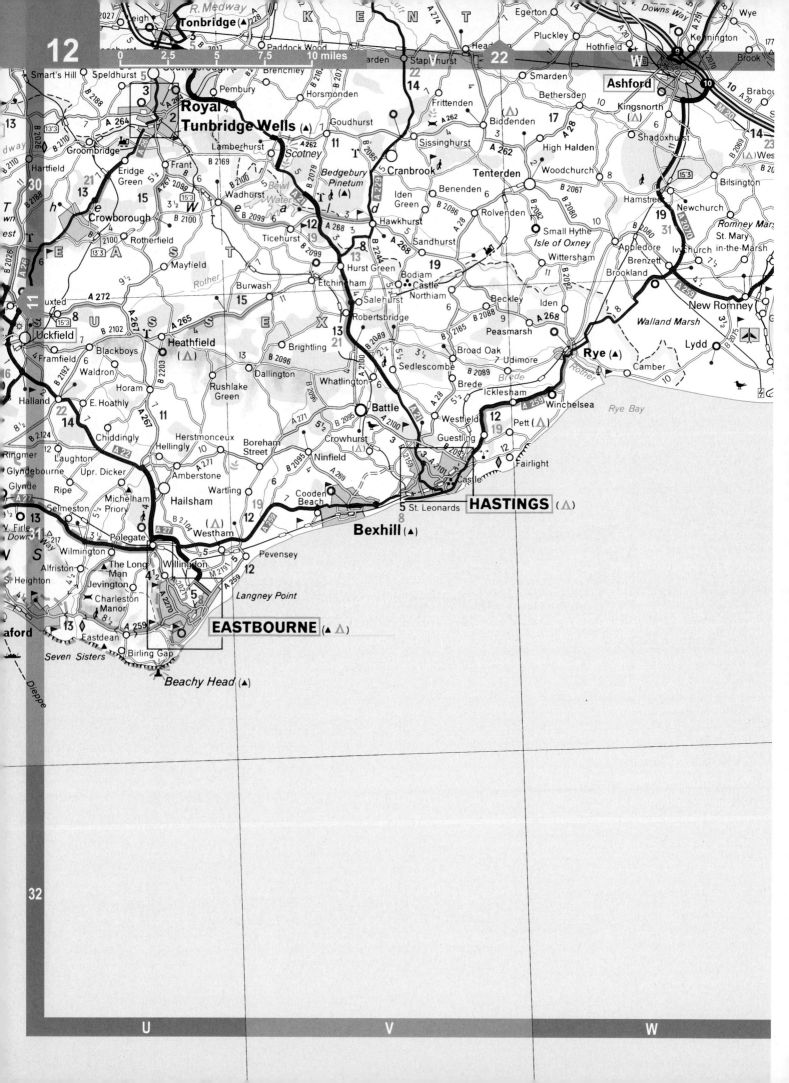

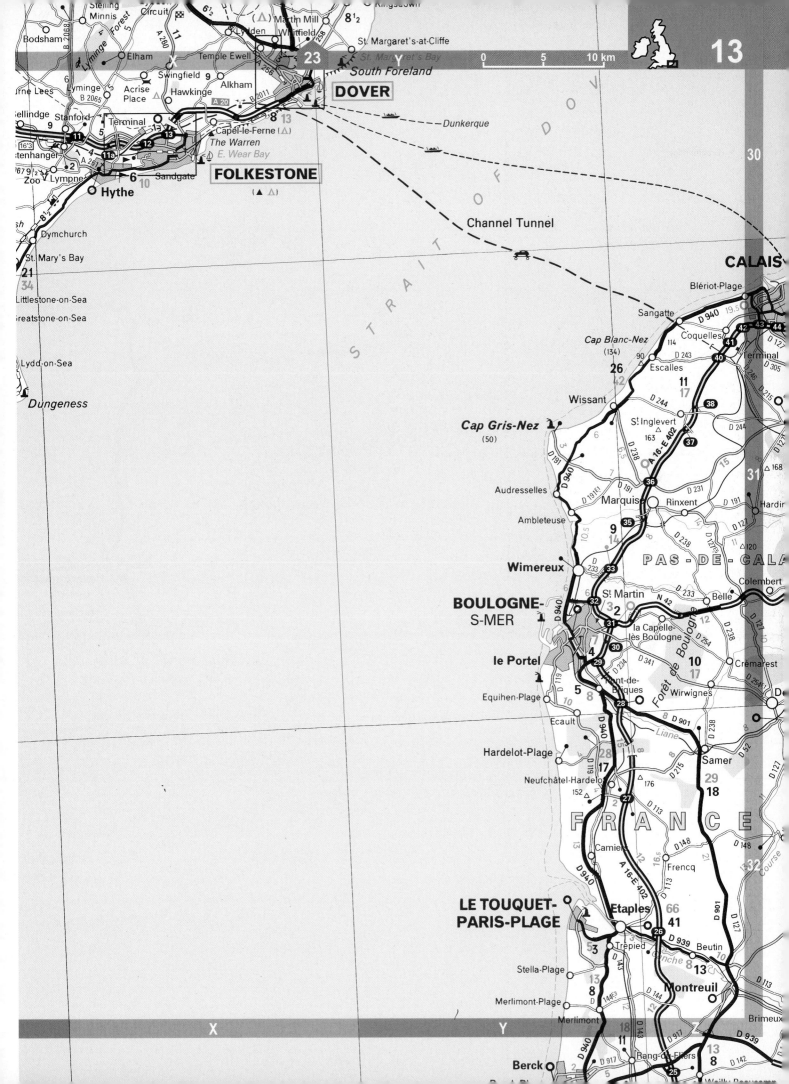

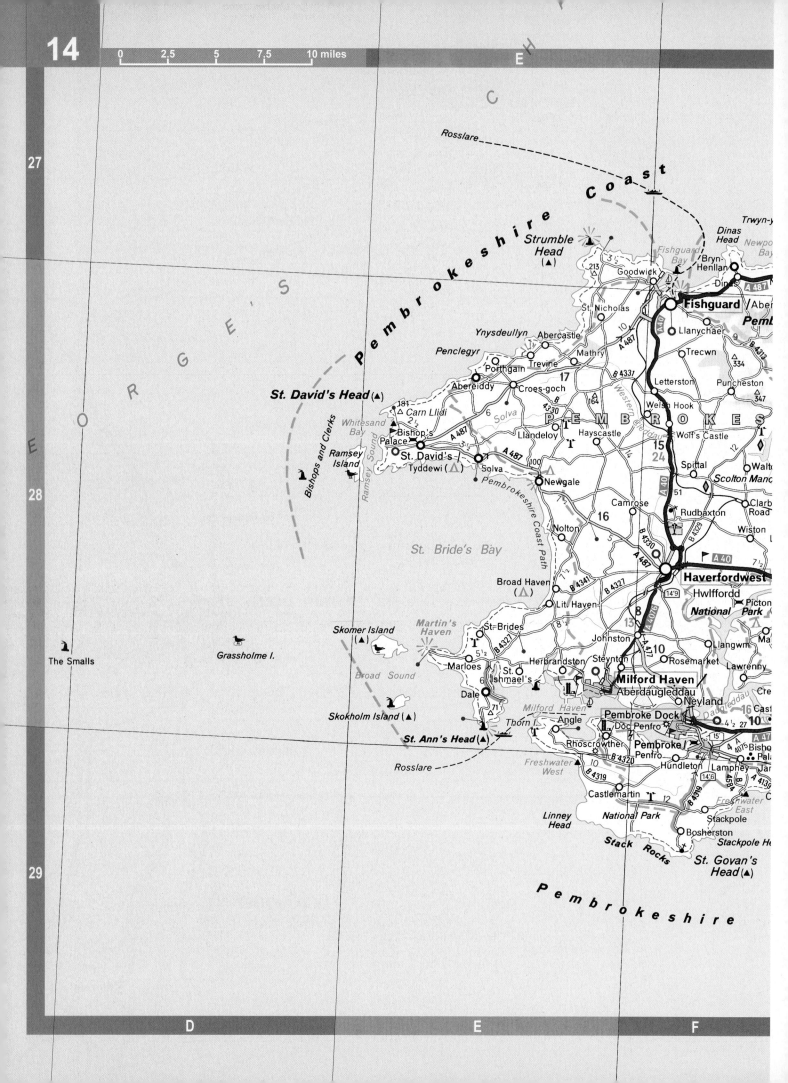

0   2.5   5   7.5   10 miles

Rosslare

Pembrokeshire Coast

Strumble
Head
(▲)

213   3½
Goodwick

*Fishguard
Bay*   Dinas
Head   *Trwyn-y*

*Newpo
Bay*

Bryn
Henllan

Dinas   A 487

St. Nicholas   **Fishguard** /Aber

Pem

10   Llanychaer

Ynysdeullyn   Abercastle   Mathry

Penclegyr   Trevine   A 487   Trecwn   334

Porthgain   17   Letterston   Puncheston

St. David's Head (▲)   Abereiddy   Croes-goch   B 4331   Welsh Hook   347

181   B   164   *Western Cleddau*

△ Carn Llidi   6   *Solva*   **P E M B R O K E S**   Wolf's Castle   12

2½   Bishops and Clerks   *Whitesand
Bay*   Bishop's   A 487   Llandeloy   Hayscastle   **15
24**   Spital   Walt

Palace   3½   Scolton Mano

St. David's /   A 487   100   51   Clarb
Road

*Ramsey
Island*   Tyddewi (△)   Solva   △   Camrose   Rudbaxton   Wiston

*Ramsey
Sound*   Newgale   **16**   5   Wiston

28   7½

St. Bride's Bay   A 40   7½

The Smalls   *Grassholme I.*   Broad Haven
(△)   B 4341   B 4327   **Haverfordwest**
Hwlffordd

14'9   Picton

Lit. Haven   8   8½   **National Park**

Skomer Island
(▲)   *Martin's
Haven*   St-Brides   Johnston   A 477   **8
13**   10   Llangwm   Ma

St. Ishmael's   B 4327   Steynton   Rosemarket   Lawrenny

Broad   Sound   Marloes   5½   Herbrandston   **Milford Haven**
Aberdaugleddau   Neyland

6   St.   **Pembroke Dock**   *Daugleddau*   **16** Cast

Skokholm Island (▲)   Dale   71   *Milford Haven*   Angle   Dôc Penfro   4½ 27 **10**

Thorn I.   Rhoscrowther   15'   4075 Bisho

St. Ann's Head (▲)   **Pembroke**   Pala
Penfro   Hundleton   Lamphey   Jar

Rosslare   *Freshwater
West*   B 4320   14'6   A 458   A 413

Freshwater
East

Castlemartin   12   B 4319   B

Linney
Head   **National   Park**   Stackpole

Stack   Rocks   Bosherston   Stackpole H

29   **St. Govan's
Head** (▲)

P e m b r o k e s h i r e

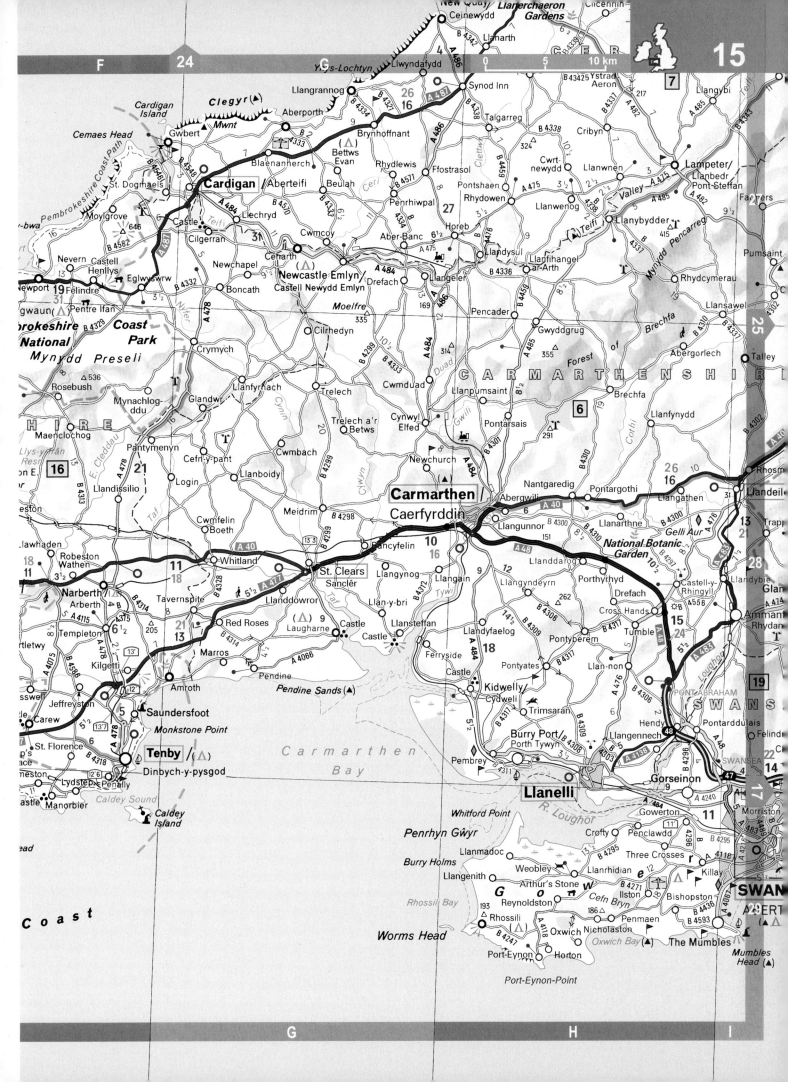

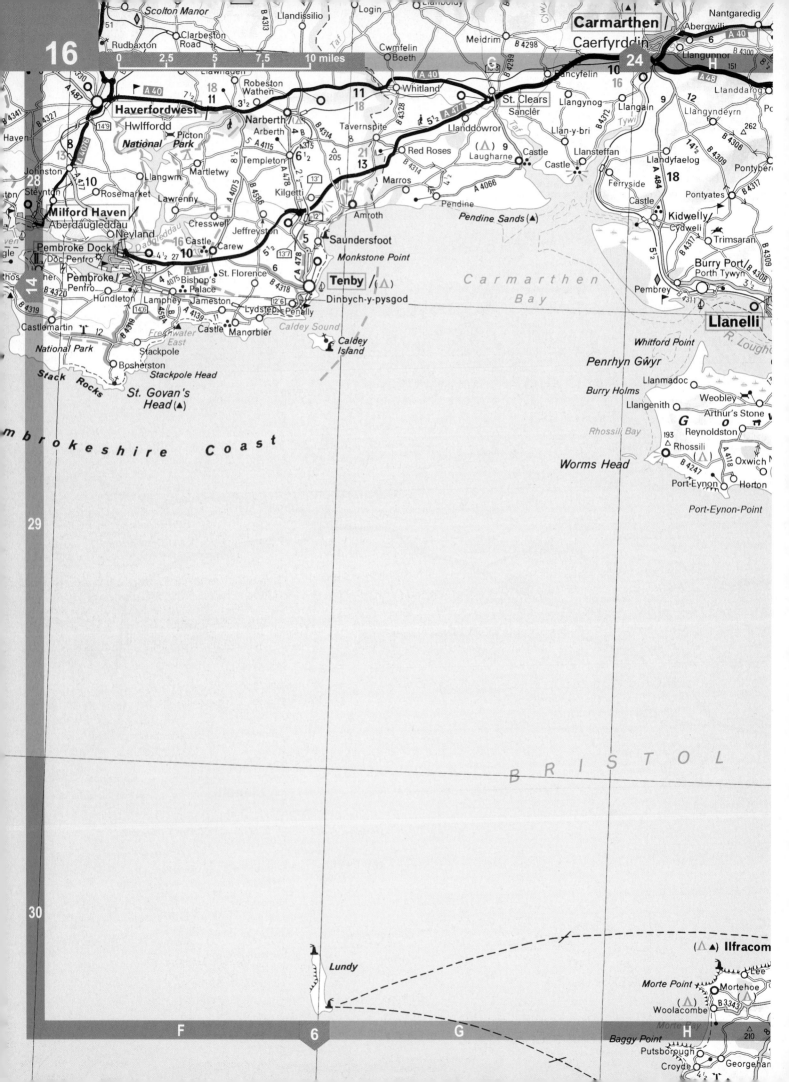

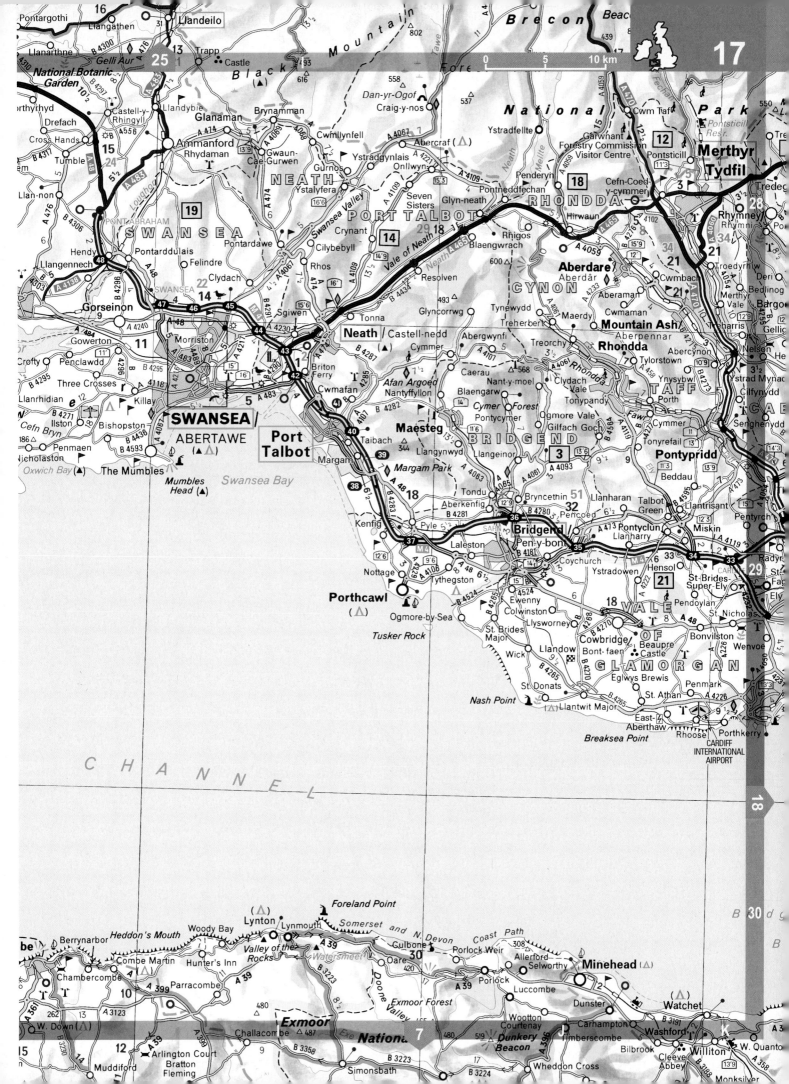

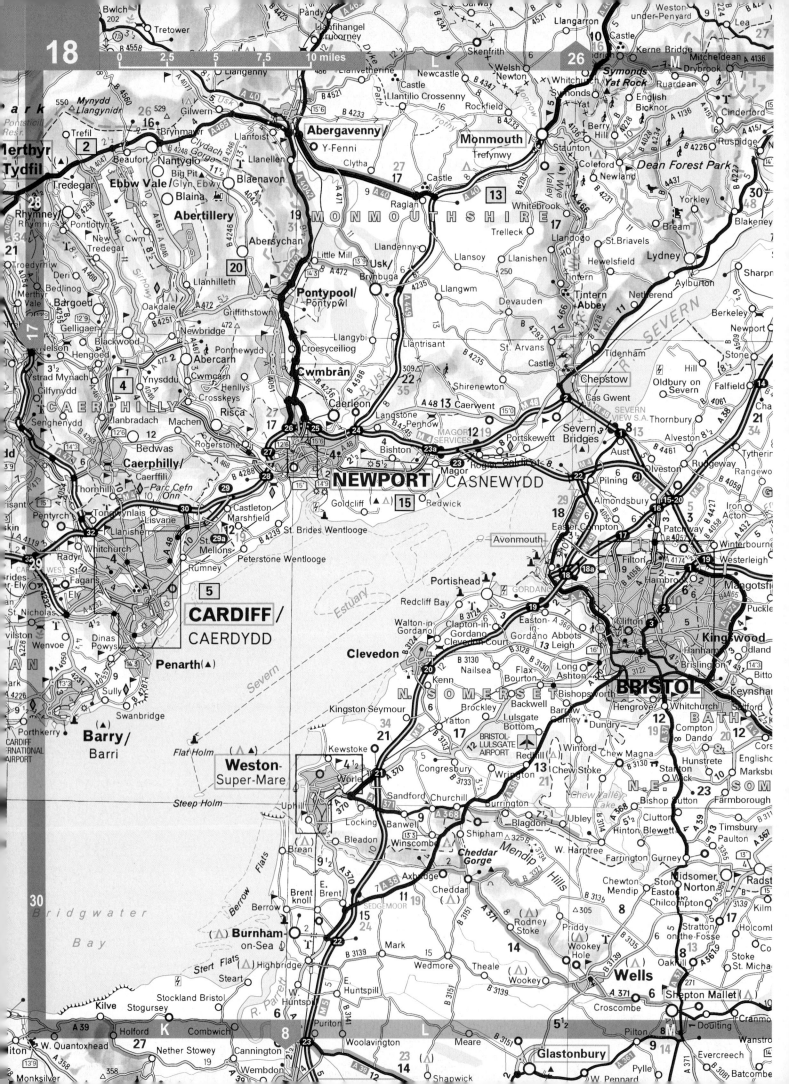

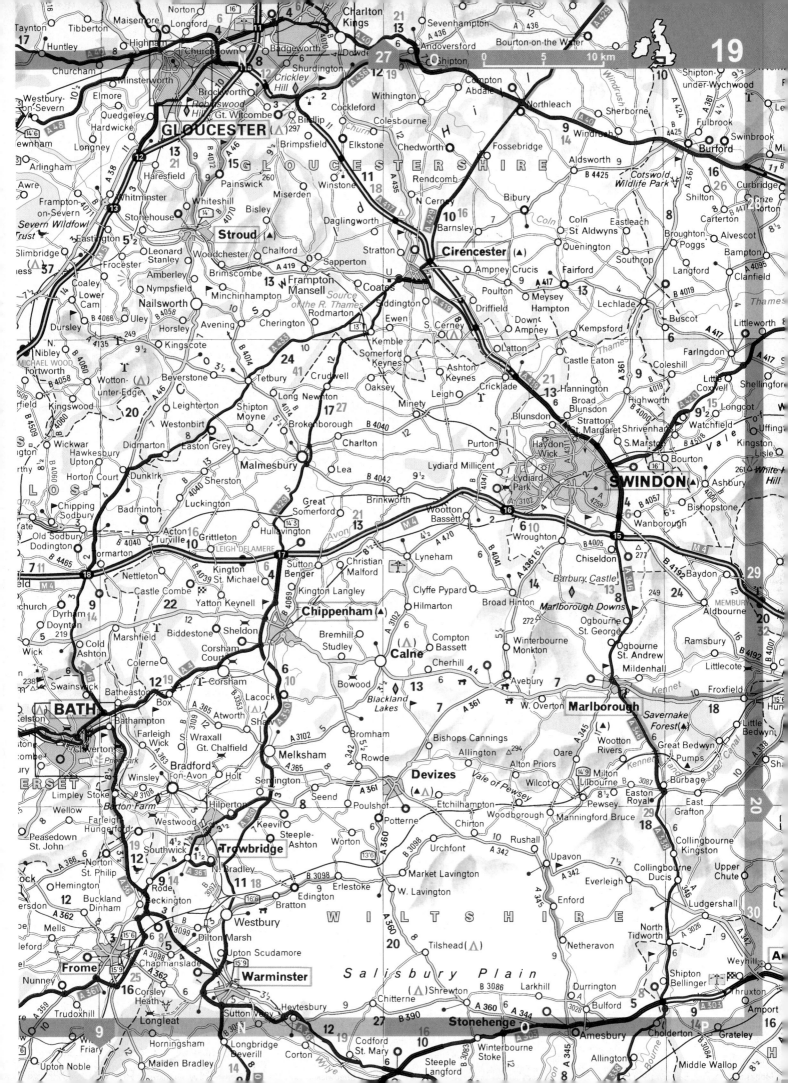

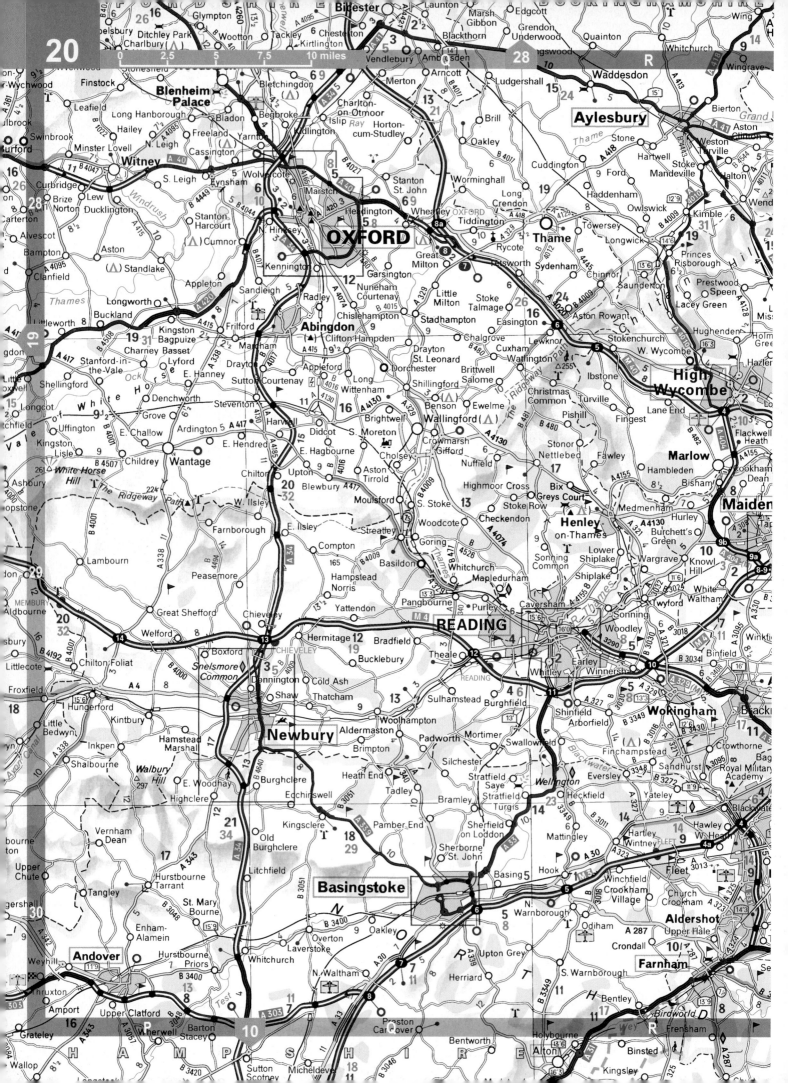

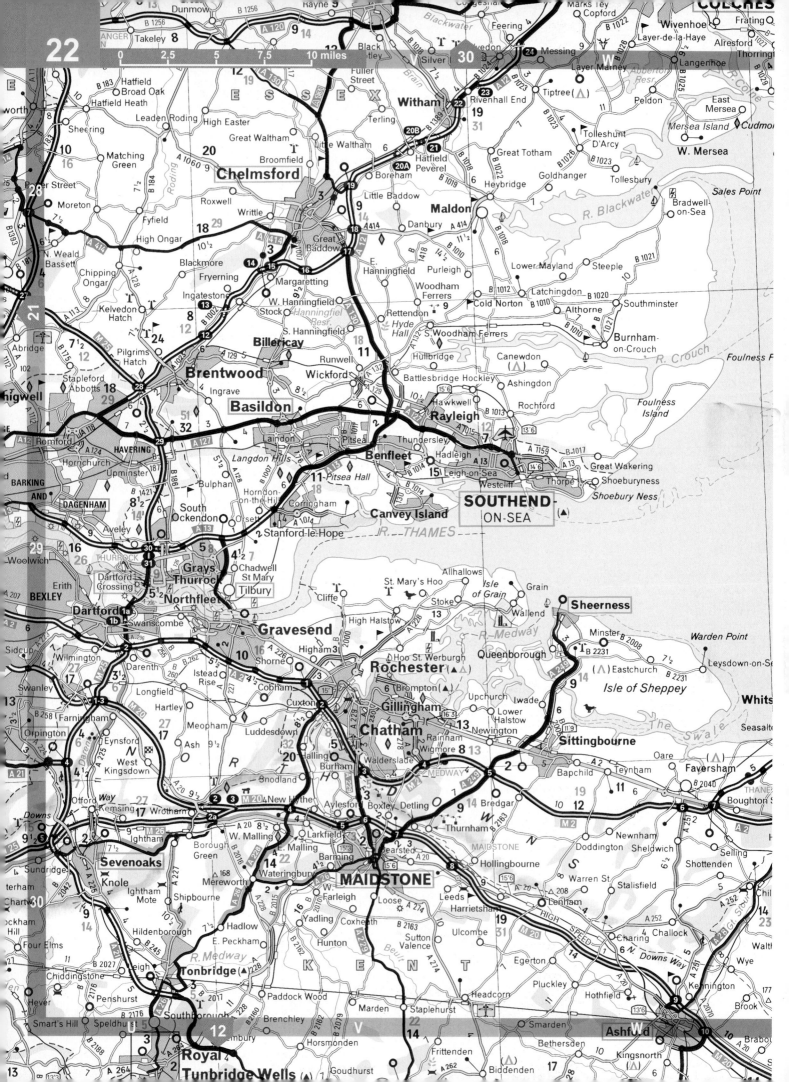

0 5 10 km

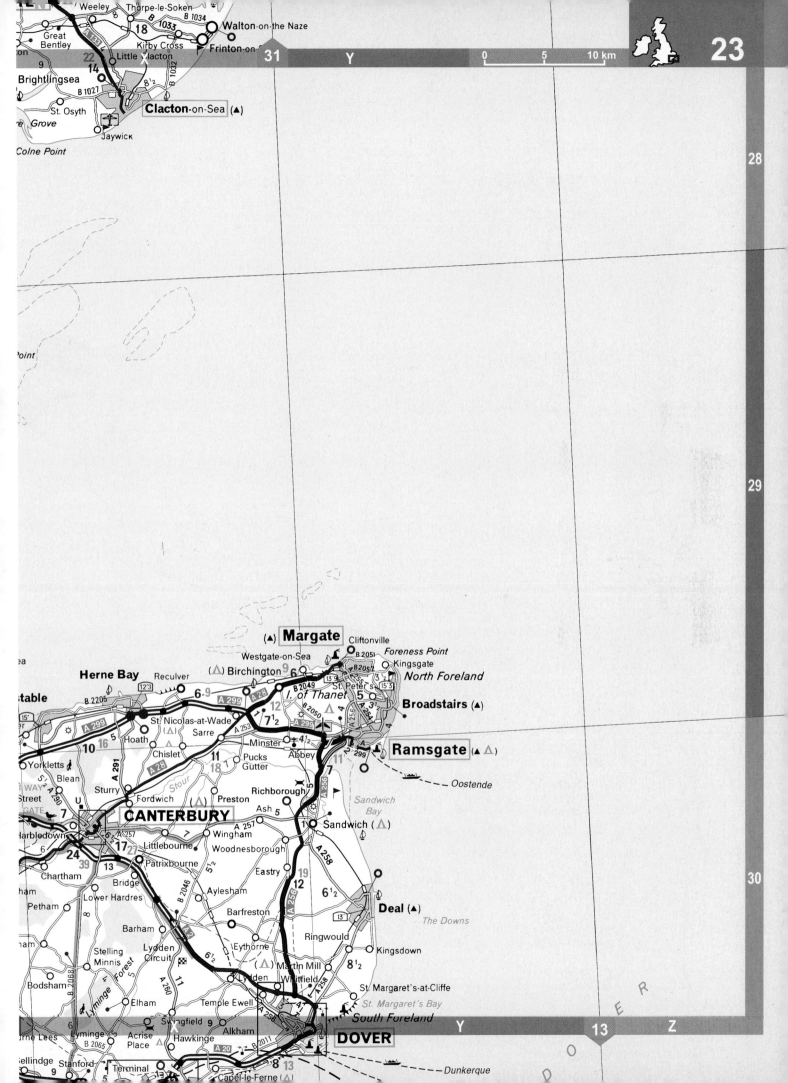

Weeley Thorpe-le-Soken
Great Bentley 18 B 1034
Kirby Cross Walton-on-the Naze
A 133 Little Clacton Frinton-on-Sea 31 Y
22 14
9
Brightlingsea
B 1027 8½
St. Osyth Clacton-on-Sea (▲)
Grove Jaywick
Colne Point

28

Point

29

Margate (▲) Cliftonville
Westgate-on-Sea Foreness Point
Herne Bay Reculver (△) Birchington 9 6 B 2051 Kingsgate
12'3 B 2205 6 9 A 299 A 28 B 2049 North Foreland
stable 15' A 299 St. Nicolas-at-Wade 12 B 2050 5 Broadstairs (▲)
10 16 5 Hoath (△) Sarre 7½ I. of Thanet 4 A 256
Yorkletts Chislet A 28 11 Minster 4½ Ramsgate (▲ △)
5½ A 291 18 Pucks Abbey 11 A 299 Oostende
Blean Gutter 7
Street Sturry Fordwich Preston Richborough 5 Sandwich Bay
GATE 7 (△) Ash 5 1 A 256 Sandwich (△)
Harbledown CANTERBURY Wingham A 258
6 A 257 17 27 Littlebourne Woodnesborough
24 39 13 Patrixbourne Eastry 19
Chartham Bridge 5½ 12 6½ Deal (▲)
Petham Lower Hardres B 2046 Aylesham A 256 13 The Downs
Barfreston Ringwould
8 Barham A 2 Eythorne Kingsdown
Stelling Minnis Lydden 8½
Bodsham Circuit (△) Martin Mill
B 2068 A 260 4½ Lydden Whitfield A 258 St. Margaret's-at-Cliffe
Elham Temple Ewell St. Margaret's Bay
11 Swingfield 9 South Foreland
rne Lees Lyminge Acrise Alkham A 258 Y 13 Z
llindge Stanford Place Hawkinge A 20 B 2011 DOVER
9 B 2065 Terminal 8 13 Dunkerque
Capel-le-Ferne (△)

30

D O V E R

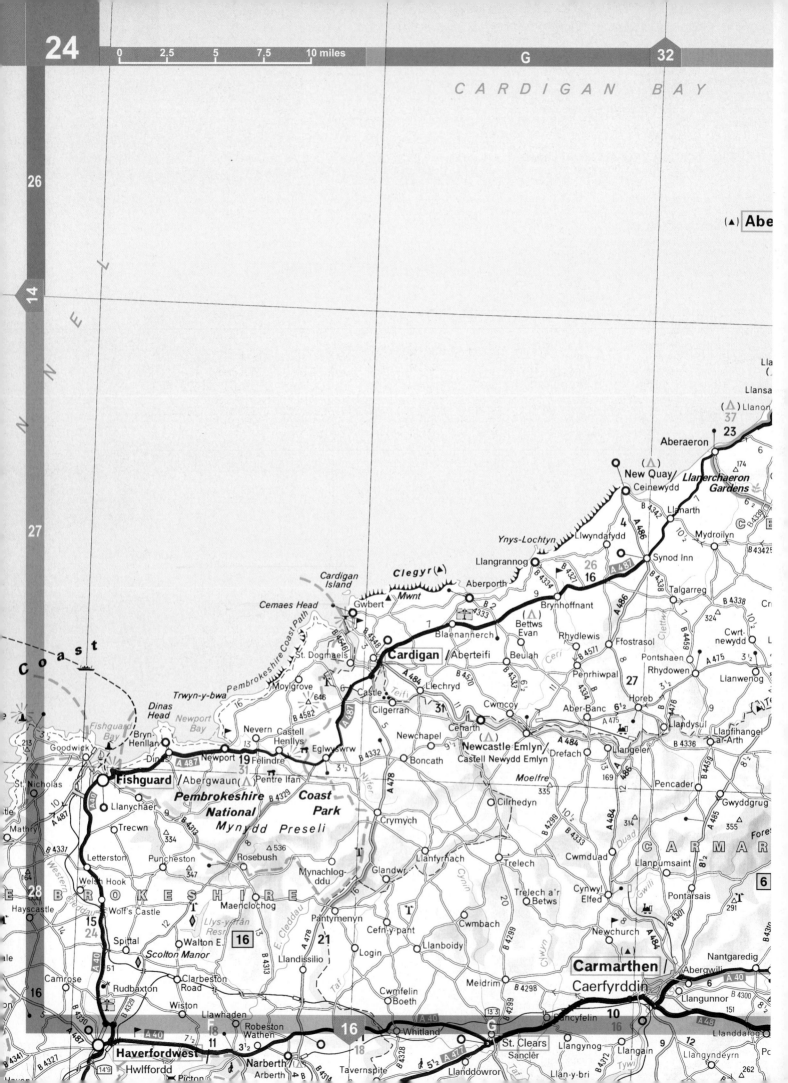

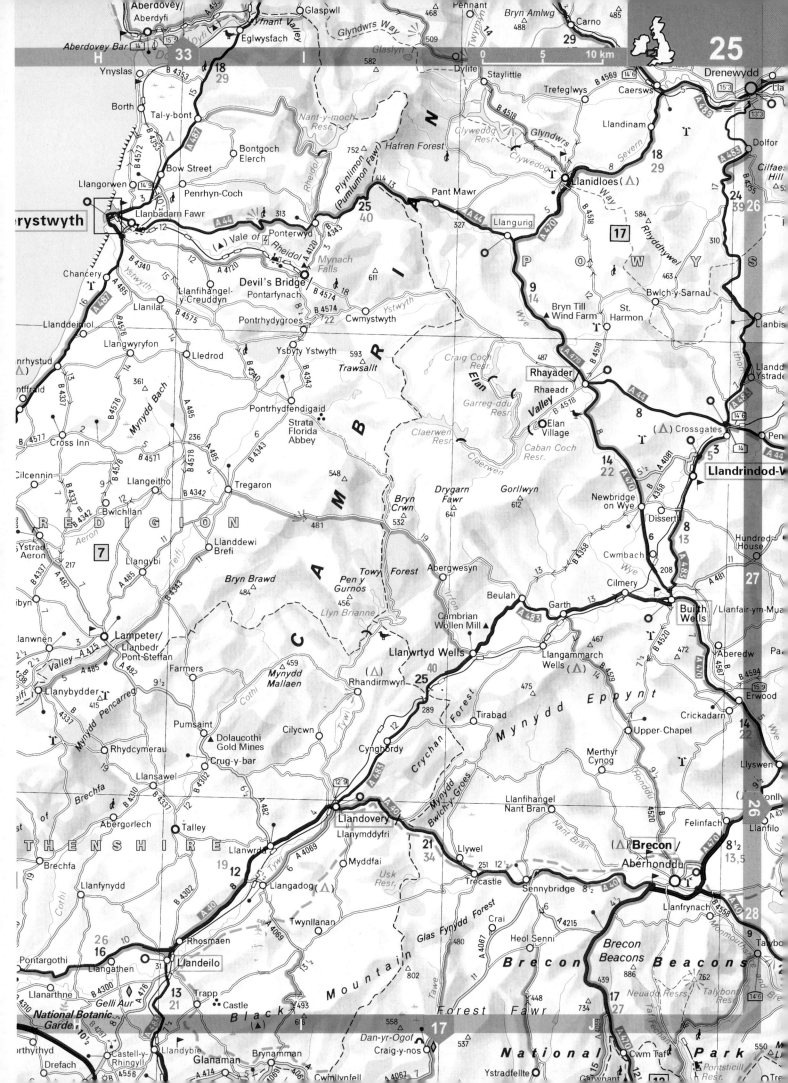

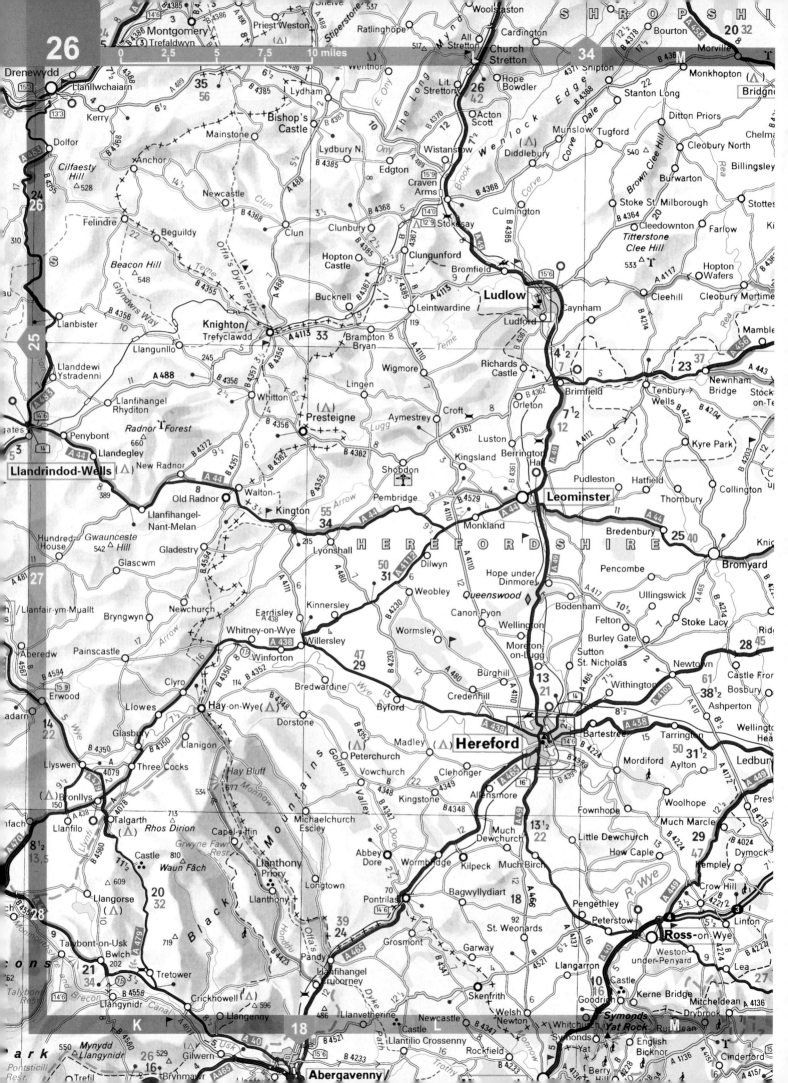

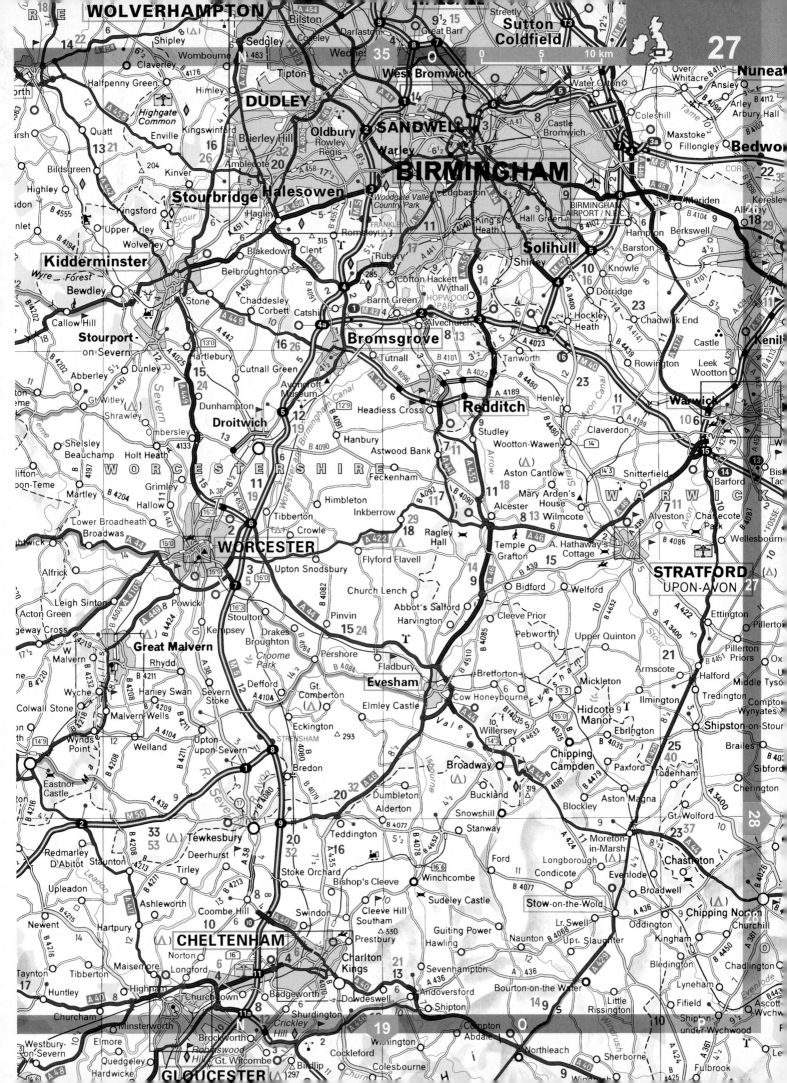

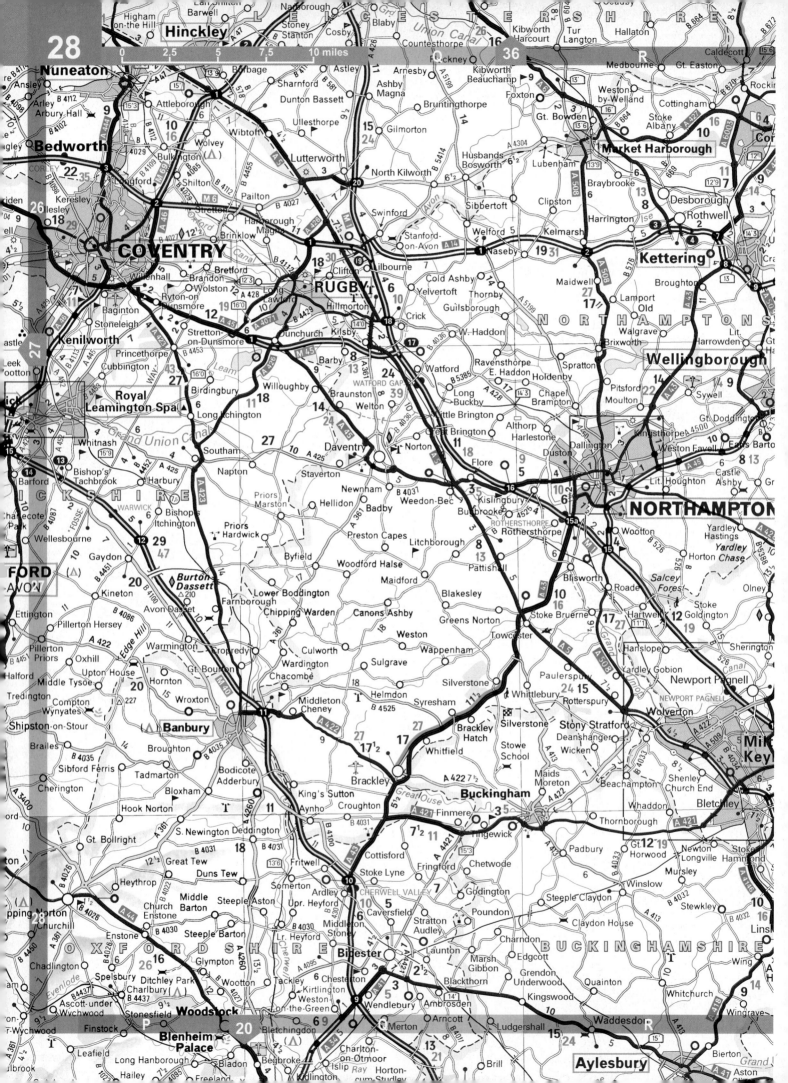

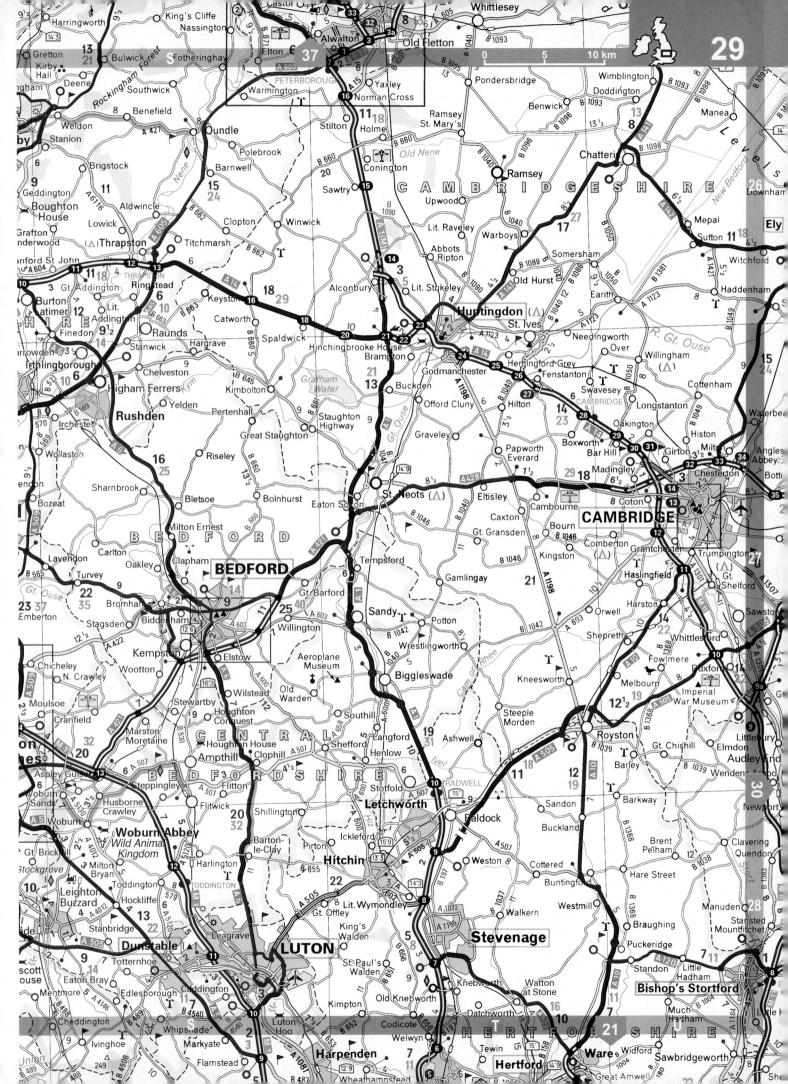

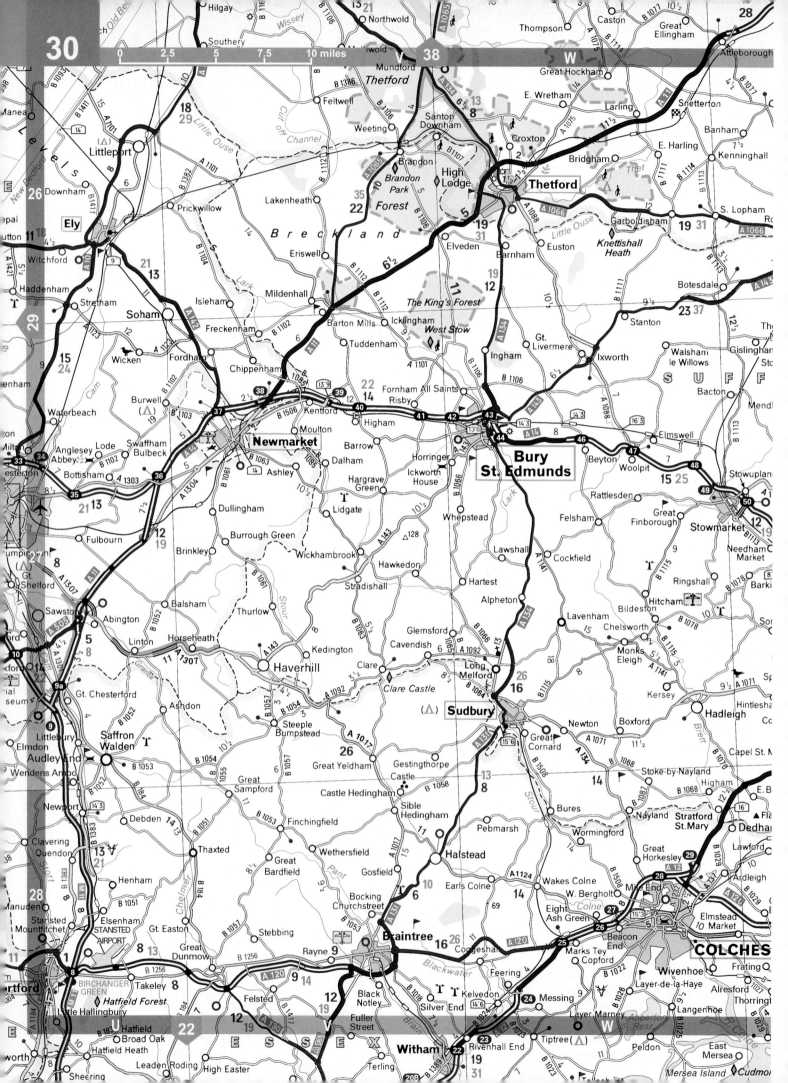

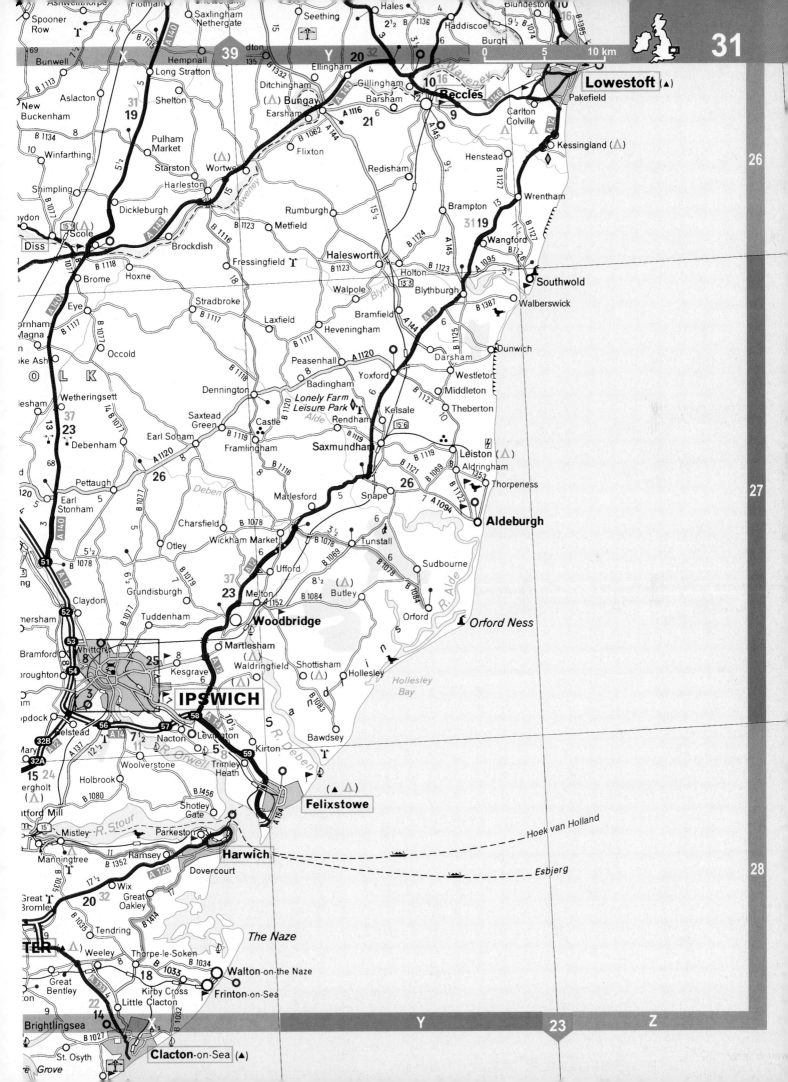

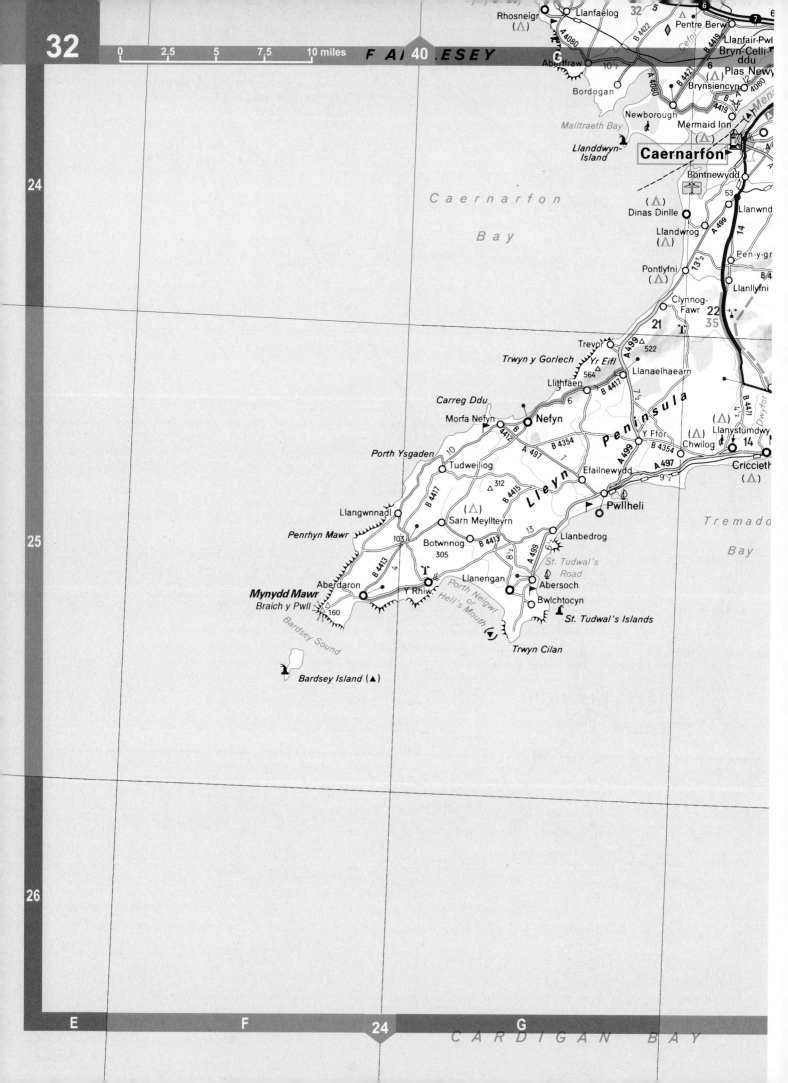

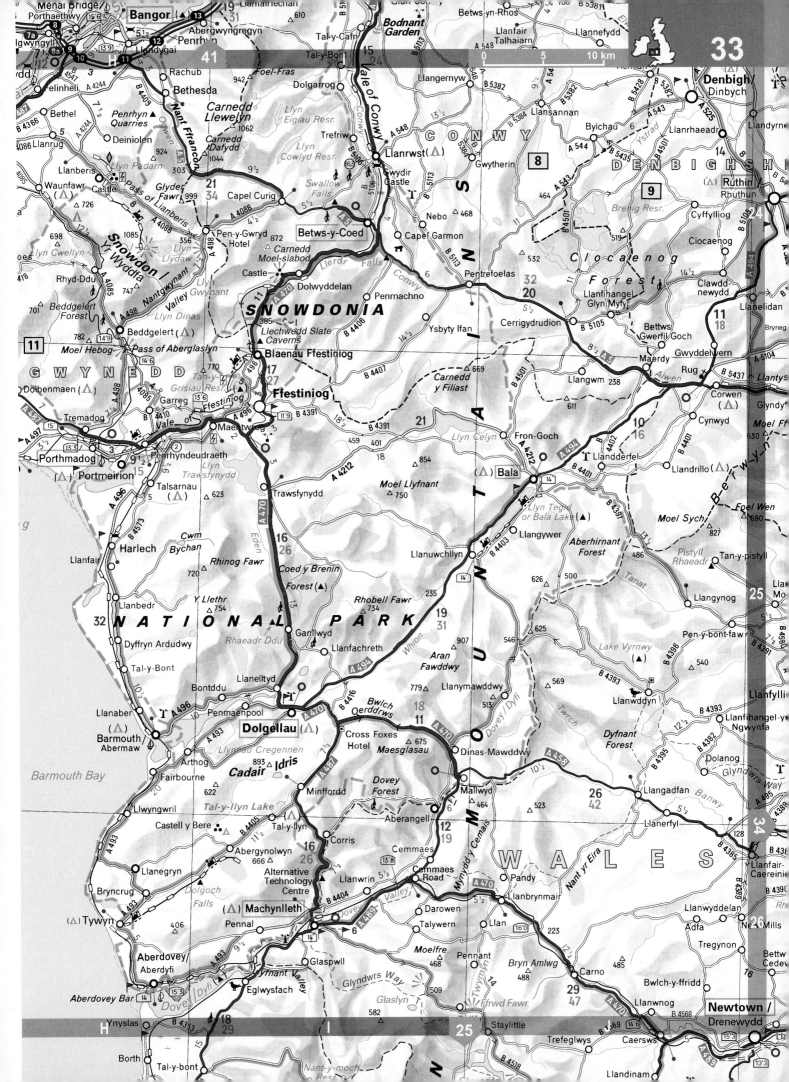

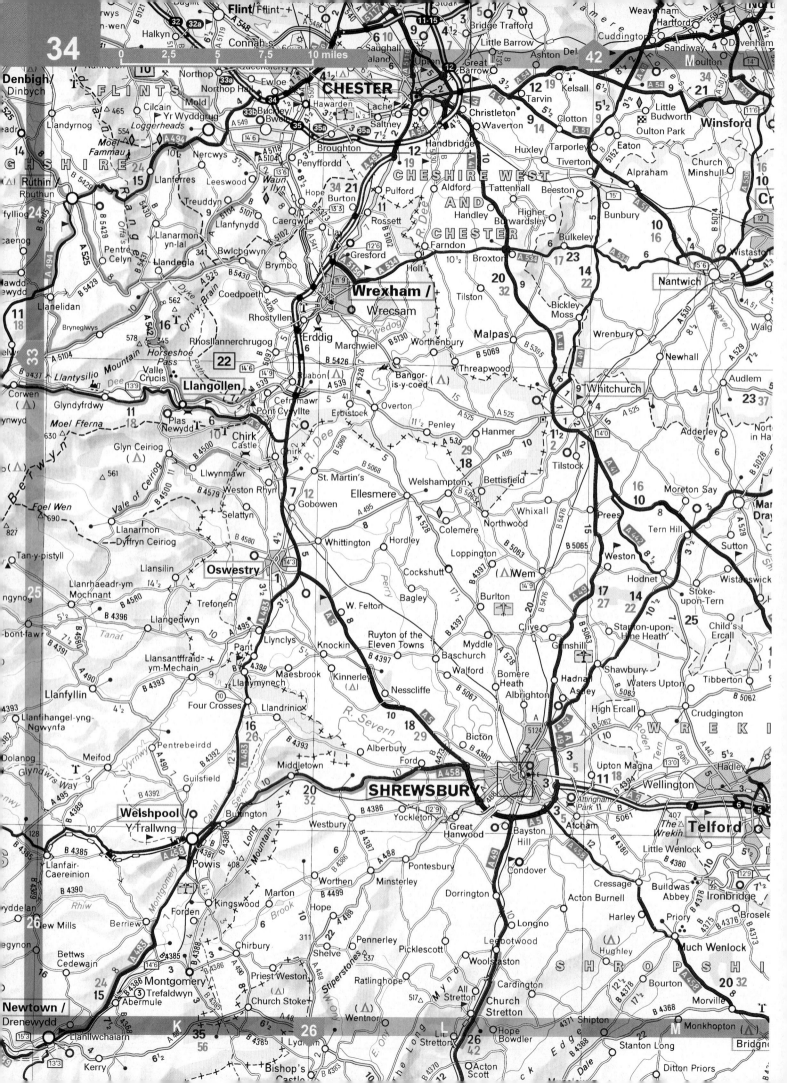

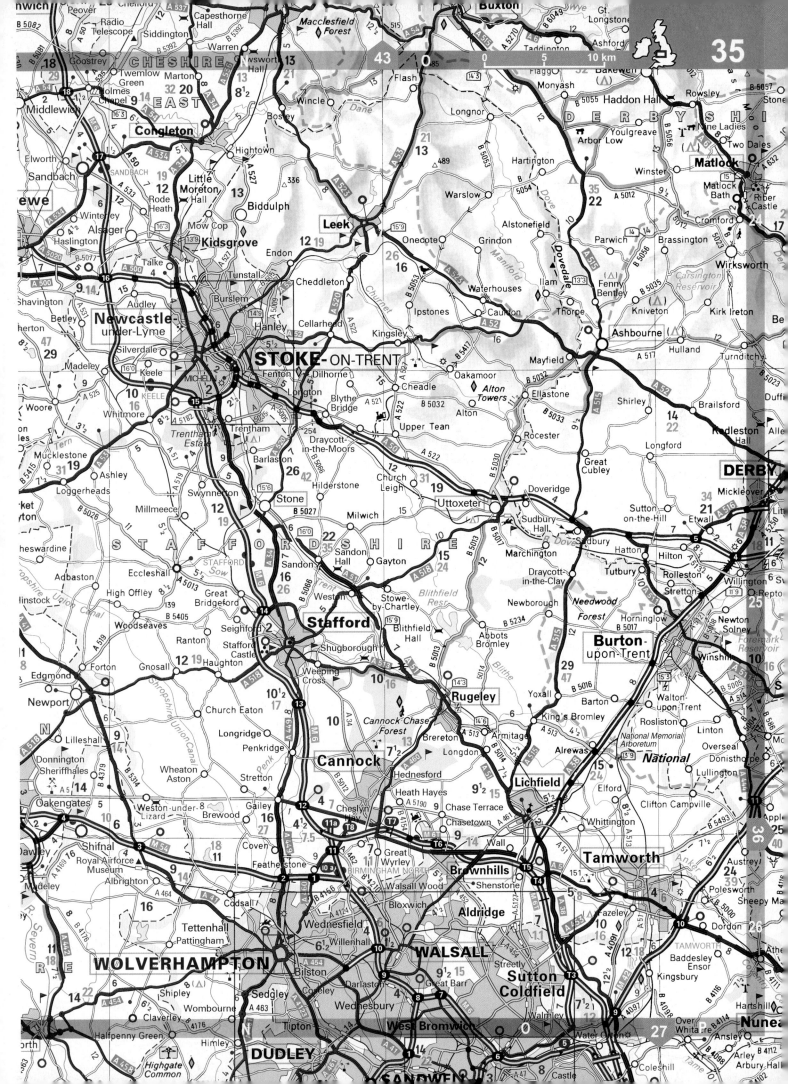

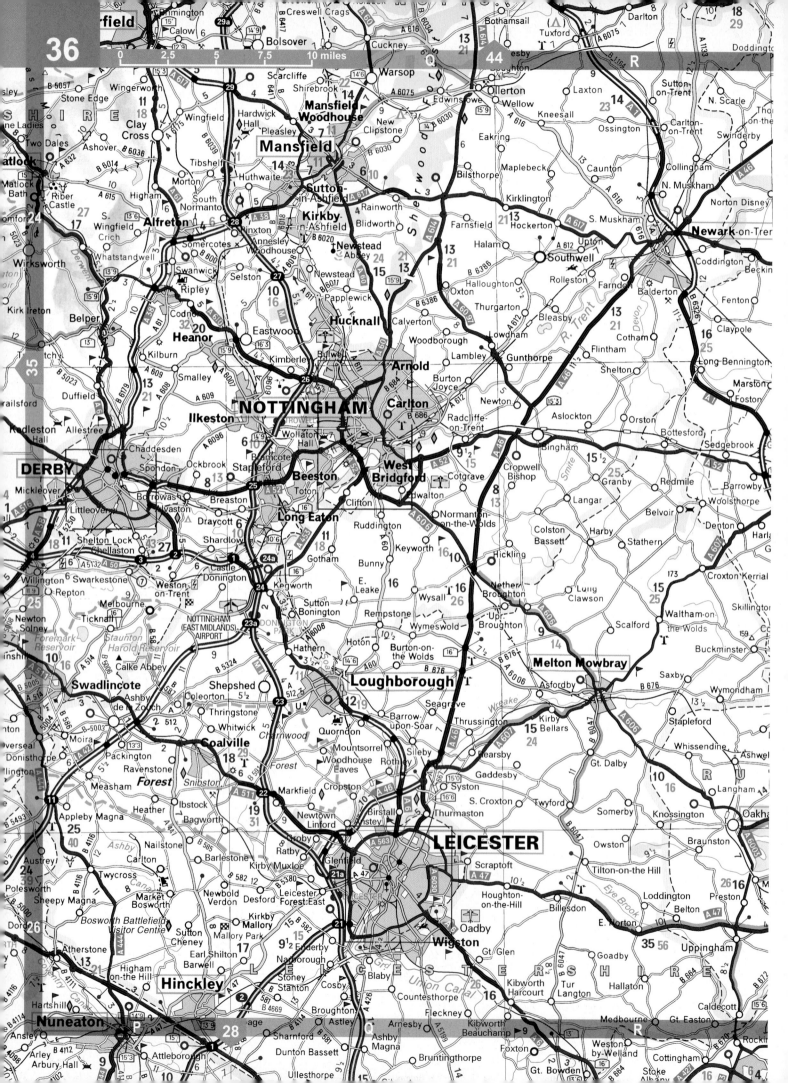

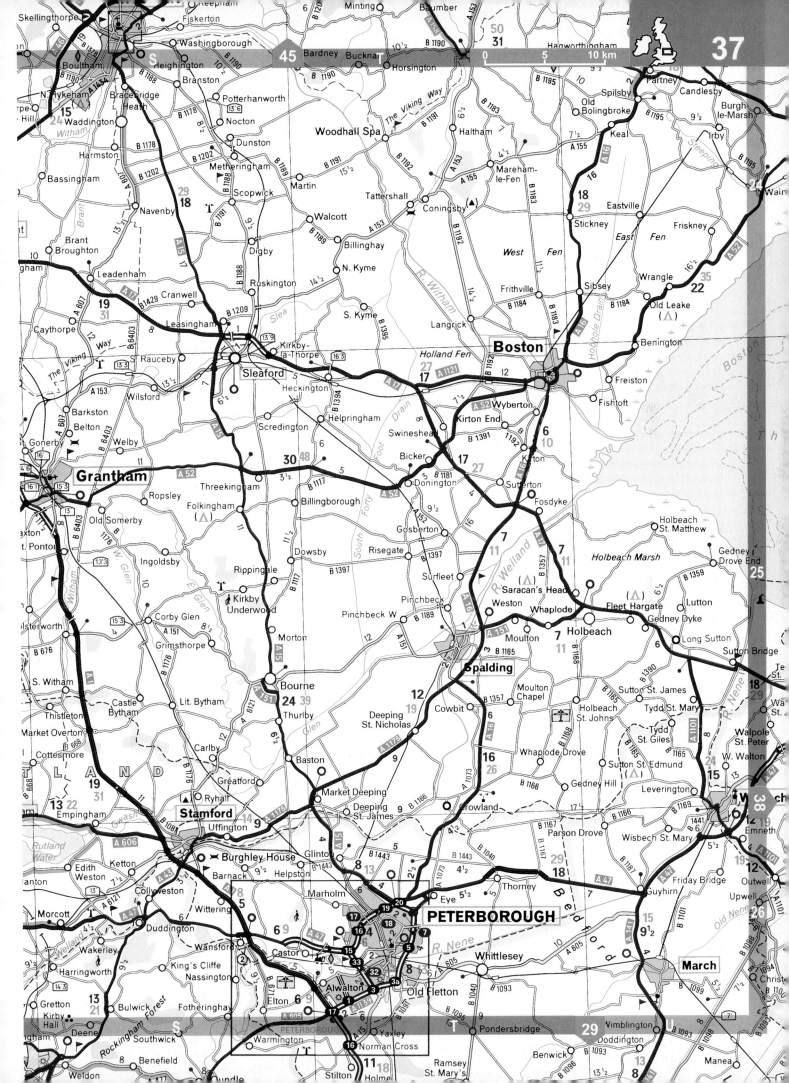

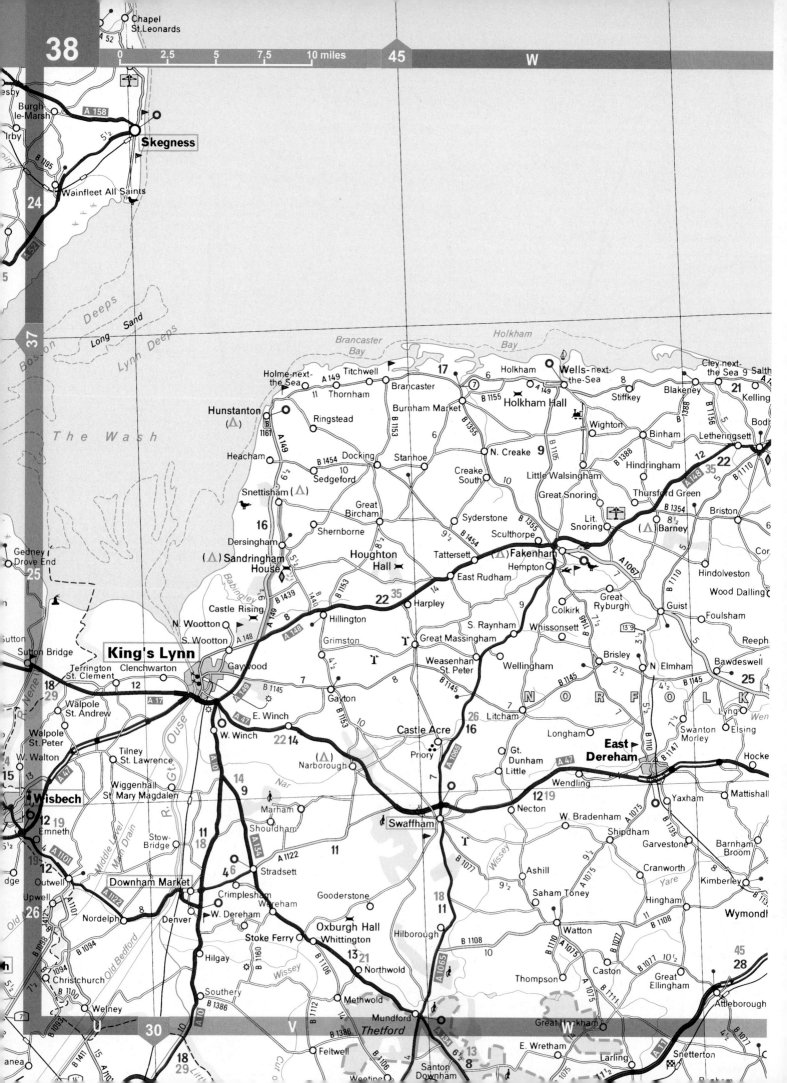

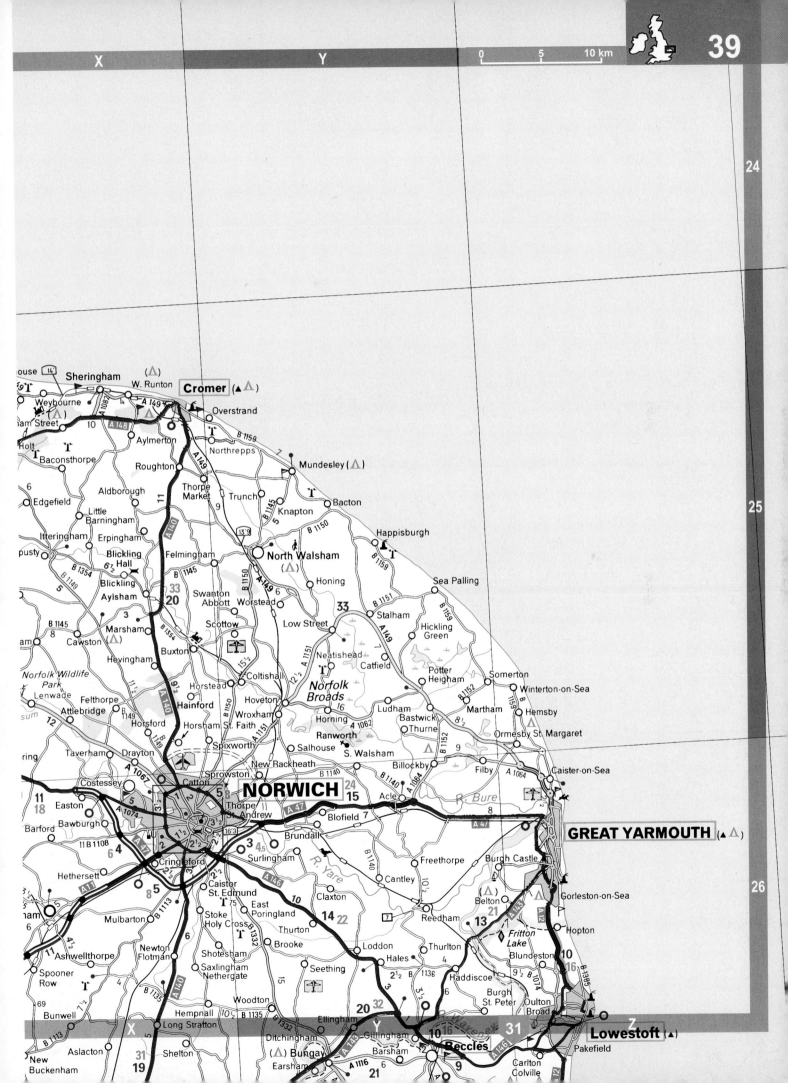

0   2.5   5   7.5   10 miles

G   H

22

The Skerries

Cemlyn Bay

A 5025   Amlwch

Carmel Head   Cemaes   Point Lynas

B 5111

Llanfairynghornwy   Llanfechell   Penysarn

Holyhead Bay   *Church Bay*   128   *Dulas Bay*

Dublin   A 5025   6   *Lligwy Bay*

Dún Laoghaire   Llanfaethlu   Rhosybol   A 5025   12   Moelfre

Llanddeusant   *Llyn Alaw*   B 5111

Llanfwrog   Marian - glas

S. Stack   220   Llanerchymedd   Benllech   B 5108

Holyhead   Caergybi   Llanfachraeth   112   6   Brynteg   B 5110   *Red Wharf Bay*

Holyhead   A N G L E S E Y   Penmon

Mountain   Llanynghenedl   Trefor   Pentraeth   Penmon

Penrhyn Mawr   B 5109   B 5110   Llanddona   B 5109

A 5025   Valley   1   B 5111   Castle

Trearddur Bay   B 4545   Bodedern   B 5112   B 5109   Beauma

Holy Island   Bryngwran   Bodffordd   Talwrn   A 5025   B 5109

Llanfair-   Gwalchmai   *Cefni Rest*   Llangefni   A 545   Beauma

Rhoscolyn   yn-Neubwll   4   5   A 5   20   32   5   A 5114   13'3   6   Porthaethwy   Bangor

Cymyran Bay   9'6   A 55   6   Pentre Berw   Menai Bridge   15'6'3   Bangor

Llanfaelog   A 4422   7   7a   8   9'1   13'9

Rhosneigr   Cefni   Llanfair-Pwllgwyngyll   7a   8a   9   13'9   Llandygai

(△)   A 4080   Pentre Berw   Bryn-Celli   7 1   10   11

ISLE OF ANGLESEY   B 4422   Llanfair   ddu   A 5   12   3   Rac

Aberffraw   10 1/2   B 4421   Plas Newydd   A 5047   B 4409   Be

A 4080   Brynsiencyn   Felinheli   A 4244

Bordogan   4419   *Mena*   B 4409

Penrhyn   924   303

Malltraeth Bay   Newborough   Bethel   Quarries

Mermaid Inn   B 4366   5   Deiniolen

Llanddwyn-   A 437   A 4244

Island   **Caernarfon**   A 4086   Llanrug   A 4086

C a e r n a r f o n   Bontnewydd   53   Llanberis   *Llyn Padarn*

Waunfawr   Castle   726   Glyder

B a y   (△)   A 499   Fawr   A 4086

Dinas Dinlle   14   Llanwnda   698   12 1/2   1085

Llandwrog   A 499   Pen-y-groes   *Llyn Cwellyn*   Yr Wyddfa

(△)   Snowdon /

Pontllyfni   13 1/2   Beddgelert   701   747

(△)   Llanllyfni   B 4418   Rhyd-Ddu   Forest   A 4085

Clynnog-   A 4085

Fawr   22   782   14'9

21   35   Beddgelert

Trevor   A 499   11   Moel Hebog   Pass of Aber

Trwyn y Gorlech   Yr Eifl   522   G W Y N E D D

Llithfaen   564   Llanaelhaearn   Dolbenmaen   H

Carreg Ddu   B 4417   7 1/2   *Dwyfor*   Tremadog   14'6

Morfa Nefyn   6   *ninsula*   A 487   15   Vale

Nefyn   A 4410

F   32   G

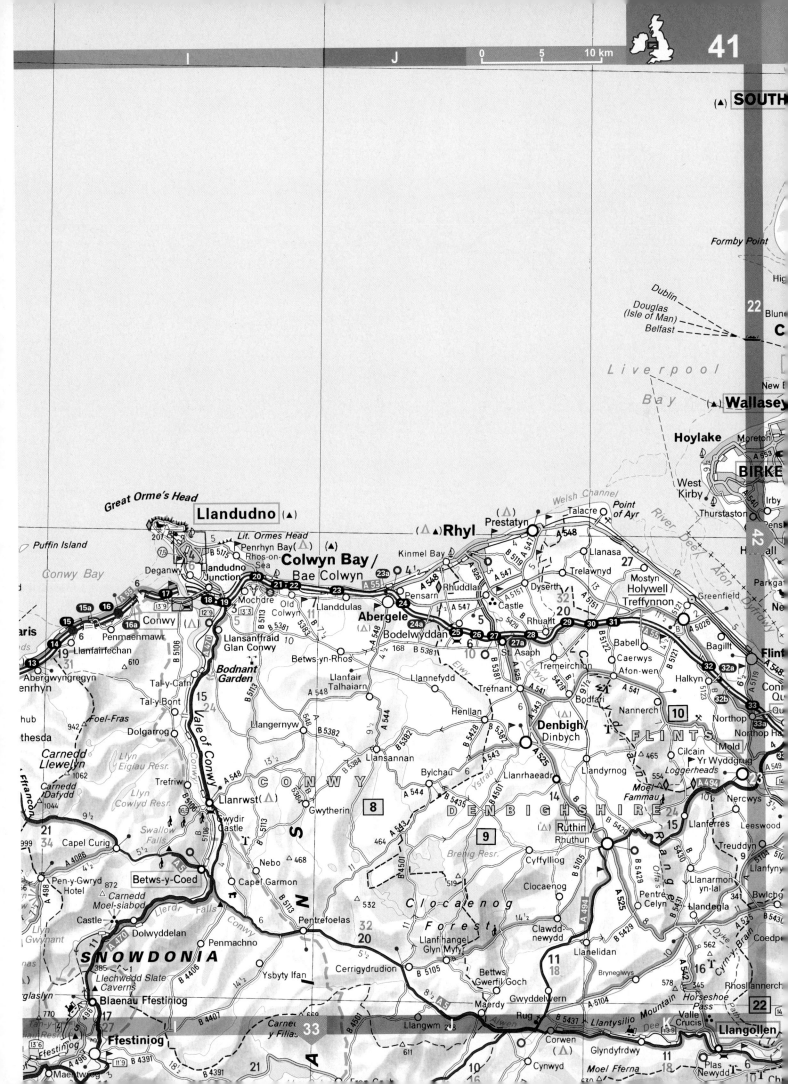

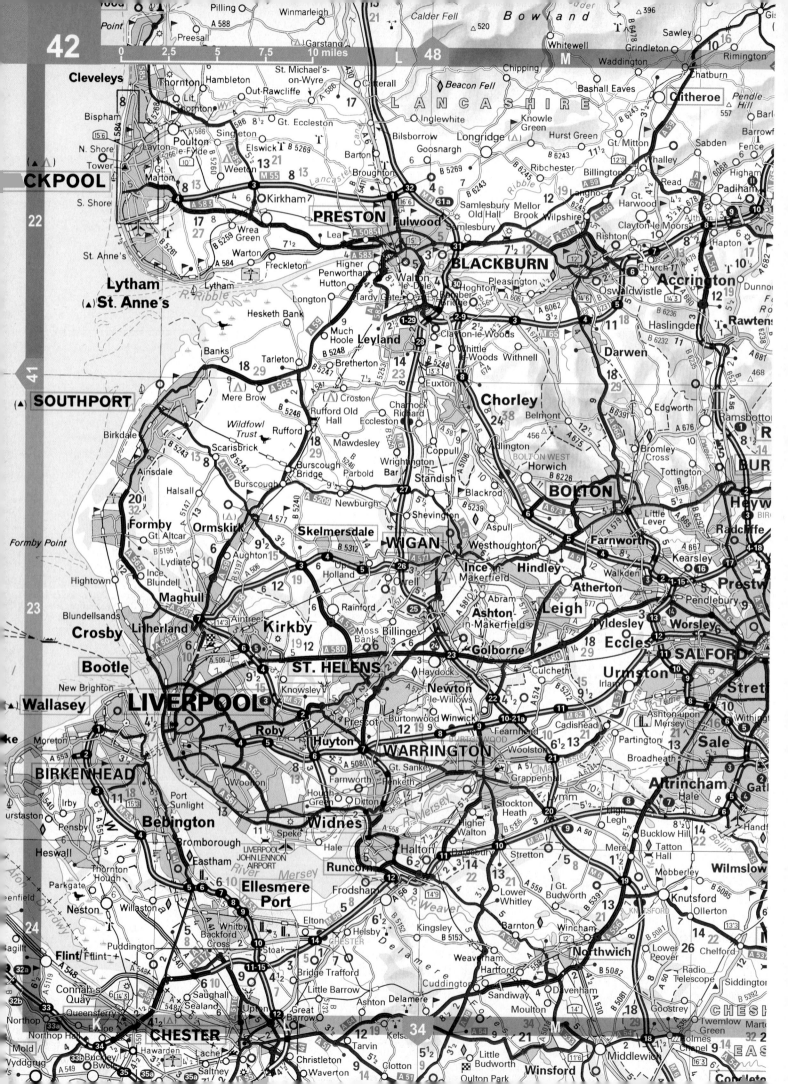

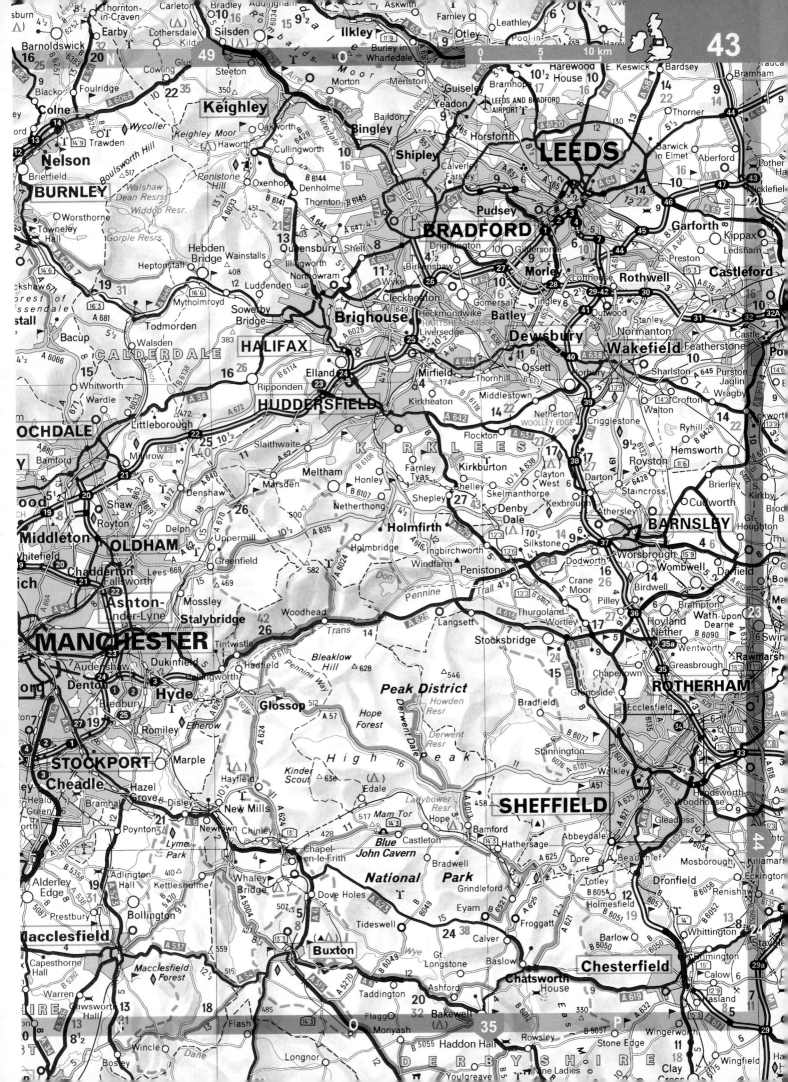

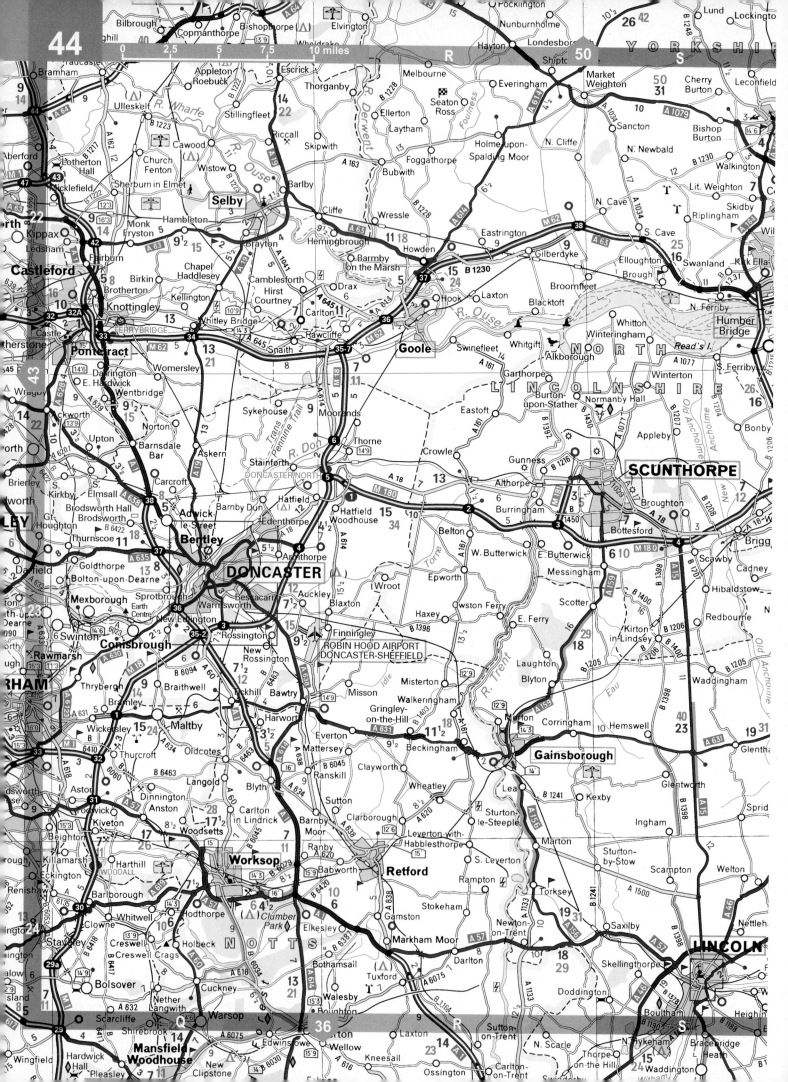

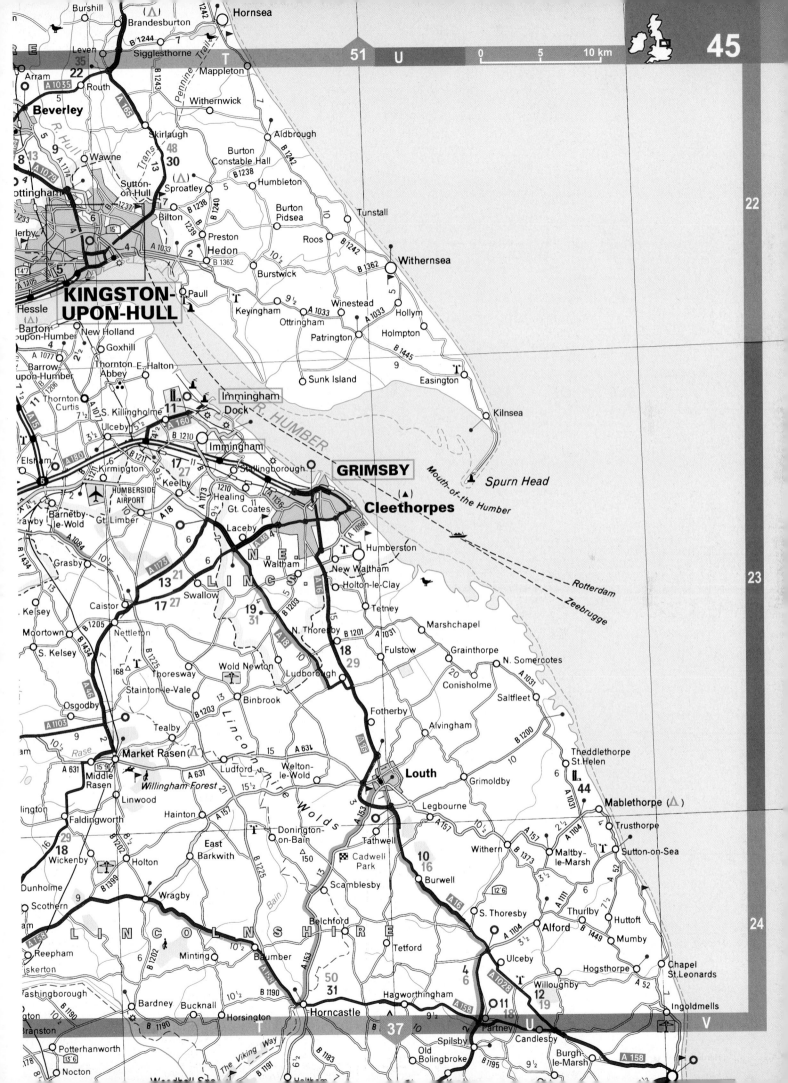

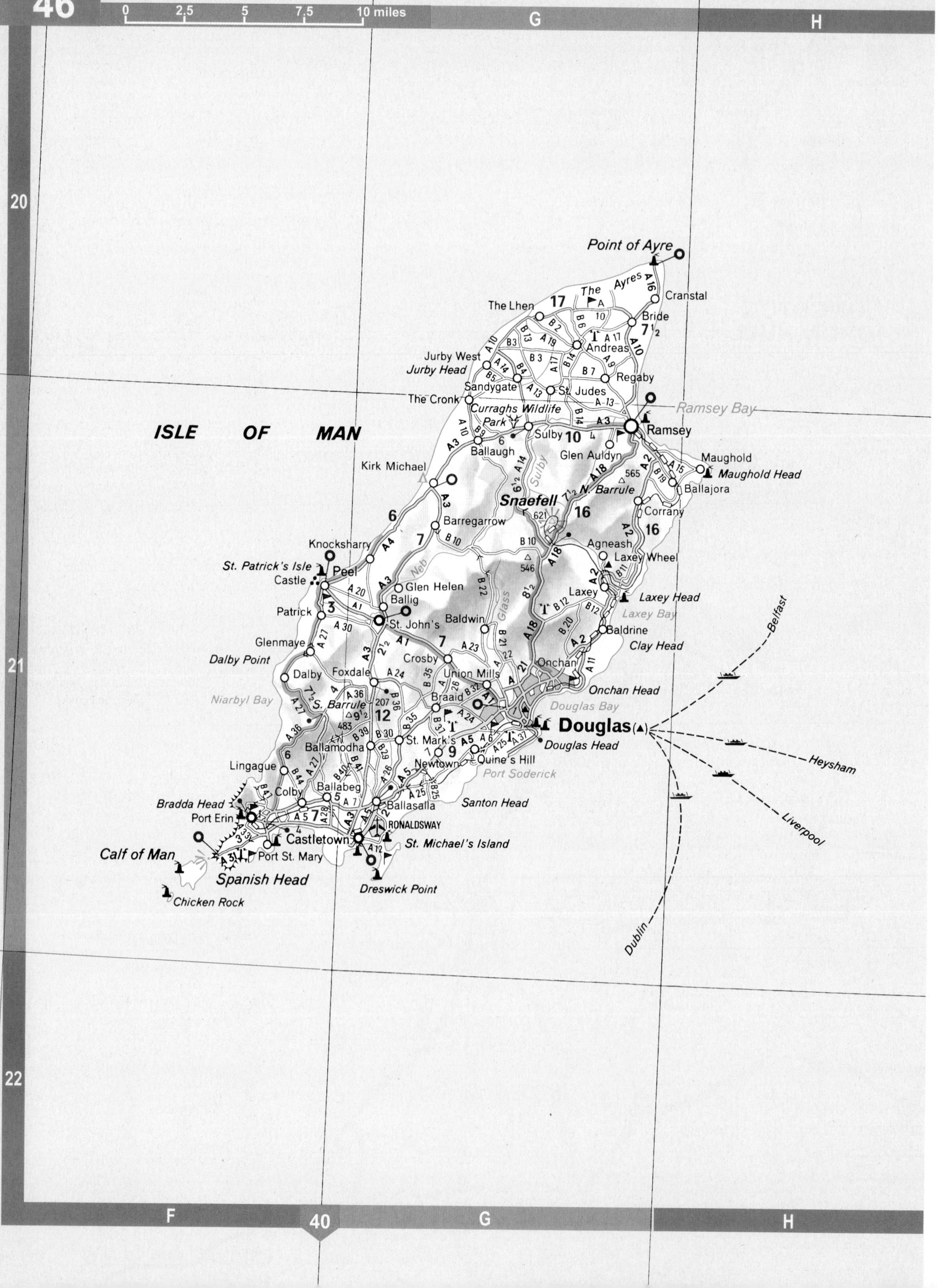

0   2.5   5   7.5   10 miles

G

H

20

Point of Ayre

The *Ayres* A16

The Lhen   **17**   ▶A   Cranstal

Bride
A16   **7**½
B2   B6   10
B3   A19   A17   A11   A10
Jurby West   A10   B4   Andreas   A9
Jurby Head   B5   A14   B3   B7   Regaby
Sandygate   A13   St. Judes   A-13
The Cronk   **Curraghs Wildlife**   B14   A3
Park   6   **10**   *Ramsey Bay*
A10   Sulby   4   Ramsey

ISLE   OF   MAN

A3   Ballaugh   Glen Auldyn   A2   A15   Maughold
Kirk Michael   6½ A14   N. Barrule   A18   565   **Maughold Head**
Sulby   Ballajora

A3   **Snaefell**   **16**   Corrany
6   621   A2   **16**
Barregarrow   B10   Agneash   Laxey Wheel
Knocksharry   **7**   A18   B11
B10   B10   546   A2   Laxey
St. Patrick's Isle   Peel   A3   Glen Helen   *Glass*   B12   *Laxey Head*
Castle   A20   Ballig   B22   B1½   B12   *Laxey Bay*
Patrick   **3**   A1   St. John's   Baldwin   A18   B20   Baldrine
Glenmaye   A21   A30   **7**   A23   B21   A2   *Clay Head*
Dalby Point   A3   2½   Crosby   A22   Onchan   A11
Dalby   Foxdale   A24   B5   Union Mills   A21   *Onchan Head*
Niarbyl Bay   4   A36   207   B36   Braaid   A1   A41   *Douglas Bay*
7½ S. *Barrule*   9½   B35   A24   **Douglas**(▲)
A21   483   **12**   B39   B30   St. Mark's   A5   A6   *Douglas Head*
A36   6   B40   A41   Newtown   **9**   A25   Quine's Hill
Ballamodha   A27   B29   1   A5   *Port Soderick*
Lingague   B44   B26   A5   A25   *Santon Head*
Colby   Ballabeg   5   A7   Ballasalla
Bradda Head   A41   A7   *St. Michael's Island*
Port Erin   **5** **7**   A29   **RONALDSWAY**
A5   A12
Calf of Man   A3   Castletown
Port St. Mary
Spanish Head   *Dreswick Point*
Chicken Rock

Belfast

Heysham

Liverpool

Dublin

21

22

F

40

G

H

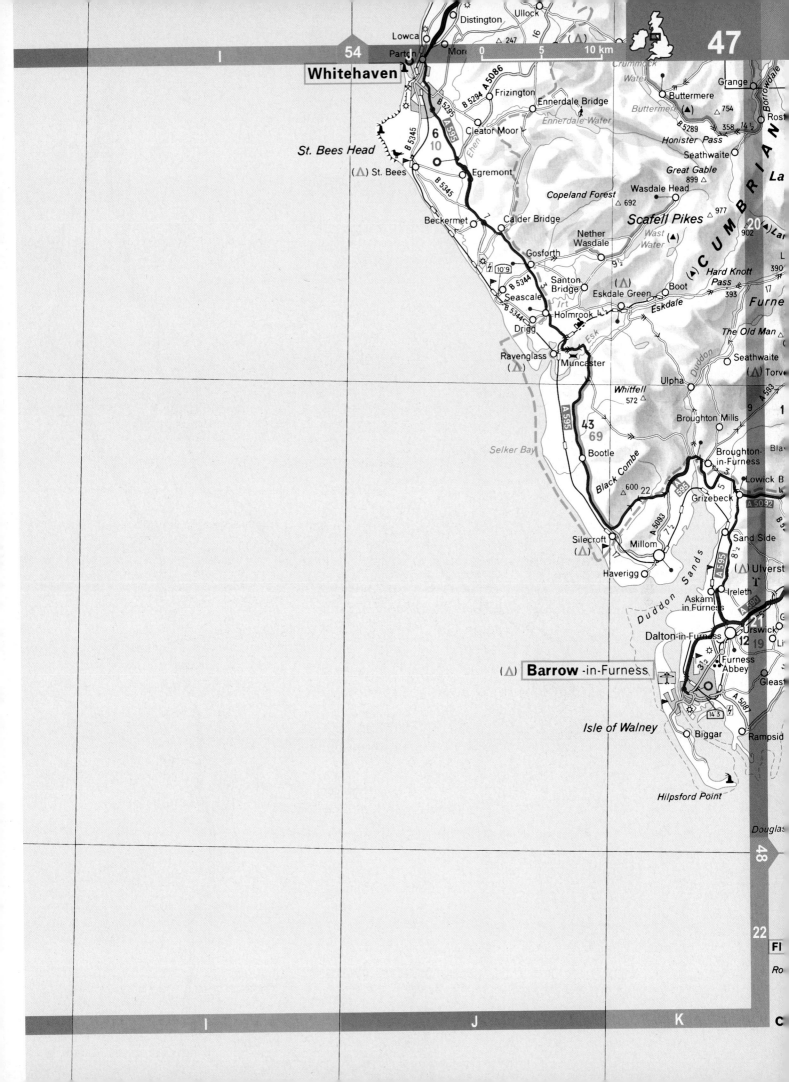

I | | | J | | | K | | | C

Distington
Ullock
△ 247
16
(△)

Lowca
Mor
0   5   10 km

Partch

Whitehaven

Frizington
B 5294 A 5086
Ennerdale Bridge
Grange
Buttermere
Crummock Water

B 5295
Cleator Moor
△ 754
B 5289
358 14½
Ros

A 595
6
10
Ennerdale Water
Ehen
Honister Pass

St. Bees Head
Egremont
Seathwaite

(△) St. Bees
B 5345
Great Gable
899 △
977

B 5345
7
Calder Bridge
Copeland Forest
Wasdale Head
△ 692
Scafell Pikes
20
902
(△) Lar

Beckermet
Nether Wasdale
West Water
△
L

Gosforth
9½
Hard Knott Pass
390

7 10·9
B 5344
Santon Bridge
Eskdale Green Boot
393
17
Furne

Seascale
(△)
Irt
Eskdale

B 5344
Holmrook
Esk
The Old Man

Drigg
B 5344
Seathwaite

Ravenglass
Muncaster
Duddon
(△) Torv
(△)

A 595
Ulpha

Whitfell
572 △
A 593

A 595
43
69
9

Broughton Mills
1

Selker Bay
Broughton-
in-Furness
Bla

Bootle
3
Lowick B

△ 600
22
Grizebeck
A 5092

Black Combe
A 595
5

A 5093
Sand Side

Silecroft
Millom
7½

(△)
8½
A 595
(△) Ulverst

Haverigg
Duddon Sands
Ireleth
A 590
21

Askam
in Furness
12 19
Urswick
Li

Dalton-in-Furness
3½

(△) **Barrow** -in-Furness
Furness Abbey
Gleas

14·3
A 5087

Isle of Walney

Biggar
Rampsid

Hilpsford Point

Douglas

Fl
Ro

I | | | J | | | K | | | C

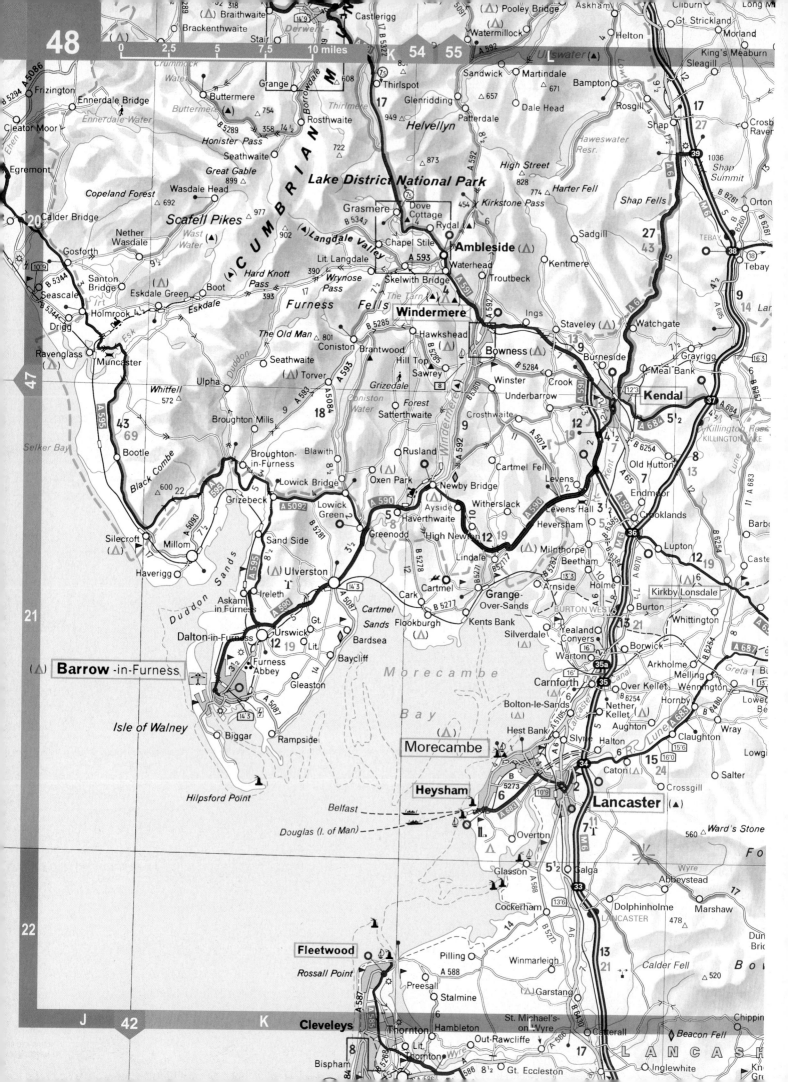

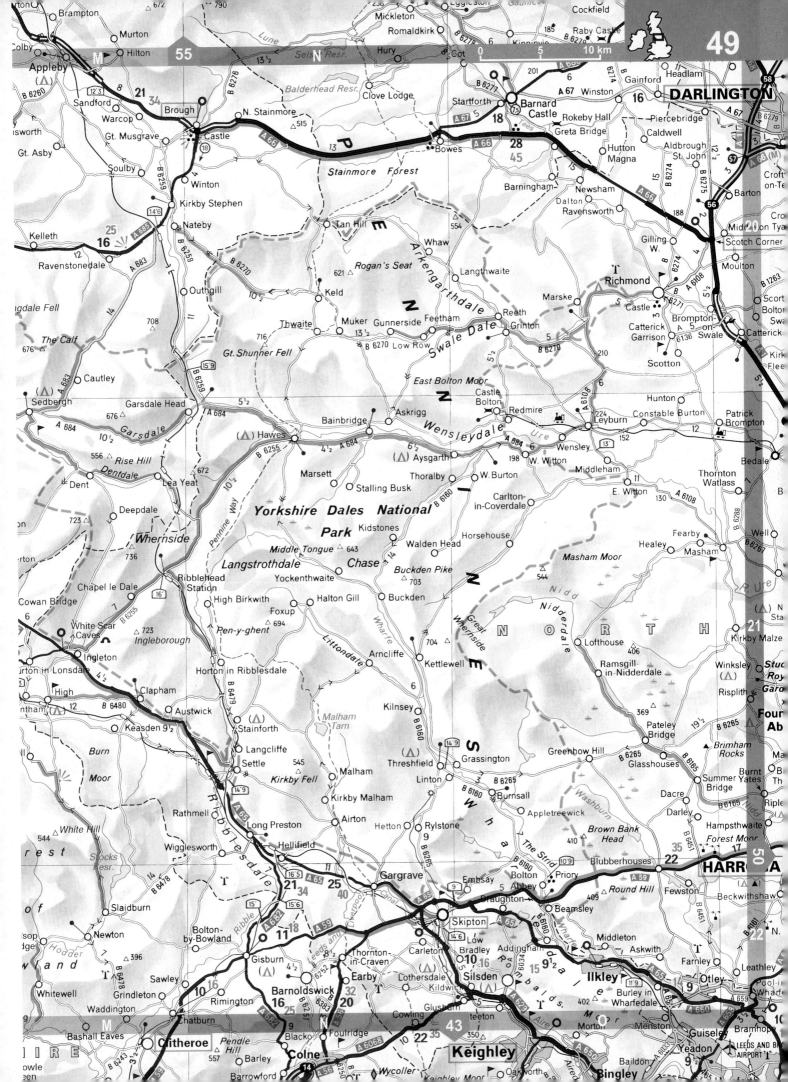

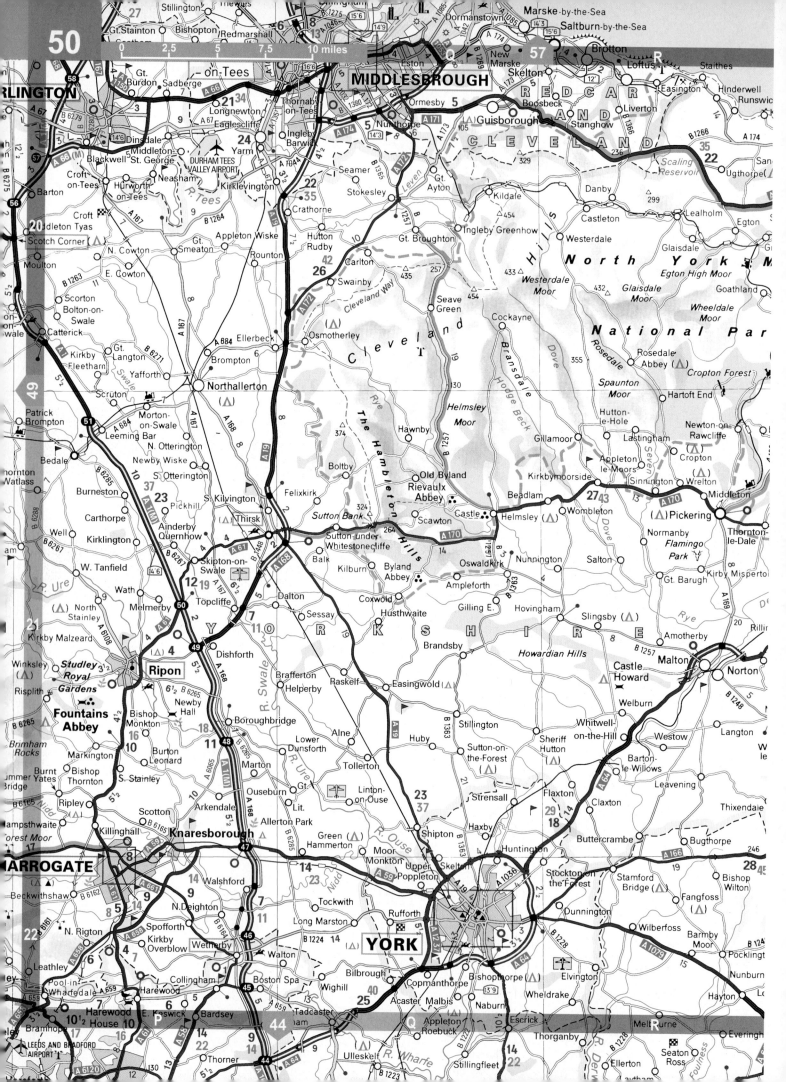

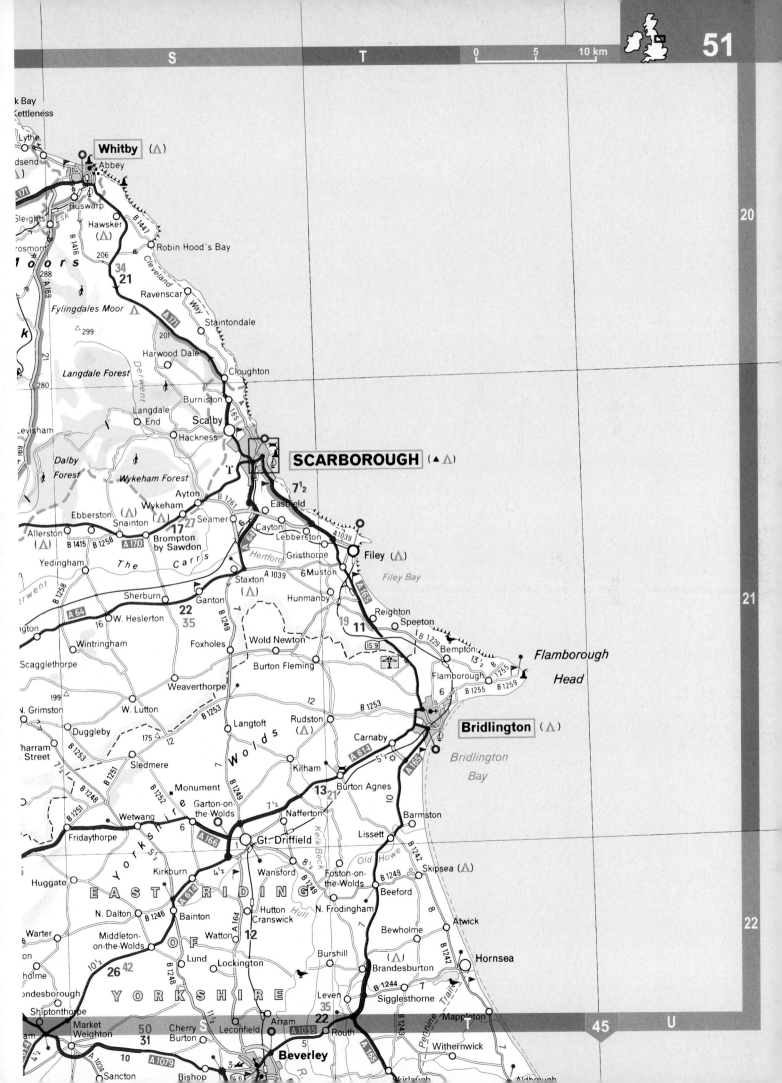

0 5 10 km

20

S   T

Whitby (Λ)

k Bay
Kettleness
Lythe
dsend
Abbey
Sleights
Ruswarp
A171
Hawsker (Λ)
Grosmont
B 1416
B 1447
Robin Hood's Bay
oors
A 169
206
34
21
288
Ravenscar
Fylingdales Moor
A171
Cleveland Way
Staintondale
299
201
k
21
Harwood Dale
280
Langdale Forest
Cloughton
levisham
Burniston
Langdale End
Scalby
Dalby Forest
Hackness
A165
Wykeham Forest
Ayton
SCARBOROUGH (▲ Λ)
Ebberston (Λ)
Wykeham
B 1261
7½
Snainton
17 27
Seamer
Eastfield
Allerston (Λ)
Brompton by Sawdon
Cayton
A 1039
B 1415 B 1258 A 170
A 64
Lebberston
Yedingham
Hertford
Gristhorpe
Filey (Λ)
The Carrs
6 Muston
Staxton
A 1039
Sherburn
Hunmanby
Filey Bay
Derwent
B 1258
Ganton
22
Reighton
ngton
16 W. Heslerton
35
B 1249
19 11
Speeton
Wintringham
Foxholes
Wold Newton
15'9
B 1229
Bempton
Scagglethorpe
Burton Fleming
13½ B
Flamborough
Flamborough Head
199
Weaverthorpe
12
6
B 1255
B 1253
B 1255 B 1259
N. Grimston
W. Lutton
Langtoft
Rudston (Λ)
B 1253
Duggleby
175 12
Wolds
Carnaby
Bridlington (Λ)
Tharram Street
B 1253
Sledmere
Kilham
A 614
5½
A165
Bridlington Bay
B 1251
B 1248
Monument
B 1252
B 1249
Garton-on-the-Wolds
13 21
Burton Agnes
Wetwang
7½
Nafferton
Barmston
Fridaythorpe
6
A 166
Yorksh
Gt. Driffield
Lissett
Huggate
5½
1
Kelk Beck
B 1242
Kirkburn
4½
Wansford
8½
Skipsea (Λ)
N. Dalton
B 1246
Bainton
Foston-on-the-Wolds
B 1249
Warter
A 614
Hutton
Cranswick
N. Frodingham
Beeford
8
Middleton-on-the-Wolds
A 164
Watton
12
Bewholme
Atwick
holme
10½
Lund
Lockington
Burshill
(Λ)
B 1242
Hornsea
ndesborough
26 42
B 1248
Brandesburton
YORKSHIRE
Leven
Sigglesthorne
Mappleton
Shiptonthorpe
35
B 1244
7
Pennine Trail
am
Market Weighton
50
Cherry
Leconfield
Arram
22
Withernwick
31
Burton
A 1035
Routh
A 165
45
U
A 1079
5
A 164
Beverley
Sancton
Bishop
Skirlaugh
Aldbrough

21

22

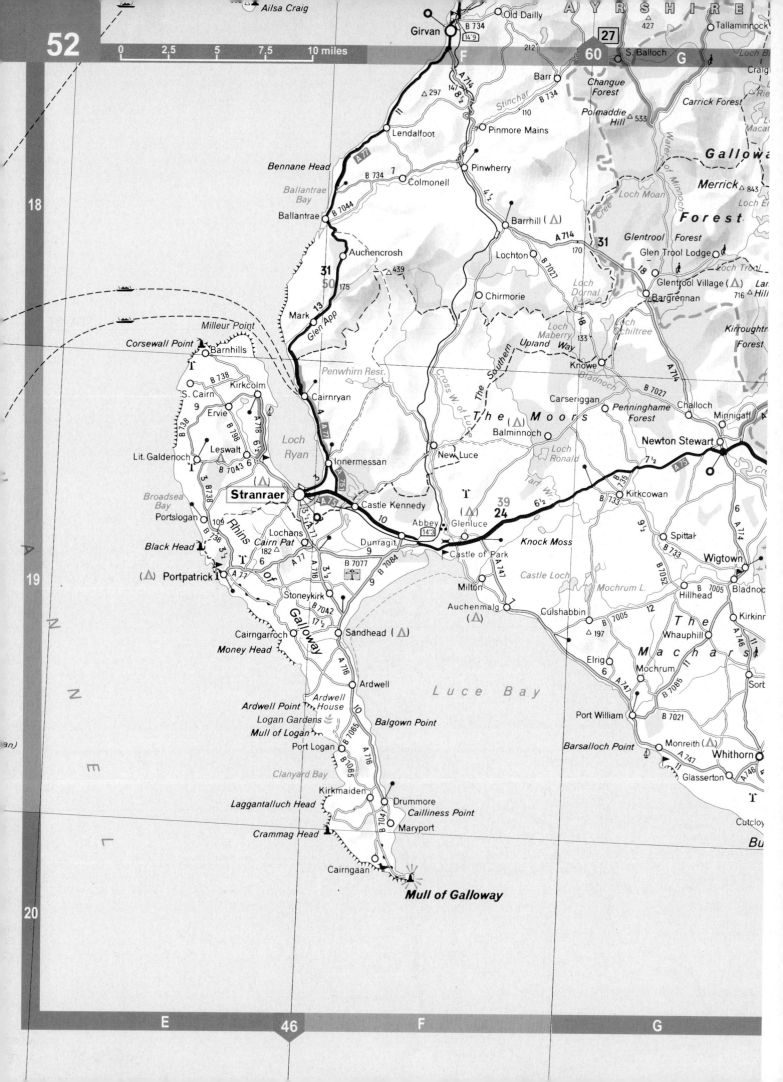

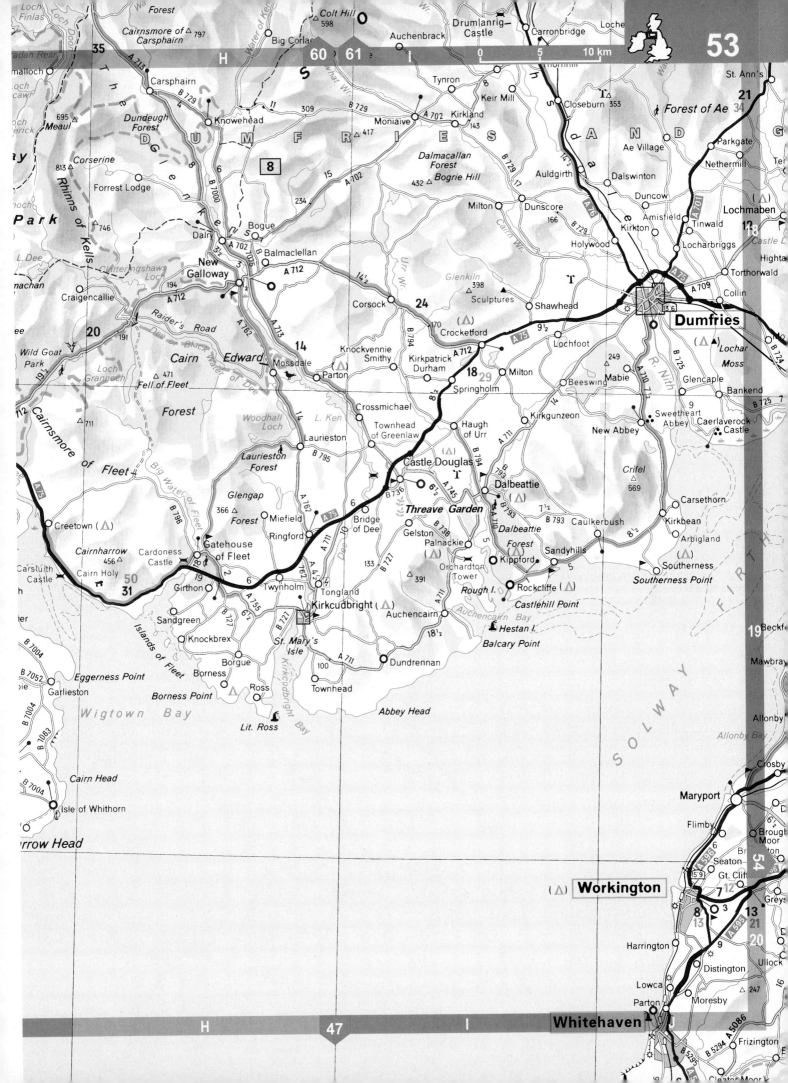

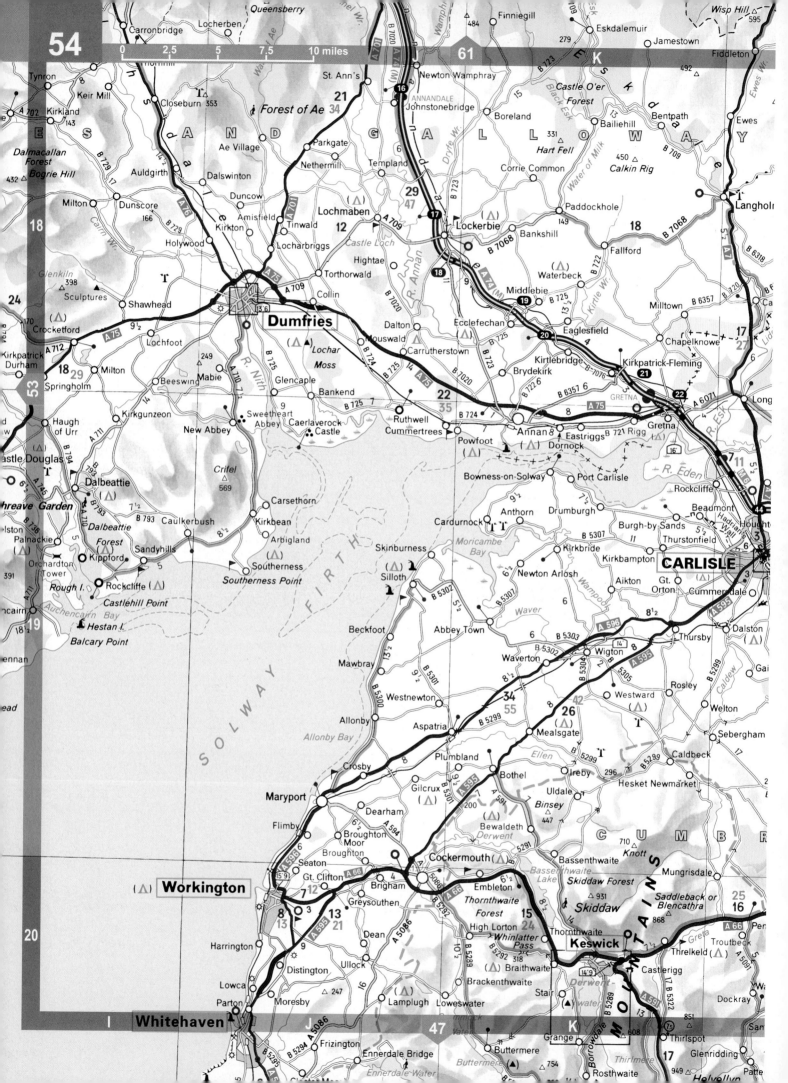

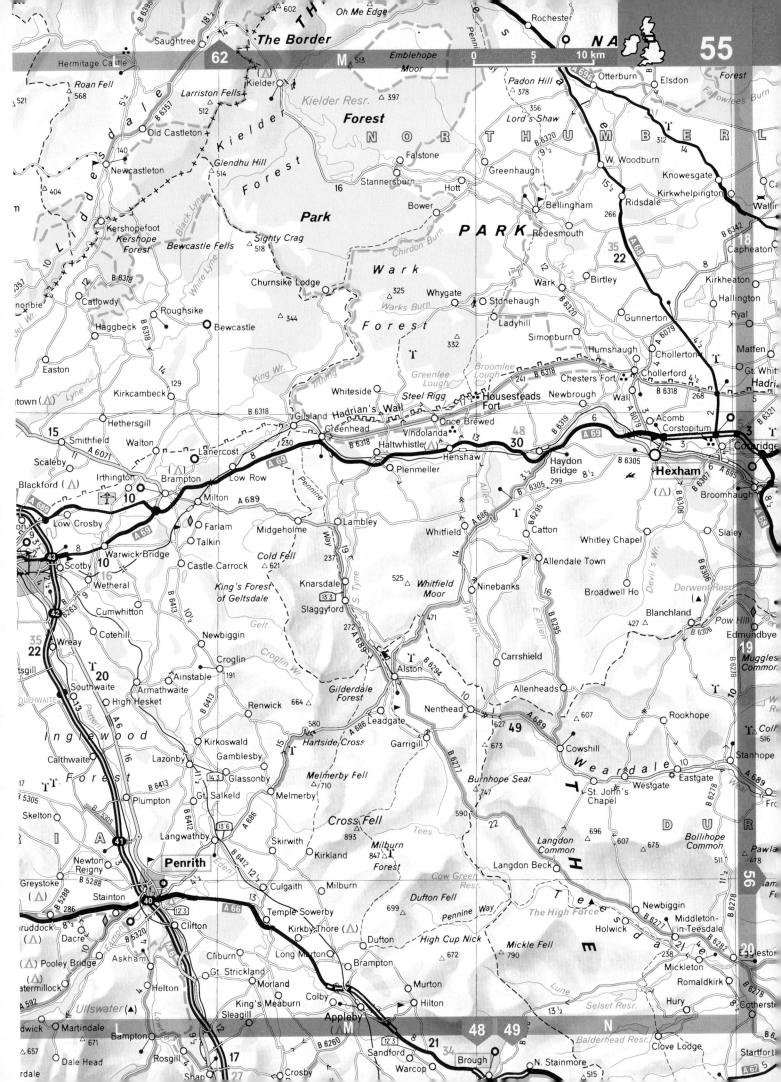

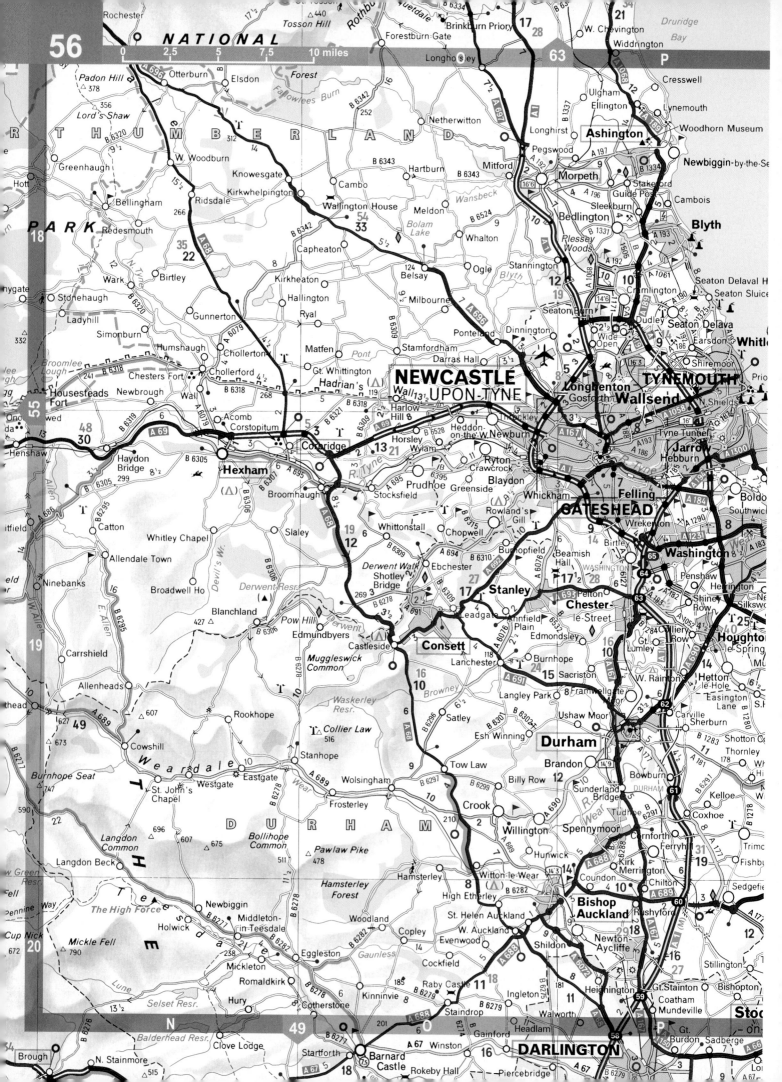

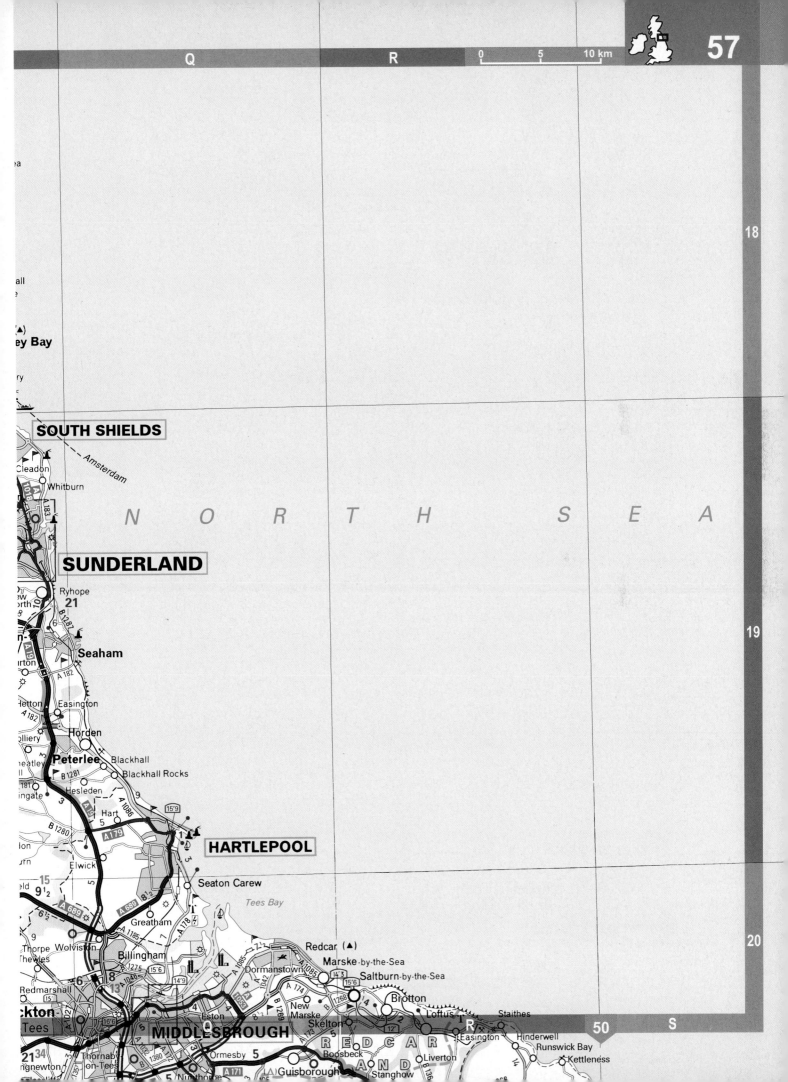

18

SOUTH SHIELDS

Amsterdam

Cleadon

Whitburn

N O R T H S E A

SUNDERLAND

Ryhope
21

B 1287

Seaham

A 182

19

Hetton
A 182

Easington

Horden
olliery

Peterlee Blackhall
B 1281 Blackhall Rocks

eatley
ll

B 181

ingate Hesleden

3

9

B 1280 A 1086 Hart
5

A 179 15'9

on

Elwick 5 1

HARTLEPOOL

eld **15** 3
9½

Seaton Carew

A 689 A 689 8½

Tees Bay

20

A 689
6½

Greatham

A 1185 A 178

Thorpe Wolviston

Thewles Billingham Redcar (▲)

B 1275 15'6

Redmarshall A 1046 Marske-by-the-Sea

13 14'9 A 1085 14'3 Saltburn-by-the-Sea

ckton Eston A 174

Tees 16'6 New Skelton B 1268 Brotton

Marske 12' Loftus Staithes

MIDDLESBROUGH B 1269 4 Easington Hinderwell

21 34 Ormesby **5** R E D C A R Liverton Runswick Bay

gnewton on-Tees Thornaby B 1380 Boosbeck A N D Kettleness

Numthorpe A 171 (A) Guisborough Stanghow B 136

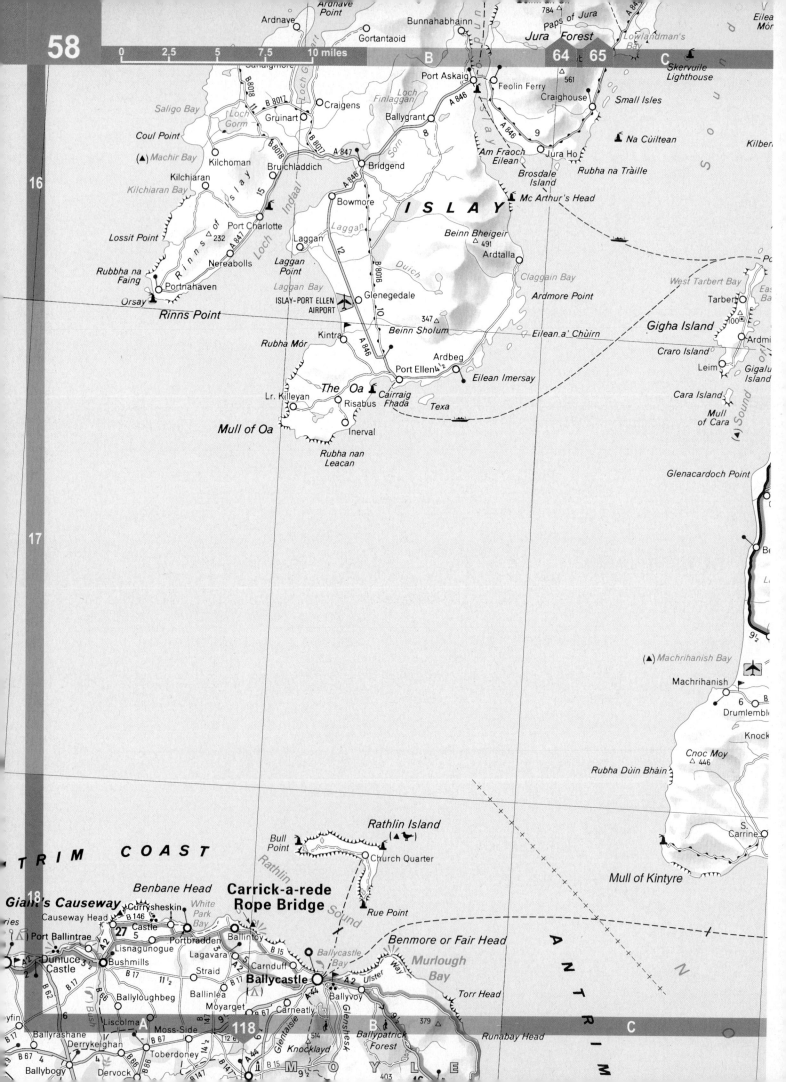

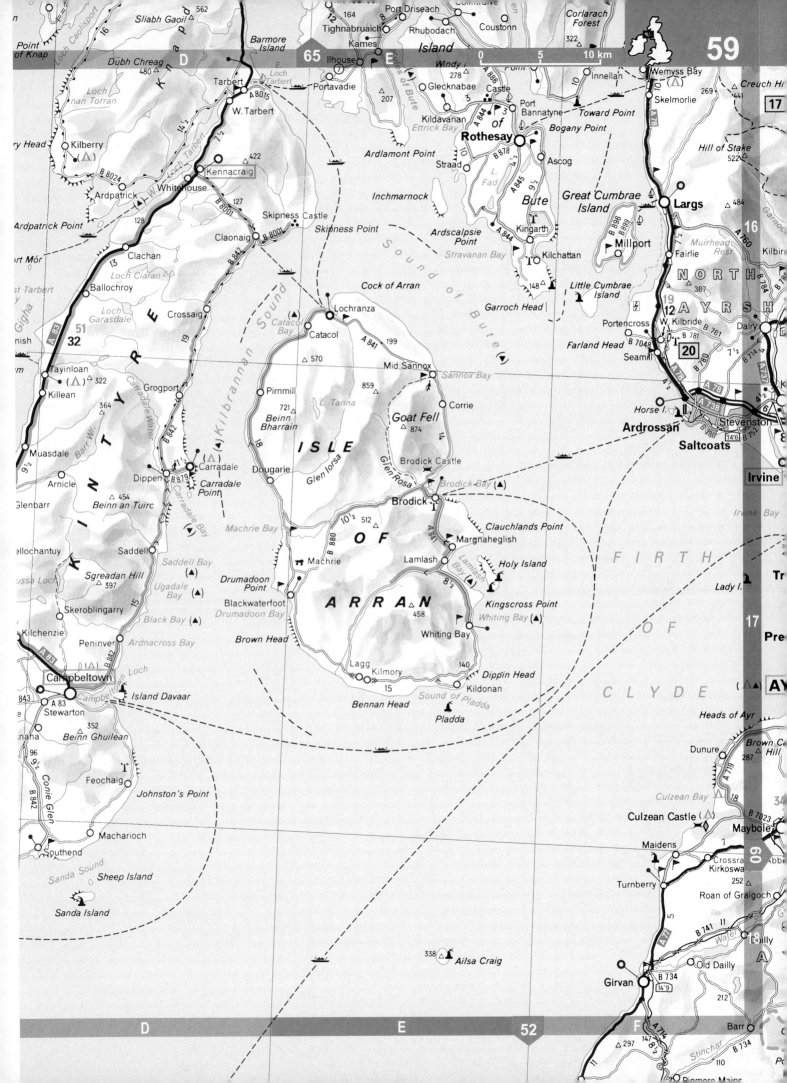

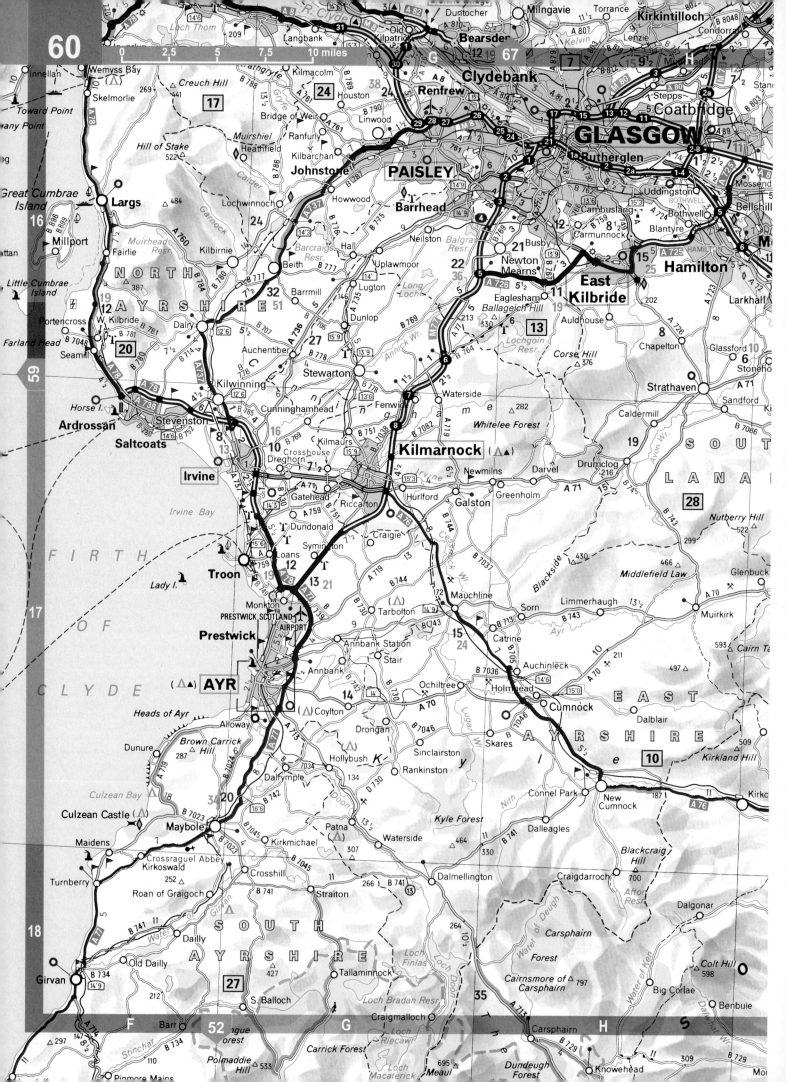

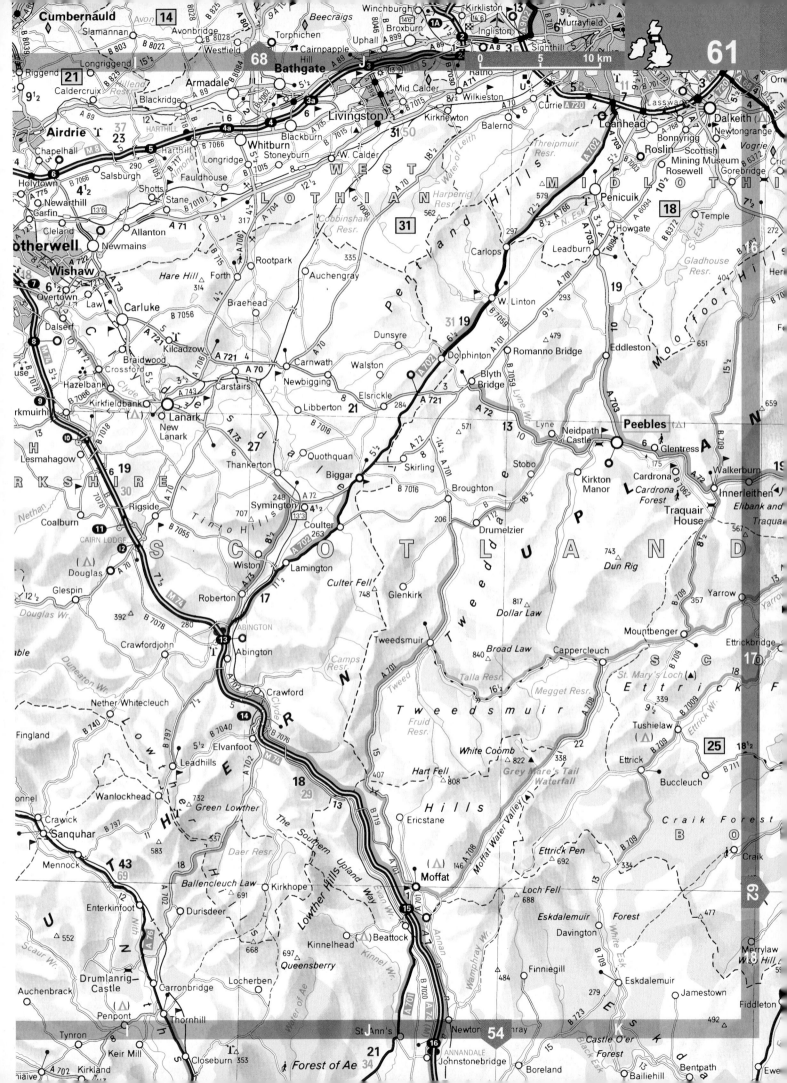

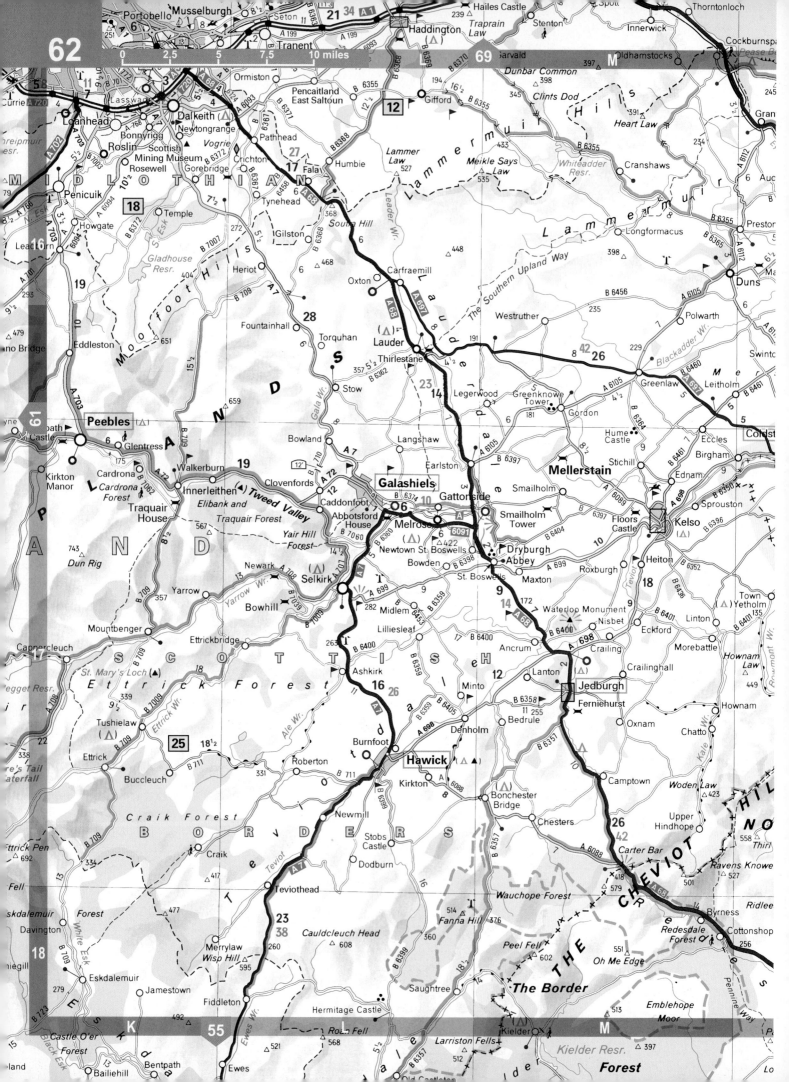

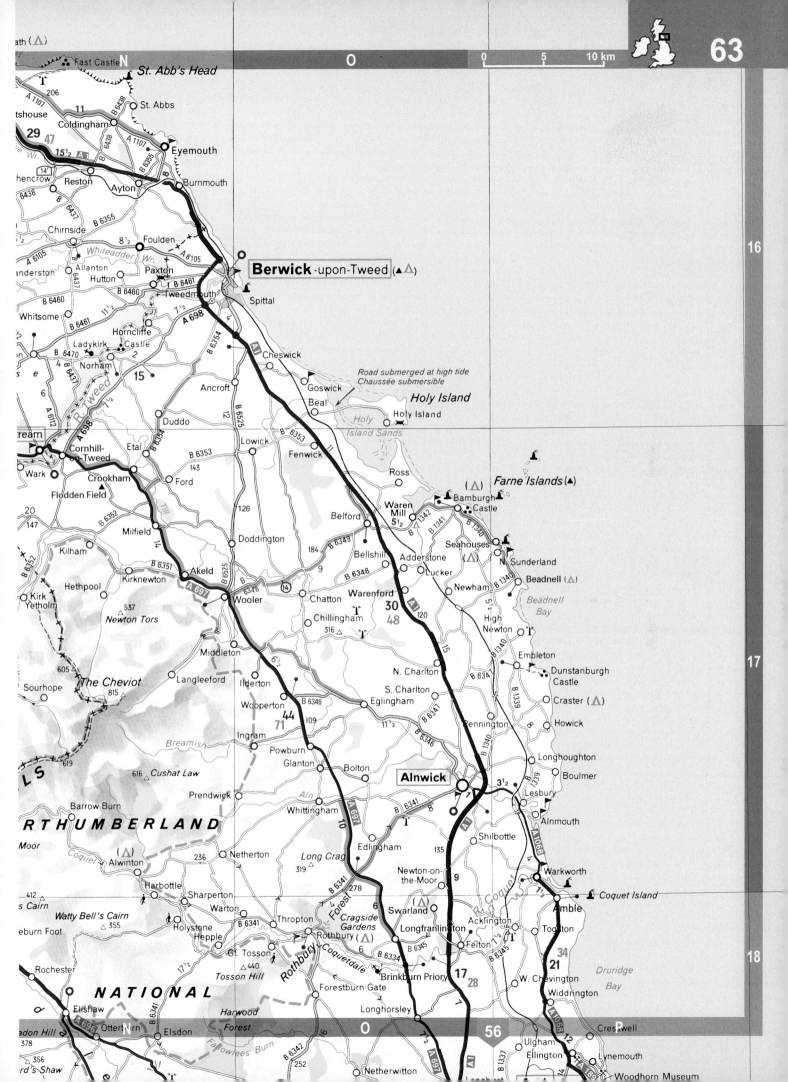

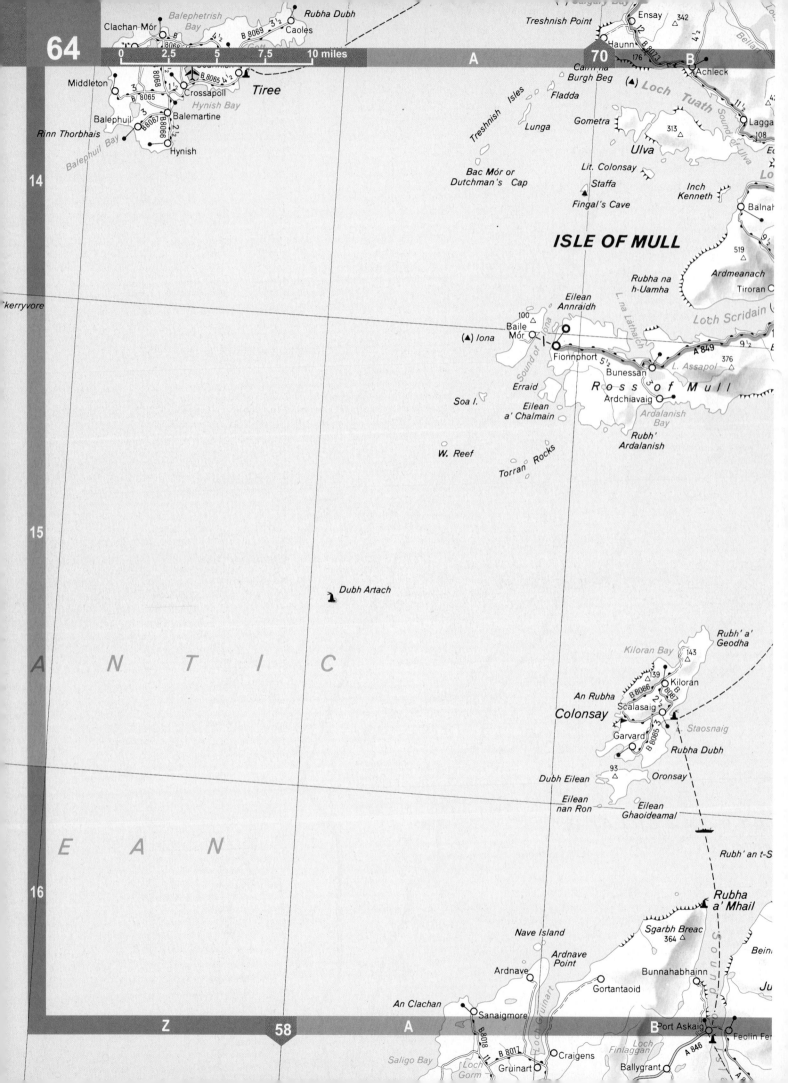

Balephetrish Bay
Clachan-Mór
Rubha Dubh
Caoles
B 8069

0   2.5   5   7.5   10 miles

Middleton
Crossapoll
Hynish Bay
Tiree
B 8068
B 8065

Balephuil
Balemartine
Balemartine
B 8067
B 8066
Rinn Thorbhais
Hynish
Balephuil Bay

'kerryvore

14

Treshnish Point
Ensay   342
Haunn   176
Càrn na
Burgh Beg
Achleck
(▲)   Loch Tuath
Treshnish Isles
Fladda
Lagga   108
Sound of Ulva
Lunga
Gometra
313
Ulva
Bac Mór or
Dutchman's Cap
Lit. Colonsay
Inch
Kenneth
Staffa
Balnah
Fingal's Cave

ISLE OF MULL

Rubha na
h-Uamha
Ardmeanach
Tiroran
519
Eilean
Annraidh
L. na Làthaich
Loch Scridain
100
Baile
Mór
(▲) Iona
A 849   9½
Fionnphort   5½
L. Assapol   376
Bunessan
Sound of Iona
R o s s   of   M u l l
Erraid
Ardchiavaig
Soa I.
Eilean
a' Chalmain
Ardalanish
Bay
Rubh'
Ardalanish
W. Reef
Torran Rocks

15

A   N   T   I   C

Dubh Artach

Rubh' a'
Geodha
Kiloran Bay   143
139
Kiloran
An Rubha
B 8086
Scalasaig
B 8087
Colonsay
Staosnaig
Garvard
B 8085   3
Rubha Dubh
Dubh Eilean   93
Oronsay
Eilean
nan Ron
Eilean
Ghaoideamal
Rubh' an t-S

E   A   N

16

Rubha
a' Mhail
Nave Island
Sgarbh Breac   364
Bein
Ardnave
Point
Bunnahabhainn
Ardnave
Gortantaoid
Ju
An Clachan
Sanaigmore
Port Askaig
Feolin Fer
B 8018
B 8017
Craigens
Loch
Finlaggan
A 846
Saligo Bay
Loch
Gorm
Gruinart
Ballygrant

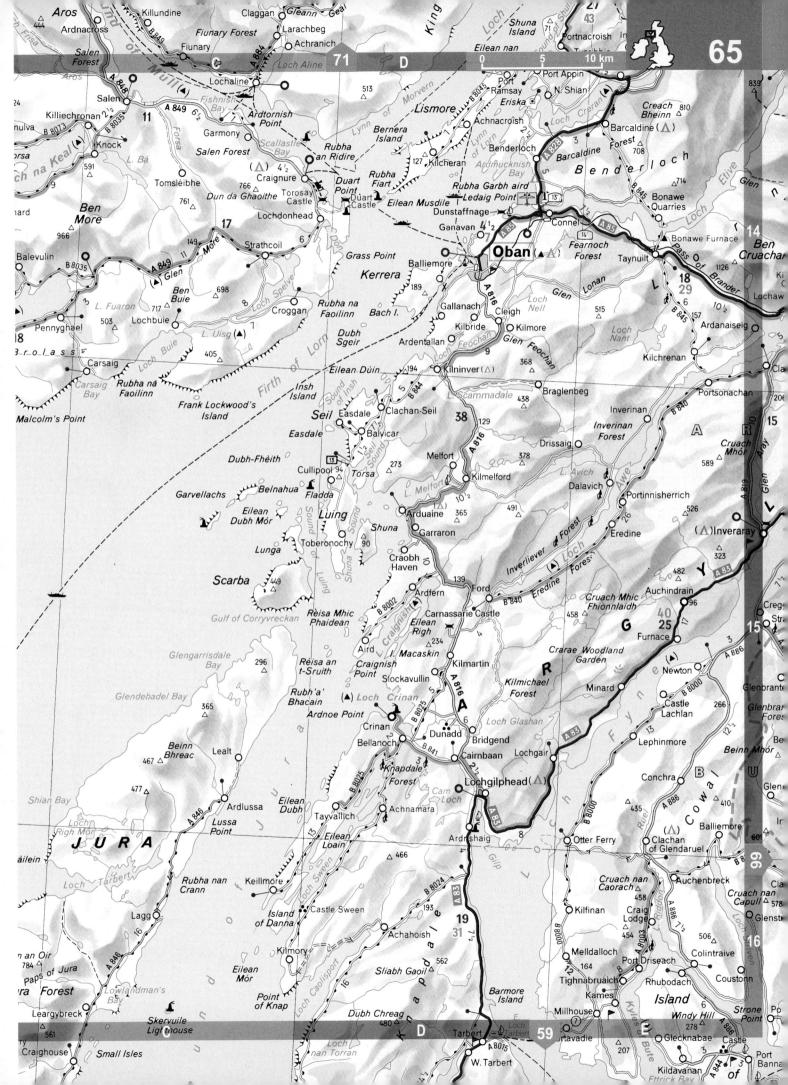

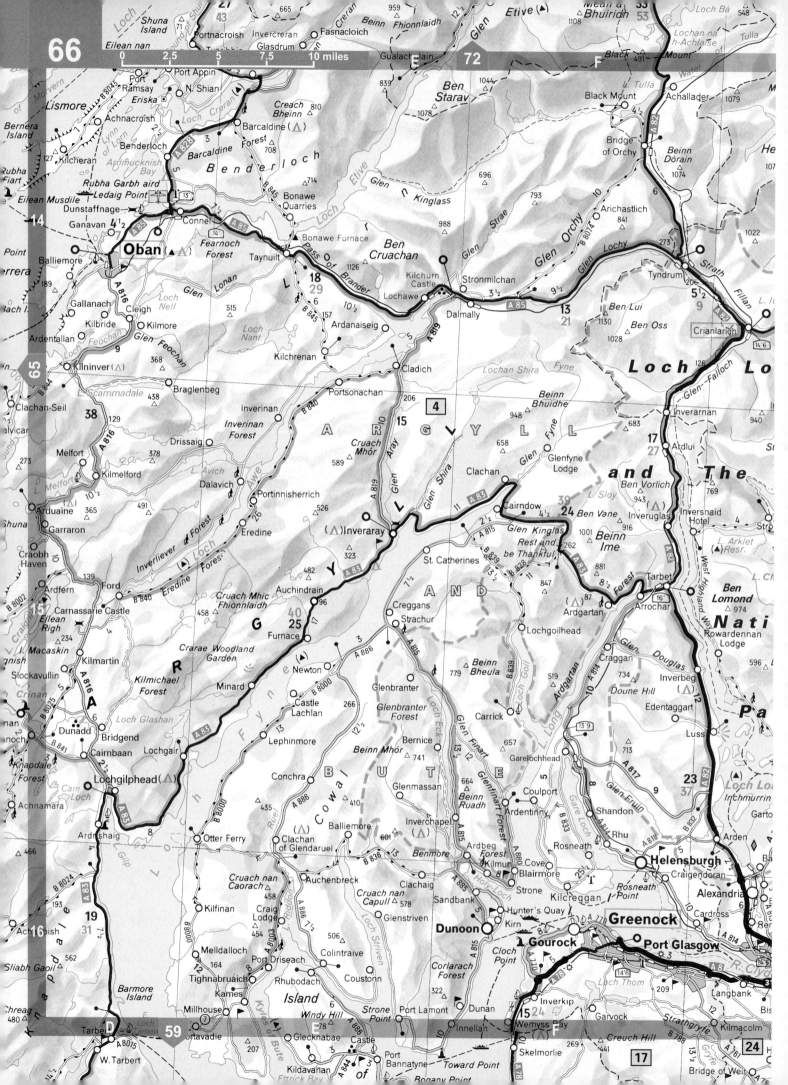

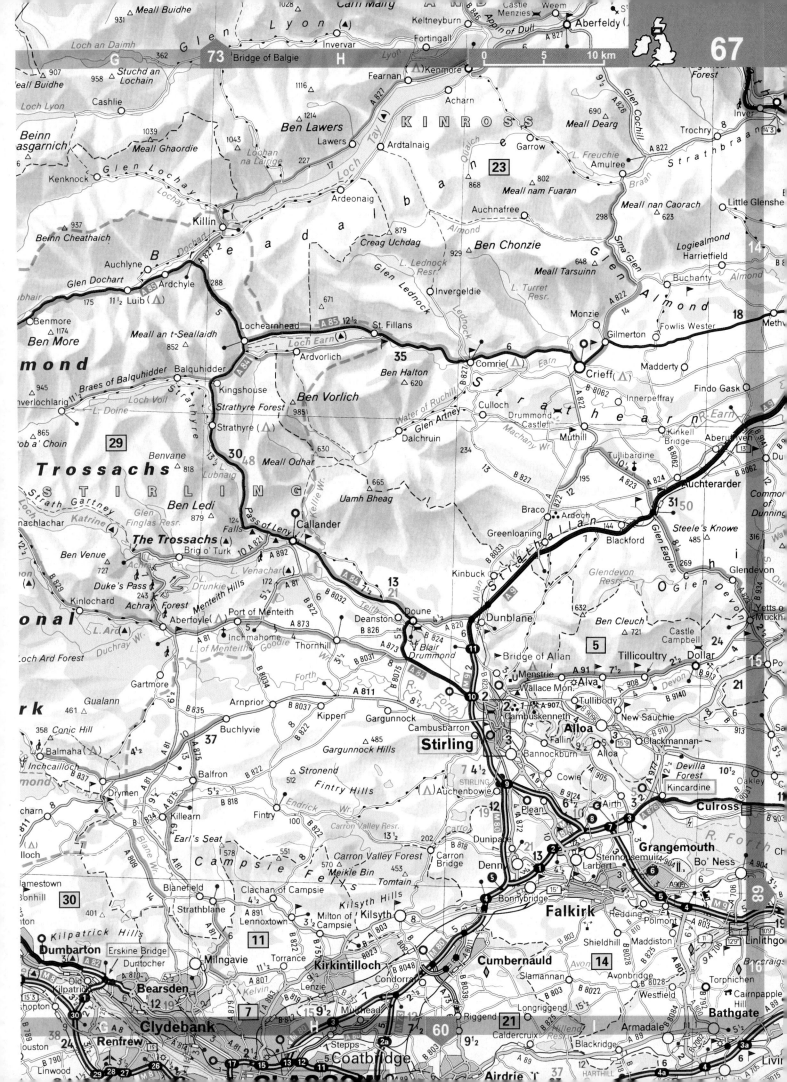

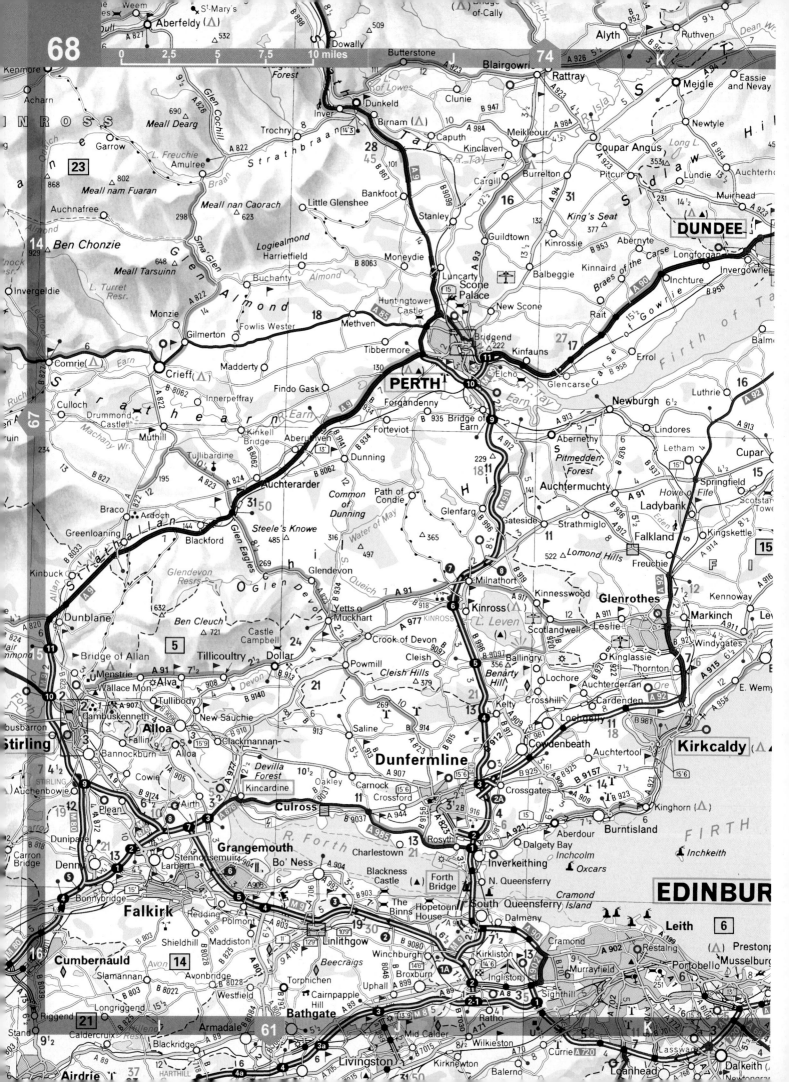

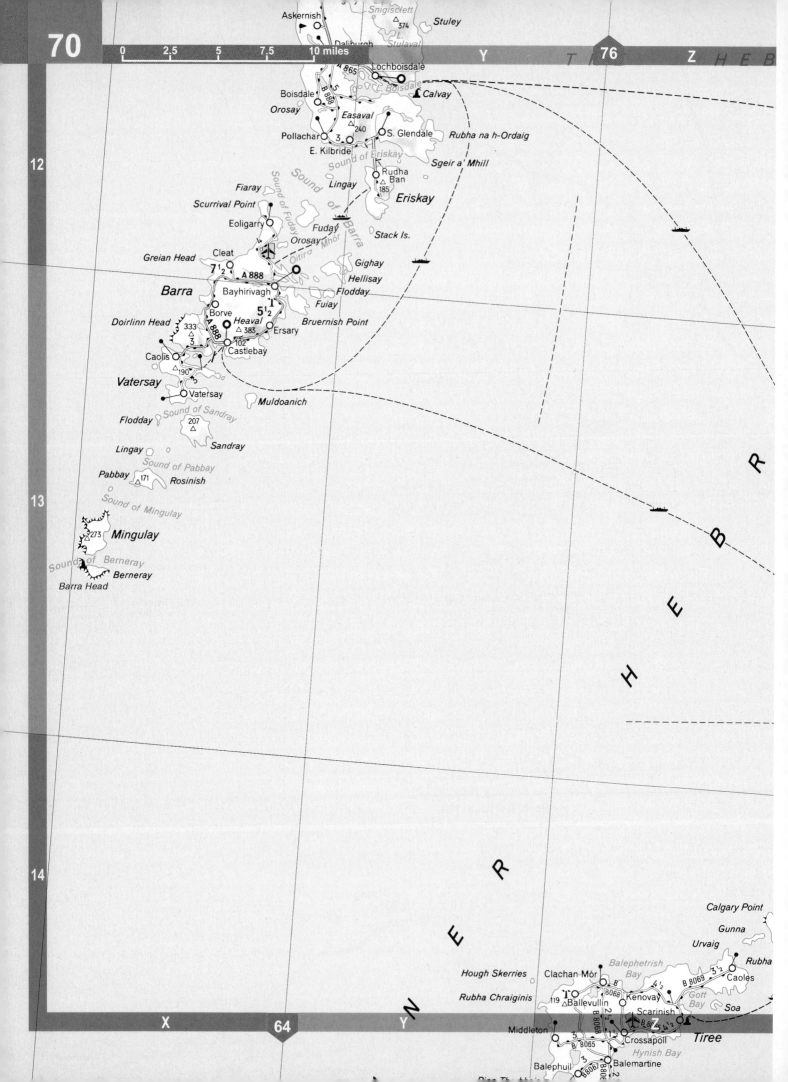

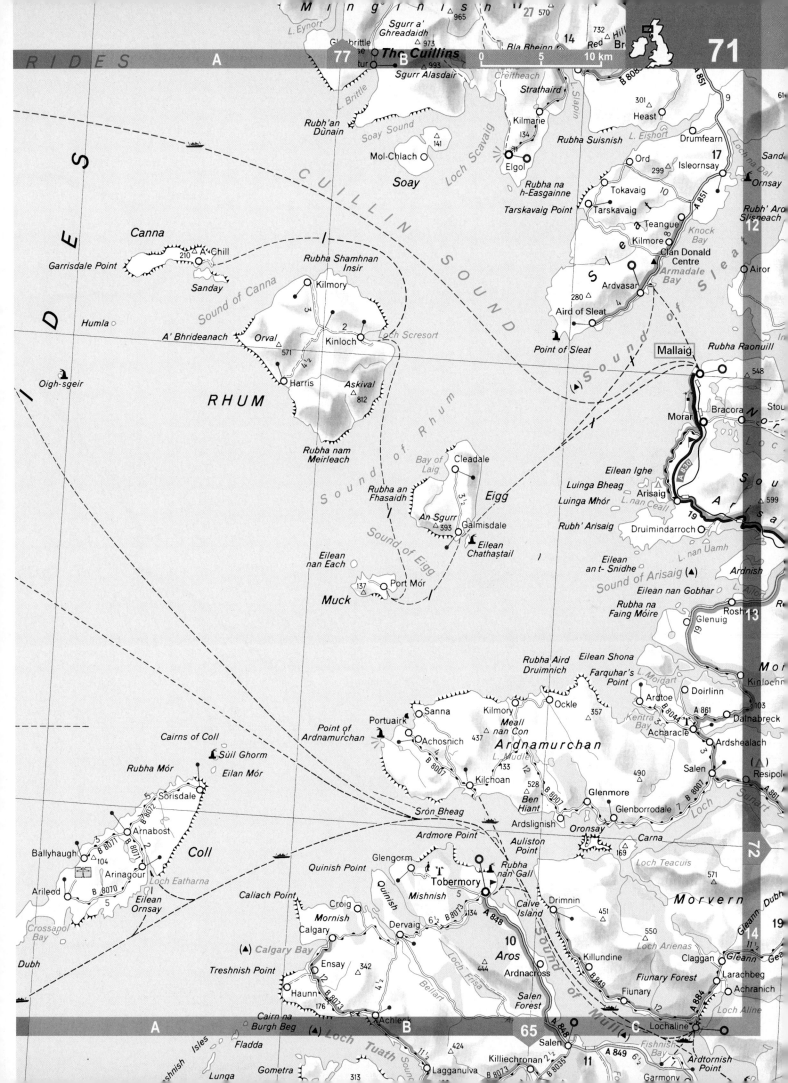

RIDES

A
77
B **The Cuillins**

M i n g i n i s h
27 570
L. Eynort
Sgurr a'
Ghreadaidh
965
973
Glenbrittle
993
Sgurr Alasdair
L. Brittle
Sgurr Alasdair
14 Red Hill Br
732
B 808
9
61

0 5 10 km

Rubh'an
Dùnain
Soay Sound
Soay
141
Mol-Chlach
Loch Scavaig
Crèitheach
Strathaird
Kilmarie
134
Elgol
Rubha na
h-Easgainne
Tarskavaig Point
Tarskavaig
Rubha Suisnish
L. Eishort
Ord
299
Isleornsay
Tokavaig
10
Teangue
Kilmore
Knock Bay
Clan Donald
Centre
Ardvasar
Aird of Sleat
280
Point of Sleat
Heast
301
Drumfearn
17
A 851
Ornsay
Rubh' Aro
Slisneach
12
Airor
I s l e   o f   S l e a t
Sound of Sleat

Canna
210
A' Chill
Garrisdale Point
Sanday
Sound of Canna
Humla
A' Bhrideanach
Oigh-sgeir
Rubha Shamhnan
Insir
Kilmory
3
2
Orval
571
Kinloch
Loch Scresort
4½
Harris
Askival
812
RHUM
Rubha nam
Meirleach
Sound of Rhum
Mallaig
Rubha Raonuill
548
Morar
Bracora
Eilean Ighe
Luinga Bheag
Luinga Mhór
Arisaig
L. nan Ceall
19
Rubh' Arisaig
Druimindarroch
A 830
599
L. nan Uamh
No r
Loc
Sou
Aris
9

Bay of
Laig
Cleadale
Rubha an
Fhasaidh
3½
Eigg
An Sgurr
393
Galmisdale
Eilean
Chathastail
Eilean nan Each
Port Mór
137
Muck
Eilean
an t- Snidhe
Sound of Arisaig
Eilean nan Gobhar
Rubha na
Faing Móire
Glenuig
Roshv
13
Ardnish
Aloi
R

I
D
E
S

Sound of Eigg

Rubha Aird
Druimnich
Eilean Shona
Farquhar's
Point
L. Moidart
Ardtoe
Doirlinn
Kinlochn
Mor
Mo
103
A 861
Dalnabreck
Kentra
Bay
Acharacle
Ardshealach
Resipol
Salen
B 8007
A 861
Sunart
Kilmory
Ockle
357
Sanna
Portuairk
Achosnich
Meall
nan Con
Ardnamurchan
437
L. Mudle
133
Kilchoan
528
Ben
Hiant
Glenmore
Glenborrodale
490
Oronsay
Carna
169
Loch Teacuis
571
Point of
Ardnamurchan
B 8007
B 8007
7
B 8007
Loch
Point of Ardnamurchan
Sron Bheag
Ardslignish
Ardmore Point
Auliston
Point
Rubha
nan Gall
Drimnin
451
Morvern
14
19

Cairns of Coll
Súil Ghorm
Rubha Mór
Eilan Mór
5
Sorisdale
B 8072
Arnabost
B 8071
2
Ballyhaugh
B 8071
3
104
Arinagour
Arileod
B 8070
5
Eilean Ornsay
Loch Eatharna
Coll
Crossapol
Bay
Dubh

Glengorm
Quinish Point
Tobermory
Mishnish
5
Calve
Island
Sound of Mull
72
65
10
Aros
Ardnacross
Killundine
B 849
550
Claggan
Gleann Dubh
Larachbeg
Achranich
A 884
Loch Aline
Gleann
Ge
Fiunary
Fiunary Forest
Salen
Forest
A 848
Quinish
Dervaig
Croig
Mornish
Calgary
Caliach Point
Ensay
342
Haunn
176
B 8073
4½
Treshnish Point
Cairn na
Burgh Beg
Fladda
Gometra
Lunga
313
Achleck
424
Lagganulva
Killiechronan
2½
11
Salen
A 848
A 849
Garmony
Lochaline
Ardtornish
Point
Fishnish
Bay
B 8035
6½
12
Calgary Bay
Loch Tuath
Loch Frisa
Bellart
Drimnin
Glenmore
A 848
6½
B 8073
134
Ardncross
444
Isles
Dubh
B 8070

A
B
C
A

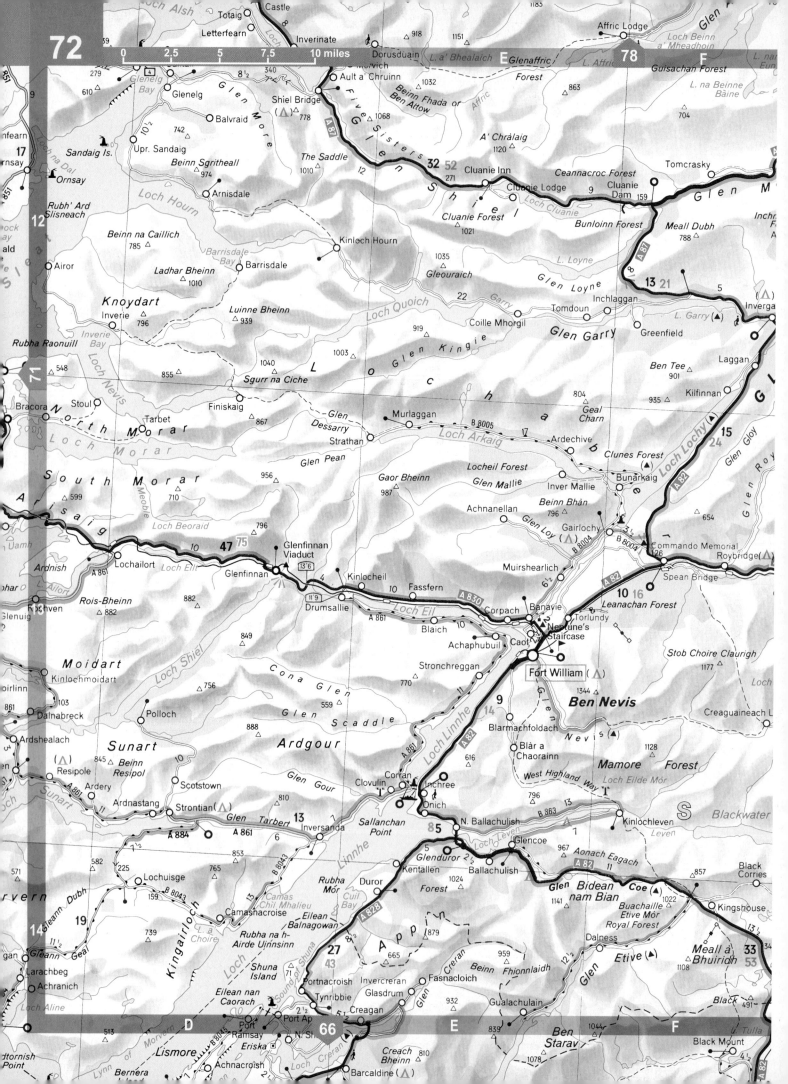

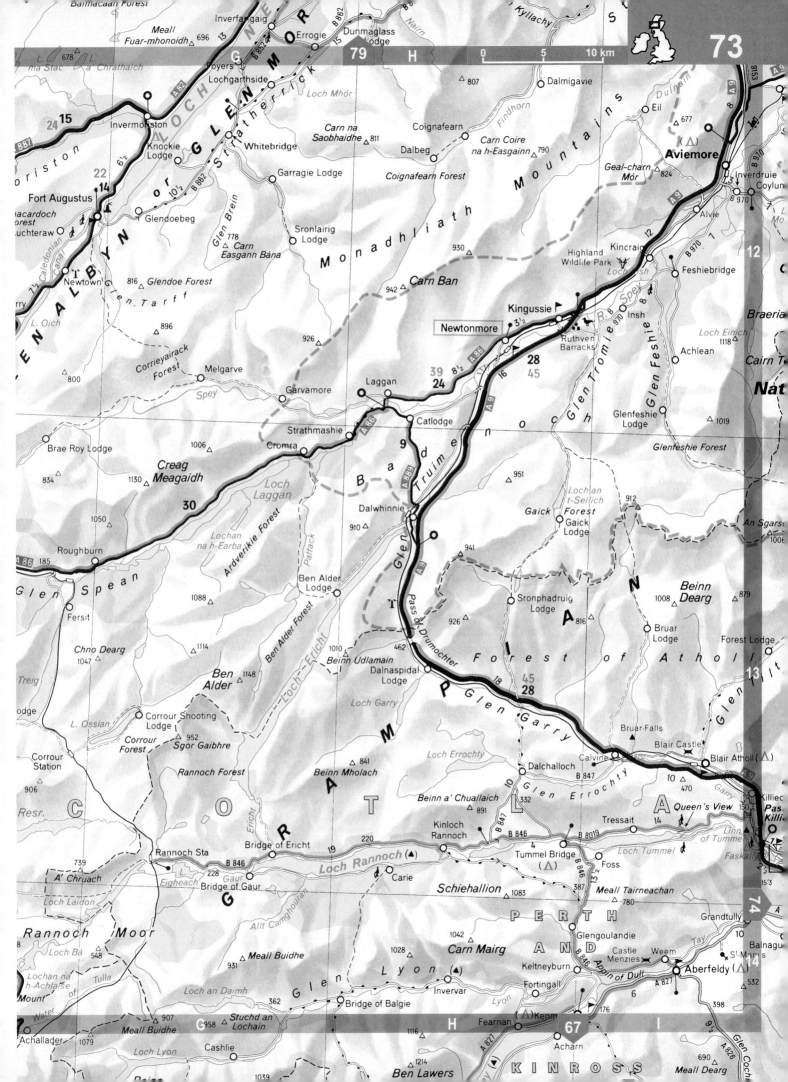

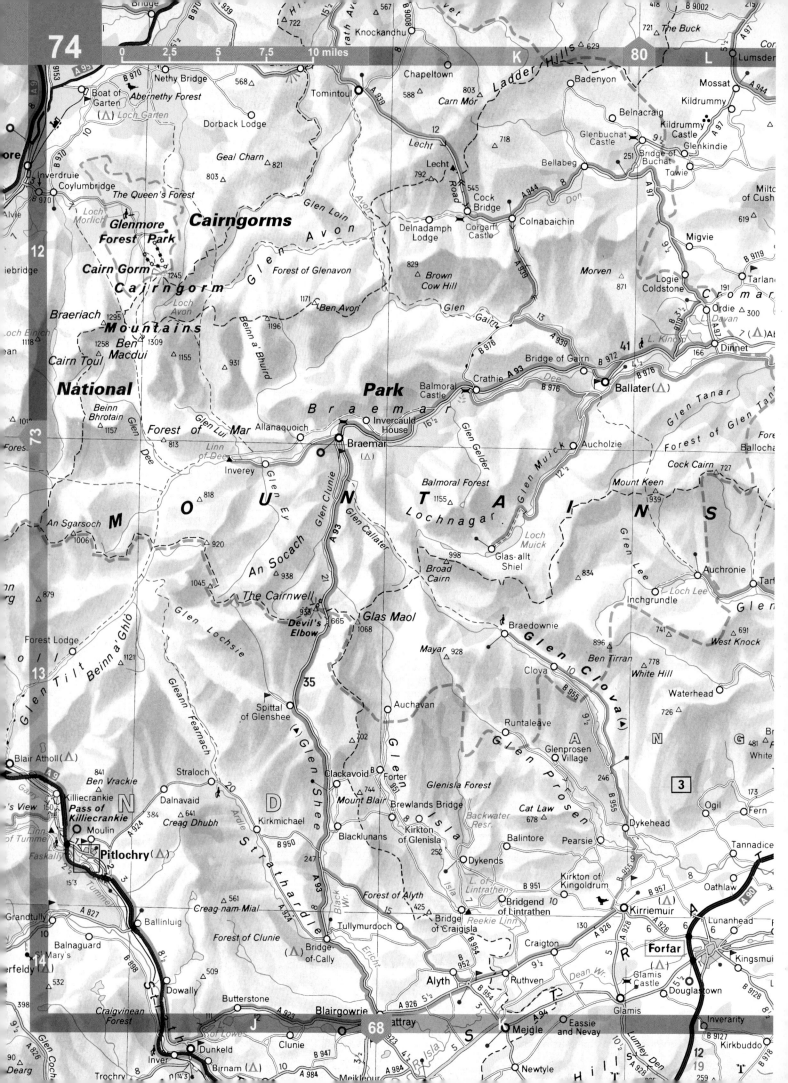

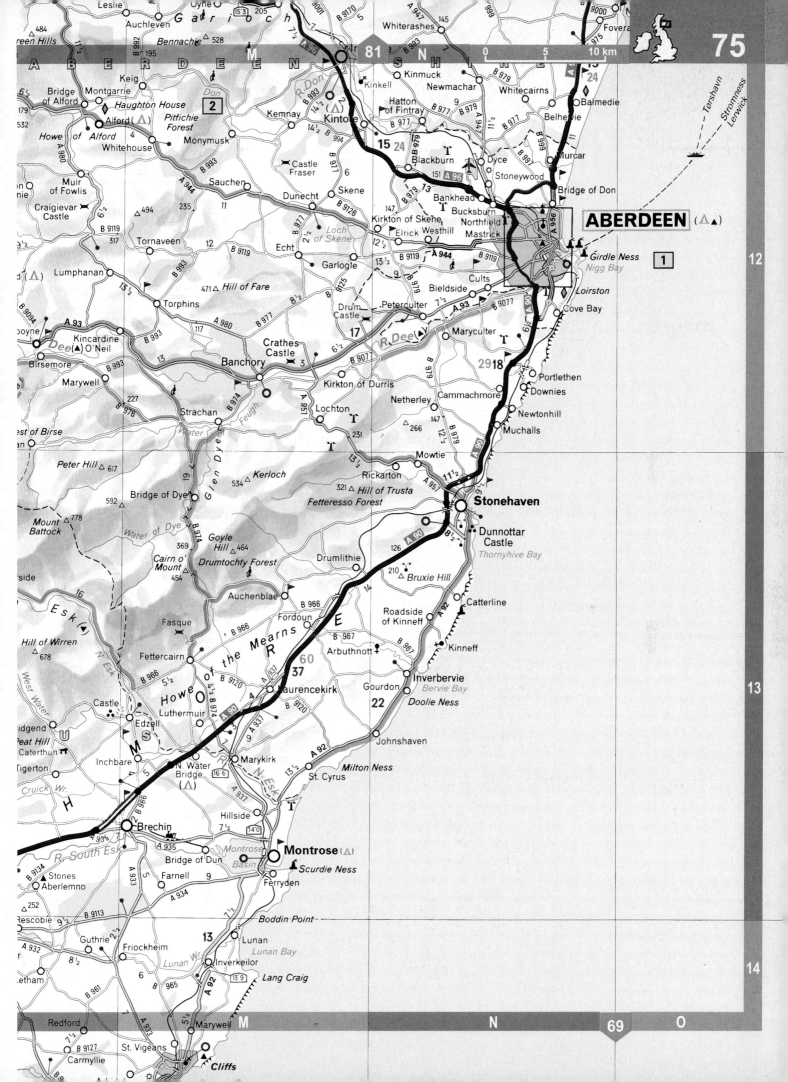

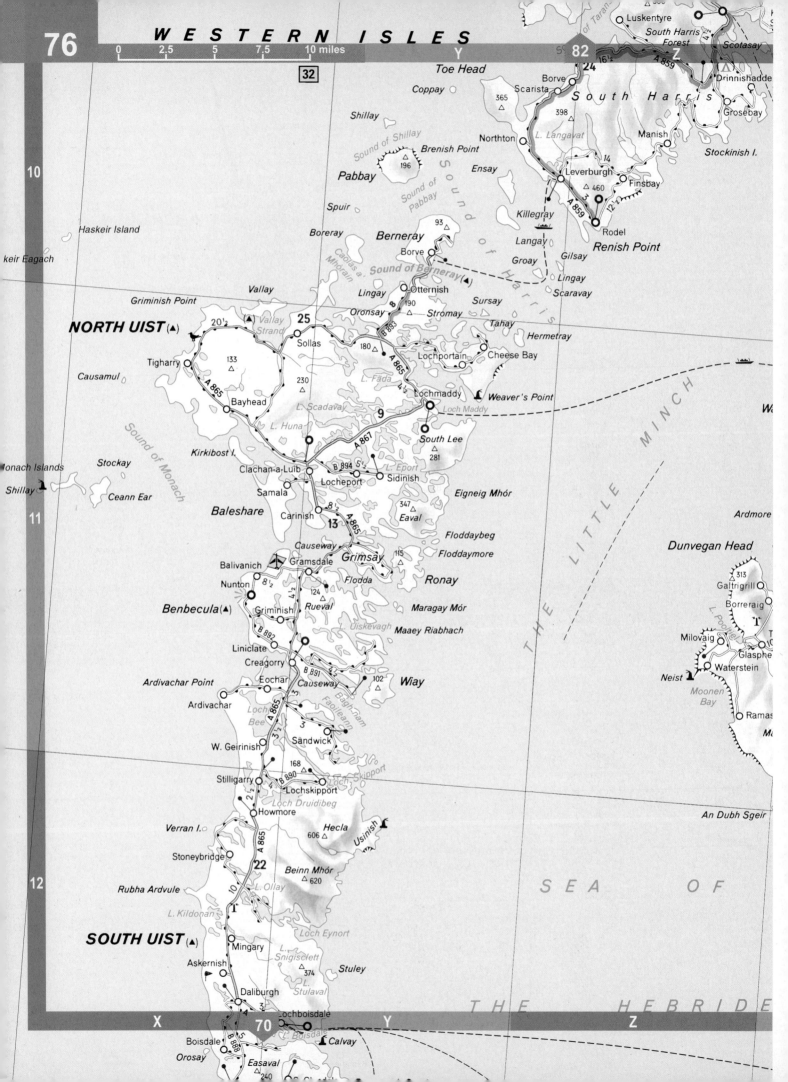

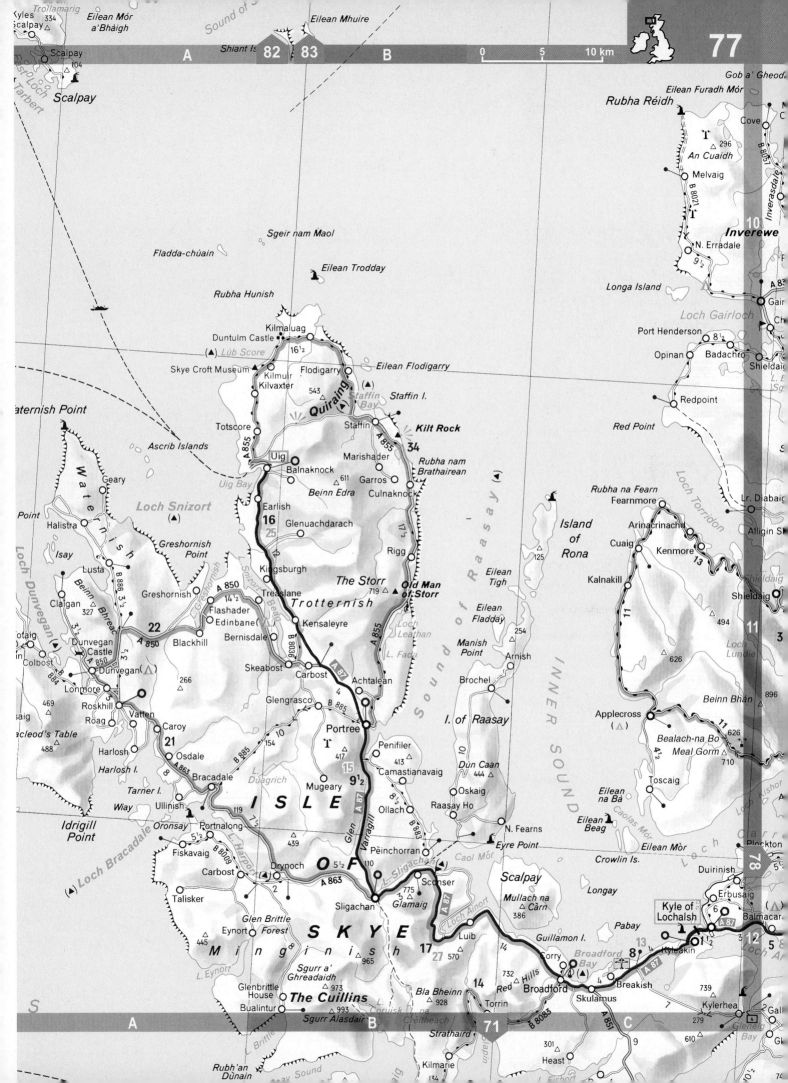

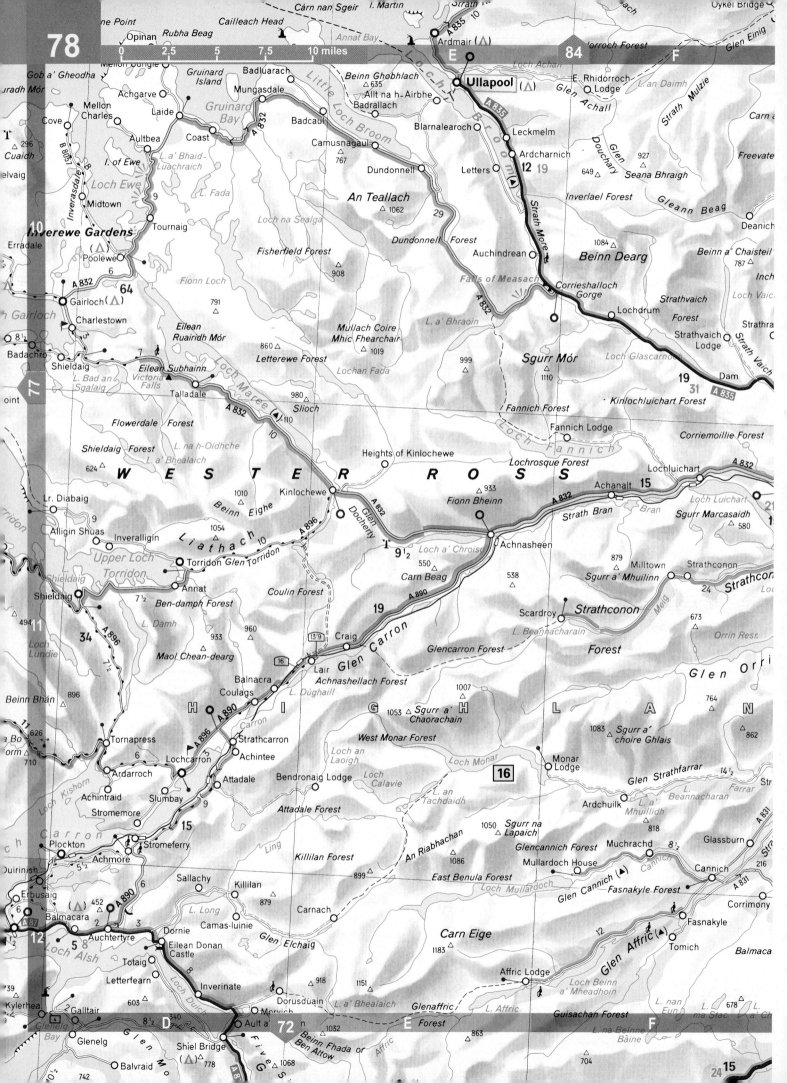

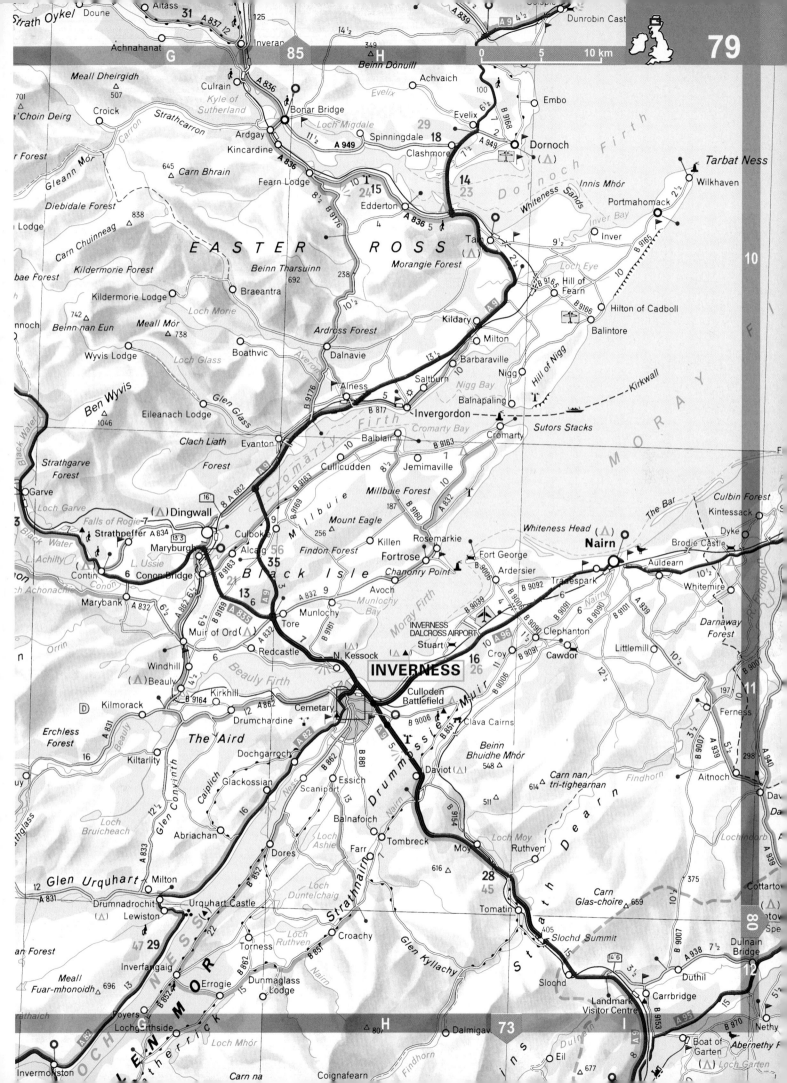

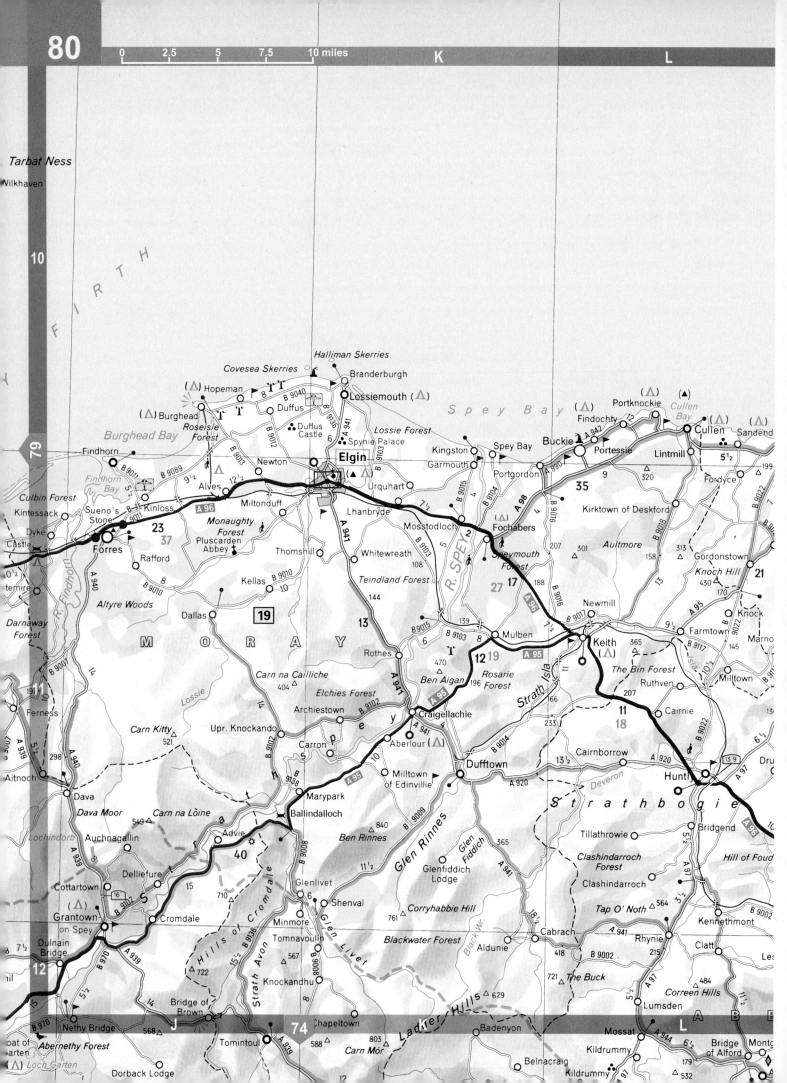

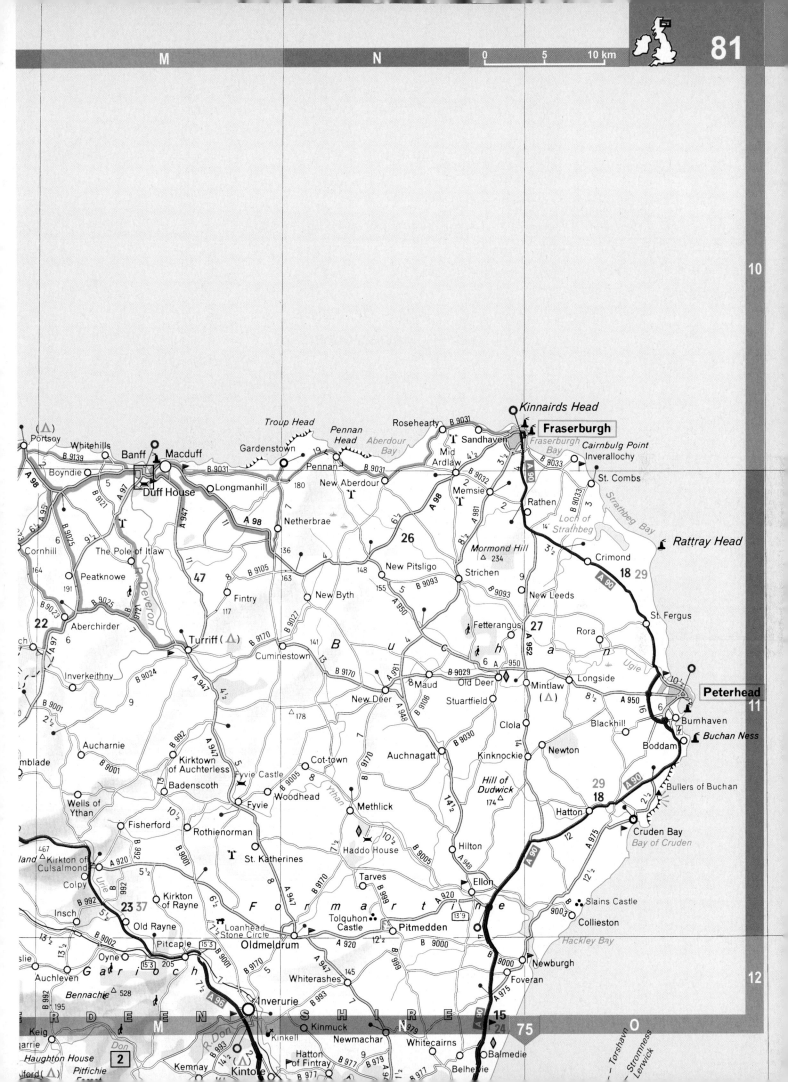

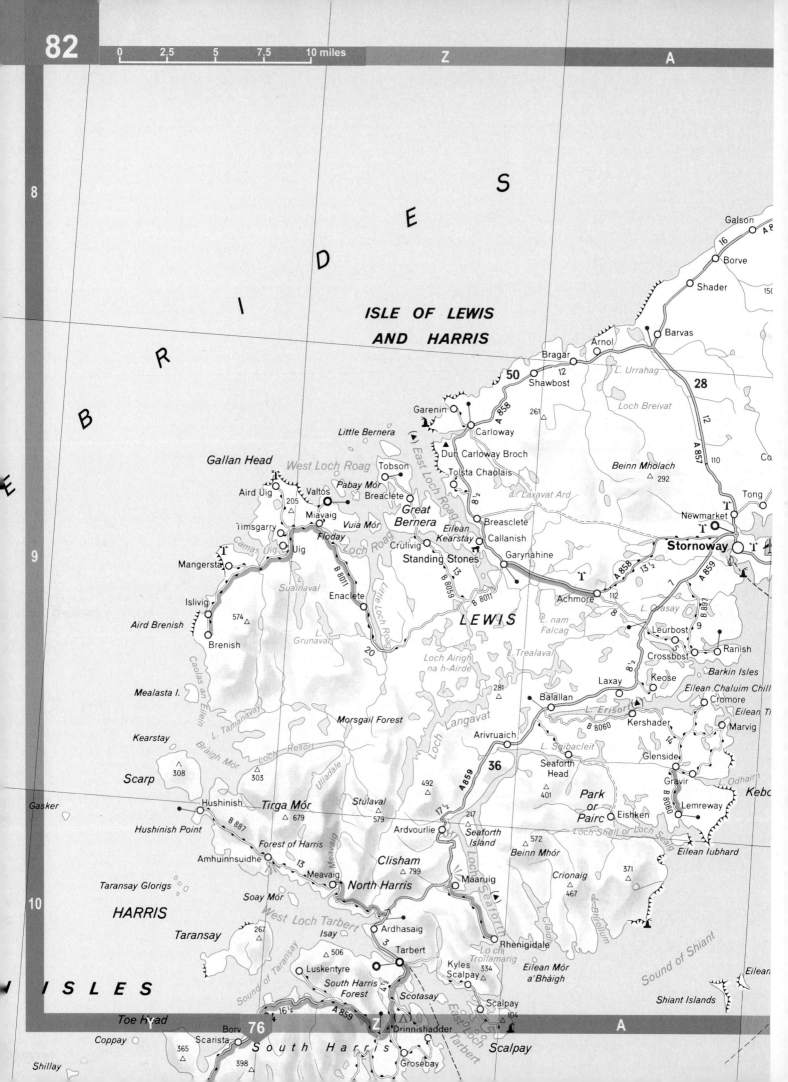

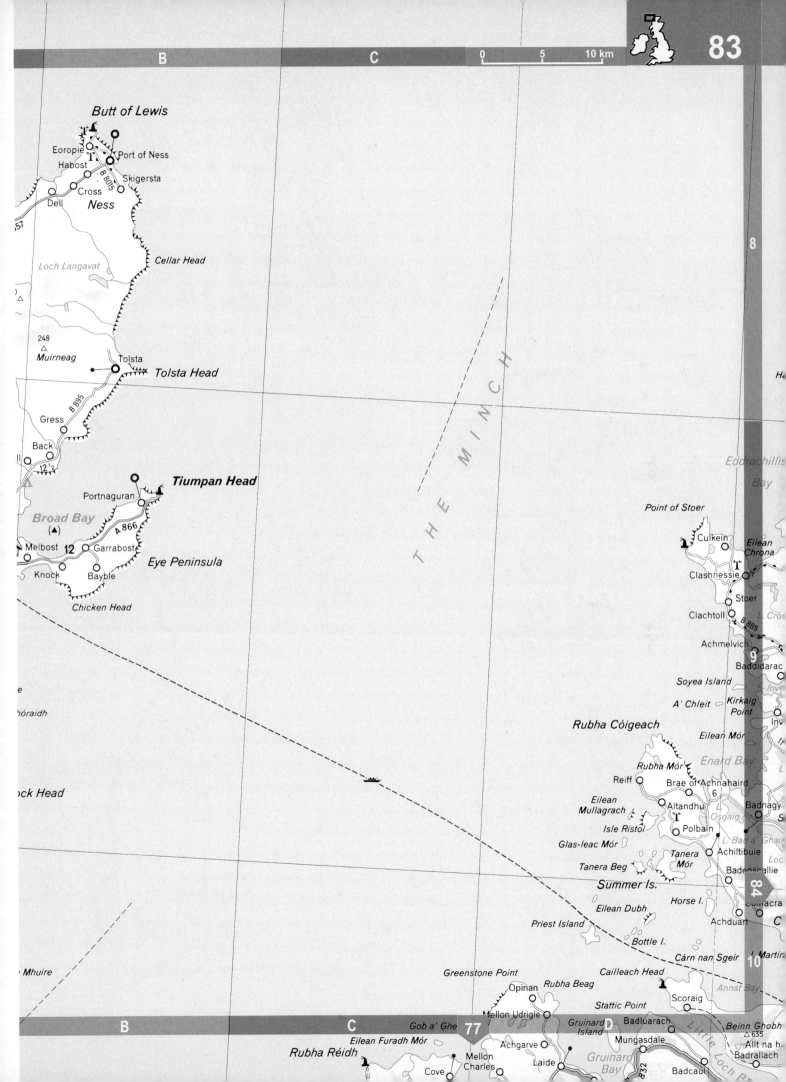

0   5   10 km

B

C

Butt of Lewis

Eoropie
Port of Ness
Habost
Skigersta
B 8015
Cross
Dell
Ness

Loch Langavat

Cellar Head

248
Muirneag
Tolsta
Tolsta Head

B 895

Gress

Back

12 ²

Tiumpan Head

Portnaguran

Broad Bay

(▲)

A 866

Melbost
12
Garrabost

Knock
Bayble
Eye Peninsula

Chicken Head

THE MINCH

8

Eddrachillis Bay

Point of Stoer

Culkein
Eilean Chrona

Clashnessie

Stoer
Clachtoll
B 869

Achmelvich

9

Baddidarac

Soyea Island

A' Chleit
Kirkaig Point

Rubha Còigeach

Eilean Mòr

Enard Bay

Rubha Mòr

Reiff
Brae of Achnahaird
6

Eilean Mullagrach
Altandhu
Badnagy

Isle Ristol
Polbain

Glas-leac Mór
L. Bad a' Ghair

Tanera Mór
Achiltibuie

Tanera Beg
Badenscallie

Summer Is.
84

Eilean Dubh
Horse I.

Priest Island
Achduart

Bottle I.

Càrn nan Sgeir

10

ock Head

Mhuire

Greenstone Point
Cailleach Head

Annat Bay

Opinan
Rubha Beag

Mellon Udrigle
Stattic Point
Scoraig

B

C
77

Gob a' Ghe

Eilean Furadh Mór
Gruinard Island
Badluarach

D

Rubha Réidh

Achgarve
Mungasdale

Cove
Mellon Charles
Laide
Badcaul

Gruinard Bay
B 832

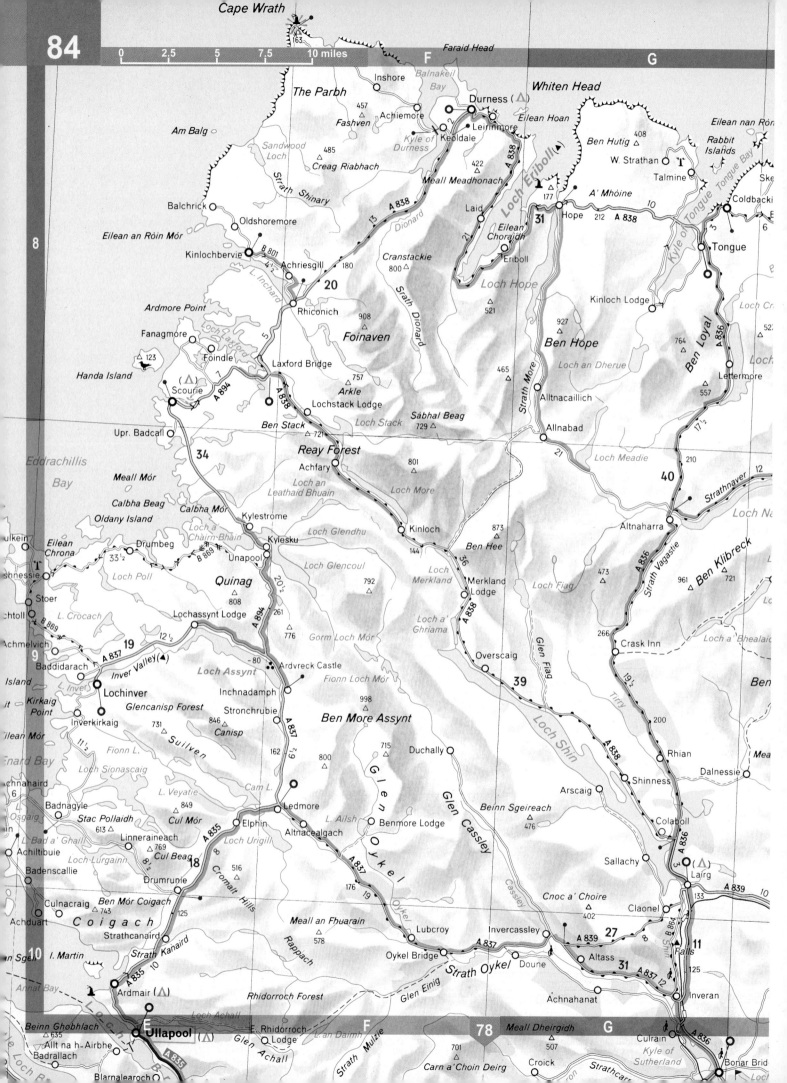

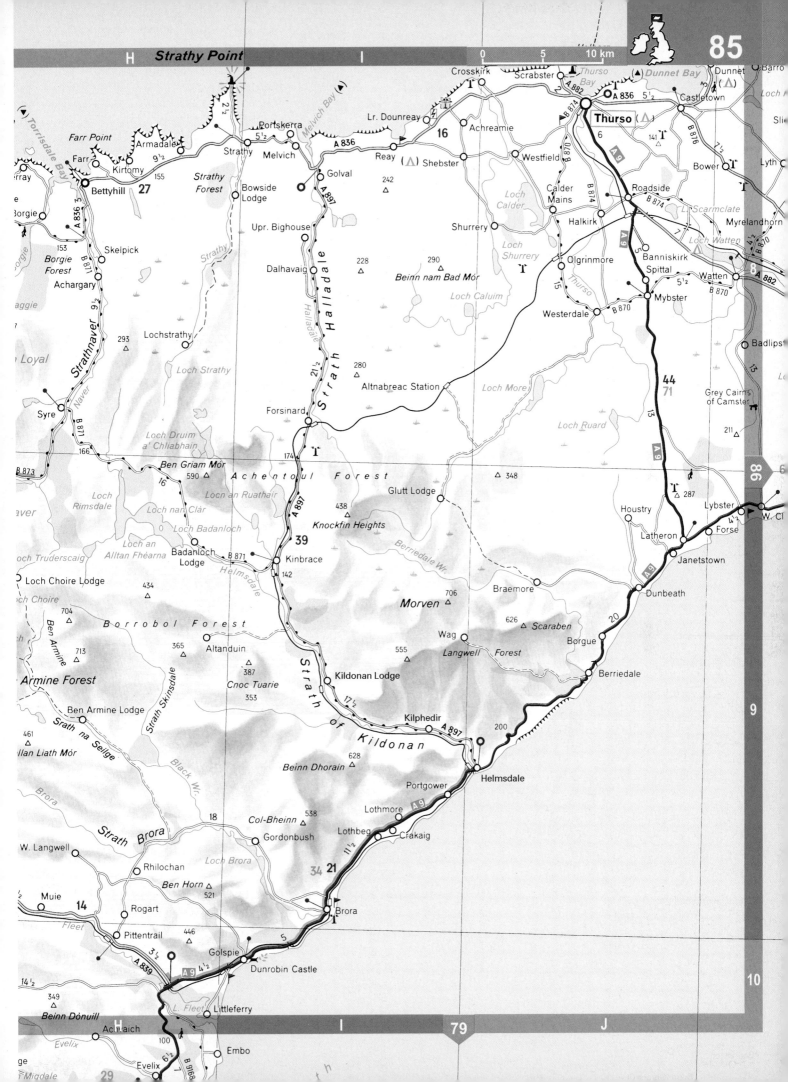

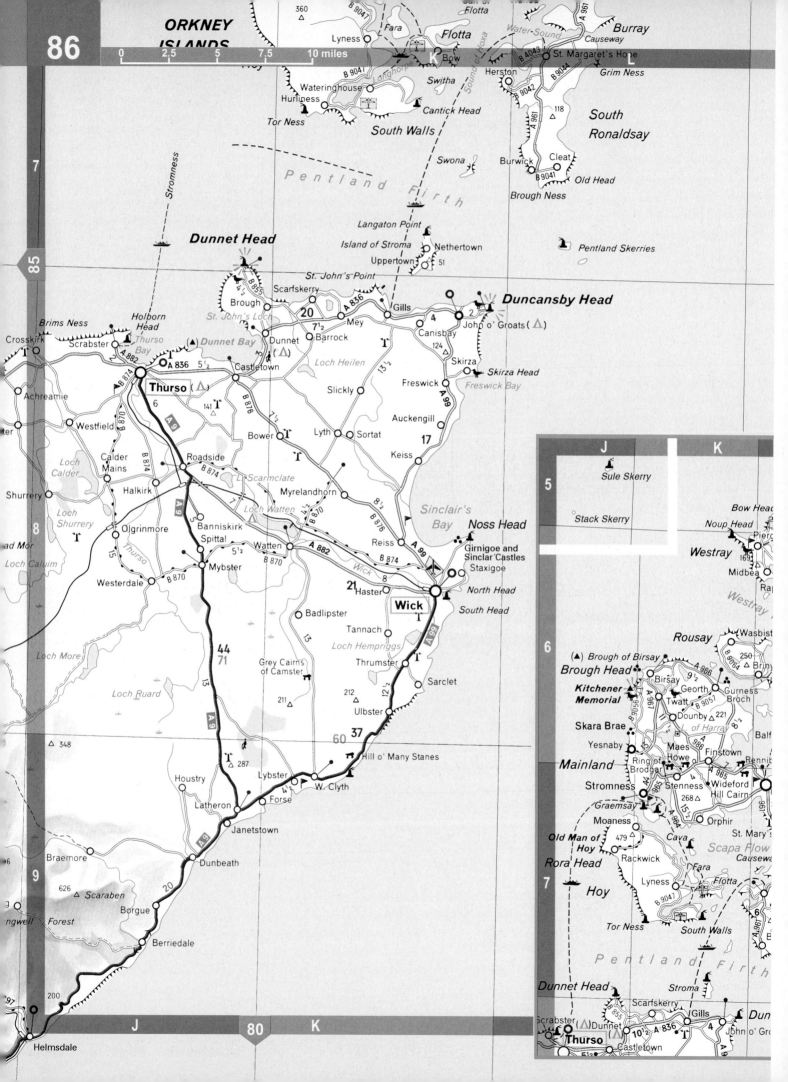

0   2.5   5   7.5   10 miles

7

85

8

9

J   **80**   **K**

Burray

South Ronaldsay

Fara
Flotta
Lyness
Flotta
Bow
St. Margaret's Hope
Herston
Grim Ness
Causeway
Wateringhouse
Hurliness
Tor Ness
Cantick Head
South Walls
Switha
Burwick
Cleat
Old Head
Brough Ness

Pentland   *Firth*
Swona
Pentland Skerries

Langaton Point
Island of Stroma
Nethertown
Uppertown   51

Dunnet Head
St. John's Point
Scarfskerry
Brough
20
Mey
Gills
Duncansby Head
4
2
John o' Groats (△)
Canisbay
124
Brims Ness
Holborn Head
Thurso Bay
Dunnet Bay
Dunnet
Barrock
Loch Heilen
Skirza
Skirza Head
Crosskirk
Scrabster
Achreamie
Westfield
Thurso (△)
Castletown
Slickly
Freswick
Freswick Bay
Calder Mains
Roadside
Bower
Lyth
Sortat
Auckengill
Shurrery
Halkirk
Keiss
17
Loch Calder
Myrelandhorn
Olgrinmore
Banniskirk
Spittal
Watten
Reiss
Sinclair's Bay
Noss Head
ad Mor
Loch Caluim
Loch Shurrery
Westerdale
Mybster
A 882
Wick
Girnigoe and Sinclair Castles
Staxigoe
21
Haster
Wick
North Head
Badlipster
Tannach
South Head
Loch More
Loch Ruard
Grey Cairns of Camster
Loch Hempriggs
Thrumster
44 71
Sarclet
211
212
Ulbster
348
287
60 37
Hill o' Many Stanes
Houstry
Lybster
W. Clyth
Latheron
Forse
Scaraben
Braemore
626
Janetstown
Borgue
Dunbeath
Berriedale
200
Helmsdale

J
5
Sule Skerry
Stack Skerry

K

Bow Head
Noup Head
Pierc
Westray
169
Midbea
Rap

Westray

6
(△) Brough of Birsay
Brough Head
Kitchener Memorial
Birsay
250
Rousay
Wasbist
A 966
Georth
Gurness Broch
Twatt
Dounby
221
Skara Brae
Yesnaby
Maes Howe
Finstown
Mainland
Ring of Brodgar
Stenness
268
Wideford Hill Cairn
Stromness
Graemsay
Orphir
St. Mary's
Old Man of Hoy
Moaness
479
Cava
Scapa Flow
Rora Head
Rackwick
Fara
Flotta
Causewa
7
Hoy
Lyness
Tor Ness
South Walls
Pentland   *Firth*

Dunnet Head
Stroma
Scarfskerry
Gills
Scrabster (△) Dunnet (△)
Dun
John o' Gro
Thurso
Castletown

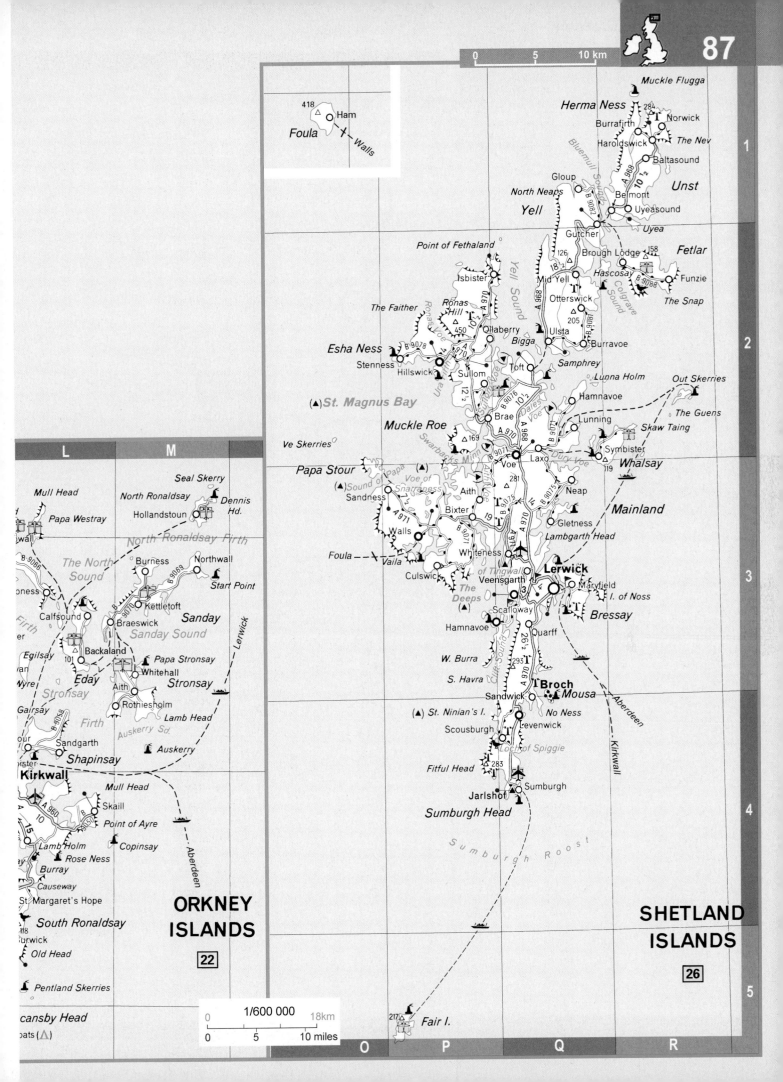

0   5   10 km

Foula

418 △ Ham
Walls

Muckle Flugga
Herma Ness   284
Burrafirth   Norwick
Haroldswick   *The Nev*
Baltasound
Gloup   Belmont   **Unst**
North Neaps   A 968 10½
Uyeasound
Yell   *Uyea*
Gutcher
126   Brough Lodge   158   **Fetlar**
18½
Point of Fethaland   Mid Yell   Hascosay   Funzie
Isbister   Otterswick   *The Snap*
The Faither   *Ronas*   Ulsta
Hill   Bigga   Burravoe
450 10½   Ollaberry   *Samphrey*
Esha Ness   205   *Lunna Holm*   *Out Skerries*
Stenness   B 9078   *The Guens*
Hillswick   Sullom   Toft   Hamnavoe
12½   Brae   Lunning   *Skaw Taing*
(▲)*St. Magnus Bay*   10½   Symbister
Muckle Roe   Laxo   119   **Whalsay**
Ve Skerries   169   Voe   *Dury Voe*
Papa Stour   281   **Mainland**
(▲)*Sound of Papa*   Aith   Neap
Voe of   Bixter   19
Snarraness   Gletness
Sandness   14   *Lambgarth Head*
A 971   Whiteness
Foula   Walls   L. of Tingwall   **Lerwick**
Vaila   Veensgarth   Maryfield
Culswick   *The*   3   *I. of Noss*
Deeps   Scalloway   **Bressay**
(▲)   Hamnavoe   Quarff
W. Burra   26½
S. Havra   293
Broch   *Mousa*
Sandwick
St. Ninian's I.   *No Ness*
Scousburgh   Levenwick
283
Fitful Head   *Loch of Spiggie*
Jarlshof   Sumburgh
Sumburgh Head

Sumburgh Roost

217   *Fair I.*

SHETLAND
ISLANDS

26

ORKNEY
ISLANDS

22

Seal Skerry
Mull Head   *North Ronaldsay*   Dennis
Papa Westray   Hollandstoun   Hd.
North Ronaldsay Firth
The North   Burness   Northwall
Sound   *Start Point*
Calfsound   Kettletoft   **Sanday**
Braeswick   *Sanday Sound*
Backaland
101   Whitehall   *Papa Stronsay*
Eday   Aith   **Stronsay**
Rothiesholm   *Lamb Head*
Stronsay   *Auskerry Sd.*   Auskerry
Firth
Sandgarth
Shapinsay   *Mull Head*
Kirkwall   Skaill   Point of Ayre   Copinsay
A 960   B   15
10   *Lamb Holm*
Burray   *Rose Ness*
Causeway
St. Margaret's Hope
418
South Ronaldsay   *Old Head*

Pentland Skerries

...cansby Head
...oats (△)

1/600 000   18km
0
0   5   10 miles

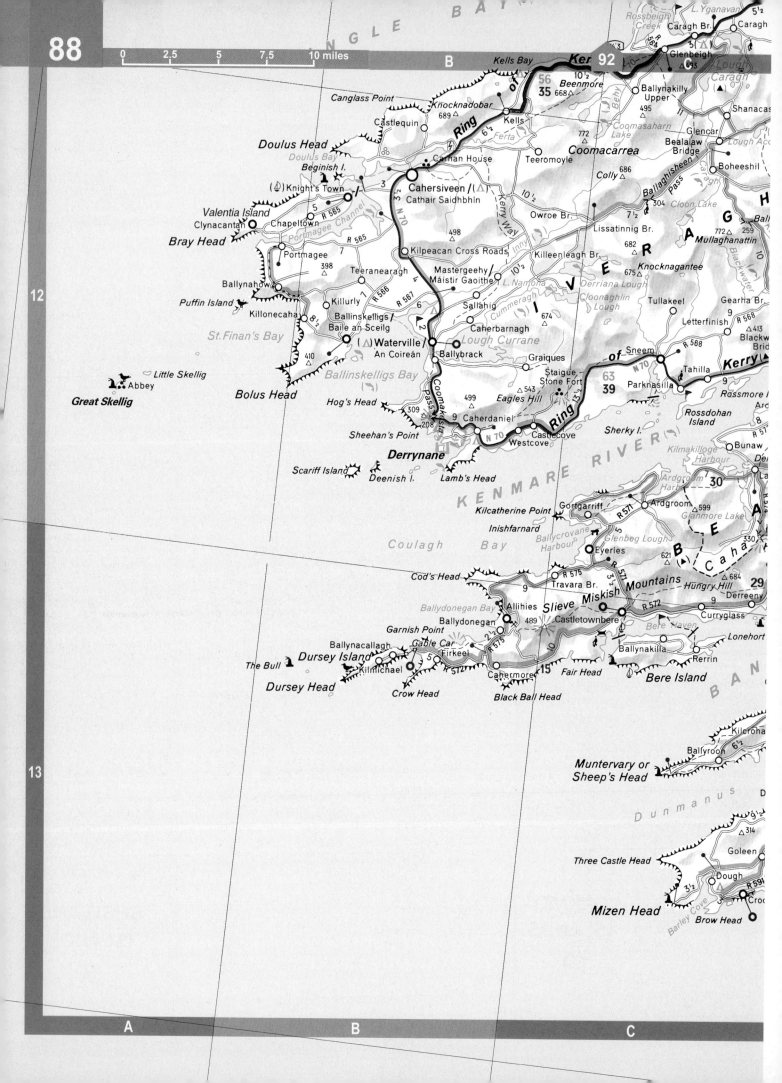

0   2.5   5   7.5   10 miles

NGLE BAY
Rossbeigh
Creek   Caragh Br.   Caragh
L. Yganavan
5½

Kells Bay   Ker   Glenbeigh   Caragh
R 554   Lough

Canglass Point   Ring   56   Beenmore   Ballynakilly
35   668 △   Upper
Knocknadobar   Kells   495   Shanacas
Castlequin   689 △   Beby
Doulus Head   Ferta   6½   Coomasaharn
Doulus Bay   Carhan House   772 △   Lake   Glencar
Beginish I.   Coomacarrea   Bealalaw   Lough Acc
Teeromoyle   Bridge
Knight's Town   Cahersiveen /(△)   Colly   686 △   Boheeshil
Valentia Island   Cathair Saidhbhín   304   Cloon Lake
Clynacantan   Chapeltown   Owroe Br.   7½
Bray Head   R 565   Kerry Way   Lissatinnig Br.   772 △   259
498   682 △   Mullaghanattin
Portmagee   R 565   Kilpeacan Cross Roads   Inny   Killeenleagh Br.   675 △   Knocknagantee
398   7   Mastergeehy /   L. Namona   Derriana Lough   Tullakeel   Gearha Br.
Ballynahow   R 566   Máistir Gaoithe   4   Cloonaghlin   △ 413   Blackw
Teeranearagh   Lough   Letterfinish   R 568   Brid
Killurly   R 567   6   Sallahig   Cummeragh   674 △
Puffin Island   Ballinskelligs /   Caherbarnagh   Sneem   R 568
Killonecaha   8½   Baile an Sceilg   Lough Currane   of   Tahilla   KERRY
St.Finan's Bay   410   (△) Waterville /   63   N70   Parknasilla
An Coireán   Ballybrack   39   Rossmore
Little Skellig   Graiques   Staigue   Rossdohan
Abbey   Stone Fort   Island
Great Skellig   Bolus Head   Hog's Head   309   9   Caherdaniel   Eagles Hill   13½   Sherky I.   Bunaw
499   △ 543   Ring
208   N70   Castlecove
Sheehan's Point   Westcove   KENMARE RIVER   Kilmakilloge
Derrynane   Harbour
Scariff Island   Deenish I.   Lamb's Head   30
Kilcatherine Point   Gortgarriff   Ardgroom   599 △   Glanmore Lake   330
Inishfarnard   R 571   B   Caha
Coulagh   Bay   Ballycrovane   Eyeries   621 △
Harbour   Glenbeg Lough   Hungry Hill
Cod's Head   R 575   Travara Br.   Miskish Mountains   684 △   29
9   Slieve   R 572   Derreeny
Ballydonegan Bay   Allihies   489   Castletownbere   Curryglass
Garnish Point   Ballydonegan   Bere Haven   Lonehort
Ballynacallagh   Cable Car   Ballynakilla   Rerrin
The Bull   Dursey Island   Firkeel   2½   Bere Island   BAN
Kilmichael   5   R 572   Cahermore   15   Fair Head   Kilcroha
Dursey Head   Crow Head   Black Ball Head   Ballyroon   6½
Muntervary or   Sheep's Head
DUNMANUS
△ 314   Goleen
Three Castle Head   Dough   R 591
Mizen Head   Brow Head   Croc
Barley Cove

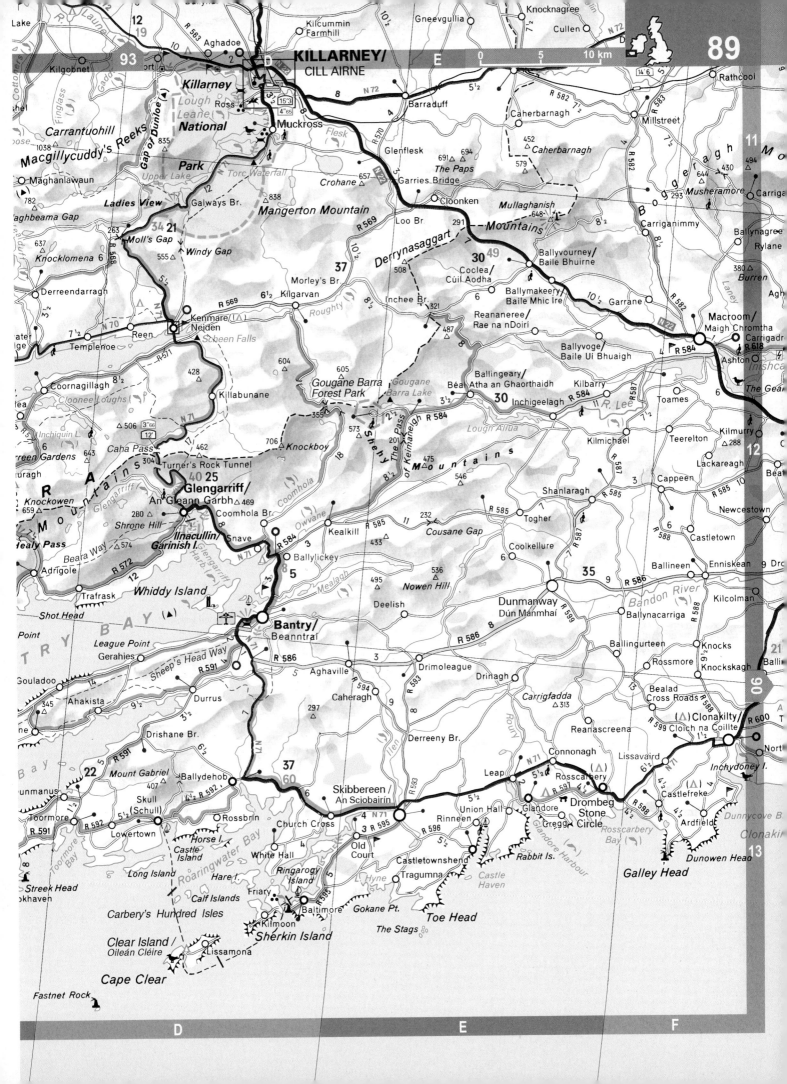

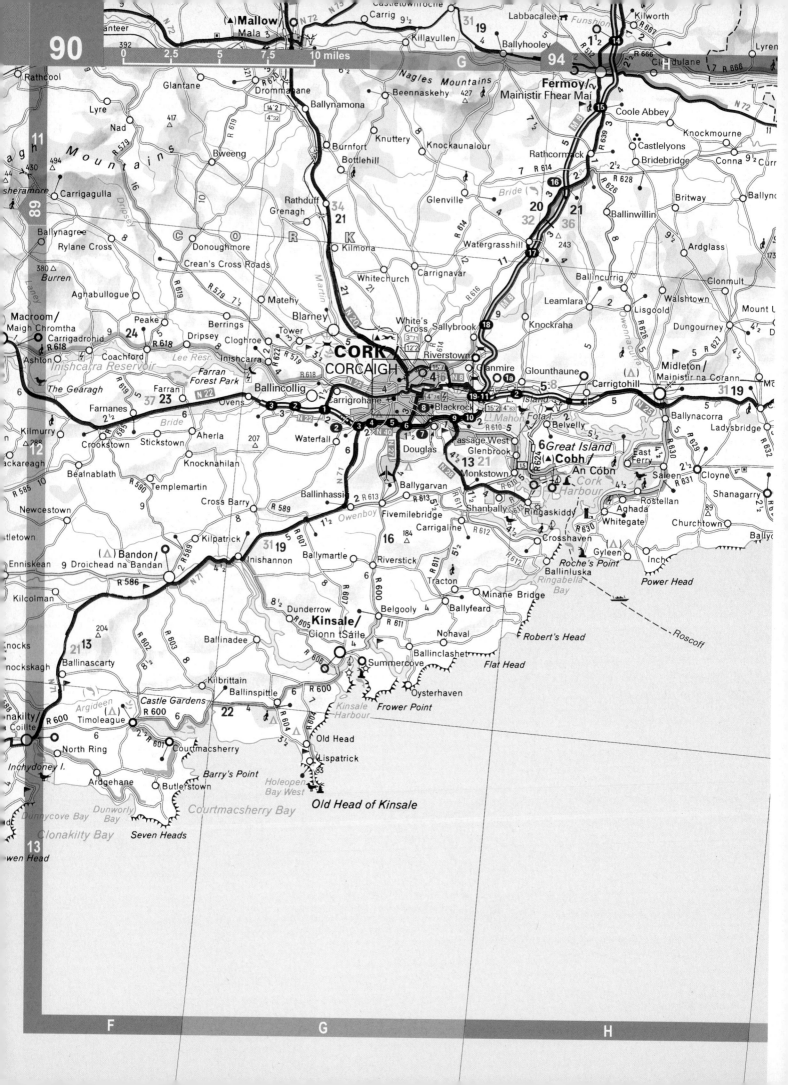

Feagarrid
Mt. Melleray Monastery
Ballynamult
Knockboy 725
△ Seefin
Mahon Bridge
Fews
Newtow
Kilmacthomas
aglogh
9
Ballynaguilkee
W A T E R F
8½
Ballyduff
R 668
R 666
5
R 669
4
Cappoquin/
Ceapach Choinn
Millstreet
22
95
25
Boolatt
J
0
5
10 km
8½
R 681
24
39
Lismore/
Lios Mór
5½
6½
R 671
Modelligo
N 72
Colligan
9
484
△
Lemybrien
N25
Ballylaneen
R 675
Kill
Dunhill
R 675
Fennor
R 882
Tallowbridge
Ballinaspick
3½
4½
7½
12
Kilgobnet
6
The Pike
25
12½
4½
Annestown
Tramore/
Trá Mhór
△
R 628
Tallow
River Bride
Villierstown
R 672
2 3
R 675
Stradbally
Bunmahon
(△)
Dunabrattin
Head
Gt. Newtown
Head
aglass
6½
Keereen
3
Ballyvoyle Head
11
R 634
The Pike
Aglish
7½
(△) Dungarvan
Dún Garbhán
Clonea Bay
Ballynacourty
Dungarvan Harbour
River Blackwater
17
Drum
2½
6
R 674
Ballynagaul
Helvick Head
Uniacke
Inch
Boola
Toung
7½
R 634
301
△
17
27
Hills
Ringville
An Rinn
Muggort's Bay
angan
Cross
Licky
N25
5½
9½
Loskeran
Clashmore
Grange
R 673
1
Killeagh
6
N25
Kinsalebeg
7½
4½
Mine Head
Gortaroo
Moord
2½
4½
Curragh
astlemartyr
Youghal/
Eochaill
R 673
Ardmore/Aird Mhór
58
Ram Head
Womanagh
Ballymadog
(△ ▲ ≫)
Whiting Bay
R 633
Youghal
Bay
Kilcredan
Ballymacoda
Knockadoon Head
Garryvoe
Ballymakeagh
Ballycotton Bay
cotton

I
J
K
12
13

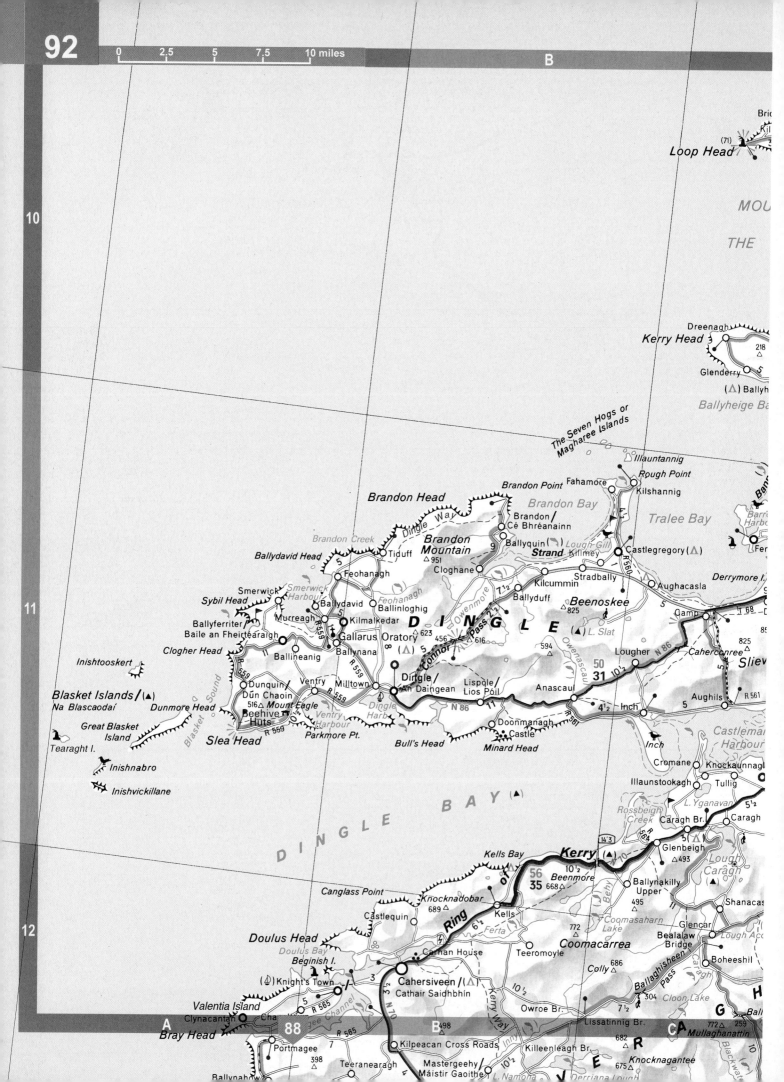

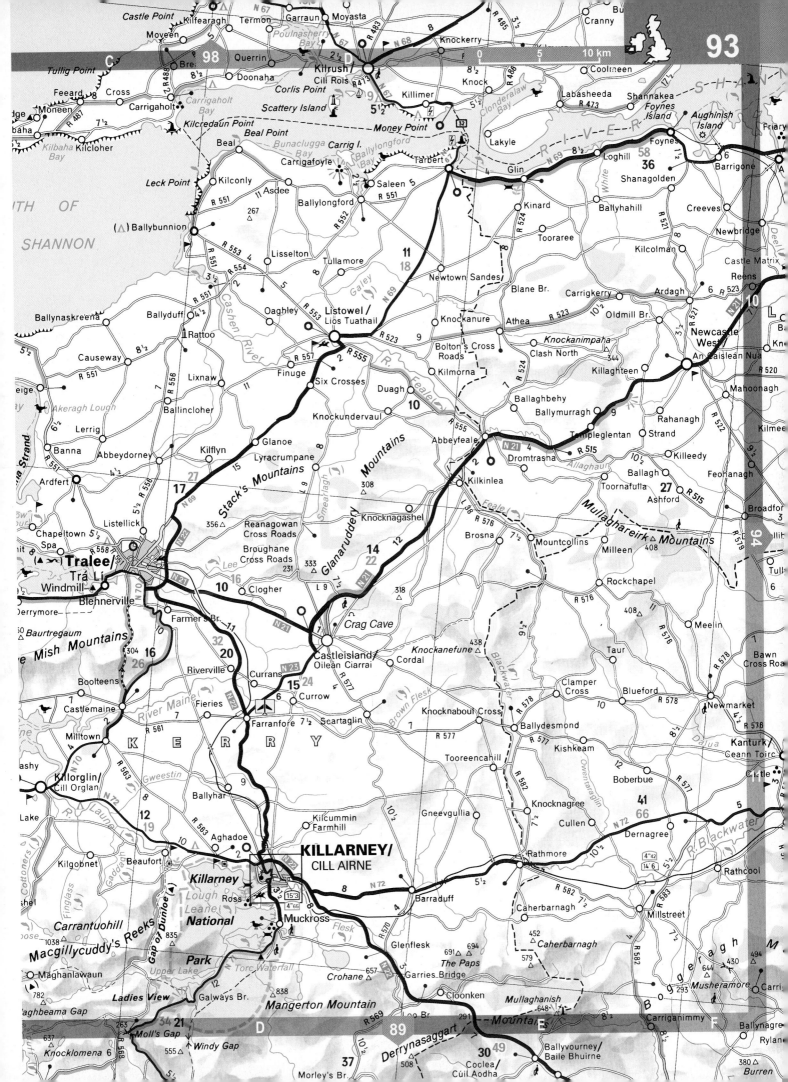

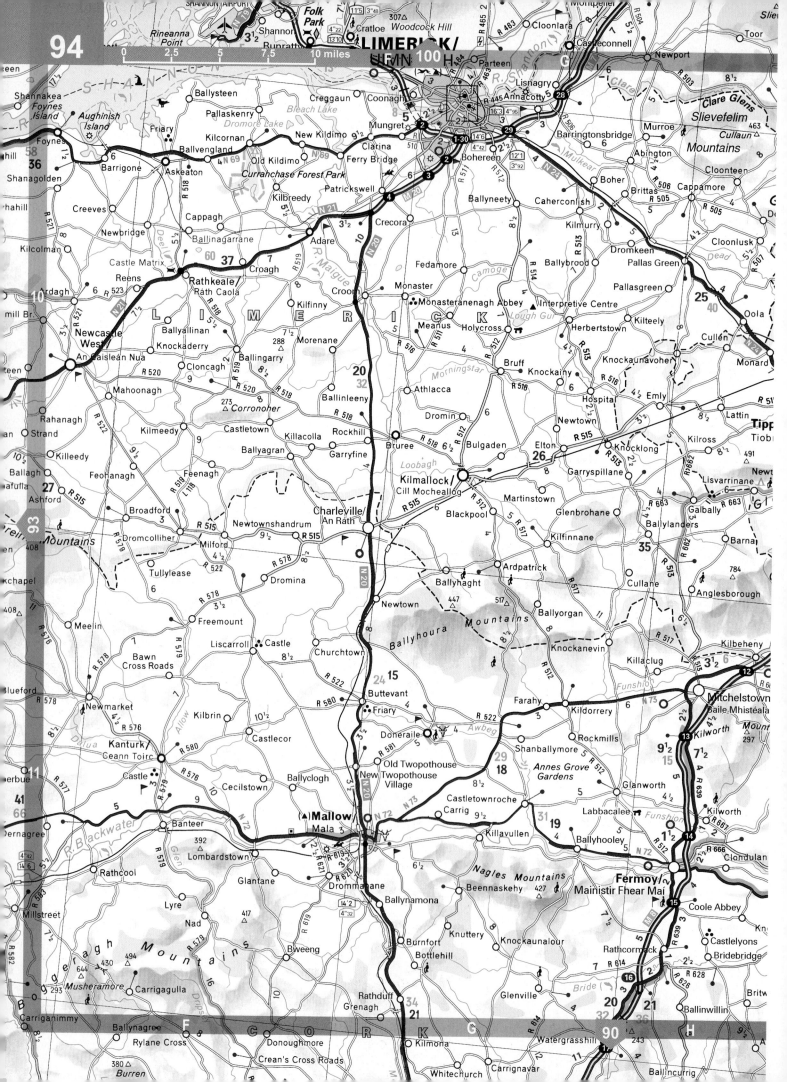

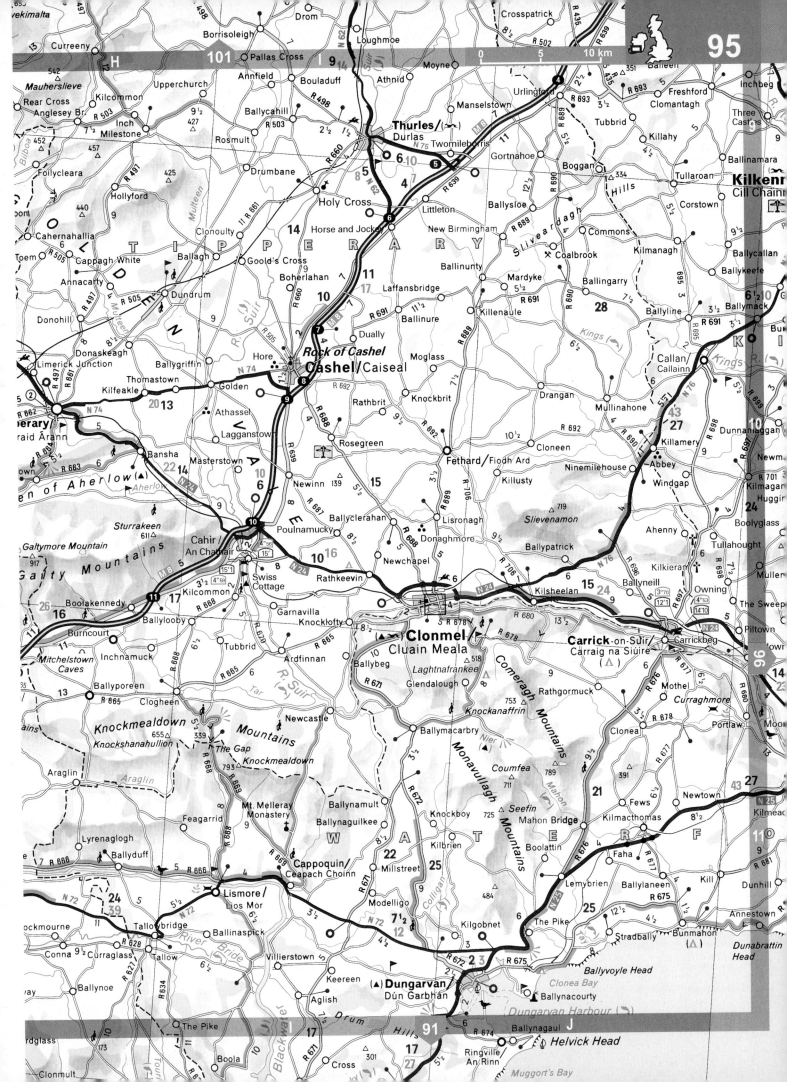

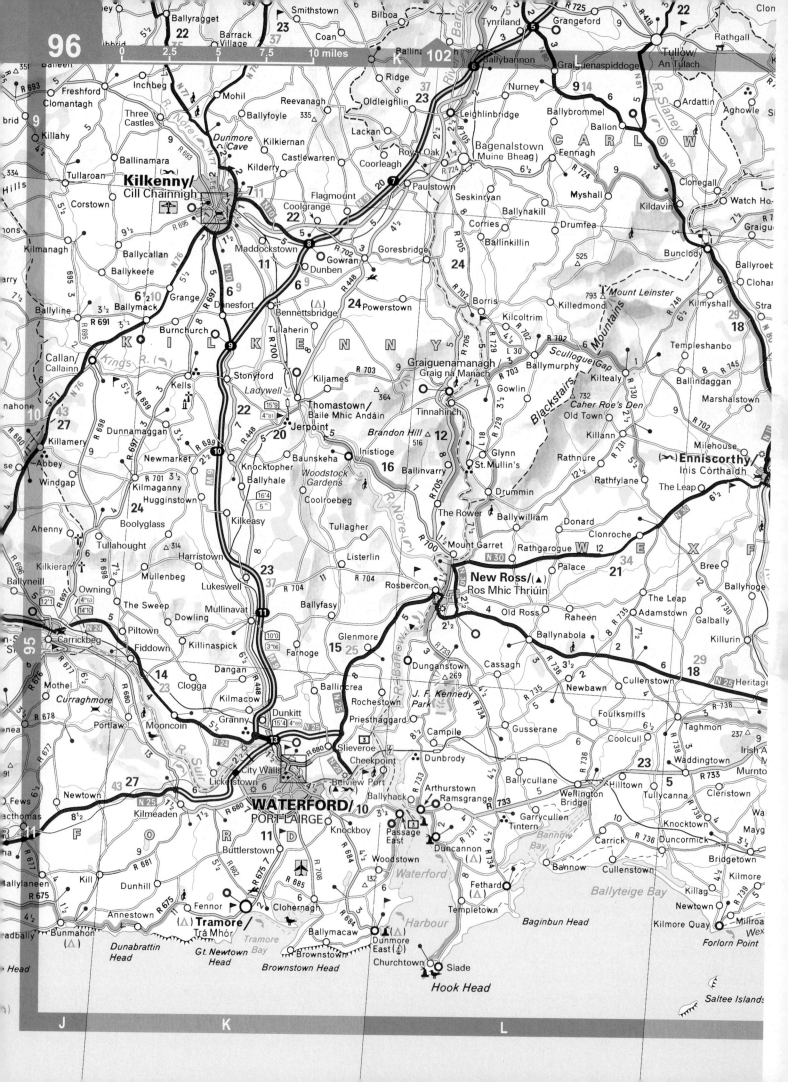

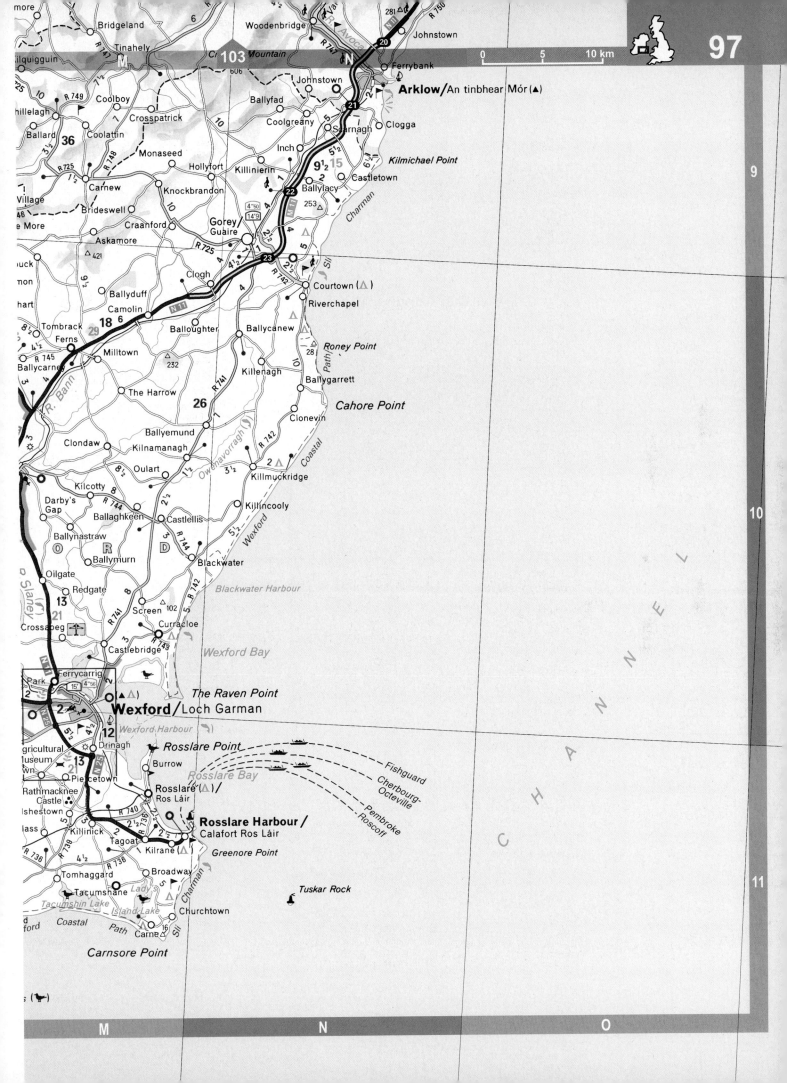

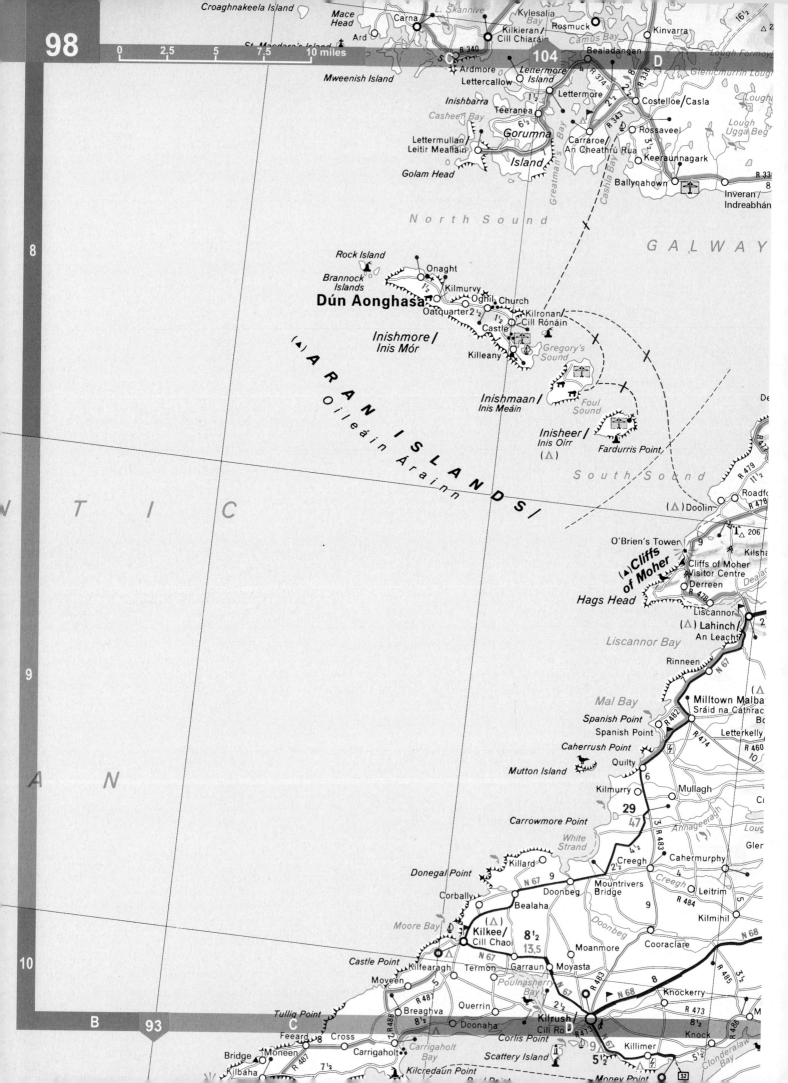

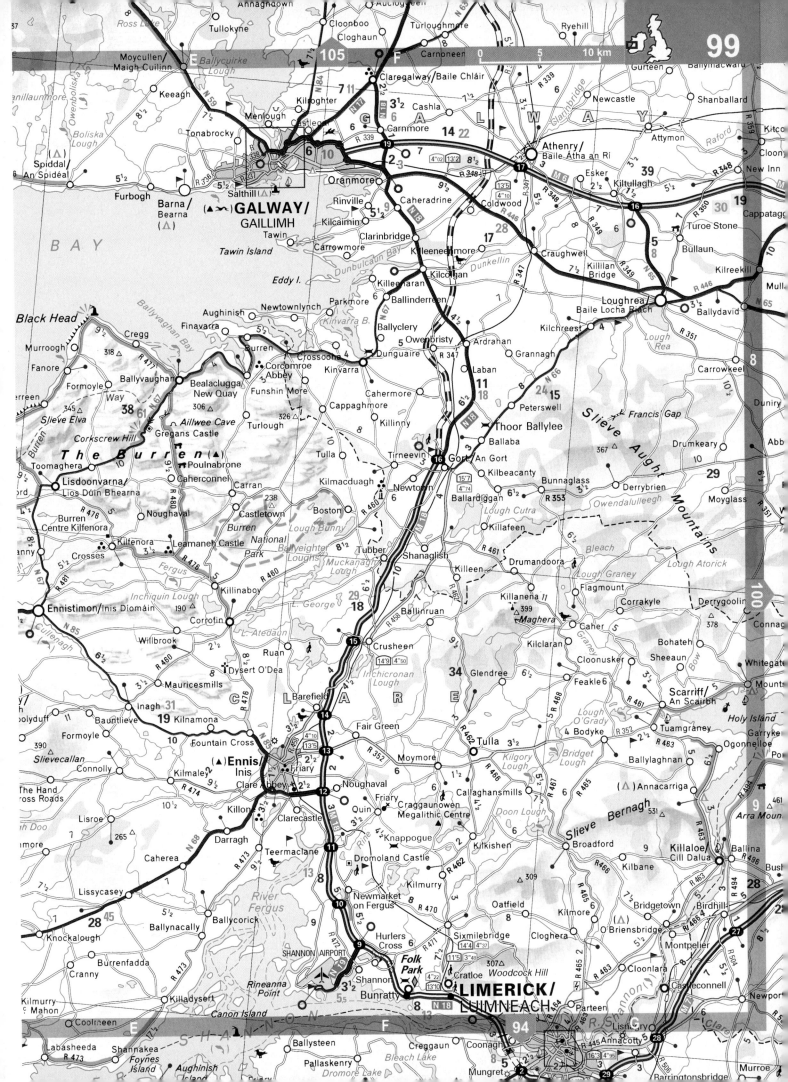

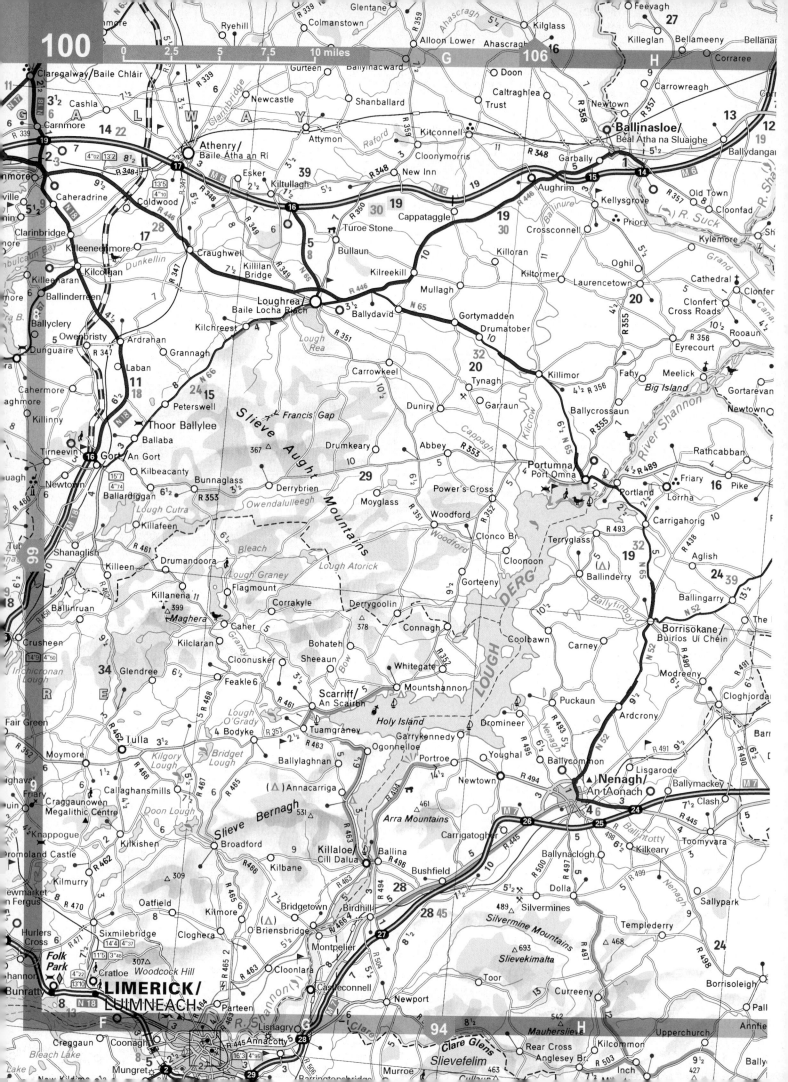

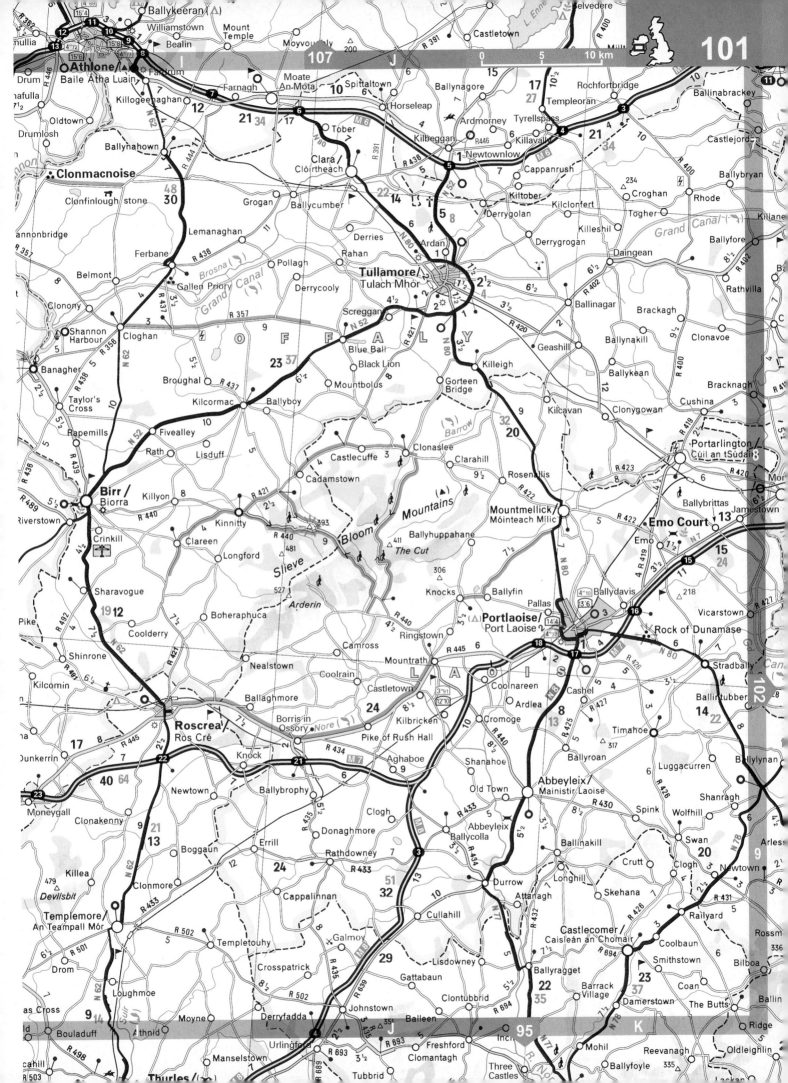

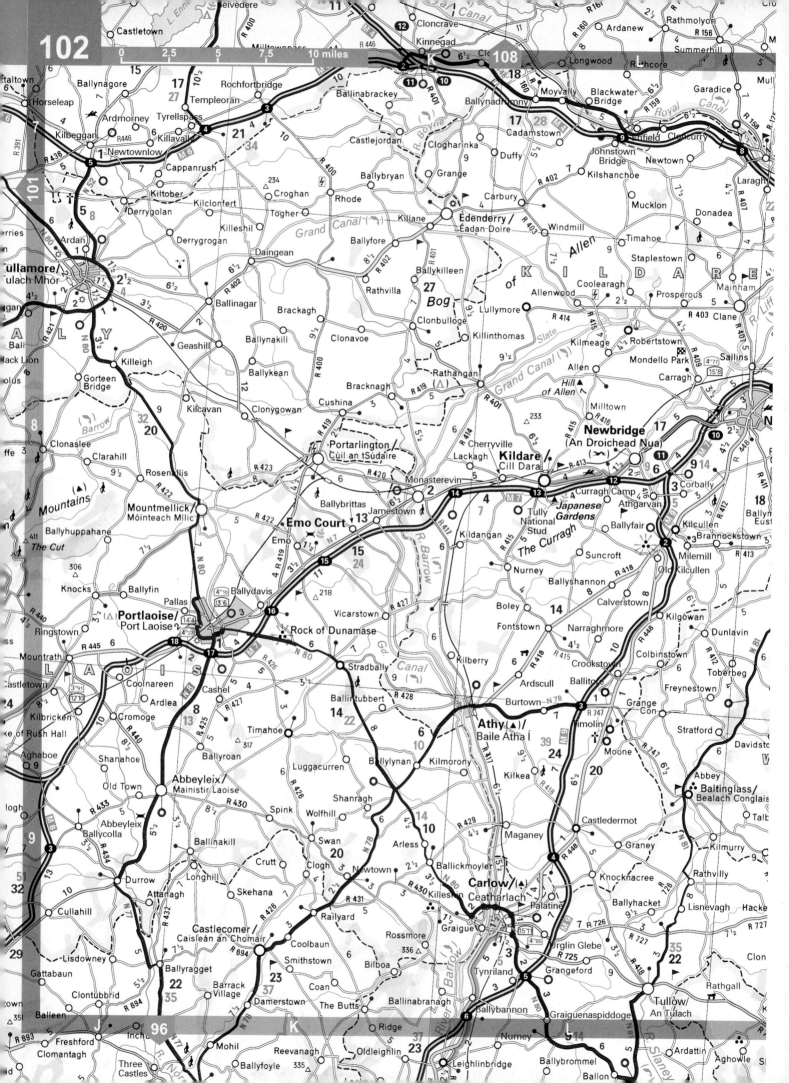

7

8

9

0 5 10 km

DUBLIN / BAILE ÁTHA CLIATH

Howth / Binn Éadair

Dublin Bay

Douglas (I. of Man)
Holyhead
Liverpool

Dún Laoghaire
Holyhead

Dalkey
Killiney
Killiney Bay
Ballybrack
Loughlinstown
Shankill
Little Bray

Bray / Bré
Bray Head
Killruddery
Kilmacanoge
Great Sugar Loaf
The Downs
Carriggower
Greystones / Na Clocha Liatha
Delgany
Kilpedder
Newtown Mt. Kennedy
Kilcoole

Leamore Strand
Newcastle
Killiskey
Mount Usher
Ashford
Ballinalea
Rathnew

Wicklow / Cill Mhantáin
Wicklow Head

Kilpoole
Ardmore Point
Kilbride
Brittas Bay
Ardanairy
Mizen Head
Johnstown
Ferrybank

Arklow / An tinbhear mor

FINGAL

Rush / An Ros
Portrane
Donab
Newbridge
Malahide / Mullach Íde
Portmarnock
Ireland's Eye
Baldoyle
Kinsaley
Santry
Artane
Clontarf
Nose of Howth

Swords / Sord
Ward
St. Margaret's
Kils
Mulhuddart
Finglas
Rathmines

Ashbourne
Corduff
Ratoath
Donaghmore
Fairyhouse
Kilbride
Clonee
Dunboyne
Clonsilla
Blanchardstown
Mulhuddart
Phoenix Park

Batterstown
Ballynare
Dunboyne
Maynooth / Maigh Nuad
Leixlip
Lucan
Castletown House
Celbridge
Milltown
Straffan
Clondalkin
Newcastle
Rathcoole
Russborough House
Blessington
Hollywood
Valleymount
Ballyknockan
Poulaphouca Reservoir
Lackan
Kilcock
Kilbride
Kill
Johnstown
Furness
aas / An Nás
Punchestown
Kilteel
Brittas
Saggart
Tallaght
Dundrum
Stillorgan
Sandyford
Stepaside
Kiltiernan
Glencullen
Three Rock Mt.
Killakee
Enniskerry
Powerscourt Demesne
Killough
Killoge

Kippure
WICKLOW
Glencree
Sally Gap
Waterfall
Dargle
Lough Tay
Mullaghcleevaun
Glenbridge Lodge
Granabeg
MOUNTAINS
Sraghmore
Lough Dan
Roundwood
Vartry Reservoir

Donard
Table Mountain
Wicklow Gap
NATIONAL PARK
Glendalough
Upper Lake
Lower Lake
Laragh
Annamoe
Tomdarragh
The Devil's Glen

Ballinclea
Lugnaquilla Mountain
Ballycullen
Clara
Glenealy
Drumgoff
Ballinderry
Rathdrum / Ráth Droma
Vale of Clara
Rathdangan
Aghavannagh
Greenan
Kilmacurragh
Avondale Forest Park
Kilbride
Kiltegan
Sheeanamore
Ballinaclash
Kilmacoo
Ballinacor
Knockananna
Askanagap
Motte Stone
Redcross
Moyne
Craffield
Aughrim
Avoca
Meeting of the Waters
Bridgeland
Tinahely
Woodenbridge
Croghan Mountain
Johnstown
Coolboy
Ballyfad
R 749
Crosspatrick
Coolgreany
Clogga

Grand Canal
Tolka
Liffey
Avonmore
Avonbeg
Glenmalur

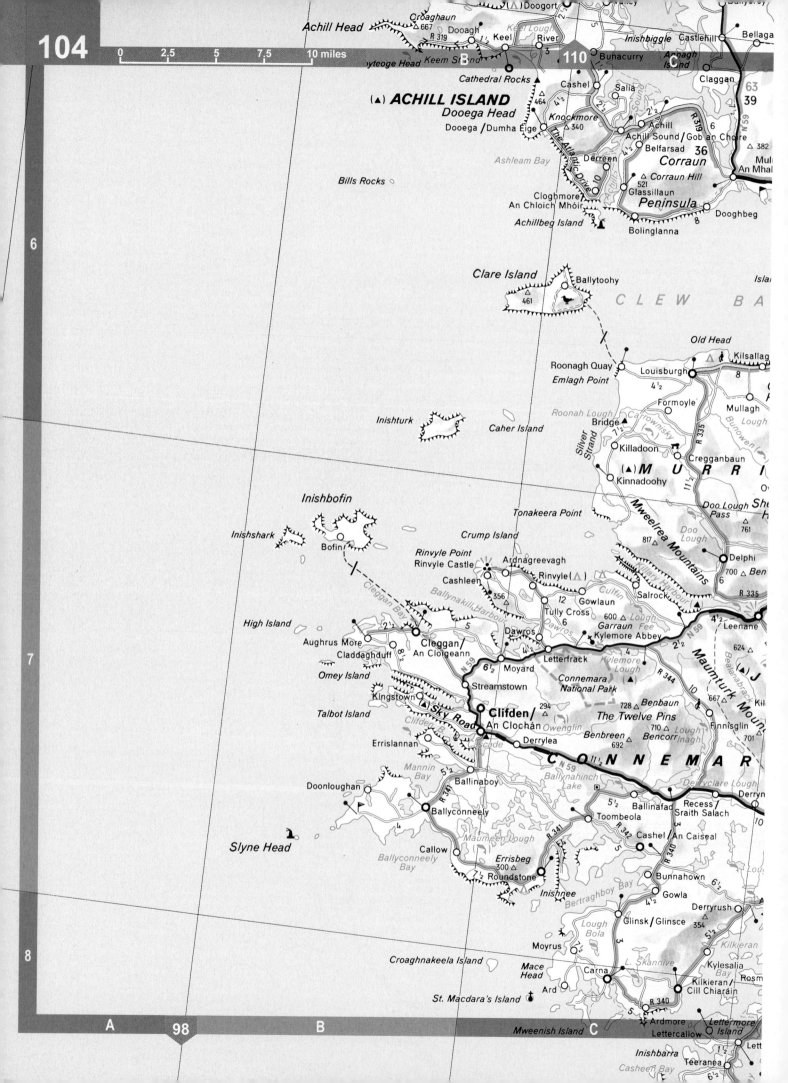

0   2.5   5   7.5   10 miles

Achill Head
Croaghaun
△ 667   Doogort
Dooagh
R 319   1½   Keel   Keel Lough
yteoge Head   Keem Strand   River   Inishbiggle   Castlehill   Bellaga
B   5   Bunacurry   C   Annagh
Cathedral Rocks ▲   Cashel   Island   Claggan   63
(▲) ACHILL ISLAND   △ 464   4½   Salia   39
Dooega Head   Knockmore   2½   Achill   △ 382   Mul
Dooega / Dumha Éige   △ 340   Achill Sound / Gob an Choire   An Mhai
Derreen   4½   Belfarsad   36
Ashleam Bay   **Corraun**
△ 521   △ Corraun Hill
Bills Rocks ○   Cloghmore   Glassillaun
An Chloich Mhóir   **Peninsula**   Dooghbeg
Achillbeg Island   8
Bolinglanna

Clare Island   Ballytoohy   Islan
△ 461   **C L E W   B A**   6

Old Head
Roonagh Quay   Kilsallag
Emlagh Point   Louisburgh   8
4½   Formoyle
Roonah Lough   Carrownisky   Mullagh   Lough
Inishturk   Bridge   1½   R 335   Bunowen
Caher Island   Silver Strand   Killadoon   Cregganbaun
(▲) M U R R I
Kinnadoohy   11½   Ov
7

Inishbofin   Doo Lough   Sh
Tonakeera Point   Doo Lough   Pass
Inishshark   Crump Island   817 △   Lough   761
Bofin /   Rinvyle Point   Ardnagreevagh   Mweelrea Mountains   Delphi
Rinvyle Castle   Rinvyle (▲)   700 △ Ben
Cashleen   △ 356   Salrock   R 335
High Island   12   Gowlaun   Cuilfin   Leenane
Ballynakill Harbour   Tully Cross   600 △   Lough   4½   624 △
Aughrus More   2½   5   Dawros   6   Garraun   Fee   N 59
Claddaghduff   8½   Cleggan /   4½   Kylemore Abbey   2½
Omey Island   An Cloigeann   Dawros   Letterfrack   Kylemore   10   667 △   Kil
Kingstown   6½   Moyard   Lough   R 344
Talbot Island   Sky Road   Streamstown   Connemara   (▲)
Errislannan   294 △   National Park   728 △   Benbaun   Finnisglin
Clifden /   The Twelve Pins   701
An Clochán   Benbreen   710 △ Lough
Cascade   Derrylea   692   Bencorr   Inagh
Doonloughan   Ballinaboy   **C O N N E M A R**   Derryclare Lough   Derryn
Mannin   Ballynahinch   N 59   11½
Bay   R 341   Lake   5½   Ballinafad   Recess /
Ballyconneely   Toombeola   Sraith Salach
4   R 342   Cashel / An Caiseal
Slyne Head   Maumeen Lough   Bunnahown   6½
Ballyconneely   Callow   Errisbeg   R 341   Gowla
Bay   300 △   Derryrush
1½   Roundstone   354
Inishnee   Bertraghboy   Bay   Glinsk / Glinsce
Lough   5½
Croaghnakeela Island   Bola   Kilkieran
Mace   L. Skannive   Kylesalia
Head   Carna   Kilkieran /
Ard   R 340   Cill Chiaráin   Rosm
St. Macdara's Island   Lette
Ardmore   Lettercallow   Island
A   98   B   Mweenish Island   C   Inishbarra   Teeranea
Casheen Bay

8

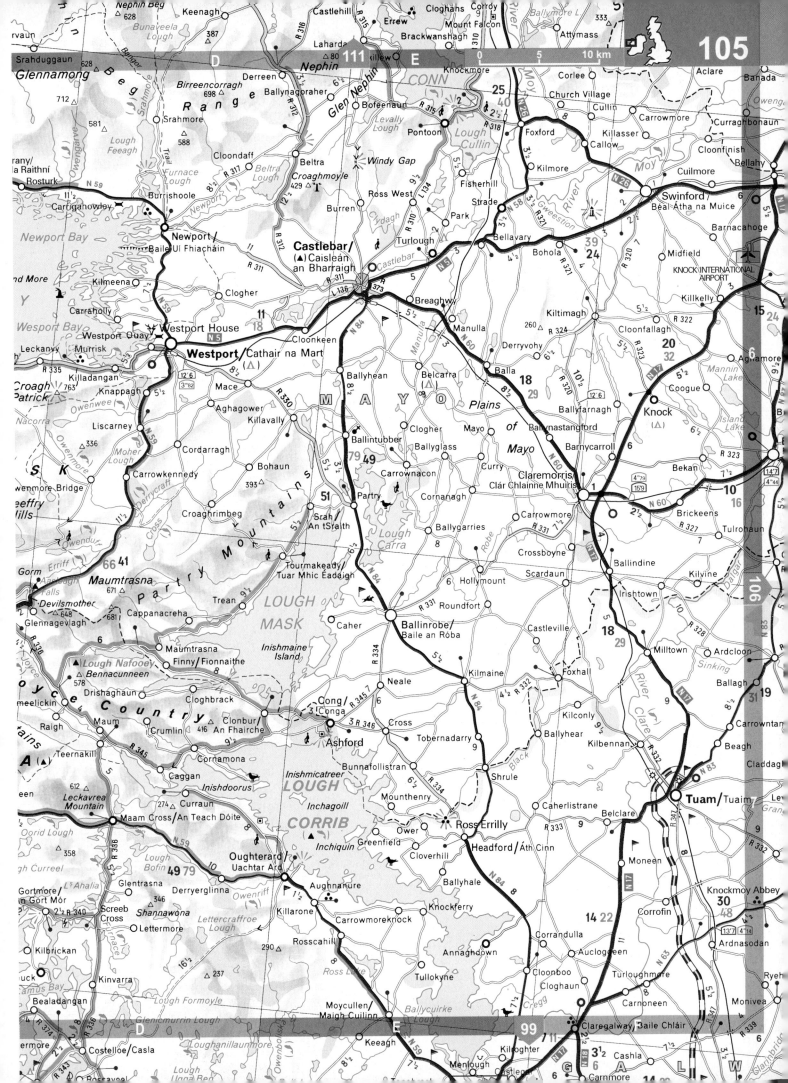

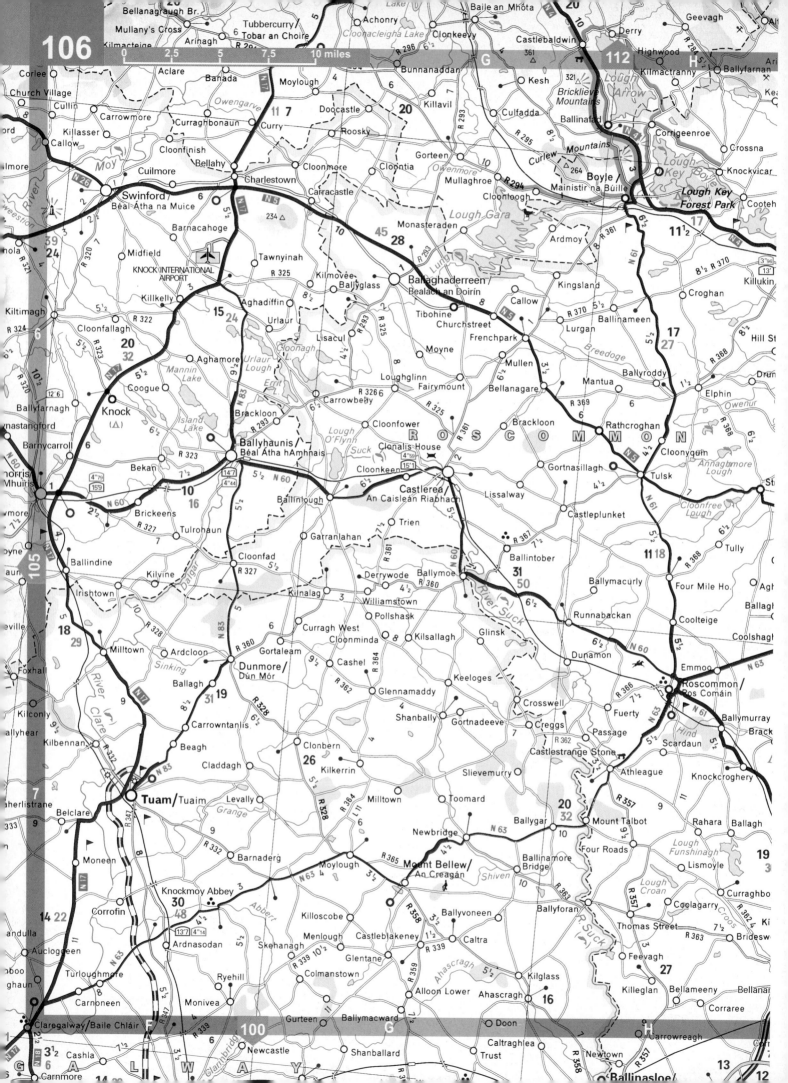

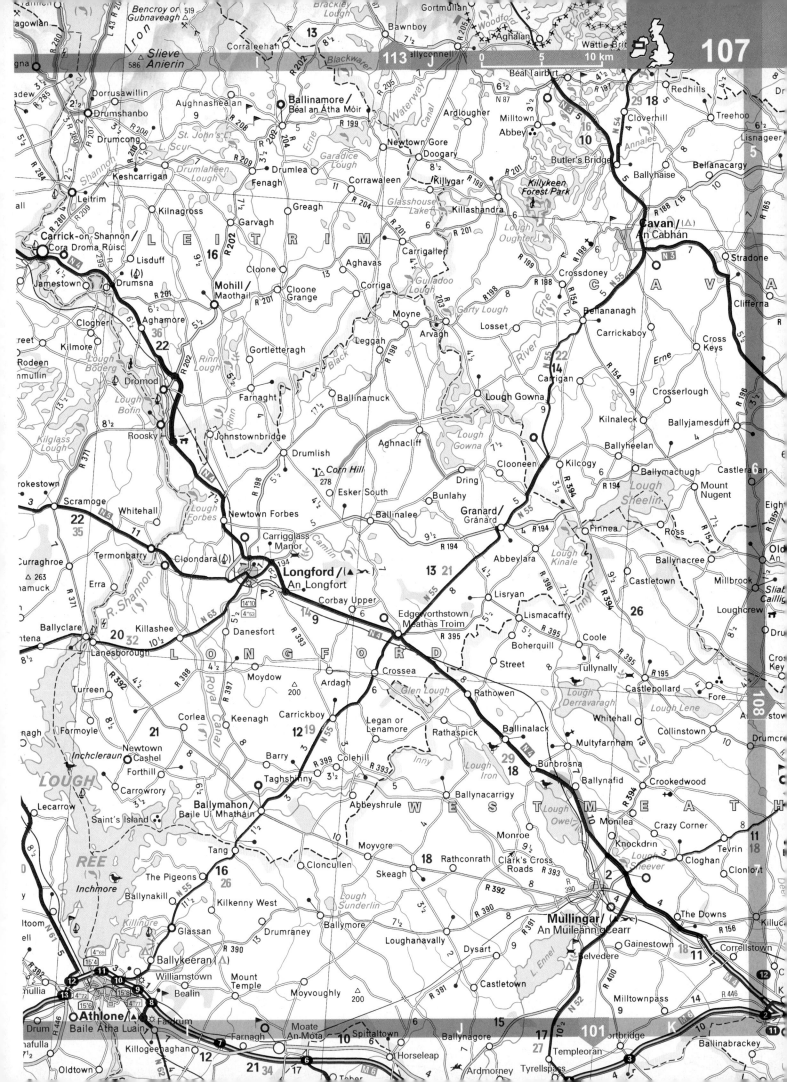

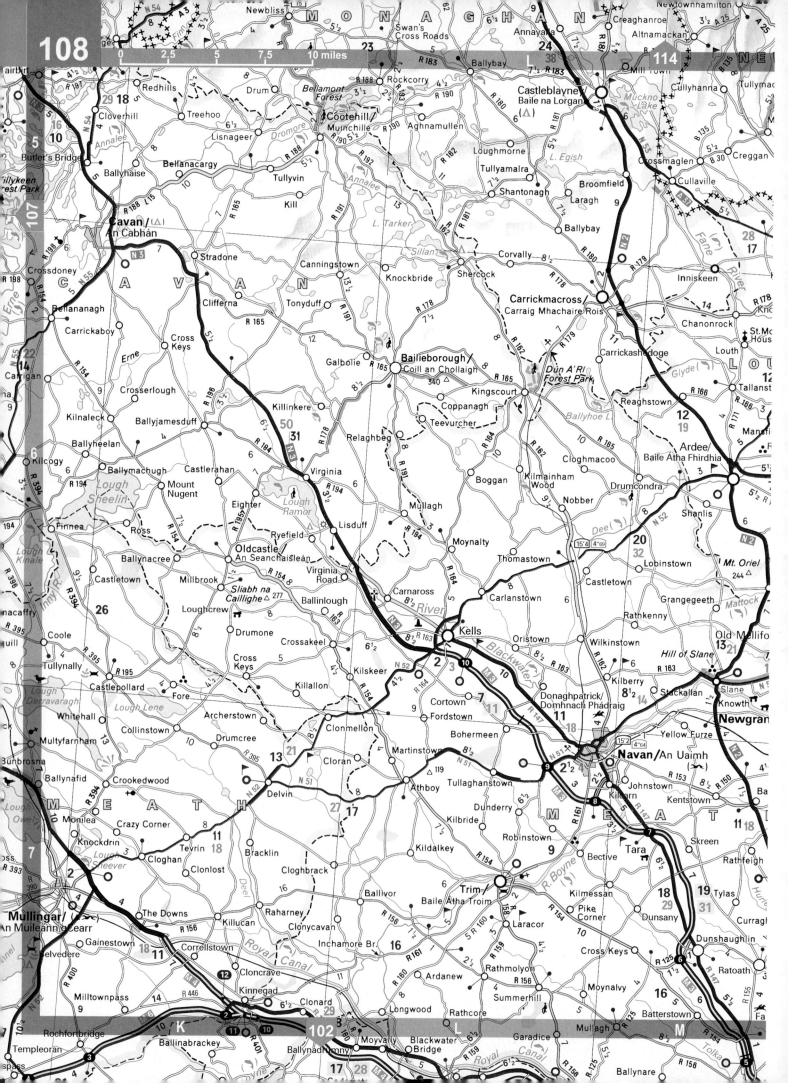

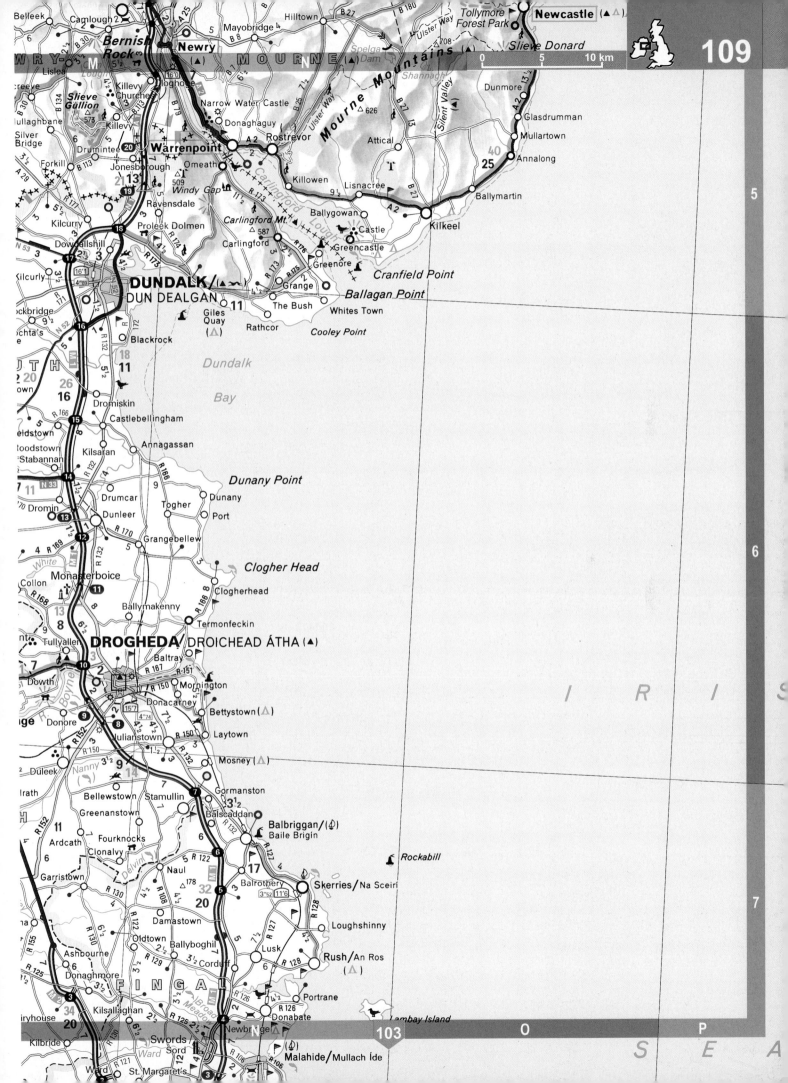

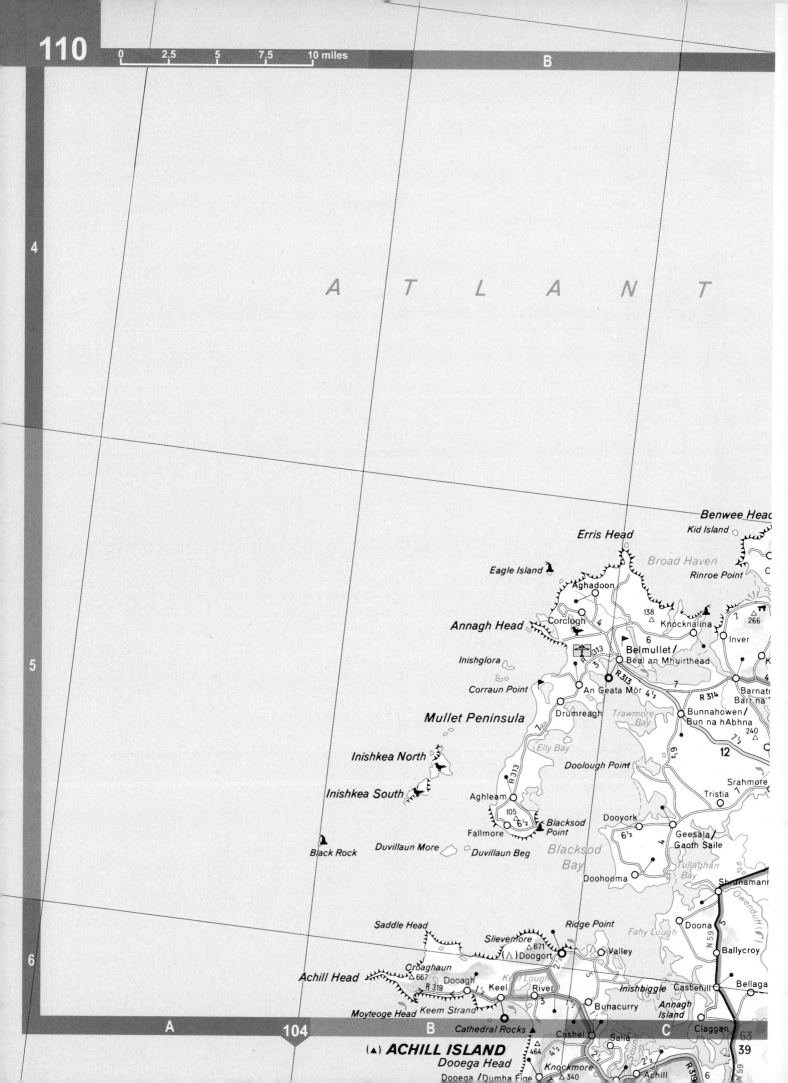

0 2.5 5 7.5 10 miles

A T L A N T

4

B

104

A

B

C

5

6

Benwee Head
Erris Head   Kid Island
Eagle Island   Broad Haven   Rinroe Point
Aghadoon
Annagh Head   Corclogh   138   Knocknalina   266
4
Belmullet /   6   Inver
Inishglora   R 313   Béal an Mhuirthead
5
Corraun Point   An Geata Mór 4½   R 313
Mullet Peninsula   Drumreagh   7   R 314   Barnatr
Trawmore   Bart na
7½   Bay   Bunnahowen /
Elly Bay   Bun na hAbhna   240
6½   12
Doolough Point
Inishkea North   Srahmore
Tristia
Inishkea South   Aghleam   Dooyork
105   6½   Dooyork   6½   Geesala /
Fallmore   6½   Blacksod   Gaoth Saile
Point   4
Black Rock   Duvillaun More   Duvillaun Beg   Blacksod   Tullaghan
Bay   Bay
Doohooma   Shranamann

Saddle Head   Ridge Point   Doona   5
Slievemore   Fahy Lough   N 59
Croaghaun   △ 671   Valley   Ballycroy
△ 667   (△) Doogort 2½   5
Achill Head   Dooagh   Keel   River   Inishbiggle   Castlehill   Bellaga
R 319   1½   Keel   Lough   3   Bunacurry   Annagh   Claggan
Moyteoge Head   Keem Strand   1½   Island   63
Cathedral Rocks ▲   Cashel   Salia   39
(▲) ACHILL ISLAND   464   R 319   6
Dooega Head   Knockmore
Dooega / Dumha Éige   △ 340   Achill

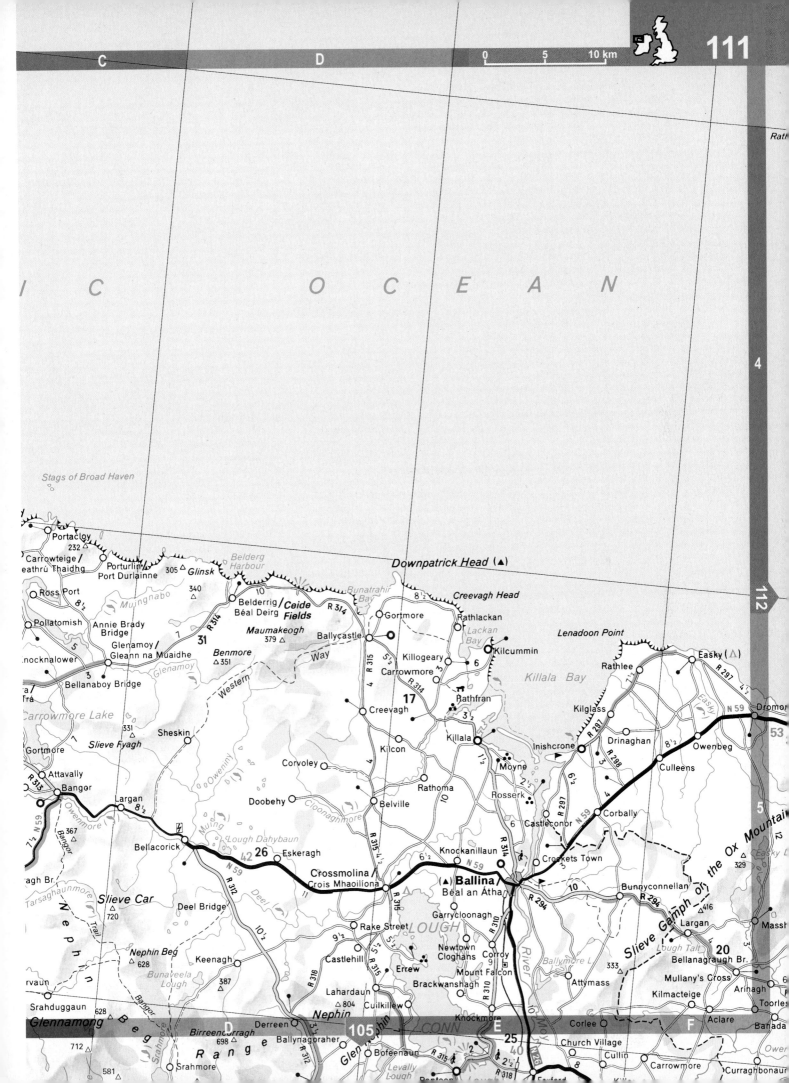

0   5   10 km

ATLANTIC OCEAN

4

112

Stags of Broad Haven

Portacloy
232
Carrowteige /
eathrú Thaidhg
Porturlin /
Port Durlainne
305 *Glinsk*
340
Ross Port
Belderg Harbour
Downpatrick Head (▲)
Pollatomish
Muingnabo
Belderrig
Béal Deirg
Ceide Fields
R 314
Bunatrahir Bay
Creevagh Head
Lenadoon Point
Annie Brady Bridge
7
31
R 314
Maumakeogh
379 △
Gortmore
8½
Rathlackan
Easky (△)
R 297
Glenamoy /
Gleann na Muaidhe
3
Benmore
△ 351
Ballycastle
R 315
Killogeary
Carrowmore
6
Kilcummin
Rathlee
Killala Bay
N 59
Dromor
nocknalower
Glenamoy
Western
Way
4
R 314
5½
3
7½
53
Bellanaboy Bridge
331
Creevagh
17
Lackan Bay
Rathfran
Kilglass
R 297
Drinaghan
8½
Carrowmore Lake
Sheskin
Slieve Fyagh
7
Kilcon
1½
Killala
Inishcrone
R 298
Owenbeg
Gortmore
Corvoley
2½
Moyne
6½
Culleens
R 313
Attavally
Doobehy
Rathoma
Rosserk
R 297
N 59
4
Bangor
Owenmore
Belville
10
6
Castleconor
Corbally
367
Lough Dahybaun
Knockanillaun
Crockets Town
3
329
Largan
8½
42
26
Eskeragh
6½
N 59
Bellacorick
R 315
Crossmolina /
Crois Mhaoilíona
Ballina
Béal an Átha
10
Bunnyconnellan
R 294
Slieve Car
720
Deel Bridge
11
R 312
Garrycloonagh
R 310
416
Largan
20
Slieve Gamph on the Ox Mountai
333
Bellanagraugh Br.
Nephin Beg
△ 628
Keenagh
387
Rake Street
9½
Castlehill
5½
Newtown Cloghans
Corroy
9
Mount Falcon
Attymass
Mullany's Cross
Arinagh
Srahduggaun
628
Bunaveela Lough
Lahardaun
Cuilkillew
Brackwanshagh
Kilmacteige
Toorles
Glennamong
712
△
△ 804
Nephin
Derreen
Knockmore
Corlee
Aclare
Banada
Range
698 △
Ballynagoraher
105
CONN
E
25
40
Church Village
581 △
Srahmore
Bofeenaun
R 315
R 318
Cullin
Carrowmore
Curraghbonaur

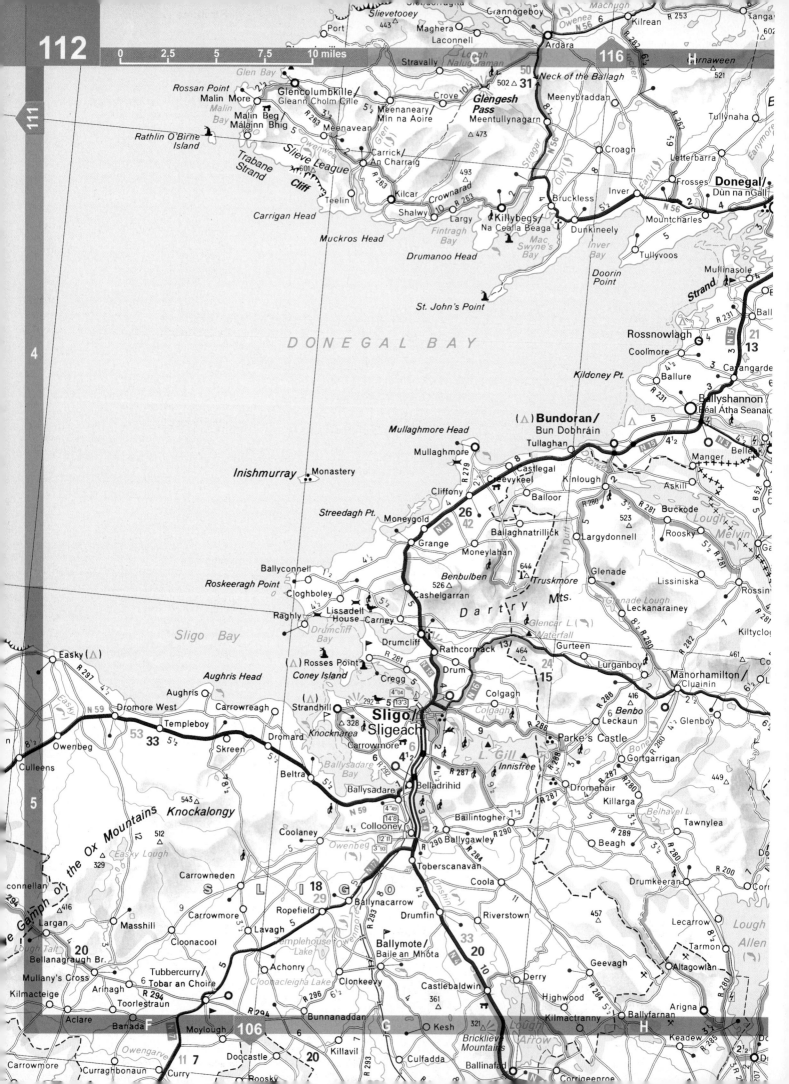

Slievetooey
443
Port
Maghera
Laconnell
Grannogeboy
Owenea N 56 6
Kilrean
R 253
Machugh
Tanga
602

Stravally
Lough
Nalughraman
Ardara
Hirnaween
521
H

0   2.5   5   7.5   10 miles

Glen Bay
Rossan Point
Malin More
Glencolumbkille/
Gleann Cholm Cille
Crove
502 △ 31
50
Neck of the Ballagh
Meenybradden
R 262
Tullynaha
Letterbarra

Malin Beg/
Málainn Bhig
Meenaneary/
Mín na Aoire
Glengesh
Pass
Meentullynagarn
△ 473
Croagh
Rathlin O'Birne
Island
Meenavean
R 263
Carrick/
An Charraig
493
Bruckless
Inver
Frosses
Donegal/
Dún na nGall

Trabane
Strand
Slieve League
601
Cliff
Kilcar
Crownarad
Killybegs/
Na Cealla Beaga
Dunkineely
Mountcharles
R 262

Teelin
Shalwy
10
R 263
Largy
Mac
Swyne's
Bay
Inver
Bay
Tullyvoos

Carrigan Head
Muckros Head
Fintragh
Bay
Drumanoo Head
Doorin
Point
Mullinasole
Strand

St. John's Point

D O N E G A L   B A Y
Rossnowlagh
Coolmore
N15
21
13

Kildoney Pt.
Ballure
Carrangarde
R 231

Ballyshannon
Béal Átha Seanaidh
N 3

Mullaghmore Head
(△) Bundoran/
Bun Dobhráin
Tullaghan
Manger
Bella

Mullaghmore
Castlegal
Kinlough
Askill
R 52

Inishmurray
Monastery
Cliffony
R 279
Ceevykeel
Balloor
R 280
Buckode
Lough
Melvin

Streedagh Pt.
Moneygold
26
42
N15
Ballaghnatrillick
523
Roosky
Ga

Grange
Moneylahan
Largydonnell
Glenade
Rossin

Ballyconnell
Roskeeragh Point
Cloghboley
Benbulben
526 △
644
Truskmore
Dartry   Mts.
Leckanarainey
Lissiniska

Raghly
Lissadell
House
Carney
Glencar L.
Waterfall
Glenade Lough
Kiltyclog

Sligo Bay
Drumcliff
Rathcormack
13
464
Gurteen
Lurganboy
R 282
461

Easky (△)
R 297
Rosses Point
Coney Island
Drum
24
15
Manorhamilton/
Cluainín
L

Aughris Head
Cregg
Colgagh
R 286
416
Benbo
Glenboy

Dromore West
Aughris
Carrowreagh
Strandhill
292
Sligo/
Sligeach
Colgagh
Leckaun
Parke's Castle
Gortgarrigan

Templeboy
53
33
Dromard
Knocknarea
328
L. Gill
Innisfree
Dromahair

Owenbeg
Skreen
Carrowmore
Belladrihid
R 287
Killarga

Culleens
Beltra
Ballysadare
Bay
Ballintogher
Tawnylea
Belhavel L.

Knockalongy
543 △
N 59
Colooney
Ballygawley
R 290
Beagh
R 280

connellan
Carrowneden
512
329
Coolaney
Owenbeg
Toberscanavan
Coola
Drumkeeran
Lough
Allen

Largan
416
S   L   I   18   G
29
Ballynacarrow
Drumfin
Riverstown
457
Lecarrow
Tarmon

Mullany's Cross
Carrowmore
Ropefield
Lavagh
Templehouse
Lake
Ballymote/
Baile an Mhóta
33
20
Derry
Geevagh
Altagowlan

Kilmacteige
Arinagh
Tubbercurry/
Tobar an Choire
Achonry
Clonkeevy
Castlebaldwin
361
Highwood
Kilmactranny
Arigna

Aclare
Banada
F
106
Moylough
Bunnanaddan
G
Kesh
Culfadda
Brickleve
Mountains
Kilmacranny
Ballyfarnan
Keadew
H

Carrowmore
Curraghbonaun
Curry
11 7
Doocastle
20
Killavil
Roosky
R 293
Ballinafad
Corrigeenroe

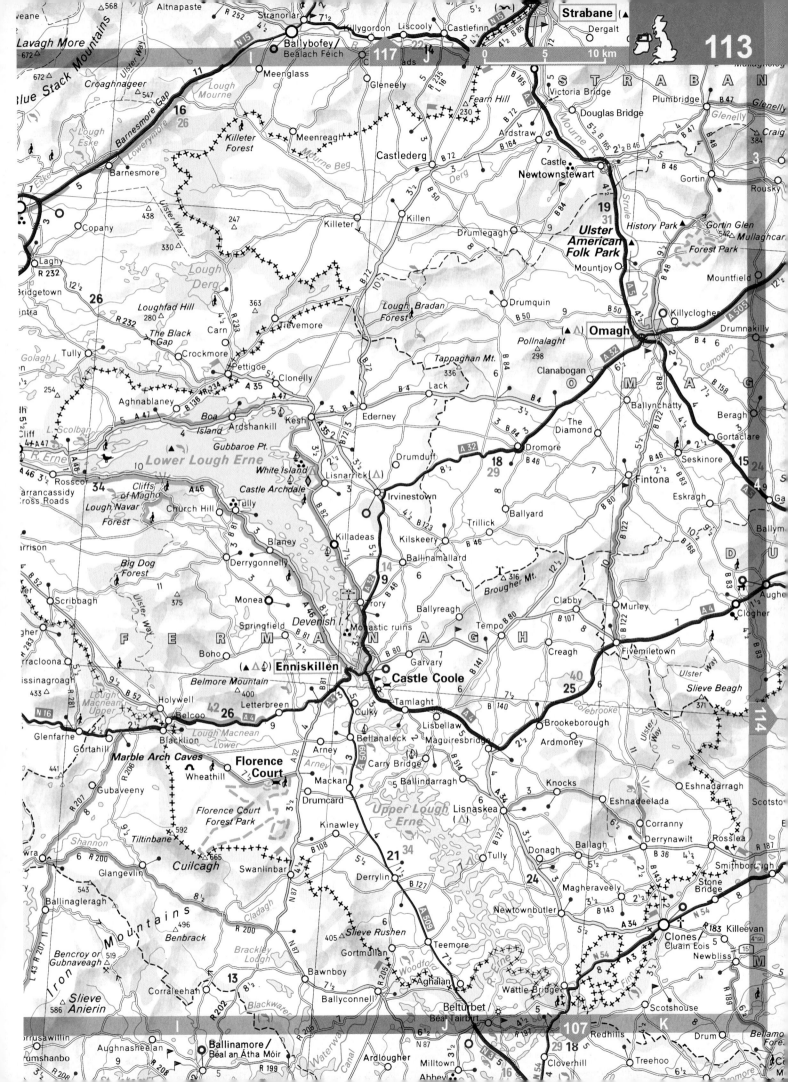

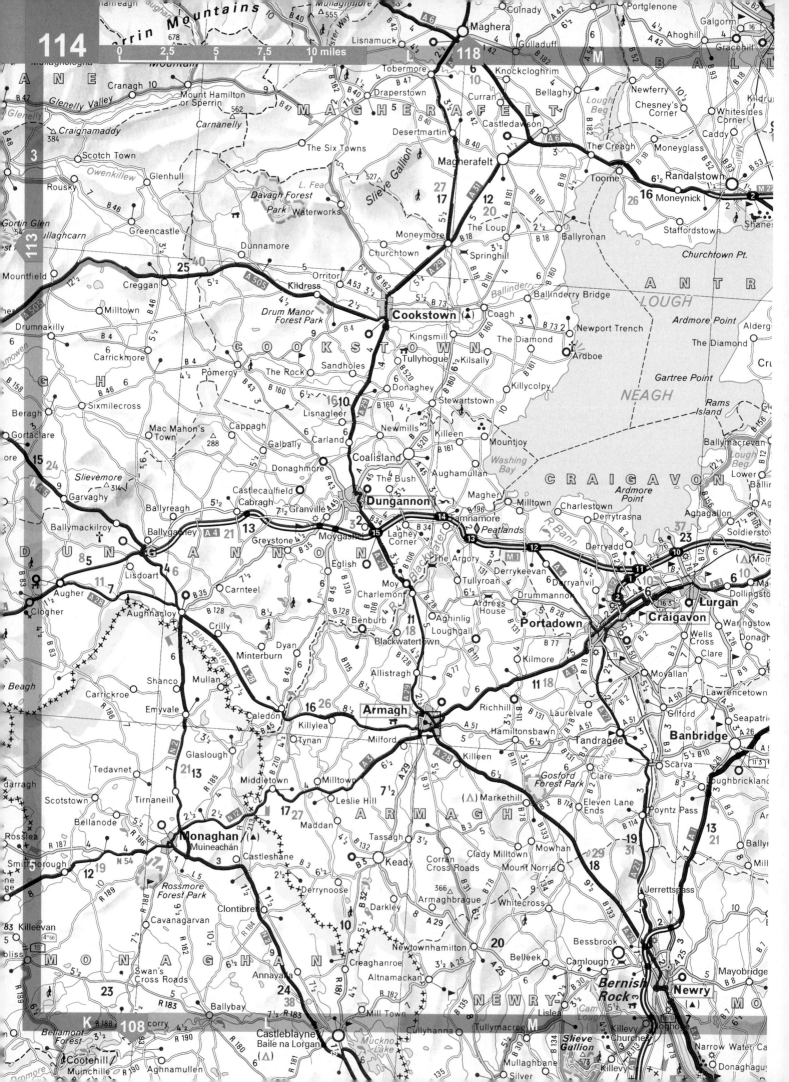

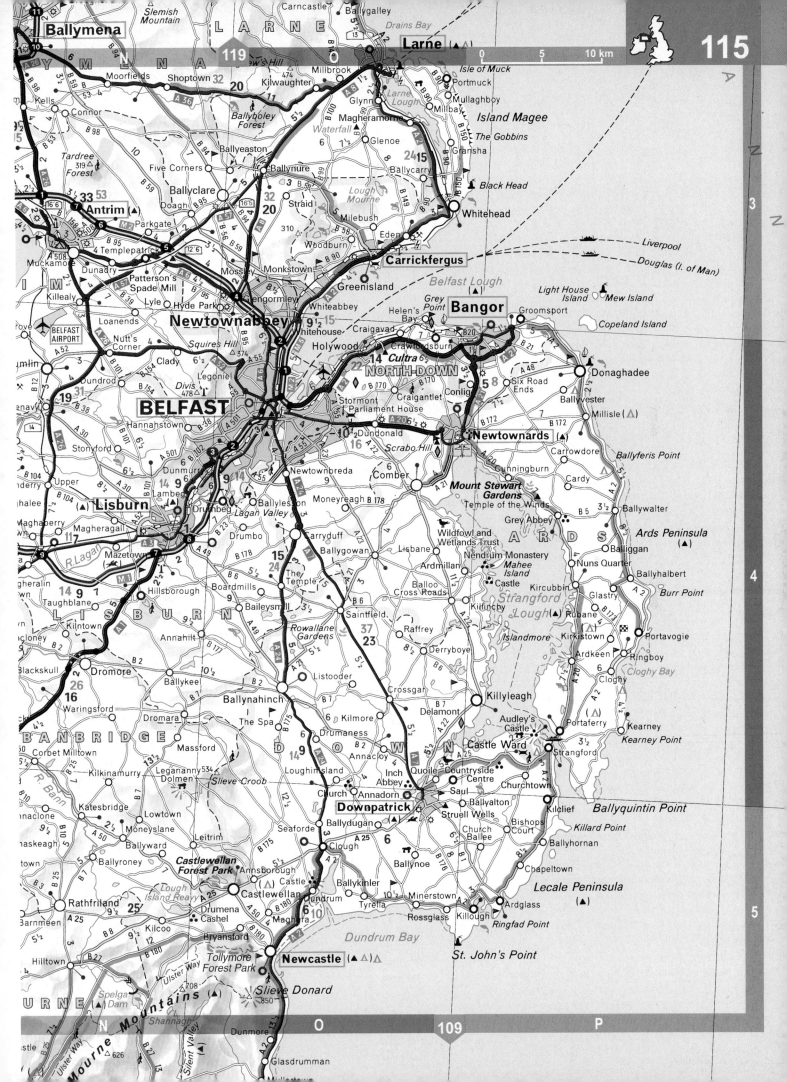

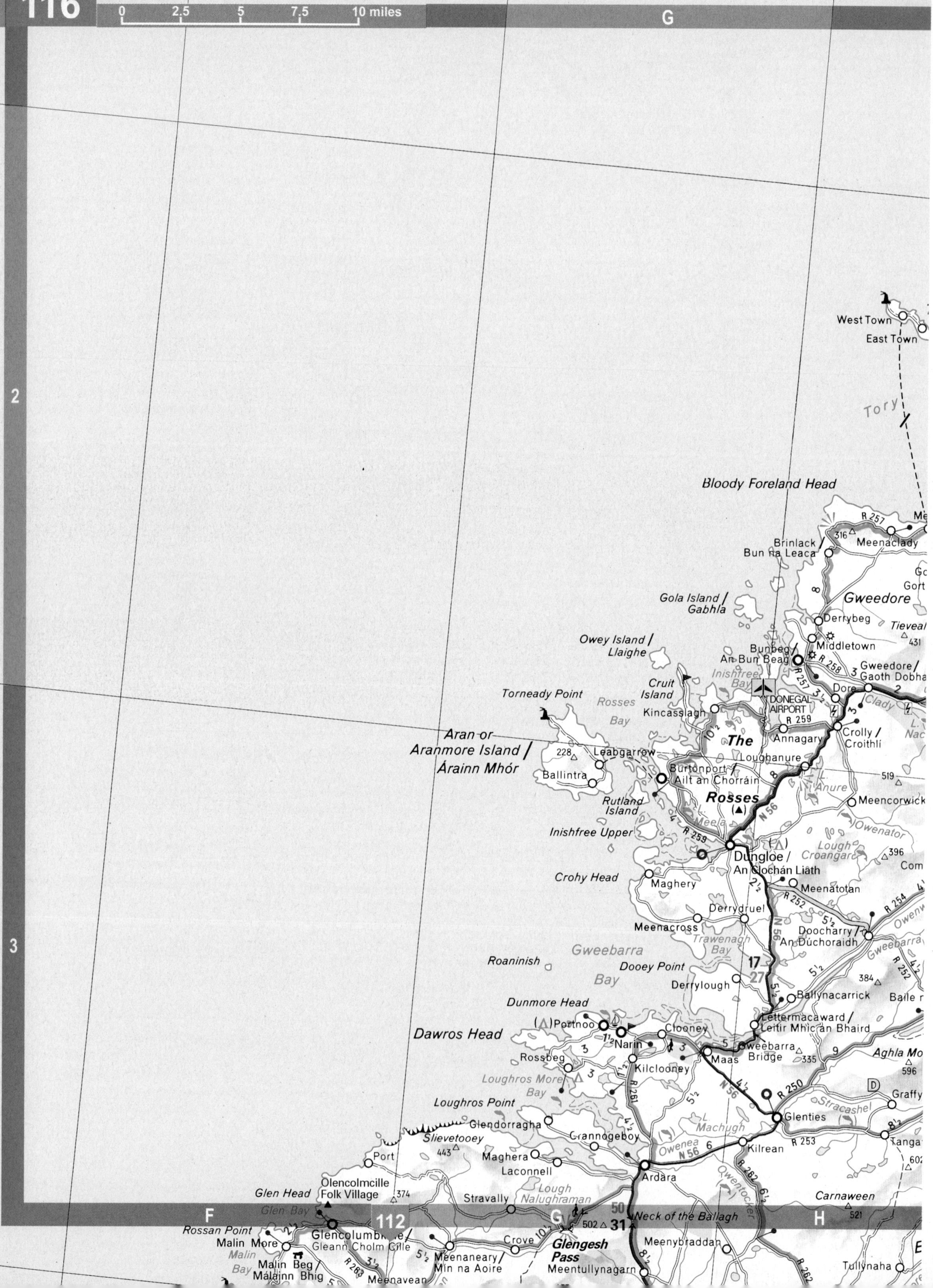

0 2.5 5 7.5 10 miles

2

West Town
East Town

Tory

Bloody Foreland Head

R 257
316 △ Me
Brinlack
Bun na Leaca
Meenaclady

*Gola Island /
Gabhla*
Derrybeg
Tieveal
△ 431

Gweedore

Go
Gort

Middletown

*Owey Island /
Laighe*
Bunbeg /
An Bun Beag
Gweedore /
Gaoth Dobha
R 258 3
Dore
Clady
L.
Nac

*Cruit
Island*
Torneady Point
*Rosses
Bay*
DONEGAL
AIRPORT
R 259
Kincasslagh

The

Crolly /
Croithlí
Annagary

Aran or
**Aranmore Island /
Árainn Mhór**
228 △ Leabgarrow
Loughanure
519

Ballintra
Burtonport /
Ailt an Chorráin
Anure

*Rutland
Island*
Rosses
(▲)
N 56
Meencorwick

Inishfree Upper
R 259
Meela
(△)
*Lough
Croangar*
△ 396
Com

3

Crohy Head
Maghery
**Dungloe /
An Clochán Liath**
R 252
Meenatotan
R 254

Derrydruel
Owenx

Meenacross
Doocharry /
An Dúchoraidh
R 252

Gweebarra
Bay
*Trawenagh
Bay*
N 56
384 △
Roaninish
Dooey Point
**17
27**
Ballynacarrick
Baile n
Derrylough
Aghla Mo
596 △
Dunmore Head
(△) Portnoo
Clooney
Lettermacaward /
Leitir Mhic an Bhaird
Dawros Head
Narin
1½
Gweebarra
Bridge
335 △
Rossbeg
3
Maas
R 250
D
Graffy
Kilclooney
3
*Loughros More
Bay*
R 261
5½
N 56
Stracashel
Loughros Point
Glenties
R 253
Tanga
*L.
Machugh*
Kilrean
602
Glendorragha
Owenea
N 56
Grannogeboy
6
Port
Slievetooey
443 △
Maghera
Laconnell
Ardara
Carnaween
Owentocker
521 △

Olencolmcille
Folk Village
374 △
Stravally
*Lough
Nalughraman*
50
502 △ **31**
Neck of the Ballagh
Meenybraddan
Glen Head
Glen Bay

E

Rossan Point
Malin More
Glencolumbk
Gleann Cholm Cille
Crove
**Glengesh
Pass**
R 262
*Malin
Bay*
Malin Beg /
Málainn Bhig
R 263
3½
Meenaneary /
Mín na Aoire
5½
Meenavean
Meentullynagarn
8½
Tullynaha

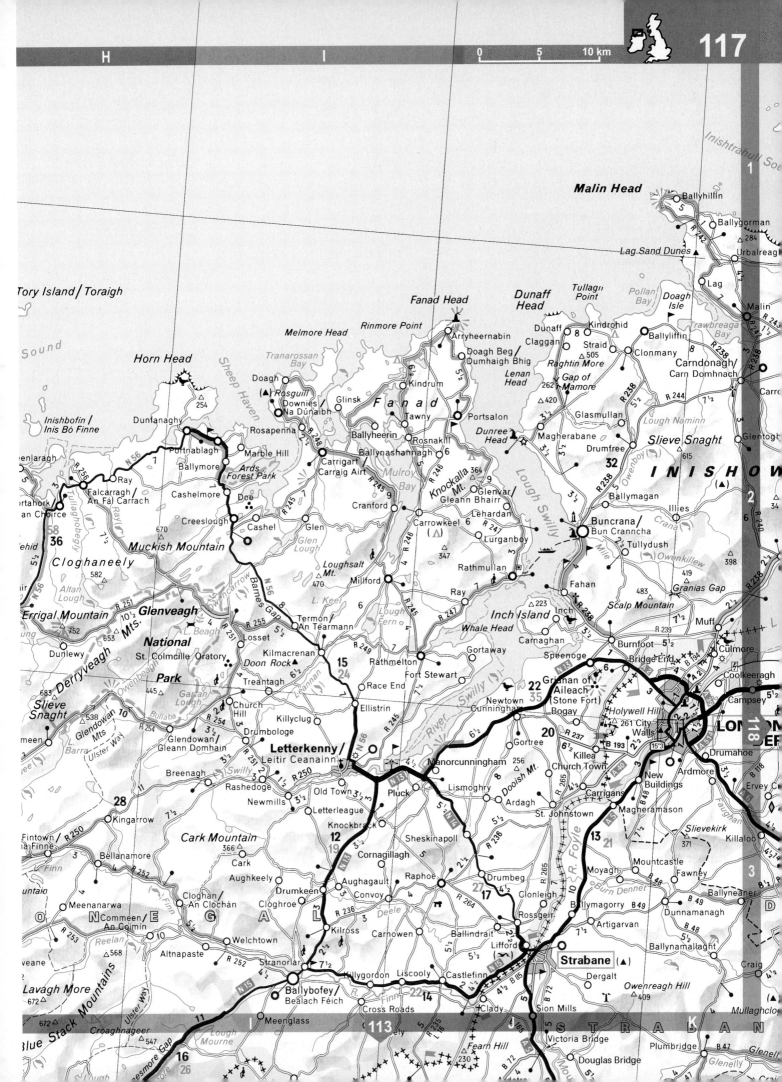

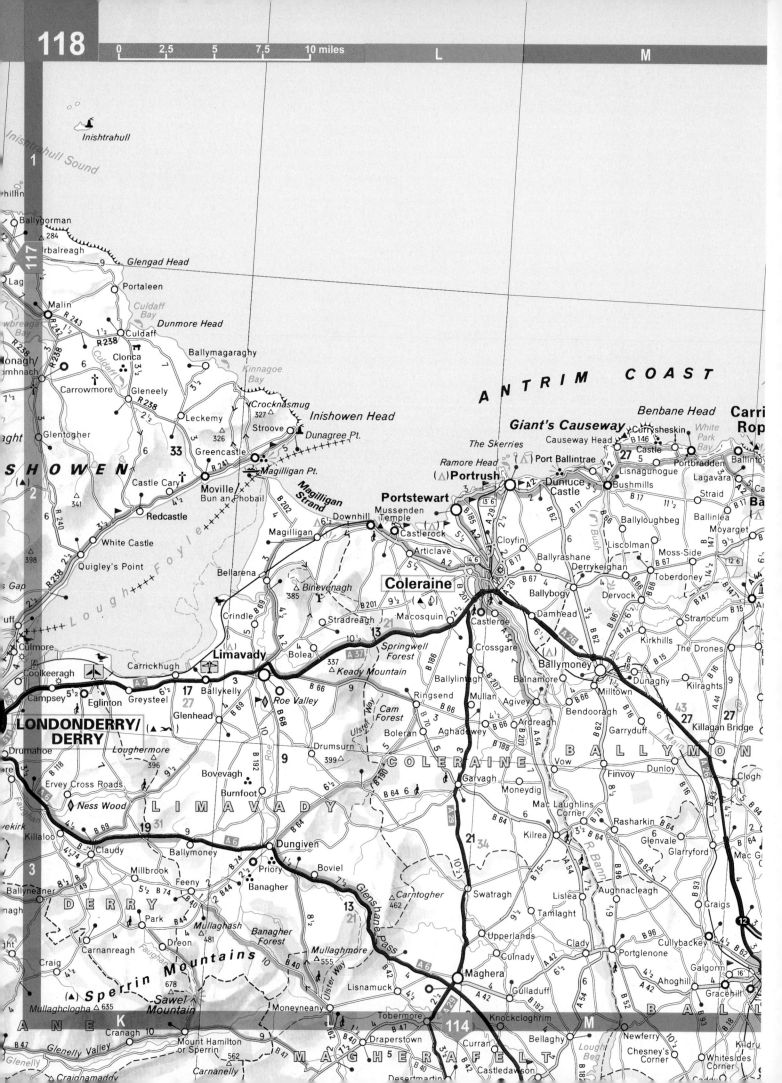

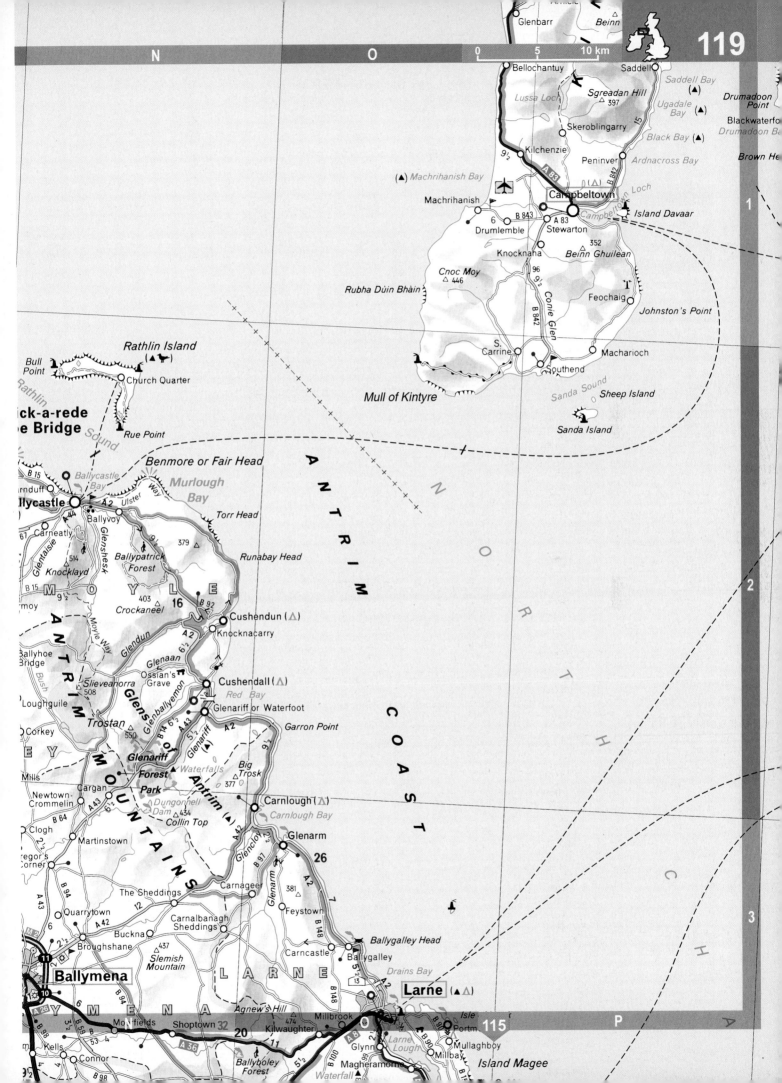

0   5   10 km

Glenbarr
Beinn
Bellochantuy
Saddell
Saddell Bay
Lussa Loch
Sgreadan Hill
△ 397
Ugadale Bay
Drumadoon Point
Skeroblingarry
Black Bay
Blackwaterf
Drumadoon B
9½
Kilchenzie
Peninver
Ardnacross Bay
Brown He
A 83
Campbeltown Loch
Machrihanish Bay
Machrihanish
Campbeltown
Island Davaar
6   B 843
A 83   Stewarton
Drumlemble
Knocknaha
352
Beinn Ghuilean
96
9½   Conie Glen
B 842
Cnoc Moy
△ 446
Feochaig
Rubha Dùin Bhàin
Johnston's Point
S. Carrine
Macharioch
Southend

Mull of Kintyre
Sanda Sound
Sheep Island

Sanda Island

Rathlin Island
Bull Point
Church Quarter
ck-a-rede
e Bridge   Sound   Rue Point

Benmore or Fair Head
B 15   Ballycastle Bay
Murlough Bay
nduff
Ballycastle   A 2   Ulster   Way
Torr Head
llycastle   A 44
Ballyvoy
Carneatly   Glenshesk   9½   379
Runabay Head
Glentaisie   514
Knocklayd
Ballypatrick Forest
moy   B 15   M   9½   O   403   16   Y   B 92   L   E
Crockaneel
Cushendun (△)
Ballyhoe Bridge   A 2
Knocknacarry
A   Glendun
N   Glenaan   Ossian's Grave
Slieveanorra   508   Glens   Glenballyemon
Cushendall (△)
Loughguile   Trostan   Red Bay
Corkey   Glenariff or Waterfoot
550   B 14 6½   A 43
Garron Point
Mills   Glenariff   5½   A 2
M   Glenariff (△)
Cargan   Forest   Waterfalls   Big Trosk
Park   377
Newtown-   A 43   O   Dungonnell
Cromelin   6½   Dam   434   Collin Top
Clogh   B 64   U   A 42   Carnlough (△)
Martinstown   N   Carnlough Bay
regor's   T   Glencloy 2½   Glenarm
Corner   A   Glenarm   B 97   26
B 94   I   A 2
Quarrytown   N   381
The Sheddings   S   Carnageer   A 2   7
A 42   12   Carnalbanagh   Glenarm   Feystown   B 148
A 43   Sheddings
6   Buckna   437
2½   A 42   Broughshane   Slemish   Carncastle   Ballygalley Head
11   Mountain   L   A   R   Ballygalley
Ballymena   N   E   5½   Drains Bay
10   B 94   13
2½   Y   M   E   N   A   Larne (▲ △)
M2   Agnew's Hill   Isle
Mon fields   Shoptown 32   Millbrook   B 148   Portm
20   Kilwaughter   A 8   Larne   Mullaghboy
Kells   B 59   B   A 36   11   Glynn   Millbay
Connor   53   4   Ballyboley   B 100   Magheramorne   Island Magee
Forest   Waterfall
115

A
B
C
D
E
F
G
H
I
J
K
L
M
N
O
P
Q
R
S
T
U
V
W
X
Y
Z

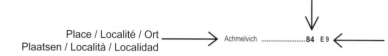

Page number / Numéro de page / Seitenzahl
Paginanummer / Numero di pagina / Número de Página

Place / Localité / Ort ——————> Achmelvich ....84 E 9 <—— Grid coordinates / Coordonnées de carroyage
Plaatsen / Località / Localidad   Koordinatenangabe / Verwijstekens ruitsysteem
                                                                                               Coordinate riferite alla quadrettatura
                                                                                               Coordenadas en los mapas

A

A Chill ....71 A 12
A La Ronde ....4 J 32
Abbas Combe ....9 M 30
Abberley ....27 M 27
Abbey ....23 X 30
Abbey Dore ....26 L 28
Abbey Town ....54 K 19
Abbeydale ....43 P 23
Abbeystead ....48 L 22
Abbots Bromley ....35 O 25
Abbots Langley ....21 S 28
Abbots Leigh ....18 M 29
Abbots Ripton ....29 T 26
Abbotsbury ....5 M 32
Abbotsford House ....62 L 17
Abbotskerswell ....4 J 32
Aber Banc ....15 G 27
Aberaeron ....24 H 27
Aberaman ....17 J 28
Aberangell ....33 I 25
Abercarn ....18 K 29
Abercastle ....14 E 28
Aberchirder ....81 M 11
Abercynon ....17 J 29
Aberdâr / Aberdare ....17 J 28
Aberdare / Aberdâr ....17 J 28
Aberdaron ....32 F 25
Aberdaugleddau /
  Milford Haven ....14 E 28
Aberdeen ....75 N 12
Aberdour ....68 K 15
Aberdour Bay ....81 N 10
Aberdovey / Aberdyfi ....33 H 26
Aberdyfi / Aberdovey ....33 H 26
Aberedw ....25 J 27
Abereiddy ....14 E 28
Aberfeldy ....73 I 14
Aberffraw ....32 G 24
Aberford ....43 P 22
Aberfoyle ....67 G 15
Abergavenny / Y-Fenni ....18 K 28
Abergele ....41 J 23
Abergolech ....15 H 28
Abergwaun / Fishguard ....24 F 28
Abergwesyn ....25 I 27
Abergwili ....15 H 28
Abergwynfi ....17 J 29
Abergwyngregyn ....41 H 23
Abergynolwyn ....33 I 26
Aberhonddu / Brecon ....25 J 28
Aberkenfig ....17 J 29
Aberlady ....69 L 15
Aberlemno ....75 L 13
Aberlour ....80 K 11
Abermaw / Barmouth ....33 H 25
Abermule ....34 K 26
Abernethy ....68 K 15
Abernyte ....68 K 14
Aberpennar / Mountain Ash ....17 J 28
Aberporth ....15 G 27
Abersoch ....32 G 25
Abersychan ....18 K 28
Abertawe / Swansea ....17 I 29
Aberteifi / Cardigan ....15 G 27
Abertillery ....18 K 28
Aberuthven ....67 J 15
Aberystwyth ....25 H 26
Abingdon ....20 Q 28
Abinger Common ....21 S 30
Abinger Hammer ....21 S 30
Abington Cambs. ....30 U 27
Abington South Lanarkshire ....61 I 17
Aboyne ....75 L 12
Abriachan ....79 G 11
Abridge ....21 U 29
Accrington ....42 M 22
Achahoish ....65 D 16
Achallader ....66 F 14
Achanalt ....78 F 11
Achaphubuil ....72 E 13
Acharacle ....71 C 13
Achargary ....85 H 8
Acharn ....67 H 14

Achduart ....83 E 10
Achgarve ....78 D 10
Achiemore ....84 F 8
Achiltibuie ....83 D 9
Achintee ....78 D 11
Achintraid ....78 D 11
Achlean ....73 I 12
Achleck ....64 B 14
Achmelvich ....84 E 9
Achmore ....78 D 11
Achnahanat ....84 G 10
Achnamara ....65 D 15
Achnanellan ....72 E 13
Achnasheen ....78 E 11
Achnashellach Forest ....78 E 11
Achosnich ....71 B 13
Achranich ....71 C 14
Achray (Loch) ....67 G 15
Achreamie ....85 I 8
Achriesgill ....84 F 8
Achtalean ....77 B 11
Achvaich ....79 H 10
Acklington ....63 P 18
Ackworth ....44 P 23
Acle ....39 Y 26
Acomb ....55 N 19
Acrise Place ....13 X 30
Acton Burnell ....34 L 26
Acton Scott ....26 L 26
Acton Turville ....19 N 29
Adbaston ....35 M 25
Adderbury ....28 Q 27
Adderley ....34 M 25
Adderstone ....63 O 17
Addingham ....49 O 22
Addlestone ....21 S 29
Adfa ....33 J 26
Adlington ....42 M 23
Adlington Hall ....43 N 24
Advie ....80 J 11
Adwick-le-Street ....44 Q 23
Ae (Forest of) ....53 J 18
Ae Village ....53 J 18
Afan Argoed ....17 J 29
Affric (Glen) ....78 F 12
Affric Lodge ....78 E 12
Afon Dyfrdwy / Dee (River) ....34 K 24
Afon Dyfrdwy (River) /
  Dee Wales ....41 K 23
Afon-wen ....41 K 23
Agneash ....46 G 21
Aighton ....30 W 27
Aikton ....54 K 19
Ailort (Loch) ....72 C 13
Ailsa Craig ....59 E 18
Ainderby Quernhow ....50 P 21
Ainort (Loch) ....77 B 12
Ainsdale ....42 K 23
Air Uig ....82 Y 9
Aird ....65 D 15
Aird (The) ....79 G 11
Aird of Sleat ....71 C 12
Airdrie ....61 I 16
Airigh na h-Airde (Loch) ....82 Z 9
Airor ....72 C 12
Airth ....67 I 15
Airton ....49 N 21
Aith Orkney Is. ....87 M 6
Aith Shetland Is. ....87 P 3
Aitnoch ....80 I 11
Akeld ....63 N 17
Albourne ....11 T 31
Albrighton ....35 N 26
Albyn or Mor (Glen) ....73 F 12
Alcaig ....79 G 11
Alcester ....27 O 27
Alconbury ....29 T 26
Aldborough ....39 X 25
Aldbourne ....19 P 29
Aldbrough ....45 T 22
Aldbrough St. John ....49 O 20
Aldbury ....21 S 28
Alde (River) ....31 Y 27
Aldeburgh ....31 Y 27
Aldenham ....21 S 28
Alderbury ....9 O 30

Alderholt ....9 O 31
Alderley Edge ....43 N 24
Alderney Channel I. 5
Aldershot ....20 R 30
Alderton ....27 N 28
Aldford ....34 L 24
Aldingbourne ....11 R 31
Aldridge ....35 O 26
Aldringham ....31 Y 27
Aldsworth ....19 O 28
Aldunie ....80 K 12
Aldwick ....11 R 31
Alexandria ....66 G 16
Alfold Crossways ....11 S 30
Alford Aberdeenshire ....75 L 12
Alford Lincs. ....45 U 24
Alfreton ....36 P 24
Alfrick ....27 M 27
Alfriston ....12 U 31
Alkborough ....44 S 22
Alkham ....13 X 30
All Stretton ....34 L 26
Allanaquoich ....74 J 12
Allanton
  North Lanarkshire ....61 I 16
Allanton Scottish Borders ....63 N 16
Allendale Town ....55 N 19
Allenheads ....55 N 19
Allensmore ....26 L 27
Allerford ....17 J 30
Allerston ....51 S 21
Allestree ....36 P 25
Allhallows ....22 V 29
Alligin Shuas ....78 D 11
Allington Kennet ....19 O 29
Allington Salisbury ....9 O 30
Allnabad ....84 G 8
Alloa ....67 I 15
Allonby ....54 J 19
Alloway ....60 G 17
Allt na h-Airbhe ....78 E 10
Alltan Fhèarna (Loch an) ....85 H 9
Alltnacaillich ....84 G 8
Almond (Glen) ....67 I 14
Almondbank ....68 J 14
Almondsbury ....18 M 29
Alness ....79 H 10
Alnham ....63 N 17
Alnmouth ....63 P 17
Alnwick ....63 O 17
Alpheton ....30 W 27
Alphington ....4 J 31
Alpraham ....34 M 24
Alresford ....30 X 28
Alrewas ....35 O 25
Alsager ....35 N 24
Alsh (Loch) ....78 D 12
Alston ....55 M 19
Alstonefield ....35 O 24
Alswear ....7 I 31
Altandduin ....85 H 9
Altandhu ....83 D 9
Altarnun ....3 G 32
Altass ....84 G 10
Alternative Technology
  Centre ....33 I 26
Althorne ....22 W 29
Althorpe ....44 R 23
Altnabreac Station ....85 I 8
Altnacealgach ....84 F 9
Altnaharra ....84 G 9
Alton Hants. ....10 R 30
Alton Staffs. ....35 O 25
Alton Pancras ....9 M 31
Alton Priors ....19 O 29
Alton Towers ....35 O 25
Altrincham ....42 M 23
Alum Bay ....10 P 31
Alva ....67 I 15
Alvaston ....36 P 25
Alvechurch ....27 O 26
Alvediston ....9 N 30
Alverdiscott ....7 H 31
Alves ....80 J 11
Alvescot ....19 P 28

Alvie ....73 I 12
Alvingham ....45 U 23
Alwinton ....63 N 17
Alyth ....74 K 14
Amberley ....11 S 31
Amble ....63 P 18
Amblecote ....27 N 26
Ambleside ....48 L 20
Ambrosden ....28 Q 28
Amersham ....21 S 29
Amesbury ....9 O 30
Amhuinnsuidhe ....82 Y 10
Amisfield ....53 J 18
Amlwch ....40 G 22
Ammanford / Rhydaman ....15 I 28
Amotherby ....50 R 21
Ampleforth ....50 Q 21
Amport ....20 P 30
Ampthill ....29 S 27
Amroth ....15 G 28
Amulree ....67 I 14
An Riabhachan ....78 E 11
An Socach ....74 J 13
An Teallach ....78 E 10
Anchor ....26 K 26
Ancroft ....63 O 16
Ancrum ....62 M 17
Andover ....20 P 30
Andoversford ....27 O 28
Andreas ....46 G 20
Angle ....14 E 28
Anglesey (Isle of) 40
Anglesey Abbey ....30 U 27
Angmering ....11 S 31
Annan ....54 K 19
Annan (River) ....61 J 18
Annat ....78 D 11
Annat Bay ....83 E 10
Annbank ....60 G 17
Annbank Station ....60 G 17
Anne Hathaway's Cottage ....27 O 27
Annesley-Woodhouse ....36 Q 24
Annfield Plain ....56 O 19
Ansley ....28 P 26
Anstey ....36 Q 25
Anston ....44 Q 23
Anstruther ....69 L 15
Antony House ....3 H 32
Appin ....72 E 14
Appleby Eden ....55 M 20
Appleby
  North Lincolnshire ....44 S 23
Appleby Magna ....36 P 25
Applecross ....77 C 11
Appledore Devon ....6 H 30
Appledore Kent ....12 W 30
Appleford ....20 Q 29
Appleton ....20 P 28
Appleton Roebuck ....44 Q 22
Appleton Wiske ....50 P 20
Appletreewick ....49 O 21
Aran Fawddwy ....33 I 25
Arberth / Narberth ....15 F 28
Arbigland ....53 J 19
Arbirlot ....69 M 14
Arbor Low ....35 O 24
Arborfield ....20 R 29
Arbroath ....69 M 14
Arbuthnott ....75 N 13
Archiestown ....80 K 11
Ard (Loch) ....67 G 15
Ardanaiseig ....66 E 14
Ardarroch ....78 D 11
Ardcharnich ....78 E 10
Ardchiavaig ....64 B 15
Ardchuilk ....78 F 11
Ardchyle ....67 G 14
Archive ....72 E 13
Ardeley ....36 R 25
Ardeonaig ....67 H 14
Ardersier ....79 H 11
Ardery ....72 C 13

Ardfern ....65 D 15
Ardgartan ....66 F 15
Ardgay ....79 G 10
Ardgour ....72 D 13
Ardhasaig ....82 Z 10
Ardingly ....11 T 30
Ardington ....20 P 29
Ardivachar ....76 X 11
Ardleigh ....30 W 28
Ardler ....68 Q 28
Ardley ....28 Q 28
Ardlui ....66 F 15
Ardlussa ....65 C 15
Ardmair ....84 E 10
Ardminish ....58 C 16
Ardmore Point Isle of Skye ....77 A 11
Ardnacross ....71 C 14
Ardnamurchan ....71 B 13
Ardnastang ....72 D 13
Ardpatrick ....59 D 16
Ardrishaig ....65 D 15
Ardrossan ....59 F 17
Ardshealach ....71 C 13
Ardslignish ....71 C 13
Ardtalla ....58 B 16
Ardtalnaig ....67 H 14
Ardtoe ....71 C 13
Ardvasar ....71 C 12
Ardverikie Forest ....73 G 13
Ardvorlich ....67 H 14
Ardwell ....52 F 19
Argyll ....65 D 15
Argyll Forest Park ....66 F 15
Arichastlich ....66 F 14
Arienas (Loch) ....71 C 14
Arileod ....71 A 14
Arinacrinachd ....77 C 11
Arinagour ....71 A 14
Arisaig ....71 C 13
Arivruaich ....82 Z 9
Arkaig (Loch) ....72 E 13
Arkendale ....50 P 21
Arkengarthdale ....49 O 20
Arkholme ....48 M 21
Arklet (Loch) ....66 G 15
Arley ....27 P 26
Arlingham ....19 M 28
Arlington Court ....7 I 30
Armadale Highland ....85 H 8
Armadale West Lothian ....61 I 16
Armadale Bay ....71 C 12
Armathwaite ....55 O 19
Armitage ....35 O 25
Armston ....44 Q 23
Arnabost ....71 A 14
Arncliffe ....49 N 21
Arncott ....20 Q 28
Arncroach ....69 L 15
Arne ....9 N 31
Arnesby ....28 Q 26
Arnicle ....59 D 17
Arnisdale ....72 D 12
Arnish ....77 B 11
Arnol ....82 A 8
Arnold ....36 Q 25
Arnprior ....67 H 15
Arnside ....48 L 21
Aros ....65 B 14
Arrad Foot ....48 K 21
Arran (Isle of) ....59 E 17
Arreton ....10 Q 31
Arrochar ....66 F 15
Arscaig ....84 G 9
Arundel ....11 S 31
Ascog ....59 E 16
Ascot ....21 R 29
Ascott House ....20 R 28
Ascott-under-Wychwood ....28 P 28
Ascrib Islands ....77 A 11
Asfordby ....36 R 25
Ash Kent ....23 X 30
Ash Surrey ....20 R 30
Ash Mill ....7 I 31
Ashbourne ....35 O 24
Ashburton ....4 I 32

Ashbury ....19 P 29
Ashby de la Zouch ....36 P 25
Ashby Magna ....28 Q 26
Ashcott ....8 L 30
Ashdon ....30 U 27
Ashford Kent ....12 W 30
Ashford Surrey ....21 S 29
Ashford-in-the-Water
  Derbs. ....43 O 24
Ashie (Loch) ....79 H 11
Ashill Breckland ....38 W 26
Ashill South Somerset ....8 L 31
Ashington Northumb. ....56 P 18
Ashington West Sussex ....11 S 31
Ashkirk ....62 L 17
Ashleworth ....27 N 28
Ashley
  East Cambridgeshire ....30 V 27
Ashley
  Newcastle-under-Lyme ....35 M 25
Ashley Torridge ....7 I 31
Ashley Green ....21 S 28
Ashmore ....9 N 31
Ashover ....36 P 24
Ashperton ....26 M 27
Ashreigney ....7 I 31
Ashtead ....21 T 30
Ashton ....34 L 24
Ashton-in-Makerfield ....42 M 23
Ashton Keynes ....19 O 29
Ashton-under-Lyne ....43 N 23
Ashton-upon-Mersey ....42 M 23
Ashurst ....10 P 31
Ashwell North Hertfordshire ....29 T 27
Ashwell Rutland ....36 R 25
Ashwellthorpe ....39 X 26
Askam in Furness ....47 K 21
Askernish ....76 X 12
Askerswell ....5 L 31
Askham ....55 L 20
Askrigg ....49 N 21
Askwith ....49 O 22
Aslacton ....31 X 26
Aslockton ....36 R 25
Aspatria ....54 K 19
Aspley Guise ....29 S 27
Assynt (Loch) ....84 E 9
Astley ....34 L 25
Aston West Oxfordshire ....20 P 28
Aston Clinton ....20 R 28
Aston Magna ....27 O 27
Aston Rowant ....20 R 28
Aston Tirrold ....20 Q 29
Astwood Bank ....27 O 27
Atcham ....34 L 25
Athelhampton Hall ....9 N 31
Athelney ....8 L 30
Athelstaneford ....69 L 16
Atherington ....7 H 31
Athersley ....43 P 23
Atherstone ....36 P 26
Atherton ....42 M 23
Atholl (Forest of) ....73 H 13
Attadale ....78 D 11
Attleborough Breckland ....38 X 26
Attleborough
  Nuneaton and Bedworth ....28 P 26
Attlebridge ....39 X 25
Atwick ....51 T 22
Atworth ....19 N 29
Aucharnie ....81 M 11
Auchavan ....74 K 13
Auchenblae ....75 M 13
Auchenbowie ....67 I 15
Auchenbrack ....61 I 18
Auchenbreck ....65 E 16
Auchencairn ....53 I 19
Auchencrosh ....52 F 18
Auchencrow ....63 N 16
Auchengray ....61 J 16
Auchenmalg ....52 F 19
Auchentiber ....60 G 16

Great Britain 121

Auchindrean 78 E 10
Auchinleck 60 H 17
Auchleven 81 M 12
Auchlyne 67 G 14
Auchnafree 67 I 14
Auchnagallin 80 J 11
Auchnagatt 81 N 11
Aucholzie 74 K 12
Auchronie 74 L 13
Auchterarder 67 I 15
Auchteraw 73 F 12
Auchterderran 68 K 15
Auchterhouse 68 K 14
Auchtermuchty 68 K 15
Auchtertyre 78 D 12
Auckengill 86 K 8
Auckley 44 Q 23
Audenshaw 43 N 23
Audlem 34 M 25
Audley 35 N 24
Audley End 30 U 27
Aughton *near Lancaster* 48 L 21
Aughton *near Ormskirk* 42 L 23
Auldearn 79 I 11
Auldgirth 53 I 18
Auldhouse 60 H 16
Ault a' Chruinn 72 D 12
Aultbea 78 D 10
Aust 18 M 29
Austrey 35 P 26
Austwick 49 M 21
Avebury 19 O 29
Aveley 22 U 29
Avening 19 N 28
Aveton Gifford 4 I 33
Aviemore 73 I 12
Avoch 79 H 11
Avon (Glen) 74 J 12
Avon (River) *R. Severn* 28 Q 26
Avon (River) *Wilts.* 9 O 31
Avonbridge 67 I 16
Avonmouth 18 L 29
Avonwick 4 I 32
Awe (Loch) 65 E 15
Awliscombe 8 K 31
Awre 19 M 28
Axbridge 18 L 30
Axminster 8 L 31
Axmouth 5 K 31
Aylburton 18 M 28
Aylesbury 20 R 28
Aylesford 22 V 30
Aylesham 23 X 30
Aylsham 39 X 25
Aylton 26 M 27
Aymestrey 26 L 27
Aynho 28 Q 28
Ayr 60 G 17
Aysgarth 49 O 21
Ayside 48 L 21
Ayton *Scarborough* 51 S 21
Ayton *Scottish Borders* 63 N 16

B

Bà (Loch) 65 C 14
Babbacombe Bay 4 J 32
Babcary 8 M 30
Babell 41 K 23
Babworth 44 R 24
Back 83 B 9
Backaland 87 L 6
Backmuir of New Gilston 69 L 15
Backwater Reservoir 74 K 13
Backwell West Town 18 L 29
Baconsthorpe 39 X 25
Bacton *Mid Suffolk* 30 X 27
Bacton *North Norfolk* 39 Y 25
Bacup 43 N 22
Bad a' Ghaill (Loch) 84 E 9
Bad an Sgalaig (Loch) 78 D 10
Badachro 77 C 10
Badanloch (Loch) 85 H 9
Badanloch Lodge 85 H 9
Badcaul 78 D 10
Baddesley Ensor 35 P 26
Baddidarach 84 E 9
Badenoch 73 H 13
Badenscallie 83 E 9
Badenyon 74 K 12
Badlipster 86 K 8
Badluarach 78 D 10
Badminton 19 N 29
Badrallach 78 E 10
Bae Colwyn / Colwyn Bay 41 I 23
Bagh nam Faoileann 76 Y 11
Bagillt 41 K 23
Bagley 34 L 25
Bagshot 21 R 29
Bagworth 36 P 25
Bagwyllydiart 26 L 28
Baile Mór 64 A 15
Bailiehill 54 K 18
Bainbridge 49 N 21
Bainton 51 S 22
Bakewell 35 O 24
Bala 33 J 25
Balallan 82 A 9
Balbeggie 68 J 14
Balblair 79 H 10
Balcary Point 53 I 19
Balchrick 84 E 8
Balcombe 11 T 30
Balderton 36 R 24
Baldock 29 T 28
Baldrine 46 G 21
Baldwin 46 G 21
Balemartine 64 Z 14
Balephetrish Bay 70 Z 14
Balephuil 64 Z 14
Balephuil Bay 64 Z 14
Balerno 61 J 16
Baleshare 76 X 11
Balevulin 65 B 14
Balfour 87 L 6
Balfron 67 H 15
Balgray 69 L 14
Balintore *Angus* 74 K 13
Balintore *Highland* 79 I 10
Balivanich 76 X 11
Balk 50 Q 21
Ballabeg 46 F 21
Ballachulish 72 E 13
Ballajora 46 G 21
Ballamodha 46 G 21
Ballantrae 52 E 18
Ballasalla 46 G 21
Ballater 74 K 12
Ballaugh 46 G 21
Ballevullin 70 Z 14
Balliemore *near Dunoon* 65 E 15
Balliemore *near Oban* 65 D 14
Ballig 46 G 21
Ballingry 68 K 15
Ballinluig 74 J 14
Ballochan 75 L 12
Ballochroy 59 D 16
Ballyhaugh 71 A 14
Balmaclellan 53 H 18
Balmaha 67 G 15
Balmedie 75 N 12
Balminnoch 52 F 19
Balmoral Castle 74 K 12
Balmullo 69 L 14
Balnacra 78 D 11
Balnafoich 79 H 11
Balnaguard 74 I 14
Balnahard 64 B 14
Balnakeil Bay 84 F 8
Balnaknock 77 B 11
Balnapaling 79 H 10
Baltonsborough 8 M 30
Balvicar 65 D 15
Balvraid 72 D 12
Bamburgh Castle 63 O 17
Bamford 43 O 23
Bampton *Cumbria* 48 L 20
Bampton *Devon* 7 J 31
Bampton *Oxon.* 20 P 28
Banavie 72 E 13
Banbury 28 P 27
Banchory 75 M 12
Bancyfelin 15 G 28
Bandenscoth 81 M 11
Banff 81 M 10
Bangor 40 H 23
Bankend 53 J 18
Bankfoot 68 J 14
Bankhead 75 N 12
Banks 42 L 22
Bankshill 54 K 18
Banniskirk 85 J 8
Bannockburn 67 I 15
Banstead 21 T 30
Banwell 18 L 30
Bapchild 22 W 30
Bar Hill 29 U 27
Barbaraville 79 H 10
Barbon 48 M 21
Barcaldine 65 E 14
Barcombe Cross 11 U 31
Bardney 45 T 24
Bardsea 48 K 21
Bardsey 43 P 22
Bardsey Island 32 F 25
Barford 39 X 26
Barford-St. Martin 9 O 30
Barfreston 23 X 30
Bargoed 18 K 28
Bargrennan 52 G 18
Barham 23 X 30
Barking 30 X 27
Barking and Dagenham
London Borough 21 U 29
Barkston 37 S 25
Barkway 29 U 28
Barlaston 35 N 25
Barlborough 44 Q 24
Barlestone 36 P 26
Barley *North Hertfordshire* 29 U 27
Barley *Pendle* 42 N 22
Barlow 43 P 24
Barmby on the Marsh 44 R 22
Barming 22 V 30
Barmouth / Abermaw 33 H 25
Barmouth Bay 33 H 25
Barmston 51 T 21
Barnack 37 S 26
Barnard Castle 49 O 20
Barnby Dun 44 Q 23
Barnby Moor
East Riding of Yorks. 50 R 22
Barnby Moor *Notts.* 44 Q 23
Barnet *London Borough* 21 T 29
Barnetby-le-Wold 45 S 23
Barney 38 W 25
Barnham 30 W 26
Barnham Broom 38 X 26
Barnhill 80 J 11
Barnhills 52 E 18
Barningham 49 O 20
Barnoldswick 49 N 22
Barnsley 43 P 23
Barnstaple 7 H 30
Barnton 42 M 24
Barnwell 29 S 26
Barr 52 F 18
Barra 70 X 13
Barra (Sound of) 70 X 12
Barra Head 70 X 13
Barregarrow 46 G 21
Barrhead 60 G 16
Barrhill 52 F 18
Barri / Barry 18 K 29
Barrington 8 L 31
Barrisdale 72 D 12
Barrisdale Bay 72 D 12
Barrmill 60 G 16
Barrock 86 K 8
Barrow 30 V 27
Barrow Burn 63 N 17
Barrow Gurney 18 L 29
Barrow-in-Furness 47 K 21
Barrow-upon-Humber 45 S 22
Barrow-upon-Soar 36 Q 25
Barrowby 36 R 25
Barrowford 43 N 22
Barry *Angus* 69 L 14
Barry / Barri
Vale of Glamorgan 18 K 29
Barsham 31 Y 26
Barston 27 O 26
Bartestree 26 M 27
Barton *Eden* 49 P 20
Barton *Lancs.* 42 L 22
Barton-le-Clay 29 S 28
Barton le Willows 50 R 21
Barton Mills 30 V 26
Barton-on-Sea 9 P 31
Barton-under-Needwood 35 O 25
Barton-upon-Humber 44 S 22
Barvas 82 A 8
Barwell 36 P 26
Barwick-in-Elmet 43 P 22
Baschurch 34 L 25
Bashall Eaves 42 M 22
Basildon *Berks.* 20 Q 29
Basildon *Essex* 22 V 29
Basing 20 Q 30
Basingstoke 20 Q 30
Baslow 43 P 24
Bass Rock 69 M 15
Bassenthwaite 54 K 19
Bassingham 37 S 24
Baston 37 S 25
Bastwick 39 Y 25
Batcombe 8 M 31
Bath 19 M 29
Bathampton 19 N 29
Batheaston 19 N 29
Bathgate 61 J 16
Batley 43 P 22
Battle 12 V 31
Baumber 45 T 24
Bawburgh 39 X 26
Bawdeswell 38 X 25
Bawdsey 31 Y 27
Bawtry 44 Q 23
Bayble 83 B 9
Baycliff 48 K 21
Baydon 19 P 29
Bayhead 76 X 11
Bayston Hill 34 L 25
Beachampton 28 R 27
Beachy Head 12 U 31
Beacon (The) 2 E 33
Beacon End 30 W 28
Beaconsfield 21 S 29
Beadlam 50 R 21
Beadnell Bay 63 P 17
Beaford 7 H 31
Beal 63 O 16
Beaminster 8 L 31
Beamish Hall 56 P 19
Beamsley 49 O 22
Bearsden 67 G 16
Bearsted 22 V 30
Beattock 61 J 18
Beauchief 43 P 24
Beaufort 18 K 28
Beaulieu 10 P 31
Beauly 79 G 11
Beauly Firth 79 G 11
Beaumaris 40 H 23
Beaumont 54 K 19
Beaupré Castle 17 J 29
Bebington 42 L 23
Beccles 31 Y 26
Beckfoot 54 J 19
Beckingham 44 R 23
Beckington 19 N 30
Beckley 12 V 31
Beckton 21 U 29
Bedale 50 P 21
Beddau 17 J 29
Beddgelert 33 H 24
Beddingham 11 U 31
Bedford 29 S 27
Bedgebury Pinetum 12 V 30
Bedlington 56 P 18
Bedlinog 17 K 28
Bedrule 62 M 17
Bedwas 18 K 29
Bedworth 28 P 26
Bee (Loch) 76 X 11
Beer 5 K 31
Beeston 36 Q 25
Beeswing 53 I 18
Begdbroke 20 Q 28
Beguildy 26 K 26
Beighton 44 P 23
Beinn a' Ghlò 74 I 13
Beinn a' Mheadhoin (Loch) 78 F 12
Beinn Dearg *Highland* 78 F 10
Beinn Dearg
Perthshire and Kinross 73 I 13
Beinn Heasgarnich 67 G 14
Beinn Ime 66 F 15
Beith 60 G 16
Belbroughton 27 N 26
Belchford 45 T 24
Belford 63 O 17
Belhelvie 75 N 12
Bellabeg 74 K 12
Bellingham 55 N 18
Bellshill
Berwick-upon-Tweed 63 O 17
Bellshill *North Lanarkshire* 60 H 16
Belmont 87 R 1
Belnacraig 74 K 12
Belnahua 65 C 15
Belper 36 P 24
Belsay 56 O 18
Belstead 31 X 27
Belstone 4 I 31
Belton *Lincs.* 37 S 25
Belton *Norfolk* 39 Y 26
Belton *North Lincs.* 44 R 23
Belton *Rutland* 36 R 26
Belvoir 36 R 25
Bembridge 10 Q 31
Bempton 51 T 21
Ben Alder 73 G 13
Ben Alder Lodge 73 G 13
Ben Armine Forest 85 H 9
Ben Armine Lodge 85 H 9
Ben Chonzie 67 I 14
Ben Cruachan 65 E 14
Ben-damph Forest 78 D 11
Ben Hope 84 G 8
Ben Klibreck 84 G 9
Ben Lawers 67 H 14
Ben Ledi 67 H 15
Ben Lomond 66 G 15
Ben Loyal 84 G 8
Ben Macdui 74 I 12
Ben More *Argyll and Bute* 65 B 14
Ben More *Stirling* 67 G 14
Ben More *Assynt* 84 F 9
Ben Nevis 72 E 13
Ben Starav 66 E 14
Ben Vorlich 67 H 14
Ben Wyvis 79 G 10
Benbecula 76 X 11
Benbuie 60 H 18
Benderloch *Argyll and Bute* 65 D 14
Benderloch *Mountain* 65 E 14
Bendronaig Lodge 78 E 11
Benenden 12 V 30
Benfleet 22 V 29
Benigton 37 U 25
Benllech 40 H 23
Benmore 67 G 14
Benmore Lodge 84 F 9
Benson 20 Q 29
Bentley *Doncaster* 44 Q 23
Bentley *East Hampshire* 20 R 30
Bentpath 54 K 18
Bentworth 10 Q 30
Benwick 29 T 26
Beoraid (Loch) 72 D 13
Bere Alston 3 H 32
Bere Ferrers 3 H 32
Bere Regis 9 N 31
Berkeley 18 M 28
Berkhamsted 21 S 28
Berneray *near Barra* 70 X 13
Berneray *near North Uist* 76 Y 10
Bernice 66 E 15
Bernisdale 77 B 11
Berriew 34 K 26
Berrington Hall 26 L 27
Berrow 18 K 30
Berry Head 4 J 32
Berry Hill 18 M 28
Berry Pomeroy 4 J 32
Berrynarbor 17 H 30
Bervie Bay 75 N 13
Berwick-St. John 9 N 31
Berwick-upon-Tweed 63 O 16
Berwyn 33 J 25
Bessacarr 44 Q 23
Bethel 33 H 24
Bethersden 12 W 30
Bethesda 33 H 24
Betley 35 M 24
Bettisfield 34 L 25
Bettws Cedewain 34 K 26
Bettws Evan 15 G 27
Bettws Gwerfil Goch 33 J 24
Bettyhill 85 H 8
Betws-y-Coed 33 I 24
Betws yn Rhos 41 J 23
Beulah *near Cardigan* 15 G 27
Beulah
near Llandrindod-Wells 25 J 27
Beverley 45 S 22
Beverstone 19 N 29
Bewaldeth 54 K 19
Bewcastle 55 L 18
Bewdley 27 N 26
Bewholme 51 T 22
Bexhill 12 V 31
Bexley *London Borough* 21 U 29
Beyton 30 W 27
Bhaid-Luachraich (Loch) 78 D 10
Bhealaich (Loch a') 84 G 9
Bhraoin (Loch a') 78 E 10
Bhrollum (Loch) 82 A 10
Bibury 19 O 28
Bicester 28 Q 28
Bicker 37 T 25
Bickington 4 I 32
Bickleigh *Mid Devon* 7 J 31
Bickleigh *South Hams* 4 H 32
Bicton 34 L 25
Bicton gardens 5 K 31
Biddenden 12 V 30
Biddenham 29 S 27
Biddestone 19 N 29
Biddulph 35 N 24
Bidean nam Bian 72 E 14
Bideford 6 H 30
Bidford 27 O 27
Bieldside 75 N 12
Bierton 20 R 28
Big Corlae 60 H 18
Bigbury 4 I 33
Bigbury-on-Sea 4 I 33
Biggar *Barrow-in-Furness* 47 K 21
Biggar *South Lanarkshire* 61 J 17
Biggin Hill 21 U 30
Biggleswade 29 T 27
Bignor 11 S 31
Bildeston 30 W 27
Bildsgreen 27 M 26
Bill of Portland 8 M 32
Billericay 22 V 29
Billesdon 36 R 26
Billingborough 37 S 25
Billinge 42 L 23
Billingham 57 Q 20
Billinghay 37 T 24
Billingshurst 11 S 30
Billingsley 27 M 26
Billington 42 M 22
Billockby 39 Y 26
Billy Row 56 O 19
Bilsington 12 W 30
Bilsthorpe 36 Q 24
Bilston 35 N 26
Bilton 45 T 22
Binbrook 45 T 23
Binfield 20 R 29
Bingham 36 R 25
Bingley 43 O 22
Binham 38 W 25
Binns (The) 68 J 16
Binsted 10 R 30
Birchington 23 X 29
Birdham 10 R 31
Birdingbury 28 P 27
Birdwell 43 P 23
Birdworld 10 R 30
Birgham 62 N 17
Birkdale 42 K 23
Birkenhead 42 K 23
Birkin 44 Q 22
Birling Gap 12 U 31
Birmingham 27 O 26
Birnam 68 J 14
Birsay 86 K 6
Birsemore 75 L 12
Birstall 36 Q 25
Birtley *Gateshead* 56 P 19
Birtley *Tynedale* 55 N 18
Birtsmorton Court 27 N 27
Bisham 20 R 29
Bishop Auckland 56 P 20
Bishop Burton 44 S 22
Bishop Monkton 50 P 21
Bishop Sutton 18 M 29
Bishop Thornton 50 P 21
Bishop Wilton 50 R 22
Bishops Cannings 19 O 29
Bishop's Castle 26 L 26
Bishop's Caundle 9 M 31
Bishop's Cleeve 27 N 28
Bishop's Itchington 28 P 27
Bishops Lydeard 8 K 30
Bishops Nympton 7 I 31
Bishop's Palace
near St. David's 14 E 28
Bishop's Palace *near Tenby* 16 F 28
Bishop's Stortford 30 U 28
Bishop's Tachbrook 28 P 27
Bishop's Tawton 7 H 30
Bishop's Waltham 10 Q 31
Bishopsteignton 4 J 32
Bishopstocke 10 Q 31
Bishopston 15 H 29
Bishopstone *Salisbury* 9 O 30
Bishopstone *Swindon* 19 P 29
Bishopthorpe 50 Q 22
Bishopton *Darlington* 56 P 20
Bishopton *Renfrewshire* 67 G 16
Bishton 18 L 29
Bisley 19 N 28
Bispham 42 K 22
Bix 20 R 29
Bixter 87 P 3
Blaby 36 Q 26
Black Bay 59 D 17
Black Corries 72 F 13
Black Down Hills 8 K 31
Black Isle 79 G 11
Black Mount 66 F 14
Black Mountain 25 I 28
Black Mountains 26 K 28
Black Notley 30 V 28
Black Torrington 6 H 31
Black Water Valley 78 F 11
Blackawton 4 I 32

A B C D E F G H I J K L M N O P Q R S T U V W X Y Z

A
B
C
D
E
F
G
H
I
J
K
L
M
N
O
P
Q
R
S
T
U
V
W
X
Y
Z

Blackburn *Aberdeenshire* ...75 N 12
Blackburn *Lancs.* ...42 M 22
Blackburn *West Lothian* ...61 J 16
Blackfield ...10 P 31
Blackford *Cumbria* ...54 L 19
Blackford *Perthshire and Kinross* ...67 I 15
Blackhall ...57 Q 19
Blackhall Rocks ...57 Q 19
Blackhill *Aberdeenshire* ...81 O 11
Blackhill *Highland* ...77 A 11
Blacklunans ...74 J 13
Blackmoor Gate ...17 I 30
Blackmore ...22 U 28
Blackness Castle ...68 J 15
Blacko ...43 N 22
Blackpool ...42 K 22
Blackridge ...61 I 16
Blackthorn ...28 Q 28
Blacktoft ...44 R 22
Blackwater *Hart* ...20 R 30
Blackwater *Isle of Wight* ...10 Q 31
Blackwater (River) ...22 W 28
Blackwater Reservoir ...72 F 13
Blackwaterfoot ...59 D 17
Blackwell ...50 P 20
Blackwood ...18 K 29
Bladnoch ...52 G 19
Bladon ...20 P 28
Blaenannherch ...15 G 27
Blaenau Ffestiniog ...33 I 25
Blaenavon ...18 K 28
Blaengarw ...17 J 29
Blaengrwrach ...17 J 28
Blagdon ...18 L 30
Blaich ...72 E 13
Blaina ...18 K 28
Blair Atholl ...73 I 13
Blair Castle ...73 I 13
Blairgowrie ...68 J 14
Blairmore ...66 F 16
Blakeney *Glos.* ...18 M 28
Blakeney *Norfolk* ...38 X 25
Blakesley ...28 Q 27
Blamerino ...68 K 14
Blandford Forum ...9 N 31
Blanefield ...67 H 16
Blàr a Chaorainn ...72 E 13
Blarmachfoldach ...72 E 13
Blarnalearoch ...78 E 10
Blawith ...48 K 21
Blaxton ...44 R 23
Blaydon ...56 O 19
Bleadon ...18 L 30
Bleaklow Hill ...43 O 23
Blean ...23 X 30
Bleasby ...36 R 24
Blenheim Palace ...20 P 28
Bletchingdon ...20 Q 28
Bletchley ...28 R 27
Bletsoe ...29 S 27
Blewbury ...20 Q 29
Blickling ...39 X 25
Blickling Hall ...39 X 25
Blidworth ...36 Q 24
Blindley Heath ...21 T 30
Blisland ...3 F 32
Blisworth ...28 R 27
Blithe ...35 O 25
Blithfield Hall ...35 O 25
Blithfield Reservoir ...35 O 25
Blockley ...27 O 27
Blofield ...39 Y 26
Bloxham ...28 P 27
Blubberhouses ...49 O 22
Blue John Cavern ...43 O 23
Bluemull Sound ...87 Q 1
Blundellsands ...42 K 23
Blundeston ...39 Z 26
Blyth *Northumb.* ...56 P 18
Blyth *Notts.* ...44 Q 23
Blythburgh ...31 Y 27
Blythe Bridge ...35 N 25
Blyton ...44 R 23
Bo' Ness ...68 J 15
Boarhills ...69 L 15
Boat of Garten ...74 I 12
Boathvic ...79 G 10
Bocking Churchstreet ...30 V 28
Boddam ...81 O 11
Bodedern ...40 G 23
Bodelwyddan ...41 J 23
Bodenham ...26 L 27
Bodfari ...41 J 23
Bodfordd ...40 G 23
Bodham Street ...39 X 25
Bodiam Castle ...12 V 30

Bodicote ...28 Q 27
Bodmin ...3 F 32
Bodmin Moor ...3 G 32
Bodnant Garden ...41 I 23
Bognor Regis ...11 R 31
Bogue ...53 H 18
Boisdale ...70 X 12
Boisdale (Loch) ...70 Y 12
Boldon ...56 P 19
Bolham ...7 J 31
Bollin (River) ...42 N 23
Bollington ...43 N 24
Bolney ...11 T 31
Bolnhurst ...29 S 27
Bolsover ...44 Q 24
Boltby ...50 Q 21
Bolton *Alnwick* ...63 O 17
Bolton *Bolton* ...42 M 23
Bolton Abbey ...49 O 22
Bolton-by-Bowland ...49 N 22
Bolton-le-Sands ...48 L 21
Bolton on Swale ...50 P 20
Bolton-upon-Dearne ...44 Q 23
Bomere Heath ...34 L 25
Bonar Bridge ...79 G 10
Bonawe Quarries ...65 E 14
Bonby ...44 S 23
Boncath ...15 G 27
Bonchester Bridge ...62 M 17
Bonhill ...66 G 16
Bonnybridge ...67 I 16
Bonnyrigg ...61 K 16
Bont-faen / Cowbridge ...17 J 29
Bontgoch Elerch ...25 I 26
Bontnewydd ...32 H 24
Boosbeck ...50 R 20
Boot ...47 K 20
Bootle *Cumbria* ...47 J 21
Bootle *Merseyside* ...42 K 23
Border Forest Park (The) ...55 M 18
Bordogan ...32 G 24
Boreham ...22 V 28
Boreham Street ...12 V 31
Borehamwood ...21 T 29
Boreland ...54 K 18
Borgue *Dumfries and Galloway* ...53 H 19
Borgue *Highland* ...85 J 9
Borness ...53 H 19
Borough Green ...22 U 30
Boroughbridge ...50 P 21
Borreraig ...77 Z 11
Borrobol Forest ...85 H 9
Borrowash ...36 P 25
Borth ...25 H 26
Borve *Barra Isle* ...70 X 13
Borve *Eilean Siar* ...70 X 13
Borve *Isle of Lewis* ...82 A 8
Borve *South Harris* ...76 Y 10
Borwick ...48 L 21
Bosbury ...26 M 27
Boscastle ...6 F 31
Boscombe ...9 O 31
Bosham ...10 R 31
Bosherston ...16 F 29
Bosley ...35 N 24
Boston ...37 T 25
Boston Spa ...50 P 22
Boswinger ...3 F 33
Botesdale ...30 W 26
Bothamsall ...44 R 24
Bothel ...54 K 19
Bothwell ...60 H 16
Botley ...10 Q 31
Bottesfor *Melton* ...36 R 25
Bottesford *North Lincolnshire* ...44 S 23
Bottisham ...30 U 27
Botwnnog ...32 G 25
Boughton ...36 Q 24
Boughton House ...29 R 26
Boughton Street ...22 W 30
Boulmer ...63 P 17
Boultham ...44 S 24
Bourn ...29 T 27
Bourne ...37 S 25
Bournemouth ...9 O 31
Bourton *North Dorset* ...9 N 30
Bourton *Vale of White Horse* ...19 P 29
Bourton-on-the-Water ...27 O 28
Bovey Tracey ...4 I 32
Bovingdon ...21 S 28
Bow ...7 I 31
Bow Street ...25 H 26
Bowden ...62 L 17
Bower *Highland* ...85 K 8

Bower *Tynedale* ...55 M 18
Bowerchalke ...9 O 30
Bowes ...49 N 20
Bowhill ...62 L 17
Bowland ...62 L 17
Bowland (Forest of) ...49 M 22
Bowmore ...58 B 16
Bowness ...48 L 20
Bowness-on-Solway ...54 K 19
Bowood House ...19 N 29
Box ...19 N 29
Box Hill ...21 T 30
Boxford *Babergh* ...30 W 27
Boxford *West Berkshire* ...20 P 29
Boxley ...22 V 30
Boxworth ...29 T 27
Boyton ...6 G 31
Bozeat ...29 R 27
Braaid ...46 G 21
Brabourne Lees ...12 W 30
Bracadale (Loch) ...77 A 12
Bracebridge Heath ...37 S 24
Brackley ...28 Q 27
Brackley Hatch ...28 Q 27
Bracknell ...20 R 29
Braco ...67 I 15
Bracora ...72 C 13
Bradan Resr (Loch) ...60 G 18
Bradfield *Sheffield* ...43 P 23
Bradfield *West Berkshire* ...20 Q 29
Bradford *Bradford* ...43 O 22
Bradford *Taunton Deane* ...8 K 31
Bradford Abbas ...8 M 31
Bradford-on-Avon ...19 N 29
Brading ...10 Q 31
Bradninch ...7 J 31
Bradpole ...5 L 31
Bradwell ...43 O 24
Bradwell-on-Sea ...22 W 28
Bradworthy ...6 G 31
Brae ...87 P 2
Brae of Achnahaird ...83 D 9
Brae Roy Lodge ...73 F 13
Braeantra ...79 G 10
Braehead ...61 J 16
Braemar ...74 J 12
Braemore ...85 J 9
Braeriach ...74 I 12
Braeswick ...87 L 6
Brafferton Helperby ...50 Q 21
Bragar ...82 A 8
Braglenbeg ...65 D 15
Braich y Pwll ...32 F 25
Braidwood ...61 I 16
Bràigh Mór ...82 Y 9
Brailes ...28 P 27
Brailsford ...35 P 25
Braintree ...30 V 28
Braishfield ...10 P 30
Braithwell ...44 Q 23
Bramcote ...36 Q 25
Bramfield ...31 Y 27
Bramford ...31 X 27
Bramhall ...43 N 23
Bramham ...43 P 22
Bramley *Basingstoke and Deane* ...20 Q 30
Bramley *South Yorks.* ...44 Q 23
Bramley *Surrey* ...21 S 30
Brampton *Cambs.* ...29 T 27
Brampton *Cumbria* ...55 L 19
Brampton *Eden* ...55 M 20
Brampton *Rotherham.* ...43 P 23
Brampton *Suffolk* ...31 Y 26
Brampton Bryan ...26 L 26
Brancaster ...38 V 25
Branderburgh ...80 K 10
Brandesburton ...51 T 22
Brandon *Durham* ...56 P 19
Brandon *Suffolk* ...30 V 26
Brandsby ...50 Q 21
Branscombe ...5 K 31
Bransgore ...9 O 31
Branston ...37 S 24
Brant Broughton ...37 S 24
Brassington ...35 P 24
Bratton ...19 N 30
Bratton Clovelly ...6 H 31
Bratton Fleming ...7 I 30
Braughing ...29 U 28
Braunston *Daventry* ...28 Q 27
Braunston *Rutland* ...36 R 26
Braunton ...6 H 30
Bray-on-Thames ...21 R 29

Bray Shop ...3 G 32
Braybrooke ...28 R 26
Brayford ...7 I 30
Brayton ...44 Q 22
Breaclete ...82 Z 9
Breadalbane ...67 G 14
Breage ...2 D 33
Breamore House ...9 O 31
Brean ...18 K 30
Breasclete ...82 Z 9
Breaston ...36 Q 25
Brechin ...75 M 13
Breckland ...30 V 26
Brecon / Aberhonddu ...25 J 28
Brecon Beacons National Park ...25 J 28
Bredbury ...43 N 23
Brede ...12 V 31
Bredenbury ...26 M 27
Bredgar ...22 W 30
Bredon ...27 N 27
Bredwardine ...26 L 27
Bremhill ...19 N 29
Brenchley ...12 V 30
Brendon Hills ...7 J 30
Brenig Reservoir ...33 J 24
Brenish ...82 Y 9
Brent *London Borough* ...21 T 29
Brent Knoll ...18 L 30
Brent Pelham ...29 U 28
Brentwood ...22 U 29
Brenzett ...12 W 30
Brereton ...35 O 25
Bressay ...87 Q 3
Bretford ...28 P 26
Bretherton ...42 L 22
Brewham ...9 M 30
Brewlands Bridge ...74 K 13
Brewood ...35 N 25
Bride ...46 G 20
Bridestowe ...4 H 31
Bridge ...23 X 30
Bridge of Alford ...75 L 12
Bridge of Allan ...67 I 15
Bridge of Avon ...80 J 11
Bridge of Balgie ...73 H 14
Bridge of Buchat ...74 L 12
Bridge of Craigisla ...74 K 13
Bridge of Dee ...53 I 19
Bridge of Don ...75 N 12
Bridge of Dun ...75 M 13
Bridge of Dye ...75 M 13
Bridge of Earn ...68 J 14
Bridge of Ericht ...73 G 13
Bridge of Gairn ...74 K 12
Bridge of Gaur ...73 G 13
Bridge of Orchy ...66 F 14
Bridge of Weir ...60 G 16
Bridgemary ...10 Q 31
Bridgend *Aberdeenshire* ...80 L 11
Bridgend *Angus* ...75 L 13
Bridgend *Argyll and Bute* ...65 D 15
Bridgend *Islay* ...58 B 16
Bridgend *Perthshire and Kinross* ...68 J 14
Bridgend / Pen-y-bont ...17 J 29
Bridgend of Lintrathen ...74 K 13
Bridgerule ...6 G 31
Bridgham ...30 W 26
Bridgnorth ...27 M 26
Bridgwater ...8 L 30
Bridlington ...51 T 21
Bridport ...5 L 31
Brierfield ...43 N 22
Brierley ...43 P 23
Brierley Hill ...27 N 26
Brigham ...54 J 20
Brighouse ...43 O 22
Brighstone ...10 P 32
Brighstone Forest ...10 P 32
Brightling ...12 V 31
Brightlingsea ...22 X 28
Brighton ...11 T 31
Brightwell ...20 Q 29
Brigstock ...29 S 26
Brimfield ...26 L 27
Brimham Rocks ...49 O 21
Brimington ...43 P 24
Brimpsfield ...19 N 28
Brimpton ...20 Q 29
Brinkburn Priory ...63 O 18
Brinkley ...30 V 27

Brinklow ...28 P 26
Brinkworth ...19 O 29
Brinyan ...86 L 6
Brisley ...38 W 25
Brislington ...18 M 29
Bristol ...18 M 29
Briston ...38 X 25
Briton Ferry ...17 I 29
Brittle (Loch) ...71 B 12
Brittwell Salome ...20 Q 29
Brixham ...4 J 32
Brixton ...4 H 32
Brixworth ...28 R 27
Brize Norton ...20 P 28
Broad Bay ...83 B 9
Broad Blunsdon ...19 O 29
Broad Chalke ...9 O 30
Broad Haven ...14 E 28
Broad Hinton ...19 O 29
Broad Law ...61 J 17
Broad Oak ...12 V 31
Broadbrige Heath ...11 S 30
Broadclyst ...7 J 31
Broadford ...77 C 12
Broadlands ...10 P 31
Broadmayne ...9 M 31
Broadstairs ...23 Y 29
Broadstone ...9 O 31
Broadwas ...27 M 27
Broadway ...27 O 27
Broadwey ...8 M 32
Broadwindsor ...8 L 31
Broadwoodwidger ...6 H 31
Brockdish ...31 X 26
Brockenhurst ...10 P 31
Brockley ...18 L 29
Brockworth ...19 N 28
Brodick ...59 E 17
Brodick Bay ...59 E 17
Brodick Castle ...59 E 17
Brodie Castle ...79 I 11
Brodsworth ...44 Q 23
Brodsworth Hall ...44 Q 23
Brokenborough ...19 N 29
Brolass ...65 B 14
Bromborough ...42 L 24
Brome ...31 X 26
Bromfield ...26 L 26
Bromham *Bedford* ...29 S 27
Bromham *Kennet* ...19 N 29
Bromley *London Borough* ...21 U 29
Brompton *Kent* ...22 V 29
Brompton *near Northallerton* ...50 P 20
Brompton-by-Sawdon ...51 S 21
Brompton on Swale ...49 O 20
Brompton Ralph ...7 K 30
Brompton Regis ...7 J 30
Bromsgrove ...27 N 26
Bromyard ...26 M 27
Bronllys ...26 K 27
Brook ...22 W 30
Brooke ...39 Y 26
Brookmans Park ...21 T 28
Broom (Loch) ...78 E 10
Broomfield *Chelmsford* ...22 V 28
Broomfield *Sedgemoor* ...8 K 30
Broomfleet ...44 S 22
Broomhaugh ...56 O 19
Brora ...85 I 9
Broseley ...34 M 26
Brotherton ...44 Q 22
Brotton ...57 R 20
Brough *East Riding of Yorkshire* ...44 S 22
Brough *Eden* ...49 N 20
Brough *Highland* ...86 J 8
Brough Head ...86 J 6
Brough Lodge ...87 R 2
Brough of Birsay ...86 J 6
Broughton *Cumbria* ...54 J 19
Broughton *Flintshire / Sir y Fflint* ...34 L 24
Broughton *Hants.* ...10 P 30
Broughton *Lancs.* ...42 L 22
Broughton *North Lincs.* ...44 S 23
Broughton *Northants.* ...28 R 26
Broughton *Oxon.* ...28 P 27
Broughton *Scottish Borders* ...61 J 17
Broughton-in-Furness ...47 K 21
Broughton Mills ...47 K 21
Broughton Moor ...54 J 19
Broughton Poggs ...19 P 28
Broughty Ferry ...69 L 14
Brownhills ...35 O 26
Brownsea Island ...9 O 31

Broxbourne ...21 T 28
Broxburn ...68 J 16
Bruar Lodge ...73 I 13
Bruichladdich ...58 A 16
Brundall ...39 Y 26
Brushford ...7 J 30
Bruton ...8 M 30
Brydekirk ...54 K 18
Brymbo ...34 K 24
Bryn-Henllan ...24 F 27
Brynamman ...17 I 28
Brynbuga / Usk ...18 L 28
Bryncethin ...17 J 29
Bryneglwys ...34 K 24
Bryngwran ...40 G 23
Bryngwyn ...26 K 27
Brynhoffnant ...15 G 27
Brynmawr ...18 K 28
Brynsiencyn ...32 H 24
Brynteg ...40 H 23
Bualintur ...71 B 12
Bubwith ...44 R 22
Buccleuch ...61 K 17
Buchanty ...67 I 14
Buchlyvie ...67 H 15
Buckden *Cambs.* ...29 T 27
Buckden *North Yorks.* ...49 N 21
Buckfast ...4 I 32
Buckfast Abbey ...4 I 32
Buckfastleigh ...4 I 32
Buckhaven ...68 K 15
Buckhorn Weston ...9 M 30
Buckie ...80 L 10
Buckingham ...28 R 27
Buckland *Herts.* ...29 T 28
Buckland *Oxon.* ...20 P 28
Buckland Abbey ...4 H 32
Buckland Brewer ...6 H 31
Buckland Dinham ...19 M 30
Buckland in-the-Moor ...4 I 32
Buckland Newton ...8 M 31
Buckland St. Mary ...8 K 31
Bucklebury ...20 Q 29
Bucklers Hard ...10 P 31
Buckley / Bwcle ...34 K 24
Buckminster ...36 R 25
Bucknall ...37 T 24
Bucknell ...26 L 26
Bucks green ...11 S 30
Buckshurn ...75 N 12
Bude ...6 G 31
Budleigh Salterton ...5 K 32
Bugbrooke ...28 Q 27
Bugle ...3 F 32
Bugthorpe ...50 R 21
Buildwas Abbey ...34 M 26
Builth Wells / Llanfair-ym-Muallt ...25 J 27
Bulford ...19 O 30
Bulkéley ...34 L 24
Bulkington ...28 P 26
Bulwell ...36 Q 24
Bulwick ...37 S 26
Bunarkaig ...72 F 13
Bunessan ...64 B 15
Bungay ...31 Y 26
Bunnahabhainn ...64 B 16
Bunny ...36 Q 25
Buntingford ...29 T 28
Burbage *Leics.* ...28 P 26
Burbage *Wilts.* ...19 O 29
Burchett's Green ...20 R 29
Bures ...30 W 28
Burford ...19 P 28
Burgess Hill ...11 T 31
Burgh-by-Sands ...54 K 19
Burgh Castle ...39 Y 26
Burgh-le-Marsh ...38 U 24
Burgh-St. Peter ...39 Y 26
Burghead ...80 J 10
Burghfield ...20 Q 29
Burghill ...26 L 27
Burghley House ...37 S 26
Burham ...22 V 30
Burley ...9 O 31
Burley-in-Wharfedale ...49 O 22
Burlton ...34 L 25
Burneside ...48 L 20
Burneston ...50 P 21
Burnfoot ...62 L 17
Burnham ...21 S 29
Burnham Market ...38 W 25
Burnham-on-Crouch ...22 W 29
Burnham-on-Sea ...18 L 30
Burnhaven ...81 O 11
Burnhope ...56 O 19
Burniston ...51 S 21

Burnley 43 N 22
Burntisland 68 K 15
Burrafirth 87 R 1
Burravoe 87 Q 2
Burray 87 L 7
Burrelton 68 K 14
Burringham 44 R 23
Burrington *North Devon* 7 I 31
Burrington *North Somerset* 18 L 30
Burrough Green 30 V 27
Burrow Head 53 G 19
Burry Port /Porth Tywyn 15 H 28
Burscough 42 L 23
Burscough Bridge 42 L 23
Burshill 51 S 22
Bursledon 10 Q 31
Burslem 35 N 24
Burstwick 45 T 22
Burton *Christchurch* 9 O 31
Burton *Ellesmere*
  Port and Neston 48 L 21
Burton *South Lakeland* 48 L 21
Burton *Wrecsam / Wrexham* 34 L 24
Burton Agnes 51 T 21
Burton Bradstock 5 L 31
Burton Constable Hall 45 T 22
Burton Fleming 51 S 21
Burton in Lonsdale 49 M 21
Burton Joyce 36 Q 25
Burton Latimer 29 R 26
Burton Leonard 50 P 21
Burton Pidsea 45 T 22
Burton-upon-Stather 44 R 23
Burton-upon-Trent 35 O 25
Burwarton 26 M 26
Burwash 12 V 31
Burwell *Cambs.* 30 U 27
Burwell *Lincs.* 45 U 24
Bury *Bury* 42 N 23
Bury *Chichester* 11 S 31
Bury St. Edmunds 30 W 27
Busby 60 H 16
Buscot 19 P 28
Bushey 21 S 29
Bute (Island of) 59 E 16
Bute (Kyles of) 59 E 16
Bute (Sound of) 59 E 16
Butleigh 8 L 30
Butley 31 Y 27
Butt of Lewis 83 B 8
Buttercrambe 50 R 21
Buttermere 47 K 20
Butterstone 68 J 14
Buttington 34 K 25
Buxted 12 U 31
Buxton *Derbs.* 43 O 24
Buxton *Norfolk* 39 X 25
Bwcle / Buckley 34 K 24
Bwlch 26 K 28
Bwlch Oerddrws 33 I 25
Bwlch y Ffridd 33 J 26
Bwlch-y-Groes 25 I 28
Bwlch-y-Sarnau 25 J 26
Bwlchgwyn 34 K 24
Bwlchllan 25 H 27
Byfield 28 Q 27
Byfleet 21 S 30
Byland Abbey 50 Q 21
Byrness 62 M 18

C

Cabrach 80 K 12
Cadair Idris 33 I 25
Caddington 29 S 28
Caddonfoot 62 L 17
Cadhay 5 K 31
Cadishead 42 M 23
Cadnam 10 P 31
Cadney 44 S 23
Cadwell Park 45 T 24
Caerau 17 J 29
Caerdydd / Cardiff 18 K 29
Caerffili / Caerphilly 18 K 29
Caerfyrddin / Carmarthen 15 H 28
Caergwrle 34 K 24
Caergybi / Holyhead 40 G 23
Caerlaverock Castle 53 J 19
Caerleon 18 L 29
Caernarfon 32 H 24
Caernarfon Bay 32 G 24
Caerphilly / Caerffili 18 K 29
Caersws 25 J 26
Caerwent 18 L 29
Caerwys 41 K 23
Cailliness Point 52 F 19
Cairn Edward Forest 53 H 18
Cairn Gorm 74 J 12

Cairn Table 60 H 17
Cairn Toul 74 I 12
Cairnborrow 80 L 11
Cairndow 66 F 15
Cairngaan 52 F 20
Cairngarroch 52 E 19
Cairnie 80 L 11
Cairnpapple Hill 67 J 16
Cairnryan 52 E 19
Cairnsmore of Carsphairn 60 H 18
Cairnsmore of Fleet 53 G 19
Cairraig Fhada 58 B 17
Caister-on-Sea 39 Z 26
Caistor 45 T 23
Calbourne 10 P 31
Caldbeck 54 K 19
Caldecott 36 R 26
Calder (Loch) 85 J 8
Calder Bridge 47 J 20
Calder Mains 85 J 8
Caldercruix 61 I 16
Calderdale 43 N 22
Caldermill 60 H 17
Caldey Island 15 F 29
Caldicot 18 L 29
Caldwell 49 O 20
Calf of Man 46 F 21
Calfsound 87 L 6
Calgary 71 B 14
Calgary Bay 71 B 14
Caliach Point 71 B 14
Calke Abbey 36 P 25
Callander 67 H 15
Callater (Glen) 74 J 13
Callington 3 H 32
Callow 19 N 29
Calne 19 N 29
Calow 43 P 24
Calstock 3 H 32
Calthwaite 55 L 19
Calvay 70 Y 12
Calver 43 P 24
Calverton 36 Q 24
Calvine 73 I 13
Cam 29 U 27
Cam Loch 84 E 9
Camas Chil Mhalieu 72 D 14
Camas-luinie 78 D 12
Camasnacroise 72 D 14
Camastianavaig 77 B 11
Camber 12 W 31
Camberley 20 R 30
Camblesforth 44 Q 22
Cambo 56 O 18
Cambois 56 P 18
Camborne 2 E 33
Cambrian Mountains 25 I 27
Cambridge 29 U 27
Cambusbarron 67 I 15
Cambuskenneth 67 I 15
Camden *London Borough* 21 T 29
Camelford 6 F 32
Cammachmore 75 N 12
Campbeltown 59 D 17
Campsie Fells 67 H 15
Camptown 62 M 17
Campville 35 P 25
Camrose 24 E 28
Camusnagaul 78 E 10
Candlesby 37 U 24
Canewdon 22 W 29
Canisbay 86 K 8
Canna 71 A 12
Cannich 78 F 11
Cannich (Glen) 78 F 11
Cannington 8 K 30
Cannock 35 N 25
Canonbie 54 L 18
Canons Ashby 28 Q 27
Canterbury 23 X 30
Cantley 39 Y 26
Canvey Island 22 V 29
Caol 72 E 13
Caolas a' Mhòrain 76 Y 10
Caoles 70 Z 14
Caolis 70 X 13
Caolisport (Loch) 65 D 16
Cape Cornwall 2 C 33
Cape Wrath 84 E 8
Capel 11 T 30
Capel Curig 33 I 24
Capel Garmon 33 I 24
Capel Le Ferne 13 X 30
Capel St. Mary 31 X 27
Capel-y-Ffin 26 K 28
Capesthorne Hall 43 N 24
Capheaton 56 O 18
Cappercleuch 61 K 17

Caputh 68 J 14
Cara Island 58 C 17
Carbis Bay 2 D 33
Carbost *Minginish* 77 A 12
Carbost *Trotternish* 77 B 11
Cardenden 68 K 15
Cardiff / Caerdydd 18 K 29
Cardigan / Aberteifi 15 G 27
Cardigan Bay 24 G 26
Cardington 34 L 26
Cardinham 3 G 32
Cardrona 61 K 17
Cardross 66 G 16
Cardurnock 54 K 19
Carew 15 F 28
Carfraemill 62 L 16
Cargill 68 J 14
Carhampton 7 J 30
Carie 73 H 13
Carinish 76 Y 11
Carisbrooke 10 Q 31
Cark 48 L 21
Carlbt 37 S 25
Carleen 2 D 33
Carleton 49 N 22
Carlecotie 55 L 19
Carlops 61 J 16
Carlton *Bedford* 29 S 27
Carlton *Hambleton* 50 Q 20
Carlton
  Hinckley and Bosworth 36 P 26
Carlton *North Yorks.* 44 Q 22
Carlton *Notts.* 36 Q 25
Carlton Colville 31 Z 26
Carlton in Lindrick 44 Q 23
Carlton-on-Trent 36 R 24
Carluke 61 I 16
Carmarthen / Caerfyrddin 15 H 28
Carmel Head 40 G 22
Carmunnock 60 H 16
Carmyllie 69 L 14
Carn Ban 73 H 12
Carn Coire na h-Easgainn 73 H 12
Carn Eige 78 E 12
Carn Glas-choire 79 I 11
Carn Mairg 73 H 14
Carnaby 51 T 21
Carnach 78 E 12
Carnassarie Castle 65 D 15
Carnedd Llewelyn 33 I 24
Carnforth 48 L 21
Carno 33 J 26
Carnock 68 J 15
Carnoustie 69 L 14
Carnwath 61 J 16
Carradale 59 D 17
Carradale Bay 59 D 17
Carrbridge 79 I 12
Carrick 66 F 15
Carrick Roads 2 E 33
Carron 80 K 11
Carron (Loch) 77 C 11
Carron Bridge 67 I 15
Carrshield 55 N 19
Carrutherstown 54 J 18
Carsaig 65 C 15
Carse of Gowrie 68 K 14
Carsethorn 53 J 19
Carseriggan 52 G 19
Carsluith 53 G 19
Carsphairn 53 H 18
Carstairs 61 I 16
Carterton 19 P 28
Carterway Heads 56 O 19
Carthew 3 F 32
Carthorpe 50 P 21
Cartmel 48 L 21
Carville 56 P 19
Cas-Gwent / Chepstow 18 M 29
Cashlie 67 G 14
Casnewydd / Newport 18 L 29
Cassington 20 P 28
Cassley (Glen) 84 F 9
Castell-Nedd / Neath 17 I 29
Castell Newydd Emlyn /
  Newcastle Emlyn 15 G 27
Castell-y-Rhingyll 15 H 28
Castle Acre 38 W 25
Castle Ashby 28 R 27
Castle Bolton 49 O 21
Castle Bytham 37 S 25
Castle Campbell 67 I 15
Castle Cary 8 M 30
Castle Combe 19 N 29
Castle Donington 36 P 25
Castle Douglas 53 I 19

Castle Drogo 4 I 31
Castle Eaton 19 O 29
Castle Fraser 75 M 12
Castle frome 26 M 27
Castle Hedingham 30 V 28
Castle Howard 50 R 21
Castle Kennedy 52 F 19
Castle Lachlan 65 E 15
Castle Loch 52 F 19
Castle Rising 38 V 25
Castlebay 70 X 13
Castleford 43 P 22
Castlemartin 16 E 29
Castlerigg 54 K 20
Castleton
  Casnewydd / Newport 18 K 29
Castleton *Derbs.* 43 O 23
Castleton *North Yorks.* 50 R 20
Castletown *Highland* 85 J 8
Castletown *Isle of Man* 46 G 21
Caston 38 W 26
Catacol 59 E 16
Catacol Bay 59 D 16
Caterham 21 T 30
Catfield 39 Y 25
Catlodge 73 H 12
Caton 48 L 21
Catrine 60 H 17
Catterall 42 L 22
Catterick 50 P 20
Catterick Garrison 49 O 20
Catterline 75 N 13
Cattistock 8 M 31
Catton *Broadland* 39 X 26
Catton *Tynedale* 55 N 19
Catworth 29 S 26
Cauldcleuch Head 62 L 18
Cauldon 35 O 24
Caulkerbush 53 I 19
Cautley 49 M 20
Cava 86 K 7
Cavendish 30 V 27
Caversfield 28 Q 28
Caversham 20 R 29
Cawdor 79 I 11
Cawood 44 Q 22
Caxton 29 T 27
Caynham 26 M 26
Caythorpe 37 S 24
Cayton 51 S 21
Ceall (Loch nan) 71 C 13
Cefn Bryn 15 H 29
Cefn-Coed-y-cymmer 17 J 28
Cefn-mawr 34 K 25
Cefn-y-Pant 15 G 28
Ceinewydd / New Quay 24 G 27
Ceiriog (Vale of) 34 K 25
Cemaes 40 G 22
Cemaes Head 15 F 27
Cemmaes 33 I 26
Cemmaes road 33 I 26
Cenarth 15 G 27
Ceres 69 L 15
Cerne Abbas 8 M 31
Cerrigydrudion 33 J 24
Chacewater 2 E 33
Chacombe 28 Q 27
Chadderton 43 N 23
Chaddesden 36 P 25
Chadlington 28 P 28
Chadwell St. Mary 22 V 29
Chagford 4 I 31
Chailey 11 T 31
Chàirn Bhain (Loch a') 84 E 9
Chalfont St. Giles 21 S 29
Chalfont St. Peter 21 S 29
Chalford 19 N 28
Chalgrove 20 Q 29
Challacombe 7 I 30
Challoch 52 G 19
Challock 22 W 30
Chambercombe Manor 17 H 30
Chandler's Ford 10 P 31
Channel Islands 5
Chapel Brampton 28 R 27
Chapel-en-le-Frith 43 O 24
Chapel Haddlesey 44 Q 22
Chapel le Dale 49 M 21
Chapel St. Leonards 45 V 24
Chapel Stile 48 K 20
Chapelhall 61 I 16
Chapelknowe 54 K 18
Chapeltown *Moray* 74 K 12
Chapeltown *Sheffield* 43 P 23
Chapmanslade 19 N 30
Chard 8 L 31

Chardstock 8 L 31
Charfield 19 M 29
Charing 22 W 30
Charlbury 28 P 28
Charlecote *Park* 27 P 27
Charleston *Manor* 12 U 31
Charlestown *Highland* 78 C 10
Charlestown *Restormel* 3 F 33
Charlton 19 N 29
Charlton Horethorne 8 M 30
Charlton Kings 27 N 28
Charlton Marshall 9 N 31
Charlton Musgrove 9 M 30
Charlton on Otmoor 20 Q 28
Charlwood 11 T 30
Charminster 8 M 31
Charmouth 5 L 31
Charney Basset 20 P 29
Charsfield 31 X 27
Chartham 23 X 30
Chartridge 21 S 28
Chartwell 21 U 30
Chastleton 27 P 28
Chatburn 42 M 22
Chatham 22 V 29
Chatsworth House 43 P 24
Chatteris 29 U 26
Chatto 62 M 17
Chawleigh 7 I 31
Cheadle *Gtr. Mches.* 43 N 23
Cheadle *Staffs.* 35 O 25
Checkendon 20 Q 29
Cheddar 18 L 30
Cheddar Gorge 18 L 30
Cheddington 21 S 28
Cheddleton 35 N 24
Chedington 8 L 31
Chedworth 19 O 28
Cheese Bay 76 Y 11
Chelford 42 N 24
Chellaston 36 P 25
Chelmarsh 27 M 26
Chelmsford 22 V 28
Cheltenham 27 N 28
Chelveston 29 S 27
Chelwood Gate 11 U 30
Chepstow / Cas-Gwent 18 L 29
Cherhill 19 O 29
Cherington *Cotswold* 19 N 28
Cherington
  Stratford-on-Avon 27 P 27
Cheriton 10 Q 30
Cheriton Bishop 4 I 31
Cheriton Fitzpaine 7 J 31
Cherry Burton 44 S 22
Chertsey 21 S 29
Cherwell (River) 28 Q 28
Cheselbourne 9 M 31
Chesham 21 S 28
Chesham Bois 21 S 28
Cheshunt 21 T 28
Chesil Beach 8 M 32
Cheslyn Hay 35 N 26
Chester 34 L 24
Chester-le-Street 56 P 19
Chesterfield 43 P 24
Chesters 62 M 17
Chesters Fort 55 N 18
Chesterton *Cambridge* 29 U 27
Chesterton *Cherwell* 28 Q 28
Cheswardine 35 M 25
Cheswick 63 O 16
Cheviot (The) 63 N 17
Cheviot Hills (The) 62 M 17
Chew Magna 18 M 29
Chew Stoke 18 M 29
Chewton Mendip 18 M 30
Chicheley 29 R 27
Chichester 10 R 31
Chickerell 5 M 32
Chicklade 9 N 30
Chiddingfold 11 S 30
Chiddingly 12 U 31
Chiddingstone 22 U 30
Chideock 5 L 31
Chieveley 20 Q 29
Chigwell 21 U 29
Chilcompton 18 M 30
Child Okeford 9 N 31
Childrey 20 P 29
Child's Ercall 34 M 25
Chilham 22 W 30
Chillingham 63 O 17
Chilmark 9 N 30
Chilton *Sedgefield* 56 P 20

Chilton
  Vale of White Horse 20 Q 29
Chilton Folia 20 P 29
Chippenham
  East Cambridgeshire 30 V 27
Chippenham
  North Wiltshire 19 N 29
Chipping 42 M 22
Chipping Campden 27 O 27
Chipping Norton 28 P 28
Chipping Ongar 22 U 28
Chipping Sodbury 19 M 29
Chipping Warden 28 Q 27
Chirbury 34 K 26
Chirk 34 K 25
Chirk Castle 34 K 25
Chirmorie 52 F 18
Chirnside 63 N 16
Chirton 19 O 30
Chiseldon 19 O 29
Chislet 23 X 30
Chiswell Green 21 S 28
Chitterne 19 N 30
Chittlehamholt 7 I 31
Chittlehampton 7 I 30
Chobham 21 S 29
Choire (Loch) 84 H 9
Cholderton 9 O 30
Cholesbury 21 S 28
Chollerton 55 N 18
Cholsey 20 Q 29
Chon (Loch) 67 G 15
Chopwell 56 O 19
Chorley 42 M 23
Chorleywood 21 S 29
Christchurch *Christchurch* 9 O 31
Christchurch *Fenland* 38 U 26
Christian Malford 19 N 29
Christleton 34 L 24
Christmas Common 20 R 29
Christow 4 J 32
Chroisg (Loch a') 78 E 11
Chudleigh 4 J 32
Chulmleigh 7 I 31
Church 42 M 22
Church Crookham 20 R 30
Church Eaton 35 N 25
Church Enstone 28 P 28
Church Fenton 44 Q 22
Church Knowle 9 N 32
Church Leigh 35 O 25
Church Lench 27 O 27
Church Minshull 34 M 24
Church Stoke 34 K 26
Church Stretton 34 L 26
Churcham 19 M 28
Churchdown 27 N 28
Churchill *North Somerset* 18 L 29
Churchill *Oxon.* 27 P 28
Churchingford 8 K 31
Churnet 35 N 24
Churnsike Lodge 55 M 18
Churston Ferrers 4 J 32
Churt 10 R 30
Chwilog 32 H 25
Cifynydd 17 K 29
Cilcain 34 K 24
Cilcennin 25 H 27
Cilgerran 15 G 27
Cilmery 25 J 27
Cilrhedyn 15 G 28
Cilybebyll 17 I 28
Cilycwn 25 I 27
Cinderford 18 M 28
Cirencester 19 O 28
City of London
  London Borough 21 T 29
Clachaig 66 E 16
Clachan *Argyl* 66 F 15
Clachan *Kintyre* 59 D 16
Clachan Mòr 70 Z 14
Clachan of Campsie 67 H 16
Clachan of Glendaruel 65 E 15
Clachtoll 83 E 9
Clackavoid 74 J 13
Clackmannan 67 I 15
Clacton-on-Sea 23 X 28
Claggain Bay 58 B 16
Claggan 71 C 14
Claidh (Loch) 82 A 10
Claigan 77 A 11
Clandon Park 21 S 30
Clanfield 10 Q 31
Claonel 84 G 9
Clapham *Beds.* 29 S 27
Clapham *North Yorks.* 49 M 21
Clapton-in-Gordano 18 L 29

A B C D E F G H I J K L M N O P Q R S T U V W X Y Z

A
B
C
D
E
F
G
H
I
J
K
L
M
N
O
P
Q
R
S
T
U
V
W
X
Y
Z

Clàr (Loch nan) ....85 H 9
Clarbeston Road ....24 F 28
Clare ....30 V 27
Clashindarroch ....80 L 11
Clashmore ....79 H 10
Clashnessie ....84 E 9
Clatt ....80 L 12
Clatteringshaws (Loch) .....53 H 18
Clauchlands Point ....59 E 17
Clavering ....29 U 28
Claverley ....27 N 26
Claverton Manor ....19 N 29
Clawdd-newydd ....33 J 24
Clawton ....6 G 31
Claxton *Ryedale* ....50 R 21
Claxton *South Norfolk* ...39 Y 26
Clay Cross ....36 P 24
Claydon ....31 X 27
Claydon House ....28 R 28
Claypole ....36 R 24
Clayton ....11 T 31
Clayton-le-Moors ....42 M 22
Clayton West ....43 P 23
Cleadale ....71 B 13
Cleadon ....57 P 19
Cleat ....70 X 12
Cleator Moor ....47 J 20
Cleckheaton ....43 O 22
Cleedownton ....26 M 26
Cleehill ....26 M 26
Cleethorpes ....45 T 23
Cleeve Abbey ....7 J 30
Cleeve Prior ....27 O 27
Clehonger ....26 L 27
Cleigh ....65 D 14
Clenchwarton ....38 V 25
Clent ....27 N 26
Cleobury Mortimer ....26 M 26
Cleobury North ....26 M 26
Clephanton ....79 I 11
Clevedon ....18 L 29
Clevedon-Court ....18 L 29
Cleveland Hills ....50 Q 20
Cleveleys ....42 K 22
Cley Next the Sea ....38 X 25
Cliburn ....55 M 20
Cliffe *Edway* ....22 V 29
Cliffe *Selby* ....44 R 22
Clifton
  City of Nottingham .....36 Q 25
Clifton *Eden* ....55 L 20
Clifton *Rugby* ....28 Q 26
Clifton Hampden ....20 Q 29
Clifton-upon-Teme ....27 M 27
Clipston ....28 R 26
Clisham ....82 Z 10
Clitheroe ....42 M 22
Clive ....34 L 25
Cliveden House ....21 R 29
Clocaenog ....33 J 24
Clocaenog Forest ....33 J 24
Clola ....81 O 11
Clophill ....29 S 27
Clopton ....29 S 26
Closeburn ....53 I 18
Clotton ....34 L 24
Clouds Hill ....9 N 31
Cloughton ....51 S 20
Clova ....74 K 13
Clova (Glen) ....74 K 13
Clove Lodge ....49 N 20
Clovelly ....6 G 31
Clovenfords ....62 L 17
Clovulin ....72 E 13
Clowne ....44 Q 24
Cluanie Loch ....72 E 12
Cluanie Lodge ....72 E 12
Clumber Park ....44 Q 24
Clun ....26 K 26
Clunbury ....26 L 26
Clunes Forest ....72 F 13
Clungunford ....26 L 26
Clunie ....68 J 14
Clutton ....18 M 30
Clwydian Range ....34 K 24
Clydach ....17 I 28
Clyde (Firth of) ....59 F 17
Clyde (River) ....61 J 17
Clydebank ....60 G 16
Clydesdale ....61 I 16
Clyffe Pypard ....19 O 29
Clynnog-Fawr ....32 G 24
Clyro ....26 K 27
Clyst Honiton ....4 J 31
Clyst Hydon ....7 J 31
Clytha ....18 L 28
Clywedog Resr. ....25 J 26

Coalburn ....61 I 17
Coaley ....19 N 28
Coalville ....36 P 25
Coast ....78 D 10
Coatbridge ....60 H 16
Coates ....19 N 28
Cobham ....21 S 30
Cock Bridge ....74 K 12
Cockayne ....50 Q 20
Cockburnspath ....69 M 16
Cockenzie and Port Seton ...69 L 16
Cockerham ....48 L 22
Cockermouth ....54 J 20
Cockfield *Babergh* ....30 W 27
Cockfield *Teesdale* ....56 O 20
Cocking ....10 R 31
Cockleford ....19 N 28
Cockshutt ....34 L 25
Coddington ....36 R 24
Codford St. Mary ....9 N 30
Codicote ....21 T 28
Codnor ....36 P 24
Codsall ....35 N 26
Coe (Glen) ....72 F 14
Coed y Brenin Forest ....33 I 25
Coedpoeth ....34 K 24
Coggeshall ....30 W 28
Coigach ....84 E 10
Coignafearn ....73 H 12
Coignafearn Forest ....73 H 12
Coille Mhorgil ....72 E 12
Colaboll ....84 G 9
Colbost ....77 A 11
Colby *Eden* ....55 M 20
Colby *Isle of Man* ....46 F 21
Colchester ....30 W 28
Cold Ash ....20 Q 29
Cold Ashby ....28 Q 26
Cold Ashton ....19 M 29
Cold Fell ....55 M 19
Cold Norton ....22 W 28
Coldbackie ....84 G 8
Coldean ....11 T 30
Coldingham ....63 N 16
Coldstream ....63 N 17
Colebrooke ....7 I 31
Coleford *Glos.* ....18 M 28
Coleford *Somerset* ....18 M 30
Colemere ....34 L 25
Coleorton ....36 P 25
Coleshill
  North Warwickshire .....27 O 26
Coleshill
  Vale of White Horse ....19 P 29
Colgrave Sound ....87 R 2
Colkirk ....38 W 25
Coll *Argyll and Bute* ....71 A 14
Coll *Eilean Siar* ....83 B 9
Colliery Row ....56 P 19
Collieston ....81 O 11
Collin ....53 J 18
Collingbourne Ducis ....19 P 30
Collingbourne Kingston ....19 P 30
Collingham *Notts.* ....36 R 24
Collingham *West Yorks.* ....50 P 22
Collington ....26 M 27
Collyweston ....37 S 26
Colmonell ....52 F 18
Coln (River) ....19 O 28
Colnabaichin ....74 K 12
Colne ....43 N 22
Colne (River) ....22 X 28
Colonsay ....64 B 15
Colpy ....81 M 11
Colsterworth ....37 S 25
Coltishall ....39 Y 25
Colwall Stone ....27 M 27
Colwinston ....17 J 29
Colwyn Bay / Bae Colwyn ...41 I 23
Colyton ....5 K 31
Combe Florey ....8 K 30
Combe Martin ....17 H 30
Combe-St. Nicholas ....8 L 31
Comberton ....29 U 27
Combwich ....8 K 30
Come-to-Good ....2 E 33
Compton *Berks.* ....20 Q 29
Compton *Guildford* ....21 S 30
Compton *West Sussex* ....10 R 31
Compton Abdale ....19 O 28
Compton Basset ....19 O 29
Compton Castle ....4 J 32
Compton Dando ....18 M 29
Compton Wynyates ....28 P 27
Comrie ....67 I 14
Cona Glen ....72 D 13

Conchra ....65 E 15
Condicote ....27 O 28
Condover ....34 L 26
Congleton ....35 N 24
Congresbury ....18 L 29
Coningsby ....37 T 24
Conington ....29 T 26
Conisbrough ....44 Q 23
Coniston ....48 K 20
Connah's Quay ....42 K 24
Connel ....65 D 14
Connel Park ....60 H 17
Conon Bridge ....79 G 11
Consett ....56 O 19
Constantine Bay ....2 E 32
Contin ....79 G 11
Convinth (Glen) ....79 G 11
Conway Falls ....33 I 24
Conwy ....41 I 23
Conwy (River) ....33 I 24
Conwy (Vale of) ....33 I 24
Cooden Beach ....12 V 31
Cookham ....21 R 29
Coolham ....11 S 31
Coombe Bissett ....9 O 30
Copdock ....31 X 27
Copford ....30 W 28
Copley ....56 O 20
Copmanthorpe ....50 Q 22
Copplestone ....7 I 31
Coppull ....42 M 23
Copthorne ....11 T 30
Coquet (River) ....63 N 17
Corbridge ....55 N 19
Corby ....28 R 26
Corby Glen ....37 S 25
Corfe Castle ....9 N 32
Corfe Mullen ....9 N 31
Corgarff Castle ....74 K 12
Corhampton ....10 Q 31
Cornforth ....56 P 19
Cornhill ....81 L 11
Cornhill-on-Tweed ....63 N 17
Cornwood ....4 I 32
Cornworthy ....4 J 32
Corpach ....72 E 13
Corpusty ....39 X 25
Corran ....72 E 13
Corrany ....46 G 21
Corrie ....59 E 17
Corrie Common ....54 K 18
Corrimony ....78 F 11
Corringham *Thurrock* ....22 V 29
Corringham *West Lindsey* ...44 R 23
Corris ....33 I 26
Corry ....77 C 12
Corryvreckan (Gulf of) ....65 C 15
Corscombe ....8 L 31
Corsham ....19 N 29
Corsham Court ....19 N 29
Corsley Heath ....19 N 30
Corsock ....53 I 18
Corstopitum ....55 N 19
Corton ....9 N 30
Corwen ....33 J 25
Cosby ....36 Q 26
Cosham ....10 Q 31
Costessey ....39 X 26
Cot-town ....81 N 11
Cotehill ....55 L 19
Cotgrave ....36 Q 25
Cotham ....36 R 24
Cotherstone ....49 O 20
Cothi River ....25 H 28
Coton ....29 U 27
Cotswold Wildlife Park ....19 O 28
Cottenham ....29 U 27
Cottered ....29 T 28
Cottesmore ....37 S 25
Cottingham
  East Riding of Yorks. ...45 S 22
Cottingham *Northants.* .....28 R 26
Cottisford ....28 Q 28
Cottonshopeburn Foot ....62 M 18
Coulags ....78 D 11
Coulport ....66 F 15
Coulter ....61 J 17
Coundon ....56 P 20
Countesthorpe ....36 Q 26
Coupar Angus ....68 K 14
Coustonn ....66 E 16
Cove *Argyll and Bute* ....66 F 15
Cove *Highland* ....78 C 10
Cove Bay ....75 N 12
Coventry ....28 P 26
Coverack ....2 E 33
Cow Honeybourne ....27 O 27

Cowal ....65 E 15
Cowan Bridge ....48 M 21
Cowbit ....37 T 25
Cowbridge / Bont-faen ....17 J 29
Cowden ....60 H 15
Cowdenbeath ....68 J 15
Cowdray House ....10 R 31
Cowes *Isle of Wight* ....10 Q 31
Cowfold ....11 T 31
Cowie ....67 I 15
Cowling ....43 N 22
Cowplain ....10 Q 31
Coxheath ....22 V 30
Coxhoe ....56 P 19
Coxwold ....50 Q 21
Coylton ....60 G 17
Coylumbridge ....74 I 12
Crackington Haven ....6 G 31
Crafthole ....3 H 32
Craggan ....66 F 15
Cragside Gardens ....63 O 18
Crai ....25 J 28
Craig ....78 E 11
Craig Lodge ....65 E 16
Craig-y-nos ....17 I 28
Craigdarroch ....60 H 18
Craigellachie ....80 K 11
Craigencallie ....53 G 18
Craigendoran ....66 F 16
Craigens ....58 B 16
Craighead ....69 M 15
Craighouse ....58 C 16
Craigievar Castle ....75 L 12
Craigmalloch ....53 G 18
Craignish (Loch) ....65 D 15
Craignure ....65 C 14
Craigrothie ....69 L 15
Craigton ....74 K 14
Craik ....62 K 17
Crail ....69 M 15
Crailing ....62 M 17
Crailinghall ....62 M 17
Crakaig ....85 I 9
Cramlington ....56 P 18
Cramond ....68 K 16
Cranborne ....9 O 31
Cranbrook ....12 V 30
Cranford St. John ....29 S 26
Cranleigh ....11 S 30
Cranshaws ....62 M 16
Cranstal ....46 G 20
Cranwell ....37 S 24
Cranworth ....38 W 26
Crask Inn ....84 G 9
Craster ....63 P 17
Crathes Castle ....75 M 12
Crathie ....74 K 12
Crathorne ....50 Q 20
Craven Arms ....26 L 26
Crawcrock ....56 O 19
Crawford ....61 J 17
Crawfordjohn ....61 I 17
Crawick ....61 I 17
Crawley *Hants.* ....10 P 30
Crawley *West Sussex* ....11 T 30
Crawley Down ....11 T 30
Creag Meagaidh ....73 G 13
Creagan ....65 E 14
Creagorry ....76 Y 11
Creake South ....38 W 25
Credenhill ....26 L 27
Crediton ....7 J 31
Creech St. Michael ....8 K 30
Creetown ....53 G 19
Creggans ....66 E 15
Creran (Loch) ....65 D 14
Cressage ....34 M 26
Cresswell Castle Morpeth ....56 P 18
Cresswell *Pembrokeshire /
  Sir Benfro* ....15 F 28
Creswell ....44 Q 24
Crewe ....35 M 24
Crewkerne ....8 L 31
Crianlarich ....66 G 14
Cribyn ....15 H 27
Criccieth ....33 H 25
Crich ....36 P 24
Crichton ....62 L 16
Crick ....28 Q 26
Crickadarn ....25 K 27
Cricket St. Thomas ....8 L 31
Crickhowell ....26 K 28
Cricklade ....19 O 29
Crickley Hill ....19 N 28
Crieff ....67 I 14

Crimond ....81 O 11
Crimplesham ....38 V 26
Crinan ....65 D 15
Crinan (Loch) ....65 D 15
Cringleford ....39 X 26
Croachy ....79 H 12
Crocketford ....53 I 18
Crockham Hill ....21 U 30
Croes-goch ....14 E 28
Croesyceiliog ....18 L 29
Croft Herefordshire ....26 L 27
Croft *Richmondshire* ....50 P 20
Croft-on-Tees ....50 P 20
Crofty ....15 H 29
Croggan ....65 C 14
Croglin ....55 M 19
Croick ....79 G 10
Croig ....71 B 14
Cromalt Hills ....84 E 9
Cromar ....74 L 12
Cromarty ....79 H 10
Cromarty Bay ....79 H 10
Cromarty Firth ....79 H 11
Cromdale ....80 J 11
Cromdale (Hills of) ....80 J 12
Cromer ....39 X 25
Cromford ....35 P 24
Cromore ....82 A 9
Cromra ....73 G 13
Crondall ....20 R 30
Cronk (The) ....46 G 21
Crook *South Lakeland* ....48 L 20
Crook *Wear Valley* ....56 O 19
Crook of Devon ....68 J 15
Crookham ....63 N 17
Crookham Village ....20 R 30
Crooklands ....48 L 21
Cropredy ....28 Q 27
Cropston ....36 Q 25
Cropwell Bishop ....36 R 25
Crosby *Allerdale* ....54 J 19
Crosby *Isle of Man* ....46 G 21
Crosby *Sefton* ....42 K 23
Crosby Ravensworth ....48 M 20
Croscombe ....18 M 30
Cross ....83 B 8
Cross Fell ....55 M 19
Cross Hands ....15 H 28
Cross Inn ....25 H 27
Crossaig ....59 D 16
Crossapoll ....64 Z 14
Crossbost ....82 A 9
Crossford ....61 I 16
Crossgates ....68 J 15
Crossgill ....48 L 21
Crosshill *Fife* ....68 K 15
Crosshill *South Ayrshire* ..60 G 18
Crosshouse ....60 G 17
Crosskeys ....18 K 29
Crosskirk ....85 J 8
Crossmichael ....53 I 19
Crossraguel Abbey ....60 F 18
Crossways ....9 N 31
Croston ....30 W 26
Crouch (River) ....22 W 29
Croughton ....28 Q 28
Crow Hill ....26 M 28
Crowborough ....12 U 30
Crowcombe ....8 K 30
Crowhurst ....12 V 31
Crowland ....37 T 25
Crowle *Doncaster* ....44 R 23
Crowle *Wychavon* ....27 N 27
Crowlin Island ....77 C 11
Crowmarsh Gifford ....20 Q 29
Crowthorne ....20 R 29
Croxley Green ....21 S 29
Croxton ....30 W 26
Croxton Kerrial ....36 R 25
Croy ....79 H 11
Croyde ....6 H 30
Croydon *London Borough* ...21 T 29
Cruden Bay ....81 O 11
Crudgington ....34 M 25
Crudwell ....19 N 29
Crug-y-bar ....25 I 27
Crulivig ....82 Z 9
Crymmych ....15 G 28
Crynant ....17 I 28
Cuaig ....77 C 11
Cubbington ....28 P 27
Cubert ....2 E 32
Cuckfield ....11 T 30
Cucklington ....9 M 30
Cuckney ....44 Q 24
Cuddington *Aylesbury* ....20 R 28
Cuddington *Vale Royal* .....42 M 24

Cudworth ....43 P 23
Cuffley ....21 T 28
Cuhxham ....20 Q 29
Cuilicudden ....79 H 11
Cuillin Sound ....71 B 12
Cuillins (The) ....77 B 12
Culbokie ....79 G 11
Culdrose ....2 E 33
Culgaith ....55 M 20
Culkein ....83 D 9
Cullen ....80 L 10
Cullen Bay ....80 L 10
Cullingworth ....43 O 22
Cullipool ....65 D 15
Culloch ....67 I 14
Cullompton ....7 J 31
Culmington ....26 L 26
Culmstock ....8 K 31
Culnacraig ....84 E 10
Culrain ....79 G 10
Culross ....68 J 15
Culshabbin ....52 G 19
Culswic ....87 P 3
Culter Fell ....61 J 17
Cults ....75 N 12
Culzean Castle ....59 F 17
Cumbernauld ....67 I 16
Cumbrian Moutains ....48 K 20
Cuminestown ....81 N 11
Cummersdale ....54 L 19
Cummertrees ....54 J 19
Cumnock ....60 H 17
Cumnor ....20 P 28
Cumwhitton ....55 L 19
Cunninghamhead ....60 G 17
Cupar ....69 K 15
Curbridge ....20 P 28
Curdridge ....10 Q 31
Currie ....61 K 16
Curry Rivel ....8 L 30
Cutcloy ....53 G 19
Cutnall green ....27 N 27
Cuxton ....22 V 29
Cwm ....18 K 28
Cwm Bychan ....33 H 25
Cwm Taf ....17 J 28
Cwmafan ....17 I 29
Cwmaman ....17 J 28
Cwmbach *Carmarthenshire /
  Sir Gaerfyrddin* ....15 G 28
Cwmbach *Powys / Powys* ...25 J 27
Cwmbach *Rhondda, Cynon, Taf /
  Rhondda, Cynon, Taff* ....17 J 28
Cwmbrân ....18 L 29
Cwmcarn ....18 K 29
Cwmcoy ....15 G 27
Cwmllynfell ....17 I 28
Cwmystwyth ....25 I 26
Cwnduad ....15 G 28
Cwnfelin Boeth ....15 G 28
Cwrt-Newydd ....15 H 27
Cydweli / Kidwelly ....15 H 28
Cyffylliog ....33 J 24
Cymmer ....17 J 29
Cymyran Bay ....40 G 23
Cynwyl Elfed ....15 G 28

D

Dacre *Eden* ....55 L 20
Dacre *Harrogate* ....49 O 21
Daglingworth ....19 N 28
Dailly ....60 F 18
Daimh (Loch an) ....73 G 14
Dairsie or Osnaburgh ....69 L 14
Dalavich ....65 E 15
Dalbeattie ....53 I 19
Dalbeg ....73 H 12
Dalblair ....60 H 17
Dalby ....46 F 21
Dalchalloch ....73 H 13
Dalchruin ....67 H 15
Dale ....14 E 28
Dale Head ....48 L 20
Dalgonar ....60 H 18
Dalham ....30 V 27
Dalhavaig ....85 I 8
Daliburgh ....76 X 12
Dalkeith ....61 K 16
Dallas ....80 J 11
Dalleagles ....60 H 17
Dallington *Northampton* ....28 R 27
Dallington *Rother* ....12 V 31
Dalmally ....66 F 14
Dalmellington ....60 G 18
Dalmeny ....68 J 16
Dalmigavie ....73 H 12
Dalnabreck ....71 C 13

Dalnaspidal Lodge ....73 H 13
Dalnavaid ....74 J 13
Dalnavie ....79 H 10
Dalness ....72 F 14
Dalry
 Dumfries and Galloway ....53 H 18
Dalry *North Ayrshire* ....60 F 16
Dalrymple ....60 G 17
Dalston ....54 L 19
Dalswinton ....53 I 18
Dalton
 Dumfries and Galloway ....54 J 18
Dalton *North Yorks.* ....50 P 21
Dalton in Furness ....47 K 21
Damerham ....9 O 31
Damh (Loch) ....78 D 11
Dan-yr-Ogof ....17 I 28
Danbury ....22 V 28
Danby ....50 R 20
Dane ....35 N 24
Danehill ....11 U 30
Darenth ....22 U 29
Darfield ....43 P 23
Darlington ....50 P 20
Darowen ....33 I 26
Darras Hall ....56 O 18
Darrington ....44 Q 22
Darsham ....31 Y 27
Dartford ....22 U 29
Dartford Tunnel ....22 U 29
Dartington ....4 I 32
Dartmeet ....4 I 32
Dartmoor National Park ....4 I 32
Dartmouth ....4 J 32
Darton ....43 P 23
Darvel ....60 H 17
Darwen ....42 M 22
Datchet ....21 S 29
Datchworth ....29 T 28
Dava ....80 J 11
Daventry ....28 Q 27
Davidstow ....6 G 32
Davington ....61 K 18
Daviot ....79 H 11
Dawley ....34 M 26
Dawlish ....4 J 32
Deal ....23 Y 30
Dean ....54 J 20
Dean Forest Park ....18 M 28
Deanich Lodge ....78 F 10
Deanston ....67 H 15
Dearham ....54 J 19
Debden ....30 U 28
Deben (River) ....31 X 27
Debenham ....31 X 27
Deddington ....28 Q 28
Dedham ....30 W 28
Dee / Afon Dyfrdwy (River)
 Wales ....41 K 23
Dee (River) *Scotland* ....75 N 12
Dee (River) / Afon Dyfrdwy ..34 K 24
Deene ....29 S 26
Deepcut ....21 R 30
Deepdale ....49 M 21
Deeping-St. James ....37 T 25
Deeping St. Nicholas ....37 T 25
Deeps (The) ....87 P 3
Defford ....27 N 27
Deinielon ....33 H 24
Delabole ....6 F 32
Delamere ....34 M 24
Delamere Forest ....42 L 24
Dell ....83 B 8
Dellifure ....80 J 11
Delnadamph Lodge ....74 K 12
Delph ....43 N 23
Denbigh / Dinbych ....33 J 24
Denby Dale ....43 P 23
Denchworth ....20 P 29
Denham ....21 S 29
Denholm ....62 L 17
Denmead ....10 Q 31
Dennington ....31 Y 27
Denny ....67 I 15
Dent ....49 M 21
Denton *South Kesteven* ..36 R 25
Denton *Stockport* ....43 N 23
Denver ....38 V 26
Derby ....36 P 25
Deri ....18 K 28
Dersingham ....38 V 25
Dervaig ....71 B 14
Derwent (River) *R. Ouse* ....44 R 22
Derwent (River) *R. Trent* ..36 P 24
Derwent (River) *R. Tyne* ..56 O 19
Derwent Dale ....43 O 23
Derwent Reservoir *Derbs.* ..43 O 23

Derwent Reservoir
 Northumb. ....56 N 19
Derwent Water ....54 K 20
Desborough ....28 R 26
Desford ....36 Q 26
Detling ....22 V 30
Devauden ....18 L 28
Deveron (River) ....81 M 11
Devil's Beef Tub ....61 J 17
Devil's Bridge / Pontarfynach 25 I 26
Devil's Elbow ....74 J 13
Devil's Punch Bowl ....10 R 30
Devizes ....19 O 29
Devonport ....3 H 32
Dewsbury ....43 P 22
Dherue (Loch an) ....84 G 8
Dial Post ....11 S 31
Dickleburgh ....31 X 26
Didcot ....20 Q 29
Diddlebury ....26 L 26
Digby ....37 S 24
Dilhorne ....35 N 25
Dilton Marsh ....19 N 30
Dilwyn ....26 L 27
Dinas ....24 F 27
Dinas Dinlle ....32 G 24
Dinas Head ....24 F 27
Dinas-Mawddwy ....33 I 25
Dinas Powys ....18 K 29
Dinbych / Denbigh ....33 J 24
Dinbych-y-pysgod / Tenby ..15 F 28
Dingwall ....79 G 11
Dinnet ....74 L 12
Dinnington
 Newcastle upon Tyne ......56 O 18
Dinnington *Rotherham* ......44 Q 23
Dinsdale ....50 P 20
Dinton ....9 O 30
Diptford ....4 I 32
Dirleton ....69 L 15
Dishforth ....50 P 21
Diss ....31 X 26
Disserth ....25 J 27
Distington ....53 J 20
Ditcheat ....8 M 30
Ditchingham ....31 Y 26
Ditchley Park ....28 P 28
Ditchling ....11 T 31
Ditton Priors ....26 M 26
Doc Penfro /
 Pembroke Dock ....16 F 28
Docherty (Glen) ....78 E 11
Dochgarroch ....79 H 11
Docking ....38 V 25
Dockray ....54 L 20
Dodburn ....62 L 17
Doddington *Cambs.* ....29 U 26
Doddington *Kent* ....22 W 30
Doddington *Lincs.* ....44 S 24
Doddington *Northumb.* ......63 O 17
Dodington ....19 M 29
Dodman Point ....3 F 33
Dodworth ....43 P 23
Doirlinn ....71 C 13
Dolanog ....33 J 25
Dolbenmaen ....33 H 25
Dolfor ....26 K 26
Dolgarrog ....33 I 24
Dolgellau ....33 I 25
Dolgoch Falls ....33 I 26
Dollar ....67 I 15
Dolphinholme ....48 L 22
Dolton ....7 H 31
Don (River) *R. Ouse* ....44 Q 23
Don (River) *R. Spey* ....74 K 12
Doncaster ....44 Q 23
Donhead-St. Andrew ....9 N 30
Donhead-St. Mary ....9 N 30
Donington ....37 T 25
Donington-on-Bain ....45 T 24
Donington Park Circuit ..36 P 25
Donisthorpe ....36 P 25
Donnington *Berks.* ....20 Q 29
Donnington *Salop* ....35 M 25
Donyatt ....8 L 31
Doon (Loch) ....60 G 18
Dorback Lodge ....74 J 12
Dorchester *Dorset* ....8 M 31
Dorchester *Oxon.* ....20 Q 29
Dordon ....35 P 26
Dore ....43 P 24
Dores ....79 H 11
Dorking ....21 T 30
Dormansland ....11 U 30
Dormanstown ....57 Q 20
Dornie ....78 D 12
Dornoch ....79 H 10

Dornoch Firth ....79 H 10
Dornock ....54 K 19
Dorrington ....34 L 26
Dorstone ....26 K 27
Dorusduain ....78 D 12
Douchary (Glen) ....78 F 10
Dougarie ....59 D 17
Douglas *Isle of Man* ....46 G 21
Douglas
 South Lanarkshire ....61 I 17
Douglastown ....74 L 14
Dounby ....86 K 6
Doune *Highland* ....84 G 10
Doune *Stirling* ....67 H 15
Dove (River) ....35 O 24
Dove Cottage ....48 K 20
Dove Holes ....43 O 24
Dovedale ....35 O 24
Dover ....13 X 30
Dovercourt ....31 X 28
Doveridge ....35 O 25
Dovey / Dyfi (River) ....33 I 26
Dowally ....74 J 14
Dowdeswell ....27 N 28
Dowlish Wake ....8 L 31
Down Ampney ....19 O 28
Downderry ....3 G 32
Downham ....30 U 26
Downham Market ....38 V 26
Downies ....75 N 12
Downton ....9 O 31
Dowsby ....37 S 25
Doynton ....19 M 29
Drakes Broughton ....27 N 27
Draughton ....49 O 22
Drax ....44 R 22
Draycott ....36 P 25
Draycott-in-the-Clay ....35 O 25
Draycott-in-the-Moors ....35 N 25
Drayton *Norfolk* ....39 X 25
Drayton *Oxon.* ....20 Q 29
Drayton-St. Leonard ....20 Q 29
Drefach *near Carmarthen* ..15 H 28
Drefach
 near Newcastle-Emlyn ....15 G 27
Dreghorn ....60 G 17
Drem ....69 L 15
Drenewydd / Newtown ....26 K 26
Dreswick Point ....46 G 21
Driffield ....19 O 28
Drigg ....47 J 20
Drighlington ....43 P 22
Drimnin ....71 C 14
Drinnishadder ....76 Z 10
Drissaig ....65 E 15
Droitwich ....27 N 27
Dronfield ....43 P 24
Drongan ....60 G 17
Droxford ....10 Q 31
Druidibeg (Loch) ....76 Y 12
Druim a' Chliabhain (Loch) ..85 H 8
Druimindarroch ....71 C 13
Drum Castle ....75 M 12
Drumbeg ....84 E 9
Drumblade ....81 L 11
Drumburgh ....54 K 19
Drumchardine ....79 G 11
Drumclog ....60 H 17
Drumelzier ....61 J 17
Drumfearn ....71 C 12
Drumlanrig Castle ....61 I 18
Drumlemble ....58 C 17
Drumlithie ....75 M 13
Drummond Castle ....67 I 14
Drummore ....52 F 19
Drummossie Muir ....79 H 11
Drumnadrochit ....79 G 11
Drumuie ....84 E 9
Drumsallie ....72 D 13
Drumtochty Forest ....75 M 13
Druridge Bay ....63 P 18
Drybrook ....18 M 28
Dryburgh Abbey ....62 M 17
Drygarn Fawr ....25 J 27
Drymen ....67 G 15
Drynoch ....77 B 12
Duchally ....84 F 9
Ducklington ....20 P 28
Duddington ....37 S 26
Duddo ....63 N 16
Dudley *Dudley* ....27 N 26
Dudley *North Tyneside* ..56 P 18
Duff House ....81 M 11
Duffield ....36 P 25
Dufftown ....80 K 11
Duffus ....80 J 10
Dufton ....55 M 20

Duggleby ....51 S 21
Duich (Loch) ....78 D 12
Duirinish ....77 C 12
Duke's Pass ....67 G 15
Dukinfield ....43 N 23
Dullingham ....30 V 27
Dulnain Bridge ....80 J 12
Duloe ....3 G 32
Dulverton ....7 J 30
Dumbarton ....67 G 16
Dumbleton ....27 O 27
Dumfries ....53 J 18
Dun Carloway Broch ....82 Z 9
Dunan ....66 F 16
Dunbar ....69 M 15
Dunbeath ....85 J 9
Dunblane ....67 I 15
Duncansby Head ....86 K 8
Dunchurch ....28 Q 26
Duncow ....53 J 18
Duncton ....11 S 31
Dundee ....69 K 14
Dundonald ....60 G 17
Dundrennan ....53 I 19
Dundry ....18 M 29
Dunecht ....75 M 12
Dunfermline ....68 J 15
Dungeness ....13 W 31
Dunholme ....44 S 24
Dunino ....69 L 15
Dunipace ....67 I 15
Dunkeld ....68 J 14
Dunkerton ....18 M 30
Dunkery Beacon ....7 J 30
Dunkeswell ....8 K 31
Dunkirk ....19 N 29
Dunley ....27 N 27
Dunlop ....60 G 16
Dunmaglass Lodge ....79 H 12
Dunnet ....85 J 8
Dunnet Bay ....85 J 8
Dunnet Head ....86 J 7
Dunning ....68 J 15
Dunnington ....50 R 22
Dunnockshaw ....42 N 22
Dunnottar Castle ....75 N 13
Dunoon ....66 F 16
Dunragit ....52 F 19
Dunrobin Castle ....85 I 10
Duns ....62 M 16
Duns Tew ....28 P 28
Dunscore ....53 I 18
Dunsdale ....57 Q 20
Dunsfold ....11 S 30
Dunsford ....4 I 31
Dunsop Bridge ....49 M 22
Dunstable ....29 S 28
Dunstaffnage Castel ....65 D 14
Dunstanburgh Castle ....63 P 17
Dunster ....17 J 30
Dunston ....37 S 24
Dunstone ....4 I 32
Dunsyre ....61 J 16
Duntelchaig (Loch) ....79 H 11
Dunton bassett ....28 Q 26
Dunure ....59 F 17
Dunvegan ....77 A 11
Dunvegan (Loch) ....77 A 11
Dunvegan Castle ....77 A 11
Dunvegan Head ....76 Z 11
Dunwich ....31 Y 27
Durdle Door ....9 N 32
Durham ....56 P 19
Durisdeer ....61 I 18
Durleigh ....8 K 30
Durlston Head ....9 O 32
Durness ....84 F 8
Durrington ....19 O 30
Dursley ....19 M 28
Dury Voe ....87 Q 2
Duston ....28 R 27
Duthil ....79 I 12
Duxford ....29 U 27
Dyce ....75 N 12
Dyfi / Dovey (River) ....33 I 26
Dyke ....80 I 11
Dykehead ....74 K 13
Dykends ....74 K 13
Dymchurch ....13 W 30
Dymock ....27 M 28
Dyrham ....19 M 29
Dyserth ....41 J 23

E

Eaglescliffe ....50 P 20
Eaglesfield ....54 K 18
Eaglesham ....60 H 16
Eakring ....36 R 24
Ealing *London Borough* ..21 T 29
Earba (Lochan na h-) ....73 G 13

Duggleby ....51 S 21
Duich (Loch) ....78 D 12

Earby ....49 N 22
Eardisley ....26 K 27
Earl Shilton ....36 Q 26
Earl Soham ....31 X 27
Earl Stonham ....31 X 27
Earley Winnersh ....20 R 29
Earlish ....77 A 11
Earls Barton ....28 R 27
Earls Colne ....30 W 28
Earlsferry ....69 L 15
Earlston ....62 L 17
Earn (Loch) ....67 H 14
Earn (River) ....67 J 14
Earsdon ....56 P 18
Earsham ....31 Y 26
Easdale ....65 D 15
Easebourne ....10 R 31
Easington *Easington* ....57 P 19
Easington
 East Riding of Yorkshire ..45 U 23
Easington
 Redcar and Cleveland ..50 R 20
Easington
 South Oxfordshire ..20 Q 28
Easington Lane ....56 P 19
Easingwold ....50 Q 21
Eassie and Nevay ....68 K 14
East Aberthaw ....17 J 29
East Barkwith ....45 T 24
East Bergholt ....30 X 28
East Brent ....18 L 30
East Budleigh ....5 K 32
East Butterwick ....44 R 23
East-Challow ....20 P 29
East Chinnock ....8 L 31
East-Coker ....8 M 31
East Cowes ....10 Q 31
East Cowton ....50 P 20
East Dereham ....38 W 25
East Ferry ....44 R 23
East Glen (River) ....37 S 25
East Grafton ....19 P 29
East Grinstead ....11 T 30
East Hagbourne ....20 Q 29
East-Halton ....45 T 23
East Hanney ....20 P 29
East Hardwick ....44 Q 23
East Harling ....30 W 26
East Haven ....69 L 14
East Hendred ....20 P 29
East Hoathly ....12 U 31
East Horsley ....21 S 30
East Huntspill ....18 L 30
East Ilsley ....20 Q 29
East Keswick ....50 P 22
East Kilbride *Eilean Siar* ..70 X 12
East Kilbride
 South Lanarkshire ..60 H 16
East-Knoyle ....9 N 30
East Knoyle ....9 N 30
East Lambrook ....8 L 31
East Leake ....36 Q 25
East Linton ....69 M 16
East Loch Roag ....82 Z 9
East Loch Tarbet ....77 Z 10
East Lulworth ....9 N 32
East-Malling ....22 V 30
East Markham ....44 R 24
East Meon ....10 Q 31
East Mersea ....22 W 28
East Midlands Airport ..36 Q 25
East Moor ....35 P 24
East Norton ....36 R 26
East-Poringland ....39 Y 26
East Portlemouth ....4 I 33
East Rhidorroch Lodge ..78 F 10
East-Rudham ....38 W 25
East-Saltoun ....62 L 16
East Tisted ....10 R 30
East Wemyss ....68 K 15
East-Winch ....38 V 25
East Wittering ....10 R 31
East Witton ....49 O 21
East-Woodhay ....20 P 29
East-Wretham ....30 W 26
Eastbourne ....12 U 31
Eastchurch ....22 W 29
Eastdean ....12 U 31
Easter-Compton ....18 M 29
Easter Ross ....79 G 10
Eastergate ....11 S 31
Eastfield ....51 S 21
Eastgate ....55 N 19
Eastham ....42 L 24
Eastington ....19 N 28

Eastleach ....19 O 28
Eastleigh ....10 P 31
Eastoft ....44 R 23
Easton *Carlisle* ....55 L 18
Easton *Dorset* ....8 M 32
Easton *Norfolk* ....39 X 26
Easton-Grey ....19 N 29
Easton-in-Gordano ....18 L 29
Easton-Royal ....19 O 29
Eastriggs ....54 K 19
Eastrington ....44 R 22
Eastry ....23 X 30
Eastville ....37 U 24
Eastwood ....36 Q 24
Eaton ....34 M 24
Eaton Bray ....29 S 28
Eaton Socon ....29 T 27
Ebbw Vale / Glyn Ebwy ..18 K 28
Ebchester ....56 O 19
Ebrington ....27 O 27
Eccels ....62 M 17
Ecchinswell ....20 Q 29
Ecclefechan ....54 K 18
Eccles ....42 M 23
Eccleshall ....35 N 25
Echt ....75 M 12
Eckford ....62 M 17
Eckington *Derbs.* ....43 P 24
Eckington *Worc.* ....27 N 27
Edale ....43 O 23
Eday ....87 L 6
Eddelston ....61 K 16
Edderton ....79 H 10
Eddrachillis Bay ....84 E 9
Edderton ....79 H 10
Edenbridge ....21 U 30
Edentaggart ....66 F 15
Edenthorpe ....44 Q 23
Edgefield ....39 X 25
Edgmond ....35 M 25
Edgton ....26 L 26
Edinample ....77 A 11
Edinbane ....77 A 11
Edinburgh ....68 K 16
Edington ....19 N 30
Edith Weston ....37 S 26
Edlesborough ....29 S 28
Edmondsley ....56 P 19
Edmundbyers ....56 O 19
Edmundbyers ....56 O 19
Ednaston ....36 Q 25
Edwalton ....36 Q 25
Edwinstowe ....36 Q 24
Edzell ....75 M 13
Efailnewydd ....32 G 25
Egerton ....22 W 30
Eggerness Point ....53 G 19
Eggleston ....56 N 20
Egham ....21 S 29
Egilsay ....87 L 6
Eglingham ....63 O 17
Egloskerry ....6 G 32
Eglwys Brewis ....17 J 29
Eglwysfach ....33 I 26
Eglwyswrw ....15 F 27
Egremont ....47 J 20
Egton ....50 R 20
Eigg ....71 B 13
Eigheach (Loch) ....73 G 13
Eight Ash Green ....30 W 28
Eil ....73 I 12
Eil (Loch) ....72 E 13
Eilde Mòr (Loch) ....72 F 13
Eildon ....62 L 13
Eilean a' Chalmain ....64 A 15
Eilean Beag ....77 C 11
Eilean Chathastail ....71 B 13
Eilean Donan Castle ....78 D 12
Eilean Flodigarry ....77 B 10
Eilean Mhuire ....82 A 10
Eilean Mòr ....77 C 11
Eilean Mullagrach ....83 D 9
Eilean na Bà ....77 C 11
Eilean nan Each ....71 B 13
Eilean Trodday ....77 B 10
Eileanach Lodge ....79 G 10
Eilt (Loch) ....72 D 13
Eishken ....82 A 9
Eishort (Loch) ....71 C 12
Elan Valley ....25 J 27
Elan Village ....25 J 27
Elcho ....68 J 14
Elgin ....80 K 11
Elgol ....71 B 12
Elham ....23 X 30
Elie ....69 L 15
Eling ....10 P 31
Elkesley ....44 R 24
Elkstone ....19 N 28

Place	Ref.
Elland	43 O 22
Ellastone	35 O 25
Ellen's Green	11 S 30
Ellerbeck	50 P 20
Ellerton	44 R 22
Ellesmere	34 L 25
Ellesmere Port	42 L 24
Ellingham	31 Y 26
Ellington	56 P 18
Ellon	81 N 11
Elloughton	44 S 22
Elmdon	29 U 27
Elmley Castle	27 N 27
Elmore	19 N 28
Elmstead Market	30 W 28
Elmswell	30 W 27
Elphin	84 E 9
Elrick	75 N 12
Elrig	52 G 19
Elsdon	55 N 18
Elsenham	30 U 28
Elsham	45 S 23
Elsrickle	61 J 16
Elstead	21 R 30
Elstree	21 T 29
Elswick	42 L 22
Eltisley	29 T 27
Elton	37 S 26
Elveden	30 W 26
Elvington	50 R 22
Elwick	57 Q 19
Elworth	35 M 24
Ely	30 U 26
Emberton	28 R 27
Embleton *Allerdale*	54 K 20
Embleton *Alnwick*	63 P 17
Embo	79 I 10
Embsay	49 O 22
Emneth	37 U 26
Empingham	37 S 25
Emsworth	10 R 31
Enaclete	82 Z 9
Enard Bay	83 D 9
Enderby	36 Q 26
Endmoor	48 L 21
Endon	35 N 24
Enfield *London Borough*	21 T 29
Enford	19 O 30
Englefield Green	21 S 29
English Bicknor	18 M 28
Englishcombe	19 M 29
Enham Alamein	20 P 30
Enmore	8 K 30
Ensay	71 B 14
Enstone	28 P 28
Enterkinfoot	61 I 18
Enville	27 N 26
Eochar	76 X 11
Eoligarry	70 X 12
Eoropie	83 B 8
Eorsa	65 B 14
Eport (Loch)	76 Y 11
Epping	21 U 28
Epping Forest	21 U 29
Epsom	21 T 30
Epworth	44 R 23
Erddig	34 K 24
Eredine	65 E 15
Eredine Forest	65 D 15
Eriboll	84 F 8
Eriboll (Loch)	84 F 8
Ericht (Loch)	73 G 13
Ericstane	61 J 17
Eridge Green	12 U 30
Eriska	65 D 14
Eriskay	70 Y 12
Erisort (Loch)	82 A 9
Eriswell	30 V 26
Erlestoke	19 N 30
Ermington	4 I 32
Erpingham	39 X 25
Erraid	64 A 15
Errochty (Loch)	73 H 13
Errogie	79 G 12
Errol	68 K 14
Ersary	70 X 13
Erskine Bridge	67 G 16
Ervie	52 E 19
Erwood	25 K 27
Esh Winning	56 O 19
Esha Ness	87 P 2
Esher	21 S 29
Esk (Glen)	75 L 13
Esk (River)	54 K 19
Eskdale	54 K 18
Eskdalemuir	61 K 18
Essendon	21 T 28
Essich	79 H 11
Eston	57 Q 20
Etal	63 N 17
Etchilhampton	19 O 29
Etchingham	12 V 30
Etherow (River)	43 N 23
Etherow Park	43 N 23
Etive (Glen)	72 F 14
Etive (Loch)	65 E 14
Eton	21 S 29
Ettington	27 P 27
Ettrick	61 K 17
Ettrick Forest	62 K 17
Ettrick Pen	61 K 17
Etwall	35 P 25
Euston	30 W 26
Euxton	42 L 22
Evanton	79 G 11
Evelix	79 H 10
Evenlode	27 O 28
Evenwood	56 O 20
Evercreech	8 M 30
Everingham	44 R 22
Everleigh	19 O 30
Evershot	8 M 31
Eversley	20 R 29
Everton	44 R 23
Evesham	27 O 27
Evesham (Vale of)	27 O 27
Ewe (Isle of)	78 D 10
Ewell	21 T 29
Ewelme	20 Q 29
Ewenny	17 J 29
Ewes	54 L 18
Ewhurst	11 S 30
Exbourne	7 I 31
Exe (River)	7 J 31
Exebridge	7 J 30
Exeter	4 J 31
Exford	7 J 30
Exminster	4 J 31
Exmoor National Park	7 I 30
Exmouth	4 J 32
Exton	7 J 30
Eyam	43 O 24
Eye *Cambs.*	37 T 26
Eye *Suffolk*	31 X 27
Eye Peninsula	83 B 9
Eyemouth	63 N 16
Eynort (Loch) *Highland*	77 A 12
Eynort (Loch) *Western Isles*	76 Y 12
Eynsford	22 U 29
Eynsham	20 P 28
Eyre Point	77 B 12
Eythorne	23 X 30

F

Place	Ref.
Fada (Loch)	76 Y 11
Failsworth	43 N 23
Fair Isle	87 P 5
Fair Oak	10 Q 31
Fairbourne	33 H 25
Fairburn	44 Q 22
Fairford	19 O 28
Fairlie	59 F 16
Fairlight	12 V 31
Fakenham	38 W 25
Fala	62 L 16
Faldingworth	45 S 23
Falfield	18 M 29
Falkirk	67 I 16
Falkland	68 K 15
Fallford	54 K 18
Fallin	67 I 15
Falmer	11 T 31
Falmouth	2 E 33
Falstone	55 M 18
Fanagmore	84 E 8
Fangfoss	50 R 22
Fannich (Loch)	78 E 11
Fannich Lodge	78 F 11
Fara	86 K 7
Fareham	10 Q 31
Faringdon	19 P 29
Farleigh-Hungerford	19 N 30
Farley	9 O 30
Farley Mount	10 P 30
Farlow	26 M 26
Farmborough	18 M 29
Farmers	25 I 27
Farmtown	80 L 11
Farnborough *Hants.*	20 R 30
Farnborough *Warw.*	28 P 27
Farnborough *West Berkshire*	20 P 29
Farndon *Chester*	34 L 24
Farndon *Newark and Sherwood*	36 R 24
Farne Islands	63 P 17
Farnell	75 M 13
Farnham *Dorset*	9 N 31
Farnham *Surrey*	20 R 30
Farnham Royal	21 S 29
Farningham	22 U 29
Farnley	49 O 22
Farnsfield	36 Q 24
Farnworth	42 M 23
Farr	85 H 8
Farrington Gurney	18 M 30
Farway	5 K 31
Fasnakyle	78 F 12
Fasnakyle Forest	78 F 11
Fasque	75 M 13
Fassfern	72 E 13
Fauldhouse	61 I 16
Faversham	22 W 30
Fawley	10 P 31
Fazeley	35 O 26
Fearby	49 O 21
Fearn Lodge	79 H 10
Fearnan	67 H 14
Fearnmore	77 C 11
Featherstone *Staffs.*	35 N 26
Featherstone *West Yorks.*	43 P 22
Feetham	49 N 20
Felbridge	11 T 30
Felindre *Carmarthenshire / Sir Gaerfyrddin*	25 I 28
Felindre *Powys*	26 K 26
Felinfach	25 K 28
Felinheli	33 H 24
Felixkirk	50 Q 21
Felixstowe	31 Y 28
Felling	56 P 19
Felmingham	39 Y 25
Felpham	11 S 31
Felsham	30 W 27
Felsted	30 V 28
Feltham	21 S 29
Felthorpe	39 X 25
Felton	63 O 18
Feltwell	30 V 26
Fence	42 N 22
Feniton	8 K 31
Fenny Bentley	35 O 24
Fenstanton	29 T 27
Fenton *Stoke-on-Trent*	35 N 25
Fenton *West Lindsey*	44 R 24
Fenwick *Berwick-upon-Tweed*	63 O 17
Fenwick *East Ayrshire*	60 G 17
Feochaig	59 D 17
Feochan (Loch)	65 D 14
Feock	2 E 33
Feolin Ferry	58 B 16
Fern	74 L 13
Ferndown	9 O 31
Ferness	79 I 11
Fernhurst	11 R 30
Ferryden	75 M 13
Ferryhill	56 P 19
Ferryside	15 G 28
Fersit	73 F 13
Feshie (Glen)	73 I 12
Feshiebridge	73 I 12
Fetcham	21 S 30
Fetlar	87 R 2
Fetterangus	81 N 11
Fettercairn	75 M 13
Fewston	49 O 22
Ffestiniog	33 I 25
Ffestiniog (Vale of)	33 H 25
Fflint / Flint	42 K 24
Fforest Fawr	17 J 28
Ffostrasol	15 G 27
Fiaray	70 X 12
Fiddleton	62 L 18
Fifield	27 P 28
Filby	39 Y 26
Filey	51 T 21
Fillongley	27 P 26
Filton	18 M 29
Finchampstead	20 R 29
Finchingfield	30 V 28
Findhorn	80 J 11
Findhorn (River)	73 H 12
Findhorn Bay	80 J 11
Findo Gask	68 J 14
Findochty	80 L 10
Findon	11 S 31
Finedon	29 S 26
Fingest	20 R 29
Fingland	60 I 17
Finiskaig	72 D 13
Finmere	28 Q 28
Finningley	44 R 23
Finsbay	76 Z 10
Finstock	20 P 28
Finstown	86 K 6
Fintry *Aberdeenshire*	81 M 11
Fintry *Stirling*	67 H 15
Fionn Loch	78 D 10
Fionn Loch Mór	84 F 9
Fionnphort	64 A 15
Fishbourne *Chichester*	10 R 31
Fishbourne *Isle of Wight*	10 Q 31
Fishburn	56 P 19
Fisherfield Forest	78 D 10
Fisherford	81 M 11
Fishguard / Abergwaun	24 F 28
Fishnish Bay	65 B 14
Fishtoft	37 U 25
Fiskavaig	77 A 12
Fiskerton	44 S 24
Fittleworth	11 S 31
Fiunary	71 C 14
Fivehead	8 L 30
Flackwell Heath	21 R 29
Fladbury	27 N 27
Fladda-Chùain	77 A 10
Flagg	35 O 24
Flamborough	51 T 21
Flamborough Head	51 T 21
Flamingo Park	50 R 21
Flamstead	21 S 28
Flash	35 O 24
Flashader	77 A 11
Flatford Mill	30 X 28
Flax Bourton	18 L 29
Flaxton	50 R 21
Fleckney	36 Q 26
Fleet	20 R 30
Fleet (Islands of)	53 H 19
Fleet Hargate	37 U 25
Fleetwood	48 K 22
Flimby	53 J 19
Flint / Fflint	42 K 24
Flintham	36 R 24
Flitwick	29 S 27
Flixton	31 Y 26
Flodday *near Hellisay*	70 X 13
Flodday *near Sandray*	70 X 13
Flodden Field	63 N 17
Flodigarry	77 B 11
Flookburgh	48 L 21
Floors Castle	62 M 17
Flotta	86 K 7
Flowerdale Forest	78 D 11
Flyford Flavell	27 N 27
Fochabers	80 K 11
Foggathorpe	44 R 22
Foindle	84 E 8
Folke	9 M 31
Folkestone	13 X 30
Folkingham	37 S 25
Folly Gate	7 H 31
Fontmell Magna	9 N 31
Ford *Argyll and Bute*	65 D 15
Ford *Arun*	11 S 31
Ford *Berwick-upon-Tweed*	63 N 17
Ford *Buckinghamshire*	20 R 28
Ford *Cotswold*	27 O 28
Ford *Shrewsbury and Atcham*	34 L 25
Forcett Abbey	8 L 31
Forden	34 K 26
Fordham	30 V 27
Fordingbridge	9 O 31
Fordoun	75 M 13
Fordwich	23 X 30
Fordyce	80 L 11
Foreland Head	10 Q 31
Foreland Point	17 I 30
Foremark Reservoir	36 P 25
Forest Lodge	74 I 13
Forest Row	11 U 30
Forestburn Gate	63 O 18
Forfar	74 L 14
Forres	80 J 11
Forrest Lodge	53 H 18
Forse	85 K 9
Forsinard	85 I 8
Fort Augustus	73 F 12
Fort George	79 H 11
Fort Victoria	10 P 31
Fort William	72 E 13
Forter	74 K 13
Forteviot	68 J 14
Forth	61 I 16
Forth (Firth of)	68 K 15
Forth (River)	67 G 15
Forth Bridges	68 J 15
Fortingall	73 H 14
Forton	35 M 25
Fortrose	79 H 11
Fortuneswell	8 M 32
Fosdyke	37 T 25
Foston	36 R 25
Foston on the Wolds	51 T 22
Fotherby	45 T 23
Fotheringhay	29 S 26
Foulden	63 N 16
Foulness Point	22 W 29
Foulridge	43 N 22
Fountainhall	62 L 16
Fountains Abbey	50 P 21
Four Crosses	34 K 25
Four Elms	21 U 30
Four Marks	10 Q 30
Fovant	9 O 30
Foveran	81 N 12
Fowey	3 G 32
Fowlmere	29 U 27
Fownhope	26 M 27
Foxdale	46 G 21
Foxholes	51 S 21
Foxton	28 R 26
Foxup	49 N 21
Foyers	73 G 12
Fraddon	3 F 32
Framfield	12 U 31
Framlingham	31 Y 27
Frampton-on-Severn	19 M 28
Framwellgate Moor	56 P 19
Frant	12 U 30
Fraserburgh	81 O 10
Fraserburgh Bay	81 O 10
Freckenham	30 V 27
Freckleton	42 L 22
Freeland	20 P 28
Freethorpe	39 Y 26
Freevater Forest	79 F 10
Freiston	37 U 25
Fremington	7 H 30
Frensham	10 R 30
Freshwater	10 P 31
Freshwater Bay	10 P 31
Freshwater East	16 F 29
Freshwater West	14 E 29
Fressingfield	31 X 26
Freswick	86 K 8
Freuchie	68 K 15
Freuchie (Loch)	67 I 14
Friday Bridge	37 U 26
Fridaythorpe	51 S 21
Frimley	21 R 30
Fringford	28 Q 28
Frinton-on-Sea	31 X 28
Friockheim	75 M 14
Frisa (Loch)	71 B 14
Friskney	37 U 24
Frithville	37 T 24
Frittenden	12 V 30
Fritwell	28 Q 28
Frizington	47 J 20
Frocester	19 N 28
Frodsham	42 L 24
Froggatt	43 P 24
Frome	19 N 30
Frosterley	56 O 19
Froxfield	20 P 29
Fuday	70 X 12
Fuiay	70 X 13
Fulbourn	30 U 27
Fulking	11 T 31
Fuller Street	22 V 28
Fulwood	42 M 22
Funtington	10 R 31
Funzie	87 R 2
Furness Abbey	47 K 21
Furness Fells	48 K 20
Fyfield	22 U 28
Fyvie	81 M 11

G

Place	Ref.
Gaddesby	36 R 25
Gaick Lodge	73 H 13
Gainford	49 O 20
Gainsborough	44 R 23
Gairloch	78 C 10
Gairlochy	72 F 13
Gairsay	87 L 6
Galashiels	62 L 17
Galgate	48 L 22
Gallan Head	82 Y 9
Gallanach	65 D 14
Galloway Forest Park	52 G 18
Galltair	72 D 12
Galmisdale	71 B 13
Galmpton	4 J 32
Galson	82 A 8
Galston	60 G 17
Galtrigill	76 Z 11
Gamblesby	55 M 19
Gamlingay	29 T 27
Gamston	44 R 24
Ganavan	65 D 14
Ganton	51 S 21
Garboldisham	30 W 26
Gardenstown	81 N 10
Garelochhead	66 F 15
Garenin	82 Z 9
Garforth	43 P 22
Gargrave	49 N 22
Gargunnock	67 H 15
Garioch	81 M 12
Garlieston	53 G 19
Garlogte	75 M 12
Garmony	65 C 14
Garmouth	80 K 11
Garrabost	83 B 9
Garragie Lodge	73 G 12
Garraron	65 D 15
Garreg	33 H 25
Garrigill	55 M 19
Garrisdale Point	71 A 12
Garros	77 B 11
Garrow	67 I 14
Garry (Glen) *Highland*	72 E 12
Garry (Glen) *Perthshire and Kinross*	73 H 13
Garry (Loch)	72 F 12
Garsington	20 Q 28
Garten (Loch)	74 I 12
Garth	25 J 27
Garthorpe	44 R 23
Gartmore	67 G 15
Gartocharn	67 G 15
Garton-on-The-Wolds	51 S 21
Garvald	69 M 16
Garvamore	73 G 12
Garve	79 F 11
Garvellachs	65 C 15
Garvestone	38 W 26
Garvock	66 F 16
Garway	26 L 28
Garynahine	82 Z 9
Gatehouse of Fleet	53 H 19
Gateshead	56 P 19
Gateside	68 K 15
Gatley	42 N 23
Gatwick Airport	11 T 30
Gaulden Manor	8 K 30
Gavard	64 B 15
Gaydon	28 P 27
Gayton *King's Lynn and West Norfolk*	38 V 25
Gayton *Stafford*	35 N 25
Gaywood	38 V 25
Geary	77 A 11
Geddington	29 R 26
Gedney Drove End	37 U 25
Gedney Hill	37 T 25
Gelligaer	18 K 29
Gelston	53 I 19
Georgeham	6 H 30
Georth	86 K 6
Gerrards Cross	21 S 29
Gestingthorpe	30 V 27
Gifford	62 L 16
Gigha (Sound of)	58 C 17
Gigha Island	58 C 16
Gighay	70 Y 12
Gilberdyke	44 R 22
Gilcrux	54 J 19
Gildersome	43 P 22
Gilfach Goch	17 J 29
Gillamour	50 R 21
Gilling East	50 Q 21

Gilling West ....49 O 20
Gillingham *Dorset* ....9 N 30
Gillingham *Kent* ....22 V 29
Gillingham *South Norfolk* ....31 Y 26
Gills ....86 K 8
Gilmerton ....67 I 14
Gilmorton ....28 Q 26
Gilston ....62 L 16
Gilwern ....18 K 28
Girthon ....53 H 19
Girton ....29 U 27
Girvan ....59 F 18
Gisburn ....49 N 22
Gisland ....55 M 19
Gittisham ....8 K 31
Gladestry ....26 K 27
Glaisdale ....50 R 20
Glamis ....74 K 14
Glamis Castle ....74 L 14
Glanaman ....17 I 28
Glandwr ....15 G 28
Glanton ....63 O 17
Glas-allt-Shiel ....74 K 13
Glas-leac Mór ....83 D 9
Glas Maol ....74 J 13
Glasbury ....26 K 27
Glascarnoch (Loch) ....78 F 10
Glascwm ....26 K 27
Glasdrum ....72 E 14
Glasgow ....60 H 16
Glasphein ....76 Z 11
Glaspwll ....33 I 26
Glass (Loch) ....79 G 10
Glassburn ....78 F 11
Glasserton ....52 G 19
Glassford ....60 H 16
Glasshouses ....49 O 21
Glasson ....48 L 22
Glassonby ....55 M 19
Glastonbury ....8 L 30
Gleadless ....43 P 23
Gleann Beag ....78 F 10
Gleann Mór ....79 G 10
Gleaston ....48 K 21
Glecknabae ....59 E 16
Glemsford ....30 V 27
Glen auldyn ....46 G 21
Glen Brittle Forest ....77 B 12
Glen Finglas Reservoir ....67 G 15
Glen More Forest Park ....74 I 12
Glen Shee ....74 J 13
Glen Trool Lodge ....52 G 18
Glenbarr ....59 C 17
Glenborrodale ....71 C 13
Glenbranter ....66 E 15
Glenbrittle House ....77 B 12
Glenbuchat Castle ....74 K 12
Glenbuck ....60 I 17
Glencaple ....53 J 18
Glencarse ....68 K 14
Glencoe ....72 E 13
Glencoul (Loch) ....84 F 9
Glendoebeg ....73 G 12
Glendurgan Garden ....2 E 33
Glenegedale ....58 B 16
Glenelg ....72 D 12
Glenelg Bay ....72 D 12
Glenfarg ....68 J 15
Glenfeshie Lodge ....73 I 12
Glenfiddich Lodge ....80 K 11
Glenfield ....36 Q 26
Glenfinnan ....72 D 13
Glenforsa Airport ....65 C 14
Glenfyne Lodge ....66 F 15
Glengorm ....71 B 14
Glengoulandie ....73 H 14
Glengrasco ....77 B 11
Glenkens (The) ....53 H 18
Glenkin die ....74 L 12
Glenkirk ....61 J 17
Glenlivet ....80 J 11
Glenluce ....52 F 19
Glenmassan ....66 E 15
Glenmaye ....46 F 21
Glenmore ....71 C 13
Glenprosen Village ....74 K 13
Glenridding ....48 L 20
Glenrothes ....68 K 15
Glenside ....82 A 9
Glenstriven ....66 E 16
Glentham ....44 S 23
Glentress ....61 K 17
Glentrool Village ....52 G 18
Glenworth ....44 S 23
Glenuachdarach ....77 B 11
Glenuig ....71 C 13
Glespin ....61 I 17

Gletness ....87 Q 3
Glinton ....37 T 26
Glossop ....43 O 23
Gloucester ....27 N 28
Gloup ....87 Q 1
Glusburn ....49 O 22
Glutt Lodge ....85 I 9
Glympton ....28 P 28
Glyn Ceiriog ....34 K 25
Glyn-Ebwy / Ebbw Vale ..18 K 28
Glyn-neath ....17 J 28
Glynde ....11 U 31
Glyndebourne ....11 U 31
Glyndyfrdwy ....34 K 25
Gnosall ....35 N 25
Goadby ....36 R 26
Goat Fell ....59 E 17
Goathland ....50 R 20
Gobowen ....34 K 25
Godalming ....21 S 30
Godmanchester ....29 T 27
Godmanstone ....8 M 31
Godshill ....10 Q 32
Godstone ....21 T 30
Goil (Loch) ....66 F 15
Golborne ....42 M 23
Goldcliff ....18 L 29
Goldhanger ....22 W 28
Goldthorpe ....44 Q 23
Golspie ....85 I 10
Gomersal ....43 O 22
Gometra ....64 B 14
Gomshall ....21 S 30
Gooderstone ....38 V 26
Goodleigh ....7 I 30
Goodrich ....26 M 28
Goodrington ....4 J 32
Goodwick ....24 F 27
Goodwood House ....10 R 31
Goole ....44 R 22
Goonhavern ....2 E 32
Goostrey ....42 M 24
Gordon ....62 M 16
Gordonbush ....85 I 9
Gordonstown ....80 L 11
Gorebridge ....61 K 16
Goring ....20 Q 29
Gorm Loch Mór ....84 F 9
Gorran Haven ....3 F 33
Gorseinon ....15 H 29
Gorsleston-on-Sea ....39 Z 26
Gortantaoid ....64 B 16
Gosberton ....37 T 25
Gosfield ....30 V 28
Gosforth *Cumbria* ....47 J 20
Gosforth
Newcastle upon Tyne ..56 P 18
Gosport ....10 Q 31
Goswick ....63 O 16
Gotham ....36 Q 25
Gott Bay ....70 Z 14
Goudhurst ....12 V 30
Gourdon ....75 N 13
Gourock ....66 F 16
Gowerton ....15 H 29
Goxhill ....45 T 22
Graemsay ....86 K 7
Grafton Underwood ....29 S 26
Grain ....22 W 29
Grainthorpe ....45 U 23
Granby ....36 R 25
Grandtully ....74 I 14
Grange-over-Sands ....48 L 21
Grangemouth ....67 I 15
Grantchester ....29 U 27
Grantham ....37 S 25
Grantown-on-Spey ....80 J 12
Grantshouse ....62 N 16
Grasby ....45 S 23
Grasmere ....48 K 20
Grassington ....49 O 21
Grateley ....9 P 30
Graveley ....29 T 27
Gravesend ....22 V 29
Gravir ....82 A 9
Grayrigg ....48 M 20
Grays Thurrock ....22 V 29
Grayshott ....10 R 30
Grayswood ....11 R 30
Greasbrough ....43 P 23
Great Addington ....29 S 26
Great Altcar ....42 K 23
Great Amwell ....21 T 28
Great Asby ....49 M 20
Great Ayton ....50 Q 20
Great Baddow ....22 V 28

Great Bardfield ....30 V 28
Great Barford ....29 S 27
Great Barr ....35 O 26
Great Barrow ....34 L 24
Great Barugh ....50 R 21
Great Bedwyn ....19 P 29
Great Bentley ....31 X 28
Great Bernera ....82 Z 9
Great Bircham ....38 V 25
Great-Bollright ....28 P 28
Great Bookham ....21 S 30
Great Bourton ....28 Q 27
Great Bowden ....28 R 26
Great Brickhill ....29 R 28
Great Bridgeford ....35 N 25
Great Bromley ....30 X 28
Great Broughton ....50 Q 20
Great-Budworth ....42 M 24
Great Burdon ....50 P 20
Great Chalfield ....19 N 29
Great Chesterford ....30 U 27
Great Chishill ....29 U 27
Great Clifton ....53 J 20
Great Coates ....45 T 23
Great-Comberton ....27 N 27
Great Cornard ....30 W 27
Great Cubley ....35 O 25
Great Cumbrae Island ..59 F 16
Great-Dalby ....36 R 25
Great Doddington ....28 R 27
Great Driffield ....51 S 21
Great-Dunham ....38 W 25
Great Dunmow ....30 V 28
Great Easton *Essex* ....30 U 28
Great Easton *Leics.* ....28 R 26
Great Eccleston ....42 L 22
Great Ellingham ....38 W 26
Great Finborough ....30 W 27
Great Glen ....36 Q 26
Great Gonerby ....37 S 25
Great Gransden ....29 T 27
Great Harrowden ....28 R 27
Great Harwood ....42 M 22
Great Hockham ....30 W 26
Great Horkesley ....30 W 28
Great Horwood ....28 R 28
Great Houghton ....43 P 23
Great Langton ....50 P 20
Great-Limber ....45 T 23
Great Livermere ....30 W 27
Great Lumley ....56 P 19
Great Malvern ....27 N 27
Great Marton ....42 K 22
Great Massingham ....38 W 25
Great Milton ....20 Q 28
Great Missenden ....21 R 28
Great Mitton ....42 M 22
Great Musgrave ....49 M 20
Great Oakley ....31 X 28
Great Ormes Head ....41 I 22
Great Orton ....54 K 19
Great Ouse (River) ....38 V 25
Great Ouseburn ....50 Q 21
Great Ponton ....37 S 25
Great Ryburgh ....38 W 25
Great Salkeld ....55 L 19
Great Sampford ....30 V 28
Great Shefford ....20 P 29
Great Shelford ....29 U 27
Great Smeaton ....50 P 20
Great Somerford ....19 N 29
Great Stainton ....56 P 20
Great Strickland ....55 L 20
Great Torrington ....6 H 31
Great Tosson ....63 O 18
Great Totham ....22 W 28
Great Urswick ....48 K 21
Great Wakering ....22 W 29
Great Waltham ....22 V 28
Great Whernside ....49 O 21
Great Whittington ....56 O 18
Great Witley ....27 M 27
Great Wolford ....27 P 27
Great Wyrley ....35 N 26
Great Yarmouth ....39 Z 26
Great Yeldham ....30 V 27
Greatford ....37 S 25
Greatham *Cleveland* ....57 Q 20
Greatham *Hants.* ....10 R 30
Greatstone-on-Sea ....12 W 31
Green Hammerton ....50 Q 21
Greenfield
Flintshire / Sir y Fflint ..41 K 23
Greenfield *Highland* ....72 F 12
Greenhaugh ....55 N 18
Greenhead ....55 M 19
Greenholm ....60 H 17

Greenhow Hill ....49 O 21
Greenlaw ....62 M 16
Greenloaning ....67 I 15
Greenock ....66 F 16
Greenodd ....48 K 21
Greens Norton ....28 Q 27
Greenside ....56 O 19
Greenwich
London Borough ....21 U 29
Grendon ....28 R 27
Grendon Underwood ....28 Q 28
Gresford ....34 L 24
Greshornish ....77 A 11
Greshornish (Loch) ....77 A 11
Gress ....83 B 9
Gretna ....54 K 19
Gretton ....37 R 26
Greys Court ....20 R 29
Greysouthen ....54 J 20
Greystoke ....55 L 19
Griffithstown ....18 K 28
Griminish ....76 X 11
Grimley ....27 N 27
Grimoldby ....45 U 23
Grimsay ....76 Y 11
Grimsby ....45 T 23
Gringley on the Hill ....44 R 23
Grinshill ....34 L 25
Grinton ....49 O 20
Gristhorpe ....51 T 21
Grittleton ....19 N 29
Groby ....36 Q 26
Grogport ....59 D 17
Groombridge ....12 U 30
Grosebay ....76 Z 10
Grosmont *Monmouthshire /
Sir Fynwy* ....26 L 28
Grosmont *Scarborough* ....50 R 20
Grove ....20 P 29
Gruinard Bay ....78 D 10
Gruinard Island ....78 D 10
Gruinart ....58 B 16
Gruinart (Loch) ....64 B 16
Grunavat (Loch) ....82 Z 9
Grundisburgh ....31 X 27
Gualachulain ....66 E 14
Guardbridge ....69 L 14
Guernsey *Channel I.* 5
Guesting ....12 V 31
Guildford ....21 S 30
Guildtown ....68 J 14
Guilsborough ....28 Q 26
Guisborough ....50 Q 20
Guiseley ....43 O 22
Guist ....38 W 25
Gullane ....69 L 15
Gunna ....70 Z 14
Gunnerside ....49 N 20
Gunnerton ....55 N 18
Gunness ....44 R 23
Gunnislake ....3 H 32
Gunthorpe ....36 R 25
Gurnard ....10 Q 31
Gurness Broch ....86 K 6
Gurnos ....17 I 28
Gussage All Saints ....9 O 31
Gutcher ....87 Q 1
Guthrie ....75 L 14
Guyhirn ....37 U 26
Gwalchmai ....40 G 23
Gwaun-Cae-Gurwen ....17 I 28
Gwbert-on-Sea ....15 F 27
Gweek ....2 E 33
Gwennap ....2 E 33
Gwithian ....2 D 33
Gwyddelwern ....33 J 24
Gwyddgrug ....15 H 28
Gwydir Castle ....33 I 24
Gwytherin ....33 I 24

H

Habost ....83 B 8
Hackney *London Borough* ..21 T 29
Haddenham *Bucks.* ....20 R 28
Haddenham *Cambs.* ....29 U 26
Haddington ....69 L 16
Haddiscoe ....39 Y 26
Haddo House ....81 N 11
Haddon Hall ....35 P 24
Hadfield ....43 O 23
Hadleigh *Essex* ....22 V 29
Hadleigh *Suffolk* ....30 W 27
Hadley ....34 M 25
Hadlow ....22 V 30
Hadnall ....34 L 25
Hadrian's Wall ....55 M 18
Haggbeck ....55 L 18

Hagley ....27 N 26
Hagworthingham ....45 U 24
Hailsham ....12 U 31
Hainford ....39 X 25
Hainton ....45 T 23
Halam ....36 R 24
Halberton ....7 J 31
Hale ....42 M 23
Hales ....39 Y 26
Halesowen ....27 N 26
Halesworth ....31 Y 26
Halford ....27 P 27
Halifax ....43 O 22
Halistra ....77 A 11
Halkirk ....85 J 8
Hall ....60 G 16
Halland ....12 U 31
Hallaton ....36 R 26
Halling ....22 V 29
Hallington ....55 N 18
Halloughton ....36 R 24
Hallow ....27 N 27
Hallsands ....4 J 33
Halsall ....42 L 23
Halse ....8 K 30
Halsetown ....2 D 33
Halstead ....30 V 28
Halstock ....8 M 31
Haltham ....37 T 24
Halton *Aylesbury Vale* ....20 R 28
Halton *Lancaster* ....48 L 21
Halton Gill ....49 N 21
Haltwhistle ....55 M 19
Halwell ....4 I 32
Halwill Junction ....6 H 31
Hamble ....10 Q 31
Hambleden ....20 R 29
Hambledon *Hants.* ....10 Q 31
Hambledon *Surrey* ....11 S 30
Hambleton *Lancs.* ....42 L 22
Hambleton *North Yorks.* ..44 Q 22
Hambleton Hills (The) ....50 Q 21
Hambridge ....8 L 31
Hamilton ....60 H 16
Hammersmith and Fulham
London Borough ....21 T 29
Hamnavoe *near Brae* ....87 Q 2
Hamnavoe *near Scallway* ..87 P 3
Hampreston ....9 O 31
Hampstead Norris ....20 Q 29
Hampsthwaite ....50 P 21
Hampton Court ....21 S 29
Hampton in Arden ....27 O 26
Hamstead Marshall ....20 P 29
Hamsterley ....56 O 19
Hamstreet ....12 W 30
Hamworthy ....9 N 31
Hanbridge ....34 L 24
Handbury ....27 N 27
Handcross ....11 T 30
Handforth ....43 N 23
Handley ....34 L 24
Handsworth ....43 P 23
Hanham ....18 M 29
Hanley ....35 N 24
Hanley Swan ....27 N 27
Hanningfield ....22 V 28
Hannington ....19 O 29
Hanslope ....28 R 27
Happisburgh ....39 Y 25
Hapton ....42 N 22
Harberton ....4 I 32
Harbertonford ....4 I 32
Harbledown ....23 X 30
Harborough Magna ....28 Q 26
Harbottle ....63 N 17
Harbury ....28 P 27
Harby ....36 R 25
Hardham ....11 S 31
Hardwick ....44 Q 24
Hardwick Hall ....36 Q 24
Hardwicke ....19 N 28
Hardy Monument ....5 M 31
Hardy's Cottage ....9 M 31
Hare Street ....29 U 28
Haresfield ....19 N 28
Harewood House ....50 P 22
Hargrave ....29 S 27
Hargrave Green ....29 S 27
Haringey *London Borough* ..21 T 29
Harlaxton ....36 R 25
Harlech ....33 H 25
Harleston ....31 X 26
Harlestone ....28 R 27
Harley ....34 M 26
Harlington ....29 S 28

Harlosh ....77 A 11
Harlow ....21 U 28
Harlow Hill ....56 O 18
Harmston ....37 S 24
Haroldswick ....87 R 1
Harpenden ....21 S 28
Harpley ....38 V 25
Harport (Loch) ....77 A 12
Harray (Loch of) ....86 K 6
Harrietfield ....67 J 14
Harrington *Allerdale* ....53 J 20
Harrington *Kettering* ....28 R 26
Harringworth ....37 S 26
Harris *Highland* ....71 A 13
Harris *Western Isles* ....82 Y 10
Harris (Sound of) ....76 Y 10
Harrogate ....50 P 22
Harrow *London Borough* ..21 S 29
Harston ....29 U 27
Hartburn ....56 O 18
Hartest ....30 W 27
Hartfield ....11 U 30
Harthill *North Lanarkshire* ..61 I 16
Harthill *Rotherham* ....44 Q 23
Harting ....10 R 31
Hartington ....35 O 24
Hartland ....6 G 31
Hartland Quay ....6 G 31
Hartlebury ....27 N 26
Hartlepool ....57 Q 19
Hartley ....22 U 29
Hartley Wintney ....20 R 30
Hartpury ....27 N 28
Hartshill ....36 P 26
Hartwell ....20 R 28
Hartwell ....28 R 27
Harvington ....27 O 27
Harwell ....20 Q 29
Harwich ....31 X 28
Harwood Dale ....51 S 20
Harworth ....44 Q 23
Hascosay ....87 R 2
Haselbury Plucknett ....8 L 31
Hasland ....43 P 24
Haslemere ....11 R 30
Haslingden ....42 N 22
Haslingfield ....29 U 27
Haslington ....35 M 24
Hassocks ....11 T 31
Haster ....86 K 8
Hastings ....12 V 31
Hatch Court ....8 L 31
Hatfield
County of Herefordshire ..26 M 27
Hatfield *Herts.* ....21 T 28
Hatfield *South Yorks.* ....44 Q 23
Hatfield Broad Oak ....22 U 28
Hatfield Heath ....22 U 28
Hatfield Peverel ....22 V 28
Hatfield Woodhouse ....44 R 23
Hatherleigh ....7 H 31
Hathern ....36 Q 25
Hathersage ....43 P 24
Hatton *Aberdeenshire* ..81 O 11
Hatton *Derbs.* ....35 O 25
Hatton of Fintray ....75 N 12
Haugh of Urr ....53 I 19
Haughton ....35 N 25
Haunn ....71 B 14
Havant ....10 R 31
Havenstreet ....10 Q 31
Haverfordwest / Hwlffordd ..16 F 28
Haverhill ....30 V 27
Havering *London Borough* ..22 U 29
Haverthwaite ....48 K 21
Hawarden ....34 K 24
Hawes ....49 N 21
Hawick ....62 L 17
Hawkchurch ....8 L 31
Hawkedon ....30 V 27
Hawkesbury Upton ....19 M 29
Hawkhurst ....12 V 30
Hawkridge ....7 J 30
Hawkshead ....48 L 20
Hawkwell ....22 V 29
Hawley ....20 R 30
Hawling ....27 O 28
Haworth ....43 O 22
Hawsker ....51 S 20
Haxby ....50 Q 21
Haxey ....44 R 23
Hay-on-Wye ....26 K 27
Haydock ....42 M 23
Haydon Bridge ....55 N 19
Haydon Wick ....19 O 29
Hayfield ....43 O 23

128 Great Britain

Hayle 2 D 33
Hayling Island 10 R 31
Hayscastle 14 E 28
Hayton 50 R 22
Haywards Heath 11 T 31
Hazel Grove 43 N 23
Hazelbank 61 I 16
Hazelbury Bryan 9 M 31
Hazlemere 21 R 29
Heacham 38 V 25
Headcorn 22 V 30
Headington 20 Q 28
Headless Cross 27 O 27
Headley 10 R 30
Heads of Ayr 60 F 17
Healey 49 O 21
Healing 45 T 23
Heanor 36 P 24
Heast 71 C 12
Heath End 20 Q 29
Heath Hayes 35 O 25
Heather 36 P 25
Heathfield *Renfrewshire* 60 F 16
Heathfield *Wealden* 12 U 31
Heathrow Airport 21 S 29
Hebburn 56 P 19
Hebden Bridge 43 N 22
Hebrides (Sea of the) 76 Z 12
Heckfield 20 R 29
Heckington 37 T 25
Heddon on the Wall 56 O 19
Hedge End 10 Q 31
Hednesford 35 O 25
Hedon 45 T 22
Heighington *Durham* 56 P 20
Heighington *Lincs.* 44 S 24
Heights of Kinlochewe 78 E 11
Helensburgh 66 F 15
Helford 2 E 33
Hellifield 49 N 22
Hellingly 12 U 31
Hellisay 70 X 12
Hell's Mouth or Porth Neigwl 32 G 25
Helmdon 28 Q 27
Helmsdale 85 J 9
Helmsley 50 Q 21
Helpringham 37 T 25
Helpston 37 S 26
Helsby 42 L 24
Helston 2 E 33
Helton 55 L 20
Helvellyn 48 K 20
Hemel Hempstead 21 S 28
Hemingbrough 44 R 22
Hemingford Grey 29 T 27
Hemington 19 M 30
Hempnall 39 X 26
Hempton 38 W 25
Hemsby 39 Z 25
Hemswell 44 S 23
Hemsworth 43 P 23
Hemyock 8 K 31
Hendy 15 H 28
Henfield 11 T 31
Hengoed 18 K 29
Henham 30 U 28
Henley 27 O 27
Henley-on-Thames 20 R 29
Henllan 33 J 24
Henllys 18 K 29
Henlow 29 T 27
Hennock 4 J 32
Henshaw 55 M 19
Henstead 31 Y 26
Henstridge 9 M 31
Heol Senni 25 J 28
Hepple 63 N 18
Heptonstall 43 N 22
Herbrandston 14 E 28
Hereford 26 L 27
Heriot 62 L 16
Herm *Channel I.* 5
Herma Ness 87 R 1
Hermitage 20 Q 29
Hermitage Castle 62 L 18
Herne Bay 23 X 29
Herriard 20 Q 30
Herrington 56 P 19
Herstmonceux 12 U 31
Hertford 21 T 28
Hesket Newmarket 54 K 19
Hesketh Bank 42 L 22
Hesleden 57 Q 19
Hessenford 3 G 32
Hessle 45 S 22
Hest Bank 48 L 21
Heswall 42 K 24
Hethersgill 55 L 19
Hethpool 63 N 17
Hetton-le-Hole 56 P 19
Heveningham 31 Y 27
Hever 21 U 30
Heversham 48 L 21
Hevingham 39 X 25
Hewelsfield 18 M 28
Hexham 55 N 19
Heybridge 22 W 28
Heysham 48 L 21
Heyshott 11 R 31
Heytesbury 9 N 30
Heythrop 28 P 28
Heywood 43 N 23
Hibaldstow 44 S 23
Hickling 36 R 25
Hickling Green 39 Y 25
Hidcote Manor Garden 27 O 27
High Bentham 49 M 21
High Bickington 7 I 31
High Birkwith 49 N 21
High Easter 22 V 28
High Ercall 34 M 25
High Etherley 56 O 20
High Force (The) 55 N 20
High Halden 12 W 30
High Halstow 22 V 29
High Ham 8 L 30
High Hesket 55 L 19
High Newton *Alnwick* 63 P 17
High Newton *South Lakeland* 48 L 21
High Offley 35 N 25
High Ongar 22 U 28
High Peak 43 O 23
High Willhays 4 I 31
High Wycombe 20 R 29
Higham *Kent* 22 V 29
Higham *Lancs.* 42 N 22
Higham *North East Derbyshire* 36 P 24
Higham *Suffolk* 30 V 27
Higham Ferrers 29 S 27
Higham on the Hill 36 P 26
Highbridge 18 L 30
Highclere 20 P 29
Highcliffe 9 O 31
Higher Penwortham 42 L 22
Highland Wildlife Park 73 I 12
Highley 27 M 26
Highmoor Cross 20 R 29
Highnam 27 N 28
Hightae 54 J 18
Hightown *Congleton* 35 N 24
Hightown *Sefton* 42 K 23
Highworth 19 O 29
Hilborough 38 W 26
Hildenborough 22 U 30
Hilderstone 35 N 25
Hilgay 38 V 26
Hill 18 M 29
Hill of Fearn 79 I 10
Hill of Tarvit 69 L 15
Hillhead 52 G 19
Hillingdon *London Borough* 21 S 29
Hillington 38 V 25
Hillside 75 M 13
Hillswick 87 P 2
Hilmarton 19 O 29
Hilperton 19 N 30
Hilpsford Point 47 K 21
Hilton *Aberdeenshire* 81 N 11
Hilton *Eden* 55 M 20
Hilton *Huntingdonshire* 29 T 27
Hilton *North Dorset* 9 N 31
Hilton *South Derbyshire* 35 P 25
Hilton of Cadboll 79 I 10
Himbleton 27 N 27
Hinchingbrooke House 29 T 27
Hinckley 36 P 26
Hinderwell 50 R 20
Hindhead 10 R 30
Hindley 42 M 23
Hindolveston 38 X 25
Hindon 9 N 30
Hingham 38 W 26
Hinstock 34 M 25
Hintlesham 31 X 27
Hinton-Blewett 18 M 30
Hirst Courtney 44 Q 22
Hirwaun 17 J 28
Histon 29 U 27
Hitcham 30 W 27
Hitchin 29 T 28
Hockering 38 X 25
Hockerton 36 R 24
Hockley 22 V 29
Hockley Heath 27 O 26
Hockliffe 29 S 28
Hoddesdon 21 T 28
Hodnet 34 M 25
Hodthorpe 44 Q 24
Hogsthorpe 45 U 24
Holbeach 37 U 25
Holbeach-St. Johns 37 T 25
Holbeach-St. Matthew 37 U 25
Holbeck 44 Q 24
Holbrook 31 X 28
Holbury 10 P 31
Holcombe 18 M 30
Holcombe Rogus 7 J 31
Holdenby 28 R 27
Holford 8 K 30
Holkam Hall 38 W 25
Hollandstoun 87 M 5
Hollesley 31 Y 27
Hollesley Bay 31 Y 27
Hollingbourne 22 V 30
Hollingworth 43 O 23
Hollybush 60 G 17
Hollym 45 U 22
Holmbridge 43 O 23
Holme *Huntingdonshire* 29 T 26
Holme *South Lakeland* 48 L 21
Holme-next-the-Sea 38 V 25
Holme upon Spalding-Moor 44 R 22
Holmer Green 21 R 29
Holmes Chapel 35 M 24
Holmesfield 43 P 24
Holmfirth 43 O 23
Holmhead 60 H 17
Holmpton 45 U 22
Holnest 8 M 31
Holsworthy 6 G 31
Holt *Dorset* 9 O 31
Holt *Norfolk* 38 X 25
Holt *Wilts.* 19 N 29
Holt *Wrexham* 34 L 24
Holt Heath 27 N 27
Holton *Lincs.* 45 T 24
Holton *Norfolk* 31 Y 26
Holton *South Somerset* 8 M 30
Holton Heath 9 N 31
Holton-le-Clay 45 T 23
Holwick 55 N 20
Holy Island *Anglesey* 40 F 23
Holy Island *North Ayrshire* 59 E 17
Holy Island *Northumb.* 63 O 16
Holybourne 10 R 30
Holyhead / Caergybi 40 G 23
Holystone 63 N 18
Holywell 2 E 32
Holywell / Treffynnon 41 K 23
Holywell Bay 2 E 32
Holywood 53 J 18
Honing 39 Y 25
Honiton 8 K 31
Hoo St. Werburgh 22 V 29
Hook *Basingstoke and Deane* 20 R 30
Hook *East Riding of Yorkshire* 44 R 22
Hook Norton 28 P 28
Hooke 8 M 31
Hope *Derbs.* 43 O 23
Hope *Flintshire* 34 K 24
Hope *Highland* 84 G 8
Hope *South Shropshire* 34 L 26
Hope (Loch) 84 G 8
Hope Bowdler 26 L 26
Hope under Dinmore 26 L 27
Hopeman 80 J 10
Hopetoun House 68 J 16
Hopton 39 Z 26
Horam 12 U 31
Horbury 43 P 23
Horden 57 Q 19
Hordley 34 L 25
Horeb 15 G 27
Horley 21 T 30
Hornby 48 M 21
Horncastle 45 T 24
Hornchurch 22 U 29
Horncliffe 63 N 16
Horning 39 Y 25
Horninglow 35 P 25
Horn's Cross 6 H 31
Hornsea 51 T 22
Hornton 28 P 27
Horrabridge 4 H 32
Horseheath 30 V 27
Horsehouse 49 O 21
Horsell 21 S 30
Horsford 39 X 25
Horsforth 43 P 22
Horsham 11 T 30
Horsham St. Faith 39 X 25
Horsington *East Lindsey* 37 T 24
Horsington *South Somerset* 9 M 30
Horsley *Stroud* 19 N 28
Horsley *Tynedale* 56 O 19
Horsmonden 12 V 30
Horstead 39 Y 25
Horsted Keynes 11 T 30
Horton *Abertawe / Swansea* 15 H 29
Horton *East Dorset* 9 O 31
Horton *South Somerset* 8 L 31
Horton Court 19 M 29
Horton-in-Ribblesdale 49 N 21
Horwich 42 M 23
Hoton 36 Q 25
Hott 55 M 18
Houghton 10 P 30
Houghton Hall 38 V 25
Houghton House 29 S 27
Houghton-le-Spring 56 P 19
Houghton-on-the-Hill 36 R 26
Hougton 55 L 19
Hounslow *London Borough* 21 S 29
Hourn (Loch) 72 D 12
Housesteads Fort 55 N 18
Houston 60 G 16
Houstry 85 J 9
Hove 11 T 31
Hoveton 39 Y 25
Hovingham 50 R 21
How Caple 26 M 28
Howden 44 R 22
Howe of the Mearns 75 M 13
Howick 63 P 17
Howmore 76 X 12
Hownam 62 M 17
Howwood 60 G 16
Hoxa (Sound of) 86 K 7
Hoxne 31 X 26
Hoy 86 J 7
Hoylake 41 K 22
Hoyland Nether 43 P 23
Huby 50 Q 21
Hucknall 36 Q 24
Huddersfield 43 O 23
Huggate 51 S 22
Hugh Town *I. of Scilly* 2
Hughenden 20 R 29
Hughley 34 M 26
Huish Champflower 7 J 30
Huish Episcopi 8 L 30
Hull (River) 45 S 22
Hulland 35 P 24
Hullavington 19 N 29
Hullbridge 22 V 29
Humber (River) 45 T 23
Humber Bridge 44 S 22
Humberston 45 T 23
Humbleton 45 T 22
Hume Castle 62 M 17
Humshaugh 55 N 18
Hundleton 16 F 28
Hundred House 26 K 27
Hungerford 20 P 29
Hunmanby 51 T 21
Hunstanton 38 V 25
Hunter's Inn 17 I 30
Hunter's Quay 66 F 16
Huntingdon 29 T 26
Huntington 50 Q 22
Huntingtower Castle 68 J 14
Huntly 80 L 11
Hunton 49 O 21
Huntspill 18 L 30
Hunwick 56 O 19
Hurlford 60 G 17
Hurn 9 O 31
Hursley 10 P 30
Hurst Green 12 V 30
Hurstbourne Priors 20 P 30
Hurstbourne Tarrant 20 P 30
Hurstpierpoint 11 T 31
Hurworth-on-Tees 50 P 20
Hury 55 N 20
Husbands Bosworth 28 Q 26
Huthwaite 36 Q 24
Huttoft 45 U 24
Hutton *Scottish Borders* 63 N 16
Hutton *South Ribble* 42 L 22
Hutton Cranswick 51 S 22
Hutton Rudby 50 Q 20
Huxley 34 L 24
Huyton 42 L 23
Hwlffordd / Haverfordwest 16 F 28
Hyde 43 N 23
Hynish 64 Z 14
Hynish Bay 64 Z 14
Hythe *Hants.* 10 P 31
Hythe *Kent* 13 X 30

I

Ibsley 9 O 31
Ibstock 36 P 25
Ickleford 29 T 28
Icklingham 30 V 27
Ickworth House 30 V 27
Iddesleigh 7 H 31
Ideford 4 J 32
Iden 12 W 31
Iden Green 12 V 30
Idmiston 9 O 30
Idrigill Point 77 A 12
Ightham 22 U 30
Ightham Mote 22 U 30
Ilchester 8 L 30
Ilderton 63 O 17
Ilfracombe 17 H 30
Ilkeston 36 Q 25
Ilkley 49 O 22
Illogan 2 E 33
Ilmington 27 O 27
Ilminster 8 L 31
Ilsington 4 I 32
Ilton 8 L 31
Immingham 45 T 23
Immingham Dock 45 T 23
Ince Blundell 42 K 23
Ince-in-Makerfield 42 M 23
Inch Kenneth 64 B 14
Inchard (Loch) 84 E 8
Inchbare 75 M 13
Inchgrundle 74 L 13
Inchkeith 68 K 15
Inchlaggan 72 E 12
Inchmarnock 59 E 16
Inchnadamph 84 F 9
Inchture 68 K 14
Indaal (Loch) 58 A 16
Inerval 58 B 17
Ingatestone 22 V 28
Ingbirchworth 43 P 23
Ingham 30 W 27
Ingleby Barwick 50 Q 20
Ingleton *Durham* 56 O 20
Ingleton *North Yorks.* 49 M 21
Inglewhite 42 L 22
Inglewood Forest 55 L 19
Ingliston 68 J 16
Ingoldmells 38 V 24
Ingoldsby 37 S 25
Ingram 63 O 17
Ings 48 L 20
Inkpen 20 P 29
Innellan 59 F 16
Inner Hebrides 70 Y 14
Inner Sound 77 C 11
Innerleithen 61 K 17
Innerpeffray 67 I 14
Innerwick 69 M 16
Insch 81 M 11
Insh 73 I 12
Inshore 84 F 8
Instow 6 H 30
Inver *Highland* 79 I 10
Inver *Perth and Kinross* 68 J 14
Inver (Loch) 84 E 9
Inver Bay 79 I 10
Inver Mallie 72 E 13
Inver Valley 84 E 9
Inveralligin 78 D 11
Inverallochy 81 O 10
Inveran 84 G 10
Inveraray 66 E 15
Inverarity 69 L 14
Inverarnan 66 F 15
Inverbeg 66 G 15
Inverbervie 75 N 13
Invercassley 84 G 10
Invercauld House 74 J 12
Inverchapel 66 F 15
Invercreran 72 E 14
Inverdruie 73 I 12
Inverewe Gardens 78 C 10
Inverey 74 J 13
Inverfarigaig 79 G 12
Invergarry 72 F 12
Invergeldie 67 H 14
Invergordon 79 H 10
Invergowrie 68 K 14
Inverie 72 C 12
Inverinan 65 E 15
Inverinate 78 D 12
Inverkeithing 68 J 15
Inverkeithny 81 M 11
Inverkip 66 F 16
Inverkirkaig 84 E 9
Inverliever Forest 65 D 15
Inverlochlarig 67 G 15
Invermoriston 73 G 12
Inverness 79 H 11
Inversanda 72 D 13
Inversnaid Hotel 66 F 15
Inveruglas 66 F 15
Inverurie 81 M 12
Invervar 73 H 14
Inwardleigh 7 H 31
Iona 64 A 15
Ipplepen 4 J 32
Ipstones 35 O 24
Ipswich 31 X 27
Irby *East Lindsey* 37 U 24
Irby *Wirral* 42 K 23
Irchester 29 S 27
Ireby 54 K 19
Ireleth 47 K 21
Irlam 42 M 23
Iron Acton 18 M 29
Ironbridge 34 M 26
Irthington 55 L 19
Irthlingborough 29 S 27
Irvine 60 F 17
Irwell (River) 42 N 23
Isbyty Ystwyth 25 I 27
Isla (Glen) 74 K 13
Islay (Sound of) 64 B 16
Isle of Whithorn 53 G 19
Isleham 30 V 26
Isleornsay 71 C 12
Isleworth 21 S 29
Islington *London Borough* 21 T 29
Islip 20 Q 28
Islivig 82 Y 9
Itchingfield 11 S 30
Ithon (River) 25 K 27
Itteringham 39 X 25
Iver 21 S 29
Iver Heath 21 S 29
Ivinghoe 21 S 28
Ivybridge 4 I 32
Ivychurch 12 W 30
Iwade 22 W 29
Iwerne Minster 9 N 31
Ixworth 30 W 27

J

Jacobstow 6 G 31
Jacobstowe 7 H 31
Jameston 15 F 29
Jamestown *Dumfries and Galloway* 61 K 18
Jamestown *West Dunbartonshire* 66 G 16
Janetstown 85 J 9
Jarrow 56 P 19
Jaywick 23 X 28
Jedburgh 62 M 17
Jedburgh Abbey 62 M 17
Jeffreyston 15 F 28
Jemimaville 79 H 11
Jersey *Channel I.* 5
Jevington 12 U 31
John Muir 69 M 15
John o' Groats 86 K 8
Johnshaven 75 N 13
Johnston 16 F 28
Johnstone 60 G 16
Johnstonebridge 54 J 18
Jura (Isle of) 58 B 16
Jura (Sound of) 65 C 16
Jura Forest 65 B 16
Jura Ho 58 B 16
Jurby West 46 G 20

K

Kainakill 77 C 11
Kames 65 E 16
Katrine (Loch) 67 G 15
Kea 2 E 33
Keal 37 U 24
Keal (Loch na) 65 B 14
Kearsley 42 M 23
Keasden 49 M 21

A B C D E F G H I J K L M N O P Q R S T U V W X Y Z

Kebock Head 82 A 9
Kedington 30 V 27
Kedleston Hall 36 P 25
Keelby 45 T 23
Keevil 19 N 30
Kegworth 36 Q 25
Keig 75 M 12
Keighley 43 O 22
Keillmore 65 C 16
Keinton Mandeville 8 M 30
Keir Mill 53 I 18
Keiss 86 K 8
Keith 80 L 11
Keld 49 N 20
Kellas *Angus* 69 L 14
Kellas *Moray* 80 J 11
Kellieth 49 M 20
Kellie Castle 69 L 15
Kellington 44 Q 22
Kelloe 56 P 19
Kelly Bray 3 H 32
Kelmarsh 28 R 26
Kelsall 34 L 24
Kelso 62 M 17
Kelston 19 M 29
Keltneyburn 73 H 14
Kelty 68 J 15
Kelvedon 30 W 28
Kelvedon Hatch 22 U 29
Kemble 19 N 28
Kemnay 75 M 12
Kempley 26 M 28
Kempsey 27 N 27
Kempsford 19 O 28
Kempston 29 S 27
Kemsing 22 U 30
Kendal 48 L 21
Kenfig 17 I 29
Kenilworth 27 P 26
Kenknock 67 G 14
Kenmore *Highland* 77 C 11
Kenmore
  Perthshire and Kinross 67 I 14
Kenn 18 L 29
Kennet (River) 19 O 29
Kennethmont 80 L 11
Kenninghall 30 X 26
Kennington *Kent* 22 W 30
Kennington *Oxon.* 20 Q 28
Kennoway 68 K 15
Kenovay 70 Z 14
Kensaleyre 77 B 11
Kentallen 72 E 13
Kentford 30 V 27
Kentisbeare 7 K 31
Kentmere 48 L 20
Kenton 4 J 32
Kents Bank 48 L 21
Keoldale 84 F 8
Keresley 28 P 26
Kerrera 65 D 14
Kerry 26 K 26
Kersey 30 W 27
Kershader 82 A 9
Kershopefoot 55 L 18
Kesgrave 31 X 27
Kessingland 31 Z 26
Keswick 54 K 20
Kettering 28 R 26
Kettleness 50 R 20
Kettleshulme 43 N 24
Kettletoft 87 M 6
Kettlewell 49 N 21
Ketton 37 S 26
Kew 21 T 29
Kewstoke 18 L 29
Kexbrough 43 P 23
Kexby 44 R 23
Keyingham 45 T 22
Keymer 11 T 31
Keynsham 18 M 29
Keyworth 36 Q 25
Kibworth Harcourt 36 R 26
Kidderminster 27 N 26
Kidermorie Lodge 79 G 10
Kidlington 20 Q 28
Kidsgrove 35 N 24
Kidstones 49 N 21
Kidwelly / Cydweli 15 H 28
Kielder 55 M 18
Kielder Forest 55 M 18
Kielder Reservoir 55 M 18
Kiiphedir 85 I 9
Kilamarsh 44 Q 24
Kilbarchan 60 G 16
Kilbirnie 60 F 16
Kilbrannan Sound 59 D 17

Kilbride 65 D 14
Kilburn *Amber Valley* 36 P 24
Kilburn *Hambleton* 50 Q 21
Kilchattan 59 E 16
Kilchenzie 59 C 17
Kilcheran 65 D 14
Kilchiaran 58 A 16
Kilchoan 71 B 13
Kilchoman 58 A 16
Kilchrenan 65 E 14
Kilconquhar 69 L 15
Kilcreggan 66 F 16
Kildale 50 Q 20
Kildary 79 H 10
Kildavanan 59 E 16
Kildonan 59 E 17
Kildonan Lodge 85 I 9
Kildrummy 74 L 12
Kildrummy Castle 74 L 12
Kilfinnan 72 F 12
Kilgetti 15 F 28
Kilham
  Berwick-upon-Tweed 63 N 17
Kilham
  East Riding of Yorkshire 51 S 21
Kilkhampton 6 G 31
Killay 15 H 29
Killean 59 D 17
Killearn 67 G 15
Killen 79 H 11
Killerton 7 J 31
Killiechronan 65 C 14
Killilan 78 D 12
Killin 67 H 14
Killinghall 50 P 21
Killundine 71 C 14
Kilmacolm 60 G 16
Kilmaluag 77 B 10
Kilmany 69 L 14
Kilmarie 71 B 12
Kilmarnock 60 G 17
Kilmartin 65 D 15
Kilmaurs 60 G 17
Kilmelford 65 D 15
Kilmersdon 19 M 30
Kilmington *East Devon* 8 K 31
Kilmington *Salisbury* 9 N 30
Kilmorack 79 G 11
Kilmore 71 C 12
Kilmory *Ardnamurchan* 71 B 13
Kilmory *Argyll and Bute* 65 C 16
Kilmory *I. Rhum* 71 A 12
Kilmory *North Ayrshire* 59 E 17
Kilmuir 77 A 11
Kilmun 66 F 16
Kilncadzow 61 I 16
Kilninver 65 D 14
Kilnsey 49 N 21
Kiloran 64 B 15
Kilpeck 26 L 28
Kilrenny 69 L 15
Kilsby 67 H 16
Kilsyth 67 H 16
Kiltarlity 79 G 11
Kilvaxter 77 A 11
Kilwinning 60 F 17
Kimberley *Broxtowe* 36 Q 25
Kimberley *South Norfolk* 38 X 26
Kimble 20 R 28
Kimbolton 29 S 27
Kimmeridge 9 N 32
Kimpton 21 T 28
Kinbrace 85 I 9
Kinbuck 67 I 15
Kincardine *Fife* 67 I 15
Kincardine *Highland* 79 G 10
Kincardine *O'Neil* 75 L 12
Kinclaven 68 J 14
Kincraig 73 I 12
Kineton 28 P 27
Kinfauns 68 J 14
Kingairloch 72 D 14
Kingarth 59 E 16
Kinghorn 68 K 15
Kinglassie 68 K 15
King's Bromley 35 O 25
King's Cliffe 37 S 26
Kings Langley 21 S 28
King's Lynn 38 V 25
King's Meaburn 55 M 20
King's Somborne 10 P 30
King's Sutton 28 Q 27
King's Walden 29 T 28
Kings Worthy 10 Q 30
Kingsbarns 69 M 15
Kingsbridge 4 I 33
Kingsburgh 77 A 11

Kingsbury Episcopi 8 L 31
Kingsclere 20 Q 30
Kingscote 19 N 29
Kingsdon 8 L 30
Kingsdown 23 Y 30
Kingsgate 23 Y 29
Kingshouse *Highland* 72 F 14
Kingshouse *Stirling* 67 H 14
Kingskerswell 4 J 32
Kingskettle 68 K 15
Kingsland 26 L 27
Kingsley *East Hampshire* 10 R 30
Kingsley
  Staffordshire Moorlands 35 O 24
Kingsmuir 74 L 14
Kingsnorth 12 W 30
Kingsteignton 4 J 32
Kingsthorpe 28 R 27
Kingston *Devon* 4 I 33
Kingston *East Hampshire* 69 L 15
Kingston *Moray* 80 K 10
Kingston
  South Cambridgeshire 29 T 27
Kingston Bagpuize 20 P 28
Kingston Deverill 9 N 30
Kingston Lacy 9 N 31
Kingston Lisle 20 P 29
Kingston Seymour 18 L 29
Kingston-St. Mary 8 K 30
Kingston-upon-Hull 45 S 22
Kingston-upon-Thames
  London Borough 21 T 29
Kingstone 26 L 27
Kingswear 4 J 32
Kingswinford 27 N 26
Kingswood 19 M 29
Kingswood *Powys* 34 K 26
Kingswood *South Glos.* 18 M 29
Kington 26 K 27
Kington Langley 19 N 29
Kington-St. Michael 19 N 29
Kingussie 73 H 12
Kinkell 75 M 12
Kinkell Bridge 67 I 15
Kinknockie 81 O 11
Kinlet 27 M 26
Kinloch 71 B 12
Kinloch Hourn 72 D 12
Kinloch Lodge 84 G 8
Kinloch Rannoch 73 H 13
Kinlochard 67 G 15
Kinlochbervie 84 E 8
Kinlocheil 72 E 13
Kinlochewe 78 E 11
Kinlochleven 72 F 13
Kinlochmoidart 71 C 13
Kinloss 80 J 11
Kinmuck 75 N 12
Kinnaird 68 K 14
Kinneff 75 N 13
Kinnelhead 61 J 18
Kinnerley 34 L 25
Kinnersley 26 L 27
Kinnesswood 68 K 15
Kininvie 56 O 20
Kinross 68 J 15
Kinrossie 68 K 14
Kintbury 20 P 29
Kintessack 80 I 11
Kintore 75 M 12
Kintra 58 B 17
Kintyre (Peninsula) 59 D 17
Kinver 27 N 26
Kippax 43 P 22
Kippen 67 H 15
Kippford 53 I 19
Kirby Bellars 36 R 25
Kirby Cross 31 X 28
Kirby Hall 29 S 26
Kirby Misperton 50 R 21
Kirby Muxloe 36 Q 26
Kirby Underwood 37 S 25
Kirdford 11 S 30
Kirk Ella 45 S 22
Kirk Ireton 35 P 24
Kirk Merrington 56 P 19
Kirk Michael 46 G 21
Kirk Yetholm 63 N 17
Kirkbampton 54 K 19
Kirkbean 53 I 19
Kirkbride 54 K 19
Kirkbuddo 69 L 14
Kirkburn 51 S 22
Kirkburton 43 O 23
Kirkby 42 L 23
Kirkby Fleetham 50 P 20
Kirkby-in-Ashfield 36 Q 24

Kirkby-la-Thorpe 37 S 25
Kirkby Lonsdale 48 M 21
Kirkby Malham 49 N 21
Kirkby Mallory 36 Q 26
Kirkby Malzeard 49 P 21
Kirkby Overblow 50 P 22
Kirkby Stephen 49 M 20
Kirkby Thore 55 M 20
Kirkbymoorside 50 R 21
Kirkcaldy 68 K 15
Kirkcolm 52 E 19
Kirkconnel 60 I 17
Kirkcowan 52 G 19
Kirkcudbright 53 H 19
Kirkcudbright Bay 53 H 19
Kirkfieldbank 61 I 16
Kirkgunzeon 53 I 19
Kirkham 42 L 22
Kirkheaton 56 O 18
Kirkhill 79 G 11
Kirkhope 61 J 18
Kirkinner 52 G 19
Kirkintilloch 67 H 16
Kirkland
  Dumfries and Galloway 53 I 18
Kirkland *Eden* 55 M 19
Kirklees 43 O 23
Kirklevington 50 P 20
Kirklington
  North Yorkshire 50 P 21
Kirklington
  Nottinghamshire 36 R 24
Kirkliston 68 J 16
Kirkmaiden 52 F 19
Kirkmichael
  Perthshire and Kinross 74 J 13
Kirkmichael
  South Ayrshire 60 G 17
Kirkmuirhill 61 I 17
Kirknewton
  Berwick-upon-Tweed 63 N 17
Kirknewton
  West Lothian 61 J 16
Kirkoswald 59 F 18
Kirkpatrick Durham 53 I 18
Kirkpatrick-Fleming 54 K 18
Kirkstone Pass 48 L 20
Kirkton
  Dumfries and Galloway 53 J 18
Kirkton *Scottish Borders* 62 L 17
Kirkton Manor 61 K 17
Kirkton of Culsalmond 81 M 11
Kirkton of Durris 75 M 12
Kirkton of Glenisla 74 K 13
Kirkton of Kingoldrum 74 K 13
Kirkton of Largo 69 L 15
Kirkton of Skene 75 N 12
Kirkton of Strathmartine 69 K 14
Kirktown of Auchterless 81 M 11
Kirktown of Deskford 80 L 11
Kirkwall 86 L 7
Kirkwhelpington 56 N 18
Kirmington 45 T 23
Kirn 66 F 16
Kirriemuir 74 K 13
Kirtlebridge 54 K 18
Kirtlington 28 Q 28
Kirtomy 85 H 8
Kirton *Boston* 37 T 25
Kirton *Suffolk Coastal* 31 X 27
Kirton End 37 T 25
Kirton-in-Lindsey 44 S 23
Kishorn (Loch) 78 D 11
Kislingbury 28 R 27
Kitchener Memorial 86 J 6
Kiveton 44 Q 23
Knaresborough 50 P 21
Knarsdale 55 M 19
Knebworth 29 T 28
Kneesall 36 R 24
Kneesworth 29 T 27
Knighton / Trefyclawdd 26 K 26
Knightshayes Court 7 J 31
Kniveton 35 O 24
Knock *Argyll and Bute* 65 C 14
Knock *Moray* 80 L 11
Knock *Western Isles* 83 B 9
Knockandhu 80 K 12
Knockbrex 53 H 19
Knockie Lodge 73 G 12
Knockin 34 L 25
Knocknaha 59 D 17
Knocksharry 46 G 21
Knockvennie Smithy 53 I 18
Knole 22 U 30
Knossington 36 R 25
Knottingley 44 Q 22

Knowe 52 G 18
Knowehead 53 H 18
Knowesgate 55 N 18
Knowle 27 O 26
Knowsley 42 L 23
Knoydart 72 D 12
Knutsford 42 M 24
Kyle of Durness 84 F 8
Kyle of Lochalsh 77 C 12
Kyle of Sutherland 79 G 10
Kyle of Tongue 84 G 8
Kyleakin 77 C 12
Kylerhea 72 C 12
Kyles Scalpay 82 Z 10
Kylestrome 84 E 9
Kynance Cove 2 E 34
Kyre park 26 M 27

L

La Rocque *Jersey I.* 5
Laceby 45 T 23
Lacey Green 20 R 28
Lache 34 L 24
Lacock 19 N 29
Ladder Hills 74 K 12
Ladock 3 F 33
Ladybank 68 K 15
Ladybower Reservoir 43 O 23
Ladyhill 55 N 18
Lagg 65 C 16
Laggan *Argyll and Bute* 58 B 16
Laggan *near Invergarry* 72 F 12
Laggan
  near Newtonmore 73 H 12
Laggan (Loch) 73 G 13
Laggan Point 58 B 16
Lagganulva 64 B 14
Laide 78 D 10
Lair 78 E 11
Lairg 84 G 9
Lake District National Park 48 K 20
Lakenheath 30 V 26
Lamanva 2 E 33
Lamberhurst 12 V 30
Lambeth *London Borough* 21 T 29
Lambley *Gedling* 36 Q 24
Lambley *Tynedale* 55 M 19
Lambourn 20 P 29
Lamerton 3 H 32
Lamington 61 J 17
Lamlash 59 E 17
Lamlash Bay 59 E 17
Lammermuir Hills 62 L 16
Lampeter /
  Llanbedr Pont Steffan 15 H 27
Lamplugh 54 J 20
Lamport 28 R 26
Lanark 61 I 16
Lancaster 48 L 21
Lanchester 56 O 19
Lancing 11 S 31
Landmark Visitor Centre 79 I 12
Landrake 3 H 32
Land's End 2 C 33
Landulph 3 H 32
Lane End 20 R 29
Laneast 6 G 32
Lanercost 55 L 19
Langar 36 R 25
Langavat (Loch) *Lewis* 82 Z 9
Langavat (Loch)
  South Harris 76 Z 10
Langbank 66 G 16
Langcliffe 49 N 21
Langdale End 51 S 21
Langdale Valley 48 K 20
Langdon Beck 55 N 19
Langenhoe 30 W 28
Langford
  Mid Bedfordshire 29 T 27
Langford
  West Oxfordshire 19 P 28
Langford Budville 8 K 31
Langham 36 R 25
Langholm 54 L 18
Langleeford 63 N 17
Langley 21 S 29
Langley Park 56 O 19
Langold 44 Q 23
Langport 8 L 30
Langrick 37 T 24
Langrish 10 Q 30
Langsett 43 O 23
Langshaw 62 L 17
Langstrothdale
  Chase 49 N 21

Langthwaite 49 O 20
Langtoft 51 S 21
Langton 50 R 21
Langton Matravers 9 O 32
Langwathby 55 L 19
Lanhydrock 3 F 32
Lanivet 3 F 32
Lanlivery 3 F 32
Lanreath 3 G 32
Lansallos 3 G 32
Lanton 62 M 17
Lapford 7 I 31
Larachbeg 71 C 14
Larbert 67 I 15
Largs 59 F 16
Larkhall 61 I 16
Larkhill 19 O 30
Larling 30 W 26
Lasswade 61 K 16
Lastingham 50 R 21
Latchingdon 22 W 28
Latton 19 O 29
Lauder 62 L 16
Lauderdale 62 L 16
Laugharne 15 G 28
Laughton *Wealden* 12 U 31
Laughton *West Lindsey* 44 R 23
Launcells 6 G 31
Launceston 6 G 32
Launton 28 Q 28
Laurencekirk 75 M 13
Laurieston 53 H 19
Lauriston Castle 68 K 16
Lavendon 29 S 27
Lavenham 30 W 27
Laverstock 9 O 30
Laverstoke 20 Q 30
Lawford 30 X 28
Lawrenny 16 F 28
Lawshall 30 W 27
Laxay 82 A 9
Laxey 46 G 21
Laxey Bay 46 G 21
Laxfield 31 Y 27
Laxford (Loch) 84 E 8
Laxford Bridge 84 E 8
Laxo 87 Q 2
Laxton
  East Riding of Yorkshire 44 R 22
Laxton
  Newark and Sherwood 36 R 24
Layer-de-la-Haye 30 W 28
Layer Marney 22 W 28
Laytham 44 R 22
Layton 42 K 22
Lazonby 55 L 19
Lea *Herefordshire* 26 M 28
Lea *North Wiltshire* 19 N 29
Lea *West Lindsey* 44 R 23
Leaden Roding 22 U 28
Leadenham 37 S 24
Leadgate *Derwentside* 56 O 19
Leadgate *Eden* 55 M 19
Leadhills 61 I 17
Leafield 20 P 28
Leagrave 29 S 28
Lealholm 50 R 20
Lealt 65 C 15
Leargybreck 65 C 16
Leasingham 37 S 24
Leathaid Bhuain (Loch an) 84 F 9
Leatherhead 21 T 30
Leathley 49 P 22
Leavening 50 R 21
Lebberston 51 S 21
Lechlade 19 O 28
Lecht Road 74 K 12
Leckmelm 78 E 10
Leconfield 44 S 22
Ledbury 27 M 27
Ledmore 84 F 9
Ledsham 44 Q 22
Lee 16 H 30
Lee-on-the-Solent 10 Q 31
Leebotwood 34 L 26
Leeds *Kent* 22 V 30
Leeds *West Yorks.* 43 P 22
Leedstown 2 D 33
Leek 35 N 24
Leek Wootton 27 P 27
Leeming Bar 50 P 21
Leeswood 34 K 24
Legbourne 45 U 23
Legerwood 62 M 16
Leicester 36 Q 26
Leicester Forest East 36 Q 26
Leigh 42 M 23

A B C D E F G H I J **K L** M N O P Q R S T U V W X Y Z

A B C D E F G H I J K L M N O P Q R S T U V W X Y Z

Leigh *Mole Valley* .....21 T 30
Leigh *North Wiltshire* .....19 O 29
Leigh *Sevenoaks* .....22 U 30
Leigh *West Dorset* .....8 M 31
Leigh-on-Sea .....22 V 29
Leigh Sinton .....27 N 27
Leighterton .....19 N 29
Leighton Buzzard .....29 S 28
Leim .....58 C 17
Leintwardine .....26 L 26
Leirinmore .....84 F 8
Leiston .....31 Y 27
Leith .....68 K 16
Leitholm .....62 M 16
Lemreway .....82 A 9
Lendalfoot .....52 F 18
Lenham .....22 W 30
Lennoxtown .....67 H 16
Leominster .....26 L 27
Leonard Stanley .....19 N 28
Lepe .....10 P 31
Lephinmore .....65 E 15
Lerwick .....87 Q 3
Lesbury .....63 P 17
Leslie *Aberdeenshire* .....81 L 12
Leslie *Fife* .....68 K 15
Lesmahagow .....61 I 17
Leswalt .....52 E 19
Letchworth .....29 T 28
Letham *Angus* .....75 L 14
Letham *Fife* .....68 K 15
Letheringsett .....38 X 25
Letterewe Forest .....78 D 10
Letterfearn .....78 D 12
Lettermore .....84 G 8
Letters .....78 E 10
Letterston .....24 F 28
Leuchars .....69 L 14
Leurbost .....82 A 9
Leven
  East Riding of Yorks. .....51 T 22
Leven *Fife* .....69 K 15
Leven (Loch) .....72 E 13
Leven (River) .....72 F 13
Levens .....48 L 21
Levens Hall .....48 L 21
Levenwick .....87 Q 4
Leverington .....37 U 25
Leverton
  with Habblesthorpe .....44 R 24
Levington .....31 X 27
Levisham .....50 R 21
Lewannick .....3 G 32
Lewdown .....6 H 32
Lewes .....11 U 31
Lewis (Isle of) .....82 Z 9
Lewis and Harris (Isle of) .....82 Z 8
Lewisham
  London Borough .....21 T 29
Lewknor .....20 R 28
Leyburn .....49 O 21
Leyland .....42 L 22
Leysdown-on-Sea .....22 W 29
Lezant .....3 G 32
Lhanbryde .....80 K 11
Lhen (The) .....46 G 20
Liathach .....78 D 11
Libberton .....61 J 16
Lichfield .....35 O 25
Liddesdale .....55 L 18
Lidgate .....30 V 27
Lifton .....6 H 32
Ligger or Perran Bay .....2 E 32
Lilbourne .....28 Q 26
Lilleshall .....35 M 25
Lilliesleaf .....62 L 17
Limmerhaugh .....60 H 17
Limpsfield .....21 U 30
Linchmere .....10 R 30
Lincoln .....44 S 24
Lincolnshire Wolds .....45 T 23
Lindfield .....11 T 30
Lindores .....68 K 14
Lingague .....46 F 21
Lingay *near Eriskay* .....70 X 12
Lingay *near Pabbay* .....70 X 13
Lingen .....26 L 27
Lingfield .....21 T 30
Liniclate .....76 X 11
Linlithgow .....67 J 16
Linn of Dee .....74 J 13
Linn of Tummel .....74 I 13
Linneraineach .....84 E 9
Linney Head .....14 E 29
Linnhe (Loch) .....72 D 14
Linslade .....29 R 28
Lintmill .....80 L 10

Linton *Craven* .....49 N 21
Linton *Herefordshire* .....26 M 28
Linton *Scottish Borders* .....62 M 17
Linton
  South Cambridgeshire .....30 U 27
Linton *South Derbyshire* .....35 P 25
Linton-on-Ouse .....50 Q 21
Lintrathen (Loch of) .....74 K 13
Linwood *Renfrewshire* .....60 G 16
Linwood *West Lindsey* .....45 T 23
Liphook .....10 R 30
Liskeard .....3 G 32
Lismore .....65 D 14
Liss .....10 R 30
Lisset .....51 T 21
Lisvane .....18 K 29
Litcham .....38 W 25
Litchborough .....28 Q 27
Litchfield .....20 P 30
Litherland .....42 L 23
Little-Baddow .....22 V 28
Little-Barningham .....39 X 25
Little Berkhamsted .....21 T 28
Little Brington .....28 Q 27
Little Budworth .....34 M 24
Little Bytham .....37 S 25
Little Chalfont .....21 S 28
Little Clacton .....31 X 28
Little Colonsay .....64 B 14
Little-Coxwell .....19 P 29
Little Cumbrae Island .....59 F 16
Little Dewchurch .....26 L 28
Little Galdenoch .....52 E 19
Little Glenshee .....67 J 14
Little Hadham .....29 U 28
Little Hallingbury .....22 U 28
Little Harrowden .....28 R 27
Little Houghton .....28 R 27
Little Loch Broom .....78 D 10
Little Loch Roag .....82 Z 9
Little Mill .....18 L 28
Little-Milton .....20 Q 28
Little Minch (The) .....76 Z 11
Little Moreton Hall .....35 N 24
Little Ouse (River) .....30 V 26
Little Ouseburn .....50 Q 21
Little-Raveley .....29 T 26
Little Snoring .....38 W 25
Little-Stretton .....26 L 26
Little-Stukeley .....29 T 26
Little Torrington .....6 H 31
Little Urswick .....48 K 21
Little Walsingham .....38 W 25
Little Waltham .....22 V 28
Little Wenlock .....34 M 26
Littleborough .....43 N 23
Littlebourne .....23 X 30
Littlebury .....30 U 27
Littlecote House .....20 P 29
Littleferry .....79 H 10
Littleham .....4 J 32
Littlehampton .....11 S 31
Littlemill .....79 I 11
Littleport .....30 U 26
Littlestone-on-Sea .....12 W 31
Littleton .....10 P 30
Littleworth .....20 P 28
Litton Cheney .....5 M 31
Liverpool .....42 L 23
Liverton .....50 R 20
Livet (Glen) .....80 K 12
Livingston .....61 J 16
Lizard .....2 E 34
Lizard Peninsula .....2 E 33
Llam .....35 O 24
Llan .....33 J 26
Llan-non .....15 H 28
Llan-y-Bri .....15 G 28
Llanarmon-yn-Ial .....34 K 24
Llanarthne .....24 H 28
Llanarthney .....15 H 28
Llanasa .....41 J 23
Llanbadarn Fawr .....25 H 26
Llanbedr .....33 H 25
Llanbedr Pont Steffan /
  Lampeter .....15 H 27
Llanbedrog .....32 G 25
Llanberis .....33 H 24
Llanberis (Pass of) .....33 H 24
Llanbister .....26 K 26
Llanboidy .....15 G 28
Llanbradach .....18 K 29
Llanbrynmair .....33 J 26
Llanddarog .....15 H 28
Llanddeiniol .....25 H 27
Llandderfel .....33 J 25
Llanddeusant .....40 G 22

Llanddewi Brefi .....25 I 27
Llanddewi Ystradenni .....26 K 27
Llanddona .....40 H 23
Llanddowror .....15 G 28
Llanddulas .....41 J 23
Llandegla .....34 K 24
Llandeilo .....15 I 28
Llandenny .....18 L 28
Llandinam .....25 J 26
Llandissilio .....15 F 28
Llandogo .....18 L 28
Llandovery / Llanymddyfri .....25 I 28
Llandrindod Wells .....25 J 27
Llandrinio .....34 K 25
Llandudno .....41 I 23
Llandudno Junction .....41 I 23
Llandwrog .....32 H 24
Llandybie .....15 H 28
Llandyfaelog .....15 H 28
Llandygai .....40 H 23
Llandysul .....15 H 27
Llanegryn .....33 H 26
Llanelidan .....34 K 24
Llanellen .....18 K 28
Llanelli .....15 H 28
Llanelltyd .....33 I 25
Llanengan .....32 G 25
Llanerchymedd .....40 G 23
Llanerfyl .....33 J 25
Llanfachraeth .....40 G 23
Llanfaethlu .....40 G 22
Llanfair .....33 H 25
Llanfair-Caereinion .....34 K 26
Llanfair-Pwllgwyngyll .....40 H 23
Llanfair-ym-Muallt /
  Builth Wells .....25 J 27
Llanfair-yn-Neubwll .....40 G 23
Llanfairfechan .....41 I 23
Llanfairynghornwy .....40 G 22
Llanfechell .....40 G 22
Llanferres .....34 K 24
Llanfihangel-ar-arth .....15 H 27
Llanfihangel Glyn Myfyr .....33 J 24
Llanfihangel Nant Bran .....25 J 28
Llanfihangel Rhyditon .....26 K 27
Llanfihangel-y-Creuddyn .....25 I 26
Llanfilo .....26 K 28
Llanfoist .....18 K 28
Llanfrynach .....25 J 28
Llanfwrog .....40 G 23
Llanfyllin .....34 K 25
Llanfynydd *Carmarthenshire /
  Sir Gaerfyrddin* .....15 H 28
Llanfynydd *Flintshire /
  Sir y Fflint* .....34 K 24
Llanfyrnach .....15 G 28
Llangadfan .....33 J 25
Llangadog .....25 I 28
Llangain .....15 G 28
Llangammarch Wells .....25 J 27
Llangarron .....26 L 28
Llangathen .....15 H 28
Llangedwyn .....34 K 25
Llangefni .....40 H 23
Llangeinor .....17 J 29
Llangeitho .....25 H 27
Llangeler .....15 G 27
Llangenith .....15 H 29
Llangennech .....15 H 28
Llangernyw .....33 I 24
Llangoed .....40 H 23
Llangollen .....34 K 25
Llangorse .....26 K 28
Llangorwen .....25 H 26
Llangrannog .....15 G 27
Llangunllo .....26 K 27
Llangunnor .....15 H 28
Llangurig .....25 J 26
Llangwm *Monmouthshire /
  Sir Fynwy* .....18 L 28
Llangwm *Pembrokeshire /
  Sir Benfro* .....16 F 28
Llangwyryfon .....25 H 27
Llangybi .....15 H 27
Llangyndeyrn .....15 H 28
Llangynidr .....26 K 28
Llangynog *Carmarthenshire /
  Sir Gaerfyrddin* .....15 G 28
Llangynog *Powys* .....33 J 25
Llangynwyd .....17 J 29
Llangywer .....33 J 25
Llanharan .....17 J 29
Llanharry .....17 J 29
Llanhilleth .....18 K 28
Llanidloes .....25 J 26

Llanilar .....25 H 26
Llanishen .....18 K 28
Llanllwchaiarn .....26 K 26
Llanllyfni .....32 H 24
Llanmadoc .....15 H 29
Llannefydd .....41 J 23
Llanon .....25 H 27
Llanpumsaint .....15 H 28
Llanrhaeadr .....33 J 24
Llanrhaeadr-ym-
  Mochnant .....34 K 25
Llanrhidian .....15 H 29
Llanrhystud .....25 H 27
Llanrug .....33 H 24
Llanrwst .....33 I 24
Llansanffraid Glan Conwy .....41 I 23
Llansannan .....33 J 24
Llansantffraid .....25 H 27
Llansantffraid-ym-Mechain .....34 K 25
Llansawel .....15 H 27
Llansilin .....34 K 25
Llansoy .....18 L 28
Llansteffan .....15 G 28
Llanthony .....26 K 28
Llanthony Priory .....26 K 28
Llantilio Crossenny .....18 L 28
Llantrisant .....17 J 29
Llantwit Major .....17 J 29
Llanuwchllyn .....33 I 25
Llanvetherine .....18 L 28
Llanwddyn .....33 J 25
Llanwenog .....15 H 27
Llanwnda .....32 H 24
Llanwnen .....15 H 27
Llanwnog .....25 J 26
Llanwrda .....25 I 28
Llanwrin .....33 I 26
Llanwrtyd Wells .....25 J 27
Llanwyddelan .....33 J 26
Llanybydder .....15 H 27
Llanychaer .....24 F 28
Llanymawddwy .....33 J 25
Llanymddyfri / Llandovery .....25 I 28
Llanymynech .....34 K 25
Llanynghenedl .....40 G 23
Llanystumdwy .....32 H 25
Llawhaden .....15 F 28
Llechryd .....15 G 27
Lledrod .....25 I 27
Lleyn Peninsula .....32 G 25
Llithfaen .....32 G 25
Llowes .....26 K 27
Llston .....15 H 29
Llwydafydd .....24 G 27
Llwyngwril .....33 H 25
Llwynmawr .....34 K 25
Llyfnant Valley .....33 I 26
Llyn Brianne .....25 I 27
Llyn Celyn .....33 I 25
Llyn Tegid or Bala Lake .....33 J 25
Llyswen .....26 K 27
Llysworney .....17 J 29
Llywel .....25 J 28
Loanhead .....61 K 16
Lochailort .....72 D 13
Lochaline .....65 C 14
Lochans .....52 E 19
Locharbriggs .....53 J 18
Lochawe .....66 E 14
Lochay (Glen) .....67 G 14
Lochboisdale .....70 Y 12
Lochbuie .....65 C 14
Lochcarron .....78 D 11
Lochdonhead .....65 C 14
Lochdrum .....78 F 10
Lochearnhead .....67 H 14
Locheport .....76 Y 11
Locherben .....61 J 18
Lochfoot .....53 I 18
Lochgair .....65 D 15
Lochgarthside .....73 G 12
Lochgelly .....68 K 15
Lochgilphead .....65 D 15
Lochgoilhead .....66 F 15
Lochinver .....84 E 9
Lochluichart .....78 F 11
Lochmaben .....54 J 18
Lochmaddy .....76 Y 11
Lochore .....68 K 15
Lochportain .....76 Y 11
Lochranza .....59 E 16
Lochsie (Glen) .....74 J 13
Lochstack .....84 F 8
Lochton *Aberdeenshire* .....75 M 12
Lochton *South Ayrshire* .....52 F 18
Lochtyn / Ynys .....15 G 27

Lochuisge .....72 D 14
Lochwinnoch .....60 G 16
Lochy (Loch) .....72 F 13
Lockerbie .....54 J 18
Lockerley .....9 P 30
Locking .....18 L 30
Loddington .....28 R 26
Loddon .....39 Y 26
Lode .....30 U 27
Lodsworth .....11 R 31
Lofthouse .....49 O 21
Loftus .....50 R 20
Logan Gardens .....52 F 19
Loggerheads .....35 M 25
Logie Coldstone .....74 L 12
Logiealmond .....67 I 14
Login .....15 F 28
Lomond (Loch) .....66 G 15
Londesborough .....51 R 22
London .....21 T 29
London Colney .....21 T 28
Long (Loch) *Angus* .....68 K 14
Long (Loch)
  Argyll and Bute .....66 F 15
Long Ashton .....18 M 29
Long Bennington .....36 R 25
Long Bredy .....5 M 31
Long Buckby .....28 Q 27
Long Clawson .....36 R 25
Long Crendon .....20 R 28
Long Eaton .....36 Q 25
Long Hanborough .....20 P 28
Long Itchington .....28 P 27
Long Lawford .....28 Q 26
Long Man (The) .....12 U 31
Long Marston .....50 Q 22
Long Marton .....55 M 20
Long Melford .....30 W 27
Long Mountain .....34 K 26
Long Mynd (The) .....26 L 26
Long Preston .....49 N 21
Long Stratton .....31 X 26
Long Sutton *Lincs.* .....37 U 25
Long Sutton *Somerset* .....8 L 30
Long Wittenham .....20 Q 29
Longay .....77 C 12
Longbenton .....56 P 18
Longborough .....27 O 28
Longbridge Deverill .....9 N 30
Longburton .....8 M 31
Longcot .....19 P 29
Longdon .....35 O 25
Longfield .....22 U 29
Longford
  Derbyshire Dales .....35 O 25
Longford *Tewkesbury* .....27 N 28
Longforgan .....68 K 14
Longformacus .....62 M 16
Longham .....38 W 25
Longhirst .....56 P 18
Longhorsley .....56 O 18
Longhoughton .....63 P 17
Longleat House .....19 N 30
Longmanhil .....81 M 11
Longnewton .....50 P 20
Longney .....19 M 28
Longniddry .....69 L 16
Longnor .....35 O 24
Longridge *Ribble Valley* .....42 M 22
Longridge
  South Staffordshire .....35 N 25
Longridge *West Lothian* .....61 I 16
Longside .....81 O 11
Longstanton .....29 U 27
Longton *South Ribble* .....42 L 22
Longton *Stoke-on-Trent* .....35 N 25
Longtown *Carlisle* .....54 L 18
Longtown *Herefordshire* .....26 L 28
Longwick .....20 R 28
Longworth .....20 P 28
Lonmore .....77 A 11
Loose .....22 V 30
Loppington .....34 L 25
Lorn .....65 E 14
Lorn (Firth of) .....65 D 14
Lossiemouth .....80 K 10
Lostwithiel .....3 G 32
Lothbeg .....85 I 9
Lothersdale .....49 N 22
Lothmore .....85 I 9
Loudwater .....21 R 29
Loughborough .....36 Q 25
Loughor (River) .....17 H 29
Loughton .....21 U 29
Louth .....45 U 23
Lovington .....8 M 30

Low Bradley .....49 O 22
Low Crosby .....55 L 19
Low Row *Carlisle* .....55 M 19
Low Row *Richmondshire* .....49 N 20
Low Street .....39 Y 25
Lowca .....53 J 20
Lowdham .....36 Q 24
Lower Beeding .....11 T 30
Lower Bentham .....49 M 21
Lower Boddington .....28 Q 27
Lower Broadheath .....27 N 27
Lower Cam .....19 M 28
Lower Diabaig .....78 C 11
Lower Dounreay .....85 I 8
Lower Dunsforth .....50 Q 21
Lower Halstow .....22 W 29
Lower Hardres .....23 X 30
Lower Heyford .....28 Q 28
Lower Killeyan .....58 B 17
Lower Largo .....69 L 15
Lower Mayland .....22 W 28
Lower Peover .....42 M 24
Lower Upham .....10 Q 31
Lower-Whitley .....42 M 24
Lowestoft .....31 Z 26
Lowgill .....49 M 21
Lowick
  Berwick-upon-Tweed .....63 O 17
Lowick
  East Northamptonshire .....29 S 26
Lowick Bridge .....48 K 21
Lowther .....55 L 20
Lowther Hills .....61 J 18
Loxwood .....11 S 30
Loyal (Loch) .....84 G 8
Lùb Score .....77 A 10
Lubcroy .....84 F 10
Lubenham .....28 R 26
Lubnaig (Loch) .....67 H 15
Luccombe .....17 J 30
Luce Bay .....52 F 19
Lucker .....63 O 17
Luddesdown .....22 V 29
Ludford *East Lindsey* .....45 T 23
Ludford *South Shropshire* .....26 L 26
Ludgershall *Bucks* .....20 Q 28
Ludgershall *Wilts* .....19 P 30
Ludgvan .....2 D 33
Ludham .....39 Y 25
Ludlow .....26 L 26
Luib *Highland* .....77 B 12
Luib *Stirling* .....67 G 14
Luichart (Loch) .....78 F 11
Luing .....65 D 15
Lullington .....35 P 25
Lulsgate Bottom .....18 L 29
Lulworth Cove .....9 N 32
Lumphanan .....75 L 12
Lumsden .....80 L 12
Lunan .....75 M 14
Lunanhead .....74 L 14
Luncarty .....68 J 14
Lund .....51 S 22
Lundie .....68 K 14
Lundie (Loch) .....78 C 11
Lundin Links .....69 L 15
Lundy .....16 G 30
Lunning .....87 Q 2
Lurgainn (Loch) .....84 E 9
Lurgashall .....11 S 30
Luskentyre .....82 Z 10
Luss .....66 G 15
Lusta .....77 A 11
Lustleigh .....4 I 32
Luston .....26 L 27
Luthermuir .....75 M 13
Luthrie .....68 K 14
Luton .....29 S 28
Luton Hoo .....21 S 28
Lutterworth .....28 Q 26
Lutton .....37 U 25
Luxborough .....7 J 30
Lybster .....86 K 9
Lydbury North .....26 L 26
Lydd .....12 W 31
Lydd-on-Sea .....12 W 31
Lydden .....23 X 30
Lydeard-St. Lawrence .....8 K 30
Lydford *Mendip* .....8 M 30
Lydford *West Devon* .....4 H 32
Lydiard Millicent .....19 O 29
Lydiard Park .....19 O 29
Lydiate .....42 L 23
Lydlinch .....9 M 31

Lydney .... 18 M 28
Lydstep .... 15 F 29
Lyme Bay .... 5 L 32
Lyme Park .... 43 N 23
Lyme Regis .... 5 L 31
Lyminge .... 13 X 30
Lymington .... 10 P 31
Lymm .... 42 M 23
Lympne .... 13 X 30
Lympstone .... 4 J 32
Lyndhurst .... 10 P 31
Lyne .... 61 K 17
Lyneham *North Wiltshire* ..... 19 O 29
Lyneham
    West Oxfordshire ....27 P 28
Lynemouth .... 56 P 18
Lyness .... 86 K 7
Lynmouth .... 17 I 30
Lynton .... 17 I 30
Lyon (Glen) .... 73 H 14
Lyonshall .... 26 L 27
Lytchett Matravers .... 9 N 31
Lytchett Minster .... 9 N 31
Lytes Cary .... 8 L 30
Lyth .... 86 K 8
Lytham .... 42 L 22
Lytham St. Anne's ....42 K 22
Lythe .... 51 R 20

M

Maaruig .... 82 Z 10
Mabie .... 53 J 18
Mablethorpe .... 45 U 23
Macaskin (Island) ....65 D 15
Macclesfield .... 43 N 24
Macduff .... 81 M 10
Machars (The) .... 52 G 19
Machen .... 18 K 29
Machir Bay .... 58 A 16
Machrihanish .... 58 C 17
Machrihanish Bay ....58 C 17
Machynlleth .... 33 I 26
Madderty .... 67 I 14
Maddiston .... 67 I 16
Maddy (Loch) .... 76 Y 11
Madeley *Staffs* .... 35 M 24
Madeley
    Telford and Wrekin ....35 M 26
Madingley .... 29 U 27
Madron .... 2 D 33
Maenclochog .... 15 F 28
Maentwrog .... 33 I 25
Maerdy *Conwy* .... 33 J 25
Maerdy
    Rhondda, Cynon, Taf ..17 J 28
Maes Howe .... 86 K 7
Maesbrook .... 34 K 25
Maesteg .... 17 J 29
Maghull .... 42 L 23
Magor .... 18 L 29
Maiden Bradley .... 9 N 30
Maiden Castle .... 8 M 31
Maiden Newton .... 8 M 31
Maidenhead .... 20 R 29
Maidens .... 59 F 17
Maidford .... 28 Q 27
Maids Morelon .... 28 R 27
Maidstone .... 22 V 30
Maidwell .... 28 R 26
Mainland *Orkney Islands* ..86 J 6
Mainland *Shetland Islands* .87 R 3
Mainstone .... 26 K 26
Maisemore .... 27 N 28
Malborough .... 4 I 33
Maldon .... 22 W 28
Malham .... 49 N 21
Mallaig .... 71 C 12
Mallory Park Circuit ....36 P 26
Mallwyd .... 33 I 25
Malmesbury .... 19 N 29
Malpas .... 34 L 24
Maltby .... 44 Q 23
Maltby-le-Marsh .... 45 U 24
Malton .... 50 R 21
Malvern Wells .... 27 N 27
Mamble .... 26 M 26
Mamore Forest .... 72 F 13
Man (Isle of) .... 46 G 21
Manaccan .... 2 E 33
Manaton .... 4 I 32
Manchester .... 43 N 23
Manderston .... 62 N 16
Manea .... 29 U 26
Mangersta .... 82 Y 9
Mangotsfield .... 18 M 29
Manish .... 76 Z 10
Manningford Bruce ....19 O 30

Mannings Heath .... 11 T 30
Manningtree .... 31 X 28
Manorbier .... 15 F 29
Mansfield .... 36 Q 24
Mansfield Woodhouse ....36 Q 24
Manstone .... 9 N 31
Manton .... 36 R 26
Manuden .... 30 U 28
Maplebeck .... 36 R 24
Mapledurham .... 20 Q 29
Mappleton .... 45 T 22
Mappowder .... 9 M 31
Mar (Forest of) .... 74 J 12
Marazion .... 2 D 33
March .... 37 U 26
Marcham .... 20 P 29
Marchington .... 35 O 25
Marchwood .... 10 P 31
Marden .... 22 V 30
Maree (Loch) .... 78 D 10
Mareham-le-Fen .... 37 T 24
Maresfield .... 11 U 31
Margam .... 17 I 29
Margaretting .... 22 V 28
Margate .... 23 Y 29
Margnaheglish .... 59 E 17
Marham .... 38 V 26
Marhamchurch .... 6 G 31
Marholm .... 37 T 26
Marian-Glas .... 40 H 22
Marishader .... 77 B 11
Mark *Sedgemoor* .... 18 L 30
Mark *South Ayrshire* ....52 E 18
Market Bosworth .... 36 P 26
Market Deeping .... 37 T 25
Market Drayton .... 34 M 25
Market Harborough ....28 R 26
Market Lavington ....19 O 30
Market Overton .... 36 R 25
Market Rasen .... 45 T 23
Market Weighton .... 44 S 22
Markfield .... 36 Q 25
Markinch .... 68 K 15
Marks Tey .... 30 W 28
Marksbury .... 18 M 29
Markyate .... 21 S 28
Marlborough .... 19 O 29
Marldon .... 4 J 32
Marlesford .... 31 Y 27
Marloes .... 14 E 28
Marlow .... 20 R 29
Marnhull .... 9 N 31
Marple .... 43 N 23
Marros .... 15 G 28
Marsden .... 43 O 23
Marsett .... 49 N 21
Marsh Gibbon .... 28 Q 28
Marsham .... 39 X 25
Marshaw .... 48 M 22
Marshchapel .... 45 U 23
Marshfield
    Casnewydd / Newport ..18 K 29
Marshfield
    South Gloucestershire ..19 N 29
Marshwood .... 8 L 31
Marske .... 49 O 20
Marske-by-the-Sea ....57 Q 20
Marston .... 20 Q 28
Marston .... 37 R 25
Marston Magna .... 8 M 31
Marston Moretaine ....29 S 27
Martham .... 39 Y 25
Martin *New Forest* .... 9 O 31
Martin *North Kesteven* ..37 T 24
Martin (Isle) .... 84 E 10
Martin Mill .... 23 Y 30
Martindale .... 48 L 20
Martinstown .... 5 M 31
Martlesham .... 31 X 27
Martletwy .... 15 F 28
Martley .... 27 M 27
Martock .... 8 L 31
Marton *Harrogate* .... 50 P 21
Marton *Macclesfield* ....35 N 24
Marvig .... 82 A 9
Marwell Zoological Park ..10 Q 31
Mary Arden's House ....27 O 27
Mary Tavy .... 4 H 32
Marybank .... 79 G 11
Maryburgh .... 79 G 11
Maryculter .... 75 N 12
Maryfield .... 87 Q 3
Marykirk .... 75 M 13
Marypark .... 80 J 11
Maryport *Allerdale* .... 53 J 19
Maryport
    Dumfries and Galloway ..52 F 19

Marywell *Aberdeenshire* ..75 L 12
Marywell *Angus* .... 69 M 14
Masham .... 49 P 21
Matching Green .... 22 U 28
Mathry .... 14 E 28
Matlock .... 36 P 24
Matlock Bath .... 35 P 24
Mattersey .... 44 R 23
Mattingley .... 20 R 30
Mattishall .... 38 X 26
Mauchline .... 60 G 17
Maud .... 81 N 11
Maughold .... 46 H 21
Maughold Head .... 46 H 21
Mawbray .... 54 J 19
Mawnan .... 2 E 33
Maxstoke .... 27 P 26
Maxton .... 62 M 17
Maybole .... 60 F 17
Mayfield *East Sussex* ....12 U 30
Mayfield *Staffs* .... 35 O 24
Mc Arthur's Head ....58 B 16
Meadie (Loch) .... 84 G 9
Meal Bank .... 48 L 20
Mealsgate .... 54 K 19
Meare .... 8 L 30
Measach (Falls of) .... 78 E 10
Measham .... 36 P 25
Meavaig .... 82 Z 10
Meavy .... 4 H 32
Medbourne .... 28 R 26
Medmenham .... 20 R 29
Medstead .... 10 Q 30
Medway (River) .... 22 W 29
Meidrim .... 15 G 28
Meifod .... 34 K 25
Meigle .... 68 K 14
Meikleour .... 68 J 14
Meikle Ferry .... 79 H 10
Melbost .... 83 B 9
Melbourne
    East Riding of Yorkshire ..44 R 22
Melbourne
    South Derbyshire ....36 P 25
Melbury Osmond .... 8 M 31
Meldon .... 56 O 18
Melfort .... 65 D 15
Melgarve .... 73 G 12
Melksham .... 19 N 29
Melldalloch .... 65 E 16
Mellerstain .... 62 M 17
Melling .... 48 M 21
Mellon Charles .... 78 D 10
Mellon Udrigle .... 78 D 10
Mells .... 19 M 30
Melmerby *Eden* .... 55 M 19
Melmerby *Harrogate* ....50 P 21
Melrose .... 62 L 17
Meltham .... 43 O 23
Melton .... 31 X 27
Melton Mowbray .... 36 R 25
Melvaig .... 77 C 10
Melvich .... 85 I 8
Memsie .... 81 N 11
Menai Bridge /
    Porthaethwy .... 40 H 23
Menai Strait .... 33 H 24
Mendip Hills .... 18 L 30
Mendlesham .... 31 X 27
Menheniot .... 3 G 32
Mennock .... 61 I 17
Menston .... 43 O 22
Menstrie .... 67 I 15
Menteith Hills .... 67 H 15
Mentmore .... 29 R 28
Meonstoke .... 10 Q 31
Meopham .... 22 V 29
Mepal .... 29 U 26
Mere *Cheshire* .... 42 M 24
Mere *Wilts* .... 9 N 30
Mereworth .... 22 V 30
Meriden .... 27 P 26
Merkland Lodge .... 84 F 9
Mermaid Inn .... 32 H 24
Merrick .... 52 G 18
Merriott .... 8 L 31
Merrow .... 62 K 18
Mersey (River) .... 42 M 23
Merthyr Cynog .... 25 J 27
Merthyr Tydfil .... 17 J 28
Merton *Cherwell* .... 20 Q 28
Merton *Devon* .... 7 H 31
Merton *London Borough* ..21 T 29
Meshaw .... 7 I 31
Messing .... 30 W 28
Messingham .... 44 S 23
Metfield .... 31 Y 26

Metheringham .... 37 S 24
Methil .... 69 K 15
Methlick .... 81 N 11
Methven .... 68 J 14
Methwold .... 38 V 26
Mevagissey .... 3 F 33
Mexborough .... 44 Q 23
Mhòr (Loch) .... 73 G 12
Miavaig .... 82 Z 9
Michaelchurch Escley ..26 L 27
Michaelstow .... 3 F 32
Micheldever .... 10 Q 30
Michelham Priory .... 12 U 31
Micklefield .... 44 Q 22
Mickleover .... 36 P 25
Mickleton *Cotswold* ....27 O 27
Mickleton *Teesdale* ....55 N 20
Mid Ardlaw .... 81 N 10
Mid Calder .... 61 J 16
Mid Lavant .... 10 R 31
Mid Sannox .... 59 E 17
Mid Yell .... 87 Q 2
Middle Barton .... 28 P 28
Middle Rasen .... 45 S 23
Middle Tysoe .... 28 P 27
Middle Wallop .... 9 P 30
Middle Woodford .... 9 O 30
Middleham .... 49 O 21
Middlebie .... 54 K 18
Middlesbrough .... 57 Q 20
Middlestown .... 43 P 23
Middleton *Argyll and Bute* ..64 Z 14
Middleton
    Berwick-upon-Tweed ..63 O 17
Middleton *Bradford* ....49 O 22
Middleton *Gtr. Mches* ..43 N 23
Middleton Cheney ....28 Q 27
Middleton-in-Teesdale ..55 N 20
Middleton-on-Sea ....11 S 31
Middleton on the Wolds ..51 S 22
Middleton St. George ..50 P 20
Middleton Tyas .... 49 P 20
Middletown *Powys* ....34 K 25
Middlewich .... 35 M 24
Middlegeholme .... 55 M 19
Midhurst .... 10 R 31
Midlem .... 62 L 17
Midsomer Norton .... 18 M 30
Midtown .... 78 C 10
Miefield .... 53 H 19
Migdale (Loch) .... 79 H 10
Milborne Port .... 8 M 31
Milborne St. Andrew ..9 N 31
Milbourne .... 56 O 18
Milburn .... 55 M 20
Mildenhall *Forest Heath* ..30 V 26
Mildenhall *Kennet* ....19 O 29
Mile End .... 30 W 28
Milfield .... 63 N 17
Milford .... 11 S 30
Milford Haven /
    Aberdaugleddau ....14 E 28
Milford-on-Sea .... 9 P 31
Milland .... 10 R 30
Millbrook .... 3 H 32
Millhouse .... 59 E 16
Millmeece .... 35 N 25
Millom .... 47 K 21
Millport .... 59 F 16
Milltown
    Dumfries and Galloway ..54 K 18
Milltown *Highland* .... 78 F 11
Milltown *Moray* .... 80 L 11
Milnathort .... 68 J 15
Milngavie .... 67 H 16
Milnrow .... 43 N 23
Milnthorpe .... 48 L 21
Milovaig .... 76 Z 11
Milton .... 79 H 10
Milton *Cambs* .... 29 U 27
Milton *Carlisle* .... 55 L 19
Milton *Dumfries* .... 53 I 18
Milton *Highland* .... 79 G 11
Milton *Stranraer* .... 52 F 19
Milton Abbas .... 9 N 31
Milton Abbot .... 3 H 32
Milton Bryan .... 29 S 28
Milton Ernest .... 29 S 27
Milton Keynes .... 28 R 27
Milton Libourne .... 19 O 29
Milton of Campsie ....67 H 16
Milton of Cushnie ....75 L 12
Milton-on-Stour .... 9 N 30
Miltonduff .... 80 J 11
Miltown of Edinvillie ..80 K 11
Milverton .... 8 K 30

Milwich .... 35 N 25
Minard .... 65 E 15
Minch (The) .... 83 C 9
Minehead .... 17 J 30
Minety .... 19 O 29
Mingary .... 76 X 12
Minginish .... 77 B 12
Mingulay .... 70 X 13
Minnigaff .... 52 G 19
Minster *near Sheerness* ..22 W 29
Minster *near Ramsgate* ..23 X 29
Minsterley .... 34 L 26
Minsterworth .... 19 N 28
Minting .... 45 T 24
Mintlaw .... 81 O 11
Minto .... 62 L 17
Mirfield .... 43 O 22
Miserden .... 19 N 28
Misson .... 44 R 23
Misterton *Notts* .... 44 R 23
Misterton *Somerset* ....8 L 31
Mistley .... 31 X 28
Mitcham .... 21 T 29
Mitcheldean .... 26 M 28
Mitchell .... 2 E 32
Mitford .... 56 O 18
Mithcam .... 21 T 29
Mithian .... 2 E 33
Moaness .... 86 K 7
Mochdre .... 41 I 23
Mochrum .... 52 G 19
Modbury .... 4 I 32
Moelfre .... 40 H 22
Moffat .... 61 J 17
Moidart .... 72 C 13
Moira .... 36 P 25
Mol-Chlach .... 71 B 12
Mold / Yr Wyddgrug ....34 K 24
Molland .... 7 I 30
Monach Islands .... 76 W 11
Monadhliath Mountains ..73 H 12
Monar (Loch) .... 78 E 11
Monaughty Forest ....80 J 11
Moneydie .... 68 J 14
Moniaive .... 53 I 18
Monifieth .... 69 L 14
Monikie .... 69 L 14
Monk Fryston .... 44 Q 22
Monkland .... 26 L 27
Monkokehampton ....7 H 31
Monks Eleigh .... 30 W 27
Monksilver .... 7 K 30
Monkton .... 60 G 17
Monmouth / Trefynwy ..18 L 28
Monreith .... 52 G 19
Montacute .... 8 L 31
Montgarrie .... 75 L 12
Montgomery / Trefaldwyn ..34 K 26
Montrose .... 75 M 13
Monyash .... 35 O 24
Monymusk .... 75 M 12
Monzie .... 67 I 14
Moonen Bay .... 76 Z 11
Moor Monkton .... 50 Q 21
Moorends .... 44 R 23
Moorfoot Hills .... 61 K 16
Moors (The) .... 52 F 19
Moortown .... 45 S 23
Morar .... 71 C 13
Moray Firth .... 79 H 11
Morchard Bishop .... 7 I 31
Morcott .... 37 S 26
Morden .... 9 N 31
Mordiford .... 26 M 27
More (Glen) .... 65 C 14
More (Loch) *near Kinloch* ..84 F 9
More (Loch)
    near Westerdale .... 85 J 8
Morebath .... 7 J 30
Morebattle .... 62 M 17
Morecambe .... 48 L 21
Morecambe Bay .... 48 L 21
Moresby .... 53 J 20
Moreton *Epping Forest* ..22 U 28
Moreton *Purbeck* .... 9 N 31
Moreton-in-Marsh ....27 O 28
Moreton-on-lugg .... 26 L 27
Moreton Say .... 34 M 25
Moretonhampstead ....4 I 32
Morfa Nefyn .... 32 G 25
Moricambe Bay .... 54 K 19
Morie (Loch) .... 79 G 10
Moriston (Glen) .... 72 F 12
Morland .... 55 M 20
Morley .... 43 P 22
Morlich (Loch) .... 74 I 12

Morpeth .... 56 O 18
Morriston .... 17 I 29
Morte Bay .... 6 H 30
Mortehoe .... 16 H 30
Mortimer .... 20 Q 29
Morton *near Bourne* ....37 S 25
Morton
    near Gainsborough ....44 R 23
Morton
    North East Derbyshire ..36 P 24
Morton on Swale ....50 P 21
Morval .... 3 G 32
Morven .... 85 I 9
Morvern .... 71 C 14
Morvich .... 72 D 12
Morville .... 34 M 26
Morwelham .... 3 H 32
Morwenstow .... 6 G 31
Mosborough .... 43 P 24
Moss Bank .... 42 L 23
Mossdale .... 53 H 18
Mossend .... 60 H 16
Mossley .... 43 N 23
Mosstodloch .... 80 K 11
Mostyn .... 41 K 23
Motherwell .... 61 I 16
Moulin .... 74 I 13
Moulton *Forest Heath* ..30 V 27
Moulton *Lincs* .... 37 T 25
Moulton *Northants* ....28 R 27
Moulton Chapel .... 37 T 25
Mount Pleasant .... 9 P 31
Mount's Bay .... 2 D 33
Mountsorrel .... 36 Q 25
Mousa .... 87 Q 4
Mousehole .... 2 D 33
Mouswald .... 54 J 18
Mow Cop .... 35 N 24
Mowtie .... 75 N 13
Moy .... 79 H 11
Muasdale .... 59 C 17
Much Dewchurch ....26 L 28
Much Hadham .... 29 U 28
Much Hoole .... 42 L 22
Much Marcle .... 26 M 28
Much Wenlock .... 34 M 26
Muchalls .... 75 N 12
Muchelney .... 8 L 30
Muchrachd .... 78 F 11
Muck .... 71 B 13
Muckle Roe .... 87 P 2
Mucklestone .... 35 M 25
Muddiford .... 7 H 30
Mudford .... 8 M 31
Mugeary .... 77 B 11
Muick (Loch) .... 74 K 13
Muie .... 85 H 9
Muir of Fowlis .... 75 L 12
Muir of Ord .... 79 G 11
Muirhead .... 69 L 14
Muirhead .... 60 H 16
Muirkirk .... 60 H 17
Muirshearlich .... 72 E 13
Muker .... 49 N 20
Mulbarton .... 39 X 26
Mull (Isle of) .... 64 B 14
Mull (Sound of) .... 71 C 14
Mull of Galloway ....52 F 20
Mull of Oa .... 58 A 17
Mullardoch (Loch) ....78 E 12
Mullardoch House ....78 F 11
Mullion .... 2 E 33
Mumbles (The) .... 15 H 29
Mumby .... 45 U 24
Mundesley .... 39 Y 25
Mundford .... 30 V 26
Mundham .... 10 R 31
Munlochy .... 79 H 11
Munlochy Bay .... 79 H 11
Munslow .... 26 L 26
Murlaggan .... 72 E 13
Murrayfield .... 68 K 16
Mursley .... 28 R 28
Murton *Easington* .... 57 P 19
Murton *Eden* .... 55 M 20
Musbury .... 5 K 31
Musselburgh .... 68 K 16
Muston .... 51 T 21
Muthill .... 67 I 15
Mwnt .... 15 G 27
Mybster .... 85 J 8
Myddfai .... 25 I 28
Myddle .... 34 L 25

A B C D E F G H I J K L M N O P Q R S T U V W X Y Z

A B C D E F G H I J K L M N O P Q R S T U V W X Y Z

Mydroilyn 15 H 27
Mynach Falls 25 I 26
Mynachlog-ddu 15 F 28
Mynydd Eppynt 25 J 27
Mynydd Mawr 32 F 25
Mynydd Preseli 15 F 28
Myrelandhorn 86 K 8
Mytchett 21 R 30
Mytholmroyd 43 O 22

N

Na Cùiltean 58 C 16
Naburn 50 Q 22
Nacton 31 X 27
Nafferton 51 S 21
Nailsea 18 L 29
Nailstone 36 P 26
Nailsworth 19 N 28
Nairn 79 I 11
Nant (Loch) 65 E 14
Nant-y-Moch Reservoir 25 I 26
Nant-y-moel 17 J 29
Nantgwynant Valley 33 H 24
Nantwich 34 M 24
Nantyglo 18 K 28
Napton 28 Q 27
Narberth / Arberth 15 F 28
Narborough *Blaby* 36 Q 26
Narborough *Breckland* 38 V 25
Naseby 28 R 26
Nash Point 17 J 29
Nassington 37 S 26
Nateby 49 M 20
National Exhibition Centre 27 O 26
National Motor Museum 10 P 31
Naunton 27 O 28
Navenby 37 S 24
Naver (Loch) 84 G 9
Nayland 30 W 28
Naze (The) 31 X 28
Neap 87 Q 3
Neath / Castell-nedd 17 I 29
Neath (River) 17 I 28
Nebo 33 I 24
Necton 38 W 26
Needham Market 31 X 27
Needingworth 29 T 27
Needles (The) 10 P 32
Nefyn 32 G 25
Neidpath Castle 61 K 17
Neilston 60 G 16
Neist Point 76 Z 11
Nelson
Caerffili / Caerphilly 18 K 29
Nelson *Pendle* 43 N 22
Nene (River) 37 T 26
Nenthead 55 M 19
Nercwys 34 K 24
Nereabolls 58 A 16
Ness 83 B 8
Ness (Loch) 73 G 12
Nesscliffe 34 L 25
Nestley Marsh 10 P 31
Neston 42 K 24
Nether Broughton 36 R 25
Nether Kellet 48 L 21
Nether Langwith 44 Q 24
Nether Stowey 8 K 30
Nether Wasdale 47 J 20
Nether Whitecleuch 61 I 17
Netheravon 19 O 30
Netherbrae 81 M 11
Netherbury 8 L 31
Netherend 18 M 28
Netherhampton 9 O 30
Nethermill 54 J 18
Netherthong 43 O 23
Netherton 63 N 17
Nethertown 86 K 7
Netherwitton 56 O 18
Nethy Bridge 74 J 12
Netley 10 P 31
Nettlebed 20 R 29
Nettleham 44 S 24
Nettleton 45 T 23
Nevern 15 F 27
Nevis (Glen) 72 E 13
Nevis (Loch) 72 C 12
New Abbey 53 J 19
New Aberdour 81 N 11
New Alresford 10 Q 30
New Buckenham 31 X 26
New Byth 81 N 11
New Clipstone 36 Q 24
New Cumnock 60 H 17
New Deer 81 N 11
New Edlington 44 Q 23
New Forest National Park 9 P 31
New Galloway 53 H 18
New Holland 45 S 22
New Hythe 22 V 30
New Leeds 81 N 11
New Luce 52 F 19
New Marske 57 Q 20
New Mills 43 O 23
New Mills *Powys* 33 K 26
New Milton 9 P 31
New Pitsligo 81 N 11
New Quay / Ceinewydd 24 G 27
New Rackheat 39 Y 26
New Radnor 26 K 27
New Romney 12 W 31
New Rossington 44 Q 23
New Sauchie 67 I 15
New Scone 68 J 14
New Silksworth 57 P 19
New Tredegar 18 K 28
New Waltham 45 T 23
Newark-on-Trent 36 R 24
Newbiggin *Eden* 55 L 19
Newbiggin *Teesdale* 55 N 20
Newbiggin-by-the-Sea 56 P 18
Newbigging *Angus* 69 L 14
Newbigging
South Lanarkshire 61 J 16
Newbold Verdon 36 P 26
Newborough
East Staffordshire 35 O 25
Newborough
Isle of Anglesey 32 G 24
Newbridge *Caerffili /*
Caerphilly 18 K 29
Newbridge *Isle of Wight* 10 P 31
Newbridge-on-Wye 25 J 27
Newbrough 55 N 18
Newburgh *Aberdeenshire* 81 N 12
Newburgh *Fife* 68 K 14
Newburgh *Lancashire* 42 L 23
Newburn 56 O 19
Newbury 20 Q 29
Newby Bridge 48 L 21
Newby Hall 50 P 21
Newcastle *Monmouthshire /*
Sir Fynwy 18 L 28
Newcastle
South Shropshire 26 K 26
Newcastle Emlyn /
Castell Newydd Emlyn 15 G 27
Newcastle-under-Lyme 35 N 24
Newcastle-upon-Tyne 56 P 19
Newcastle-upon-Tyne
Airport 56 O 18
Newcastleton 55 L 18
Newchapel 15 G 27
Newchurch *Carmarthenshire /*
Sir Gaerfyrddin 15 G 28
Newchurch *Isle of Wight* 10 Q 32
Newchurch *Powys* 26 K 27
Newchurch *Shepway* 12 W 30
Newdigate 11 T 30
Newent 27 M 28
Newgale 14 E 28
Newhall 34 M 24
Newham *Isle of Wight* 63 O 17
Newham *London Borough* 21 U 29
Newhaven 11 U 31
Newick 11 U 31
Newington 22 V 29
Newland 18 M 28
Newlyn 2 D 33
Newmachar 75 N 12
Newmains 61 I 16
Newmarket *Isle of Lewis* 82 A 9
Newmarket *Suffolk* 30 V 27
Newmill *Moray* 80 L 11
Newmill *Scottish Borders* 62 L 17
Newmilns 60 G 17
Newnham *Daventry* 28 Q 27
Newnham *Glos.* 18 M 28
Newnham *Kent* 22 W 30
Newnham *Bridge* 26 M 27
Newport *Essex* 30 U 28
Newport *I.O.W.* 10 Q 31
Newport *Pembrokes* 15 F 27
Newport *Stroud* 19 M 28
Newport
Telford and Wrekin 35 M 25
Newport /
Casnewydd *Newport* 18 L 29
Newport-on-Tay 69 L 14
Newport Pagnell 28 R 27
Newquay 2 E 32
Newsham 49 O 20
Newstead 36 Q 24
Newstead Abbey 36 Q 24
Newton *Aberdeenshire* 81 O 11
Newton *Argyll and Bute* 65 E 15
Newton *Babergh* 30 W 27
Newton *Moray* 80 J 11
Newton *Ribble Valley* 49 M 22
Newton *Rushcliffe* 36 R 25
Newton Abbot 4 J 32
Newton Arlosh 54 K 19
Newton-Aycliffe 56 P 20
Newton Ferrers 4 H 33
Newton Flotman 39 X 26
Newton-le-Willows 42 M 23
Newton Longville 28 R 28
Newton Mearns 60 H 16
Newton-on-Rawcliffe 50 R 21
Newton-on-Trent 44 R 24
Newton Poppleford 5 K 31
Newton Reigny 55 L 19
Newton St. Cyres 7 J 31
Newton Stewart 52 G 19
Newton Tracey 7 H 30
Newton Wamphray 54 J 18
Newtongrange 61 K 16
Newtonhill 75 N 12
Newtonmore 73 H 12
Newtown *Cheshire* 43 N 23
Newtown *Heref.* 26 M 27
Newtown *Highland* 73 F 12
Newtown *Isle of Man* 46 G 21
Newtown /
Drenewydd *Powys* 26 K 26
Newtown Linford 36 Q 25
Newtown St. Boswells 62 L 17
Newtyle 68 K 14
Neyland 16 F 28
Nicholaston 15 H 29
Nigg 79 H 10
Nigg Bay 79 H 10
Nine Ladies 35 P 24
Ninebanks 55 M 19
Ninfield 12 V 31
Nisbet 62 M 17
Nith (River) 53 J 19
Niths 61 I 18
Niton 10 Q 32
Nocton 37 S 24
Nolton 14 E 28
Nordelph 38 U 26
Norfolk Broads 39 Y 25
Norham 63 N 16
Normanby 50 R 21
Normandy 21 S 30
Normanton 43 P 22
Normanton-on-the-Wolds 36 Q 25
North Baddesley 10 P 31
North Ballachulish 72 E 13
North Berwick 69 L 15
North Bovey 4 I 32
North Bradley 19 N 30
North Brentor 4 H 32
North Cadbury 8 M 30
North Cave 44 S 22
North-Cerney 19 O 28
North-Charlton 63 O 17
North Cliffe 44 R 22
North Cowton 50 P 20
North Crawley 29 S 27
North Creake 38 W 25
North Curry 8 L 30
North Dalton 51 S 22
North Deighton 50 P 22
North Erradale 77 C 10
North Esk (Riv.) 75 L 13
North Fearns 77 B 11
North Foreland 23 Y 29
North Frodingham 51 T 22
North Grimston 51 R 21
North Harris 82 Z 10
North Hill 3 G 32
North Hinksey 20 Q 28
North Holmwood 21 T 30
North Hykeham 37 S 24
North Kelsey 45 S 23
North Kessock 79 H 11
North Kyme 37 T 24
North Leigh 20 P 28
North-Molton 7 I 30
North Morar 72 C 13
North Newbald 44 S 22
North Nibley 19 M 29
North Otterington 50 P 21
North Petherton 8 K 30
North Petherwin 6 G 31
North Rigton 50 P 22
North Ronaldsay 87 M 5
North-Scarle 36 R 24
North-Shian 65 D 14
North Shields 56 P 18
North Shore 42 K 22
North Somercotes 45 U 23
North Sound (The) 87 L 6
North Stainley 50 P 21
North Stainmore 49 N 20
North Sunderland 63 P 17
North Tamerton 6 G 31
North-Tawton 7 I 31
North Thoresby 45 T 23
North Tidworth 19 P 30
North Uist 76 X 11
North Walsham 39 Y 25
North Warnborough 20 R 30
North Water Bridge 75 M 13
North Weald Bassett 22 U 28
North Wootton 38 V 25
North York Moors
National Park 50 R 20
Northallerton 50 P 20
Northam 6 H 30
Northampton 28 R 27
Northaw 21 T 28
Northchapel 11 S 30
Northchurch 21 S 28
Northfleet 22 V 29
Northiam 12 V 31
Northleach 19 O 28
Northleigh 5 K 31
Northlew 7 H 31
Northop 34 K 24
Northrepps 39 Y 25
Northton 76 Y 10
Northumberland
National Park 63 N 18
Northwich 42 M 24
Northwold 38 V 26
Northwood 34 L 25
Norton *Daventry* 28 Q 27
Norton *Doncaster* 44 Q 23
Norton *Ryedale* 50 R 21
Norton *Tewkesbury* 27 N 28
Norton Disney 36 R 24
Norton Fitzwarren 8 K 30
Norton in Hales 35 M 25
Norton St. Philip 19 N 30
Norwich 39 X 26
Norwick 87 R 1
Noss (Isle of) 87 Q 3
Noss Head 86 K 8
Nottingham 36 Q 25
Nuffield 20 Q 29
Nunburnholme 51 R 22
Nuneaton 28 P 26
Nuneham Courtenay 20 Q 28
Nunney 19 M 30
Nunthorpe 50 Q 20
Nunton 76 X 11
Nutley 11 U 30
Nympsfield 19 N 28

O

Oa (The) 58 B 17
Oadby 36 Q 26
Oakamoor 35 O 24
Oakdale 18 K 28
Oakengates 35 M 25
Oakford 7 J 31
Oakham 36 R 25
Oakhill 18 M 30
Oakington 29 U 27
Oakley *Aylesbury Vale* 20 Q 28
Oakley *Bedfordshire* 29 S 27
Oakley *Fife* 68 J 15
Oaksey 19 N 29
Oakworth 43 O 22
Oare *Kennet* 19 O 29
Oare *Swale* 22 W 30
Oare *West Somerset* 17 I 30
Oathlaw 74 L 13
Oban 65 D 14
Occold 31 X 27
Ochil Hills 68 I 15
Ochiltree 60 G 17
Ockbrook 36 P 25
Ockle 71 C 13
Ockley 11 S 30
Odiham 20 R 30
Odland 18 M 29
Odstock 9 O 30
Offa's Dyke Path 26 K 26
Offord Cluny 29 T 27
Ogbourne St. Andrew 19 O 29
Ogbourne St. George 19 O 29
Ogil 74 L 13
Ogle 56 O 18
Ogmore-by-Sea 17 J 29
Ogmore Vale 17 J 29
Oich (Loch) 73 F 12
Oidhche (Loch na h-) 78 D 11
Oigh-Sgeir 71 Z 13
Okeford Fitzpaine 9 N 31
Okehampton 4 H 31
Old Alresford 10 Q 30
Old Bolingbroke 37 U 24
Old Burghclere 20 Q 30
Old Castleton 55 L 18
Old Colwyn 41 I 23
Old Dailly 59 F 18
Old Deer 81 N 11
Old Fletton 37 T 26
Old Harry Rocks 9 O 32
Old Head 87 L 7
Old Hurst 29 T 26
Old Hutton 48 L 21
Old Kilpatrick 67 G 16
Old Knebworth 29 T 28
Old Leake 37 U 24
Old Man of Hoy 86 J 7
Old Man of Storr 77 B 11
Old Radnor 26 K 27
Old Rayne 81 M 11
Old' Sarum 9 O 30
Old Sodbury 19 M 29
Old Somerby 37 S 25
Old Warden 29 S 27
Old Windsor 21 S 29
Oldany Island 84 E 9
Oldbury 27 N 26
Oldbury on Severn 18 M 29
Oldcotes 44 Q 23
Oldham 43 N 23
Oldhamstocks 69 M 16
Oldmeldrum 81 N 11
Oldshoremore 84 E 8
Olgrinmore 85 J 8
Ollaberry 87 P 2
Ollach 77 B 11
Ollay (Loch) 76 X 12
Ollerton *Macclesfield* 42 M 24
Ollerton
Newark and Sherwood 36 Q 24
Olney 28 R 27
Olveston 18 M 29
Ombersley 27 N 27
Once Brewed 55 M 19
Onchan 46 G 21
Onecote 35 O 24
Onich 72 E 13
Onllwyn 17 I 28
Opinan 83 D 10
Orchy (Glen) 66 F 14
Ord 71 C 12
Ordie 74 L 12
Orford 31 Y 27
Orford Ness 31 Y 27
Orkney Islands 87
Orleton 26 L 27
Ormesby 50 Q 20
Ormesby St. Margaret 39 Z 25
Ormiston 62 L 16
Ormskirk 42 L 23
Oronsay 64 B 15
Orosay *near Fuday* 70 X 12
Orosay *near Lochboisdale* 70 X 12
Orphir 86 K 7
Orrin (Glen) 78 F 11
Orrin Reservoir 78 F 11
Orsay 58 A 16
Orsett 22 V 29
Orston 36 R 25
Orton 48 M 20
Orwell 29 T 27
Orwell (River) 31 X 28
Osborne House 10 Q 31
Osdale 77 A 11
Osgaig (Loch) 83 E 9
Osgodby 45 S 23
Oskaig 77 B 11
Osmington 9 M 32
Ossett 43 P 22
Ossington 36 R 24
Oswaldtwistle 42 M 22
Oswestry 34 K 25
Otford 22 U 30
Othery 8 L 30
Otley *Suffolk* 31 X 27
Otley *West Yorks.* 49 O 22
Otterbourne 10 P 30
Otterburn 55 N 18
Otternish 76 Y 10
Otterswick 87 Q 2
Otterton 5 K 32
Ottery St. Mary 5 K 31
Ottringham 45 T 22
Oulton Broad 39 Z 26
Oulton Park Circuit 34 M 24
Oundle 29 S 26
Ouse (River)
English Channel 11 T 30
Ouse (River) *North Sea* 50 Q 21
Out-Rawcliffe 42 L 22
Out Skerries 87 R 2
Outer Hebrides 82 Y 9
Outhgill 49 M 20
Outwell 38 U 26
Over 29 U 27
Over Compton 8 M 31
Overseal 35 P 25
Overstrand 39 Y 25
Overton *Hants.* 20 Q 30
Overton *Lancs.* 48 L 21
Overton *Wrexham* 34 L 25
Overtown 61 I 16
Ower 10 P 31
Owermoigne 9 N 32
Owlswick 20 R 28
Owslebury 10 Q 30
Owston 36 R 26
Owston Ferry 44 R 23
Oxburgh Hall 38 V 26
Oxen Park 48 K 21
Oxenhope 43 O 22
Oxford 20 Q 28
Oxnam 62 M 17
Oxted 21 T 30
Oxton
Newark and Sherwood 36 Q 24
Oxton *Scottish Borders* 62 L 16
Oxwich 15 H 29
Oxwich Bay 15 H 29
Oykel (Glen) 84 F 9
Oykel Bridge 84 F 10
Oyne 81 M 12

P

Pabay 77 C 12
Pabbay *near Harris* 76 Y 10
Pabbay *near Mingulay* 70 X 13
Pabbay (Sound of) 76 Y 10
Packington 36 P 25
Padbury 28 R 28
Paddock Wood 22 V 30
Paddockhole 54 K 18
Padiham 42 N 22
Padstow 3 F 32
Pagham 10 R 31
Paignton 4 J 32
Pailton 28 Q 26
Painscastle 26 K 27
Painswick 19 N 28
Paisley 60 G 16
Pakefield 31 Z 26
Palnackie 53 I 19
Pamber End 20 Q 30
Pandy
Monmouthshire / Sir Fynwy 26 L 28
Pandy *Powys* 33 J 26
Pangbourne 20 Q 29
Pant 34 K 25
Pantymenyn 15 F 28
Papa Stour 87 O 3
Papa Westray 87 L 5
Papplewick 36 Q 24
Paps of Jura 65 B 16
Papworth Everard 29 T 27
Parbh (The) 84 F 8
Parbold 42 L 23
Parc Cefn Onn 18 K 29
Parham House 11 S 31
Park Gate 10 Q 31
Park of Pairc 82 A 9
Parkeston 31 X 28
Parkgate 53 J 18
Parkhurst 10 Q 31
Parnham House 8 L 31
Parracombe 17 I 30
Parrett (River) 8 K 30
Parson Drove 37 U 26
Partney 37 U 24
Parton *Copeland* 54 J 20
Parton
Dumfries and Galloway 53 H 18
Partridge Green 11 T 31
Parwich 35 O 24
Patchway 18 M 29
Pateley Bridge 49 O 21
Path of Condie 68 J 15
Pathhead 62 L 16
Patna 60 G 17

Patrick .....46 F 21
Patrington .....45 T 22
Patrixbourne .....23 X 30
Patterdale .....48 L 20
Pattingham .....35 N 26
Pattishall .....28 Q 27
Paulerspury .....28 R 27
Paull .....45 T 22
Paulton .....18 M 30
Paxton .....63 N 16
Peacehaven .....11 T 31
Peak District
  National Park .....43 O 23
Pearsie .....74 K 13
Peasedown St. John .....19 M 30
Peasemore .....20 P 29
Peasenhall .....31 Y 27
Peaslake .....21 S 30
Peasmarsh .....12 W 31
Peat Inn .....69 L 15
Peatknowe .....81 M 11
Pebmarsh .....30 W 28
Pebworth .....27 O 27
Peebles .....61 K 17
Peel .....46 F 21
Peel Fell .....62 M 18
Pegswood .....56 P 18
Pegwell Bay .....23 Y 30
Peinchorran .....77 B 12
Peldon .....22 W 28
Pelton .....56 P 19
Pelynt .....3 G 32
Pembrey .....15 H 28
Pembridge .....26 L 27
Pembroke / Penfro .....16 F 28
Pembroke Dock /
  Doc Penfro .....16 F 28
Pembrokeshire Coast
  National Park .....15 F 29
Pembury .....12 V 30
Pen-y-bont / Bridgend .....17 J 29
Pen-y-groes .....32 H 24
Penalun .....15 F 29
Penarth .....18 K 29
Pencader .....15 H 27
Pencaitland .....62 L 16
Pencarrow .....3 F 32
Penclawdd .....15 H 29
Pencombe .....26 M 27
Penderyn .....17 J 28
Pendine .....15 G 28
Pendine Sands .....15 G 28
Pendlebury .....42 N 23
Pendoylan .....17 J 29
Penelewey .....2 E 33
Penfro / Pembroke .....16 F 28
Pengethley .....26 M 28
Penhow .....18 L 29
Penicuik .....61 K 16
Penifiler .....77 B 11
Peninver .....59 D 17
Penistone .....43 P 23
Penketh .....42 L 23
Penkridge .....35 N 25
Penley .....34 L 25
Penmaen .....15 H 29
Penmaenmawr .....41 I 23
Penmaenpool .....33 I 25
Penmark .....17 J 29
Penmon .....40 H 23
Pennal .....33 I 26
Pennant .....33 J 26
Pennerley .....34 L 26
Pennines (The) .....49 N 20
Pennyghael .....65 B 14
Penpont .....53 I 18
Penrhiwpal .....15 G 27
Penrhyn .....40 H 23
Penrhyn Bay .....41 I 23
Penrhyndeudraeth .....33 H 25
Penrith .....55 L 19
Penruddock .....55 L 20
Penryn .....2 E 33
Pensarn .....41 J 23
Penshaw .....56 P 19
Penshurst .....22 U 30
Pensilva .....3 G 32
Pentewan .....3 F 33
Pentire Point .....3 F 32
Pentland Firth .....86 K 7
Pentland Hills .....61 J 16
Pentland Skerries .....87 L 7
Pentraeth .....40 H 23
Pentre-Berw .....40 H 23
Pentre-Celyn .....34 K 24
Pentrebeirdd .....34 K 25
Penwith .....2 D 33

Penybont .....26 K 27
Penysarn .....40 H 22
Penzance .....2 D 33
Pernrhyn-Coch .....25 I 26
Perranaworthal .....2 E 33
Perranporth .....2 E 32
Perranzabuloe .....2 E 33
Pershore .....27 N 27
Pertenhall .....29 S 27
Perth .....68 J 14
Peterborough .....37 T 26
Peterculter .....75 N 12
Peterhead .....81 O 11
Peterlee .....57 P 19
Petersfield .....10 R 30
Peterstone Wentlooge .....18 K 29
Peterstow .....26 M 28
Petham .....23 X 30
Petrockstowe .....7 H 31
Pett .....12 V 31
Pettaugh .....31 X 27
Petworth .....11 S 31
Pevensey Bay .....12 V 31
Pewsey .....19 O 29
Pickering .....50 R 21
Picklescott .....34 L 26
Picton Castle .....16 F 28
Piddlehinton .....9 M 31
Piddletrenthide .....9 M 31
Piercebridge .....49 O 20
Pierowall .....86 L 6
Pilgrims Hatch .....22 U 29
Pillerton Hersey .....28 P 27
Pillerton Priors .....27 P 27
Pilley .....43 P 23
Pilling .....48 L 22
Pilning .....18 M 29
Pilton .....8 M 30
Pinchbeck .....37 T 25
Pinchbeck-West .....37 T 25
Pinhoe .....4 J 31
Pinmore Mains .....52 F 18
Pinner .....21 S 29
Pinvin .....27 N 27
Pinwherry .....52 F 18
Pirbright .....21 S 30
Pirnmill .....59 D 17
Pirton .....29 T 28
Pishill .....20 R 29
Pitcaple .....81 M 12
Pitcombe .....8 M 30
Pitcur .....68 K 14
Pitlochry .....74 I 13
Pitmedden .....81 N 11
Pitminster .....8 K 31
Pitscottie .....69 L 15
Pitsford .....28 R 27
Pittentrail .....85 H 10
Pittenweem .....69 L 15
Pladda .....59 E 17
Plaistow .....11 S 30
Plas Newydd *Anglesey* .....33 H 24
Plas Newydd
  Denbighshire .....34 K 25
Plean .....67 I 15
Pleasington .....42 M 22
Pleasley .....36 Q 24
Plenmeller .....55 M 19
Plockton .....78 D 11
Pluckley .....22 W 30
Plumbland .....54 K 19
Plumpton .....11 T 31
Plymouth .....4 H 32
Plympton .....4 H 32
Plymstock .....4 H 32
Plymtree .....7 J 31
Plynlimon
  (Pumlumon Fawr) .....25 I 26
Pocklington .....50 R 22
Point Lynas .....40 H 22
Point of Ayr *Flintshire* .....41 K 22
Point of Ayre *Isle of Man* .....46 G 20
Polbain .....83 D 9
Pole of Itlaw (The) .....81 M 11
Polebrook .....29 S 26
Polegate .....12 U 31
Polesden Lacey .....21 S 30
Polesworth .....35 P 26
Polkerris .....3 F 32
Polloch .....72 D 13
Pollock House .....60 H 16
Polmont .....67 I 16
Polperro .....3 G 33
Polruan .....3 G 33
Polwarth .....62 M 16
Pondersbridge .....29 T 26

Pont-ar-Gothi .....15 H 28
Pontardawe .....17 I 28
Pontarddulais .....15 H 28
Pontarfynach /
  Devil's Bridge .....25 I 26
Pontargothi .....15 H 28
Pontarsais .....15 H 28
Pontefract .....44 Q 22
Ponteland .....56 O 18
Ponterwyd .....25 I 26
Pontesbury .....34 L 26
Pontlottyn .....18 K 28
Pontlyfni .....32 G 24
Pontneddfechan .....17 J 28
Pontrhydfendigaid .....25 I 27
Pontrhydygroes .....25 I 26
Pontrilas .....26 L 28
Pontsticill .....17 J 28
Pontyates .....15 H 28
Pontyberem .....15 H 28
Pontyclun .....17 J 29
Pontycymer .....17 J 29
Pontypool / Pontypwl .....18 K 28
Pontypridd .....17 J 29
Pontypwl / Pontypool .....18 K 28
Poole .....9 O 31
Poole Bay .....9 O 31
Poolewe .....78 D 10
Pooley Bridge .....55 L 20
Pooltiel (Loch) .....76 Z 11
Porlock .....17 J 30
Port Appin .....65 D 14
Port Askaig .....58 B 16
Port Bannatyne .....59 E 16
Port Carlisle .....54 K 19
Port Charlotte .....58 A 16
Port Driseach .....65 E 16
Port Ellen .....58 B 17
Port Erin .....46 F 21
Port-Eynon .....15 H 29
Port-Eynon Point .....15 H 29
Port Gaverne .....3 F 32
Port Glasgow .....66 F 16
Port Henderson .....77 C 10
Port Isaac .....3 F 32
Port Lamont .....59 E 16
Port Logan .....52 F 19
Port Mór .....71 B 13
Port of Menteith .....67 H 15
Port of Ness .....83 B 8
Port Ramsay .....65 D 14
Port St. Mary .....46 F 21
Port Talbot .....17 I 29
Port William .....52 G 19
Portavadie .....59 E 16
Portchester .....10 Q 31
Portencross .....59 F 16
Portesham .....5 M 31
Portgordon .....80 K 11
Portgower .....85 I 9
Porth .....17 J 29
Porth Neigwl
  or Hell's Mouth .....32 G 25
Porth Tywyn /Burry Port .....15 H 28
Porthaethwy /
  Menai Bridge .....40 H 23
Porthcawl .....17 I 29
Porthcothan .....2 E 32
Porthcurno .....2 D 33
Porthgwarra .....2 C 33
Porthkerry .....17 K 29
Porthleven .....2 E 33
Porthmadog .....33 H 25
Porthtowan .....2 E 33
Porthyrhyd .....15 H 28
Portinnisherrich .....65 E 15
Portishead .....18 L 29
Portknockie .....80 L 10
Portland (Isle of) .....8 M 32
Portlethen .....75 N 12
Portmahomack .....79 I 10
Portmeirion .....33 H 25
Portnacroish .....72 D 14
Portnaguran .....83 B 9
Portnahaven .....58 A 16
Portnalong .....77 A 12
Portobello .....68 K 16
Portreath .....2 E 33
Portree .....77 B 11
Portscatho .....3 F 33
Portskerra .....85 I 8
Portskewett .....18 L 29
Portslade .....11 T 31
Portslogan .....52 E 19
Portsmouth .....10 Q 31
Portsoy .....81 L 10
Portuairk .....71 B 13

Postbridge .....4 I 32
Potten End .....21 S 28
Potter Heigham .....39 Y 25
Potter Street .....21 U 28
Potterhanworth .....37 S 24
Potterne .....19 N 30
Potters Bar .....21 T 28
Potton .....29 T 27
Poughill .....6 G 31
Poulshot .....19 N 29
Poulton .....19 O 28
Poulton-le-Fylde .....42 L 22
Poundstock .....6 G 31
Powburn .....63 O 17
Powerstock .....8 L 31
Powick .....27 N 27
Powis .....34 K 26
Powmill .....68 J 15
Poynings .....11 T 31
Poynton .....43 N 23
Praa Sands .....2 D 33
Prawle Point .....4 I 33
Praze-an-Beeble .....2 E 33
Prees .....34 M 25
Preesall .....48 L 22
Prendwick .....63 O 17
Prestatyn .....41 J 22
Prestbury *Cheltenham* .....27 N 28
Prestbury *Macclesfield* .....43 N 24
Presteigne .....26 K 27
Preston
  East Riding of Yorks. .....45 T 22
Preston *Kent* .....23 X 30
Preston *Lancs.* .....42 L 22
Preston *Rutland* .....36 R 26
Preston *West Sussex* .....11 S 31
Preston Candover .....10 Q 30
Preston Capes .....28 Q 27
Prestonpans .....69 L 16
Prestwich .....42 N 23
Prestwick .....60 G 17
Prestwood .....20 R 28
Prickwillow .....30 V 26
Priest Island .....83 D 10
Priest Weston .....34 K 26
Princes Risborough .....20 R 28
Princethorpe .....28 P 26
Priors Marston .....28 Q 27
Probus .....3 F 33
Prosen (Glen) .....74 K 13
Prudhoe .....56 O 19
Puckeridge .....29 U 28
Pucklechurch .....19 M 29
Pucks Gutter .....23 X 30
Puddletown .....9 M 31
Pudsey .....43 P 22
Pulborough .....11 S 31
Pulford .....34 L 24
Pulham .....9 M 31
Pulham Market .....31 X 26
Puncnardon .....7 H 30
Puncheston .....24 F 28
Purbeck (Isle of) .....9 N 32
Purbrook .....10 Q 31
Puriton .....8 L 30
Purleigh .....22 V 28
Purley .....20 Q 29
Purse Caundle Manor .....9 M 31
Purston Jaglin .....43 P 22
Purton .....19 O 29
Putsborough .....6 H 30
Pwllheli .....32 G 25
Pyecombe .....11 T 31
Pyle .....17 I 29
Pylle .....8 M 30

Q

Quainton .....28 R 28
Quantock Hills .....8 K 30
Quarff .....87 Q 3
Quarr .....10 Q 31
Quatt .....27 M 26
Quedgeley .....19 N 28
Queen Camel .....8 M 30
Queen Elizabeth
  Forest Park .....67 G 15
Queenborough .....22 W 29
Queensbury .....43 O 22
Queensferry .....34 K 24
Quendon .....30 U 28
Quenington .....19 O 28
Quinag .....84 E 9
Quines's Hill .....46 G 21
Quinish Point .....71 B 14
Quiraing .....77 B 11

Quoich (Loch) .....72 E 12
Quorndon .....36 Q 25
Quothquan .....61 J 17

R

Raasay (Island of) .....77 B 11
Raasay (Sound of) .....77 B 11
Raasay Ho .....77 B 11
Rachub .....33 H 24
Rackenford .....7 J 31
Rackwick .....86 J 7
Radcliffe .....42 N 23
Radcliffe-on-Trent .....36 Q 25
Radlett .....21 T 28
Radley .....20 Q 28
Radnor Forest .....26 K 27
Radstock .....18 M 30
Radyr .....18 K 29
Rafford .....80 J 11
Raglan .....18 L 28
Ragley Hall .....27 O 27
Rainford .....42 L 23
Rainham .....22 V 29
Rainworth .....36 Q 24
Rait .....68 K 14
Ramasaig .....76 Z 11
Rampisham .....8 M 31
Rampside .....47 K 21
Rampton .....44 R 24
Ramsbottom .....42 N 23
Ramsbury .....19 P 29
Ramsey *Cambs.* .....29 T 26
Ramsey *Isle of Man* .....46 G 21
Ramsey Bay .....46 G 21
Ramsey Island .....14 D 28
Ramsey St. Mary's .....29 T 26
Ramsgate .....23 Y 29
Ramsgill-in-Nidderdale .....49 O 21
Ranby .....44 Q 24
Ranfurly .....60 G 16
Rangeworthy .....18 M 29
Ranish .....82 A 9
Rankinston .....60 G 17
Rannoch (Loch) .....73 H 13
Rannoch Moor .....73 F 14
Rannoch Sta .....73 G 13
Ranskill .....44 Q 23
Ranton .....35 N 25
Ranworth .....39 Y 25
Rapness .....87 L 6
Rappach .....84 F 10
Ratby .....36 Q 26
Rathen .....81 O 11
Rathmell .....49 N 21
Ratho .....68 J 16
Ratlinghope .....34 L 26
Rattlesden .....30 W 27
Rattray .....68 K 14
Rattray Head .....81 O 11
Raunds .....29 S 26
Ravenglass .....47 J 20
Ravenscar .....51 S 20
Ravensthorpe .....28 Q 27
Ravenstone .....36 P 25
Ravenstonedale .....49 M 20
Ravensworth .....49 O 20
Rawcliffe .....44 R 22
Rawreth .....22 V 29
Rawmarsh .....44 P 23
Rawtenstall .....42 N 22
Rayleigh .....22 V 29
Rayne .....30 V 28
Read .....42 M 22
Reading .....20 R 29
Rearsby .....36 Q 25
Reay .....85 I 8
Reay Forest .....84 F 9
Reculver .....23 X 29
Red Wharf Bay .....40 H 23
Redbourn .....21 S 28
Redbourne .....44 S 23
Redbridge
  London Borough .....21 U 29
Redcar .....57 Q 20
Redcliff Bay .....18 L 29
Reddding .....67 I 16
Redditch .....27 O 27
Redesmouth .....55 N 18
Redford .....69 L 14
Redhill *North Somerset* .....18 L 29
Redhill
  Reigate and Banstead .....21 T 30
Redisham .....31 Y 26
Redmarley d'Abitot .....27 M 28
Redmarshall .....57 P 20
Redmire .....49 O 21
Redpoint .....77 C 11
Redruth .....2 E 33

Redwick .....18 L 29
Reedham .....39 Y 26
Reekie Linn .....74 K 13
Reepham .....45 S 24
Reeth .....49 O 20
Regarby .....46 G 20
Reiff .....83 D 9
Reigate .....21 T 30
Reighton .....51 T 21
Reiss .....86 K 8
Relubbus .....2 D 33
Rempstone .....36 Q 25
Rendcomb .....19 O 28
Rendham .....31 Y 27
Renfrew .....60 G 16
Renish Point .....76 Z 10
Renishaw .....44 P 24
Rennington .....63 O 17
Renton .....66 G 16
Renwick .....55 M 19
Rescobie .....75 L 14
Resipole .....72 C 13
Resolven .....17 I 28
Resort (Loch) .....82 Z 9
Restalrig .....68 K 16
Reston .....63 N 16
Restormel Castle .....3 G 32
Retford .....44 R 24
Rettendon .....22 V 29
Reynoldston .....15 H 29
Rhaeadr / Rhayader .....25 J 27
Rhaeadr Ddu .....33 I 25
Rhandirmwyn .....25 I 27
Rhayader / Rhaeadr .....25 J 27
Rheidol (Vale of) .....25 I 26
Rhenigidale .....82 Z 10
Rhian .....84 G 9
Rhiconich .....84 F 8
Rhigos .....17 J 28
Rhilochan .....85 H 9
Rhinns of Galloway (The) .....52 E 19
Rhinns of Kells .....53 G 18
Rhondda .....17 J 29
Rhoose .....17 J 29
Rhos .....17 I 28
Rhoscolyn .....40 G 23
Rhoscrowther .....14 E 28
Rhosllanerchrugog .....34 K 24
Rhosmaen .....25 I 28
Rhosneigr .....40 G 23
Rhossili .....15 H 29
Rhostyllen .....34 K 24
Rhosybol .....40 G 22
Rhu .....66 F 15
Rhuddlan .....41 J 23
Rhum .....71 A 13
Rhuthun / Ruthin .....34 K 24
Rhyd-Ddu .....33 H 24
Rhydaman / Ammanford .....15 I 28
Rhydcymerau .....15 H 27
Rhydd .....27 N 27
Rhyddhywel .....25 J 26
Rhydowen .....15 H 27
Rhyl .....41 J 23
Rhymmi / Rhymney .....18 K 28
Rhymney / Rhymmi .....18 K 28
Rhynie .....80 L 12
Ribble (River) .....49 N 22
Ribblesdale .....49 N 21
Ribchester .....42 M 22
Riber Castle .....36 P 24
Riccall .....44 Q 22
Riccarton .....60 G 17
Richards Castle .....26 L 27
Richborough .....23 X 30
Richmond .....49 O 20
Richmond-upon-Thames
  London Borough .....21 T 29
Rickarton .....75 N 13
Rickmansworth .....21 S 29
Ridgeway Cross .....27 M 27
Ridgeway Path (The) .....20 P 29
Ridsdale .....55 N 18
Rievaulx Abbey .....50 Q 21
Rigg .....77 B 11
Rigside .....61 I 17
Rillington .....51 R 21
Rimington .....49 N 22
Rimsdale (Loch) .....85 H 9
Ringford .....53 H 19
Ringmer .....11 U 31
Ringshall .....30 W 27
Ringstead
  East Northamptonshire .....29 S 26
Ringstead *King's Lynn
  and West Norfolk* .....38 V 25

A B C D E F G H I J K L M N O P Q R S T U V W X Y Z

134 Great Britain

Ringwood 9 O 31
Ringwould 23 Y 30
Rinnes (Glen) 80 K 11
Rinns of Islay 58 A 16
Rinns Point 58 A 16
Ripe 12 U 31
Ripley *Derbs.* 36 P 24
Ripley *North Yorks.* 50 P 21
Ripley *Surrey* 21 S 30
Riplingham 44 S 22
Ripon 50 P 21
Rippingale 37 S 25
Ripponden 43 O 22
Risabus 58 B 17
Risby 30 V 27
Risca 18 K 29
Risegate 37 T 25
Riseley 29 S 27
Rishton 42 M 22
Risplith 50 P 21
Ristol (Isle) 83 D 9
Roadside of Kinneff 75 N 13
Roag 77 A 11
Roag (Loch) 82 Z 9
Roan of Graigoch 60 F 18
Roberton
Dumfries and Galloway 61 I 17
Roberton
Scottish Borders 62 L 17
Robertsbridge 12 V 31
Robin Hood's Bay 51 S 20
Roby 42 L 23
Rocester 35 O 25
Rochdale 43 N 23
Roche 3 F 32
Rochester 22 V 29
Rochester
Northumberland 63 N 18
Rochford 22 W 29
Rock 3 F 32
Rockcliffe *Cumbria* 54 K 19
Rockcliffe
Dumfries and Galloway 53 I 19
Rockfield 18 L 28
Rockingham 28 R 26
Rode 19 N 30
Rode Heath 35 N 24
Rodel 76 Z 10
Rodmel 11 U 31
Rodney Stoke 18 L 30
Rogart 85 H 9
Rogerstone 18 K 29
Rogiet 18 L 29
Rokeby Hall 49 O 20
Rolleston *Notts.* 36 R 24
Rolleston-on-Dove *Staffs.* 35 P 25
Rolvenden 12 V 30
Romannobridge 61 J 16
Romiley 43 N 23
Romney Marsh 12 W 30
Romsey 10 P 31
Romsley 27 N 26
Rona (Island of) 77 C 11
Ronaldsway 46 G 21
Ronas Voe 87 P 2
Ronay 76 Y 11
Rookhope 55 N 19
Roos 45 T 22
Rootpark 61 I 16
Ropley 10 Q 30
Ropsley 37 S 25
Rora 81 O 11
Rora Head 86 J 7
Rosedale Abbey 50 R 20
Rosehearty 81 N 10
Rosemarket 16 F 28
Rosemarkie 79 H 11
Rosewell 61 K 16
Rosgill 48 L 20
Roshven 71 C 13
Rosley 54 K 19
Roslin 61 K 16
Rosliston 35 P 25
Rosneath 66 F 15
Ross
Berwick-upon-Tweed 63 O 17
Ross
Dumfries and Galloway 53 H 19
Ross of Mull 64 B 15
Ross-on-Wye 26 M 28
Rossall Point 48 K 22
Rossett 34 L 24
Rosudgeon 2 D 33
Rosyth 68 J 15
Rothbury 63 O 18
Rothbury Forest 63 O 18
Rotherfield 12 U 30
Rotherham 43 P 23
Rothersthorpe 28 R 27
Rothes 80 K 11
Rothesay 59 E 16
Rothienorman 81 M 11
Rothiesholm 87 M 6
Rothwell *Leeds.* 43 P 22
Rothwell *Northamp.* 28 R 26
Rotterspury 28 R 27
Rottingdean 11 T 31
Roughburn 73 F 13
Roughsike 55 L 18
Roughton 39 X 25
Rounton 50 P 20
Rousay 86 K 6
Rousdon 5 L 31
Routh 45 S 22
Rowardennan Lodge 66 G 15
Rowington 27 O 27
Rowland's Castle 10 R 31
Rowland's Gill 56 O 19
Rownhams 10 P 31
Rowsley 35 P 24
Roxburgh 62 M 17
Roxwell 22 V 28
Roy (Glen) 72 F 13
Royal Leamington Spa 28 P 27
Royal Military Academy 20 R 29
Royal Tunbridge Wells 12 U 30
Roybridge 72 F 13
Roydon *Essex* 21 U 28
Roydon *Norfolk* 31 X 26
Royston *Herts.* 29 T 27
Royston *South Yorks.* 43 P 23
Royton 43 N 23
Ruabon 34 K 25
Ruan High Lanes 3 F 33
Ruan Minor 2 E 34
Ruardean 18 M 28
Rubbha na Faing 58 A 16
Rubha a' Mhail 64 B 16
Rubha Còigeach 83 D 9
Rubha Dubh 70 Z 14
Rubha Hunish 77 A 10
Rubha na h-Easgainne 71 B 12
Rubha Réidh 77 C 10
Rubha Suisnish 71 B 12
Rubh'an Dùnain 71 A 12
Rudbaxton 24 F 28
Ruddington 36 Q 25
Rudgeway 18 M 29
Rudgwick 11 S 30
Rudha Ban 70 Y 12
Rudston 51 T 21
Rufford Old Hall 42 L 23
Rufforth 50 Q 22
Rugby 28 Q 26
Rugeley 35 O 25
Rumburgh 31 Y 26
Rumney 18 K 29
Runcorn 42 L 23
Runswick Bay 50 R 20
Runtaleave 74 K 13
Runwell 22 V 29
Rushall 19 O 30
Rushden 29 S 27
Ruskington 37 S 24
Rusland 48 K 21
Rusper 11 T 30
Ruspidge 18 M 28
Rustington 11 S 31
Ruswarp 51 S 20
Rutherglen 60 H 16
Ruthin / Rhuthun 34 K 24
Ruthven *Aberdeenshire* 80 L 11
Ruthven *Angus* 74 K 14
Ruthven *Highland* 79 I 11
Ruthven (Loch) 79 H 12
Ruthven Barracks 73 H 12
Ruthwell 54 J 19
Rutland Water 37 S 26
Ruyton
of the Eleven Towns 34 L 25
Ryal 56 O 18
Ryan (Loch) 52 E 19
Rycote 20 Q 28
Rydal 48 L 20
Ryde 10 Q 31
Rye 12 W 31
Ryhall 37 S 25
Ryhill 43 P 23
Ryhope 57 P 19
Ryton 56 O 19

S

Sabden 42 M 22
Sacriston 56 P 19
Sadberge 50 P 20
Saddell 59 D 17
Saddell Bay 59 D 17
Sadgill 48 L 20
Saffron Walden 30 U 27
Saham Toney 38 W 26
St. Abbs 63 N 16
St. Abb's Head 63 N 16
St. Agnes 2 E 33
St. Albans 21 T 28
St. Aldhelm's Head 9 N 32
St. Andrews 69 L 14
St. Ann's 54 J 18
St. Ann's Head 14 E 28
St. Arvans 18 L 29
St. Asaph 41 J 23
St. Athan 17 J 29
St. Austell 3 F 32
St. Bees 47 J 20
St. Bees Head 47 J 20
St. Blazey 3 F 32
St. Boswells 62 M 17
St. Breock 3 F 32
St. Breward 3 F 32
St. Briavels 18 M 28
St. Brides 14 E 28
St. Bride's Bay 14 E 28
St. Brides Major 17 J 29
St. Brides-Super-Ely 17 K 29
St. Bridge-Wentlooge 18 K 29
St. Buryan 2 D 33
St. Catherine's Point 10 Q 32
St. Clears / Sanclêr 15 G 28
St. Cleer 3 G 32
St. Columb Major 3 F 32
St. Combs 81 O 11
St. Cyrus 75 M 13
St. David's / Tyddewi 14 E 28
St. David's Head 14 D 28
St. Day 2 E 33
St. Dennis 3 F 32
St. Dogmaels 15 F 27
St. Dominick 3 H 32
St. Donats 17 J 29
St. Endellion 3 F 32
St. Erth 2 D 33
St. Ewe 3 F 33
St. Fagans 18 K 29
St. Fergus 81 O 11
St. Fillans 67 H 14
St. Florence 15 F 28
St. Gennys 6 G 31
St. Germans 3 H 32
St. Giles 7 H 31
St. Giles-on-the-Heath 6 H 31
St. Govan's Head 16 F 29
St. Harmon 25 J 26
St. Helen Auckland 56 O 20
St. Helens *I.O.W.* 10 Q 31
St. Helens *Merseyside* 42 L 23
St. Helier *Jersey* 5
St. Ishmael's 14 E 28
St. Issey 3 F 32
St. Ive 3 G 32
St. Ives *Cambs.* 29 T 27
St. Ives *Cornwall* 2 D 33
St. John's 46 G 21
St. John's Chapel 55 N 19
St. John's Loch 86 J 8
St. Jude 46 G 20
St. Just 2 C 33
St. Just in Roseland 2 F 33
St. Keverne 2 E 33
St. Kew 3 F 32
St. Leonards *Dorset* 9 O 31
St. Leonards *East Sussex* 12 V 31
St. Mabyn 3 F 32
St. Magnus Bay 87 P 2
St. Margaret's at Cliffe 23 Y 30
St. Margaret's Bay 23 Y 30
St. Margaret's Hope 87 L 7
St. Mark's 46 G 21
St. Martin's 34 K 25
St. Mary in the Marsh 12 W 30
St. Mary's *Orkney Islands* 86 L 7
St. Mary's
Perth and Kinross 73 I 14
St. Mary's-Bay 13 W 30
St. Mary's-Hoo 22 V 29
St. Mary's Loch 61 K 17
St. Mawes 2 E 33
St. Mawgan 3 F 32
St. Mellion 3 H 32
St. Mellons 18 K 29
St. Merryn 3 F 32
St. Michael Penkevil 2 E 33
St. Michael's Mount 2 D 33
St. Michaels-on-Wyre 42 L 22
St. Minver 3 F 32
St. Monans 69 L 15
St. Neot 3 G 32
St. Neots 29 T 27
St. Nicholas *Pembrokes* 14 E 28
St. Nicholas
Vale of Glamorgan 17 K 29
St. Nicholas-at-Wade 23 X 29
St. Ninian's Isle 87 P 4
St. Osyth 23 X 28
St. Patrick's Isle 46 F 21
St. Paul's Walden 29 T 28
St. Peter Port *Guernsey* 5
St. Peter's 23 Y 29
St. Pool 4 I 33
St. Stephen 3 F 32
St. Teath 3 F 32
St. Tudwal's Islands 32 G 25
St. Tudy 3 F 32
St. Vigeans 69 M 14
St. Wenn 3 F 32
St. Weonards 26 L 28
Salcombe 4 I 33
Salcombe Regis 5 K 31
Sale 42 N 23
Salehurst 12 V 31
Salen *Argyll and Bute* 65 C 14
Salen *Highland* 71 C 13
Salford 42 N 23
Salfords 21 T 30
Salhouse 39 Y 25
Saline 68 J 15
Salisbury 9 O 30
Salisbury Plain 19 O 30
Sallachy
Ben More Assybt 84 G 9
Sallachy
near Kyle of Lochalsh 78 D 12
Saltash 3 H 32
Saltburn 79 H 10
Saltburn-by-the-Sea 57 R 20
Saltcoats 59 F 17
Salter 48 M 21
Saltfleet 45 U 23
Saltford 18 M 29
Salthouse 38 X 25
Saltney 34 L 24
Salton 50 R 21
Samala 76 X 11
Samlesbury Old Hall 42 M 22
Sampford Courtenay 7 I 31
Sampford Peverell 7 J 31
Sanaigmore 58 A 16
Sanclêr / St. Clears 15 G 28
Sancreed 2 D 33
Sancton 44 S 22
Sand Side 47 K 21
Sanda Island 59 D 18
Sanday *Highland* 71 A 12
Sanday *Orkney Islands* 87 M 6
Sandbach 35 M 24
Sandbank 66 F 16
Sandbanks 9 O 31
Sandend 80 L 10
Sandford *Eden* 49 M 20
Sandford *Mid Devon* 7 J 31
Sandford *North Somerset* 18 L 30
Sandford
South Lanarkshire 60 H 17
Sandford Orcas 8 M 31
Sandgate 13 X 30
Sandgreen 53 H 19
Sandhaven 81 N 10
Sandhead 52 F 19
Sandhurst *Berks.* 20 R 29
Sandhurst *Kent* 12 V 30
Sandleigh 20 Q 28
Sandlins 31 Y 27
Sandness 87 P 3
Sandon
North Hertfordshire 29 T 28
Sandon *Stafford* 35 N 25
Sandown 10 Q 32
Sandray 70 X 13
Sandridge 21 T 28
Sandringham House 38 V 25
Sandsend 51 R 20
Sandwell 27 O 26
Sandwich 23 Y 30
Sandwick *Eden* 48 L 20
Sandwick *Eilean Siar* 76 Y 11
Sandwick *Shetland Islands* 87 Q 4
Sandwood Loch 84 E 8
Sandy 29 T 27
Sandygate 46 G 20
Sandyhills 53 I 19
Sanna 71 B 13
Sanquhar 61 I 17
Santon Downham 30 W 26
Santon Head 46 G 21
Sapperton 19 N 28
Saracen's Head 37 T 25
Sarclet 86 K 8
Sarisbury 10 Q 31
Sark *Channel I.* 5
Sarn Meyllteyrn 32 G 25
Sarre 23 X 29
Satley 56 O 19
Satterthwaite 48 K 21
Sauchen 75 M 12
Saughall 42 L 24
Saughtree 62 L 18
Saundersfoot 15 F 28
Saunderton 20 R 28
Sawbridgeworth 21 U 28
Sawrey 48 L 20
Sawston 29 U 27
Sawtry 29 T 26
Saxby 36 R 25
Saxilby 44 S 24
Saxlingham Nethergate 39 X 26
Saxmundham 31 Y 27
Saxtead Green 31 X 27
Scadavay (Loch) 76 Y 11
Scaddle (Glen) 72 D 13
Scafell Pikes 47 K 20
Scagglethorpe 50 R 21
Scalasaig 64 B 15
Scalby 51 S 21
Scaleby 55 L 19
Scalford 36 R 25
Scalloway 87 Q 3
Scalpay *Highland* 77 C 12
Scalpay *Western Isles* 77 A 10
Scamblesby 45 T 24
Scampton 44 S 24
Scaniport 79 H 11
Scapa Flow 86 K 7
Scarba 65 C 15
Scarborough 51 S 21
Scarcliffe 44 Q 24
Scardroy 78 F 11
Scarfskerry 86 K 8
Scarisbrick 42 L 23
Scarista 76 Y 10
Scarp 82 Y 9
Scavaig (Loch) 71 B 12
Scawby 44 S 23
Schiehallion 73 H 13
Scilly (Isles of) 2 B 34
Scone Palace 68 J 14
Scopwick 37 S 24
Scoraig 83 D 10
Scorton 50 P 20
Scotby 55 L 19
Scotch-Corner 49 P 20
Scothern 45 S 24
Scotlandwell 68 K 15
Scotney 12 V 30
Scotstown 72 D 13
Scotter 44 S 23
Scotton *Harrogate* 50 P 21
Scotton *Richmondshire* 49 O 20
Scottow 39 Y 25
Scourie 84 E 8
Scousburgh 87 Q 4
Scrabster 85 J 8
Scraptoft 36 Q 26
Scredington 37 S 25
Scridain (Loch) 64 B 14
Scruton 50 P 21
Sculthorpe 38 W 25
Scunthorpe 44 S 23
Sea Palling 39 Y 25
Seaford 12 U 31
Seaforth (Loch) 82 Z 10
Seaforth Head 82 A 9
Seagrave 36 Q 25
Seaham 57 P 19
Seale 21 R 30
Sealga (Loch na) 78 D 10
Seamer *Hambleton* 50 Q 20
Seamer *Scarborough* 51 S 21
Seamill 59 F 16
Seasalter 23 X 29
Seascale 47 J 20
Seaton *Allerdale* 53 J 20
Seaton *East Devon* 5 K 31
Seaton Carew 57 Q 20
Seaton Delaval 56 P 18
Seaton Delaval Hall 56 P 18
Seaton Ross 44 R 22
Seaton Sluice 56 P 18
Seave Green 50 Q 20
Seaview 10 Q 31
Sebergham 54 L 19
Sedbergh 49 M 21
Sedgebrook 36 R 25
Sedgley 27 N 26
Sedlescombe 12 V 31
Seend 19 N 29
Seething 39 Y 26
Seighford 35 N 25
Seil (Isle of) 65 D 15
Seilich (Loch an t-) 73 H 13
Selattyn 34 K 25
Selborne 10 R 30
Selby 44 Q 22
Selker Bay 47 J 21
Selkirk 62 L 17
Sellindge 13 W 30
Selmeston 12 U 31
Selsey 10 R 31
Selston 36 Q 24
Selworthy 17 J 30
Semley 9 N 30
Senghenydd 18 K 29
Sennen 2 C 33
Sennybridge 25 J 28
Sessay 50 Q 21
Settle 49 N 21
Seven Sisters
East Sussex 12 U 31
Seven Sisters
Neath and Port Talbot 17 I 28
Sevenhampton 27 O 28
Sevenoaks 22 U 30
Severn (River) 27 M 28
Severn Bridge 18 M 29
Severn Stoke 27 N 27
Sgibacleit (Loch) 82 A 9
Sgiwen 17 I 29
Sgurr Mór 78 E 10
Shader 82 A 8
Shaftesbury 9 N 30
Shalbourne 20 P 29
Shaldon 4 J 32
Shalfleet 10 P 31
Shalford 21 S 30
Shandon 66 F 15
Shanklin 10 Q 32
Shap 48 L 20
Shapinsay 87 L 6
Shapwick 8 L 30
Shardlow 36 P 25
Sharlston 43 P 23
Sharnbrook 29 S 27
Sharnford 28 Q 26
Sharperton 63 N 18
Sharpness 18 M 28
Shavington 34 M 24
Shaw *Gtr. Mches.* 43 N 23
Shaw *West Berkshire* 20 Q 29
Shaw *Wilts.* 19 N 29
Shawbost 82 Z 9
Shawbury 34 M 25
Shawford 10 Q 30
Shawhead 53 I 18
Shebbear 6 H 31
Shebster 85 I 8
Sheepwash 6 H 31
Sheepy Magna 36 P 26
Sheering 22 U 28
Sheerness 22 W 29
Sheffield 43 P 23
Sheffield Park 11 T 31
Shefford 29 S 27
Sheldon 19 N 29
Sheldon Manor 19 N 29
Sheldwich 22 W 30
Shell or Sealg (Loch) 82 A 9
Shelley 43 O 23
Shellingford 20 P 29
Shelsley Beauchamp 27 M 27
Shelton *Rushcliffe* 36 R 25
Shelton *South Norfolk* 31 X 26
Shelton Lock 36 P 25
Shelve 34 L 26
Shenley Church End 28 R 27
Shenstone 27 O 26
Shenval 80 K 11
Shepley 43 O 23
Sheppey (Isle of) 22 W 29
Shepreth 29 U 27
Shepshed 36 Q 25
Shepton Mallet 18 M 30
Sherborne *Cotswold* 19 O 28
Sherborne *West Dorset* 8 M 31
Sherborne St. John 20 Q 30
Sherburn *Durham* 56 P 19

A B C D E F G H I J K L M N O P Q R S T U V W X Y Z

Sherburn *Ryedale* ....51 S 21
Sherburn-in-Elmet ....44 Q 22
Shere ....21 S 30
Sherfield English ....9 P 31
Sheriff Hutton ....50 Q 21
Sheriffhales ....35 M 25
Sheringham ....39 X 25
Sherington ....28 R 27
Shernborne ....38 V 25
Sherston ....19 N 29
Sherwood Forest ....36 Q 24
Shetland Islands 87
Shevington ....42 L 23
Shiant (Sound of) ....82 A 10
Shiant Island ....82 A 10
Shiel (Glen) ....72 D 12
Shiel (Loch) ....72 D 13
Shieldaig *Loch Gairloch* .....78 C 10
Shieldaig *Loch Torridon* .....78 D 11
Shieldaig (Loch) ....78 C 11
Shieldhill ....67 I 16
Shifnal ....35 M 25
Shilbottle ....63 O 17
Shildon ....56 P 20
Shillay ....76 W 11
Shillingford ....7 J 30
Shillingstone ....9 N 31
Shillington ....29 S 28
Shilton *Rugby* ....28 P 26
Shilton *West Oxfordshire* .....19 P 28
Shimpling ....31 X 26
Shin (Loch) ....84 G 9
Shiney Row ....56 P 19
Shinfield ....20 R 29
Shipdham ....38 W 26
Shiplake ....20 R 29
Shipley *Salop* ....35 N 26
Shipley *West Yorks.* ....43 O 22
Shipston-on-Stour ....27 P 27
Shipton *Bridgnorth* ....26 M 26
Shipton *Cotswold* ....27 O 28
Shipton *Hambleton* ....50 Q 21
Shipton Moyne ....19 N 29
Shipton-under-Wychwood ..19 P 28
Shiptonthorpe ....44 R 22
Shira (Lochan) ....66 F 14
Shirebrook ....36 Q 24
Shiremoor ....56 P 18
Shirenewton ....18 L 29
Shirley *Derbyshire* ....35 O 25
Shirley *Solihull* ....27 O 26
Shoadoxhurst ....12 W 30
Shobdon ....26 L 27
Shoeburyness ....22 W 29
Shoreham ....11 T 31
Shorne ....22 V 29
Shotesham ....39 X 26
Shotley Bridge ....56 O 19
Shotley Gate ....31 X 28
Shottenden ....22 W 30
Shottermill ....10 R 30
Shotton Colliery ....57 P 19
Shotts ....61 I 16
Shouldham ....38 V 26
Shrewsbury ....34 L 25
Shrewton ....19 O 30
Shrivenham ....19 P 29
Shuna Sound ....65 D 15
Shurdington ....27 N 28
Shurrery ....85 J 8
Sibbertoft ....28 Q 26
Sibford Ferris ....28 P 27
Sible Hedingham ....30 V 28
Sibsey ....37 U 24
Sidbury ....5 K 31
Siddington ....19 O 28
Sidlington ....43 N 24
Sidford ....5 K 31
Sidinish ....76 Y 11
Sidlaw Hills ....68 K 14
Sidlesham ....10 R 31
Sidmouth ....5 K 31
Sighthill ....68 K 16
Sileby ....36 Q 25
Silecroft ....47 K 21
Silkstone ....43 P 23
Silloth ....54 J 19
Silsden ....49 O 22
Silver End ....30 V 28
Silverdale *Lancaster* ....48 L 21
Silverdale
 Newcastle-under-Lyme ....35 N 24
Silverstone ....28 Q 27
Silverstone Circuit ....28 Q 27
Silverton ....7 J 31
Simonburn ....55 N 18
Simonsbath ....7 I 30

Sinclair's Bay ....86 K 8
Sinclairston ....60 G 17
Singleton *Chichester* ....10 R 31
Singleton *Fylde* ....42 L 22
Sionascaig (Loch) ....84 E 9
Sissinghurst ....12 V 30
Sithney ....2 E 33
Sittingbourne ....22 W 29
Sixpenny Handley ....9 N 31
Skara Brae ....86 J 6
Skares ....60 H 17
Skeabost ....77 B 11
Skegness ....38 V 24
Skellingthorpe ....44 S 24
Skelmanthorpe ....43 P 23
Skelmersdale ....42 L 23
Skelmorlie ....59 F 16
Skelpick ....85 H 8
Skelton *Cleveland* ....50 R 20
Skelton *Cumbria* ....55 L 19
Skelwith Bridge ....48 K 20
Skene ....75 M 12
Skene (Loch of) ....75 M 12
Skenfrith ....26 L 28
Skeroblingarry ....59 D 17
Skerray ....85 H 8
Skervuile Lighthouse ....65 C 16
Skidby ....44 S 22
Skiddaw ....54 K 20
Skigersta ....83 B 8
Skilgate ....7 J 30
Skillington ....37 S 25
Skinburness ....54 J 19
Skipness ....59 D 16
Skipport (Loch) ....76 Y 12
Skipsea ....51 T 22
Skipton ....49 N 22
Skipton-on-Swale ....50 P 21
Skipwith ....44 R 22
Skirlaugh ....45 T 22
Skirling ....61 J 17
Skirwith ....55 M 19
Skirza ....86 K 8
Skokholm Island ....14 E 28
Skomer Island ....14 E 28
Skye (Isle of) ....77 B 12
Slaggyford ....55 M 19
Slaidburn ....49 M 22
Slaithwaite ....43 O 23
Slamannan ....67 I 16
Slapin (Loch) ....71 B 12
Slapton ....4 J 33
Sleaford ....37 S 25
Sleagill ....48 M 20
Sleat (Sound of) ....71 C 12
Sledmere ....51 S 21
Sleekburn ....56 P 18
Sleights ....51 S 20
Slickly ....86 K 8
Sligachan ....77 B 12
Sligachan (Loch) ....77 B 12
Slimbridge ....19 M 28
Slindon ....11 S 31
Slingsby ....50 R 21
Slochd ....79 I 12
Slockavullin ....65 D 15
Slough ....21 S 29
Sloy (Loch) ....66 F 15
Slumbay ....78 D 11
Slyne ....48 L 21
Smailholm ....62 M 17
Smailholm Tower ....62 M 17
Small Dole ....11 T 31
Small Hythe ....12 W 30
Smallfield ....11 T 30
Smarden ....12 W 30
Smart'Hill ....12 U 30
Smeatharpe ....8 K 31
Smedmore ....9 N 32
Smithfield ....55 L 19
Snaefell ....46 G 21
Snainton ....51 S 21
Snaith ....44 Q 22
Snape ....31 Y 27
Snetterton Circuit ....30 W 26
Snettisham ....38 V 25
Snitterfield ....27 O 27
Snizort (Loch) ....77 A 11
Snodland ....22 V 30
Snowdon / Yr Wyddfa ....33 H 24
Snowdonia National Park ..33 I 24
Snowshill ....27 O 27
Soa ....70 Z 14
Soa Island ....64 A 15
Soar (River) ....36 Q 25
Soay ....71 B 12
Soay Sound ....71 B 12
Soham ....30 V 26

Solent (The) ....10 Q 31
Solihull ....27 O 26
Sollas ....76 X 11
Solva ....14 E 28
Solway Firth ....53 J 19
Somerby ....36 R 25
Somercotes ....36 P 24
Somerford Keynes ....19 O 29
Somersham
 Huntingdonshire ....29 U 26
Somersham *Mid Suffolk* .....31 X 27
Somerton *Norfolk* ....39 Y 25
Somerton *Oxon.* ....28 Q 28
Somerton *Somerset* ....8 L 30
Sompting ....11 S 31
Sonning Common ....20 R 29
Sopley ....9 O 31
Sorbie ....52 G 19
Sorisdale ....71 A 13
Sorn ....60 H 17
Sortat ....86 K 8
Soulby ....49 M 20
Sound (The) ....4 H 32
Sourhope ....63 N 17
South-Alloa ....67 I 15
South Balloch ....60 G 18
South Brent ....4 I 32
South Cairn ....52 E 19
South Carrine ....59 C 18
South Cave ....44 S 22
South Cerney ....19 O 28
South Charlton ....63 O 17
South Croxton ....36 R 25
South Downs ....11 R 31
South Elmsall ....44 Q 23
South Esk (River) ....75 L 13
South Ferriby ....44 S 22
South Foreland ....23 Y 30
South Glendale ....70 Y 12
South Hanningfield ....22 V 29
South Harris ....76 Z 10
South Harris Forest ....82 Z 10
South Hayling ....10 R 31
South-Heighton ....11 U 31
South Hetton ....56 P 19
South Kelsey ....45 S 23
South Killingholme ....45 T 23
South Kirkby ....44 Q 23
South Kyme ....37 T 24
South Lancing ....11 T 31
South Leverton ....44 R 24
South Lopham ....30 X 26
South-Marston ....19 O 29
South Mary Bourne ....20 P 30
South Mimms ....21 T 28
South Molton ....7 I 30
South Morar ....72 C 13
South Moreton ....20 Q 29
South Newington ....28 P 28
South-Newton ....9 O 30
South Normanton ....36 P 24
South Ockendon ....22 U 29
South Otterington ....50 P 21
South Oxhey ....21 S 29
South Petherton ....8 L 31
South Petherwin ....3 G 32
South Queensferry ....68 J 16
South Rauceby ....37 S 25
South Raynham ....38 W 25
South Ronaldsay ....87 L 7
South Shields ....56 P 19
South Shore ....42 K 22
South Stack ....40 F 23
South Stainley ....50 P 21
South Tawton ....4 I 31
South Thoresby ....45 U 24
South Uist ....70 X 12
South Walls ....86 K 7
South Warnborough ....20 R 30
South Witham ....37 S 25
South Woodham Ferrers ....22 V 29
South Wootton ....38 V 25
South Wraxall ....19 N 29
South Zeal ....4 I 31
Southam
 Stratford-on-Avon ....28 P 27
Southam *Tewkesbury* ....27 N 28
Southampton ....10 P 31
Southborough ....12 U 30
Southbourne *Dorset* ....9 O 31
Southbourne *West Sussex* ..10 R 31
Southend ....59 D 18
Southend-on-Sea ....22 W 29
Southerness ....53 J 19
Southery ....38 V 26
Southill ....29 T 27
Southminster ....22 W 29

Southport ....42 K 23
Southrop ....19 O 28
Southsea ....10 Q 31
Southwaite ....55 L 19
Southwater ....11 S 30
Southwell ....36 R 24
Southwick
 East Northamptonshire ..29 S 26
Southwick *Sunderland* ....56 P 19
Southwick *West Sussex* .....11 T 31
Southwick *Wilts.* ....19 N 30
Southwick *Widley* ....10 Q 31
Southwold ....31 Z 27
Sowerby Bridge ....43 O 22
Spalding ....37 T 25
Spaldwick ....29 S 26
Spanish Head ....46 F 21
Sparkford ....8 M 30
Spaxton ....8 K 30
Spean (Glen) ....73 F 13
Spean Bridge ....72 F 13
Speeton ....51 T 21
Speldhurst ....12 U 30
Spelsbury ....28 P 28
Spelve (Loch) ....65 C 14
Spennymoor ....56 P 19
Spey (River) ....73 G 12
Spey Bay ....80 K 10
Speymouth Forest ....80 K 11
Spilsby ....37 U 24
Spinningdale ....79 H 10
Spithead ....10 Q 31
Spittal *Dumfries
 and Galloway* ....52 G 19
Spittal *Highland* ....85 J 8
Spittal *Northumb.* ....63 O 16
Spittal *Pembrokeshire /
 Sir Benfro* ....24 F 28
Spittal of Glenshee ....74 J 13
Spixworth ....39 X 25
Spofforth ....50 P 22
Spondon ....36 P 25
Spooner Row ....39 X 26
Spott ....69 M 16
Spreyton ....7 I 31
Spridlington ....44 S 23
Springfield ....68 K 15
Springholm ....53 I 18
Sproatley ....45 T 22
Sprotbrough ....44 Q 23
Sproughton ....31 X 27
Sprouston ....62 M 17
Sprowston ....39 X 26
Spurn Head ....45 U 23
Sronlairig Lodge ....73 G 12
Sronphadruig Lodge ....73 H 13
Stack (Loch) ....84 F 8
Stack Island ....70 Y 12
Stack Rocks ....16 E 29
Staffa ....64 A 14
Staffin Bay ....77 B 11
Stagsden ....29 S 27
Staincross ....43 P 23
Staindrop ....56 O 20
Staines ....21 S 29
Stainforth *North Yorks.* .....49 N 21
Stainforth *South Yorks.* .....44 Q 23
Stainton ....55 L 20
Stainton-le-Vale ....45 T 23
Staintondale ....51 S 20
Stair *Allerdale* ....54 K 20
Stair *South Ayrshire* ....60 G 17
Staithes ....50 R 20
Stakeford ....56 P 18
Stalbridge ....9 M 31
Stalham ....39 Y 25
Stalisfield ....22 W 30
Stalling Busk ....49 N 21
Stallingborough ....45 T 23
Stalmine ....48 L 22
Stalybridge ....43 N 23
Stamford ....37 S 26
Stamford Bridge ....50 R 22
Stamfordham ....56 O 18
Stanbridge ....29 S 28
Standford-in-the-Vale ....20 P 29
Standing Stones ....82 Z 9
Standish ....42 M 23
Standlake ....20 P 28
Standon ....29 U 28
Stane ....61 I 16
Stanford ....13 X 30
Stanford-le-Hope ....22 V 29
Stanford-on-Avon ....28 Q 26
Stanghow ....50 R 20
Stanhoe ....38 W 25

Stanhope ....55 N 19
Stanion ....29 S 26
Stanley *Durham* ....56 O 19
Stanley
 Perthshire and Kinross ..68 J 14
Stanley *Wakefield* ....43 P 22
Stanmer Park ....11 T 31
Stannington ....43 P 23
Stansted Abbotts ....21 U 28
Stansted Mountfitchet ....30 U 28
Stanton ....30 W 27
Stanton Harcourt ....20 P 28
Stanton Long ....26 M 26
Stanton-upon-Hine-Heath ..34 M 25
Stanway ....27 O 28
Stanwell ....21 S 29
Stanwick ....29 S 27
Staple Fitzpaine ....8 K 31
Stapleford *Melton* ....36 R 25
Stapleford *Notts.* ....36 Q 25
Stapleford *Wilts.* ....9 O 30
Staplehurst ....22 V 30
Starcross ....4 J 32
Start Point ....4 J 33
Startforth ....49 O 20
Stathern ....36 R 25
Staughton Highway ....29 S 27
Staunton *Forest of Dean* ...27 N 28
Staunton *Monmouthshire /
 Sir Fynwy* ....18 M 28
Staveley *Cumbria* ....48 L 20
Staveley *Derbs.* ....43 P 24
Staxigoe ....86 K 8
Staxton ....51 S 21
Staylittle ....25 J 26
Steart ....18 K 30
Stebbing ....30 V 28
Stedham ....10 R 31
Steep ....10 R 30
Steeple ....22 W 28
Steeple Ashton ....19 N 30
Steeple Aston ....28 Q 28
Steeple Barton ....28 P 28
Steeple Bumpstead ....30 V 27
Steeple Claydon ....28 R 28
Steeple Langford ....9 O 30
Steeple Morden ....29 T 27
Steeton ....49 O 22
Stelling Minnis ....23 X 30
Stenhousemuir ....67 I 15
Stenness *Orkney Islands* ....86 K 7
Stenness *Shetland Islands* ..87 P 2
Stenton ....69 M 16
Steppingley ....29 S 27
Stevenage ....29 T 28
Stevenston ....60 F 17
Steventon ....20 Q 29
Stewartby ....29 S 27
Stewarton ....60 G 16
Stewkley ....28 R 28
Steyning ....11 T 31
Steynton ....16 E 28
Stichill ....62 M 17
Sticker ....3 F 33
Sticklepath ....4 I 31
Stickney ....37 U 24
Stiffkey ....38 W 25
Stilligarry ....76 X 12
Stillingfleet ....44 Q 22
Stillington *Hambleton* ....50 Q 21
Stillington
 Stockton-on-Tees ....56 P 20
Stilton ....29 T 26
Stirling ....67 I 15
Stithians ....2 E 33
Stob Choire Claurigh ....72 F 13
Stobo ....61 K 17
Stobs Castle ....62 L 17
Stock ....22 V 29
Stockbridge ....10 P 30
Stocke Talmage ....20 Q 28
Stockland ....8 K 31
Stockland Bristol ....18 K 30
Stockport ....43 N 23
Stocksbridge ....43 P 23
Stocksfield ....56 O 19
Stockton Heath ....42 M 23
Stockton-on-Tees ....50 P 20
Stockton-on-Teme ....27 M 27
Stockton on the Forest ....50 R 22
Stoer ....83 D 9
Stogumber ....7 K 30
Stogursey ....18 K 30
Stoke ....22 V 29
Stoke Albany ....28 R 26
Stoke Ash ....31 X 27
Stoke-by-Nayland ....30 W 28

Stoke Climsland ....3 H 32
Stoke Fleming ....4 J 33
Stoke Gabriel ....4 J 32
Stoke Goldington ....28 R 27
Stoke Hammond ....28 R 28
Stoke Lacy ....26 M 27
Stoke Lyne ....28 Q 28
Stoke Mandeville ....20 R 28
Stoke Orchard ....27 N 28
Stoke Poges ....21 S 29
Stoke-St. Mary ....8 K 31
Stoke-St. Michael ....18 M 30
Stoke St. Milborough ....26 M 26
Stoke sub Hamdon ....8 L 31
Stokeham ....44 R 24
Stokenchurch ....20 R 29
Stokenham ....4 I 33
Stokesay ....26 L 26
Stokesley ....50 Q 20
Stone *Bucks.* ....20 R 28
Stone *Staffs.* ....35 N 25
Stone Edge ....36 P 24
Stonehaugh ....55 N 18
Stonehaven ....75 N 13
Stonehenge ....9 O 30
Stonehouse *Glos.* ....19 N 28
Stonehouse
 South Lanarkshire ....61 I 16
Stoneleigh ....28 P 26
Stonesfield ....20 P 28
Stoney Cross ....9 P 31
Stoney Stanton ....36 Q 26
Stoneybridge ....76 X 12
Stoneykirk ....52 F 19
Stoneywood ....75 N 12
Stony Stratford ....28 R 27
Stornoway ....82 A 9
Storr (The) ....77 B 11
Storrington ....11 S 31
Stort (River) ....29 U 28
Stotfold ....29 T 27
Stottesdon ....26 M 26
Stoughton ....10 R 31
Stoul ....72 C 13
Stoulton ....27 N 27
Stour (River)
 English Channel ....9 N 31
Stour (River) *North Sea* ....30 V 27
Stour (River) *R. Severn* ....27 N 26
Stourbridge ....27 N 26
Stourhead House ....9 N 30
Stourport-on-Severn ....27 N 26
Stourton Caundle ....9 M 31
Stow ....62 L 16
Stow-on-the-Wold ....27 O 28
Stowbridge ....38 V 26
Stowe-by-Chartley ....35 O 25
Stowe School ....28 Q 27
Stowmarket ....30 W 27
Stowupland ....30 X 27
Straad ....59 E 16
Strachan ....75 M 12
Strachur ....66 E 15
Stradbroke ....31 X 27
Stradishall ....30 V 27
Stradsett ....38 V 26
Straiton ....60 G 18
Straloch ....74 J 13
Stranraer ....52 E 19
Strata Florida Abbey ....25 I 27
Stratfield Saye ....20 Q 29
Stratford St. Mary ....30 W 28
Stratford-upon-Avon ....27 O 27
Strath Brora ....85 H 9
Strath Dearn ....79 I 11
Strath Halladale ....85 I 8
Strath Isla ....80 K 11
Strath More ....78 E 10
Strath Mulzie ....78 F 10
Strath of Kildonan ....85 I 9
Strath Oykel ....84 F 10
Strath Skinsdale ....85 H 9
Strath Tay ....68 J 14
Strathallan ....67 I 15
Strathan ....72 E 13
Strathardle ....74 J 13
Strathaven ....60 H 16
Strathbeg (Loch of) ....81 O 11
Strathblane ....67 H 16
Strathbogie ....80 L 11
Strathbraan ....67 I 14
Strathcanaird ....84 E 10
Strathcarron ....78 D 11
Strathcoil ....65 C 14
Strathconon ....78 F 11
Strathconon Forest ....78 F 11

A B C D E F G H I J K L M N O P Q R S T U V W X Y Z

Strathearn 67 I14
Stratherrick 73 G12
Strathkinness 69 L14
Strathmashie 73 H13
Strathmiglo 68 K15
Strathmore 75 M13
Strathnairn 79 H11
Strathnaver 85 H8
Strathpeffer 79 G11
Strathrannoch 79 F10
Strathspey 80 J11
Strathvaich Lodge 78 F10
Strathy 85 I8
Strathy Point 85 H8
Strathyre 67 H15
Stratton Cornwall 6 G31
Stratton Glos. 19 O28
Stratton West Dorset 5 M31
Stratton Audley 28 Q28
Stratton-on-the-Fosse 18 M30
Stratton-St. Margaret 19 O29
Streatley 20 Q29
Street 8 L30
Strensall 50 Q21
Stretford 42 N23
Stretham 30 U26
Stretton Cheshire 42 M23
Stretton Staffs. 35 N25
Stretton-on-Dunsmore 28 P26
Strichen 81 N11
Striven (Loch) 66 E16
Stroma (Island of) 86 K7
Stromeferry 78 D11
Stromemore 78 D11
Stromness 86 K7
Stronachlachar 66 G15
Stronchreggan 72 E13
Stronchrubie 84 F9
Strone 66 F16
Stronmilchan 66 F14
Stronsay 87 M6
Stronsay Firth 87 L6
Strontian 72 D13
Stroud 19 N28
Strumble Head 14 E27
Stuart Castel 79 H11
Stuartfield 81 N11
Stubbington 10 Q31
Studland 9 O32
Studley Warw. 27 O27
Studley Wilts. 19 N29
Studley Royal Gardens 50 P21
Stuley 76 Y12
Sturminster Marshall 9 N31
Sturminster Newton 9 N31
Sturry 23 X30
Sturton-le-Steeple 44 R23
Suainaval (Loch) 82 Z9
Sudbourne 31 Y27
Sudbury Derbs. 35 O25
Sudbury Suffolk 30 W27
Sudbury Hall
Sudeley Castle 27 O28
Sùil Ghorm 71 A13
Sulby 46 G21
Sulgrave 28 Q27
Sulhamstead 20 Q29
Sullom 87 P2
Sullom Voe 87 P2
Sully 18 K29
Sumburgh 87 Q4
Sumburgh Roost 87 P4
Summer Island 83 D9
Summerbridge 49 O21
Summercourt 3 F32
Sunart 72 D13
Sunart (Loch) 71 C13
Sunbury 21 S29
Sunderland 57 P19
Sunderland Bridge 56 P19
Sunk Island 45 T23
Sunningdale 21 S29
Sunninghill 21 S29
Surfleet 37 T25
Surlingham 39 Y26
Sutterton 37 T25
Sutton Bassetlaw 44 R23
Sutton Cambs. 29 U26
Sutton Guildford 21 S30
Sutton London Borough 21 T29
Sutton Shrops. 34 M25
Sutton Bank 50 Q21
Sutton Benger 19 N29
Sutton Bonington 36 Q25
Sutton Bridge 37 U25
Sutton Cheney 36 P26
Sutton Coldfield 35 O26

Sutton Courtenay 20 Q29
Sutton-in-Ashfield 36 Q24
Sutton-on-Hull 45 T22
Sutton-on-Sea 45 U24
Sutton-on-the-Forest 50 Q21
Sutton-on-the-Hill 35 P25
Sutton-on-Trent 36 R24
Sutton Scotney 10 P30
Sutton St. Edmund 37 U25
Sutton St. James 37 U25
Sutton-St. Nicholas 26 L27
Sutton under Whitestonecliffe 50 Q21
Sutton Valence 22 V30
Sutton Veny 9 N30
Swadlincote 36 P25
Swaffham 38 W26
Swaffham Bulbeck 30 U27
Swainby 50 Q20
Swainswick 19 M29
Swale (River) 50 P21
Swale (The) 22 W29
Swale Dale 49 O20
Swallow 45 T23
Swallow Falls 33 I24
Swallowcliffe 9 N30
Swallowfield 20 R29
Swanage 9 O32
Swanbridge 18 K29
Swanland 44 S22
Swanley 22 U29
Swannery 5 M32
Swanscombe 22 U29
Swansea / Abertawe 17 I29
Swanton Abbot 39 Y25
Swanton Morley 38 W25
Swanwick 36 P24
Swarbacks Minn 87 P2
Swavesey 29 T27
Sway 9 P31
Swaythling 10 P31
Swimbridge 7 I30
Swinbrook 19 P28
Swinderby 36 R24
Swindon Cheltenham 27 N28
Swindon Swindon 19 O29
Swinefleet 44 R22
Swineshead 37 T25
Swinford 28 Q26
Swingfield 23 X30
Swinton Rotherham. 44 Q23
Swinton Scottish Borders 63 N16
Swynnerton 35 N25
Swyre 5 M31
Sydenham 20 R28
Syderstone 38 W25
Sydling St. Nicholas 8 M31
Sykehouse 44 Q23
Symbister 87 Q2
Symington South Ayrshire 60 G17
Symington South Lanarkshire 61 J17
Symonds Yat 18 M28
Symonds Yat Rock 18 M28
Symondsbury 5 L31
Syresham 28 Q27
Syston 36 Q25
Sywell 28 R27

T

Tackley 28 Q28
Tadcaster 44 Q22
Taddington 43 O24
Tadley 20 Q29
Tadmarton 28 P27
Tadworth 21 T30
Taff (River) 18 K29
Taibach 17 I29
Tain 79 H10
Takeley 30 U28
Tal-y-bont Dyfed 25 I26
Tal-y-Bont Gwynedd 33 H25
Tal-y-Cafn 41 I23
Tal-y-Llyn Lake 33 I25
Talacre 41 K22
Talaton 7 K31
Talgarreg 15 H27
Talgarth 26 K28
Talke 35 N24
Tall-y-llyn 33 I26
Talladale 78 D10
Talley 25 I28
Tallaminnock 60 G18
Talsarnau 33 H25
Talwrn 40 H23
Talybont-on-Usk Powys 26 K28
Talywern 33 I26

Tamanavay (Loch) 82 Y9
Tamar (River) 6 G31
Tamerton Foliot 4 H32
Tamworth 35 O26
Tan Hill 49 N20
Tan-y-pistill 33 J25
Tanera Beg 83 D9
Tanera Mòr 83 D9
Tangley 20 P30
Tangmere 11 R31
Tannach 86 K8
Tannadice 74 L13
Tannach 86 K8
Tantallon Castle 69 M15
Taransay 82 Y10
Taransay (Sound of) 82 Z10
Tarbat Ness 79 I10
Tarbert Argyll and Bute 59 D16
Tarbert Gigha Island 65 C16
Tarbert Western Isles 82 Z10
Tarbert (Loch) 65 C16
Tarbet Argyll and Bute 66 F15
Tarbet Highland 72 D13
Tarbolton 60 G17
Tardy Gate 42 L22
Tarfside 74 L13
Tarland 74 L12
Tarleton 42 L22
Tarn (The) 48 L20
Tarporley 34 M24
Tarrant Gunville 9 N31
Tarrant Hinton 9 N31
Tarrant Keyneston 9 N31
Tarrington 26 M27
Tarskavaig 71 C12
Tarskavaig Point 71 B12
Tarves 81 N11
Tarvin 34 L24
Tathwell 45 T24
Tattersett 38 W25
Tattershall 37 T24
Tatton Hall 42 M24
Taunton 8 K30
Taunton Deane 7 K30
Taverham 39 X25
Tavernspite 15 G28
Tavistock 4 H32
Taw (River) 7 I31
Tay (Firth of) 68 K14
Tay (Loch) 67 H14
Tay Road Bridge 69 L14
Taynton 27 M28
Taynuilt 65 E14
Tayport 69 L14
Tayvallich 65 D15
Teacuis (Loch) 71 C14
Tealby 45 T23
Teangue 71 C12
Tebay 48 M20
Tedburn St. Mary 4 I31
Teddington 27 N28
Tees (River) 50 P20
Teesdale 55 N20
Teifi (River) 15 G27
Teignmouth 4 J32
Telford 34 M25
Teme (River) 27 M27
Templand 54 J18
Temple 61 K16
Temple Ewell 23 X30
Temple Grafton 27 O27
Temple Sowerby 55 M20
Templeton 15 F28
Tempsford 29 T27
Tenbury Wells 26 M27
Tenby / Dinbych-y-pysgod 15 F28
Tendring 31 X28
Tenterden 12 W30
Terling 22 V28
Tern Hill 34 M25
Terrington St. Clement 38 U25
Test (River) 20 P30
Tetbury 19 N29
Tetford 45 T24
Tetney 45 T23
Tetsworth 20 Q28
Tettenhall 35 N26
Tewin 21 T28
Tewkesbury 27 N28
Texa 58 B17
Teynham 22 W30
Thakeham 11 S31
Thame 20 R28
Thame (River) 20 R28
Thames (River) 20 Q29
Thanet (Isle of) 23 Y29
Thankerton 61 J17
Thatcham 20 Q29

Thaxted 30 V28
Theale Berks. 20 Q29
Theale Somerset 18 L30
Theddlethorpe St. Helen 45 U23
Thetford 30 W26
Theviothead 62 L17
Theydon Bois 21 U28
Thirlestane 62 L16
Thirlspot 48 K20
Thirsk 50 P21
Thistleton 37 S25
Thixendale 51 R21
Thompson 38 W26
Thomshill 80 K11
Thoralby 49 N21
Thoresway 45 T23
Thorganby 44 R22
Thornaby-on-Tees 50 Q20
Thornborough 28 R28
Thornbury Heref. 26 M27
Thornbury South Glos. 18 M29
Thornbury Torridge 6 H31
Thornby 28 Q26
Thorncombe 8 L31
Thorne 44 R23
Thorner 43 P22
Thorney 37 T26
Thornford 8 M31
Thornham 38 V25
Thornhill Dumfries and Galloway 61 I18
Thornhill Stirling 67 H15
Thornton Fife 68 K15
Thornton Lancs. 42 K22
Thornton Curtis 45 S23
Thornton-in-Craven 49 N22
Thornton-le-Dale 51 R21
Thorntonloch 69 M16
Thornyhive Bay 75 N13
Thorpe Derbs. 35 O24
Thorpe Essex 22 W29
Thorpe-le-Soken 31 X28
Thorpe-on-the-Hill 37 S24
Thorpe Thewles 57 P20
Thorpeness 31 Y27
Thornington 31 X28
Thorverton 7 J31
Thrapston 29 S26
Threapwood 34 L24
Three Cocks 26 K27
Three Crosses 15 H29
Threekingham 37 S25
Threlkeld 54 K20
Thringstone 36 P25
Throckley 56 O19
Thropton 63 O18
Throwleigh 4 I31
Thrumster 86 K8
Thruxton Circuit 20 P30
Thrybergn 44 Q23
Thundersley 22 V29
Thurcroft 44 Q23
Thurgarton 36 R24
Thurgoland 43 P23
Thurlby 37 S25
Thurlestone 4 I33
Thurlow 30 V27
Thurlton 39 Y26
Thurmaston 36 Q25
Thurne 39 Y25
Thurnham 22 V30
Thurnscoe 44 Q23
Thursby 54 K19
Thurso 85 J8
Thurstaston 42 K23
Thurstonfield 54 K19
Thurton 39 Y26
Thwaite 49 N20
Tibbermore 68 J14
Tibberton Glos. 27 M28
Tibberton Salop 34 M25
Tibberton Wychavon 27 N27
Tibshelf 36 P24
Ticehurst 12 V30
Tickhill 44 Q23
Ticknall 36 P25
Tiddington 20 Q28
Tideford 3 G32
Tideswell 43 O24
Tigerton 75 L13
Tighnabruaich 65 E16
Tilbury 22 V29
Tillathrowie 80 L11
Tillicoultry 67 I15
Tilney St. Lawrence 38 U25

Tilshead 19 O30
Tilstock 34 L25
Tilt (Glen) 73 I13
Tilton-on-the-Hill 36 R26
Timberscombe 7 J30
Timsbury 18 M30
Timsgarry 82 Y9
Tingewick 28 Q28
Tingwall (Loch) 87 P3
Tintagel 6 F32
Tintern Abbey 18 L28
Tintinhull 8 L31
Tintwistle 43 O23
Tinwald 53 J18
Tipton 27 N26
Tipton-St. john 5 K31
Tiptree 22 W28
Tirabad 25 J27
Tiree 64 Z14
Tirga Mòr 82 Z10
Tirley 27 N28
Tiroran 65 B14
Tisbury 9 N30
Titchfield 10 Q31
Titchmarsh 29 S26
Tiumpan Head 83 B9
Tiverton Chester 34 L24
Tiverton Mid Devon 7 J31
Tobermory 71 B14
Toberonochy 65 D15
Tobson 82 Z9
Tockwith 50 Q22
Todber 9 N31
Toddington 29 S28
Todenham 27 P27
Todmorden 43 N22
Toe Head 76 Y10
Togston 63 P18
Tokavaig 71 C12
Toll of Birness 81 O11
Toller Porcorum 8 M31
Tollerton 50 Q21
Tollesbury 22 W28
Tolleshunt d'Arcy 22 W28
Tolpuddle 9 N31
Tolquhon Castle 81 N11
Tolsta 83 B8
Tolsta Chaolais 82 Z9
Tolsta Head 83 B8
Tomatin 79 I11
Tombreck 79 H11
Tomcrasky 72 F12
Tomdoun 72 E12
Tomich 78 F12
Tomintoul 74 J12
Tomnavoulin 80 K12
Tomsléibhe 65 C14
Tonbridge 22 U30
Tondu 17 J29
Tong 82 A9
Tongham 20 R30
Tongland 53 H19
Tongue 84 G8
Tongwynlais 18 K29
Tonna 17 I29
Tonypandy 17 J29
Tonyrefail 17 J29
Topcliffe 50 P21
Topsham 4 J31
Tor Ness 86 K7
Torbay 4 J32
Torcross 4 J33
Torksey 44 R24
Torlundy 72 E13
Tormarton 19 N29
Tornapress 78 D11
Tornaveen 75 M12
Torness 79 G12
Torphichen 67 J16
Torphins 75 M12
Torpoint 3 H32
Torquay 4 J32
Torquhan 62 L16
Torridon (Loch) 77 C11
Torrin 71 B12
Torrisdale Bay 85 H8
Torthorwald 53 J18
Tortworth 19 M29
Torver 48 K20
Toscaig 77 C11
Totaig Loch Alsh 78 D12
Totaig Loch Dunvegan 77 A11
Totland 10 P31
Totley 43 P24
Totnes 4 I32
Toton 36 Q25
Totscore 77 A11

Totternhoe 29 S28
Totton 10 P31
Tournaig 78 D10
Tow Law 56 O19
Towcester 28 R27
Tower Hamlets London Borough 21 T29
Towie 74 L12
Town Yetholm 62 N17
Towneley Hall 43 N22
Townhead 53 H19
Townhead of Greenlaw 53 I19
Tradespark 79 I11
Trallwng / Welshpool 34 K26
Tranent 69 L16
Trapp 25 I28
Traquair House 61 K17
Trawden 43 N22
Trawsfynydd 33 I25
Trealaval (Loch) 82 A9
Trearddur Bay 40 G23
Trecastle 25 J28
Trecwn 24 F28
Tredington 27 P27
Treen 2 D33
Trefaldwyn / Montgomery 34 K26
Trefeglwys 25 J26
Treffynnon / Holywell 41 K23
Trefil 18 K28
Trefnant 41 J23
Trefonen 34 K25
Trefor 40 G23
Trefyclawdd / Knighton 26 K26
Trefynwy / Monmouth 18 L28
Tregaron 25 I27
Tregony 3 F33
Tregurrian 2 E32
Tregynon 33 J26
Treharris 18 K29
Treherbert 17 J28
Treig (Loch) 73 F13
Trelawnyd 41 J23
Trelech 15 G28
Trelech a'r Betws 15 G28
Trelissick Gardens 2 E33
Trelleck 18 L28
Tremadog 33 H25
Tremadog Bay 32 H25
Trenance 2 E32
Trengwainton Garden 2 D33
Trent 8 M31
Trent (River) 36 R24
Trentham 35 N25
Treorchy 17 J29
Trerice 2 E32
Treshnish Isles 64 A14
Treshnish Point 71 A14
Tressait 73 I13
Tretower 26 K28
Treuddyn 34 K24
Trevine 14 E28
Trevone 3 F32
Trevor 32 G25
Trevose Head 2 E32
Trewithen 3 F33
Trimdon 56 P19
Trimley Heath 31 X28
Trimsaran 15 H28
Tring 21 R28
Trispen 2 E33
Trochry 67 J14
Troedyrhiw 17 J28
Trollamarig (Loch) 82 Z10
Tromie (Glen) 73 H12
Troon 60 G17
Trossachs (The) 67 G15
Trotternish 77 B11
Troutbeck Eden 54 L20
Troutbeck South Lakeland 48 L20
Trowbridge 19 N30
Trudoxhill 19 M30
Truim (Glen) 73 H13
Trull 8 K31
Trumpington 29 U27
Trunch 39 Y25
Truro 2 E33
Trusthorpe 45 U24
Trwyn Cilan 32 G25
Tuath (Loch) 64 B14
Tuddenham Forest Heath 30 V27
Tuddenham Suffolk Coastal 31 X27
Tudhoe 56 P19
Tudweiliog 32 G25
Tugford 26 M26
Tulla (Loch) 66 F14
Tullibardine 67 I15

Tullibody ....67 I 15
Tullymurdoch ....74 K 14
Tumble ....15 H 28
Tummel (Loch) ....73 I 13
Tunstall
  East Riding of Yorkshire ...45 T 22
Tunstall *Staffs.* ....35 N 24
Tunstall *Suffolk* ....31 Y 27
Tur Langton ....36 R 26
Turnberry ....59 F 18
Turnditch ....35 P 24
Turret
  (Loch and Reservoir) ......67 I 14
Turriff ....81 M 11
Turvey ....29 S 27
Tusker Rock ....17 I 29
Tutbury ....35 O 25
Tuxford ....44 R 24
Twatt ....86 K 6
Tweed (River) ....61 J 17
Tweeddale ....61 J 17
Tweedmouth ....63 N 16
Tweedsmuir Hills ....61 J 17
Twemlow Green ....35 N 24
Twickenham ....21 S 29
Two Dales ....35 P 24
Twyford *Berks.* ....20 R 29
Twyford *Hants.* ....10 Q 30
Twyford *Leics.* ....36 R 25
Twynholm ....53 H 19
Twynllanan ....25 I 28
Tydd-St. Giles ....37 U 25
Tydd St. Mary ....37 U 25
Tyddewi / St. David's ....14 E 28
Tyldesley ....42 M 23
Tylorstown ....17 J 29
Tyne (River) ....56 P 19
Tynehead ....62 L 16
Tynemouth ....56 P 18
Tynewydd ....17 J 28
Tynron ....53 I 18
Tythegston ....17 J 29
Tytherington ....18 M 29
Tywardreath ....3 F 32
Tywi (River) ....25 I 27
Tywyn ....33 H 26

U
Ubiey ....18 L 30
Uckfield ....11 U 31
Uddingston ....60 H 16
Udimore ....12 V 31
Uffculme ....7 K 31
Uffington ....37 S 26
Ufford ....31 Y 27
Ugadale Bay ....59 D 17
Ugborough ....4 I 32
Ugbrooke House ....4 J 32
Ugthorpe ....50 R 20
Uig *Highland* ....77 A 11
Uig *Western Isles* ....82 Y 9
Uisg (Loch) ....65 C 14
Uiskevagh (Loch) ....76 Y 11
Ulbster ....86 K 8
Ulceby *East Lindsey* ....45 U 24
Ulceby *North Lincolnshire* ...45 T 23
Ulcombe ....22 V 30
Uldale ....54 K 19
Uley ....19 N 28
Ulgham ....56 P 18
Ullapool ....78 E 10
Ulleskelf ....44 Q 22
Ullesthorpe ....28 Q 26
Ullinish ....77 A 11
Ullock ....54 J 20
Ullswater ....48 L 20
Ulpha ....47 K 21
Ulsta ....87 Q 2
Ulva ....64 B 14
Ulverston ....48 K 21
Union Mills ....46 G 21
Unst ....87 R 1
Upavon ....19 O 30
Upchurch ....22 V 29
Uphall ....68 J 16
Uphill ....18 L 30
Upleadon ....27 M 28
Uplyme ....5 L 31
Upottery ....8 K 31
Upper Arley ....27 M 26
Upper Badcall ....84 E 9
Upper Beeding ....11 T 31
Upper Bighouse ....85 I 8
Upper Broughton ....36 R 25
Upper Chapel ....25 J 27
Upper Chute ....20 P 30

Upper Dicker ....12 U 31
Upper Hale ....20 R 30
Upper Heyford ....28 Q 28
Upper Hindhope ....62 M 17
Upper Knockando ....80 J 11
Upper Loch Torridon ....78 D 11
Upper Poppleton ....50 Q 22
Upper Sandaig ....72 D 12
Upper Tean ....35 O 25
Uppertown ....86 K 7
Uppingham ....36 R 26
Upton *Dorset* ....9 N 31
Upton *Notts.* ....36 R 24
Upton *Vale of White Horse* ...20 Q 29
Upton *Wakefield* ....44 Q 23
Upton *West Somerset* ....7 J 30
Upton Grey ....20 Q 30
Upton House ....28 P 27
Upton Magna ....34 M 25
Upton Noble ....9 M 30
Upton Scudamore ....19 N 30
Upton-upon-Severn ....27 N 27
Upwell ....38 U 26
Upwood ....29 T 26
Urchfont ....19 O 30
Ure (River) ....50 Q 21
Urigill (Loch) ....84 F 9
Urmston ....42 M 23
Urquhart ....80 K 11
Urquhart (Glen) ....79 G 11
Urquhart Castle ....79 G 12
Urrahag (Loch) ....82 A 8
Ushaw Moor ....56 P 19
Usk / Brynbuga ....18 L 28
Usk (River) ....18 K 28
Uttoxeter ....35 O 25
Uyea ....87 R 2
Uyeasound ....87 R 1

V
Vallay Strand ....76 X 11
Valle Crucis ....34 K 25
Valley ....40 G 23
Valtos ....82 Z 9
Vatersay ....70 X 13
Vatten ....77 A 11
Ve Skerries ....87 O 2
Venachar (Loch) ....67 H 15
Ventnor ....10 Q 32
Verham Dean ....20 P 30
Verulamium ....21 S 28
Verwood ....9 O 31
Veryan ....3 F 33
Veyatie (Loch) ....84 E 9
Vindolanda ....55 M 19
Voe ....87 Q 2
Voil (Loch) ....67 G 14
Vowchurch ....26 L 27
Vyrnwy (Lake) ....33 J 25

W
Waddesdon ....20 R 28
Waddingham ....44 S 23
Waddington *Lancs.* ....42 M 22
Waddington *Lincs.* ....37 S 24
Wadebridge ....3 F 32
Wadhurst ....12 U 30
Wag ....85 I 9
Wainfleet All Saints ....38 U 24
Wainstalls ....43 O 22
Wakefield ....43 P 22
Wakerley ....37 S 26
Wakes Colne ....30 W 28
Walberswick ....31 Y 27
Walcott ....37 T 24
Walden Head ....49 N 21
Walderslade ....22 V 29
Waldringfield ....31 X 27
Waldron ....12 U 31
Walesby ....44 R 24
Walford ....34 L 25
Walgherton ....34 M 24
Walgrave ....28 R 26
Walkden ....42 M 23
Walkeringham ....44 R 23
Walkern ....29 T 28
Wall ....35 O 26
Wallace Monument ....67 I 15
Wallasey ....42 K 23
Wallend ....22 W 29
Wallingford ....20 Q 29
Wallington House ....56 O 18
Walls ....87 P 3
Wallsend ....56 P 18
Wallyford ....69 K 16
Walney (Isle of) ....47 K 21
Walpole ....31 Y 27

Walpole St. Andrew ....38 U 25
Walpole St. Peter ....38 U 25
Walsall ....35 O 26
Walsden ....43 N 22
Walsham le Willows ....30 W 27
Walshford ....50 P 22
Walston ....61 J 16
Waltham *Kent* ....23 X 30
Waltham *North East Lincs.* ...45 T 23
Waltham Abbey ....21 U 28
Waltham Forest
  London Borough ....21 T 29
Waltham-on-the-Wolds ....36 R 25
Walton *Carlisle* ....55 L 19
Walton *Leeds* ....50 Q 22
Walton *Powys* ....26 K 27
Walton-East ....24 F 28
Walton-in-Gordano ....18 L 29
Walton-le-Dale ....42 M 22
Walton-on-Thames ....21 S 29
Walton-on-the-Naze ....31 X 28
Walton-Upon-Trent ....35 O 25
Walworth ....49 P 20
Wanborough ....19 O 29
Wandsworth
  London Borough ....21 T 29
Wangford ....31 Y 26
Wanlockhead ....61 I 17
Wansford
  East Riding of Yorkshire ...51 S 22
Wansford *Peterborough* .....37 S 26
Wanstrow ....9 M 30
Wantage ....20 P 29
Wappenham ....28 Q 27
Warboys ....29 T 26
Warbstow ....6 G 31
Warcop ....49 M 20
Wardington ....28 Q 27
Wardour Castle ....9 N 30
Ware ....21 T 28
Wareham ....9 N 31
Wargrave ....20 R 29
Wark near Coldstream ....63 N 17
Wark near Hexham ....55 N 18
Wark Forest ....55 M 18
Warkworth ....63 P 17
Warley ....27 O 26
Warlingham ....21 T 30
Warmington
  East Northamptonshire ...29 S 26
Warmington
  Stratford-on-Avon ....28 P 27
Warminster ....19 N 30
Warmsworth ....44 Q 23
Warmwell ....9 M 31
Warnborough ....20 R 30
Warnford ....10 Q 30
Warnham ....11 S 30
Warren ....43 N 24
Warren (The) ....13 X 30
Warrington ....42 M 23
Warsash ....10 Q 31
Warslow ....35 O 24
Warsop ....36 Q 24
Warter ....51 R 22
Warton *Alnwick* ....63 O 18
Warton near Morecambe ....48 L 21
Warton near Preston ....42 L 22
Warwick ....27 P 27
Warwick Bridge ....55 L 19
Wasbister ....86 K 6
Wasdale Head ....47 K 20
Wash (The) ....38 U 25
Washington
  Tyne and Wear ....56 P 19
Washington *West Sussex* ...11 S 31
Wast Water ....47 K 20
Watchet ....17 K 30
Watchfield ....19 P 29
Watchgate ....48 L 20
Water Orton ....27 O 26
Waterbeach ....30 U 27
Waterbeck ....54 K 18
Watergate Bay ....2 E 32
Waterhead ....74 L 13
Waterhouses ....35 O 24
Wateringbury ....22 V 30
Waterlooville ....10 Q 31
Waternish Point ....77 A 11
Waters Upton ....34 M 25
Waterside ....60 G 17
Waterstein ....76 Z 11
Watford *Daventry* ....28 Q 27
Watford *Watford* ....21 S 29
Wath ....50 P 21
Wath-upon-Dearne ....44 P 23
Watlington ....20 Q 29

Watten ....85 K 8
Watton *Breckland* ....38 W 26
Watton
  East Riding of Yorkshire ...51 S 22
Watton at Stone ....29 T 28
Waunfawr ....33 H 24
Waveney (River) ....31 Y 26
Waverton *Allerdale* ....54 K 19
Waverton *Chester* ....34 L 24
Wawne ....45 S 22
Wear (River) ....56 O 20
Weardale ....55 N 19
Weasenham St. Peter ....38 W 25
Weaver (River) ....34 M 24
Weaverthorpe ....51 S 21
Wedmore ....18 L 30
Wednesbury ....35 N 26
Wednesfield ....35 N 26
Weedon-Bec ....28 Q 27
Week St. Mary ....6 G 31
Weeley ....31 X 28
Weem ....73 I 14
Weeting ....30 V 26
Weeton ....42 L 22
Welburn ....50 R 21
Welby ....37 S 25
Welcombe ....6 G 31
Welford *Daventry* ....28 Q 26
Welford *Stratford-on-Avon* ...27 O 27
Welford *West Berkshire* ......20 P 29
Welham Green ....21 T 28
Well ....50 P 21
Welland ....27 N 27
Welland (River) ....37 T 25
Wellesbourne ....27 P 27
Wellingborough ....29 R 27
Wellington
  Herefordshire ....26 L 27
Wellington *Salop* ....34 M 25
Wellington *Somerset* ....8 K 31
Wellow
  Bath and North East ....19 M 30
Wellow
  Newark and Sherwood ...36 R 24
Wells ....18 M 30
Wells-next-the-Sea ....38 W 25
Wells of Ythan ....81 M 11
Welney ....38 U 26
Welshampton ....34 L 25
Welshpool / Trallwng ....34 K 26
Welton *Allerdale* ....54 K 19
Welton *Daventry* ....28 Q 27
Welton *West Lindsey* ....44 S 24
Welton-le-Wold ....45 T 23
Welwyn ....21 T 28
Welwyn Garden City ....21 T 28
Wem ....34 L 25
Wembdon ....8 K 30
Wembley ....21 T 29
Wembury ....4 H 33
Wembworthy ....7 I 31
Wemyss Bay ....59 F 16
Wendens Ambo ....30 U 27
Wendlebury ....28 Q 28
Wendover ....20 R 28
Wendron ....2 E 33
Wenlock Edge ....26 L 26
Wennington ....48 M 21
Wensley ....49 O 21
Wensleydale ....49 O 21
Wentbridge ....44 Q 23
Wentnor ....26 L 26
Wentworth ....43 P 23
Wenvoe ....18 K 29
Weobley
  Hereford and Worcester ...26 L 27
Wereham ....38 V 26
Werrington ....6 G 32
West Alvington ....4 I 33
West Auckland ....56 O 20
West-Barns ....69 M 16
West Bay ....8 M 32
West Bergholt ....30 W 28
West-Bradenham ....38 W 26
West Bridgford ....36 Q 25
West Bromwich ....27 O 26
West-Buckland
  North Devon ....7 I 30
West-Buckland
  Taunton Deane ....8 K 31
West Butterwick ....44 R 23
West Calder ....61 J 16
West Camel ....8 M 30
West Charleton ....4 I 33
West Chevington ....63 P 18
West Chiltington ....11 S 31

West-Chinnock ....8 L 31
West Coker ....8 L 31
West Dean ....9 P 30
West-Dereham ....38 V 26
West Down ....7 H 30
West End ....10 Q 31
West Farleigh ....22 V 30
West-Felton ....34 L 25
West-Firle ....11 U 31
West Geirinish ....76 X 11
West-Grinstead ....11 T 31
West Hanningfield ....22 V 28
West Harptree ....18 M 30
West Heath ....20 R 30
West Heslerton ....51 S 21
West-Hill ....5 K 31
West Hoathly ....11 T 30
West-Huntspill ....18 L 30
West Kilbride ....59 F 16
West Kingsdown ....22 U 29
West Kirby ....41 K 22
West Langwell ....85 H 9
West Lavington ....19 O 30
West Linton ....61 J 16
West Loch Roag ....82 Z 9
West Loch Tarbert
  Argyll and Bute ....59 D 16
West Loch Tarbert
  Western Isles ....82 Z 10
West Looe ....3 G 32
West Lulworth ....9 N 32
West Lutton ....51 S 21
West Malling ....22 V 30
West Malvern ....27 M 27
West Meon ....10 Q 30
West Mersea ....22 W 28
West Moors ....9 O 31
West-Overton ....19 O 29
West Putford ....6 G 31
West-Quantoxhead ....8 K 30
West Rainton ....56 P 19
West Runton ....39 X 25
West-Stafford ....9 M 31
West Strathan ....84 G 8
West Tanfield ....50 P 21
West-Tarbert ....59 D 16
West Thorney ....10 R 31
West Town ....18 L 29
West-Tytherley ....9 P 30
West Walton ....37 U 25
West Wellow ....9 P 31
West Wickam ....21 T 29
West Winch ....38 V 25
West Wittering ....10 R 31
West Woodburn ....55 N 18
West Wycombe ....20 R 29
Westbourne ....10 R 31
Westbury *Cheshire* ....34 L 25
Westbury *Wilts.* ....19 N 30
Westbury-on-Severn ....19 M 28
Westcliff ....22 W 29
Westcott ....21 S 30
Westenhanger ....13 X 30
Wester Ross ....78 D 11
Westerdale *Highland* ....85 J 8
Westerdale *Scarborough* ...50 R 20
Westerham ....21 U 30
Westerleigh ....19 M 29
Western Cleddau ....24 E 28
Westfield *Highland* ....85 J 8
Westfield *Rother* ....12 V 31
Westfield *West Lothian* ......67 I 16
Westgate-on-Sea ....23 Y 29
Westham ....12 U 31
Westhoughton ....42 M 23
Westleton ....31 Y 27
Westmeston ....11 T 31
Westmill ....29 T 28
Westnewton ....54 J 19
Weston *Devon* ....8 K 31
Weston
  North Hertfordshire ......29 T 28
Weston *South Holland* ......37 T 25
Weston
  South Northamptonshire ...28 Q 27
Weston *Staffs.* ....35 N 25
Weston-by-Welland ....28 R 26
Weston Favell ....28 R 27
Weston-on-the-Green ....28 Q 28
Weston-on-Trent ....36 P 25
Weston Rhyn ....34 K 25
Weston-super-Mare ....18 L 29
Weston Turville ....20 R 28
Weston-under-Lizard ....35 N 25
Weston-under-Penyard ....26 M 28
Westonbirt ....19 N 29

Westonzoyland ....8 L 30
Westray ....86 K 6
Westruther ....62 M 16
Westward ....54 K 19
Westward Ho ....6 H 30
Westwood ....19 N 30
Wetheral ....55 L 19
Wetherby ....50 P 22
Wetheringsett ....31 X 27
Wethersfield ....30 V 28
Wetwang ....51 S 21
Wey (River) ....10 R 30
Weybourne ....39 X 25
Weybridge ....21 S 29
Weyhill ....20 P 30
Weymouth ....8 M 32
Whaddon ....28 R 28
Whaley Bridge ....43 O 24
Whalley ....42 M 22
Whalsay ....87 R 2
Whalton ....56 O 18
Whaplode ....37 T 25
Whaplode Drove ....37 T 25
Wharfe (River) ....44 Q 22
Wharfedale ....49 O 22
Whatfield ....12 V 31
Whatsandwell ....36 P 24
Whauphill ....52 G 19
Whaw ....49 N 20
Wheathampstead ....21 T 28
Wheatley *Notts.* ....44 R 23
Wheatley *Oxon.* ....20 Q 28
Wheatley Hill ....56 P 19
Wheaton Aston ....35 N 25
Wheldrake ....50 R 22
Whepstead ....30 W 27
Whernside ....49 M 21
Wherwell ....10 P 30
Whickham ....56 O 19
Whimple ....7 J 31
Whipsnade ....21 S 28
Whissendine ....36 R 25
Whissonsett ....38 W 25
Whitburn *South Tyneside* ...57 P 19
Whitburn *West Lothian* ......61 I 16
Whitby ....51 S 20
Whitchurch
  Basingstoke and Deane ...20 P 30
Whitchurch
  Bath and N.E. Somerset ..18 M 29
Whitchurch *Bucks.* ....28 R 28
Whitchurch
  Caerdydd / Cardiff ....18 K 29
Whitchurch *Devon* ....4 H 32
Whitchurch
  Heref. and Worc. ....18 M 28
Whitchurch *Oxon.* ....20 Q 29
Whitchurch *Salop* ....34 L 25
White Coomb ....61 K 17
White Horse Hill ....20 P 29
White Scarcaves ....49 M 21
White Waltham ....20 R 29
Whitebridge ....73 G 12
Whitecairns ....75 N 12
Whitchurch Canonicorum ....5 L 31
Whitefield ....42 N 23
Whitehall ....87 M 6
Whitehaven ....47 J 20
Whitehill ....10 R 30
Whitehills ....81 M 10
Whitehouse
  Aberdeenshire ....75 M 12
Whitehouse
  Argyll and Bute ....59 D 16
Whitekirk ....69 M 15
Whiten Head ....84 G 8
Whiteness Sands ....79 I 10
Whiteparish ....9 P 30
Whitewell ....81 N 12
Whitewreath ....80 K 11
Whitfield *Dover* ....23 X 30
Whitfield
  South Northamptonshire ...28 Q 27
Whitfield *Tynedale* ....55 M 19
Whitgift ....44 R 22
Whithorn ....52 G 19
Whiting Bay ....59 E 17
Whitland ....15 G 28
Whitley ....20 R 29
Whitley Bay ....56 P 18

A B C D E F G H I J K L M N O P Q R S T U V W X Y Z

A B C D E F G H I J K L M N O P Q R S T U V W X Y Z

Whitley Bridge ....44 Q 22
Whitley Chapel ....55 N 19
Whitminster ....19 N 28
Whitmore ....35 N 25
Whitnash ....28 P 27
Whitsand Bay ....3 H 32
Whitstable ....23 X 29
Whitstone ....6 G 31
Whittingham ....63 O 17
Whittington *Derbs.* ....43 P 24
Whittington *King's Lynn
    and West Norfolk* ....38 V 26
Whittington *Lancaster* ....48 M 21
Whittington *Shrops.* ....34 L 25
Whittle le Woods ....42 M 22
Whittlebury ....28 R 27
Whittlesey ....37 T 26
Whittlesford ....29 U 27
Whitton *North Lincolnshire* ..44 S 22
Whitton *Powys* ....26 K 27
Whitton *Suffolk* ....31 X 27
Whittonstall ....56 O 19
Whitwell *Derbs.* ....44 Q 24
Whitwell *I.O.W.* ....10 Q 32
Whitwell-on-the-Hill ....50 R 21
Whitwick ....36 P 25
Whitworth ....43 N 23
Whixall ....34 L 25
Whygate ....55 M 18
Wiay *Highland* ....77 A 11
Wiay *Western Isles* ....76 Y 11
Wibtoft ....28 Q 26
Wick *Bro Morgannwg /
    The Vale of Glamorgan* ...17 J 29
Wick *Highland* ....86 K 8
Wick *South Glos.* ....19 M 29
Wicken *Cambs.* ....28 R 27
Wicken *Northants.* ....30 U 27
Wickenby ....45 S 24
Wickersley ....44 Q 23
Wickford ....22 V 29
Wickham ....10 Q 31
Wickham Market ....31 Y 27
Wickhambrook ....30 V 27
Wickwar ....19 M 29
Widdrington ....63 P 18
Wide Open ....56 P 18
Widecombe-in-the-Moor ...4 I 32
Wideford Hill Cairn ....86 K 7
Widemouth Bay ....6 G 31
Widford ....21 U 28
Widnes ....42 L 23
Wigan ....42 M 23
Wiggenhall
    St. Mary Magdalen ...38 V 25
Wigglesworth ....49 N 21
Wight (Isle of) ....10 P 32
Wighton ....38 W 25
Wigmore *Herefordshire* ...26 L 27
Wigmore *Medway* ....22 V 29
Wigston ....36 Q 26
Wigton ....54 K 19
Wigtown ....52 G 19

Wigtown Bay ....53 H 19
Wilberfoss ....50 R 22
Wilcot ....19 O 29
Wild Animal Kingdom ....29 S 28
Wilkhaven ....79 I 10
Wilkieston ....61 J 16
Willand ....7 J 31
Willenhall *Coventry* ....28 P 26
Willenhall *Walsall* ....35 N 26
Willerby ....45 S 22
Willersey ....27 O 27
Willingdon ....12 U 31
Willingham ....29 U 27
Willingham Forest ....45 T 23
Willington *Beds.* ....29 S 27
Willington *Derbs.* ....35 P 25
Willington *Durham* ....56 O 19
Williton ....7 K 30
Willoughby ....28 Q 27
Wilmcote ....27 O 27
Wilmington *East Essex* ....12 U 31
Wilmington *Kent* ....22 U 29
Wilmslow ....43 N 24
Wiloughby ....45 U 24
Wilpshire ....42 M 22
Wilsford ....37 S 25
Wilstead ....29 S 27
Wilton ....9 O 30
Wimbledon ....21 T 29
Wimblington ....29 U 26
Wimborne Minster ....9 O 31
Wimborne St. Giles ....9 O 31
Wincanton ....9 M 30
Wincham ....42 M 24
Winchburgh ....68 J 16
Winchcombe ....27 O 28
Winchelsea ....12 W 31
Winchester ....10 Q 30
Winchfield ....20 R 30
Wincle ....35 N 24
Windermere ....48 L 20
Windhill ....79 G 11
Windlesham ....21 S 29
Windrush ....19 O 28
Windrush (River) ....19 O 28
Windsor ....21 S 29
Windsor Great Park ....21 S 29
Windygates ....68 K 15
Winestead ....45 T 22
Winfarthing ....31 X 26
Winford ....18 M 29
Winforton ....26 K 27
Winfrith Newburgh ....9 N 32
Wing ....28 R 28
Wingate ....57 P 19
Wingerworth ....36 P 24
Wingfield *near Alfreton* ....36 P 24
Wingfield
    near Chesterfield ....36 P 24
Wingham ....23 X 30
Wingrave ....28 R 28
Winkfield ....21 R 29
Winkleigh ....7 I 31

Winksley ....50 P 21
Winmarleigh ....48 L 22
Winnersh ....20 R 29
Winscombe ....18 L 30
Winsford *Cheshire* ....34 M 24
Winsford *Somerset* ....7 J 30
Winsham ....8 L 31
Winshill ....35 P 25
Winslow ....28 R 28
Winster *Derbyshire Dales* ....35 P 24
Winster *South Lakeland* ....48 L 20
Winston ....49 O 20
Winstone ....19 N 28
Winterborne Kingston ....9 N 31
Winterborne Stickland ....9 N 31
Winterborne Whitechurch ....9 N 31
Winterbourne ....18 M 29
Winterbourne Abbas ....5 M 31
Winterbourne Dauntsey ....9 O 30
Winterbourne Monkton ....19 O 29
Winterbourne Stoke ....9 O 30
Winteringham ....44 S 22
Winterton ....44 S 23
Winterton-on-Sea ....39 Z 25
Winton ....49 N 20
Wintringham ....51 S 21
Winwick ....29 S 26
Wirksworth ....35 P 24
Wirral ....42 K 24
Wisbech ....37 U 25
Wisbech-St. Mary ....37 U 26
Wisborough Green ....11 S 30
Wishaw ....61 I 16
Wisley ....21 S 30
Wissey (River) ....38 V 26
Wistanstow ....26 L 26
Wistanswick ....34 M 25
Wistaston ....34 M 24
Wiston
    Dumfries and Galloway ....61 J 17
Wiston *Pembrokeshire /
    Sir Benfro* ....16 F 28
Wistow ....44 Q 22
Witchampton ....9 N 31
Witchford ....30 U 26
Witham ....22 V 28
Witham (River) ....37 T 24
Witham Friary ....9 M 30
Witheridge ....7 I 31
Withern ....45 U 24
Withernsea ....45 U 22
Withernwick ....45 T 22
Withington *Cotswold* ....19 O 28
Withington *Herefordshire* .....26 M 27
Withnell ....42 M 22
Withycombe ....4 J 32
Withypool ....7 J 30
Witley ....11 S 30
Witney ....20 P 28
Witsome ....63 N 16
Wittering ....37 S 26
Wittersham ....12 W 30
Witton le Wear ....56 O 19

Wiveliscombe ....7 K 30
Wivelsfield ....11 T 31
Wivenhoe ....30 W 28
Woburn ....29 S 28
Woburn Abbey ....29 S 28
Woburn Sands ....29 S 27
Woking ....21 S 30
Wokingham ....20 R 29
Wold Newton ....45 T 23
Woldingham ....21 T 30
Wollaston ....29 S 27
Wollaton Hall ....36 Q 25
Wolsingham ....56 O 19
Wolston ....28 P 26
Wolvercote ....20 Q 28
Wolverhampton ....35 N 26
Wolverton ....28 R 27
Wolvey ....28 P 26
Wolviston ....57 Q 20
Wombleton ....50 R 21
Wombourne ....27 N 26
Wombwell ....43 P 23
Womersley ....44 Q 22
Wonersh ....21 S 30
Wood Dalling ....39 X 25
Woodborough ....36 Q 24
Woodbridge ....31 X 27
Woodbury ....4 J 31
Woodchurch ....12 W 30
Woodcote ....20 Q 29
Woodford Halse ....28 Q 27
Woodhall Spa ....37 T 24
Woodham Ferrers ....22 V 29
Woodhouse ....43 P 23
Woodhouse Eaves ....36 Q 25
Woodingdean ....11 T 31
Woodland ....56 O 20
Woodlands ....9 O 31
Woodley ....20 R 29
Woodnesborough ....23 X 30
Woodseaves ....35 N 25
Woodsetts ....44 Q 23
Woodsford ....9 M 31
Woodstock ....20 P 28
Woodton ....39 Y 26
Woody Bay ....17 I 30
Wookey ....18 L 30
Wookey Hole ....18 L 30
Wool ....9 N 31
Woolacombe ....16 H 30
Wooler ....63 N 17
Woolfardisworthy ....6 G 31
Woolhampton ....20 Q 29
Woolpit ....30 W 27
Woolsthorpe ....36 R 25
Wooperton ....63 O 17
Woore ....35 M 25
Wootton *Bedford* ....29 S 27
Wootton *Northampton* ....28 R 27
Wootton Bassett ....19 O 29
Wootton Brige ....10 Q 31
Wootton Courtenay ....17 J 30
Wootton Rivers ....19 O 29

Wootton-Wawen ....27 O 27
Worcester ....27 N 27
Workington ....53 J 20
Worksop ....44 Q 24
Worle ....18 L 29
Wormbridge ....26 L 28
Wormingford ....30 W 28
Worminghall ....20 Q 28
Wormit ....69 L 14
Worms Head ....15 H 29
Wormsley ....26 L 27
Worplesdon ....21 S 30
Worsbrough ....43 P 23
Worsley ....42 M 23
Worsthorne ....43 N 22
Worth Matravers ....9 N 32
Worthen ....34 L 26
Worthenbury ....34 L 24
Worthing ....11 S 31
Wortley ....43 P 23
Worton ....19 N 30
Wortwell ....31 Y 26
Wotton-under-Edge ....19 M 29
Wrafton ....6 H 30
Wragby *East Lindsey* ....45 T 24
Wragby *Wakefield* ....43 P 23
Wrangle ....37 U 24
Wrawby ....44 S 23
Wray ....48 M 21
Wrea Green ....42 L 22
Wreay ....55 L 19
Wrecsam / Wrexham ....34 L 24
Wrekenton ....56 P 19
Wremtham ....31 Z 26
Wrenbury ....34 M 24
Wrestlingworth ....29 T 27
Wrexham / Wrecsam ....34 L 24
Wrington ....18 L 29
Writtle ....22 V 28
Wroot ....44 R 23
Wrotham ....22 U 30
Wroughton ....19 O 29
Wroxall ....10 Q 32
Wroxham ....39 Y 25
Wroxton ....28 P 27
Wyberton ....37 T 25
Wyche ....27 M 27
Wye ....22 W 30
Wye (River) ....26 M 28
Wykeham ....51 S 21
Wylam ....56 O 19
Wylye ....9 O 30
Wymeswold ....36 Q 25
Wymondham *Leics.* ....36 R 25
Wymondham *Norfolk* ....39 X 26
Wyre ....87 L 6
Wysall ....36 Q 25
Wyvis Lodge ....79 G 10

Y

Y-Fenni / Abergavenny ....18 L 28
Y Ffor ....32 G 25
Y Llethr ....33 I 25

Y Rhiw ....32 G 25
Yafforth ....50 P 20
Yalding ....22 V 30
Yapton ....11 S 31
Yardley Gobion ....28 R 27
Yardley Hastings ....28 R 27
Yare (River) ....38 W 26
Yarm ....50 P 20
Yarmouth ....10 P 31
Yarnton ....20 Q 28
Yarrow ....62 K 17
Yate ....19 M 29
Yateley ....20 R 29
Yatton ....18 L 29
Yatton Keynell ....19 N 29
Yaxham ....38 W 26
Yaxley ....29 T 26
Yeadon ....43 O 22
Yealand Conyers ....48 L 21
Yealmpton ....4 I 32
Yedingham ....51 S 21
Yelden ....29 S 27
Yell ....87 Q 1
Yelvertoft ....28 Q 26
Yelverton ....4 H 32
Yeolmbridge ....6 G 32
Yeovil ....8 M 31
Yeovilton ....8 M 30
Yesnaby ....86 J 6
Yetminster ....8 M 31
Yetts o' Muckhart ....68 J 15
Yielden ....29 S 27
Ynys / Lochtyn ....15 G 27
Ynysddu ....18 K 29
Ynyslas ....25 H 26
Ynysybwl ....17 J 29
Yockenthwaite ....49 N 21
Yockleton ....34 L 25
York ....50 Q 22
Yorkletts ....23 X 30
Yorkley ....18 M 28
Yorkshire Dales
    National Park ....49 N 21
Yorkshire Wolds ....51 S 21
Youlgreave ....35 O 24
Yoxall ....35 O 25
Yoxford ....31 Y 27
Yr Wyddfa / Snowdon ....33 H 24
Yr Wyddgrug / Mold ....34 K 24
Ysbyty Ifan ....33 I 24
Ystalyfera ....17 I 28
Ystrad-Aeron ....25 H 27
Ystrad Mynach ....18 K 29
Ystradfellte ....17 J 28
Ystradgynlais ....17 I 28
Ystradowen ....17 J 29
Ystwyth (River) ....25 H 26

Z

Zennor ....2 D 33

A B C D E F G H I J K L M N O P Q R S T U V W X Y Z

A

Aasleagh .... 105 D 7
Abbert .... 106 F 7
Abbey .... 100 G 8
Abbeydorney ....93 C 10
Abbeyfeale ....93 E 10
Abbeylara .... 107 J 6
Abbeyleix /
   Mainistir Laoise .... 101 J 9
Abbeyshrule .... 107 J 7
Abington ....94 G 10
Achill .... 104 C 6
Achill Head ....110 B 6
Achill Island .... 104 B 6
Achill Sound .... 104 C 6
Achillbeg Island .... 104 C 6
Achonry ....112 G 5
Aclare ....112 F 5
Acoose (Lough) ....89 C 11
Adamstown ....96 L 10
Adare ....94 F 10
Adrigole ....89 C 12
Aghaboe .... 101 J 9
Aghabullogue ....90 F 12
Aghada ....90 H 12
Aghadiffin .... 106 F 6
Aghadoe ....89 D 11
Aghadoon ....110 B 5
Aghadowey ....118 M 2
Aghagallon ....114 N 4
Aghagower .... 105 D 6
Aghalane ....113 J 5
Aghalee ....114 N 4
Aghamore *Leitrim* .... 107 I 6
Aghamore *Mayo* .... 105 F 6
Aghamuck .... 106 H 6
Aghavannagh .... 103 M 9
Aghavas .... 107 I 6
Aghaville ....89 D 13
Aghinlig ....114 M 4
Aghla Mountain ....116 H 3
Aghleam ....110 B 5
Aghnablaney ....113 I 4
Aghnacliff .... 107 J 6
Aghnamullen .... 108 L 5
Aghowle ....96 M 9
Agivey ....118 M 2
Aglish *Tipperary* .... 100 H 8
Aglish *Waterford* ....91 I 11
Agnew's Hill ....115 O 3
Ahakista ....89 D 13
Ahalia (Loughs) .... 105 D 7
Ahascragh .... 106 G 7
Ahenny ....95 J 10
Aherla ....90 F 12
Aherlow ....94 H 10
Aherlow (Glen of) ....95 H 10
Ahoghill ....118 M 3
Aillwee Cave ....99 E 8
Ailt an Chorráin /
   Burtonport ....116 G 3
Aird Mhór / Ardmore ....91 I 12
Akeragh Lough ....93 C 10
Aldergrove ....115 N 4
Allaghaun ....93 E 10
Allen .... 102 L 8
Allen (Bog of) .... 102 K 8
Allen (Lough) ....112 H 5
Allenwood .... 102 L 8
Allihies ....88 B 13
Allistragh ....114 L 4
Alloon Lower .... 106 G 7
Allow ....94 F 11
Allua (Lough) ....89 E 12
Altagowlan ....112 H 5
Altan Lough ....117 H 2
Altnamackan ....114 M 5
Altnapaste ....117 I 3
An Blascaod Mór /
   Blasket Islands ....92 A 11
An Bun Beag / Bunbeg ....116 H 2
An Caisleán Nua /
   Newcastle West ....93 E 10
An Caisleán Riabhach /
   Castlerea .... 106 G 6
An Chathair / Caher ....95 I 10
An Cheathrú Rua /
   Carraroe ....98 D 8
An Chloich Mhóir /
   Cloghmore .... 104 C 6
An Clochán / Clifden ..... 104 B 7
An Clochán / Cloghan
   Donegal ....117 I 3
An Clochán Liath /
   Dunglow ....116 G 3
An Cloigeann / Cleegan ... 104 B 7

An Cóbh / Cobh ....90 H 12
An Coimín / Commeen ....117 I 3
An Coireán / Waterville .....88 B 12
An Corrán / Currane .... 104 C 6
An Creagán /
   Mount Bellew .... 106 G 7
An Daingean / Dingle .....92 B 11
An Dúchoraidh /
   Doocharry ....116 H 3
An Fál Carrach /
   Falcarragh ....117 H 2
An Fhairche / Clonbur .... 105 D 7
An Geata Mór ....110 B 5
An Gleann Garbh /
   Glengarriff ....89 D 12
An Gort / Gort ....99 F 8
An Gort Mór / Gortmore ... 105 D 7
An Leacht / Lahinch ....98 D 9
An Longfort / Longford ... 107 I 6
An Mám / Maam Cross ... 105 D 7
An Mhala Raithní /
   Mulrany .... 104 C 6
An Móta / Moate .... 101 I 7
An Muileann gCearr /
   Mullingar .... 107 J 7
An Nás / Naas .... 102 M 8
An Ráth / Charleville ....94 F 10
An Ros / Rush ....109 N 7
An Sciobairín / Skibbereen ..89 E 13
An Seanchaisleán /
   Oldcastle .... 108 K 6
An Spidéal / Spiddal ....99 E 8
An tAonach / Nenagh ..... 100 H 9
An Teampall Mór /
   Templemore .... 101 I 9
An Tearmann / Termon .....117 I 2
An tInbhear Mór / Arklow ...97 N 9
An Tulach / Tullow .... 102 L 9
An Uaimh / Navan .... 108 L 7
Anascaul ....92 B 11
Anayalla ....114 L 5
Anglesborough ....94 H 10
Anglesey Bridge ....95 H 9
Annacarriga ....99 G 9
Annacarty ....95 H 10
Annaclone ....115 N 5
Annacloy ....115 O 4
Annacotty ....94 G 9
Annadorn ....115 O 5
Annagary ....116 H 2
Annagassan .... 109 M 6
Annageeragh (River) ....98 D 9
Annagh Head ....110 B 5
Annagh Island ....110 C 6
Annaghdown .... 105 E 7
Annaghmore Lough .... 106 H 6
Annahilt ....115 N 4
Annalee .... 107 J 5
Annalong .... 109 O 5
Annamoe .... 103 N 8
Annes Grove Gardens ....94 G 11
Annestown ....91 K 11
Annfield ....95 I 9
Annie Brady Bridge ....111 C 5
Annsborough ....115 O 5
Antrim ....115 N 3
Antrim (Glens of) ....119 N 2
Antrim Coast ....119 O 2
Antrim Mountains ....119 N 2
Anure (Lough) ....116 H 3
Araglin ....95 H 11
Árainn Mhór /
   Aran or Aranmore Island 116 G 2
Aran Islands /
   Oileáin Árainn ....98 C 8
Aughagault ....117 I 3
Archdale (Castle) ....113 I 4
Archerstown .... 108 K 7
Ard .... 104 C 8
Ardagh *Donegal* ....117 J 3
Ardagh *Limerick* ....93 E 10
Ardan .... 101 J 8
Ardanairy .... 103 N 9
Ardanew .... 108 L 7
Ardara ....116 G 3
Ardattin ....96 L 9
Ardboe ....114 M 4
Ardcath .... 109 M 7
Ardcloon .... 105 F 7
Ardcrony .... 100 H 9
Ardea ....89 C 12
Arderin .... 101 J 8
Ardfert ....93 C 11
Ardfield ....89 F 13
Ardfinnan ....95 I 11
Ardgehane ....90 F 13
Ardglass ....115 P 5
Ardglass ....90 H 11

Ardgroom ....88 C 12
Ardgroom Harbour ....88 C 12
Ardkeen ....115 P 4
Ardlea .... 101 J 9
Ardlougher .... 107 J 5
Ardmillan ....115 O 4
Ardmoney ....113 J 5
Ardmore *Derry* ....117 K 3
Ardmore *Galway* .... 104 C 8
Ardmore Point *Antrim* ....114 N 4
Ardmore Point *Craigavon* ..114 M 4
Ardmore Point
   Dunganstown East ... 103 N 9
Ardmorney .... 101 J 7
Ardmoy .... 106 G 6
Ardnagreevagh .... 104 B 7
Ardnasodan .... 105 F 7
Ardpatrick ....94 G 10
Ardrahan ....99 F 8
Ardreagh ....118 M 2
Ardress House ....114 M 4
Ards Forest Park ....117 I 2
Ards Peninsula ....115 P 4
Ardscull .... 102 L 8
Ardshankill ....113 I 4
Ardstraw ....113 J 3
Argideen ....89 F 13
Argory (The) ....114 M 4
Arigna ....112 H 5
Arinagh ....112 F 5
Arless .... 102 K 9
Armagh ....114 M 4
Armaghbrague ....114 M 5
Armoy ....118 N 2
Arney ....113 I 5
Arra Mountains .... 100 G 9
Arrow (Lough) .... 106 H 5
Arryheernabin ....117 J 2
Artane .... 103 N 7
Arthurstown ....96 L 11
Articlave ....118 L 2
Artigarvan ....117 J 3
Arvagh .... 107 J 6
Asdee ....93 D 10
Ashbourne .... 109 M 7
Ashford *Gleneely* .... 103 N 8
Ashford *Limerick* ....93 E 10
Ashford Castle .... 105 E 7
Ashleam Bay .... 104 B 6
Ashton ....90 F 12
Askamore ....97 M 9
Askanagap .... 103 M 9
Askeaton ....94 F 10
Askill ....112 H 4
Atedaun (Lough) ....99 E 9
Áth Cinn / Headford .... 105 E 7
Athassel Abbey ....95 I 10
Athboy .... 108 L 7
Athea ....93 E 10
Athgarvan .... 102 L 8
Athlacca ....94 G 10
Athleague .... 106 H 7
Athnid ....95 I 9
Athy / Baile Átha Í .... 102 L 9
Atlantic Drive (The) .... 104 C 6
Atorick (Lough) ....99 G 8
Attanagh .... 101 J 9
Attavally ....111 C 5
Attea .... 109 N 5
Attical .... 109 N 5
Attymass ....111 E 5
Attymon ....99 G 8
Aucloggen .... 105 F 7
Audley's Castle ....115 P 4
Aughacasla ....92 C 11
Aughagault ....117 I 3
Aughamullan ....114 M 4
Augher ....114 K 4
Aughils ....92 C 11
Aughinish ....99 E 8
Aughinish Island ....93 E 10
Aughkeely ....117 I 3
Aughnacleagh ....118 M 3
Aughnacloy ....114 L 4
Aughnanure Castle .... 105 E 7
Aughnasheelan .... 107 I 5
Aughrim *Galway* .... 100 H 8
Aughrim *Wicklow* .... 103 N 9
Aughris ....112 F 5
Aughris Head ....112 F 5
Aughrus More .... 104 B 7
Avoca .... 103 N 9
Avoca (River) .... 103 N 9
Avoca (Vale of) .... 103 N 9
Avondale Forest Park .... 103 N 9
Avonmore (River) .... 103 N 9
Awbeg ....94 G 11

B

Baginbun Head ....96 L 11
Bailanan Fheirtéaraigh /
   Ballyferriter ....92 A 11
Baile an Mhóta /
   Ballymote ....112 G 5
Baile na Róba /
   Ballinrobe .... 105 E 7
Baile an Sceilg /
   Ballinskelligs ....88 B 12
Baile Átha an Rí / Athenry ..99 F 8
Baile Átha Cliath / Dublin . 103 N 8
Baile Átha Fhirdhia / Ardee 108 M 6
Baile Átha Luain / Athlone 107 I 7
Baile Átha Troim / Trim ... 108 L 7
Baile Brigín / Balbriggan .. 109 N 7
Baile Chláir / Claregalway ..99 F 7
Baile Locha Riach /
   Loughrea ....99 G 8
Baile Mhic Andáin /
   Thomastown ....96 K 10
Baile Mhistéala /
   Mitchelstown ....94 H 11
Baile na Finne / Fintown ...117 H 3
Baile na Lorgan /
   Castleblayney .... 108 L 5
Baile Uí Fhiacháin /
   Newport .... 105 D 6
Baile Uí Mhatháin /
   Ballymahon .... 107 I 7
Baileysmill ....115 O 4
Baldoyle .... 103 N 7
Balla .... 105 E 6
Ballaba ....99 F 8
Ballagan Point .... 109 N 5
Ballagh *Fermanagh* ....113 J 5
Ballagh *Galway* .... 106 F 7
Ballagh *Limerick* ....93 E 10
Ballagh *near Curraghroe* .. 107 H 6
Ballagh *near Nahara* .... 106 H 7
Ballagh *Tipperary* ....95 I 10
Ballagh (Neck of the) ....112 G 3
Ballaghaderreen /
   Bealach an Doirín .. 106 G 6
Ballaghbeama Gap ....89 C 12
Ballaghbehy ....93 E 10
Ballaghisheen Pass ....88 C 12
Ballaghmore .... 101 I 9
Ballaghnatrillick ....112 G 4
Ballard ....97 M 9
Ballardiggan ....99 F 8
Balleen .... 101 J 9
Ballickmoyler .... 102 K 9
Balliggan ....115 P 4
Ballina ....99 G 9
Ballina / Béal an Átha ......111 E 5
Ballinaboy .... 104 B 7
Ballinabrackey .... 102 K 7
Ballinabranagh .... 102 L 9
Ballinaclash .... 103 N 9
Ballinacor .... 103 N 9
Ballinadee ....90 G 12
Ballinafad *Aghanagh* .... 106 G 5
Ballinafad *Galway* .... 104 C 7
Ballinagar .... 101 J 8
Ballinagleragh ....113 H 5
Ballinakill .... 101 K 9
Ballinalack .... 107 J 7
Ballinalea .... 103 N 8
Ballinalee .... 107 J 6
Ballinamallard ....113 J 4
Ballinamara ....95 J 9
Ballinamore .... 107 I 5
Ballinamore Bridge .... 106 G 7
Ballinamuck .... 107 I 6
Ballinascarty ....90 F 12
Ballinaspick ....91 I 11
Ballinclashet ....90 G 12
Ballinclea .... 103 M 9
Ballincloher ....93 C 10
Ballincollig ....90 G 12
Ballincrea ....96 K 11
Ballincurrig ....90 H 12
Ballindaggan ....96 L 10
Ballindarragh ....113 J 5
Ballinderreen ....99 F 8
Ballinderry *Cookstown* .....114 M 4
Ballinderry *Terryglass* .... 100 H 8
Ballinderry *Wicklow* .... 103 N 9
Ballinderry Bridge ....114 M 4
Ballindine .... 105 F 6
Ballindrait ....117 J 3
Ballineanig ....92 A 11
Ballineen ....89 F 12
Ballingarrane ....94 F 10

Ballingarry *Galway* .... 100 H 8
Ballingarry *Limerick* ....94 F 10
Ballingarry *Tipperary* ....95 J 10
Ballingeary / Béal Átha
   an Ghaorthaidh ....89 E 12
Ballingurteen ....89 E 12
Ballinhassig ....90 G 12
Ballinkillin ....96 L 10
Ballinlea ....118 M 2
Ballinleeny ....94 F 10
Ballinlough *Meath* .... 108 K 6
Ballinlough *Roscommon* ... 106 G 6
Ballinluska ....90 H 12
Ballinriuan ....99 F 9
Ballinskelligs Bay ....88 B 12
Ballinspittle ....90 G 12
Ballintober .... 106 G 6
Ballintogher ....112 G 5
Ballintotty .... 100 H 9
Ballintoy ....118 M 2
Ballintra *Donegal* ....112 H 4
Ballintra *near Leabgarrow* .116 G 3
Ballintubber .... 105 E 6
Ballinunty ....95 I 10
Ballinure ....95 I 10
Ballinure (River) .... 100 H 8
Ballinvarry ....96 L 10
Ballitore .... 102 L 8
Ballivor .... 108 L 7
Ballon ....96 L 9
Balloo Cross Roads ....115 O 4
Balloor ....112 G 4
Ballughter ....97 M 10
Ballure ....112 H 4
Balluvengland ....94 F 10
Ballyagran ....94 F 10
Ballyallinan ....94 F 10
Ballyalton ....115 P 5
Ballyard ....113 J 4
Ballybannon .... 102 L 9
Ballybay
   near Carrickmacross ..... 108 L 5
Ballybay
   near Castelblayney ... 108 L 5
Ballybeg ....95 I 11
Ballyboghil .... 109 N 7
Ballybogy ....118 M 2
Ballyboley Forest ....115 O 3
Ballybrack *Dublin* .... 103 N 8
Ballybrack *Kerry* ....88 B 12
Ballybrittas .... 101 K 8
Ballybrommel ....96 L 9
Ballybrood ....94 G 10
Ballybrophy .... 101 J 9
Ballybryan .... 101 K 7
Ballybunnion ....93 D 10
Ballycahill ....95 I 9
Ballycallan ....95 J 10
Ballycanew ....97 N 10
Ballycarney ....97 M 10
Ballycarry ....115 O 3
Ballycastle *Mayo* ....111 D 5
Ballycastle *Moyle* ....119 N 2
Ballycastle Bay ....119 N 2
Ballyclare *Newtonabbey* ....115 N 3
Ballyclare *Roscommon* ..... 107 I 6
Ballyclerahan ....95 I 10
Ballyclery ....99 F 8
Ballycolgy ....94 F 11
Ballycolla .... 101 J 9
Ballycommon .... 100 H 9
Ballyconneely .... 104 B 7
Ballyconneely Bay .... 104 B 7
Ballyconnell *Cavan* ....113 J 5
Ballyconnell *Sligo* ....112 G 4
Ballycorick ....99 E 9
Ballycotton ....91 H 12
Ballycotton Bay ....91 H 12
Ballycrossaun .... 100 H 8
Ballycrovane Harbour ....88 C 12
Ballycroy ....110 C 5
Ballycuirke Lough ....99 E 8
Ballycullane ....96 L 11
Ballycullen .... 103 N 8
Ballycumber .... 101 I 8
Ballydangan .... 100 H 7
Ballydavid *Galway* .... 100 G 8
Ballydavid *Kilmalkedar* ....92 A 11
Ballydavid Head ....92 A 11
Ballydavis .... 101 K 8
Ballydehob ....89 D 13
Ballydesmond ....93 E 11
Ballydonegan ....88 B 13
Ballydonegan Bay ....88 B 13
Ballyduff *Dingle* ....92 B 11

Ballyduff *Kerry* ....93 D 10
Ballyduff *Waterford* ....91 H 11
Ballyduff *Wexford* ....97 M 10
Ballyeaston ....115 O 3
Ballyeighter Loughs ....99 F 9
Ballyfad ....97 N 9
Ballyfair .... 102 L 8
Ballyfarnagh .... 105 F 6
Ballyfarnan .... 106 H 5
Ballyfasy ....96 K 10
Ballyferis Point ....115 P 4
Ballyfin .... 101 J 8
Ballyfinboy .... 100 H 8
Ballyforan .... 106 H 7
Ballyfore .... 102 K 8
Ballyfoyle ....96 K 9
Ballygalley ....119 O 3
Ballygalley Head ....119 O 3
Ballygar .... 106 H 7
Ballygarrett ....97 N 10
Ballygarries .... 105 E 6
Ballygawley *Dungannon* .....114 K 4
Ballygawley *Sligo* ....112 G 5
Ballyglass
   near Cornanagh .... 105 E 6
Ballyglass near
   Kilmovee .... 106 G 6
Ballygorman ....117 K 1
Ballygowan *Ards* ....115 O 4
Ballygowan
   Newry-Mourne .... 109 N 5
Ballygriffin ....95 I 10
Ballyhack ....96 L 11
Ballyhacket .... 102 L 9
Ballyhaght ....94 G 10
Ballyhahill ....93 E 10
Ballyhaise .... 107 K 5
Ballyhalbert ....115 P 4
Ballyhale *Galway* .... 105 E 7
Ballyhale *Kilkenny* ....96 K 10
Ballyhaunis /
   Béal Átha hAmhnais .. 106 F 6
Ballyhean .... 105 E 6
Ballyhear .... 105 E 7
Ballyheelan .... 107 J 6
Ballyheerin ....117 I 2
Ballyheige ....93 C 10
Ballyheige Bay ....93 C 10
Ballyhillin ....117 J 1
Ballyhoe Bridge ....118 N 2
Ballyhoe Lough .... 108 L 6
Ballyhooly ....94 G 11
Ballyhornan ....115 P 5
Ballyhoura Mountains ....94 G 11
Ballyhuppahane .... 101 J 8
Ballyjamesduff .... 107 K 6
Ballykean .... 101 K 8
Ballykeefe ....95 J 10
Ballykeel ....115 N 4
Ballykeeran .... 107 I 7
Ballykelly ....118 K 2
Ballykilleen .... 102 K 8
Ballykinler ....115 O 5
Ballyknockan .... 103 M 8
Ballylacy ....97 N 9
Ballylaghnan ....99 G 9
Ballylanders ....94 G 10
Ballylaneen ....91 J 11
Ballylesson ....115 O 4
Ballylickey ....89 D 12
Ballyliffin ....117 J 2
Ballyline ....95 J 10
Ballylintagh ....118 L 2
Ballylongford ....93 D 10
Ballylongford Bay ....93 D 10
Ballylooby ....95 I 11
Ballyloughbeg ....118 M 2
Ballylynan .... 102 K 9
Ballymacarbry ....95 I 11
Ballymacaw ....96 K 11
Ballymachugh .... 107 K 6
Ballymack ....96 K 10
Ballymaclary .... 100 H 9
Ballymackilroy ....114 K 4
Ballymacoda ....91 I 12
Ballymacrevan ....115 N 4
Ballymacurly .... 106 H 6
Ballymacward .... 106 G 7
Ballymadog ....91 I 12
Ballymagan ....117 J 2
Ballymagaraghy ....118 K 2
Ballymagorry ....117 J 3
Ballymakeagh ....91 I 12

140 Ireland
A B C D E F G H I J K L M N O P Q R S T U V W X Y Z

Ballymakeery / Baile Mhic Íre 89 E 12
Ballymakenny 109 M 6
Ballymartin 109 O 5
Ballymartle 90 G 12
Ballymena 119 N 3
Ballymoe 106 G 6
Ballymoney *Ballymoney* 118 M 2
Ballymoney *Limavady* 118 K 3
Ballymore *Donegal* 117 I 2
Ballymore *Westmeath* 107 I 7
Ballymore Eustace 103 M 8
Ballymore Lough 111 E 5
Ballymurphy 96 L 10
Ballymurragh 93 E 10
Ballymurray 106 H 7
Ballynabola 96 L 10
Ballynacallagh 88 B 13
Ballynacally 99 E 9
Ballynacarrick 116 H 3
Ballynacarriga 89 E 12
Ballynacarrigy 107 J 7
Ballynacarrow 112 G 5
Ballynaclogh 100 H 9
Ballynacorra 90 H 12
Ballynacourty 91 J 11
Ballynadrumny 102 L 7
Ballynafid 107 J 7
Ballynagaul 91 J 11
Ballynagoraher 105 D 6
Ballynagore 101 J 7
Ballynagree 90 F 12
Ballynaguilkee 95 I 11
Ballynahinch 115 O 4
Ballynahinch Lake 104 C 7
Ballynahow 88 A 12
Ballynahown *Kilcummin* 98 D 8
Ballynahown *Westmeath* 101 I 7
Ballynakill *Carlow* 96 L 9
Ballynakill *Offaly* 101 K 8
Ballynakill *Westmeath* 107 I 7
Ballynakill Harbour 104 B 7
Ballynakilla 88 C 13
Ballynakilly Upper 88 C 11
Ballynamallaght 117 K 3
Ballynamona 90 G 11
Ballynamult 95 I 11
Ballynana 92 A 11
Ballynare 103 M 7
Ballynashannagh 117 J 2
Ballynaskeagh 114 N 5
Ballynaskreena 93 C 10
Ballynastangford 105 E 6
Ballynastraw 97 M 10
Ballynchatty 113 K 4
Ballyneaner 118 K 3
Ballyneety 94 G 10
Ballyneill 95 J 10
Ballynoe *Cork* 90 H 11
Ballynoe *Down* 115 O 5
Ballynure 115 O 3
Ballyorgan 94 G 11
Ballypatrick 95 J 10
Ballypatrick Forest 119 N 2
Ballyporeen 95 H 11
Ballyquin 92 B 11
Ballyquintin Point 115 P 5
Ballyragget 101 J 9
Ballyrashane 118 M 2
Ballyreagh *Dungannon* 114 L 4
Ballyreagh *Fermanagh* 113 J 4
Ballyroan 101 K 9
Ballyroddy 106 H 6
Ballyroebuck 97 M 10
Ballyronan 114 M 3
Ballyroney 115 N 5
Ballyroon 88 C 13
Ballysadare 112 G 5
Ballysadare Bay 112 G 5
Ballyshannon *Donegal* 112 H 4
Ballyshannon *Kildare* 102 L 8
Ballysloe 95 J 10
Ballysteen 94 F 10
Ballyteige Bay 96 L 11
Ballytoohy 104 C 6
Ballyvaughan 99 E 8
Ballyvaughan Bay 99 E 8
Ballyvester 115 P 4
Ballyvoge / Baile Uí Bhuaigh 89 E 12
Ballyvoneen 106 G 7
Ballyvourney / Baile Bhuirne 89 E 12
Ballyvoy 119 N 2
Ballyvoyle Head 91 J 11
Ballywalter 115 P 4
Ballyward 115 N 5
Ballywilliam 96 L 10
Balnamore 118 M 2
Balrath 108 M 7
Balrothery 109 N 7
Balscaddan 109 N 7
Baltimore 89 D 13
Baltray 109 N 6
Banada 106 F 5
Banagher 101 I 8
Banagher Forest 118 L 3
Banbridge 114 N 4
Bandon River 89 F 12
Bangor *Mayo* 111 C 5
Bangor *North-Down* 115 O 4
Bangor Trail 111 C 5
Bann (River) *Lough Neagh* 115 N 5
Bann (River) *River Slaney* 97 M 10
Banna 93 C 10
Banna Strand 93 C 11
Bannow 96 L 11
Bannow Bay 96 L 11
Bansha 95 H 10
Banteer 94 F 11
Bantry / Beanntrai 89 D 12
Bantry Bay 89 C 13
Barefield 99 F 9
Barley Cove 88 C 13
Barna *Limerick* 94 H 10
Barna *Offaly* 101 I 9
Barnacahoge 105 F 6
Barnaderg 106 F 7
Barnesmore 113 H 3
Barnesmore Gap 113 I 3
Barnmeen 115 N 5
Barnycarroll 105 F 6
Baronscourt Forest 113 J 3
Barr na Trá / Barnatra 110 C 5
Barra (Lough) 117 H 3
Barrack Village 101 K 9
Barraduff 89 D 11
Barrigone 93 E 10
Barringtonsbridge 94 G 10
Barrow (River) 102 K 8
Barrow Harbour 93 C 11
Barry 107 I 7
Barry's Point 90 F 13
Batterstown 108 M 7
Baunskeha 96 K 10
Bauntlieve 99 E 9
Baurtregaum 93 C 11
Bawn Cross Roads 94 F 11
Bawnboy 113 I 5
Beagh *Galway* 105 F 7
Beagh *Roscommon* 112 H 5
Beagh (Lough) 117 I 2
Beagh (Slieve) 113 K 4
Beal 93 D 10
Béal an Átha / Ballina 111 E 5
Béal an Átha Mhóir / Ballinamore 107 I 5
Béal an Mhuirthead / Belmullet 110 C 5
Béal Átha an Ghaorthaidh / Ballingeary 89 E 12
Béal Átha na Muice / Swinford 105 F 6
Béal Átha na Sluaighe / Ballinasloe 100 H 8
Béal Átha Seanaidh / Ballyshannon 112 H 4
Béal Deirg / Belderrig 111 D 5
Beal Point 93 D 10
Béal Tairbirt / Belturbet 107 J 5
Bealach Conglais / Baltinglass 102 L 9
Bealach Féich / Ballybofey 117 I 3
Bealaclugga / New Quay 99 E 8
Bealad Cross Roads 89 F 13
Bealadangan 105 D 8
Bealaha 98 D 9
Bealalaw Bridge 88 C 12
Bealanabrack 104 C 7
Bealin 107 I 7
Bealnablath 90 F 12
Beara 89 C 12
Bearna / Barna 99 E 8
Beaufort 89 D 11
Bective 108 L 7
Beehive Huts 92 A 11
Beenmore 88 B 11
Beennaskehy 90 G 11
Beenoskee 92 B 11
Beg (Lough) *Antrim* 114 N 4
Beg (Lough) *River Bann* 114 M 3
Beginish Island 88 B 12
Behy 88 C 11
Bekan 105 F 6
Belcarra 105 E 6
Belclare 105 F 7
Belcoo 113 I 5
Belderg Harbour 111 D 5
Belfarsad 104 C 6
Belfast 115 O 4
Belfast Lough 115 O 3
Belgooly 90 G 12
Belhavel Lough 112 H 5
Bellacorick 111 D 5
Belladrihid 112 G 5
Bellagarvaun 110 C 6
Bellaghy 114 M 3
Bellahy 106 F 6
Bellameeny 106 H 7
Bellamont Forest 108 K 5
Bellanaboy Bridge 111 C 5
Bellanacargy 107 K 5
Bellanagare 106 G 6
Bellanagraugh Bridge 112 F 5
Bellanaleck 113 J 5
Bellanamore 117 H 3
Bellanamullia 107 H 7
Bellananagh 107 J 6
Bellanode 114 K 5
Bellarena 118 L 2
Bellavary 105 E 6
Belleek 114 M 5
Belleek 113 H 4
Bellewstown 109 M 7
Belmont 101 I 8
Belmore Mountain 113 I 5
Beltra *Croaghmoyle* 105 D 6
Beltra *Sligo* 112 G 5
Beltra Lough 105 D 6
Belvelly 90 H 12
Belview Port 96 K 11
Belville 111 D 5
Ben Gorm 104 C 7
Benbane Head 118 M 2
Benbaun 104 C 7
Benbo 112 H 5
Benbrack 113 I 5
Benbreen 104 C 7
Benbulben 112 G 4
Benburb 114 L 4
Bencroy or Gubnaveagh 113 I 5
Bendooragh 118 M 2
Benettsbridge 96 K 10
Benmore 111 D 5
Benmore or Fair Head 119 N 2
Bennacunneen 105 D 7
Benwee Head 111 C 4
Beragh 114 K 4
Bere Haven 88 C 13
Bere Island 88 C 13
Bernish Rock 114 M 5
Berrings 90 F 12
Bertraghboy Bay 104 C 7
Bessbrook 114 M 5
Bettystown 109 N 6
Big Dog Forest 113 I 4
Big Island 100 H 8
Big Trosk 119 N 2
Bilboa 102 K 9
Bilboa (River) 95 H 10
Billis Bridge 108 K 6
Bills Rocks 104 B 6
Binevenagh 118 L 2
Binn Éadair / Howth 103 N 7
Biorra / Birr 101 I 8
Birdhill 99 G 9
Birreencorragh 105 D 6
Bishops Court 115 P 5
Black *Galway* 105 E 7
Black (River) *Longford* 107 I 6
Black Ball Head 88 B 13
Black Bull 103 M 7
Black Gap (The) 113 I 4
Black Head *Clare* 99 E 8
Black Head *Larne* 115 O 3
Black Lion 101 J 8
Black Rock 110 B 5
Blacklion 113 I 5
Blackpool 94 G 10
Blackrock *Cork* 90 G 12
Blackrock *Louth* 109 M 6
Blackrock *Rathdown* 103 N 8
Blackskull 114 N 4
Blacksod Bay 110 B 5
Blacksod Point 110 B 5
Blackstairs Mountains 96 L 10
Blackwater 97 M 10
Blackwater (River) *Cork* 89 F 11
Blackwater (River) *Lough Neagh* 114 L 4
Blackwater (River) *River Boyne* 108 L 6
Blackwater Bridge *Innfield* 102 L 7
Blackwater Bridge *Tahilla* 88 C 12
Blackwater Harbour 97 N 10
Blackwatertown 114 L 4
Blanchardstown 103 M 7
Blane Bridge 93 E 10
Blaney 113 I 4
Blarney 90 G 12
Blasket Sound 92 A 11
Bleach 99 G 8
Bleach Lake 94 F 10
Blennerville 93 C 11
Blessington 103 M 8
Bloody Foreland 116 H 2
Blue Ball 101 J 8
Blue Stack Mountains 113 H 3
Blueford 93 E 11
Boa Island 113 I 4
Boardmills 115 O 4
Boderg (Lough) 107 I 6
Bodyke 99 G 9
Bofeenaun 105 E 6
Bofin 104 B 7
Bofin (Lough) *Galway* 105 D 7
Bofin (Lough) *Roscommon* 107 I 6
Bogay 117 J 3
Boggan *Meath* 108 L 6
Boggan *Tipperary* 95 J 9
Boggaun 101 I 9
Boggeragh Mountains 89 F 11
Bohateh 99 G 9
Bohaun 105 D 6
Boheeshil 88 C 12
Boher 94 G 10
Boheraphuca 101 I 8
Boherbue 93 E 11
Bohereen 94 G 10
Boherlahan 95 I 10
Bohermeen 108 L 7
Boherquill 107 J 6
Boho 113 I 4
Bohola 105 E 6
Bola (Lough) 104 C 7
Bolea 118 L 2
Boleran 118 L 2
Boley 102 L 8
Bolinglanna 104 C 6
Boliska Lough 99 E 8
Bolton's Cross Roads 93 D 10
Bolus Head 88 A 12
Bonet 112 H 5
Boola 91 I 11
Boolakennedy 95 H 10
Boolattin 95 J 11
Boolteens 93 C 11
Boolyduff 99 E 9
Boolyglass 96 K 10
Borris 96 L 10
Borris in Ossory 101 J 9
Borrisoleigh 100 I 9
Boston 99 F 8
Bottlehill 90 G 11
Bouladuff 95 I 9
Boviel 118 L 3
Bow 99 G 9
Boyerstown 108 L 7
Boyle (River) 106 H 6
Boyne (River) 102 K 7
Brackagh 101 K 8
Brackley Lough 113 I 5
Bracklin 108 K 7
Brackloon *Mayo* 106 F 6
Brackloon *Roscommon* 106 G 6
Bracknagh *Offaly* 102 K 8
Bracknagh *Roscommon* 107 H 7
Brackwanshagh 111 E 5
Brandon Bay 92 B 11
Brandon Head 92 B 11
Brandon Hill 96 L 10
Brannock Islands 98 C 8
Brannockstown 102 L 8
Bray Head *Kerry* 88 A 12
Bray Head *Wicklow* 103 N 8
Bré / Bray 103 N 8
Breaghva 98 C 10
Breaghwy 105 E 6
Bree 96 M 10
Breenagh 117 I 3
Brickeens 105 F 6
Bricklieve Mountains 106 G 5
Bride *Cork* 89 F 12
Bride *River Blackwater* 91 I 11
Bridebridge 90 H 11
Brideswell *Ballyellis* 97 M 9
Brideswell *Ballynamona* 106 H 7
Bridge End 117 J 2
Bridgeland 103 M 9
Bridget Lough 99 G 9
Bridgetown *Cannock Chase* 96 M 11
Bridgetown *Clare* 99 G 9
Bridgetown *Donegal* 112 H 4
Briensbridge 99 G 9
Brittas *Limerick* 94 G 10
Brittas *Saggart* 103 M 8
Brittas Bay 103 N 9
Britway 90 H 11
Broad Haven 110 C 5
Broad Meadow 109 N 7
Broadford *Clare* 99 G 9
Broadford *Limerick* 94 F 10
Broadway 97 M 11
Brookeborough 113 J 5
Broomfield 108 L 5
Brosna 93 E 11
Brosna (River) 101 I 8
Broughal 101 I 8
Broughane Cross Roads 93 D 11
Brougher Mount 113 J 4
Broughshane 119 N 3
Brow Head 88 C 13
Brown Flesk 93 D 11
Brownstown 96 K 11
Brownstown Head 96 K 11
Bruckless 112 G 4
Bruff 94 G 10
Bruree 94 G 10
Bryansford 115 O 5
Buckna 119 N 3
Buckode 112 H 4
Buiriós Uí Chéin / Borrisokane 100 H 9
Bulgaden 94 G 10
Bull (The) 88 B 13
Bull Point 119 N 2
Bullaba 117 I 3
Bullaun 99 G 8
Bull's Head 92 B 11
Bun Cranncha / Buncrana 117 J 2
Bun Dobhráin / Bundoran 112 H 4
Bun na hAbhna / Bunnahowen 110 C 5
Bun na Leaca / Brinlack 116 H 2
Bunaclugga Bay 93 D 10
Bunacurry 110 C 6
Bunatrahir Bay 111 D 5
Bunaveela Lough 111 D 5
Bunaw 88 C 12
Bunbrosna 107 J 7
Bunclody 96 M 10
Bunlahy 107 J 6
Bunmahon 91 J 11
Bunnafollistran 105 E 7
Bunnaglass 99 F 8
Bunnahown 104 C 7
Bunnanaddan 112 G 5
Bunny (Lough) 99 F 8
Bunnyconnellan 111 E 5
Bunowen 105 C 6
Bunratty 99 F 9
Burnchurch 96 K 10
Burncourt 95 H 11
Burnfoot *Birdstown* 117 J 2
Burnfoot *Limavady* 118 L 3
Burnfort 90 G 11
Burr Point 115 P 4
Burren *Clare* 99 E 8
Burren *Cork* 90 F 12
Burren *Mayo* 105 E 6
Burren (The) 99 E 8
Burren Centre Kifenora 99 E 8
Burrenfadda 99 E 9
Burrishoole Abbey 105 D 6
Burrow 97 M 11
Burtown 102 L 9
Bush 118 M 2
Bush (The) *Dungannon* 114 L 4
Bush (The) *Rathcor* 109 N 6
Bushfield 100 G 9
Bushmills 118 M 2
Butler's Bridge 107 J 5
Butlerstown 90 F 13
Buttevant 94 F 11
Butts (The) 101 K 9
Bweeng 90 F 11

C

Cabragh 114 L 4
Cadamstown *Kildare* 102 L 7
Cadamstown *Offaly* 101 J 8
Caddy 114 N 3
Caggan 105 D 7
Caha Mountains 89 C 12
Caha pass 89 D 12
Caher *Clare* 99 G 9
Caher *Mayo* 105 E 7
Caher Island 104 B 6
Caher Roe's Den 96 L 10
Caheradrine 99 F 8
Caheragh 89 E 13
Caherbarnagh *Corcaigh / Cork* 89 E 11
Caherbarnagh *Kerry* 88 B 12
Caherconlish 94 G 10
Caherconnel 99 E 8
Caherconree 92 C 11
Caherdaniel 88 B 12
Caherea 99 E 9
Caherlistrane 105 E 7
Cahermore *Cork* 88 B 13
Cahermore *Galway* 99 F 8
Cahermurphy 98 D 9
Cahernahallia 95 H 10
Cahore Point 97 N 10
Caiseal / Cashel 95 I 10
Caisleán an Bharraigh / Castlebar 105 E 6
Caisleán an Chomair / Castlecomer 101 K 9
Calafort Ros Láir / Rosslare Harbour 97 M 11
Caledon 114 L 4
Calf Islands 89 D 13
Callaghansmills 99 F 9
Callainn / Callan 95 J 10
Callow *Galway* 104 B 7
Callow *Mayo* 105 E 6
Callow *Roscommon* 106 G 6
Caltra 106 G 7
Caltraghlea 100 H 7
Calverstown 102 L 8
Cam Forest 118 L 2
Camlin (River) 107 I 6
Camlough 114 M 5
Camoge 94 G 10
Camolin 97 M 10
Camowen 113 K 4
Camp 92 C 11
Campile 96 L 11
Campsey 118 K 2
Camross 101 J 8
Camus Bay 105 D 8
Canglass Point 88 B 12
Canningstown 108 K 6
Canon Island 99 E 9
Cappagh *Dungannon* 114 L 4
Cappagh *Limerick* 94 F 10
Cappagh *River* 100 G 8
Cappagh White 95 H 10
Cappaghmore 99 F 8
Cappalinnan 101 J 9
Cappamore 94 G 10
Cappanacreha 105 D 7
Cappanrush 101 J 7
Cappataggle 100 G 8
Cappeen 89 F 12
Car (Slieve) 111 D 5
Caragh (Lough) 88 C 11
Caragh (River) 89 C 12
Caragh Bridge 92 C 11
Caragh Lake 92 C 11
Carbery's Hundred Isles 89 D 13
Carbury 102 L 7
Cardy 115 P 4
Cargan 119 N 3
Carhan House 88 B 12
Cark 117 I 3
Cark Mountain 117 I 3
Carland 114 L 4
Carlanstown 108 L 6
Carlingford 109 N 5
Carlingford Lough 109 N 5
Carn 113 I 4
Carna 104 C 8
Carnageer 119 O 3
Carnaghan 117 J 2
Carnalbanagh Sheddings 119 N 3
Carnanelly 114 L 3
Carnanreagh 118 K 3
Carnaross 108 L 6
Carnaween 112 H 3
Carncastle 119 O 3
Carndonagh / Carn Domhnach 118 K 2
Carnduff 119 N 2

Carne 97 M 11
Carneatly 119 N 2
Carnew 97 M 9
Carney Sligo 112 G 4
Carney Tipperary 100 H 9
Carnlough 119 O 3
Carnlough Bay 119 O 3
Carnmore 99 F 8
Carnoneen 105 F 7
Carnowen 117 J 3
Carnsore Point 97 M 11
Carnteel 114 L 4
Carntogher 118 L 3
Carra (Lough) 105 E 6
Carracastle 106 F 6
Carragh 102 L 8
Carraholly 105 D 6
Carraig Airt / Carrigart 117 I 2
Carraig Mhachaire Rois / Carrickmacross 108 L 6
Carraig na Siúire / Carrick-on-Suir 95 J 10
Carran 99 E 8
Carrantuohill 89 C 11
Carrick Wexford 96 L 11
Carrick / An Charraig Donegal 112 G 4
Carrick-a-Rede Rope Bridge 118 M 2
Carrick-on-Shannon / Cora Droma Rúisc 107 H 6
Carrickaboy 107 K 6
Carrickashedoge 108 L 6
Carrickboy 107 I 7
Carrickfergus 115 O 3
Carrickhugh 118 K 2
Carrickmore 114 K 4
Carrickroe 114 K 4
Carrig 94 G 11
Carrig Island 93 D 10
Carrigadrohid 90 F 12
Carrigafoyle Castle 93 D 10
Carrigagulla 90 F 11
Carrigaholt 93 C 10
Carrigaholt Bay 93 C 10
Carrigahorig 100 H 8
Carrigaline 90 G 12
Carrigallen 107 J 6
Carrigan 107 J 6
Carrigan Head 112 F 4
Carriganimmy 89 E 12
Carrigans 117 J 3
Carrigatogher 100 H 9
Carrigfadda 89 E 13
Carrigglass Manor 107 I 6
Carriggower 103 N 8
Carrigkerry 93 E 10
Carrignavar 90 G 12
Carrigrohane 90 G 12
Carrigtohill 90 H 12
Carrowbehy 106 G 6
Carrowdore 115 P 4
Carrowkeel Donegal 117 J 2
Carrowkeel Galway 99 G 8
Carrowkennedy 105 D 6
Carrowmore Galway 99 F 8
Carrowmore Kilmacowen 112 G 5
Carrowmore near Cloonacool 112 F 5
Carrowmore near Crossboyne 105 E 6
Carrowmore near Killasser 105 F 6
Carrowmore near Killogeary 111 E 5
Carrowmore Lake 110 C 5
Carrowmore Point 98 D 9
Carrowmoreknock 105 E 7
Carrownacon 105 E 6
Carrowneden 112 F 5
Carrownisky 104 C 6
Carrowntanlis 105 F 7
Carrowreagh Roscommon 100 H 7
Carrowreagh Sligo 112 F 5
Carrowrory 107 I 7
Carry Bridge 113 J 5
Carrybeg 95 J 10
Carryduff 115 O 4
Casheen bay 98 C 8
Cashel Donegal 117 I 2
Cashel Mayo 104 C 6
Cashel near Glennamaddy 106 G 7
Cashel / An Caiseal Galway 104 C 7
Cashel (Rock of) 95 I 10

Cashelgarran 112 G 4
Cashelmore 117 I 2
Cashen River 93 D 10
Cashla 99 F 8
Cashla Bay 98 D 8
Cashleen 104 B 7
Casla / Costelloe 98 D 8
Casltepollard 107 K 6
Cassagh 96 L 10
Castle Carry 118 K 2
Castle Coole 113 J 4
Castle Gardens 90 F 13
Castle Haven 89 E 13
Castle Island 89 D 13
Castle Point 98 C 10
Castlebaldwin 112 G 5
Castlebar (River) 105 E 6
Castlebellingham 109 M 6
Castleblakeney 106 G 7
Castlebridge 97 M 10
Castlecaulfield 114 L 4
Castleconnell 99 G 9
Castleconor 111 E 5
Castlecor 94 F 11
Castlecove 88 B 12
Castlecuffe 101 J 8
Castledawson 114 M 3
Castlederg 113 J 3
Castledermot 102 L 9
Castlefinn 117 J 3
Castlefreke 89 F 13
Castlegal 112 G 4
Castlegar 99 E 8
Castlegregory 92 B 11
Castlehill Ballycroy South 110 C 6
Castlehill near Rake Street 111 D 5
Castlejordan 102 K 7
Castleknock 103 M 7
Castlelyons 90 H 11
Castlemaine 93 C 11
Castlemaine Harbour 92 C 11
Castlemartyr 90 H 12
Castleplunket 106 G 6
Castlequin 88 B 12
Castlerahan 108 K 6
Castlerock 118 L 2
Castleroe 118 M 2
Castleshane 114 L 5
Castletown Clare 99 E 8
Castletown Cork 89 F 12
Castletown Laois 101 J 9
Castletown Limerick 94 F 10
Castletown Meath 108 L 6
Castletown near Finnea 107 K 6
Castletown Westmeath 107 J 7
Castletown Wexford 97 N 9
Castletown House 103 M 7
Castletownbere 88 C 13
Castletownroche 94 G 11
Castletownshend 89 E 13
Castleville 105 E 7
Castleward House 115 P 4
Castlewarren 96 K 9
Castlewellan 115 O 5
Castlewellan Forest Park 115 O 5
Cathair na Mart / Westport 105 D 6
Cathair Saidhbhín / Cahersiveen 88 B 12
Cathedral Rocks 104 B 7
Causeway 93 C 10
Causeway Head 118 M 2
Cavan / An Cabhán 107 J 6
Cavanagarvan 114 L 5
Cavangarden 112 H 4
Cé Bhréanainn / Brandon 92 B 11
Ceanannas / Ceanannus Mór (Kells) 108 L 6
Ceann Toirc / Kanturk 94 F 11
Ceapach Choinn / Cappoquin 91 I 11
Ceathrarlach / Carlow 102 L 9
Ceathrú Thaidhg / Carrowteige 111 C 5
Cecilstown 94 F 11
Celbridge 103 M 7
Chanonrock 108 M 6
Chapeltown Down 115 P 5
Chapeltown near Portmagee 88 A 12
Chapeltown near Tralee 93 C 11
Charlemont 114 L 4
Charlestown Craigavon 114 M 4
Charlestown Mayo 106 F 6
Cheekpoint 96 K 11

Cherryville 102 L 8
Chesney's Corner 114 M 3
Church Ballee 115 P 5
Church Cross 89 D 13
Church Hill Donegal 117 I 3
Church Hill Fermanagh 113 I 4
Church Quarter 119 N 2
Church Town 117 J 3
Church Village 105 E 6
Churchstreet 106 G 6
Churchtown Cookstown 114 L 3
Churchtown Cork 90 H 12
Churchtown Down 115 P 4
Churchtown Wexford 96 L 11
Churchtown Point 114 M 3
Cill Airne / Killarney 89 D 11
Cill Chainnigh / Kilkenny 96 K 10
Cill Chaoi / Kilkee 98 D 9
Cill Dalua / Killaloe 99 G 9
Cill Dara / Kildare 102 L 8
Cill Mhantáin / Wicklow 103 N 9
Cill Mocheallóg / Kilmallock 94 G 10
Cill Orglan / Killorglin 93 C 11
Cill Rois / Kilrush 93 D 10
Cill Rónáin / Kilronan 98 C 8
Cionn tSáile / Kinsale 90 G 12
City Walls 96 K 11
Clabby 113 J 4
Cladagh 113 I 5
Claddagh 106 F 7
Claddaghduff 104 B 7
Clady Antrim 115 N 4
Clady Magherafelt 118 M 3
Clady Strabane 117 J 3
Clady (River) 116 H 2
Clady Milltown 114 M 5
Claggan Donegal 117 J 2
Claggan Mayo 104 C 6
Clamper Cross 93 E 11
Clanabogan 113 J 4
Clane 102 L 8
Clár Chlainne Mhuiris / Claremorris 105 F 6
Clara 103 N 9
Clara (Vale of) 103 N 9
Clarahill 101 J 8
Clare Armagh 114 M 5
Clare Craigavon 114 N 4
Clare (River) 105 F 7
Clare Island 104 B 6
Clarecastle 99 F 9
Clareen 101 I 8
Clarina 94 F 10
Clarinbridge 99 F 8
Clark's Cross Roads 107 J 7
Clash 100 H 9
Clash North 93 E 10
Clashmore 91 I 11
Claudy 118 K 3
Clear (Cape) 89 D 13
Cleggan / An Cloigeann 104 B 7
Cleggan Bay 104 B 7
Cléire (Oileán) / Clear Island 89 D 13
Cleristown 96 M 11
Clew Bay 104 C 6
Clifden Bay 104 B 7
Cliff 112 H 4
Clifferna 108 K 6
Cliffony 112 G 4
Clogga Kilkenny 96 K 11
Clogga Wicklow 97 N 9
Clogh Ballymena 119 N 3
Clogh Kilkenny 101 K 9
Clogh Laois 101 J 9
Clogh Wexford 97 M 10
Clogh Mills 118 N 3
Cloghan Offaly 101 I 8
Cloghan Westmeath 107 K 7
Cloghane 92 B 11
Cloghaneely 117 H 2
Clogharinka 102 K 7
Cloghaun 105 F 7
Cloghboley 112 G 4
Cloghbrack Cloonbur 105 D 7
Cloghbrack Meath 108 K 7
Clogheen 95 I 11
Clogher Dungannon 113 K 4
Clogher Kerry 93 D 11
Clogher near Carrownacon 105 E 6
Clogher near Westport 105 D 6
Clogher Roscommon 107 H 6
Clogher Head Kerry 92 A 11
Clogher Head Louth / Lú 109 N 6
Cloghera 99 G 9

Clogherhead 109 N 6
Cloghjordan 100 H 9
Cloghmacoo 108 L 6
Cloghmoyne 109 M 5
Cloghroe Cork 90 G 12
Cloghroe Donegal 117 I 3
Cloghy 115 P 4
Cloghy Bay 115 P 4
Clohamon 96 M 10
Clohernagh 96 K 11
Cloich na Coillte / Clonakilty 89 F 13
Clóirtheach / Clara 101 J 7
Clomantagh 95 J 9
Clonakenny 101 I 9
Clonakilty Bay 90 F 13
Clonalis House 106 G 6
Clonalvy 109 M 7
Clonard 108 K 7
Clonaslee 101 J 8
Clonavoe 101 K 8
Clonbern 106 G 7
Clonbulloge 102 K 8
Clonbur 94 F 10
Clonco Bridge 100 G 8
Cloncrave 108 K 7
Cloncullen 107 I 7
Cloncurry 102 L 7
Clondalkin 103 M 8
Clondaw 97 M 10
Clonderalaw Bay 93 E 10
Clondulane 90 H 11
Clonea 95 J 11
Clonea Bay 91 J 11
Clonee 103 M 7
Clooneen 95 J 10
Clon (Lough) 111 E 5
Clonelly 113 I 4
Clonenagh 97 N 10
Clonfert 100 H 8
Clonfert Cross Roads 100 H 8
Clonkeevy 112 G 5
Clonleigh 117 J 3
Clonlost 107 K 7
Clonmacnoise 101 I 8
Clonmany 117 J 2
Clonmellon 108 K 7
Clonmore Carlow 103 M 9
Clonmore Tipperary 101 I 9
Clonmult 90 H 12
Clonony 101 I 8
Clonoulty 95 I 10
Clonroche 96 L 10
Clonsilla 103 M 7
Clontarf 103 N 7
Clontibret 114 L 5
Clontubbrid 101 J 9
Clonycavan 108 L 7
Clonygowan 101 K 8
Cloon Lake 88 C 12
Cloonacleigha Lake 112 G 5
Cloonacool 112 F 5
Cloonagh Lough 106 F 6
Cloonaghlin Lough 88 C 12
Cloonaghmore 111 D 5
Cloonboo 105 E 7
Cloondaff 105 D 6
Cloondara 107 I 6
Cloone 107 I 6
Cloone Grange 107 I 6
Cloonee Loughs 89 C 12
Clooneen 107 J 6
Clooney 116 G 3
Cloonfad Kiltullagh 106 F 6
Cloonfad near Old Town 100 H 8
Cloonfallagh 105 F 6
Cloonfinish 105 F 6
Cloonfower 106 G 6
Cloonfree Lough 106 H 6
Cloonkeen Kerry 89 E 12
Cloonkeen Mayo 105 D 6
Cloonkeen Roscommon 106 G 6
Cloonlara 99 G 9
Cloonloogh 106 G 6
Cloonlusk 94 H 10
Cloonmore 106 F 6
Cloonoon 100 H 8
Cloonteen 94 H 10
Cloontia 106 G 6
Cloonusker 99 G 9
Cloonymorris 100 G 8
Cloonyquin 106 H 6
Cloran 108 L 7
Clough 115 O 5
Cloverhill Cavan 107 J 5
Cloverhill Galway 105 E 7
Cloyfin 118 M 2

Cloyne 90 H 12
Cluain Eois / Clones 113 K 5
Cluain Meala / Clonmel 95 I 10
Cluainin / Manorhamilton 112 H 5
Clydagh 105 E 6
Clynacantan 88 A 12
Coachford 90 F 12
Coagh 114 M 4
Coalbrook 95 J 10
Coalisland 114 L 4
Coan 101 K 9
Cod's Head 88 B 13
Coill an Chollaigh / Bailieborough 108 L 6
Colbinstown 102 L 8
Coldwood 99 F 8
Colebrooke 113 J 5
Colehill 107 I 7
Coleraine 118 L 2
Colgagh 112 G 5
Colgagh Lough 112 G 5
Colligan (River) 95 I 11
Collin Top 119 N 3
Collinstown 107 K 7
Collon 109 M 6
Collooney 112 G 5
Colly 88 C 12
Colmanstown 106 G 7
Comber 115 O 4
Comeragh Mountains 95 J 11
Commeen 117 H 3
Commons 95 J 10
Conay Island 112 G 5
Cong / Conga 105 E 7
Conlig 115 O 4
Conn (Lough) 111 E 5
Conna 90 H 11
Connagh 100 G 9
Connemara 104 C 7
Connemara National Park 104 C 7
Connolly 99 E 9
Connonagh 89 E 13
Connor 115 N 3
Connor Pass 92 B 11
Convoy 117 I 3
Coogue 105 F 6
Coola 112 G 5
Coolagarry 106 H 7
Coolaney 112 G 5
Coolattin 97 M 9
Coolbaun 101 K 9
Coolbawn 100 H 9
Coolboy 97 M 9
Coolcull 96 L 11
Coolderry 101 I 8
Coole (Castle) 113 J 4
Coole Abbey 90 H 11
Coolea / Cúil Aodha 89 E 12
Coolearagh 102 L 8
Cooley Point 109 N 6
Coolgrange 96 K 10
Coolgreany 97 N 9
Coolkeeragh 117 K 2
Coolkellure 89 E 12
Coolmeen 93 E 10
Coolmore 117 H 4
Coolnareen 101 J 9
Coolrain 101 J 9
Coolroebeg 96 K 10
Coolshaghtena 107 H 6
Coolteige 106 H 6
Coomacarrea 88 B 12
Coomakesta Pass 88 B 12
Coomasaharn Lake 88 C 12
Coomhola 89 D 12
Coomhola Bridge 89 D 12
Coonagh 94 F 10
Cooraclare 98 D 9
Coorleagh 96 K 9
Coornagillagh 89 C 12
Cootehall 106 H 6
Copany 113 H 4
Copeland Island 115 P 3
Coppanagh 108 L 6
Cora Droma Rúisc / Carrick-on-Shannon 107 H 6
Corbally Castleconor West 111 E 5
Corbally Clare 98 D 9
Corbally Kildare 102 L 8
Corbay Upper 107 I 6
Corbet Milltown 115 N 4
Corcaigh / Cork 90 G 12
Corclogh 110 B 5
Corcomroe Abbey 99 E 8

Cordal 93 D 11
Cordarragh 105 D 6
Corduff 109 N 7
Cork Harbour 90 H 12
Corkey 119 N 2
Corkscrew Hill 99 E 8
Corlea 107 I 7
Corlee 105 E 5
Corlis Point 93 D 10
Cornafulla 101 H 7
Cornagillagh 117 I 3
Cornamona 105 D 7
Cornanagh 105 E 6
Corracloona 113 H 4
Corrakyle 99 G 9
Corralkeelan 113 I 5
Corran Cross Roads 114 M 5
Corrandulla 105 F 7
Corraree 106 H 7
Corraun Hill 104 C 6
Corraun Peninsula 104 C 6
Corraun Point 110 B 5
Corrawaleen 107 I 5
Correllstown 107 K 7
Corrib (Lough) 105 E 7
Corries 96 L 10
Corrofin 99 E 9
Corronoher 94 F 10
Corroy 111 E 5
Corry 112 H 5
Corstown 95 J 10
Corvally 108 L 6
Corvoley 111 D 5
Cottoners 89 C 11
Coulagh Bay 88 B 12
Coumfea 95 J 11
Courtmacsherry 90 F 13
Courtmacsherry Bay 90 G 13
Courtown 97 N 10
Cousane Gap 89 E 12
Craanford 97 M 9
Craffield 103 M 9
Crag Cave 93 D 11
Craggaunowen Megalithic Centre 99 F 9
Craig 118 K 3
Craigantlet 115 O 4
Craigavad 115 O 4
Craigavon 114 M 4
Cragnamaddy 114 K 3
Craigs 118 M 3
Crana 117 J 2
Cranagh 114 K 3
Cranfield Point 109 N 5
Cranford 117 I 2
Crannogeboy 116 G 3
Cranny 99 E 9
Cratloe 99 F 9
Craughwell 99 F 8
Crawfordsburn 115 O 4
Crazy Corner 107 K 7
Creagh 113 J 4
Creagh (The) 114 M 3
Creaghanroe 114 L 5
Crean's Cross Roads 90 F 12
Crecora 94 F 10
Creegh 98 D 9
Creeslough 117 I 2
Creevagh 111 D 5
Creevagh Head 111 E 5
Creeves 93 E 10
Creevykeel 112 G 4
Cregg Clare 99 E 8
Cregg Cork 89 E 13
Cregg Galway 105 E 7
Cregg Sligo 112 G 5
Creggan Armagh 108 M 5
Creggan Dungannon 114 K 4
Cregganbaun 104 C 6
Creggaun 94 F 10
Creggs 106 G 7
Crilly 114 L 4
Crindle 118 L 2
Crinkill 101 I 8
Croagh Donegal 112 G 3
Croagh Limerick 94 F 10
Croagh Patrick 105 C 6
Croaghaun 110 B 6
Croaghmoyle 105 D 6
Croaghnageer 113 I 3
Croaghnakeela Island 104 C 8
Croaghrimbeg 105 D 6

A B C D E F G H I J K L M N O P Q R S T U V W X Y Z

Croan (Lough) ...106 H7
Croangar (Lough) ...116 H3
Crockaneel ...119 N2
Crockets Town ...111 E5
Crockmore ...113 I4
Crocknasmug ...118 L2
Croghan *Offaly* ...101 K7
Croghan *Roscommon* ...106 H6
Croghan Mountain ...103 N9
Crohane ...89 D12
Crohy Head ...116 G3
Crois Mhaoilíona /
  Crossmolina ...111 E5
Croithlí / Crolly ...116 H2
Cromane ...92 C11
Cromoge ...101 J9
Croob (Slieve) ...115 N4
Crookedwood ...107 K7
Crookhaven ...88 C13
Crookstown *Kildare* ...102 L8
Crookstown *Moviddy* ...90 F12
Croom ...94 F10
Croos ...106 H7
Cross *Cong* ...105 E7
Cross *Waterford* ...91 I11
Cross (River) ...105 D7
Cross Barry ...90 G12
Cross Keys *Cavan* ...107 K6
Cross Keys *Meath* ...108 K6
Cross Keys *Meath* ...108 M7
Cross Roads ...117 I3
Crossabeg ...97 M10
Crossakeel ...108 K6
Crossboyne ...105 E6
Crossconnell ...100 H8
Crossdoney ...107 J6
Crossea ...107 J7
Crosserlough ...107 K6
Crossgar ...115 O4
Crossgare ...118 L2
Crosshaven ...90 H12
Crossmaglen ...108 M5
Crossna ...106 H5
Crossooha ...99 F8
Crosspatrick *Kilkenny* ...101 J9
Crosspatrick *Wicklow* ...97 M9
Crosswell ...106 G7
Crove ...112 G3
Crow Head ...88 B13
Crownarad ...112 G4
Cruit Island ...116 G2
Crumlin *Antrim* ...115 N4
Crumlin *Cong* ...105 D7
Crusheen ...99 F9
Crutt ...101 K9
Cúil an tSúdaire /
  Portarlington ...101 K8
Cuilcagh ...113 I5
Cuilkillew ...111 E5
Cuilmore ...105 F6
Culdaff ...118 K2
Culdaff Bay ...118 K2
Culfadda ...106 G5
Culfin ...104 C7
Culky ...113 J5
Cullahill ...101 J9
Cullane ...94 G10
Cullaun ...94 H10
Cullaville ...108 M5
Culleens ...111 F5
Cullen *Cork* ...94 H10
Cullen *Tipperary* ...93 E11
Cullenagh (River) ...99 E9
Cullenstown
  near Duncormick ...96 L11
Cullenstown
  near Newbawn ...96 L10
Cullin ...105 E6
Cullin (Lough) ...105 E6
Cullybackey ...118 M3
Cullyhanna ...108 M5
Culmore ...117 K2
Culnady ...118 M3
Cummeragh ...88 B12
Cunningburn ...115 P4
Curlew Mountains ...106 G6
Curracloe ...97 M10
Curragh ...91 I12
Curragh (The) ...102 L8
Curragh Camp ...102 L8
Curragh West ...106 G7
Curragha ...109 M7
Curraghbonaun ...106 F6
Curraghboy ...106 H7
Curraghmore Gardens ...95 J11
Curraghroe ...107 H6
Curraglass ...91 H11

Currahchase Forest Park ...94 F10
Curran ...114 M3
Currane (Lough) ...88 B12
Currans ...93 D11
Curraun ...105 D7
Curreel (Lough) ...104 C7
Curreeny ...100 H9
Currow ...93 D11
Curry ...105 E6
Curryglass ...88 C12
Curryskeskin ...118 M2
Cushendall ...119 N2
Cushendun ...119 N2
Cusher ...114 M5
Cushina ...101 K8
Cut (The) ...101 J8
Cutra (Lough) ...99 F8

D
Dahybaun (Lough) ...111 D5
Daingean ...101 K8
Dalgar ...105 F7
Dalkey ...103 N8
Damastown ...109 N7
Damerstown ...101 K9
Damhead ...118 M2
Dan (Lough) ...103 N8
Danesfort *Kilkenny* ...96 K10
Danesfort *Longford* ...107 I6
Dangan *Cork* ...91 H12
Dangan *Waterford* ...96 K11
Darby's Gap ...97 M10
Dargle ...103 N8
Darkley ...114 L5
Darragh ...99 E9
Dartry Mountains ...112 G4
Davagh Forest Park ...114 L3
Davidstown ...103 M9
Dawros ...104 C7
Dawros Head ...116 G3
Dead ...94 H10
Dealagh ...98 D9
Dee ...108 L6
Deel *Limerick* ...94 F10
Deel *Mayo* ...111 D5
Deel *Westmeath* ...108 K7
Deel Bridge ...111 D5
Deele (River) ...117 I3
Deelish ...89 E12
Deenish Island ...88 B12
Delamont ...115 O4
Delgany ...103 N8
Delphi ...104 C7
Delvin ...108 K7
Delvin (River) ...109 N7
Dennet (Burn) ...117 J3
Derg ...113 J3
Derg (Lough)
  near Donegal ...113 I4
Derg (Lough)
  near Nenagh ...100 H9
Dergalt ...117 J3
Dernagree ...93 E11
Derravaragh (Lough) ...107 J7
Derreen
  near Ballynagoraher ...105 D6
Derreen near Cloghmore ...104 C6
Derreen near Formoyle ...99 E8
Derreen near Lahinch ...98 D9
Derreen Gardens ...89 C12
Derreendarragh ...89 C12
Derreeny ...88 C12
Derreeny Bridge ...89 E13
Derriana Lough ...88 C12
Derries ...101 J8
Derry ...112 G5
Derryad ...114 M4
Derryanvil ...114 M4
Derrybeg ...116 H2
Derryboye ...115 O4
Derrybrien ...99 G8
Derryclare Lough ...104 C7
Derrycooly ...101 I8
Derrycraff ...105 D6
Derrydruel ...116 G3
Derryerglinna ...105 D7
Derryfadda ...101 J9
Derrygolan ...101 J8
Derrygonnelly ...113 I4
Derrygoolin ...100 G9
Derrygrogan ...101 J8
Derrykeevan ...114 M4
Derrykeighan ...118 M2
Derrylea ...104 C7
Derrylin ...113 J5
Derrylough ...116 G3
Derrymore ...93 C11

Derrymore Island ...93 C11
Derrynane ...88 B12
Derrynane House ...88 B12
Derrynasaggart Mountains ...89 E11
Derrynawilt ...113 K5
Derryneen ...104 C7
Derrynoose ...114 L5
Derryrush ...104 C7
Derrytrasna ...114 M4
Derryveagh Mountains ...117 H3
Derryvohy ...105 E6
Derrywode ...106 G6
Dervock ...118 M2
Desertmartin ...114 L3
Devenish Island ...113 J4
Devilsbit ...101 I9
Devilsmother ...105 D7
Diamond (The) *Antrim* ...114 N4
Diamond (The)
  Cookstown ...114 M4
Diamond (The) *Omagh* ...113 J4
Dingle Bay ...92 B11
Dingle Harbour ...92 B11
Divis ...115 N4
Doagh *Newtownabbey* ...115 N3
Doagh *Rosguill* ...117 I2
Doagh Beg /
  Dumhaigh Bhig ...117 J2
Doagh Isle ...117 J2
Dodder ...103 M8
Doe Castle ...117 I2
Dolla ...100 H9
Dollingstown ...114 N4
Domhnach Phádraig /
  Donaghpatrick ...108 L6
Donabate ...109 N7
Donacarney ...109 N6
Donadea ...102 L7
Donagh ...113 J5
Donaghadee ...115 P4
Donaghaguy ...109 N5
Donaghcloney ...114 N4
Donaghey ...114 L4
Donaghmore ...114 L4
Donaghmore *Meath* ...109 M7
Donard *Wexford* ...96 L10
Donard *Wicklow* ...103 M8
Donard (Slieve) ...115 O5
Donaskeagh ...95 H10
Donegal / Dún na nGall ...113 H4
Donegal Airport ...116 G2
Donegal Bay ...112 G5
Donegal Point ...98 D9
Doneraile ...94 G11
Donohill ...95 H10
Donore ...109 M6
Donoughmore ...90 F12
Doo (Lough) ...99 E9
Doo Lough ...104 C7
Doo Lough Pass ...104 C7
Dooagh ...110 B6
Doobehy ...111 D5
Doocastle ...106 G5
Dooega Head ...104 B6
Dooey Point ...116 G3
Doogary ...107 J5
Dooghbeg ...104 C6
Doogort ...110 B5
Doohooma ...110 B5
Dooish Mount ...117 J3
Dooleeg ...110 C5
Doolough Point ...110 C5
Doon *Galway* ...100 G7
Doon *Limerick* ...94 H10
Doon Lough ...99 F9
Doona ...110 C5
Doonaha ...93 D10
Doonbeg ...98 D9
Doonloughan ...104 B7
Doonmanagh ...92 B11
Doorin Point ...112 H4
Dooyork ...110 C5
Dore ...116 H2
Dorrusawillin ...107 H5
Dough ...88 C13
Douglas ...90 G12
Douglas Bridge ...113 J3
Doulus Bay ...88 A12
Doulus Head ...88 A12
Dowdallshill ...109 M5
Dowling ...96 K10
Downhill ...118 L2
Downpatrick ...115 O5
Downpatrick Head ...111 D5
Downs (The) ...107 K7
Dowra ...113 H5
Dowth ...109 M6
Drains Bay ...119 O3

Drangan ...95 J10
Draperstown ...114 L3
Dreen ...118 K3
Dreenagh ...92 C10
Drimoleague ...89 E13
Drinagh *Cork* ...89 E13
Drinagh *Wexford* ...97 M11
Drinaghan ...111 E5
Dring ...107 J6
Dripsey (River) ...90 F12
Dripsey ...90 F11
Drishaghaun ...105 D7
Drishane Bridge ...89 D13
Droichead Átha /
  Drogheda ...109 M6
Droichead na Bandan /
  Bandon ...90 F12
Drom ...101 I9
Dromahair ...112 H5
Dromara ...115 N4
Dromcolliher ...94 F10
Dromin *Limerick* ...94 G10
Dromin *Louth* ...109 M6
Dromina ...94 G10
Dromineer ...100 H9
Dromiskin ...109 M6
Dromkeen ...94 G10
Drommahane ...90 F11
Dromod ...107 I6
Dromoland Castle ...99 F9
Dromore *Banbridge* ...115 N4
Dromore *Omagh* ...113 J4
Dromore Lake ...94 F10
Dromore West ...112 F5
Dromtrasna ...93 E10
Drones (The) ...118 M2
Drowes ...112 H4
Drum *Monaghan* ...108 K5
Drum *Roscommon* ...101 H7
Drum *Sligo* ...112 G5
Drum Hills ...91 I11
Drum Manor
  Forest Park ...114 L4
Drumahoe ...117 K3
Drumandoora ...99 F8
Drumaness ...115 O4
Drumanoo Head ...112 G4
Drumatober ...100 G8
Drumbane ...95 I10
Drumbeg *Feddyglass* ...117 J3
Drumbeg *Lisburn* ...115 O4
Drumbologe ...117 I3
Drumcar ...109 M6
Drumcard ...113 I5
Drumcliff ...112 G5
Drumcliff Bay ...112 G5
Drumcondra ...108 M6
Drumcong ...107 I5
Drumcree ...108 K7
Drumcullen ...114 M3
Drumduff ...113 J4
Drumena Cashel ...115 O5
Drumfea ...96 L10
Drumfin ...112 G5
Drumfree ...117 J2
Drumgoft ...103 M9
Drumintee ...109 M5
Drumkeary ...99 G8
Drumkeen ...117 I3
Drumkeeran ...112 H5
Drumlaheen Lough ...107 I5
Drumlea ...107 I5
Drumlegagh ...113 J4
Drumlish ...107 I6
Drumlosh ...101 I7
Drummannon ...114 M4
Drummin ...96 L10
Drummullin ...106 H6
Drumnakilly ...114 K4
Drumone ...108 K6
Drumquin ...113 J4
Drumraney ...107 I7
Drumreagh ...110 B5
Drumshanbo ...107 H5
Drumsna ...107 H6
Drumsurn ...118 L3
Duagh ...93 D10
Dually ...95 I10
Dublin Bay ...103 N7
Duff ...112 H4
Duffy ...102 L7
Dugort ...110 B5
Duleek ...109 M7
Dumha Éige / Dooega ...104 B6
Dún Aengus ...98 C8
Dún A'Rí Forest Park ...108 L6
Dún Chaoin / Dunquin ...92 A11

Dún Dealgan / Dundalk ...109 M5
Dún Garbhán /Dungarvan ..91 I11
Dun Laoghaire ...103 N8
Dún Mánmhaí /
  Dunmanway ...89 E12
Dún Mór / Dunmore ...106 F7
Dún na nGall / Donegal ...113 H4
Dunabrattin Head ...91 K11
Dunadry ...115 N3
Dunaff ...117 J2
Dunaff Head ...117 J2
Dunaghy ...118 M2
Dunagree Point ...118 L2
Dunamase (Rock of) ...101 K8
Dunamon ...106 H7
Dunany ...109 N6
Dunany Point ...109 N6
Dunbel ...96 K10
Dunboyne ...103 M7
Dunbrody Abbey ...96 L11
Dunbulcaun Bay ...99 F8
Duncannon ...96 L11
Duncormick ...96 M11
Dundalk Bay ...109 N6
Dunderrow ...90 G12
Dunderry ...108 L7
Dundonald ...115 O4
Dundrod ...115 N4
Dundrum *Down* ...115 O5
Dundrum *Dublin* ...103 N8
Dundrum *Tipperary* ...95 H10
Dundrum Bay ...115 O5
Dunfanaghy ...117 I2
Dungannon ...114 L4
Dunganstown ...96 L10
Dungarvan Harbour ...91 J11
Dungiven ...118 L3
Dungonnell Dam ...119 N3
Dungourney ...90 H12
Dunguaire Castle ...99 F8
Dunhill ...91 K11
Duniry ...100 G8
Dunkellin ...99 F8
Dunkerrin ...101 I9
Dunkineely ...112 G4
Dunkitt ...96 K11
Dunlavin ...102 L8
Dunleer ...109 M6
Dunlewy ...117 H2
Dunloe (Gap of) ...89 D11
Dunloy ...118 M2
Dunluce Castle ...118 M2
Dunmanus ...89 D13
Dunmanus Bay ...88 C13
Dunmore ...109 O5
Dunmore Cave ...96 K9
Dunmore East ...96 L11
Dunmore Head *Dunquin* ...92 A11
Dunmore Head
  near Culdaff ...118 K2
Dunmore Head
  near Portnoo ...116 G3
Dunmurry ...115 N4
Dunnamaggan ...96 K10
Dunnamanagh ...117 K3
Dunnamore ...114 L4
Dunnycove Bay ...89 F13
Dunowen Head ...89 F13
Dunree Head ...117 J2
Dunsany ...108 M7
Dunshaughlin ...108 M7
Dunworly Bay ...90 F13
Durlas / Thurles ...95 I9
Durrow ...101 J9
Durrus ...89 D13
Dursey Head ...88 B13
Dursey Island ...88 B13
Duvillaun Beg ...110 B5
Duvillaun More ...110 B5
Dyan ...114 L4
Dysart ...107 J7
Dysert O'Dea ...99 E9

E
Éadan Doire / Édenderry ...102 K7
Eagle (Mount) ...92 A11
Eagle Island ...110 B5
Eagles Hill ...88 B12
Eany ...112 H3
Eanymore ...112 H3
Easky ...111 F5
Easky Lough ...112 F5
East Ferry ...90 H12
East Town ...116 H2
Eddy Island ...99 F8
Eden ...115 O3
Ederny ...113 J4

Edgeworthstown ...107 J6
Edgeworthstown /
  Meathas Troim ...107 J6
Egish (Lough) ...108 L5
Eglinton ...118 K2
Eglish ...114 L4
Eighter ...108 K6
Eleven Lane Ends ...114 M5
Ellistrin ...117 I3
Elly Bay ...110 B5
Elphin ...106 H6
Elton ...94 G10
Elva (Slieve) ...99 E8
Emlagh Point ...104 C6
Emly ...94 G10
Emmoo ...106 H7
Emo ...101 K8
Emo Court ...101 K8
Emyvale ...114 L4
Ennel (Lough) ...107 J7
Ennis / Inis ...99 F9
Enniscorthy /
  Inis Córthaidh ...97 M10
Enniskean ...89 F12
Enniskerry ...103 N8
Enniskillen ...113 J4
Ennistimon / Inis Díomáin ...99 E9
Eochaill / Youghal ...91 I12
Erne (Lower Lough) ...113 I4
Erne (River) ...107 J6
Erne (Upper Lough) ...113 J5
Erra ...107 I6
Errew Abbey ...111 E5
Erriff (River) ...105 D7
Errigal Mountain ...117 H2
Erril ...101 I9
Erris Head ...110 B5
Errisbeg ...104 C7
Errislannan ...104 B7
Errit Lough ...106 F6
Ervey Cross Roads ...118 K3
Eshnadarragh ...113 K5
Eshnadeelada ...113 K5
Eske ...113 H3
Eske (Lough) ...113 H3
Esker ...99 F8
Esker South ...107 I6
Eskeragh ...111 D5
Eskragh ...113 K4
Eyeries ...88 C12
Eyrecourt ...100 H8

F
Faha ...91 J11
Fahamore ...92 B11
Fahan ...117 J2
Fahy ...100 H8
Fahy Lough ...110 C5
Fair Green ...99 F9
Fair Head ...88 C13
Fairyhouse ...108 M7
Fairymount ...106 G6
Fallmore ...110 B5
Fanad ...117 I2
Fanad Head ...117 J2
Fane River ...108 M5
Fanore ...99 E8
Farahy ...94 G11
Fardrum ...101 I7
Fardurris Point ...98 D8
Farmer's Bridge ...93 D11
Farnaght ...107 I6
Farnanes Cross Roads ...90 F12
Farnoge ...96 K10
Farran ...90 F12
Farran Forest Park ...90 F12
Farrancassidy
  Cross Roads ...112 H4
Farranfore ...93 D11
Fastnet Rock ...89 D13
Faughan ...118 K3
Fawney ...117 K3
Fea (Lough) ...114 L3
Feagarrid ...95 I11
Feakle ...99 G9
Feale (River) ...93 D10
Fedamore ...94 G10
Fee (Lough) ...104 C7
Feeagh (Lough) ...105 D6
Feeard ...93 C10
Feenagh ...94 F10
Feevagh ...106 H7
Fenagh ...107 I5
Fenit ...92 C11

Fennagh 96 L9
Fennor 91 K11
Feohanagh *Kerry* 92 A11
Feohanagh *Limerick* 94 F10
Feohanagh (River) 92 B11
Ferbane 101 I8
Fergus (River) 99 E9
Fern (Lough) 117 I2
Ferns 97 M10
Ferry Bridge 94 F10
Ferrybank 97 N9
Ferrycarrig 97 M10
Ferta 88 B12
Fethard 96 L11
Fews 95 J11
Feystown 119 O3
Fiddown 96 K10
Fieries 93 D11
Finavarra 99 E8
Finglas 103 N7
Finglass 89 C11
Finn (Lough) 117 H3
Finn (River) 117 J3
Finnea 107 J6
Finnisglin 104 C7
Fintona 113 K4
Fintragh Bay 112 G4
Finuge 93 D10
Finvoy 118 M2
Fiodh Ard / Fethard 95 I10
Fionnaithe / Finny 105 D7
Firkeel 88 B13
Fisherhill 105 E6
Five Corners 115 N3
Fivealley 101 I8
Fivemilebridge 90 G12
Fivemiletown 113 K4
Flagmount *Corlea* 99 G9
Flagmount *Kilkenny* 96 K10
Flat Head 90 G12
Flesk 89 D11
Florence Court 113 I5
Florence Court
    Forest Park 113 I5
Foaty Island/Fota Island ..90 H12
Foilycleara 95 H10
Folk Park 99 F9
Fontstown 102 L8
Forbes (Lough) 107 I6
Fordstown 108 L6
Fore 107 K6
Forkill 109 M11
Forlorn Point 96 M11
Formoyle *Lonford* 107 I7
Formoyle *Mayo* 104 C6
Formoyle
    near *Ballivaghan* 99 E8
Formoyle near *Inagh* 99 E9
Formoyle (Lough) 105 D7
Fort Stewart 117 J2
Forthill 107 I7
Fota Island 90 H12
Foul Sound 98 D8
Foulksmills 96 L11
Fountain Cross 99 E9
Four Mile House 106 H6
Four Roads 106 H7
Fourknocks 109 N7
Foxford 105 E6
Foxhall 105 E7
Foyle (Lough) 118 K2
Foynes 93 E10
Foynes Island 93 E10
Francis' Gap 99 G8
Freemount 94 F11
Frenchpark 106 G6
Freshford 95 J9
Freynestown 102 L8
Frosses 112 H3
Frower Point 90 G12
Fuerty 106 H7
Funshin More 99 F8
Funshinagh (Lough) 106 H7
Funshion 94 G11
Furbogh 99 E8
Furnace 105 D7
Furnace Lough 105 D6
Furness 103 M8
Fyagh (Slieve) 111 D5

G

Gabriel (Mount) 89 D13
Gaddagh 89 C11
Gaillimh / *Galway* 99 E8
Gainestown 107 K7
Galbally *Dungannon* 114 L4
Galbally *Limerick* 94 H10

Galbally *Wexford* 96 M10
Galbolie 108 K6
Galey 93 D10
Galgorm 118 N3
Gallarus Oratory 92 A11
Galley Head 89 F13
Gallion (Slieve) 114 L3
Galmoy 101 J9
Galty Mountains 95 H10
Galtymore Mountain 95 H10
Galway Bay 98 D8
Galways Bridge 89 D12
Gaoth Dobhair /
    Gweedore 116 H2
Gaoth Sáile / *Geesala* ...110 C5
Gap (The) 95 I11
Gara (Lough) 106 G6
Garadice 102 L7
Garadice Lough 107 I5
Garbally 100 H8
Garinish Island 88 C12
Garnavilla 95 I10
Garnish Point 88 B13
Garrane 89 E12
Garranlahan 106 G6
Garraun *Clare* 98 D9
Garraun *Galway* 100 G8
Garraun (Mount) 104 C7
Garries Bridge 89 D12
Garristown 109 M7
Garron Point 119 O2
Garrycloonagh 111 E5
Garrycullen 96 L11
Garryduff 118 M2
Garryfine 94 F10
Garrykennedy 100 G9
Garryspillane 94 G10
Garryvoe 91 H12
Gartan Lough 117 I3
Gartree Point 114 N4
Garty Lough 107 J6
Garvagh *Coleraine* 118 L3
Garvagh *Rowan* 107 I6
Garvaghy 114 K4
Garvary 113 J4
Gattabaun 101 J9
Gearagh (The) 90 F12
Gearha Bridge 88 C12
Geashill 101 K8
Geevagh 112 H5
George (Lough) 99 F9
Gerahies 89 D13
Giant's Causeway 118 M2
Giles Quay 109 N6
Gilford 114 M4
Gill (Lough) near *Sligo* ..112 G5
Gill (Lough) near *Tralee* ..92 B11
Glanaruddery Mountains 93 D11
Glandore 89 E13
Glandore Harbour 89 E13
Glangevlin 113 I5
Glanmire 90 G12
Glanmore Lake 89 C12
Glanoe 93 D10
Glantane 90 F11
Glanworth 94 G11
Glarryford 118 M3
Glasdrumman 109 O5
Glaslough 114 L5
Glasmullan 117 J2
Glassan 107 I7
Glasshouse Lake 107 J5
Glassillaun 104 C6
Glastry 115 P4
Gleann Cholm Cille /
    Glencolumbkille 112 F3
Gleann Domhain /
    Glendowan 117 I3
Gleann na Muaidhe /
    Glenamoy 111 C5
Glen 117 I2
Glen (River) *Cork* 90 F11
Glen (River) *Donegal* 112 G3
Glen Bay 112 F3
Glen Head 112 F3
Glen Lough *Donegal* 117 I2
Glen Lough *Westmeath* 107 J7
Glenaan 119 N2
Glenade 112 H4
Glenade Lough 112 H4
Glenamoy (River) 111 D5
Glenariff 119 N2
Glenariff Forest Park 119 N2
Glenariff or Waterfoot 119 N2
Glenarm 119 O3
Glenavy 115 N4

Glenballyemon 119 N2
Glenbeg Lough 88 C12
Glenbeigh 92 C11
Glenboy 112 H5
Glenbridge Lodge 103 M8
Glenbrohane 94 G10
Glenbrook 90 G12
Glencar 88 C12
Glencar Lough 112 G4
Glencloy 119 O3
Glencolmcille Folk Village .112 F3
Glencree 103 N8
Glencullen 103 N8
Glendalough *Brockagh* 103 M8
Glendalough *Waterford* ...95 J11
Glenderry 92 C10
Glendorragha 116 G3
Glendovan Mountains 117 H3
Glendree 99 F9
Glendun 119 N2
Glenealy 103 N9
Gleneely near *Ballybofey* ..113 I3
Gleneely near *Cardonagh* ..118 K2
Glenelly 114 K3
Glenelly Valley 114 K3
Glenfarne 113 I5
Glenflesk 89 D11
Glengad Head 118 K1
Glengarriff (River) 89 D12
Glengarriff Harbour 89 D12
Glengesh Pass 112 G3
Glengormley 115 O3
Glenhead 118 K2
Glenhull 114 K3
Glenicmurrin Lough 98 D8
Glenmacnass 103 M8
Glenmalur 103 M9
Glenmore *Clare* 99 E9
Glenmore *Kilkenny* 96 K10
Glennagevlagh 105 D7
Glennamaddy 106 G7
Glennascaul 99 F8
Glenoe 115 O3
Glenshane Pass 118 L3
Glenshesk 119 N2
Glentaisie 119 N2
Glentane 106 G7
Glenties 116 H3
Glentogher 118 K2
Glentrasna 105 D7
Glenvale 118 M3
Glenvar / Gleann Bhairr ...117 J2
Glenveagh National Park ...117 I2
Glenville 90 G11
Glin 93 E10
Glin Castle 93 E10
Glinsce / Glinsk 104 C7
Glinsk *Donegal* 117 I2
Glinsk *Mayo* 111 D5
Glounthaune 90 G12
Glyde (River) 108 M6
Glynn *Carlow* 96 L10
Glynn *Larne* 115 O3
Gneevgullia 93 E11
Gob an Choire /
    Achill Sound 104 C6
Gobbins (The) 115 O3
Gokane Point 89 E13
Gola Island / Gabhla 116 G2
Golagh Lough 113 H4
Golam Head 98 C8
Golden 95 I10
Golden Vale 95 H10
Goleen 88 C13
Goold's Cross 95 I10
Goresbridge 96 K10
Gorey / Guaire 97 N9
Gormanston 109 N7
Gort an Choirce /
    Gortahork 117 H2
Gortaclare 113 K4
Gortahill 113 I5
Gortaleam 106 F7
Gortarevan 100 H8
Gortaroo 91 I12
Gortaway 117 J2
Gorteen 106 G6
Gorteen Bridge 101 J8
Gorteeny 100 G8
Gortgarriff 88 C12
Gortgarrigan 112 H5
Gortin 113 K3
Gortin Glen Forest Park ...113 K3
Gortletteragh 107 I6
Gortmore near *Ballycastle* .111 D5
Gortmore near *Bangor* 111 C5
Gortmullan 113 J5

Gortnadeeve 106 G7
Gortnahoo 95 J9
Gortnasillagh 106 G6
Gortree 117 J3
Gortymadden 100 G8
Gorumna Island 98 C8
Gosford Forest Park 114 M5
Gougane Barra
    Forest Park 89 D12
Gougane Barra Lake 89 E12
Gouladoo 89 C13
Gowla 104 C7
Gowlaun 104 C7
Gowlin 96 L10
Gowna (Lough) 107 J6
Gowran 96 K10
Gracehill 118 N3
Graffy 116 H3
Gráig na Manach /
    Graiguenamanagh 96 L10
Graigue 102 L9
Graigue Hill 96 L9
Graigue More 96 M10
Graigues 88 B12
Granabeg 103 M8
Gránard / Granard 107 J6
Grand Canal 101 I8
Graney 102 L9
Graney (Lough) 99 G9
Graney (River) 99 G9
Grange *Kildare* 102 K7
Grange *Kilkenny* 96 K10
Grange *Louth* 109 N5
Grange *Sligo* 112 G4
Grange *Waterford* 91 I12
Grange (River) 106 F7
Grange Con 102 L9
Grangebellew 109 M6
Grangeford 102 L9
Grangegeeth 108 M6
Granias Gap 117 K2
Grannagh 99 F8
Gransha 115 O3
Granville 114 L4
Greagh 107 I6
Great Blasket Island 92 A11
Great Island 90 H12
Great Newtown Head 96 K11
Great Skellig 88 A12
Great Sugar Loaf 103 N8
Greatman's Bay 98 D8
Greenan 103 N9
Greenanstown 109 N7
Greencastle *Donegal* 118 L2
Greencastle
    Newry-Mourne 109 N5
Greencastle *Omagh* 114 K3
Greenfield 105 E7
Greenisland 115 O3
Greenore 109 N5
Greenore Point 97 N11
Gregans Castle 99 E8
Gregory's Sound 98 D8
Grenagh 90 G11
Grey Abbey 115 P4
Grey Point 115 O3
Greysteel 118 K2
Greystones 114 L4
Grianan of Aileach 117 J2
Grogan 101 I8
Groomsport 115 P3
Gubaveeny 113 I5
Gubbaroe Point 113 I4
Gulladoo Lough 107 J6
Gulladuff 118 M3
Gullion (Slieve) 109 M5
Gur (Lough) 94 G10
Gurteen *Cappalusk* 99 G7
Gurteen *Leitrim* 112 H5
Gusserane 96 L11
Gweebarra Bridge 116 H3
Gweebarra 116 H3
Gweebarra Bay 116 G3
Gweestin 93 D11
Gweestion 105 E6
Gyleen 90 H12

H

Hacketstown 103 M9
Hags Head 98 D9
Hamiltonsbawn 114 M4
Hand Cross Roads (The) 99 E9
Hannahstown 115 N4
Hare Island 89 D13
Harristown 96 K10
Harrow (The) 97 M10
Healy Pass 89 C12

Helen's Bay 115 O3
Helvick Head 91 J11
Herbertstown 94 G10
High Island 104 B7
Highwood 112 H5
Hill Street 107 H6
Hillsborough 115 N4
Hilltown *Harristown* 96 L11
Hilltown
    Newry and Mourne 115 N5
Hind 106 H7
Hog's Head 88 B12
Holeopen Bay West 90 G13
Hollyford 95 H10
Hollyfort 97 M9
Hollymount 105 E7
Hollywood 103 M8
Holy Cross 95 I10
Holy Island 99 G9
Holycross 94 G10
Holywell 113 I5
Holywell Hill 117 J2
Holywood 115 O4
Hook Head 96 L11
Hore Abbey 95 I10
Horn Head 117 I2
Horse and Jockey 95 I10
Horse Island 89 D13
Horseleap 101 J7
Hospital 94 G10
Hugginstown 96 K10
Hungry Hill 88 C12
Hurlers Cross 99 F9
Hurley 109 M7
Hyne (Lough) 89 E13

I

Ilen 89 E13
Illaunstookagh 92 C11
Illauntannig 92 B11
Illies 117 J2
Illnacullin 89 D12
Inagh 99 E9
Inagh (Lough) 104 C7
Inch *Donegal* 117 J2
Inch near *Whitegate* 90 H12
Inch near *Youghal* 91 I12
Inch *Tipperary* 95 H9
Inch *Wexford* 97 N9
Inch Abbey 115 O4
Inchagoill 105 E7
Inchamore Bridge 108 L7
Inchbeg 96 J9
Inchcleraun 107 H7
Inchee Bridge 89 D12
Inchicronan Lough 99 F9
Inchigeelagh 89 E12
Inchiquin 105 E7
Inchiquin Lough *Clare* ...99 E9
Inchiquin Lough *Kerry* ...89 D12
Inchmore 107 I7
Inchnamuck 95 H11
Inchydoney Island 90 F13
Indreabhán / Inveran 98 D8
Inis / Ennis 99 F9
Inis Bó Finne / Inishbofin ..117 H2
Inis Meáin / Inishmaan 98 D8
Inis Mór / Inishmore 98 C8
Inis Oírr / Inisheer 98 D8
Inishannon 90 G12
Inishbarra 98 C8
Inishbiggle 110 C6
Inishbofin 104 B7
Inishcarra 90 G12
Inishcarra Reservoir 90 F12
Inishcrone 111 E5
Inishdoorus 105 D7
Inishfarnard 88 B12
Inishfree Bay 116 H3
Inishfree Upper 116 G3
Inishglora 110 B5
Inishkea North 110 B5
Inishkea South 110 B5
Inishmaine Island 105 E7
Inishmicatreer 105 E7
Inishmurray 112 G4
Inishnabro 92 A11
Inishnee 104 C7
Inishowen 117 J2
Inishowen Head 118 L2
Inishshark 104 B7
Inishtooskert 92 A11
Inishtrahull 118 K1
Inishtrahull Sound 118 K1
Inishturk 104 B6

Inishvickillane 92 A11
Inistioge 96 K10
Innfield 102 L7
Innisfree 112 G5
Inniskeen 108 M5
Inny (River) 107 J6
Inver *Donegal* 112 H4
Inver *Mayo* 110 C5
Inver Bay 112 H4
Inver's Eye 103 N7
Irish Agricultural
    Museum 97 M11
Irishtown 105 F7
Iron (Lough) 107 J7
Iron Mountains 113 I5
Irvinestown 113 J4
Island Lake 106 F6
Island Reavy (Lough) 115 N5
Islandmore 115 P4
Iveragh 88 B12

J

J. F. Kennedy Park 96 L11
Jamestown *Cloonteem* 107 H6
Jamestown *Laois* 101 K8
Japanese Gardens 102 L8
Jerpoint Abbey 96 K10
Jerrettspass 114 M5
Johnstown *Kildare* 103 M8
Johnstown *Kilkenny* 101 J9
Johnstown *Meath* 108 M7
Johnstown near *Arklow* ...103 N9
Johnstown
    near *Coolgreany* 97 N9
Johnstown Bridge 107 I6
Johnstownbridge 102 L7
Jonesborough 109 M5
Joyce 105 D7
Julianstown 109 N6

K

Kanturk Castle 94 F11
Katesbridge 115 N5
Keadew 107 H5
Keady 114 L5
Keady Mountain 118 L2
Kealduff 89 C12
Kealkill 89 D12
Kearney 115 P4
Kearney Point 115 P4
Keeagh 99 E8
Keel 110 B6
Keel (Lough) 117 I2
Keel Lough 110 B6
Keeloges 106 G7
Keem Strand 110 B6
Keenagh *Longford* 107 I7
Keenagh *Mayo* 111 D5
Keeraunnagark 98 D8
Keereen 91 I11
Keimaneigh (The pass of) ..89 E12
Kells *Ballymena* 115 N3
Kells *Kerry* 88 B12
Kells *Kilkenny* 96 K10
Kells (Ceanannas Mor) /
    Ceananas *Meath* 108 L6
Kells Bay 88 B11
Kells Priory 96 K10
Kellysgrove 100 H8
Kenmare River 88 B12
Kentstown 108 M7
Kerry (Ring of) 88 B12
Kerry Head 92 C10
Kesh *Fermanagh* 113 I4
Kesh *Toomour* 106 G5
Keshcarrigan 107 I5
Key (Lough) 106 H5
Kid Island 110 C5
Kilbaha 93 C10
Kilbaha Bay 93 C10
Kilbane 99 G9
Kilbarry 89 E12
Kilbeacanty 99 F8
Kilbeggan 101 J7
Kilbeheny 94 H11
Kilbennan 105 F7
Kilberry *Bert* 108 L6
Kilberry *Kildare* 102 K8
Kilbreedy 94 F10
Kilbrickan 105 D7
Kilbricken 101 J7
Kilbride near *Blessington* ..103 M8
Kilbride near *Ratoah* 103 M7
Kilbride near *Trim* 108 L7
Kilbride near *Wicklow* ...103 N9
Kilbrien 95 J11
Kilbrin 94 F11

A B C D E F G H I J K L M N O P Q R S T U V W X Y Z

Kilbrittain ...90 F12
Kilcaimin ...99 F8
Kilcar ...112 G4
Kilcarn ...108 L7
Kilcatherine Point ...88 B12
Kilcavan ...101 J8
Kilchreest ...99 G8
Kilclaran ...99 G9
Kilclief ...115 P5
Kilcloher ...93 C10
Kilconlonfert ...101 J8
Kilclooney ...116 G3
Kilcock ...102 L7
Kilcogy ...107 J6
Kilcolgan ...99 F8
Kilcolman Cashel ...90 F12
Kilcolman
   Dunmoylan East ...93 E10
Kilcoltrim ...96 L10
Kilcomin ...101 I9
Kilcommon near Caher ...95 I10
Kilcommon near Milestone ..95 H9
Kilcon ...111 E5
Kilconly Galway ...105 F7
Kilconly Kerry ...93 D10
Kilcoo ...115 N5
Kilcoole ...103 N8
Kilcormac ...101 I8
Kilcornan ...94 F10
Kilcotty ...97 M10
Kilcredan ...91 I12
Kilcredaun Point ...93 C10
Kilcrohane ...89 C13
Kilcrow ...100 H8
Kilcullen ...102 L8
Kilcummin Kerry ...92 B11
Kilcummin Mayo ...111 E5
Kilcummin Farmhill ...93 D11
Kilcurly ...109 M5
Kilcurry ...109 M5
Kildalkey ...108 L7
Kildangan ...102 K8
Kildavin ...96 L9
Kilderry ...96 K9
Kildoney Point ...112 H4
Kildorrery ...94 G11
Kildress ...114 L4
Kildrum ...115 N3
Kilfeakle ...95 H10
Kilfearagh ...98 D10
Kilfenora ...99 E9
Kilfinnane ...94 G10
Kilfinny ...94 F10
Kiflyn ...93 D10
Kilgarvan ...89 D12
Kilglass Galway ...106 G7
Kilglass Sligo ...111 E5
Kilglass Lough ...107 H6
Kilgobnet Kerry ...89 C11
Kilgobnet Waterford ...91 J11
Kilgory Lough ...99 F9
Kilgowan ...102 L8
Kiljames ...96 K10
Kilkea ...102 L9
Kilkeary ...100 H9
Kilkeasy ...96 K10
Kilkeel ...109 N5
Kilkeeran High Crosses ...95 J10
Kilkenny West ...107 I7
Kilkerrin ...106 G7
Kilkieran / Cill Chiaráin ...104 C8
Kilkieran Bay ...104 C7
Kilkiernan ...96 K9
Kilkinamurry ...115 N5
Kilkinlea ...93 E10
Kilkishen ...99 F9
Kill Cavan ...108 K5
Kill Waterford ...91 J11
Killabunane ...89 D12
Killaclug ...94 H11
Killacolla ...94 F10
Killadangan ...105 D6
Killadeas ...113 I4
Killadoon ...104 C6
Killadysert ...99 E9
Killafeen ...99 F8
Killag ...96 M11
Killagan Bridge ...118 M2
Killaghteen ...93 E10
Killahy ...95 J9
Killakee ...103 N8
Killala ...111 E5
Killala Bay ...111 E5
Killallon ...108 K6
Killaloo ...118 K3
Killamery ...95 J10
Killane ...102 K8

Killanena ...99 F9
Killann ...96 L10
Killard ...98 D9
Killard Point ...115 P5
Killeedy ...94 F10
Killarney National Park ...89 D11
Killarone ...105 E7
Killary Harbour ...104 C7
Killashandra ...107 J5
Killashee ...107 I6
Killasser ...105 F6
Killavally Mayo ...105 D6
Killavally Westmeath ...101 J7
Killavil ...106 G5
Killavullen ...94 G11
Killea Donegal ...117 J3
Killea Tipperary ...101 I9
Killeagh ...91 H12
Killealy ...115 N3
Killeany ...98 D8
Killedmond ...96 L10
Killeedy ...93 E10
Killeen Ardamullivan ...99 F9
Killeen Armagh ...114 M5
Killeen Dungannon ...114 M4
Killeenaran ...99 F8
Killeeneenmore ...99 F8
Killeenleagh Bridge ...88 B12
Killeevan ...113 K5
Killeglan ...106 H7
Killeigh ...101 J8
Killen ...113 J3
Killenagh ...97 N10
Killenaule ...95 I10
Killeshil ...101 K8
Killeshin ...102 K9
Killinamanagh ...97 M10
Killeter ...113 I3
Killeter Forest ...113 I3
Killevy ...109 M5
Killevy Churches ...109 M5
Killian Bridge ...99 G8
Killimer ...93 D10
Killimor ...100 H8
Killinaboy ...99 E9
Killinaspick ...96 K10
Killinchy ...115 O4
Killincooly ...97 N10
Killiney Dublin ...103 N8
Killiney Kerry ...92 B11
Killiney Bay ...103 N8
Killinick ...97 M11
Killinierin ...97 N9
Killinkere ...108 K6
Killinny ...99 F8
Killinthomas ...102 K8
Killinure Lough ...107 I7
Killiskey ...103 N8
Killkelly ...105 F6
Killogeary ...111 E5
Killogeenaghan ...101 I7
Killonecaha ...88 B12
Killoran ...100 G8
Killoscobe ...106 G7
Killough ...115 P5
Killough ...103 N8
Killowen ...109 N5
Killucan ...108 K7
Killukin ...107 H6
Killurin ...96 M10
Killurly ...88 B12
Killusty ...95 J10
Killwaughter ...115 O3
Killyclogher ...113 K4
Killyclug ...117 I3
Killycolpy ...114 M4
Killygar ...107 J5
Killygordon ...117 I3
Killykeen Forest Park ...107 J5
Killylea ...114 L4
Killyleagh ...115 P4
Killyon ...101 I8
Kilmacanoge ...103 N8
Kilmacduagh Monastery ...99 F8
Kilmacoo ...103 N9
Kilmacow ...96 K11
Kilmacrenan ...117 I2
Kilmacteige ...111 F5
Kilmacthomas ...95 J11
Kilmactranny ...106 H5
Kilmacurragh ...103 N9
Kilmaganny ...96 K10
Kilmaine ...105 E7
Kilmainham Wood ...108 L6
Kilmakilloge Harbour ...88 C12
Kilmaley ...99 E9
Kilmalkedar ...92 B11

Kilmanagh ...95 J10
Kilmeadan ...96 K11
Kilmeage ...102 L8
Kilmeedy ...94 F10
Kilmeelickin ...105 D7
Kilmeena ...105 D6
Kilmessan ...108 M7
Kilmichael
   near Castletownbere ...88 B13
Kilmichael near Macroom ...89 E12
Kilmichael Point ...97 N9
Kilmihil ...98 E9
Kilmona ...90 G12
Kilmoon ...89 D13
Kilmore Armagh ...114 M4
Kilmore Clare ...99 G9
Kilmore Down ...115 O4
Kilmore Mayo ...105 E6
Kilmore Roscommon ...107 H6
Kilmore Wexford ...96 M11
Kilmore Quay ...96 M11
Kilmorna ...93 D10
Kilmorony ...102 L9
Kilmovee ...106 F6
Kilmurry Cork ...90 F12
Kilmurry Limerick ...94 G10
Kilmurry near Kilkishen ...99 F9
Kilmurry near Milltown ...98 D9
Kilmurry Wicklow ...102 L9
Kilmurry Mac Mahon ...93 E10
Kilmurvy ...98 C8
Kilmyshall ...96 M10
Kilnagross ...107 I6
Kilnalag ...106 G6
Kilnaleck ...107 K6
Kilnamanagh ...97 M10
Kilnamona ...99 E9
Kiltown ...115 N4
Kilpatrick ...90 F12
Kilpeacan Cross Roads ...88 B12
Kilpedder ...103 N8
Kilquigguin ...97 M9
Kilraghts ...118 M2
Kilrane ...97 M11
Kilrea ...118 M3
Kilrean ...116 H3
Kilreekill ...100 G8
Kilroghter ...99 E8
Kilross Donegal ...117 I3
Kilross Tipperary ...94 H10
Kilruddery ...103 N8
Kilsallagh Galway ...106 G7
Kilsallagh Mayo ...104 C6
Kilsallaghan ...103 N7
Kilsally ...114 M4
Kilsaran ...109 M6
Kilshanchoe ...102 L7
Kilshannig ...92 B11
Kilshanny ...99 E9
Kilsheelan ...95 J10
Kilskeer ...108 L6
Kilskeery ...113 J4
Kiltealy ...96 L10
Kilteel ...103 M8
Kilteely ...94 G10
Kiltegan ...103 M9
Kilternan ...103 N8
Kiltimagh ...105 E6
Kiltober ...101 J7
Kiltoom ...107 H7
Kiltormer ...100 H8
Kiltullagh ...99 G8
Kiltyclogher ...113 H4
Kilvine ...105 F7
Kilworth ...94 H11
Kilworth Mountains ...94 H11
Kinale (Lough) ...107 J6
Kinard ...93 E10
Kinawley ...113 J5
Kincasslagh ...116 G2
Kindrohid ...117 J2
Kindrum ...117 I2
Kingarrow ...117 H3
Kings River ...95 J10
Kingscourt ...108 L6
Kingsland ...106 G6
Kingsmill ...114 M4
Kingstown ...104 B7
Kinlough ...112 H4
Kinnadoohy ...104 C6
Kinnagoe Bay ...118 K2
Kinnegad ...108 K7
Kinnitty ...101 I8
Kinsale (Old Head of) ...90 G13
Kinsale Harbour ...90 G12
Kinsalebeg ...91 I12
Kinsaley ...103 N7

Kinvarra
   near Camus Bay ...105 D7
Kinvarra
   near Kinvarra Bay ...99 F8
Kinvarra Bay ...99 F8
Kippure ...103 N8
Kircubbin ...115 P4
Kirkhills ...118 M2
Kirkistown ...115 P4
Kishkeam ...93 E11
Kitconnell ...100 G8
Knappagh ...105 D6
Knappogue Castle ...99 F9
Knight's Town ...88 B12
Knock Clare ...93 E10
Knock Mayo ...105 F6
Knock Tipperary ...101 I9
Knockaderry ...94 F10
Knockadoon Head ...91 I12
Knockainy ...94 G10
Knockalla Mount ...117 J2
Knockalongy ...112 F5
Knockalough ...99 E9
Knockanaffrin ...95 J11
Knockananna ...103 M9
Knockanefune ...93 E11
Knockanevin ...94 G11
Knockanillaun ...111 E5
Knockanimpaha ...93 E10
Knockanure ...93 D10
Knockaunalour ...90 G11
Knockaunavoher ...94 G10
Knockaunnaglashy ...92 C11
Knockboy near Dungarvan ...95 I11
Knockboy near Waterford ...96 K11
Knockboy (Mount) ...89 D12
Knockbrack ...117 I3
Knockbrandon ...97 M9
Knockbridge ...108 L6
Knockbride ...109 M6
Knockbrit ...95 I10
Knockcloghrim ...114 M3
Knockdrin ...107 K7
Knockerry ...98 D10
Knockferry ...105 E7
Knocklayd ...119 N2
Knocklofty ...95 I10
Knocklomena ...89 C12
Knocklong ...94 G10
Knockmealdown ...95 I11
Knockmealdown
   Mountains ...95 H11
Knockmore (Mount) ...104 C6
Knockmourne ...90 G12
Knockmoy Abbey ...106 F7
Knocknaboul Cross ...93 E11
Knocknacarry ...119 N2
Knocknacree ...102 L9
Knocknadobar ...88 B12
Knocknagantee ...88 C12
Knocknagashel ...93 D11
Knocknagree ...93 E11
Knocknahilan ...90 F12
Knocknalina ...110 C5
Knocknalower ...110 C5
Knockowen ...89 C12
Knockraha ...90 G12
Knocks Cork ...89 F12
Knocks Fermanagh ...113 J5
Knocks Laois ...101 J8
Knockshanahullion ...95 H11
Knockskagh ...89 F12
Knocktopher ...96 K10
Knocktown ...96 M11
Knockundervaul ...93 D10
Knockvicar ...106 H5
Knowth ...108 M6
Kylemore ...100 H8
Kylemore Abbey ...104 C7
Kylemore Lough ...104 C7

L

Laban ...99 F8
Labasheeda ...93 E10
Lack ...113 J4
Lackagh ...102 K8
Lackan Carlow ...96 K9
Lackan Wicklow ...103 M8
Lackan bay ...111 E5
Lackareagh ...89 F12
Laconnell ...116 G3
Lacken ...89 D12
Ladies View ...89 D12
Ladysbridge ...90 H12
Ladywell ...96 K10

Laffansbridge ...95 I10
Lag ...117 K2
Lagan (River) ...115 N4
Lagan Valley ...115 O4
Lagavara ...118 M2
Lagganstown ...95 I10
Laghey Corner ...114 L4
Laghtnafrankee ...95 J11
Laghy ...113 H4
Lahardaun ...111 E5
Lakyle ...93 E10
Lambay Island ...109 N7
Lambeg ...115 N4
Lamb's Head ...88 B12
Lanesborough ...107 I6
Laney (River) ...89 F12
Laracor ...108 L7
Laragh Kildare ...102 L7
Laragh Monaghan ...108 L5
Laragh Wicklow ...103 N8
Largan Mayo ...111 D5
Largan Sligo ...111 F5
Largy ...112 G4
Largydonnelly ...112 H4
Larne ...115 O3
Larne Lough ...115 O3
Lattin ...94 H10
Laune (River) ...93 C11
Lauragh ...88 C12
Laurelvale ...114 M4
Laurencetown ...100 H8
Lavagh ...112 F5
Lavagh More ...117 H3
Lawrencetown ...114 N4
Leabgarrow ...116 G3
League (Slieve) ...112 F4
League Point ...89 D13
Leamaneh Castle ...99 E9
Leamlara ...90 H12
Leamore Strand ...103 N8
Leane (Lough) ...89 D11
Leannan (River) ...117 I2
Leap ...89 E13
Leap (The)
   near Enniscorthy ...96 M10
Leap (The) near New Ross .96 L10
Lecale Peninsula ...115 O5
Lecarrow Leitrim ...112 H5
Lecarrow Roscommon ...107 H7
Leckanarainey ...112 H4
Leckanvy ...105 C6
Leckaun ...112 H5
Leckavrea Mountain ...105 D7
Leckemy ...118 K2
Lee ...93 C11
Lee (River) ...90 G12
Lee Reservoir ...90 F12
Leek Point ...93 C10
Leenane ...104 C7
Leganany Dolmen ...115 N5
Leggah ...107 J6
Legoniel ...115 O4
Lehardan ...117 J2
Leighlinbridge ...96 L9
Leinster (Mount) ...96 L10
Leitir Mealláin /
   Lettermullan ...98 C8
Leitir Mhic an Bhaird /
   Lettermacaward ...116 H3
Leitrim Banbridge ...115 O5
Leitrim Creegh ...98 D9
Leitrim Leitrim ...107 I6
Leixlip ...103 M7
Lemanaghan ...101 I8
Lemybrien ...91 J11
Lenadoon Point ...111 E5
Lenan Head ...117 J2
Lene (Lough) ...107 K7
Lerrig ...93 C10
Leslie Hill ...114 L5
Letterbarra ...112 H3
Letterbreen ...113 I5
Lettercallow ...98 C8
Lettercraffroe Lough ...105 D7
Letterfinish ...88 C12
Letterfrack ...104 C7
Letterkelly ...99 E9
Letterkenny /
   Leitir Ceanainn ...117 I3
Letterleague ...117 I3
Lettermore ...98 D8
Lettermore Island ...98 C8
Levally ...106 F7
Levally Lough ...105 E6
Licketstown ...96 K11
Liffey (River) ...102 M8

Lifford ...117 J3
Light House Island ...115 P3
Limavady ...118 L2
Limerick / Luimneach ...94 G10
Limerick Junction ...95 H10
Lios Dúin Bhearna /
   Lisdoonvarna ...99 E8
Lios Mór / Lismore ...91 I11
Lios Póil / Lispole ...92 B11
Lios Tuathail / Listowel ...93 D10
Lisacul ...106 G6
Lisbane ...115 O4
Lisbellaw ...113 J5
Lisburn ...115 N4
Liscannor ...98 D9
Liscannor Bay ...98 D9
Liscarney ...105 D6
Liscarroll ...94 F11
Liscolman ...118 M2
Liscooly ...117 J3
Lisdoart ...114 K4
Lisdowney ...101 J9
Lisduff Cavan ...108 K6
Lisduff Leitrim ...107 I6
Lisduff Offaly ...101 I8
Lisgarode ...100 H9
Lisgoold ...90 H12
Lislea Magherafelt ...118 M3
Lislea Newry-Mourne ...114 M5
Lismacaffry ...107 J6
Lismoghry ...117 J3
Lismoyle ...106 H7
Lisnacree ...109 N5
Lisnageer ...114 L4
Lisnagleer ...114 L4
Lisnagry ...94 G9
Lisnagunogue ...118 M2
Lisnamuck ...118 L3
Lisnarrick ...113 I4
Lisnaskea ...113 J5
Lisnavagh ...102 L9
Lispatrick ...90 G13
Lisroe ...99 E9
Lisronagh ...95 I10
Lisryan ...107 J6
Lissadell House ...112 G4
Lissalway ...106 G6
Lissamona ...89 D13
Lissatinnig Bridge ...88 C12
Lissavaird ...89 F13
Lisselton ...93 D10
Lissinagroagh ...112 H5
Lissiniska ...112 H4
Lissycasey ...99 E9
Listellick ...93 C11
Listerlin ...96 K10
Listooder ...115 O4
Lisvarrinane ...94 H10
Little Island ...103 N8
Little Island ...90 G12
Little Skellig ...88 A12
Littleton ...95 I10
Lixnaw ...93 D10
Loanends ...115 N4
Lobinstown ...108 M6
Loch Garman / Wexford ...97 M10
Loghill ...93 E10
Lombardstown ...94 F11
Londonderry /
   Londonderry ...117 K3
Lonehort Point ...88 C13
Long Island ...89 D13
Longford ...101 I8
Longhill ...101 K9
Longwood ...108 L7
Loo Bridge ...89 D12
Loobagh ...94 G10
Loop Head ...92 C10
Lorrha ...100 H8
Loskeran ...91 J11
Losset Cavan ...107 J6
Losset Donegal ...117 I2
Lough Bradan Forest ...113 J4
Lough Gowna ...107 J6
Lough Key Forest Park ...106 H6
Lough Navar Forest ...113 I4
Loughanavally ...107 J7
Loughanillaunmore ...98 D8
Loughanure ...116 H2
Loughbrickland ...114 N5
Lougher ...92 C11
Loughermore ...118 K3
Loughfad Hill ...113 I4
Loughgall ...114 M4
Loughglinn ...106 G6
Loughguile ...119 N2
Loughinisland ...115 O4
Loughlinstown ...103 N8

Loughmoe 101 I9
Loughmorne 108 L5
Loughros More Bay 116 G3
Loughros Point 116 G3
Loughsalt Mount 117 I2
Loughshinny 109 N7
Louisburgh 104 C6
Loup (The) 114 M3
Louth 108 M6
Lowertown 89 D13
Lowerymore 113 I3
Lowtown 115 N5
Lucan 103 M7
Luggacurren 101 K9
Lugnaquillia Mountain 103 M9
Luimneach / Limerick 94 G10
Lukeswell 96 K10
Lullymore 102 L8
Lurgan *Craigavon* 114 N4
Lurgan *Frenchpark* 106 G6
Lurganboy *Donegal* 117 J2
Lurganboy *Leitrim* 112 H5
Lusk 109 N7
Lyle 115 N3
Lyracrumpane 93 D10
Lyre 90 F11
Lyrenaglogh 95 H11

M
Maas 116 G3
Mac Gregor's Corner 119 N3
Mac Laughlins Corner 118 M3
Mac Mahon's Town 114 K4
Mac Swyne's Bay 112 G4
Mace 105 D6
Mace Head 104 C8
Macgillycuddy's Reeks 89 C12
Machugh (Lough) 116 G3
Mackan 113 J5
Macnean Lower (Lough) ..113 I5
Macnean Upper (Lough) ..113 I5
Macosquin 118 L2
Macroom/
  Maigh Chromtha 89 F12
Maddan 114 L5
Maddockstown 96 K10
Maganey 102 L9
Magee (Island) 115 O3
Maghaberry 115 N4
Maghanlawaun 89 C12
Maghera *Clare* 99 F9
Maghera *Donegal* 116 G3
Maghera *Down* 115 O5
Maghera *Magherafelt* 118 L3
Magherabane 117 J2
Magherafelt 114 M3
Magheragall 115 N4
Magheralin 114 N4
Magheramason 117 J3
Magheramorne 115 O3
Magheraveely 113 K5
Maghery *near Dungannon* .114 M4
Maghery *near Dunglow* ...116 G3
Magilligan 118 L2
Magilligan Point 118 L2
Magilligan Strand 118 L2
Maguiresbridge 113 J5
Mahee Island 115 P4
Mahon 95 J11
Mahon (Lough) 90 G12
Mahoonagh 93 E10
Maigh Chromtha /
  Macroom 89 F12
Maigh Cuilinn /
  Moycullen 105 E7
Maigh Nuad / Maynooth ..103 M7
Maigue (River) 94 F10
Main 118 N3
Maine (River) 93 C11
Mainham 102 L8
Mainistir Fhear Maí /
  Fermoy 90 H11
Mainistir na Búille /
  Boyle 106 H6
Mainistir na Corann /
  Midleton 90 H12
Máistir Gaoithe /
  Mastergeehy 88 B12
Mal Bay 98 D9
Mala / Mallow 94 G11
Málainn Bhig / Malin Beg ..112 F3
Malin 118 K2
Malin Bay 112 F3
Malin Head 117 J1
Malin More 112 F3

Mallusk 115 N3
Mamore (Gap of) 117 J2
Manger 112 H4
Mangerton Mountain 89 D12
Mannin Bay 104 B7
Mannin Lake 105 F6
Manorcunningham 117 J3
Manselstown 95 I9
Mansfieldstown 109 M6
Mantua 106 H6
Manulla 105 E6
Manulla (River) 105 E6
Maothail / Mohill 107 I6
Marble Arch Caves 113 I5
Marble Hill 117 I2
Mardyke 95 J10
Markethill 114 M5
Marshalstown 96 M10
Martin 90 G12
Martinstown *Emlygrennan* ..94 G10
Martinstown
  Grennanstown 108 L7
Martinstown
  South Somerset 119 N3
Mask (Lough) 105 D7
Massford 115 N4
Masshill 112 F5
Masterstown 95 I10
Matehy 90 G12
Matrix (Castle) 94 F10
Mattock (River) 108 M6
Mauherslieve 95 H9
Maum 105 D7
Maumakeogh 111 D5
Maumeen Lough 104 B7
Maumtrasna 105 D7
Maumturk Mountains 104 C7
Mauricesmills 99 E9
Mayo 105 E6
Mayo (Plains of) 105 E6
Mayobridge 114 N5
Mazetown 115 N4
Mealagh 89 D12
Meanus 94 G10
Meathas Troim /
  Edgeworthstown 107 J6
Meela (Lough) 116 G3
Meelick 100 H8
Meelin 93 E11
Meenaclady 116 H2
Meenacross 116 G3
Meenanarwa 117 H3
Meenaneary /
  Min na Aoire 112 G3
Meenatotan 116 H3
Meenavean 112 F3
Meencorwick 116 H3
Meenglass 113 I3
Meenlaragh 117 H2
Meenreagh 113 I3
Meentullynagarn 112 G3
Meenybraddan 112 H3
Meeting of the Waters 103 N9
Mellifont Abbey 109 M6
Melmore Head 117 I2
Melvin (Lough) 112 H4
Menlough 106 G7
Mew Island 115 P3
Michelstown Caves 95 H11
Middletown 116 H2
Middletown *Armagh* 114 L5
Midfield 105 F6
Mile 117 J2
Milebush 115 O3
Milehouse 96 M10
Milemill 102 L8
Milestone 95 H9
Milford *Armagh* 114 L5
Milford *Cork* 94 F10
Mill Town 114 L5
Millbay 115 O3
Millbrook *Derry* 118 K3
Millbrook *Larne* 115 O3
Millbrook *Oldcastle* 108 K6
Milleen 93 E11
Millford 117 I2
Millisle 115 P4
Millroad 96 M11
Millstreet *Cork* 89 E11
Millstreet *Waterford* 91 I11
Milltown *Armagh* 114 L5
Milltown *Ballymoney* 118 M2
Milltown *Banbridge* 114 N5
Milltown *Cavan* 107 J5
Milltown *Craigavon* 114 M4
Milltown *Dublin* 103 M8
Milltown *Kildare* 102 L8

Milltown *near Dingle* 92 B11
Milltown
  near Mount Bellew 106 G7
Milltown *near Tralee* 93 C11
Milltown *near Tuam* 105 F7
Milltown *Omagh* 114 K4
Milltown *Wexford* 97 M10
Miltownpass 107 K7
Minane Bridge 90 G12
Minard Head 92 B11
Mine Head 91 J12
Minerstown 115 O5
Minterburn 114 L4
Mizen Head 88 C13
Moanmore 98 D9
Modelligo 91 I11
Modreeny 100 H9
Mogeely 90 H12
Moglass 95 I10
Moher (Cliffs of) 98 D9
Moher Lough 105 D6
Mohil 96 K9
Móinteach Mílic /
  Mountmellick 101 K8
Moira 115 N4
Moll's Gap 89 D12
Monard 95 H10
Monaseed 97 M9
Monaster 94 G10
Monasteraden 106 G6
Monasteranenagh Abbey ..94 G10
Monasterboice 109 M6
Monasterevin 102 K8
Monavullagh Mountains ...95 J11
Mondello Park 102 L8
Monea 113 I4
Moneen *Clare* 93 C10
Moneen *Galway* 105 F7
Money Point 93 D10
Moneydig 118 M3
Moneygall 101 I9
Moneyglass 114 M3
Moneygold 112 G4
Moneylahan 112 G4
Moneymore 114 L3
Moneyneany 118 L3
Moneyreagh 115 O4
Monilea 107 K7
Monivea 106 F7
Monkstown *Cork* 90 G12
Monkstown
  Newtownabbey 115 O3
Monroe 107 J7
Montpelier 99 G9
Mooncoin 96 K11
Moone 102 L9
Moord 91 I12
Moore Bay 98 C9
Moorfields 115 N3
More (Island) 105 D6
Morenane 94 F10
Morley's Bridge 89 D12
Morningstar 94 G10
Mornington 109 N6
Mosney 109 N7
Moss-Side 118 M2
Mossley 115 O3
Mothel 95 J11
Motte Stone 103 N9
Mount Falcon 111 E5
Mount Garret 96 L10
Mount Hamilton or Sperrin ..114 K3
Mount Melleray Monastery .95 I11
Mount Norris 114 M5
Mount Nugent 107 K6
Mount Stewart Gardens 115 P4
Mount Talbot 106 H7
Mount Temple 107 I7
Mount Uniacke 91 H12
Mount Usher Gardens 103 N8
Mountbolus 101 J8
Mountcastle 117 J3
Mountcharles 112 H4
Mountcollins 93 E11
Mountfield 114 K4
Mounthenry 105 E7
Mountjoy *Dungannon* 114 M4
Mountjoy *Omagh* 113 J4
Mountrath 101 J8
Mountrivers Bridge 98 D9
Mountshannon 100 G9
Mourne (Lough)
  near Ballybofey 113 I3
Mourne (Lough)
  near Carrickfergus 115 O3
Mourne Beg 113 I3
Mourne Mountains 109 N5

Mourne River 113 J3
Moveen 98 C10
Moville / Bun an Phobail ..118 K2
Mowhan 114 M5
Moy 114 L4
Moy (River) 111 E5
Moyagh 117 J3
Moyallan 114 M4
Moyard 104 B7
Moyarget 118 N2
Moyasta 98 D9
Moydow 107 I7
Moygashel 114 L4
Moyglass 99 G8
Moylough *Galway* 106 G7
Moylough *Sligo* 106 F5
Moynalty 108 L6
Moynalvy 108 L7
Moyne *Roscommon* 106 G6
Moyne *Tipperary* 107 J6
Moyne *Wicklow* 103 M9
Moyne Abbey 111 E5
Moyrus 104 C7
Moyteoge Head 110 B6
Moyvally 102 L7
Moyvore 107 J7
Moyvoughly 107 I7
Muck (Isle of) 115 O3
Muckamore 115 N3
Muckanagh Lough 99 F9
Muckish Mountain 117 H2
Mucklon 102 L7
Muckno Lake 108 L5
Muckros Head 112 G4
Muckross 89 D11
Muff 117 K2
Muggort's Bay 91 J11
Muinchille / Cootehill 108 K5
Muine Bheag /
  Bagenalstown 96 L9
Muineachán / Monaghan ..114 L5
Muing 111 D5
Muingnabo 111 C5
Mulhuddart 103 M7
Mulkear 94 G10
Mullach Íde / Malahide 103 N7
Mullagh *Cavan* 108 L6
Mullagh *Galway* 100 G8
Mullagh *Mayo* 104 C6
Mullagh *Meath* 103 M7
Mullaghanattin 88 C12
Mullaghanish 89 E12
Mullaghareirk Mountains ..93 E10
Mullaghash 118 K3
Mullaghbane 109 M5
Mullaghboy 115 O3
Mullaghcarn 113 K3
Mullaghcleevaun 103 M8
Mullaghclogha 114 K3
Mullaghmore
  Cliffony North 112 G4
Mullaghmore *Magherafelt* .118 L3
Mullaghmore Head 112 G4
Mullaghroe 106 G6
Mullan *Coleraine* 118 L2
Mullan *Figullar* 114 L4
Mullany'sCross 111 F5
Mullartown 109 O5
Mullen 106 G6
Mullenbeg 96 K10
Mullet Peninsula 110 B5
Mullinahone 95 J10
Mullinasole 112 H4
Mullinavat 96 K10
Mulroy Bay 117 I2
Multeen 95 H10
Multyfarnham 107 J7
Mungret 94 F10
Muntervary
  or Sheep's Head 88 C13
Murley 113 K4
Murlough Bay 119 N2
Murntown 97 M11
Murreagh 92 A11
Murrisk 105 D6
Murroe 94 G10
Murrough 99 E8
Murroogh 99 E8
Musheramore 89 F11
Mussenden Temple 118 L2
Mutton Island 98 D9
Mweelrea Mountains 104 C7
Mweenish Island 104 C8
Myshall 96 L9

N
Na Cealla Beaga /
  Killybegs 112 G4

Na Clocha Liatha /
  Greystones 103 N8
Na Dúnaibh / Downies 117 I2
Na Sceirí / Skerries 109 N7
Nacorra (Lough) 105 D6
Nacung (Lough) 117 H2
Nad 90 F11
Nafooey (Lough) 105 D7
Nagles Mountains 90 G11
Nalughraman (Lough) 116 G3
Naminn (Lough) 117 J2
Namona (Lough) 88 B12
Nanny 108 M7
Narin 116 G3
Narraghmore 102 L8
Narrow Water Castle 109 N5
Naul 109 N7
Neagh (Lough) 114 M4
Neale 105 E7
Nealstown 101 I9
Neidín / Kenmare 89 D12
Nenagh 100 H9
Nephin 111 D5
Nephin (Glen) 111 D5
Nephin Beg 111 D5
Nephin Beg Range 111 C5
New Birmingham 95 I10
New Buildings 117 J3
New Inn *Cavan* 108 K6
New Inn *Galway* 100 G8
New Kildimo 94 F10
New Quay / Bealaclugga ..99 E8
New Twopothouse Village .94 G11
Newbawn 96 L10
Newbliss 113 K5
Newbridge *Fingal* 109 N7
Newbridge *Limerick* 94 F10
Newbridge
  near Tuomard 106 G7
Newbridge /
  An Droichead Nua 102 L8
Newcastle *Down* 115 O5
Newcastle *Dublin* 103 M8
Newcastle *Galway* 99 F7
Newcastle *Tipperary* 95 I11
Newcastle *Wicklow* 103 N8
Newcestown 90 F12
Newchapel 95 I10
Newgrange 109 M6
Newinn 95 I10
Newmarket *Cork* 93 F11
Newmarket *Kilkenny* 96 K10
Newmarket on Fergus 99 F9
Newmills *Donegal* 117 I3
Newmills *Dungannon* 114 L4
Newport *Tipperary* 100 G9
Newport *Mayo* 105 C6
Newport Trench 114 M4
Newry 114 M5
Newtown *Cork* 94 G11
Newtown *Galway* 99 F8
Newtown *Kildare* 102 L7
Newtown *Laois* 101 K9
Newtown *Limerick* 94 G10
Newtown *near Knock* 101 I9
Newtown *near Nenagh* 100 H9
Newtown *Offaly* 100 H8
Newtown *Roscommon* 100 H7
Newtown *Tipperary* 95 H10
Newtown *Waterford* 95 J11
Newtown *Wexford* 96 M11
Newtown Cashel 107 I7
Newtown Cloghans 111 E5
Newtown-Crommelin 119 N3
Newtown Cunningham 117 J3
Newtown Forbes 107 I6
Newtown Gore 107 I5
Newtown
  Mount Kennedy 103 N8
Newtown Sandes 93 D10
Newtownabbey 115 O4
Newtownards 115 O4
Newtownbreda 115 O4
Newtownbutler 113 J5
Newtownhamilton 114 M5
Newtownlow 101 J7
Newtownlynch 99 E8
Newtownshandrum 94 F10
Newtownstewart 113 J3
Nier 95 J11
Ninemilehouse 95 J10
Nobber 108 L6
Nohaval 90 G12
Nore 101 J9
Nore (River) 96 K10
North Channel 119 O2

North Ring 90 F13
North Sound 98 C8
Nose of Howth 103 N7
Noughaval *Doora* 99 F9
Noughaval *Noughaval* 99 E8
Nowen Hill 89 E12
Nuns Quarter 115 O4
Nurney *Carlow* 96 L9
Nurney *Kildare* 102 L8
Nutt's Corner 115 N4

O
Oaghley 93 D10
Oatfield 99 F9
Oatquarter 98 C8
O'Brien's Tower 98 D9
O'Flynn (Lough) 106 G6
Oghil *Clare* 100 H8
Oghil *Galway* 98 C8
Ogonnelloe 99 G9
O'Grady (Lough) 99 G9
Oileán Ciarraí /
  Castleisland 93 D11
Oilgate 97 M10
Oily 112 G4
Old Court 89 E13
Old Head *Ballymackean* ...90 G13
Old Head *Louisburgh* 104 C6
Old Kilcullen 102 L8
Old Kildimo 94 F10
Old Ross 96 L10
Old Town *Donegal* 117 I3
Old Town *Laois* 101 J9
Old Town *Roscommon* 100 H8
Old Town *Wexford* 96 L10
Old Twopothouse 94 G11
Oldleighlin 96 K9
Oldmill Bridge 93 E10
Oldtown *Dublin* 109 N7
Oldtown *Roscommon* 101 I7
Omagh 113 K4
Omeath 109 N5
Omey Island 104 B7
Onaght 98 C8
Oola 94 H10
Oorid Lough 105 D7
Oranmore 99 F8
Oriel (Mount) 108 M6
Oristown 108 L6
Oritor 114 L4
Ossian's Grave 119 N2
Oughter (Lough) 107 J6
Oulart 97 M10
Ovens 90 G12
Owel (Lough) 107 J7
Owenascaul 92 B11
Owenator 116 H3
Owenavorragh 97 M10
Owenbeagh 117 H3
Owenbeg 111 F5
Owenbeg (River) 112 G5
Owenboliska 99 E8
Owenboy 90 G12
Owenbristy 99 F8
Owencarrow 117 I2
Owendalulleegh 99 G8
Owenea 116 G3
Owengarve *Clew Bay* 105 D6
Owengarve *River Moy* 106 F5
Owenglin 104 C7
Oweniny 111 D5
Owenkillew *Glenelly* 114 K3
Owenkillew *Lough Swilly* ..117 J2
Owenmore Bridge 105 D6
Owennacurra 90 H12
Owenreagh Hill 117 J3
Owenriff 105 D7
Owentaraglin 93 E11
Owentocker 116 H3
Owenur (River) 106 H6
Ower 105 E7
Owning 95 J10
Owroe Bridge 88 B12
Owvane 89 D12
Oysterhaven 90 G12

P
Palace 96 L10
Palatine 102 L9
Pallas 101 J8
Pallas Cross 100 I9
Pallas Green 94 G10
Pallaskenry 94 F10
Paps (The) 89 E11
Park *Bellavary* 105 E6
Park *Derry* 118 K3
Parke's Castle 112 H5

A
B
C
D
E
F
G
H
I
J
K
L
M
N
O
P
Q
R
S
T
U
V
W
X
Y
Z

Parkgate 115 N 3
Parkmore 99 F 8
Parkmore Point 92 A 11
Parknasilla 88 C 12
Parteen 99 G 9
Partry 105 E 6
Partry Mountains 105 D 7
Passage 106 H 7
Passage East 96 L 11
Passage West 90 G 12
Patrickswell 94 F 10
Patterson's Spade Mill 115 N 3
Paulstown 96 K 9
Peake 90 F 12
Peatlands 114 M 4
Peterswell 99 F 8
Pettigoe 113 I 4
Phoenix Park 103 M 7
Piercetown 97 M 11
Pigeons (The) 107 I 7
Pike 100 H 8
Pike (The) *near Boola* 91 I 11
Pike (The) *near Lamybrien* 91 J 11
Pike (The) *Tipperary* 100 H 8
Pike Corner 108 L 7
Pike of Rush Hall 101 J 9
Piltown 95 K 10
Pluck 117 J 3
Plumbridge 113 K 3
Pollagh 101 I 8
Pollan Bay 117 J 2
Pollatomish 111 C 5
Pollnalaght 113 J 4
Pollshask 106 G 7
Pomeroy 114 L 4
Pontoon 105 E 6
Port 116 F 3
Port Ballintrae 118 M 2
Port Durlainne / Porturlin 111 C 5
Port Láirge / Waterford 96 K 11
Port Laoise / Portlaoise 101 K 8
Port Omna / Portumna 100 H 8
Portacloy 111 C 5
Portadown 114 M 4
Portaferry 115 P 4
Portaleen 118 K 2
Portavogie 115 P 4
Portbradden 118 M 2
Portglenone 118 M 3
Portland 100 H 8
Portlaw 96 K 11
Portmagee 88 A 12
Portmagee Channel 88 A 12
Portmarnock 103 N 7
Portmuck 115 O 3
Portnablagh 117 I 2
Portnoo 116 G 3
Portrane 109 N 7
Portroe 100 G 9
Portrush 118 M 2
Portsalon 117 J 2
Portstewart 118 L 2
Poulaphouca Reservoir 103 M 8
Poulnamucky 95 I 10
Poulnasherry Bay 98 D 10
Power Head 90 H 12
Power's Cross 100 H 8
Powerscourt Demesne 103 N 8
Powerstown 96 K 10
Poyntz Pass 114 M 5
Priesthaggard 96 L 11
Prosperous 102 L 8
Puckaun 100 H 9
Puffin Island 88 A 12
Punchestown 103 M 8

Q
Quarrytown 119 N 3
Querrin 93 D 10
Quigley's Point 118 K 2
Quilty 98 D 9
Quin 99 F 9
Quoile 115 O 4

R
Rabbit Islands 89 E 13
Race End 117 I 2
Raffrey 115 O 4
Raghly 112 G 5
Raghtin More 117 J 2
Rahan 101 J 8
Rahanagh 93 E 10
Rahara 106 H 7
Raharney 108 K 7
Raheen 96 L 10
Raigh 105 D 7
Railyard 101 K 9

Rake Street 111 D 5
Ram Head 91 I 12
Ramor (Lough) 108 K 6
Ramore Head 118 M 2
Rams Island 114 N 4
Ramsgrange 96 L 11
Randalstown 114 N 3
Rapemills 101 I 8
Raphoe 117 J 3
Rasharkin 118 M 3
Rashedoge 117 I 3
Rath 101 I 8
Ráth Caola / Rathkeale 94 F 10
Ráth Droma / Rathdrum 103 N 9
Rathangan 102 L 8
Rathaspick 107 J 7
Rathbrit 95 I 10
Rathcabban 100 H 8
Rathconrath 107 J 7
Rathcool 89 F 11
Rathcoole 103 M 8
Rathcor 109 N 6
Rathcore 102 L 7
Rathcormack *near Fermoy* 90 H 11
Rathcormack *near Sligo* 112 G 5
Rathcroghan 106 H 6
Rathdangan 103 M 9
Rathdowney 101 J 9
Rathduff 90 G 11
Rathedan 96 L 9
Rathfeigh 108 M 7
Rathfriland 115 N 5
Rathfylane 96 L 10
Rathgarogue 96 L 10
Rathgormuck 95 J 11
Rathkeevin 95 I 10
Rathkenny 108 M 6
Rathlackan 111 E 5
Rathlee 111 E 5
Rathlin Island 119 N 2
Rathlin O'Birne Island 112 F 4
Rathlin Sound 119 N 2
Rathmelton 117 J 2
Rathmines 103 N 8
Rathmolyon 108 L 7
Rathmore 89 E 11
Rathmullan 117 J 2
Rathnew 103 N 9
Rathnure 96 L 10
Rathoma 111 E 5
Rathowen 107 J 7
Rathvilla 101 K 8
Rathvilly 102 L 9
Ratoath 108 M 7
Raven Point (The) 97 M 10
Ravensdale 109 M 5
Ray *near Dunfanaghy* 117 H 2
Ray *near Rathmillan* 117 J 2
Ray (River) 117 H 2
Rea (Lough) 99 G 8
Reanagowan Cross Roads 93 D 11
Reananeree /
 Rae na nDoirí 89 E 12
Reanascreena 89 E 13
Rear Cross 95 H 9
Red Bay 119 N 2
Redcastle 118 K 2
Redcross 103 N 9
Redgate 97 M 10
Redhills 107 K 5
Ree (Lough) 107 I 7
Reelan 117 H 3
Reen 89 D 12
Reens 94 F 10
Reevanagh 96 K 9
Relaghbeg 108 L 6
Rerrin 88 C 13
Rhode 101 K 7
Richhill 114 M 4
Ridge 96 K 9
Ridge Point 110 C 5
Rine (River) 99 F 9
Rineanna Point 99 F 9
Ringabella Bay 90 H 12
Ringarogy Island 89 D 13
Ringaskiddy 90 H 12
Ringboy 115 P 4
Ringfad Point 115 P 5
Ringsend 118 L 2
Ringstown 101 J 8
Ringville / An Rinn 91 J 11
Rinmore Point 117 I 2
Rinn (River) 107 I 6
Rinn Lough 107 I 6
Rinneen *Clare* 98 D 9
Rinneen *Cork* 89 E 13

Rinroe Point 110 C 5
Rinville 99 F 8
Rinvyle 104 C 7
Rinvyle Castle 104 B 7
Rinvyle Point 104 B 7
River 110 B 6
Riverchapel 97 N 10
Riverstick 90 G 12
Riverstown *Cork* 90 G 12
Riverstown *Sligo* 112 G 5
Riverstown *Tipperary* 101 I 8
Riverville 93 D 11
Roadford 98 D 8
Roaninish 116 G 3
Roaringwater Bay 89 D 13
Robe 105 E 6
Robert's Head 90 H 12
Robertstown 102 L 8
Robinstown 108 L 7
Roche's Point 90 H 12
Rochestown 96 K 11
Rochfortbridge 101 K 7
Rock (The) 114 L 4
Rock Island 98 C 8
Rockabill 109 N 7
Rockchapel 93 E 11
Rockcorry 108 K 5
Rockhill 94 F 10
Rockmills 94 G 11
Rodeen 107 H 6
Roe 118 L 3
Roe Valley 118 L 2
Roney Point 97 N 10
Rooaun 100 H 8
Roonagh Quay 104 C 6
Roonah Lough 104 C 6
Roosky *Leitrim* 112 H 4
Roosky *Mayo* 106 F 6
Roosky *Roscommon* 107 I 6
Ropefield 112 G 5
Ros an Mhil / Rossaveel 98 D 8
Ros Comáin /
 Roscommon 106 H 7
Ros Cré / Roscrea 101 I 9
Ros Láir / Rosslare 97 M 11
Ros Mhic Thriúin /
 New Ross 96 L 10
Rosapenna 117 I 2
Rosbercon 96 L 10
Rosegreen 95 I 10
Rosenallis 101 J 8
Rosguill 117 I 2
Roskeeragh Point 112 F 4
Rosmuck 105 D 7
Rosmult 95 I 9
Rosnakill 117 I 2
Ross *Lough Leane* 89 D 11
Ross *Lough Sheelin* 107 K 6
Ross Abbey 105 E 7
Ross Lake 105 E 7
Ross Port 111 C 5
Ross West 105 E 6
Rossan Point 112 F 3
Rossbeg 116 G 3
Rossbeigh Creek 92 C 11
Rossbrin 89 D 13
Rosscahill 105 E 7
Rosscarbery 89 E 13
Rosscarbery Bay 89 E 13
Rosscor 113 H 4
Rossdohan Island 88 C 12
Rosses (The) 116 G 2
Rosses Bay 116 G 2
Rosses Point 112 G 5
Rossgeir 117 J 3
Rossglass 115 O 5
Rossinver 112 H 4
Rosslare Bay 97 M 11
Rosslare Point 97 M 11
Rosslea 113 K 5
Rossmore *Cork* 89 F 12
Rossmore *Laois* 102 K 9
Rossmore Forest Park 114 L 5
Rossmore Island 88 C 12
Rossnowlagh 112 H 4
Rostellan 90 H 12
Rostrevor 109 N 5
Rosturk 105 C 6
Rough Point 92 B 11
Roughty 89 D 12
Roundfort 105 E 7
Roundstone 104 C 7
Roundwood 103 N 8
Roury 89 E 13
Rousky 114 K 3
Rowallane Gardens 115 O 4

Rower (The) 96 L 10
Royal Canal 107 I 7
Royaloak 96 L 9
Ruan 99 F 9
Rubane 115 P 4
Rue Point 119 N 2
Runabay Head 119 N 2
Runnabackan 106 H 6
Rushen (Slieve) 113 J 5
Russborough House 103 M 8
Rutland Island 116 G 3
Ryefield 108 K 6
Ryehill 106 F 7
Rylane Cross 90 F 12

S
Saddle Head 110 B 5
Saggart 103 M 8
St. Finan's Bay 88 A 12
St. John's Lough 107 I 5
St. John's Point 115 P 5
St. John's Point 112 G 4
St. Johnstown 117 J 3
St. Macdara's Island 104 C 8
St. Margaret's 103 N 7
St. Mochta's House 108 M 6
St. Mullin's 96 L 10
Saintfield 115 O 4
Saleen *Cork* 90 H 12
Saleen *Kerry* 93 D 10
Salia 104 C 6
Sallahig 88 B 12
Sallins 102 M 8
Sallybrook 90 G 12
Sallypark 100 H 9
Salrock 104 C 7
Saltee Islands 96 M 11
Salthill 99 E 8
Sandholes 114 L 4
Sandyford 103 N 8
Santry 103 N 7
Saul 115 O 4
Sawel Mountain 118 K 3
Scalp Mountain 117 J 2
Scardaun *Mayo* 105 E 7
Scardaun *Roscommon* 106 H 7
Scarnagh 97 N 9
Scarriff / An Scairbh 99 G 9
Scarriff Island 88 B 12
Scartaglin 93 D 11
Scarva 114 M 5
Scattery Island 93 D 10
Schull / Skull 89 D 13
Scolban (Lough) 113 H 4
Scotch Town 114 K 3
Scotshouse 113 K 5
Scotstown 114 K 5
Scrabo Hill 115 O 4
Scramoge 107 H 6
Screeb Cross 105 D 7
Screen 97 M 10
Screggan 101 J 8
Scribbagh 113 H 4
Scullogue Gap 96 L 10
Scur (Lough) 107 I 5
Seaforde 115 O 5
Seapatrick 114 N 4
Seefin 95 J 11
Seskinore 113 K 4
Seskinryan 96 L 9
Seven Heads 90 F 13
Seven Hogs or
 Magharee Islands (The) 92 B 11
Shalwy 112 G 4
Shanacashel 88 C 11
Shanagarry 90 H 12
Shanaglish 99 F 8
Shanagolden 93 E 10
Shanahoe 101 J 9
Shanbally *Cork* 90 G 12
Shanbally *Galway* 106 G 7
Shanballymore 94 G 11
Shanco 114 L 4
Shanes Castle 114 N 3
Shankill 103 N 8
Shanlaragh 89 E 12
Shanlis 108 M 6
Shannagh (Lough) 115 N 5
Shannawona 105 D 7
Shannon 99 F 9
Shannon (River) 100 H 8
Shannon Airport 99 F 9
Shannon Harbour 101 I 8
Shannonbridge 100 H 8

Shanragh 101 K 9
Shantonagh 108 L 5
Sharavogue 101 I 8
Sheddings (The) 119 N 3
Sheeanamore 103 M 9
Sheeaun 99 G 9
Sheeffry Hills 105 C 6
Sheehan's Point 88 B 12
Sheelin (Lough) 107 K 6
Sheep Haven 117 I 2
Sheever (Lough) 107 K 7
Shehy Mountains 89 D 12
Shercock 108 L 6
Sherkin Island 89 D 13
Sherky Island 88 C 12
Sheskin 111 D 5
Sheskinapoll 117 J 3
Shillelagh 97 M 9
Shinrone 101 I 9
Shiven 106 G 7
Shoptown 115 N 3
Shot Head 89 C 13
Shranamanragh Bridge 110 C 5
Shrule 105 E 7
Silent Valley 109 O 5
Sillan (Lough) 108 L 5
Silver Bridge 108 M 5
Silver Strand 104 C 6
Silvermine Mountains 100 H 9
Silvermines 100 H 9
Sinking 106 F 7
Sion Mills 113 J 3
Six Crosses 93 D 10
Six Road Ends 115 P 4
Six Towns (The) 114 L 3
Sixmilebridge 99 F 9
Sixmilecross 114 K 4
Skannive (Lough) 104 C 8
Skeagh 107 J 7
Skehana 101 K 9
Skehanagh 106 G 7
Skerries (The) 118 M 2
Sky Road 104 B 7
Slade 96 L 11
Slane 108 M 6
Slane (Hill of) 108 M 6
Slaney (River) 97 M 10
Slat (Lough) 92 B 11
Slate (River) 102 L 8
Slea Head 92 A 11
Slemish Mountain 119 N 3
Sliabh na Caillighe 108 K 6
Slieve Anierin 113 I 5
Slieve Aught Mountains 99 G 8
Slieve Bernagh 99 G 9
Slieve Bloom Mountains 101 J 8
Slieve Gamph
 or the Ox Mountains 111 F 5
Slieve Mish Mountains 93 C 11
Slieve Miskish Mountains 88 C 13
Slieveanorra 119 N 2
Slievecallan 99 E 9
Slievefelim Mountains 94 H 9
Slievekimalta 100 H 9
Slievekirk 117 K 3
Slievemore *Dungannon* 114 K 4
Slievemore *Mayo* 110 B 5
Slievemurry 106 G 7
Slievenamon 95 J 10
Slieveroe 96 K 11
Slievetooey 116 G 3
Sligeach / Sligo 112 G 5
Sligo Bay 112 F 5
Slyne Head 104 B 7
Smerwick 92 A 11
Smerwick Harbour 92 A 11
Smithborough 114 K 5
Smithstown 101 K 9
Snaght (Slieve)
 Derryveagh Mts. 117 H 3
Snaght (Slieve) *Inishowen* 117 J 2
Snave 89 D 12
Sneem 88 C 12
Soldierstown 115 N 4
Sord / Swords 103 N 7
South Sound 98 D 8
Spa 93 C 11
Spa (The) 115 O 4
Spanish Point *Locality* 98 D 9
Spanish Point *Mal Bay* 98 D 9
Speenoge 117 J 2
Spelga Dam 115 N 5
Sperrin Mountains 118 K 3
Spink 101 K 9

Spittaltown 101 J 7
Springfield 113 I 4
Springhill 114 M 3
Springwell Forest 118 L 2
Squires Hill 115 O 4
Sraghmore 103 N 8
Srah / An tSraith 105 E 6
Srahduggaun 111 C 6
Srahmore *near Bangor* 111 C 5
Srahmore *near Newport* 105 D 6
Srahmore River 105 D 6
Sráid na Cathrach /
 Milltown Malbay 98 D 9
Stabannan 109 M 6
Stackallan 108 M 6
Stack's Mountains 93 D 11
Staffordstown 114 M 3
Stags (The) 89 E 13
Stags of Broad Haven 111 C 4
Staigue Stone Fort 88 B 12
Stamullin 109 N 7
Staplestown 102 L 8
Stepaside 103 N 8
Stewartstown 114 L 4
Stickstown 90 F 12
Stillorgan 103 N 8
Stone Bridge 113 K 5
Stonyford *Kilkenny* 96 K 10
Stonyford *Lisburn* 115 N 4
Stormont 115 O 4
Strabane 117 J 3
Stracashel 117 H 3
Stradbally *Kerry* 92 B 11
Stradbally *Laois* 101 K 8
Stradbally *Waterford* 91 J 11
Strade 105 E 6
Stradone 107 K 6
Stradreagh 118 L 2
Straffan 103 M 8
Stragar 112 G 3
Strahart 96 M 10
Straid *Donegal* 117 J 2
Straid *Larne* 115 O 3
Straid *Moyle* 118 M 2
Straith Salach / Recess 104 C 7
Strand 93 E 10
Strandhill 112 G 5
Strangford 115 P 4
Strangford Lough 115 P 4
Stranocum 118 M 2
Stranorlar 117 I 3
Stratford 102 L 9
Stravally 112 G 3
Streamstown 104 B 7
Streedagh Point 112 G 4
Streek Head 89 C 13
Street 107 J 6
Strokestown 106 H 6
Stroove 118 L 2
Struell Wells 115 O 5
Strule 113 J 3
Sturrakeen 95 H 10
Suck (River) 106 G 6
Suir (River) 101 I 9
Summercove 90 G 12
Summerhill 108 L 7
Suncroft 102 L 8
Sunderlin (Lough) 107 I 7
Swan 101 K 9
Swanlinbar 113 I 5
Swan's Cross Roads 114 K 5
Swatragh 118 L 3
Sweep (The) 95 J 10
Swilly (Lough) 117 J 2
Swilly (River) 117 J 2
Sybil Head 92 A 11

T
Table Mountain 103 M 8
Tacumshane 97 M 11
Tacumshin Lake 97 M 11
Taghmon 96 M 11
Taghshinny 107 I 7
Tagoat 97 M 11
Tahilla 88 C 12
Talbot Island 104 B 7
Talbotstown 102 M 9
Tallaght 103 M 8
Tallanstown 108 M 6
Tallow 91 H 11
Tallowbridge 91 H 11
Talt (Lough) 111 F 5
Tamlaght *Fermanagh* 113 J 5
Tamlaght *Magherafelt* 118 M 3
Tamnamore 114 M 4
Tandragee 114 M 4
Tang 107 I 7

Tangaveane ....116 H 3
Tappaghan Mount ....113 J 4
Tara (Hill of) ....108 M 7
Tarbert ....93 D 10
Tardree Forest ....115 N 3
Tarker (Lough) ....108 L 5
Tarmon ....112 H 5
Tarsaghaunmore ....111 C 5
Tassagh ....114 L 5
Taughblane ....115 N 4
Taur ....93 E 11
Tawin ....99 E 8
Tawin Island ....99 E 8
Tawny ....117 I 2
Tawnyinah ....106 F 6
Tawnylea ....112 H 5
Tay ....95 J 11
Tay (Lough) ....103 N 8
Taylor's Cross ....101 I 8
Tearaght Island ....92 A 11
Tedavnet ....114 K 5
Teelin ....112 G 4
Teemore ....113 J 5
Teeranea ....98 D 8
Teeranearagh ....88 B 12
Teerelton ....89 F 12
Teermaclane ....99 E 9
Teernakill ....105 D 7
Teeromoyle ....88 B 12
Teevurcher ....108 L 6
Temple (The) ....115 O 4
Temple of the Winds ....115 P 4
Templeboy ....112 F 5
Templederry ....100 H 9
Templeglentan ....93 E 10
Templehouse Lake ....112 G 5
Templemartin ....90 F 12
Templenoe ....89 C 12
Templeoran ....101 J 7
Templepatrick ....115 N 3
Templeshanbo ....96 L 10
Templetouhy ....101 I 9
Templetown ....96 L 11
Tempo ....113 J 4
Terenure ....103 N 8
Termon ....98 D 10
Termonbarry ....107 I 6
Termonfeckin ....109 N 6
Terryglass ....100 H 8
Tevrin ....107 K 7
Thomas Street ....106 H 7

Thomastown *Meath* ....108 L 6
Thomastown *Tipperrary* ....95 H 10
Thoor Ballylee ....99 F 8
Three Castle Head ....88 C 13
Three Castles ....96 J 9
Three Rock ....103 N 8
Tiduff ....92 B 11
Tievealehid ....116 H 2
Tievemore ....113 I 4
Tillyvoos ....112 H 4
Tiltinbane ....113 I 5
Timahoe ....102 L 8
Timoleague ....90 F 13
Timolin ....102 L 9
Tinahely ....103 M 9
Tinnahinch ....96 L 10
Tinriland ....102 L 9
Tiobraid Árann /
   Tipperary ....95 H 10
Tirnaneill ....114 L 5
Tirneevin ....99 F 8
Toames ....89 F 12
Tobar an Choire /
   Tubbercurry ....112 F 5
Tober ....101 J 7
Toberbeg ....102 M 8
Toberdoney ....118 M 2
Tobermore ....114 L 3
Tobernadarry ....105 E 7
Toberscanavan ....112 G 5
Toe Head ....89 E 13
Toem ....95 H 10
Togher *Cork* ....89 E 12
Togher *Louth* ....109 N 6
Togher *Offaly* ....101 K 8
Tolka ....103 M 7
Tollymore Forest Park ......115 O 5
Tombrack ....97 M 10
Tomdarragh ....103 N 8
Tomhaggard ....97 M 11
Tonabrocky ....99 E 8
Tonakeera Point ....104 C 7
Tonyduff ....108 K 6
Toomaghera ....99 E 8
Toomard ....106 G 7
Toombeola ....104 C 7
Toome ....114 M 3
Toomyvara ....100 H 9
Toor ....100 H 9
Tooraree ....93 E 10
Tooreencahill ....93 E 11

Toorlestraun ....112 F 5
Toormore ....89 D 13
Toormore Bay ....89 D 13
Toornafulla ....93 E 10
Toraigh /
   Tory Island ....116 H 2
Torc Waterfall ....89 D 11
Torneady Point ....116 G 2
Torr Head ....119 N 2
Tory Sound ....117 H 2
Tourig (River) ....91 I 11
Tower ....90 G 12
Trá Lí / Tralee ....93 C 11
Trá Mhór /
   Tramore ....96 K 11
Trabane Strand ....112 F 4
Tracton ....90 G 12
Trafrask ....89 D 12
Tragumna ....89 E 13
Tralee Bay ....92 C 11
Tramore Bay ....96 K 11
Tranarossan Bay ....117 I 2
Travara Bridge ....88 C 12
Trawbreaga Bay ....117 K 2
Trawenagh Bay ....116 G 3
Trawmore Bay ....110 C 5
Trean ....105 D 7
Treantagh ....117 I 2
Treehoo ....107 K 5
Trien ....106 G 6
Trillick ....113 J 4
Tristia ....110 C 5
Trory ....113 J 4
Trostan ....119 N 2
Truskmore ....112 G 4
Trust ....100 G 7
Tuaim / Tuam ....105 F 7
Tuamgraney ....99 G 9
Tuar Mhic Éadaigh /
   Tourmakeady ....105 D 7
Tubber ....99 F 8
Tubbrid *Kilkenny* ....95 J 9
Tubbrid *Tipperary* ....95 I 11
Tulach Mhór /
   Tullamore ....101 J 8
Tulla *near Ennis* ....99 F 9
Tulla *near Gort* ....99 F 8
Tullagh Point ....117 J 2
Tullaghan ....112 G 4
Tullaghan Bay ....110 C 5
Tullaghanstown ....108 L 7

Tullagher ....96 K 10
Tullaghobegly ....117 H 2
Tullaherin ....96 K 10
Tullahought ....95 J 10
Tullakeel ....88 C 12
Tullamore ....93 D 10
Tullaroan ....95 J 10
Tullig ....92 C 11
Tullig Point ....93 C 10
Tullokyne ....105 E 7
Tully
   Lower Lough Erne ....96 K 10
   Tully *near Ballyshannon* ....113 H 4
   Tully *Upper Lough Erne* .....113 J 5
Tully Cross ....104 C 7
Tully National Stud ....102 L 8
Tullyallen ....109 M 6
Tullyamalra ....108 L 5
Tullycanna ....96 L 11
Tullydush ....117 J 2
Tullyhogue ....114 L 4
Tullylease ....94 F 11
Tullymacreeve ....109 M 5
Tullynaha ....112 H 3
Tullynally Castle ....107 J 6
Tullyroan ....114 M 4
Tullyvin ....108 K 5
Tulrohaun ....105 F 6
Tulsk ....106 H 6
Turlough ....105 E 6
Turloughmore ....105 F 7
Turner's Rock Tunnel ....89 D 12
Turreen ....107 I 7
Tuskar Rock ....97 N 11
Twelve Pins (The) ....104 C 7
Twomileborris ....95 I 9
Tylas ....108 M 7
Tynagh ....100 G 8
Tynan ....114 L 5
Tyrella ....115 O 5
Tyrellspass ....101 J 7

Uachtar Ard /
   Oughterard ....105 E 7
Uaigh / Owey Island ....116 G 2
Ugga Beg (Lough) ....98 D 8
Ulster American
   Folk Park ....113 J 4
Ulster Folk
   Museum (The) ....115 O 4

Union Hall ....89 E 13
Unshin ....112 G 5
Upper Ballinderry ....115 N 4
Upper Lake ....103 M 8
Upperchurch ....95 H 9
Upperlands ....118 M 3
Urbalreagh ....117 K 1
Urglin Glebe ....102 L 9
Urlaur ....106 F 6
Urlaur Lough ....106 F 6
Urlingford ....95 J 9

V
Valencia Island ....88 A 12
Valley ....110 C 5
Valleymount ....103 M 8
Vartry Reservoir ....103 N 8
Ventry ....92 A 11
Ventry Harbour ....92 A 11
Vicarstown ....102 K 8
Victoria Bridge ....113 J 3
Villierstown ....91 I 11
Virginia ....108 K 6
Virginia Road ....108 K 6
Vow ....118 M 3

W
Waddingtown ....96 M 11
Walshestown ....97 M 11
Walshtown ....90 H 12
Ward ....103 N 7
Ward (River) ....103 N 7
Waringsford ....115 N 4
Waringstown ....114 M 4
Warrenpoint ....109 N 5
Washing Bay ....96 M 9
Watch Ho.-Village ....90 G 12
Waterfall ....90 G 12
Waterfoot or Glenariff ......119 N 2
Waterford Harbour ....96 L 11
Watergrasshill ....90 G 11
Waterworks ....114 L 3
Wattle Bridge ....113 J 5
Welchtown ....117 I 3
Wellington Bridge ....96 L 11
Wells Cross ....114 M 4
Wesport Bay ....105 C 6
West Town ....116 H 2
Westcove ....88 B 12
Westport House ....105 D 6
Westport Quay ....105 D 6

Wexford Bay ....97 N 10
Wexford Harbour ....97 M 10
Whale Head ....117 J 2
Wheathill ....113 I 5
Whiddy Island ....89 D 12
White *Limerick* ....93 E 10
White *Louth* ....109 M 6
White Castle ....118 K 2
White Hall ....89 D 13
White Island ....113 I 4
White Park Bay ....118 M 2
White Strand ....98 D 9
Whiteabbey ....115 O 3
Whitechurch *Cork* ....90 G 12
Whitechurch *Waterford* ...91 I 11
Whitecross ....114 M 5
Whitegate ....90 H 12
Whitehall *Roscommon* ....107 I 6
Whitehall *Westmeath* ......107 K 7
Whitehead ....115 O 3
Whites Town ....109 N 6
White'sCross ....90 G 12
Whitesides Corner ....114 M 3
Wicklow Gap ....103 M 8
Wicklow Mountains ....103 N 8
Wicklow Way ....103 N 8
Wildfowl
   and Wetlands Trust ......115 O 4
Wilkinstown ....108 L 6
Willbrook ....99 E 9
Williamstown *Galway* ......106 G 6
Williamstown
   Westmeath ....107 I 7
Windgap ....95 J 10
Windmill ....102 L 7
Windy Gap *Kerry* ....89 D 12
Windy Gap *Louth* ....109 N 5
Windy Gap *Mayo* ....105 E 6
Wolfhill ....101 K 9
Womanagh ....91 I 12
Woodburn ....115 O 3
Woodcock Hill ....99 F 9
Woodenbridge ....103 N 9
Woodford (River) ....99 G 8
Woodstown ....96 L 11

Y
Yellow Furze ....108 M 6
Yganavan (Lough) ....92 C 11
Youghal ....100 H 9
Youghal Bay ....91 I 12

A B C D E F G H I J K L M N O P Q R S T U V W X Y Z

Town plans	Plans	Stadtpläne

Sights — Curiosités — Sehenswürdigkeiten

Town plans	Plans	Stadtpläne
Place of interest	Bâtiment intéressant	Sehenswertes Gebäude
Interesting place of worship	Édifice religieux intéressant	Sehenswerter Sakralbau

Roads — Voirie — Straßen

Town plans	Plans	Stadtpläne
Motorway	Autoroute	Autobahn
Numbered junctions: complete, limited	Échangeurs numérotés: complet, partiel	Nummerierte Voll - bzw. Teilanschlussstellen
Dual carriageway	Double chaussée de type autoroutier	Schnellstraße
Major thoroughfare	Grande voie de circulation	Hauptverkehrsstraße
Primary route (GB) - National route (IRL)	Itinéraire principal (GB) - Route nationale (IRL)	Fernverkehrsstraße (Primary Route: GB) - (National route: IRL)
One-way street - Unsuitable for traffic or street subject to restrictions	Sens unique - Rue réglementée ou impraticable	Einbahnstraße - Gesperrte Straße oder mit Verkehrsbeschränkungen
Pedestrian street	Rue piétonne	Fußgängerzone
Tramway	Tramway	Straßenbahn
Shopping street — Piccadilly	Rue commerçante — Piccadilly	Einkaufsstraße — Piccadilly
Car park - Park and Ride	Parking - Parking Relais	Parkplatz - Park-and-Ride-Plätze
Gateway - Street passing under arch - Tunnel	Porte - Passage sous voûte - Tunnel	Tor - Passage - Tunnel
Low headroom (16'6'' max) on major through routes	Passage bas (inférieur à 16'6'') sur les grandes voies de circulation	Unterführung (Höhe bis 16'6'') auf Hauptverkehrsstraßen
Station and railway - Motorail	Gare et voie ferrée	Bahnhof und Bahnlinie
Funicular - Cable-car	Funiculaire - Téléphérique, télécabine	Standseilbahn - Seilschwebebahn
Lever bridge - Car ferry	Pont mobile - Bac pour autos	Bewegliche Brücke - Autofähre

Various signs — Signes divers — Sonstige Zeichen

Town plans	Plans	Stadtpläne
Tourist Information Centre	Information touristique	Informationsstelle
Church/Place of worship - Mosque - Synagogue	Eglise/édifice religieux - Mosquée - Synagogue	Kirche/Gebetshaus - Moschee - Synagoge
Communications tower - Ruins	Tour ou pylône de télécommunication - Ruines	Funk-, Fernsehturm - Ruine
Garden, park, wood - Cemetery	Jardin, parc, bois - Cimetière	Garten, Park, Wäldchen - Friedhof
Stadium - Racecourse	Stade - Hippodrome	Stadion - Pferderennbahn
Golf course - Golf course (with restrictions for visitors)	Golf - Golf (réservé)	Golfplatz - Golfplatz (Zutritt bedingt erlaubt)
Skating rink	Patinoire	Eisbahn
Outdoor or indoor swimming pool	Piscine de plein air, couverte	Freibad - Hallenbad
View - Panorama	Vue - Panorama	Aussicht - Rundblick
Monument - Fountain	Monument - Fontaine	Denkmal - Brunnen
Hospital - Covered market	Hôpital - Marché couvert	Krankenhaus - Markthalle
Pleasure boat harbour - Lighthouse	Port de plaisance - Phare	Yachthafen - Leuchtturm
Airport - Underground station	Aéroport - Station de métro	Flughafen - U-Bahnstation
Coach station	Gare routière	Autobusbahnhof
Ferry services:	Transport par bateau :	Schiffsverbindungen:
passengers and cars	passagers et voitures	Autofähre
Main post office	Bureau de poste	Hauptpostamt
Public buildings located by letter:	Bâtiment public repéré par une lettre :	Öffentliches Gebäude, durch einen Buchstaben gekennzeichnet:
Country Concil Offices - Town Hall — C H	Bureau de l'Administration du Comté - Hôtel de ville — C H	Sitz der Grafschaftsverwaltung - Rathaus — C H
Law Courts — J	Palais de justice — J	Gerichtsgebäude — J
Museum - Theatre - University, College — M T U	Musée - Théâtre - Université, grande école — M T U	Museum - Theater - Universität, Hochschule — M T U
Police (in large towns police headquarters) — POL.	Police (commissariat central) — POL.	Polizei (in größeren Städten Polizeipräsidium) — POL.

London — Londres — London

Town plans	Plans	Stadtpläne
Borough — BRENT	Nom d'arrondissement (borough) — BRENT	Name des Verwaltungsbezirks (borough) — BRENT
Area — WEMBLEY	Nom de quartier (area) — WEMBLEY	Name des Stadtteils (area) — WEMBLEY
Borough boundary	Limite de «borough»	Grenze des «borough»
Congestione Zone - Charge applies Monday-Friday 07.00-18.00	Zone à péage du centre-ville Lundi-Vendredi 7h-18h	Gebührenpflichtiger Innenstadtbereich (Mo-Fr 7-18.00 Uhr)

Plattegronden	**Piante**	**Planos**

Bezienswaardigheden / Curiosità / Curiosidades

Interessant gebouw	Edificio interessante	Edificio interesante
Interessant kerkelijk gebouw	Costruzione religiosa interessante	Edificio religioso interesante

Wegen / Viabilità / Vías de circulación

Autosnelweg **M 1**	Autostrada	Autopista
Knooppunt / aansluiting: volledig, gedeeltelijk	Svincoli numerati: completo, parziale	Número del acceso: completo, parcial
Weg met gescheiden rijbanen	Doppia carreggiata tipo autostrada	Autovía
Hoofdverkeersweg	Grande via di circolazione	Vía importante de circulación
Hoofdweg (GB) - National route (IRL) **A 2**	Itinerario principale (GB) o National route (IRL)	Itinerario principal (GB) - National route (IRL)
Eenrichtingsverkeer - Onbegaanbare straat, beperkt toegankelijk	Senso unico - Via regolamentata o impraticabile	Sentido único - Calle reglamentada o impracticable
Voetgangersgebied	Via pedonale	Calle peatonal
Tramlijn	Tranvia	Tranvía
Winkelstraat Piccadilly	Via commerciale	Calle comercial
Parkeerplaats - P & R	Parcheggio - Parcheggio Ristoro	Aparcamiento - Aparcamientos «P+R»
Poort - Onderdoorgang - Tunnel	Porta - Sottopassaggio - Galleria	Puerta - Pasaje cubierto - Túnel
Vrije hoogte (onder 16'6'') op de grote verkeerswegen	Sottopassaggio (altezza inferiore a 16'6'') sulle grandi vie di circolazione	Paso a baja altura (inferior a 16'6'') en grandes itinerarios
Station, spoorweg	Stazione e ferrovia	Estación y línea férrea
Kabelspoor - Tandradbaan	Funicolare - Funivia, cabinovia	Funicular - Teleférico, telecabina
Beweegbare brug - Auto-veerpont	Ponte mobile - Traghetto per auto	Puente móvil - Barcaza para coches

Overige tekens / Simboli vari / Signos diversos

Informatie voor toeristen	Ufficio informazioni turistiche	Oficina de Información de Turismo
Kerk/kerkelijk gebouw - Moskee - Synagoge	Chiesa/edificio religioso - Moschea - Sinagoga	Iglesia/edificio religioso - Mezquita - Sinagoga
Telecommunicatietoren of -mast - Ruïne	Torre o pilone per telecomunicazioni - Ruderi	Torreta o poste de telecomunicación - Ruinas
Tuin, park, bos - Begraafplaats	Giardino, parco, bosco - Cimitero	Jardín, parque, bosque - Cementerio
Stadion - Renbaan	Stadio - Ippodromo	Estadio - Hipódromo
Golfterrein - Golfterrein (beperkt toegankelijk voor bezoekers)	Golf - Golf riservato	Golf - Golf (sólo para socios)
IJsbaan	Pista di pattinaggio	Pista de patinaje
Zwembad: openlucht, overdekt	Piscina : all'aperto, coperta	Piscina al aire libre, cubierta
Uitzicht - Panorama	Vista - Panorama	Vista - Panorama
Gedenkteken, standbeeld - Fontein	Monumento - Fontana	Monumento - Fuente
Ziekenhuis - Overdekte markt	Ospedale - Mercato coperto	Hospital - Mercado cubierto
Jachthaven - Vuurtoren	Porto turistico - Faro	Puerto deportivo - Faro
Luchthaven - Metrostation	Aeroporto - Stazione della metropolitana	Aeropuerto - Boca de metro
Busstation	Autostazione	Estación de autobuses
Vervoer per boot:	Trasporto con traghetto:	Transporte por barco:
passagiers en auto's	passeggeri ed autovetture	pasajeros y vehículos
Postkantoor	Ufficio postale centrale	Oficina de correos
Openbaar gebouw, aangegeven met een letter:	Edificio pubblico indicato con lettera:	Edificio público localizado con letra:
Administratiekantoor van het graafschap - Stadhuis C H	Sede dell'Amministrazione di Contea - Municipio C H	Oficina de Administración del Condado - Ayuntamiento C H
Gerechtsgebouw J	Palazzo di Giustizia J	Palacio de justicia J
Museum - Schouwburg - Universiteit, hogeschool M T U	Museo - Teatro - Università, grande scuola M T U	Museo - Teatro - Universidad, Escuela Superior M T U
Politie (in grote steden, hoofdbureau) POL	Polizia (Questura, nelle grandi città) POL	Policía (en las grandes ciudades: Jefatura) POL

Londen / Londra / Londres

Naam van het arrondissement (borough) **BRENT**	Nome del distretto amministrativo (borough) **BRENT**	Nombre del distrito (borough) **BRENT**
Naam van de wijk (area) WEMBLEY	Nome del quartiere (area) WEMBLEY	Nombre del barrio (area) WEMBLEY
Grens van de «borough» - van de «area»	Limite del «borough»	Límite del «borough» - del «area»
Tolgebied van het stadscentrum, maandag-vrijdag 7-18.00 u.	Area con circolazione a pagamento Lunedì-Venerdì 07.00-18.00	Zona de peaje del centro de la ciudad. Lu-vi 7:00-18:00

Plans de ville
Town plans / Stadtpläne / Stadsplattegronden
Piante di città / Planos de ciudades

GREAT BRITAIN

- Aberdeen 151
- Bath 151
- Birmingham............ 152
- Blackpool 153
- Bournemouth 153
- Brighton and Hove 154
- Bristol 155
- Cambridge............. 156
- Canterbury............. 157
- Cardiff 158
- Carlisle................ 159
- Chester 159
- Coventry............... 160
- Derby.................. 160
- Dover.................. 161
- Dundee................ 161
- Durham................ 162
- Edinburgh 163
- Exeter................. 164
- Glasgow 165
- Ipswish 166
- Kingston-upon-Hull 166
- Leeds 167
- Leicester 168
- Lincoln................ 168
- Liverpool 169
- Greater London 170-171
- London 172-173
- Manchester 174
- Newcastle-upon-Tyne ... 175
- Newport 176
- Norwich 177
- Nottingham............ 178
- Oxford 179
- Perth 180
- Plymouth 180
- Portsmouth
  and Southsea 181
- Reading................ 182
- Sheffield 182
- Southampton 183
- Stirling................ 183
- Stoke-and-Trent 184
- Stratford-upon-Avon 184
- Warwick 185
- Winchester............. 185
- Windsor................ 186
- Wolverhampton......... 187
- York 188

IRELAND

- Belfast 189
- Cork 190
- Dublin 191
- Galway................. 192
- Limerick 193

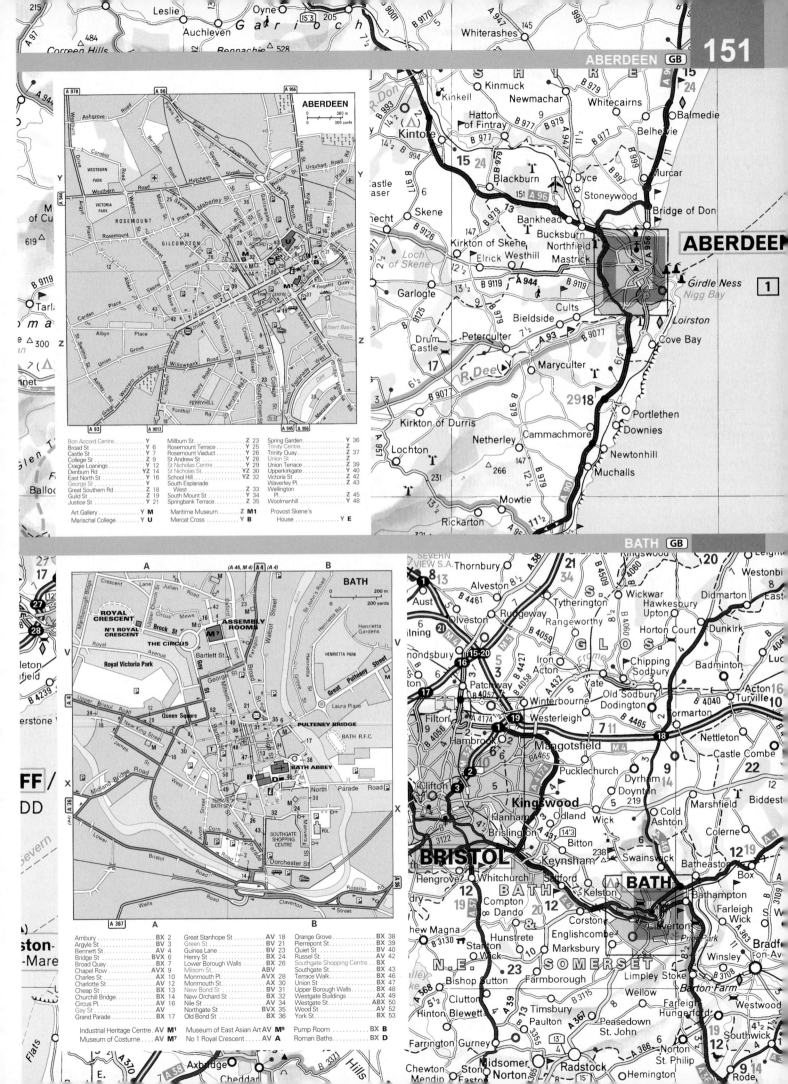

ABERDEEN

Bon Accord Centre	Y	Millburn St	Z 23
Broad St	Y 6	Rosemount Terrace	Y 25
Castle St	Y 7	Rosemount Viaduct	Y 26
College St	Z 9	St Andrew St	Y 28
Craigie Loanings	Y 12	St Nicholas Centre	Y 29
Denburn Rd	YZ 14	St Nicholas St	YZ 30
East North St	Y 16	School Hill	YZ 32
George St	Z 18	South Esplanade	
Great Southern Rd	Z 19	West	Z 33
Guild St	Z 19	South Mount St	Y 34
Justice St	Y 21	Springbank Terrace	Z 35

Spring Garden	Y 36
Trinity Centre	Z
Trinity Quay	Z 37
Union St	Z
Union Terrace	Y 39
Upperkirkgate	Y 40
Victoria St	Y 42
Waverley Pl	Z 43
Wellington	
Pl	Z 45
Woolmanhill	Y 48

Art Gallery	Y **M**	Maritime Museum	Z **M1**	Provost Skene's	
Marischal College	Y **U**	Mercat Cross	Y **B**	House	Y **E**

BATH

Ambury	BX 2	Great Stanhope St	AV 18
Argyle St	BV 3	Green St	BV 21
Bennett St	AV 4	Guinea Lane	BV 23
Bridge St	BVX 6	Henry St	BX 24
Broad Quay	BX 7	Lower Borough Walls	BX 26
Chapel Row	AVX 9	Milsom St	ABV
Charles St	AX 10	Monmouth Pl	AVX 28
Charlotte St	AV 12	Monmouth St	AV 30
Cheap St	BX 13	New Bond St	BV 31
Churchill Bridge	BX 14	New Orchard St	BX 32
Circus Pl	AV 16	Nile St	AV 34
Gay St	AV	Northgate St	BV 35
Grand Parade	BX 17	Old Bond St	BX 36

Orange Grove	BX 38
Pierrepont St	BX 39
Quiet St	BV 40
Russel St	AV 42
Southgate St	BX
Southgate Shopping Centre	BX
Southgate St	BX 43
Terrace Walk	BX 46
Union St	BX 47
Upper Borough Walls	BX 48
Westgate Buildings	AX 49
Westgate St	ABX 50
Wood St	AV 52
York St	BX 53

Industrial Heritage Centre	AV **M1**	Museum of East Asian Art	AV **M9**	Pump Room	BX **B**
Museum of Costume	AV **M7**	No 1 Royal Crescent	AV **A**	Roman Baths	BX **D**

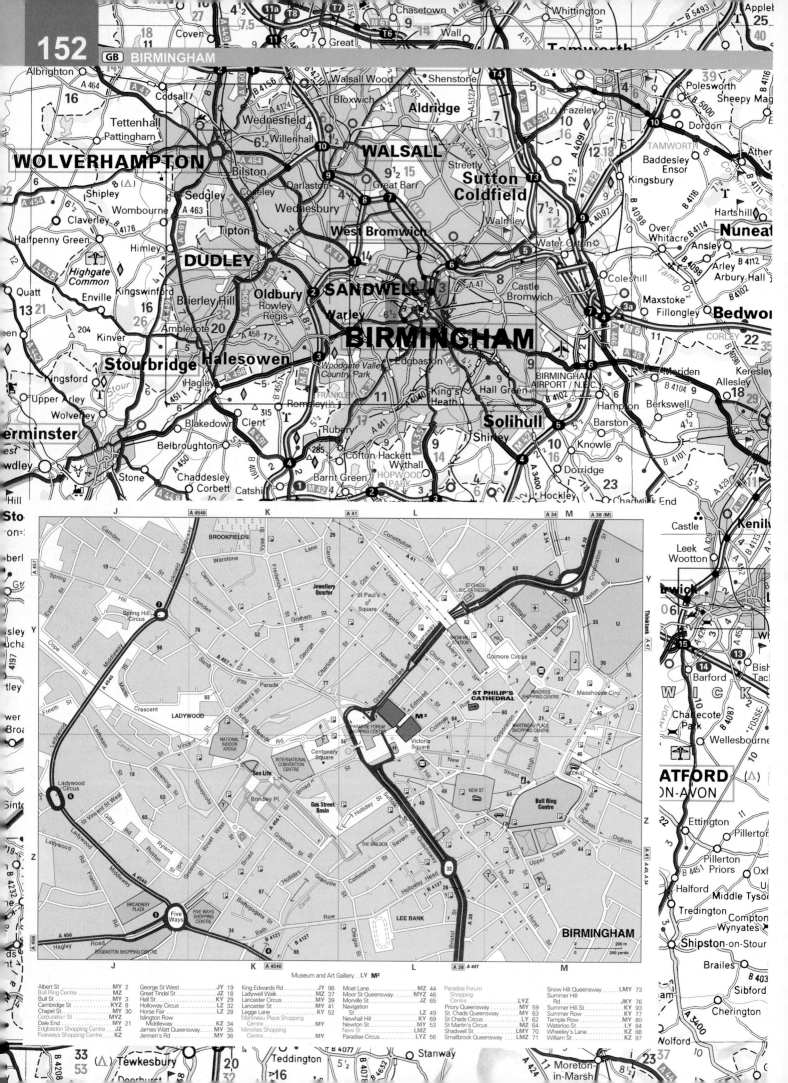

Museum and Art Gallery ..LY **M²**

Albert St ....MY 2	George St West ....JY 19	King Edwards Rd ....JY 98	Moat Lane ....MZ 44	Paradise Forum	Snow Hill Queensway......LMY 73
Bull Ring Centre ....MZ	Great Tindal St ....JZ 18	Ladywell Walk ....MZ 37	Moor St Queensway.......MYZ 46	Shopping	Summer Hill
Bull St ....MY 3	Hall St ....KY 29	Lancaster Circus ....MY 39	Morville St ....KZ 65	Centre ....LYZ	Rd.................JKY 76
Cambridge St ....KYZ 8	Holloway Circus ....LZ 32	Lancaster St ....MY 41	Navigation	Priory Queensway.........LMY 59	Summer Hill St ....KY 93
Chapel St ....MY 30	Horse Fair ....LZ 28	Legge Lane ....KY 52	St...................LY 49	St. Chads Queensway......MY 63	Summer Row ....MY 77
Corporation St ....MYZ	Islington Row		Newhall Hill ....KY 69	St Chads Circus ....LY 62	Temple Row ....MY 80
Dale End ....MY 21	Middleway ....KZ 34	Martineau Place Shopping	Newton St ....MY 53	St Martin's Circus ....MZ 64	Waterloo St ....LY 84
Edgbaston Shopping Centre ...JZ	James Watt Queensway ....MY 35	Centre ....MY	New St ....LMZ	Shadwell St ....LMY 70	Wheeley's Lane ....KZ 88
Fiveways Shopping Centre ...KZ	Jennen's Rd ....MY 36	Minories Shopping	Paradise Circus...........LYZ 56	Smallbrook Queensway .....LMZ 71	William St ....KZ 97
		Centre ....MY			

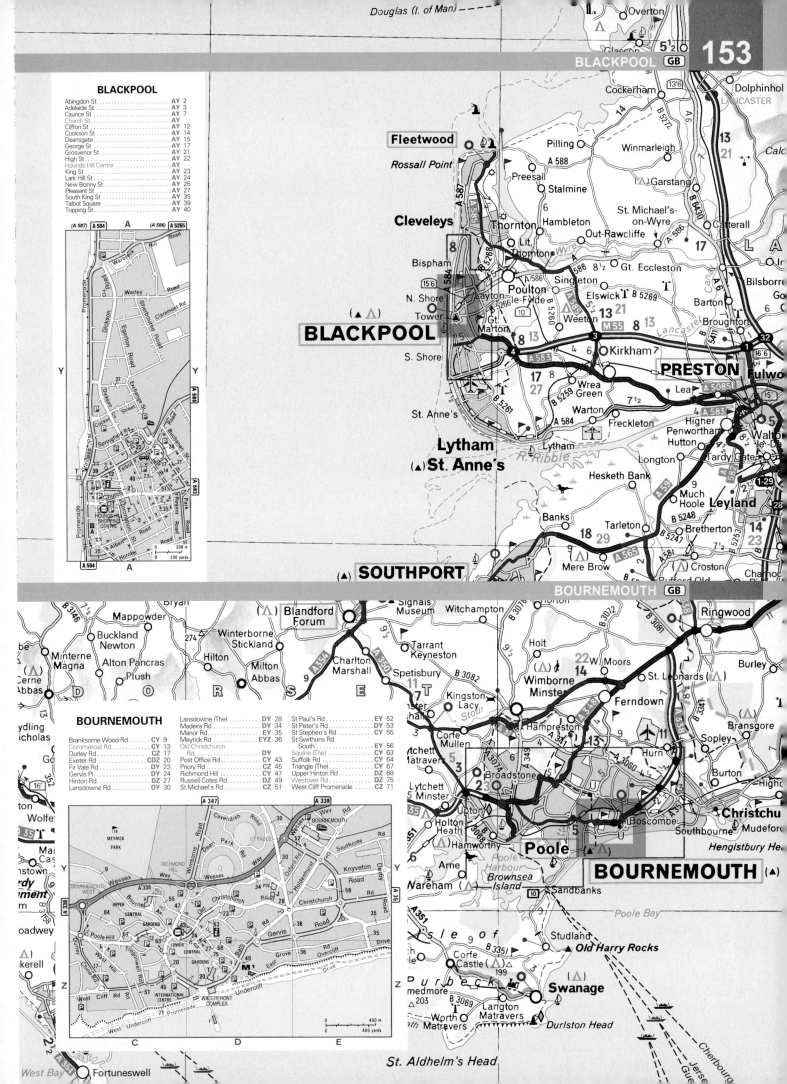

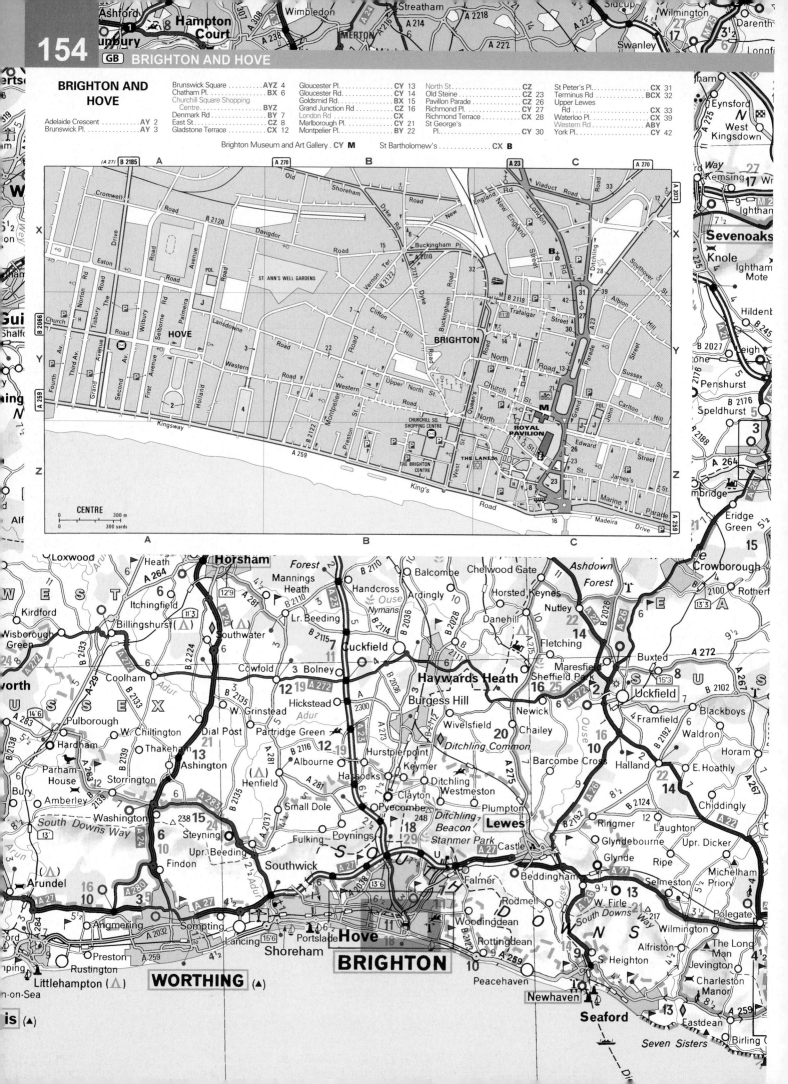

BRIGHTON AND HOVE

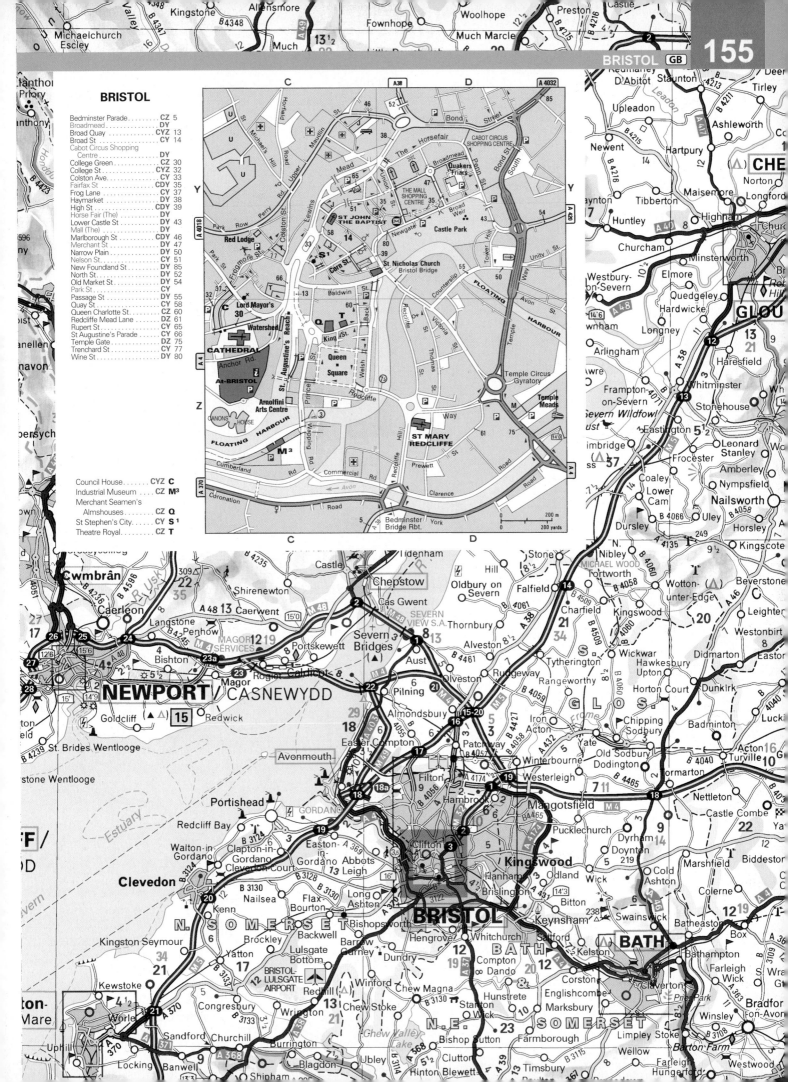

BRISTOL

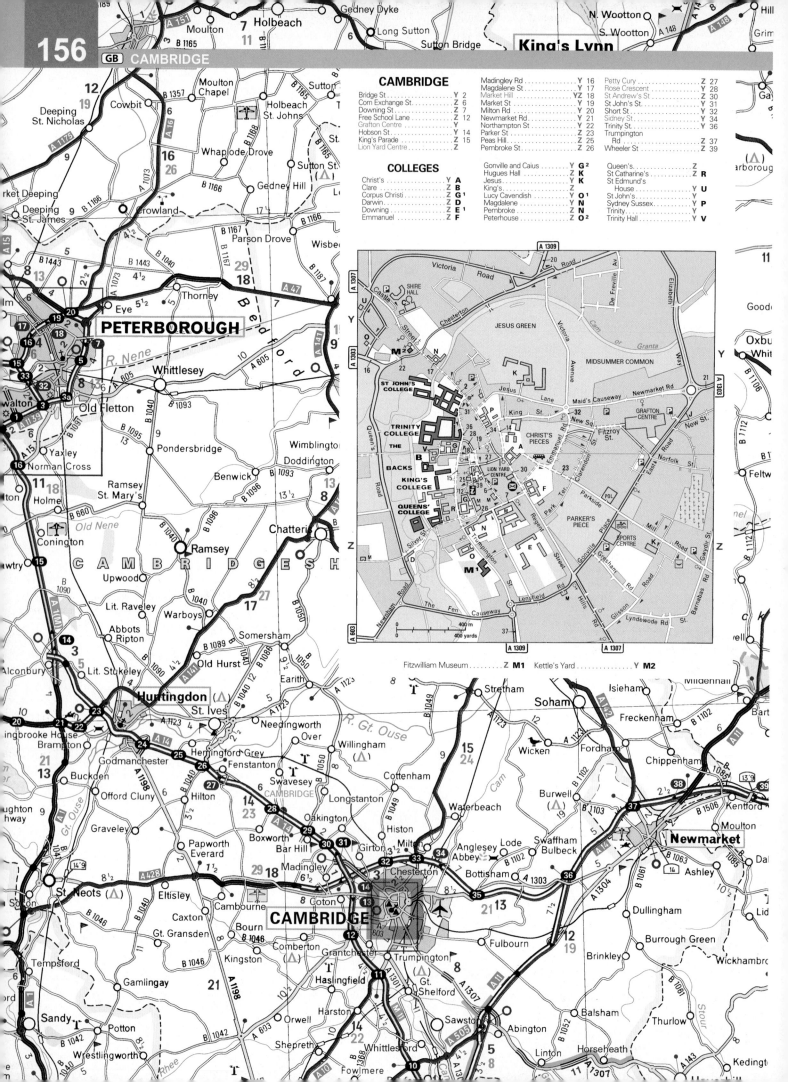

CAMBRIDGE

Bridge St	Y 2
Corn Exchange St	Z 6
Downing St	Z 7
Free School Lane	Z 12
Grafton Centre	Y
Hobson St	Y 14
King's Parade	Z 15
Lion Yard Centre	Z
Madingley Rd	Y 16
Magdalene St	Y 17
Market Hill	YZ 18
Market St	Y 19
Milton Rd	Y 20
Newmarket Rd	Y 21
Northampton St	Y 22
Parker St	Z 23
Peas Hill	Z 25
Pembroke St	Z 26
Petty Cury	Z 27
Rose Crescent	Y 28
St Andrew's St	Z 30
St John's St	Y 31
Short St	Y 32
Sidney St	Y 34
Trinity St	Y 36
Trumpington Rd	Z 37
Wheeler St	Z 39

COLLEGES

Christ's	Y A
Clare	Z B
Corpus Christi	Z D
Darwin	Z E
Downing	Z F
Emmanuel	Z F
Gonville and Caius	Y G2
Hugues Hall	Z K
Jesus	Y K
King's	Z
Lucy Cavendish	Y O1
Magdalene	Y N
Pembroke	Z O2
Peterhouse	Z
Queen's	Z
St Catharine's	Z R
St Edmund's House	Y U
St John's	Y P
Sydney Sussex	Y P
Trinity	Y V
Trinity Hall	Y V

Fitzwilliam Museum .... Z **M1**   Kettle's Yard .... Y **M2**

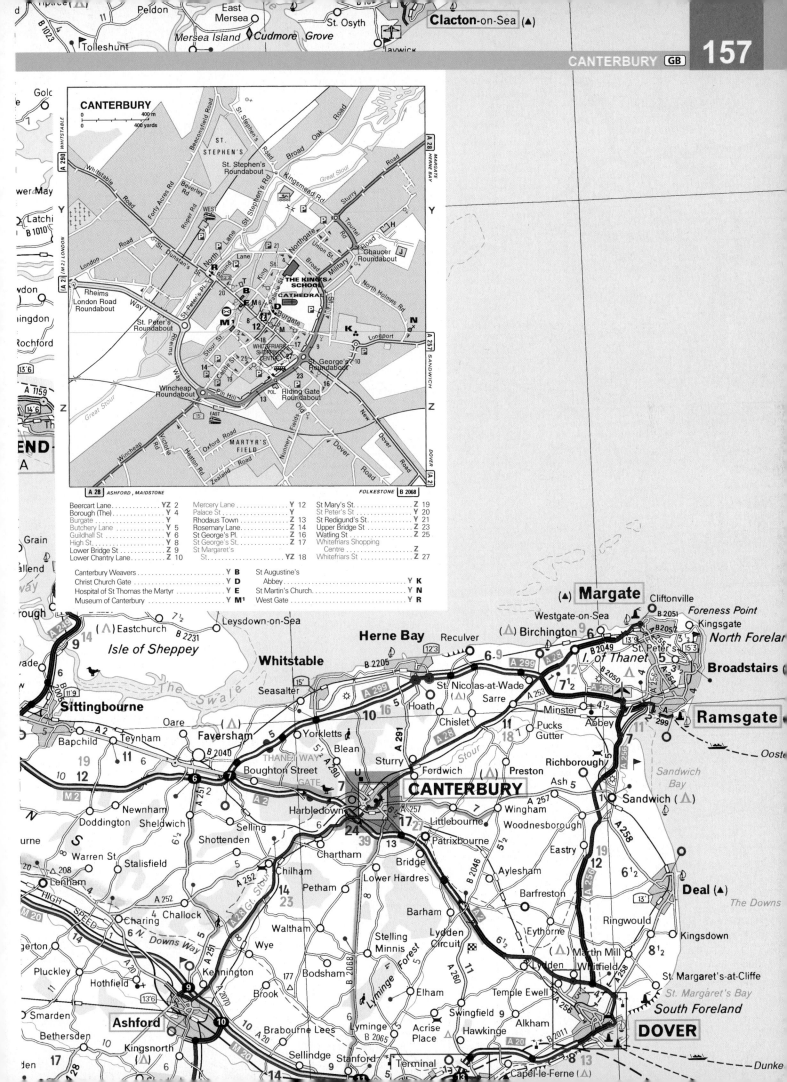

CARDIFF

Capitol Centre	. . . .	BZ
Castle St	. . . .	BZ 9
Cathays Terrace	. . . .	BY 10
Central Square	. . . .	BZ 12
Church St	. . . .	BZ 14
City Hall Rd	. . . .	BY 15
College Rd	. . . .	BY 20
Corbett Rd	. . . .	BY 21
Customhouse St	. . . .	BZ 23
David St	. . . .	BZ 25
Duke St	. . . .	BZ 26
Dumfries Pl	. . . .	BY 28
Greyfriars Rd	. . . .	BY 29
Guilford St	. . . .	BZ 30
Hayes (The)	. . . .	BZ 32
High St	. . . .	BZ
King Edward VII		
Ave.	. . . .	BY 36
Lloyd George Ave	. . . .	BZ 38
Mary Ann St	. . . .	BZ 39
Moira Terrace	. . . .	BZ 42
Nantes (Boulevard de)	. . . . . .	BY 44
Queens Arcade Shopping		
Centre	. . . .	BZ 54
Queen St	. . . .	BZ
St Andrews		
Pl.	. . . .	BY 56
St-David's 2	. . . .	BZ
St-David's Centre	. . . .	BZ
St John St	. . . .	BZ 58
St Mary St	. . . .	BZ
Station Terrace	. . . .	BZ 61
Stuttgarter		
Strasse	. . . .	BY 62
Tresilian Way	. . . .	BZ 63
Working St	. . . .	BZ 67

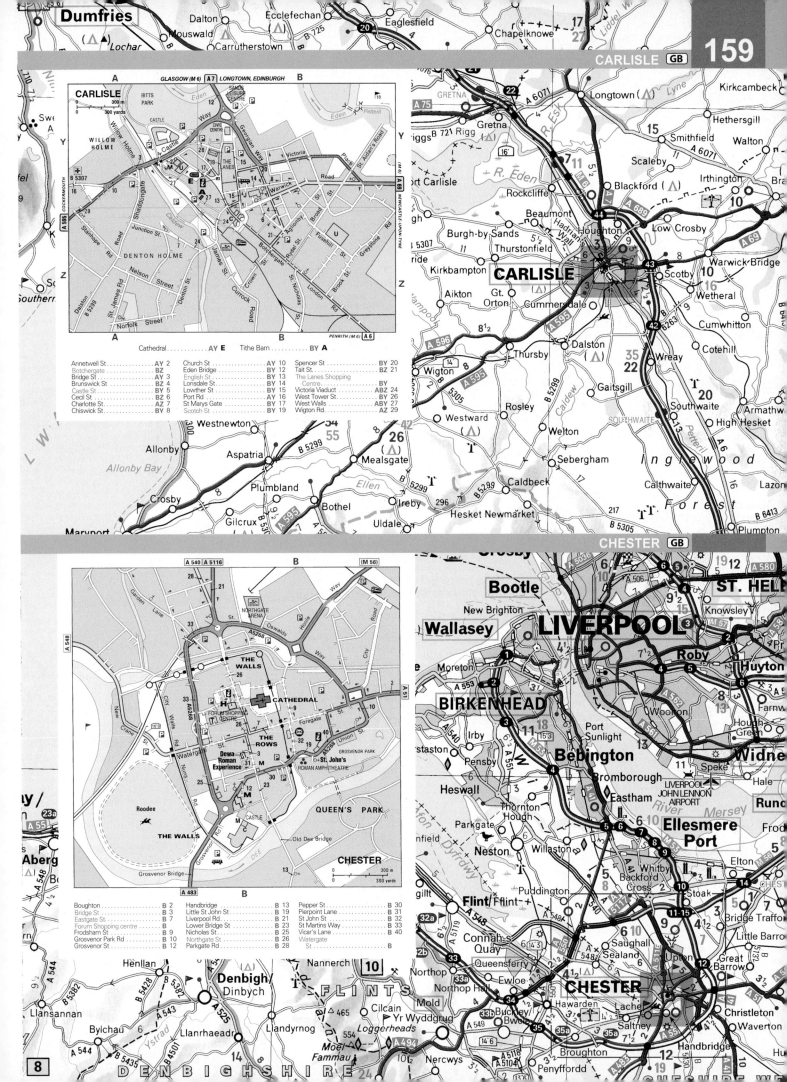

CARLISLE

300 m
300 yards

GLASGOW (M 6) A 7 LONGTOWN, EDINBURGH

Cathedral . . . . AY E   Tithe Barn . . . . BY A

Annetwell St . . . . AY 2	Church St . . . . AY 10	Spencer St . . . . BY 20
Botchergate . . . . BZ	Eden Bridge . . . . BY 12	Tait St . . . . BZ 21
Bridge St . . . . AY 3	English St . . . . BY 13	The Lanes Shopping
Brunswick St . . . . BZ 4	Lonsdale St . . . . BY 14	Centre . . . . BY
Castle St . . . . BY 5	Lowther St . . . . BY 15	Victoria Viaduct . . . . ABZ 24
Cecil St . . . . BZ 6	Port Rd . . . . BY 16	West Tower St . . . . BY 26
Charlotte St . . . . AZ 7	St Marys Gate . . . . BY 17	West Walls . . . . ABY 27
Chiswick St . . . . BY 8	Scotch St . . . . BY 19	Wigton Rd . . . . AZ 29

CHESTER

A 540 A 5116   (M 56)

300 m
300 yards

Boughton . . . . B 2	Handbridge . . . . B 13	Pepper St . . . . B 30
Bridge St . . . . B 3	Little St John St . . . . B 19	Pierpoint Lane . . . . B 31
Eastgate St . . . . B 7	Liverpool Rd . . . . B 21	St John St . . . . B 32
Forum Shopping centre . . . . B 9	Lower Bridge St . . . . B 23	St Martins Way . . . . B 33
Frodsham St . . . . B 9	Nicholas St . . . . B 25	Vicar's Lane . . . . B 40
Grosvenor Park Rd . . . . B 10	Northgate St . . . . B 26	Watergate
Grosvenor St . . . . B 12	Parkgate Rd . . . . B 28	St . . . . B

8

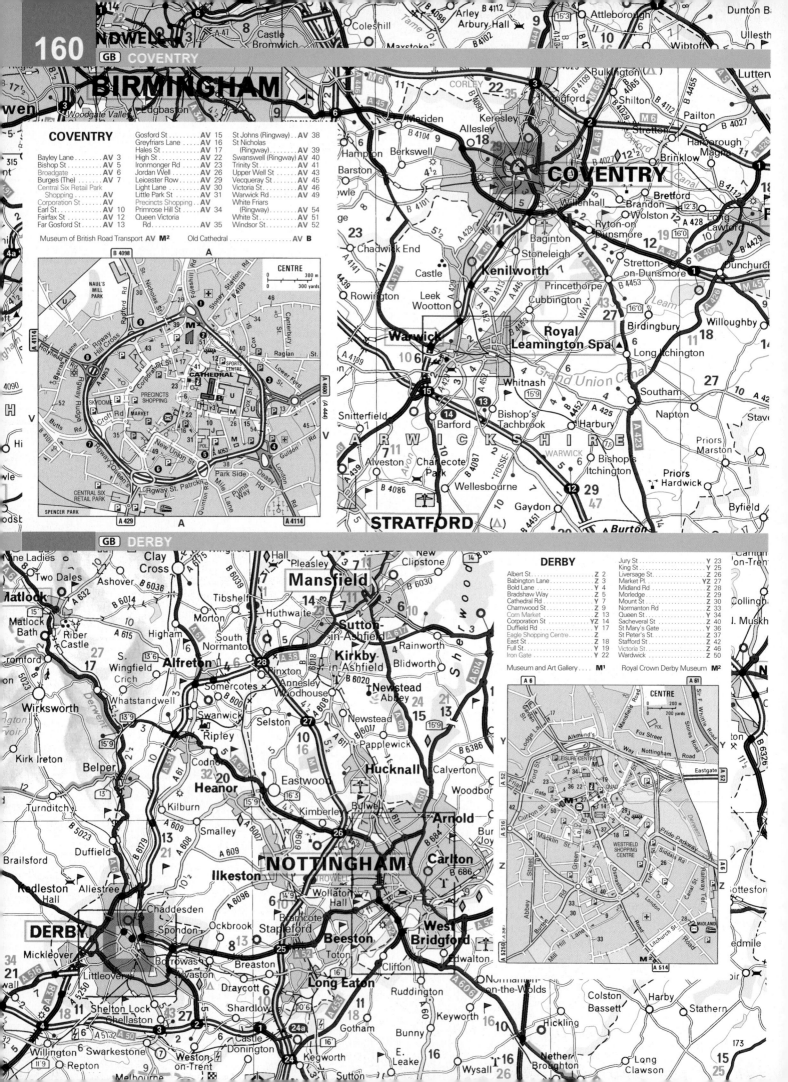

COVENTRY

Bayley Lane . . . . AV 3	Gosford St . . . . AV 15	St Johns (Ringway) . . AV 38
Bishop St . . . . AV 5	Greyfriars Lane . . . . AV 16	St Nicholas
Broadgate . . . . AV 6	Hales St . . . . AV 17	(Ringway) . . . . AV 39
Burges (The) . . . . . . AV 7	High St . . . . AV 19	Swanswell (Ringway) AV 40
Central Six Retail Park	Ironmonger Rd . . . . AV 23	Trinity St . . . . AV 41
Shopping . . . . . . AV	Jordan Well . . . . . . AV 26	Upper Well St . . . . . AV 43
Corporation St . . . . . AV	Leicester Row . . . . AV 29	Vecqueray St . . . . . AV 45
Earl St . . . . AV 10	Light Lane . . . . AV 30	Victoria St . . . . AV 46
Fairfax St . . . . AV 12	Little Park St . . . . . AV 31	Warwick Rd . . . . . . AV 49
Far Gosford St . . . . AV 13	Primrose Hill St . . . AV 34	White Friars
	Precincts Shopping . . . . AV	(Ringway) . . . . . . AV 54
	Queen Victoria	White St . . . . AV 51
	Rd . . . . AV 35	Windsor St . . . . AV 52

Museum of British Road Transport AV M²   Old Cathedral . . . . AV B

DERBY

Albert St. . . . . Z 2	Jury St . . . . Y 23	
Babington Lane . . . . Z 3	King St . . . . Y 25	
Bold Lane . . . . Y 4	Liversage St . . . . Z 26	
Bradshaw Way . . . . Z 5	Market Pl. . . . . YZ 27	
Cathedral Rd . . . . Y 7	Midland Rd . . . . Z 28	
Charnwood St . . . . Z 9	Morledge . . . . Z 29	
Corn Market . . . . Z 13	Mount St . . . . Z 30	
Corporation St . . . . YZ 14	Normanton Rd . . . . Z 33	
Duffield Rd . . . . Y 17	Queen St . . . . Y 34	
Eagle Shopping Centre . . . . . . Z	Sacheveral St . . . . Z 40	
East St . . . . Z 18	St Mary's Gate . . . . Y 36	
Full St . . . . Y 19	St Peter's St . . . . Z 37	
Iron Gate . . . . Y 22	Stafford St . . . . Z 42	
	Victoria St . . . . Z 46	
	Wardwick . . . . Z 50	

Museum and Art Gallery . . . . M¹   Royal Crown Derby Museum M²

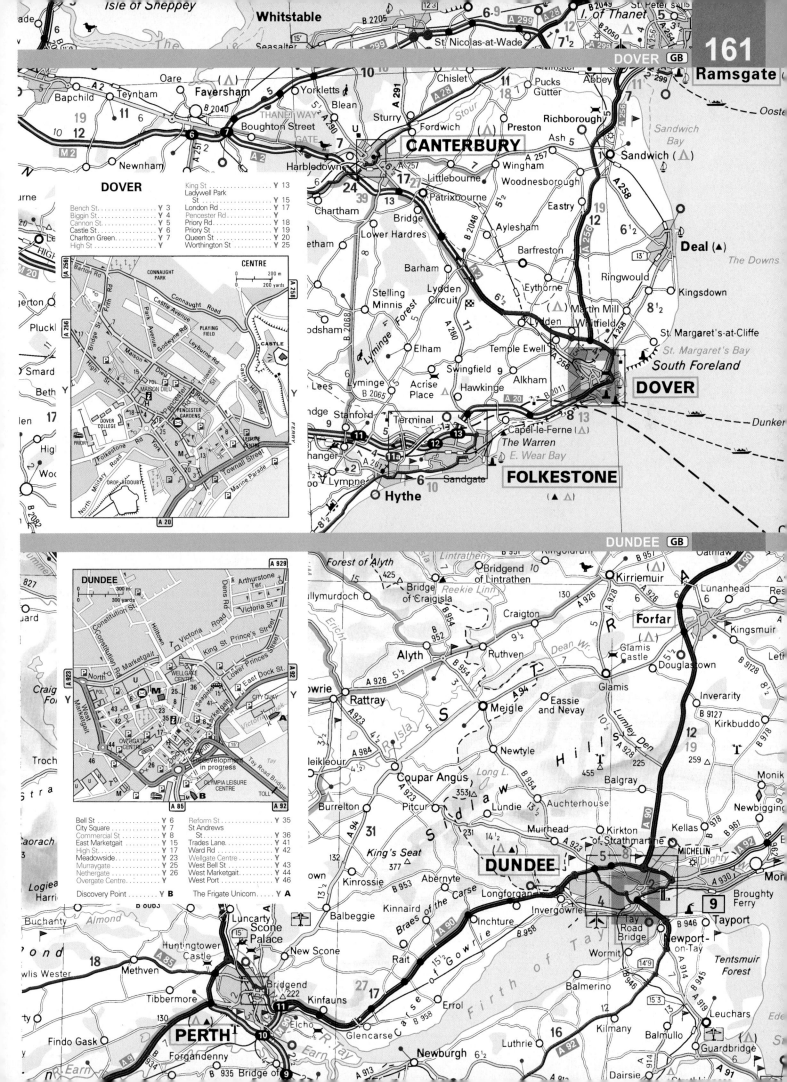

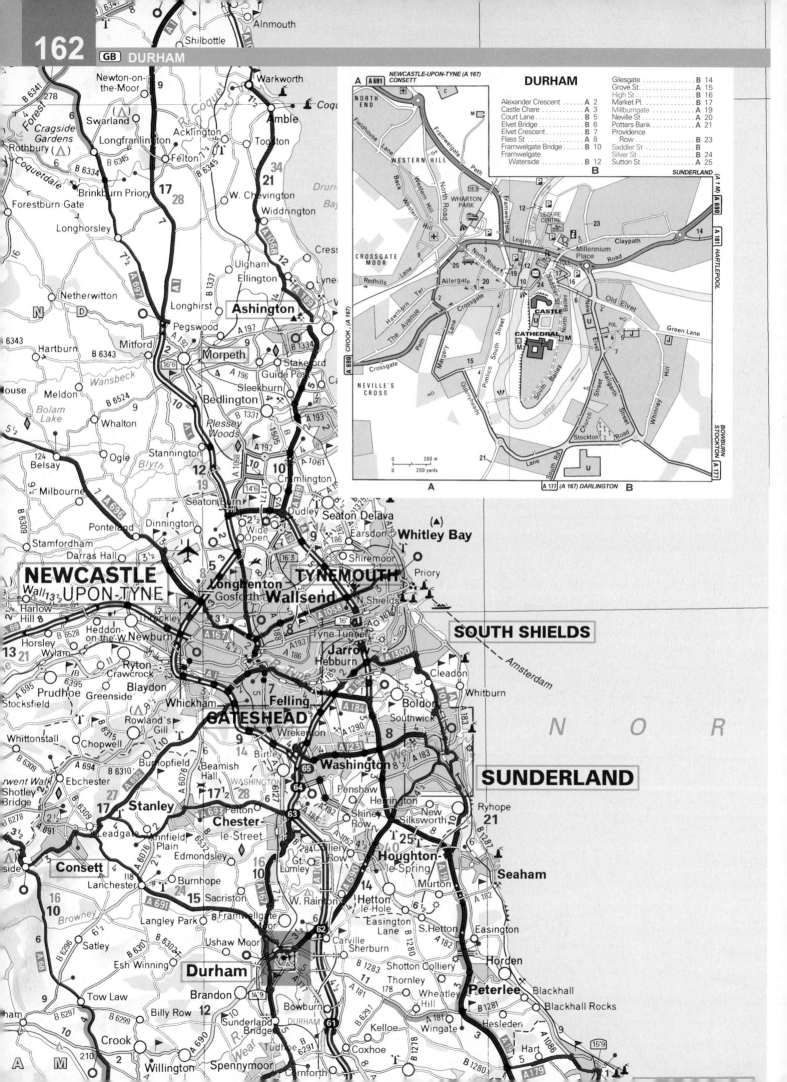

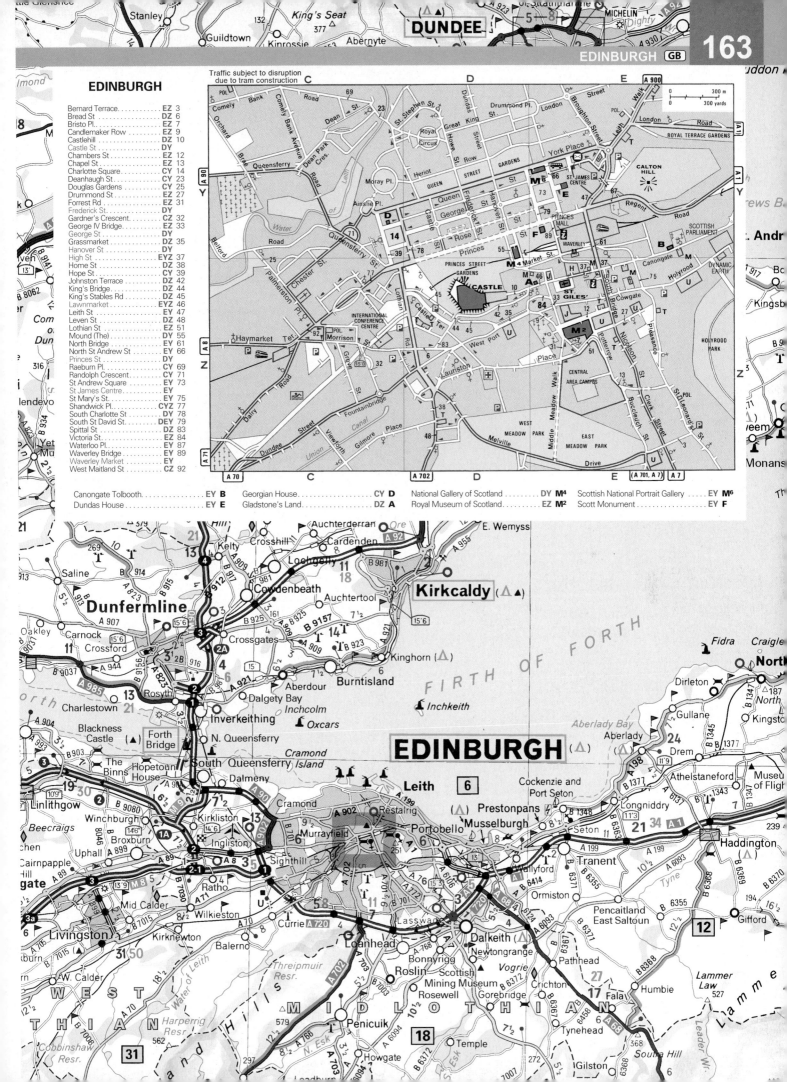

EDINBURGH

Traffic subject to disruption due to tram construction

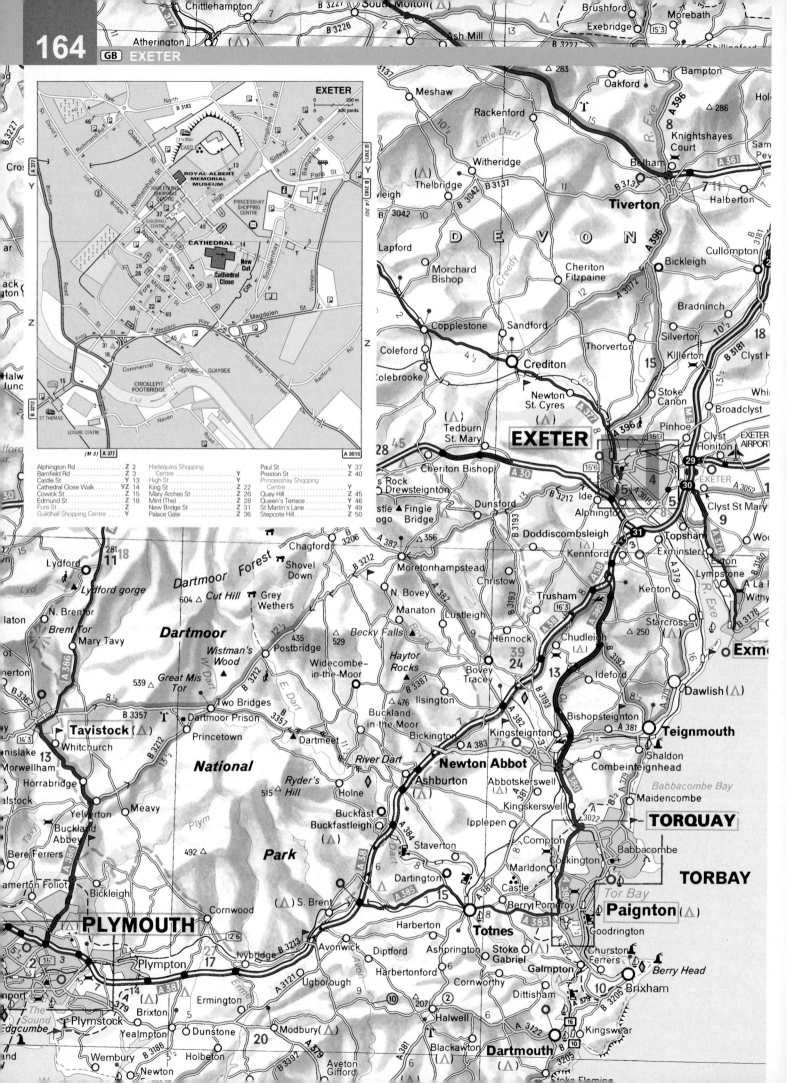

EXETER

0   200 m
0   200 yards

ROYAL·ALBERT
MEMORIAL
MUSEUM

CENTRAL
CASTLE

HARLEQUINS
SHOPPING
CENTRE

GUILDHALL
CENTRE

PRINCESSHAY
SHOPPING
CENTRE

CATHEDRAL

Cathedral
Close

New
Cut

HISTORIC QUAYSIDE

CRICKLEPIT
FOOTBRIDGE

EXE

Haven

LEISURE CENTRE

ST THOMAS

(M 5) A 371

Alphington Rd .... Z 2	Harlequins Shopping	Paul St .... Y 37
Barnfield Rd .... Z 3	Centre .... Y	Preston St .... Z 40
Castle St .... Y 13	High St .... Y	Princesshay Shopping
Cathedral Close Walk ... YZ 14	King St .... Z 22	Centre .... Y
Cowick St .... Z 15	Mary Arches St .... Z 26	Quay St .... Z 45
Edmund St .... Z 18	Mint (The) .... Z 28	Queen's Terrace .... Y 46
Fore St .... Z	New Bridge St .... Z 31	St Martin's Lane .... Y 49
Guildhall Shopping Centre .... Y	Palace Gate .... Z 36	Stepcote Hill .... Z 50

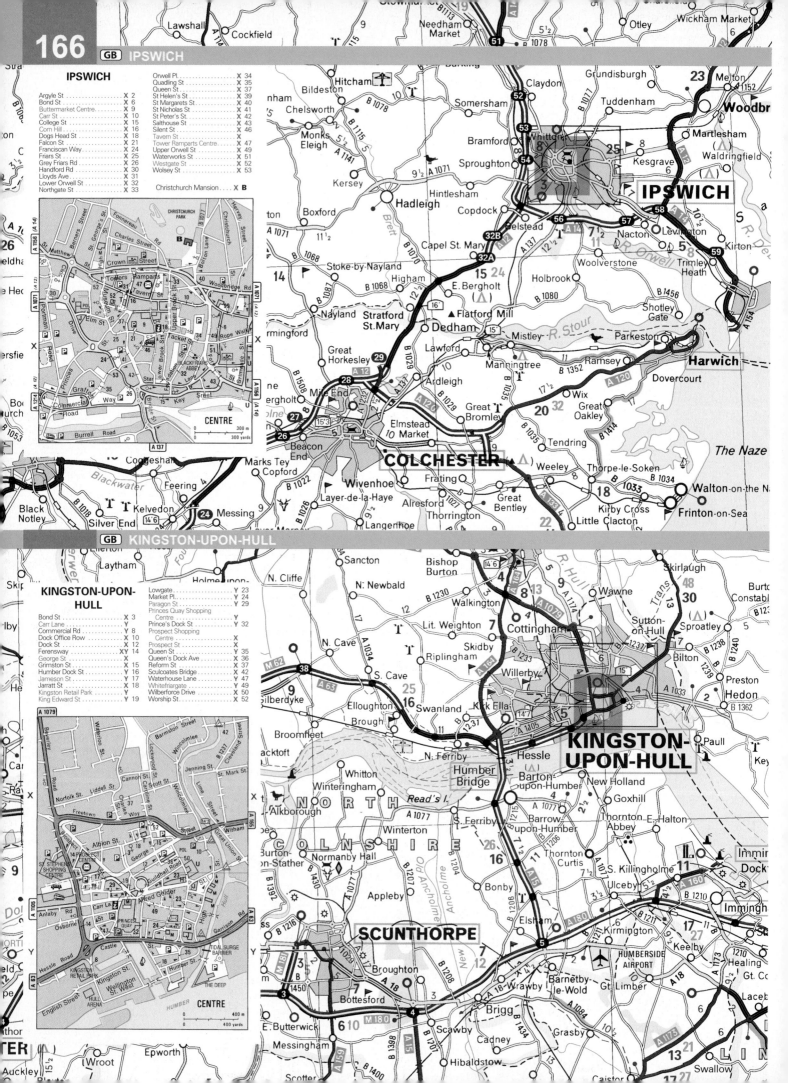

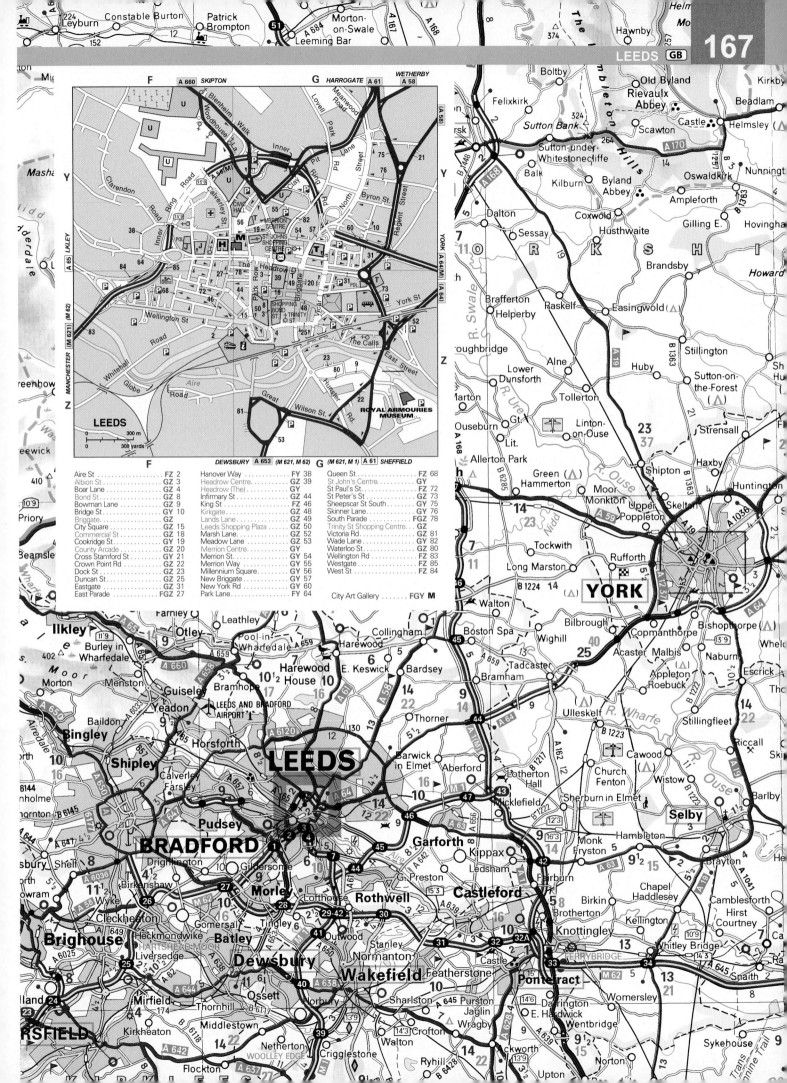

LEEDS

Aire St . . . . FZ 2	Hanover Way . . . . FY 38	Queen St . . . . FZ 68
Albion St . . . . GZ 3	Headrow Centre . . . . GZ 39	St John's Centre . . . . GY
Boar Lane . . . . GZ 4	Headrow (The) . . . . GY	St Paul's St . . . . FZ 72
Bond St . . . . GZ 8	Infirmary St . . . . GZ 44	St Peter's St . . . . GZ 73
Bowman Lane . . . . GZ 9	King St . . . . GZ 46	Sheepscar St South . . . . . . GY 75
Bridge St . . . . GY 10	Kirkgate . . . . GZ 48	Skinner Lane . . . . GY 76
Briggate . . . . GZ	Lands Lane . . . . GZ 49	South Parade . . . . FGZ 78
City Square . . . . GZ 15	Leeds Shopping Plaza . . . . GZ 50	Trinity St Shopping Centre . . GZ
Commercial St . . . . GZ 18	Marsh Lane . . . . GZ 52	Victoria Rd . . . . GY 81
Cookridge St . . . . GY 19	Meadow Lane . . . . GZ 53	Wade Lane . . . . GY 82
County Arcade . . . . GZ 20	Merrion Centre . . . . GY	Waterloo St . . . . GZ 80
Cross Stamford St . . . . . . GY 21	Merrion St . . . . GY 54	Wellington Rd . . . . GZ 83
Crown Point Rd . . . . GZ 22	Merrion Way . . . . GY 55	Westgate . . . . FZ 85
Dock St . . . . GZ 23	Millennium Square . . . . . . GY 56	West St . . . . FZ 84
Duncan St . . . . GZ 25	New Briggate . . . . GY 57	
Eastgate . . . . GZ 31	New York Rd . . . . GY 60	
East Parade . . . . FGZ 27	Park Lane . . . . FY 64	City Art Gallery . . . . FGY M

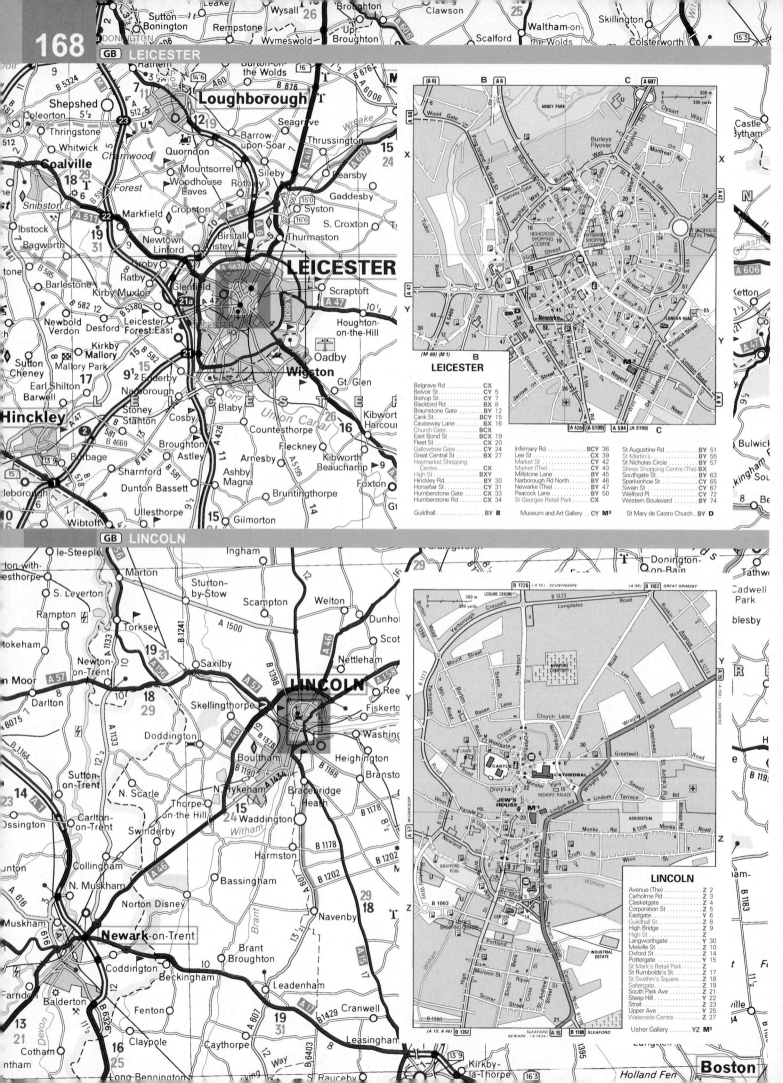

LEICESTER

Belgrave Rd	CX
Belvoir St	CY 5
Bishop St	CY 7
Blackbird Rd	BX 8
Braunstone Gate	BY 12
Cank St	BCY 15
Causeway Lane	BX 16
Church Gate	BCX
East Bond St	BCX 19
Fleet St	CX 20
Gallowtree Gate	CY 24
Great Central St	BX 27
Haymarket Shopping Centre	CX
High St	BXY
Hinckley Rd	BY 30
Horsefair St	CY 31
Humberstone Gate	CX 33
Humberstone Rd	CX 34
Infirmary Rd	BCY 36
Lee St	CX 39
Market St	CY 42
Market (The)	CY 43
Millstone Lane	BY 45
Narborough Rd North	BY 46
Newarke (The)	BY 47
Peacock Lane	BY 50
St Georges Retail Park	CX
St Augustine Rd	BY 51
St Martin's	BY 55
St Nicholas Circle	BY 57
Shires Shopping Centre (The)	BX
Southgate St	BY 63
Sparkenhoe St	CY 65
Swain St	CY 67
Welford Pl	CY 72
Western Boulevard	BY 74

Guildhall	BY	B
Museum and Art Gallery	CY	M³
St Mary de Castro Church	BY	D

LINCOLN

Avenue (The)	Z 2
Carholme Rd	Z 3
Clasketgate	Z 4
Corporation St	Z 5
Eastgate	Y 6
Guildhall St	Z 7
High Bridge	Z 8
High St	Y
Langworthgate	Y 30
Melville St	Z 10
Oxford St	Z 14
Pottergate	Y 15
St Mark's Retail Park	Z
St Rumbold's St	Z 17
St Swithin's Square	Z 18
Saltergate	Z 19
South Park Ave	Z 21
Steep Hill	Y 22
Strait	Z 23
Upper Ave	Y 25
Waterside Centre	Z 27
Usher Gallery	YZ M¹

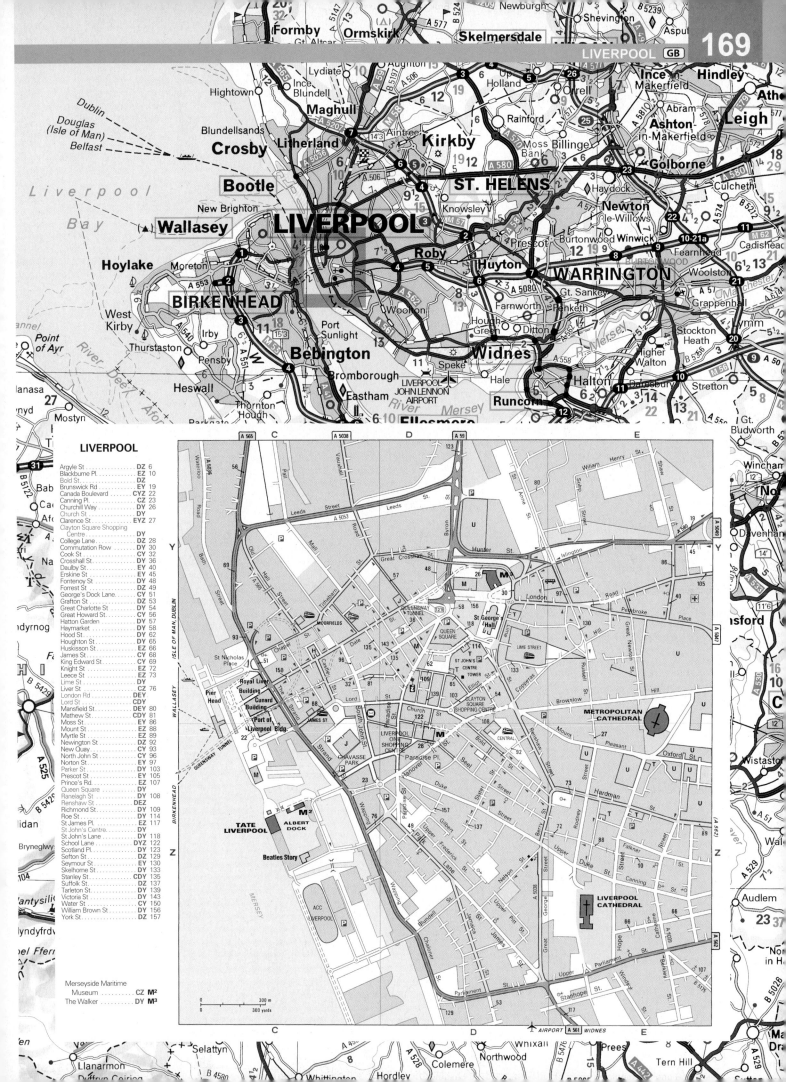

LIVERPOOL

Argyle St	DZ	6
Blackburne Pl	EZ	10
Bold St	DZ	
Brunswick Rd	EY	19
Canada Boulevard	CYZ	22
Canning Pl	CZ	23
Churchill Way	DY	26
Church St	DY	
Clarence St	EYZ	27
Clayton Square Shopping		
Centre	DY	
College Lane	DZ	28
Commutation Row	DY	30
Cook St	CY	32
Crosshall St	DY	36
Daulby St	EY	40
Erskine St	EY	45
Fontenoy St	DY	48
Forrest St	CY	49
George's Dock Lane	CY	51
Grafton St	DZ	53
Great Charlotte St	DY	54
Great Howard St	CY	56
Hatton Garden	DY	57
Haymarket	DY	58
Hood St	DY	62
Houghton St	DY	
Huskisson St	EZ	66
James St	CY	68
King Edward St	CY	69
Knight St	EZ	72
Leece St	EZ	73
Lime St	DY	
Liver St	CZ	76
London Rd	DEY	
Lord St	CDY	
Mansfield St	DEY	80
Mathew St	CDY	81
Moss St	EY	86
Mount St	EZ	88
Myrtle St	EZ	89
Newington St	DZ	92
New Quay	CY	93
North John St	CY	96
Norton St	EY	97
Parker St	DY	103
Prescot St	EY	105
Prince's Rd	EZ	107
Queen Square	DY	
Ranelagh St	DY	108
Renshaw St	DEZ	
Richmond St	DY	109
Roe St	DY	114
St James Pl	EZ	117
St John's Centre	DY	
St John's Lane	DY	118
School Lane	DYZ	122
Scotland Pl	DY	123
Sefton St	DZ	129
Seymour St	DY	130
Skelhorne St	DY	133
Stanley St	CDY	135
Suffolk St	DZ	137
Tarleton St	DY	139
Victoria St	DY	143
Water St	CY	150
William Brown St	DY	156
York St	DZ	157

Merseyside Maritime
Museum .... CZ M²
The Walker .... DY M³

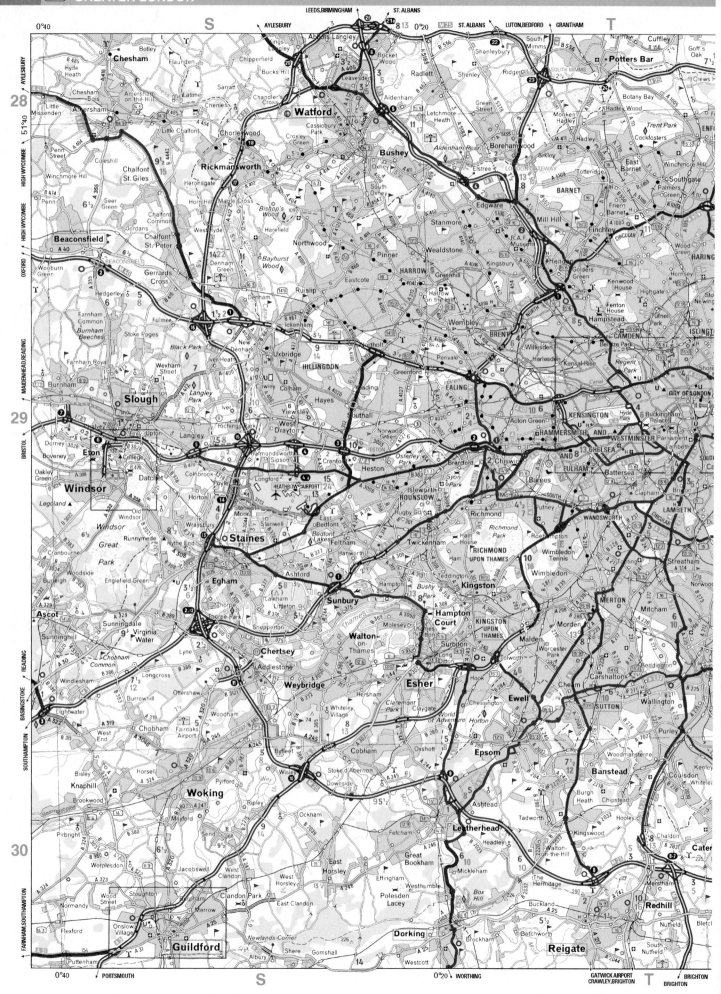

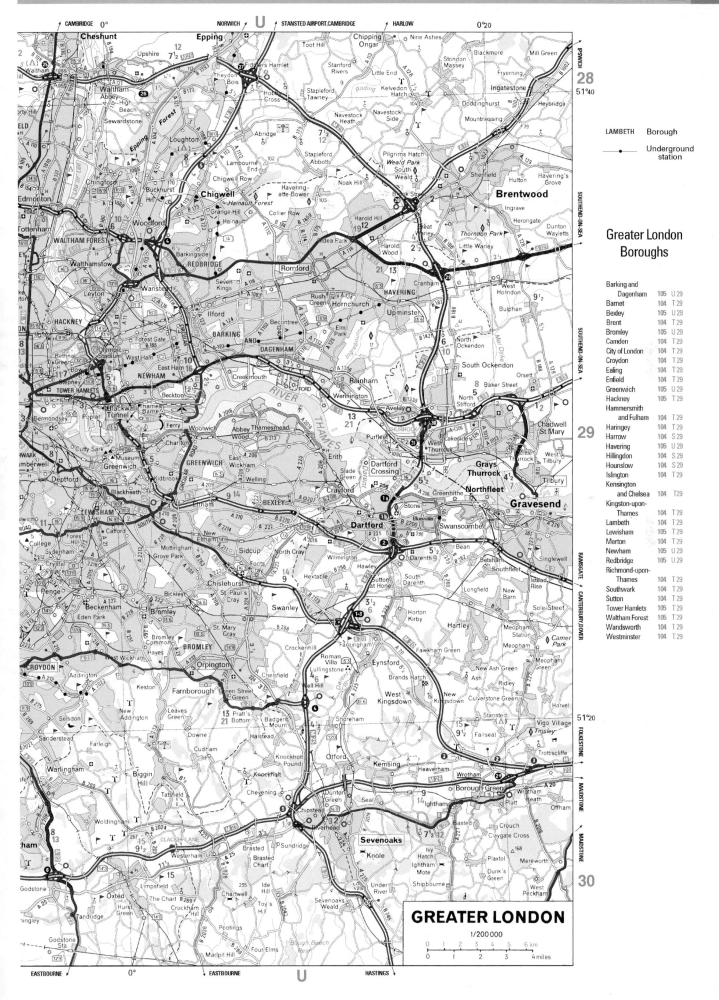

LAMBETH Borough

Underground station

GREATER LONDON

1/200 000

0 1 2 3 4 5 6 km

0 1 2 3 4 miles

LONDON

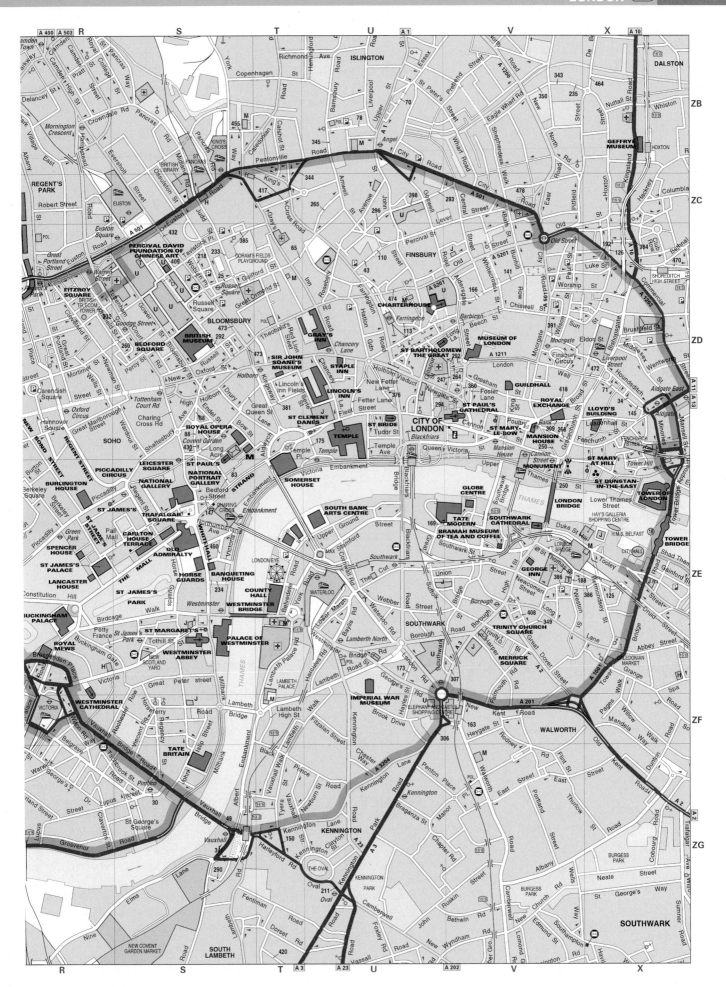

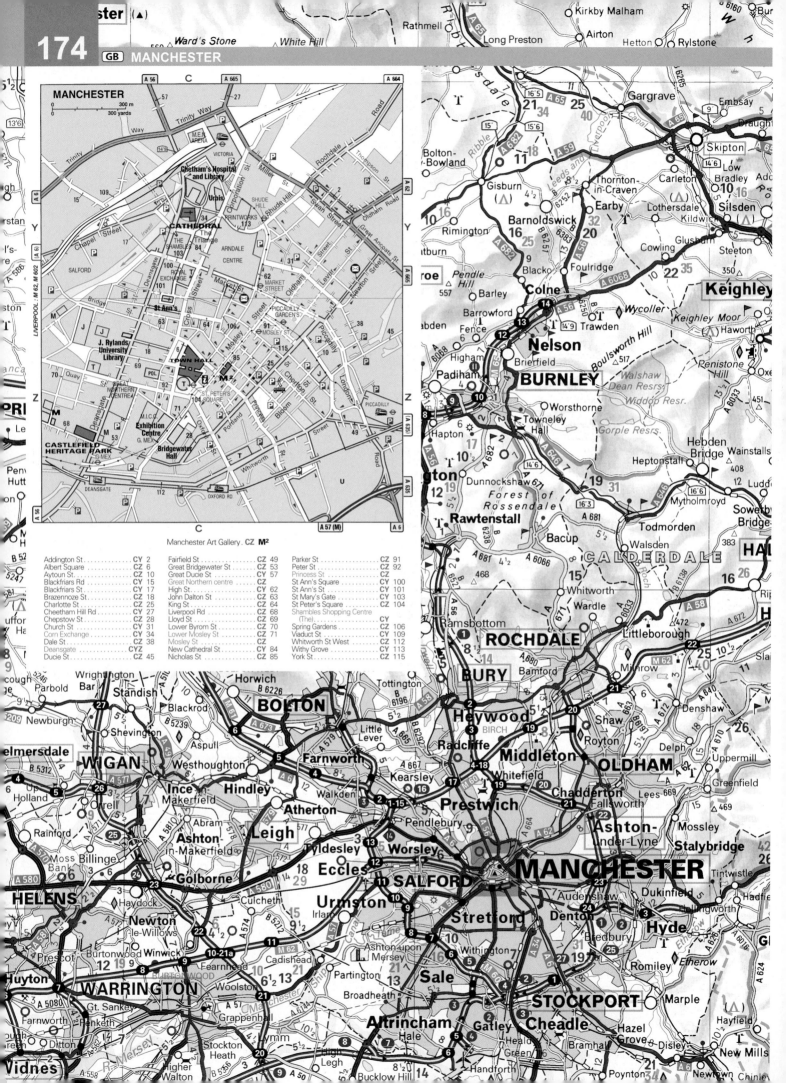

MANCHESTER

Manchester Art Gallery . CZ **M²**

Addington St . . . . CY 2	Fairfield St . . . . CZ 49	Parker St . . . . CZ 91
Albert Square . . . . CZ 6	Great Bridgewater St . . . CZ 53	Peter St . . . . CZ 92
Aytoun St . . . . CZ 10	Great Ducie St . . . . CY 57	Princess St . . . . CZ
Blackfriars Rd . . . . CY 15	Great Northern centre . . . . CZ	St Ann's Square . . . . CY 100
Blackfriars St . . . . CY 17	High St . . . . CZ 62	St Ann's St . . . . CY 101
Brazennoze St . . . . CZ 18	John Dalton St . . . . CZ 63	St Mary's Gate . . . . CY 103
Charlotte St . . . . CZ 25	King St . . . . CZ 64	St Peter's Square . . . . . . CZ 104
Cheetham Hill Rd . . . . . . CY 27	Liverpool Rd . . . . CZ 68	Shambles Shopping Centre
Chepstow St . . . . CZ 28	Lloyd St . . . . CZ 69	(The) . . . . CY
Church St . . . . CY 31	Lower Byrom St . . . . CZ 70	Spring Gardens . . . . CY 106
Corn Exchange . . . . CY 34	Lower Mosley St . . . . . . CZ 71	Viaduct St . . . . CZ 109
Dale St . . . . CZ 38	Mosley St . . . . CZ	Whitworth St West . . . . . CZ 112
Deansgate . . . . CYZ	New Cathedral St . . . . . . CY 84	Withy Grove . . . . CY 113
Ducie St . . . . CZ 45	Nicholas St . . . . CZ 85	York St . . . . CZ 115

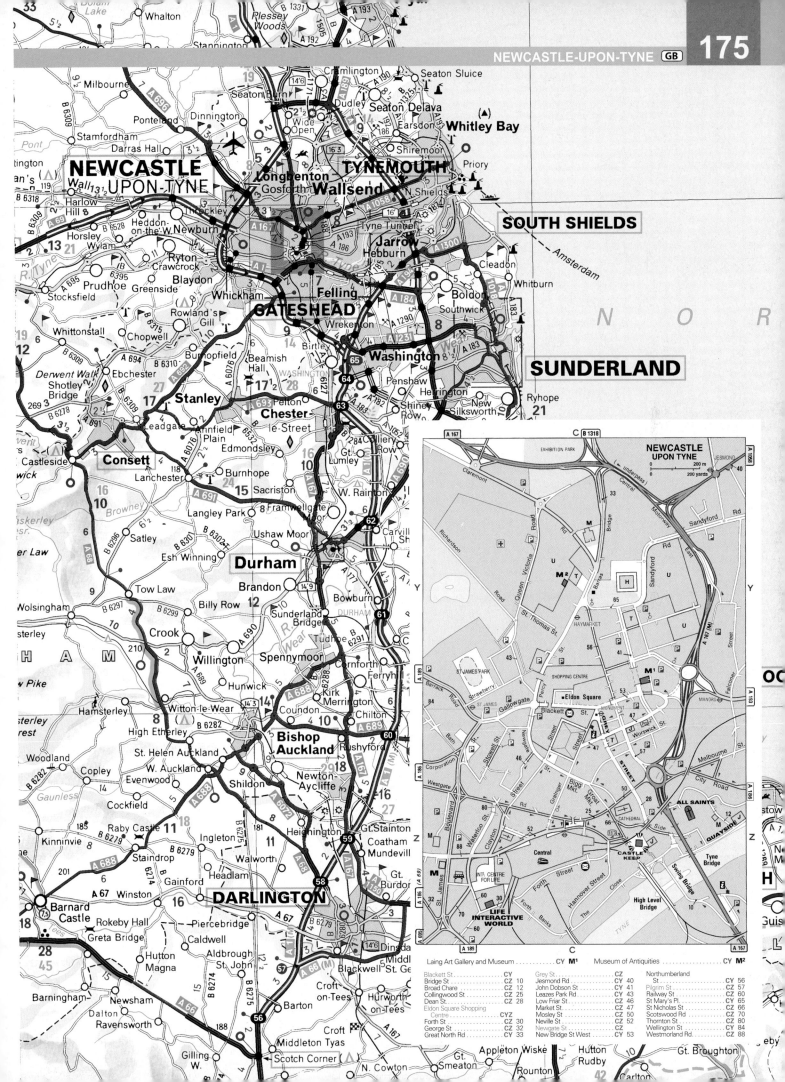

NEWCASTLE UPON TYNE

Laing Art Gallery and Museum .... CY M¹   Museum of Antiquities .... CY M²

Blackett St.	CY		Grey St.	CZ	Northumberland	
Bridge St.	CZ 10		Jesmond Rd.	CY 40	St.	CY 56
Broad Chare	CZ 12		John Dobson St.	CY 41	Pilgrim St.	CZ 57
Collingwood St.	CZ 25		Leazes Park Rd.	CY 43	Railway St.	CZ 60
Dean St.	CZ 28		Low Friar St.	CZ 46	St Mary's Pl.	CY 65
Eldon Square Shopping			Market St.	CZ 47	St Nicholas St.	CZ 66
Centre	CYZ		Mosley St.	CZ 50	Scotswood Rd	CZ 70
Forth St.	CZ 30		Neville St.	CZ 52	Thornton St.	CZ 80
George St.	CZ 32		Newgate St.	CZ	Wellington St.	CY 84
Great North Rd.	CY 33		New Bridge St West	CY 53	Westmorland Rd.	CZ 88

NEWPORT

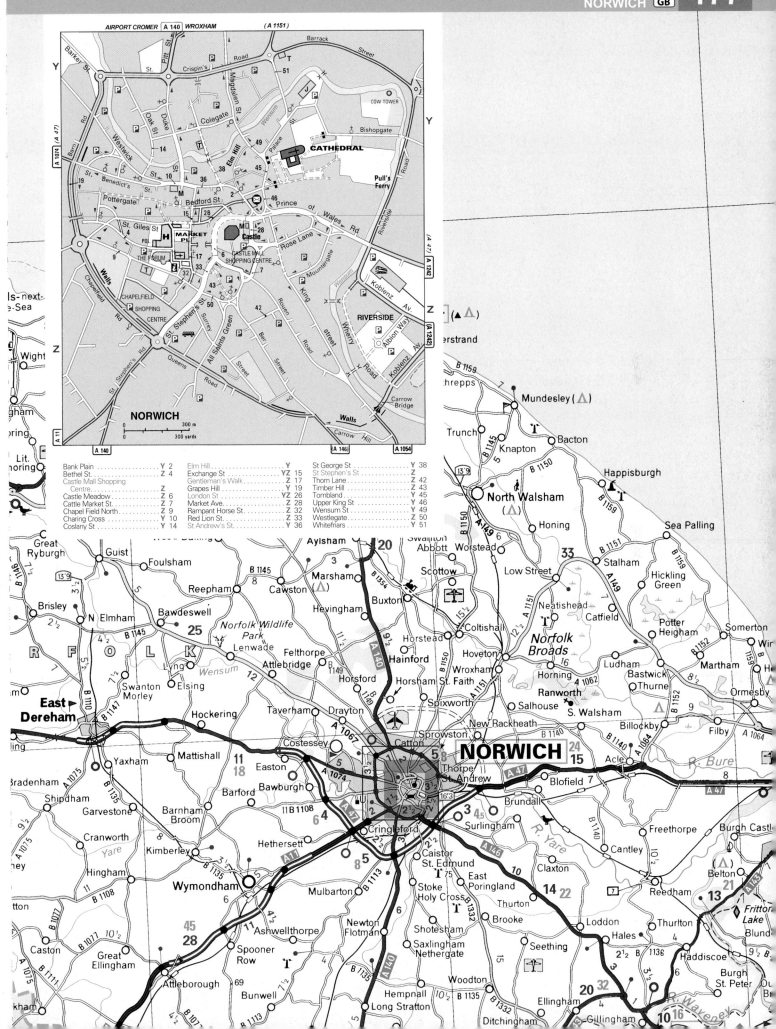

NORWICH

AIRPORT CROMER A 140 WROXHAM (A 1151)

CATHEDRAL

Pull's Ferry

CASTLE MALL SHOPPING CENTRE

Castle

MARKET PL.

THE FORUM

CHAPELFIELD SHOPPING CENTRE

RIVERSIDE

Carrow Bridge

Walls

Walls

300 m
300 yards

A 11 · A 140 · (A 146) · A 1054

Bank Plain .... Y 2	Elm Hill .... Y	St George St .... Y 38
Bethel St. .... Z 4	Exchange St .... YZ 15	St Stephen's St .... Z
Castle Mall Shopping	Gentleman's Walk .... Z 17	Thorn Lane .... Z 42
Centre .... Z	Grapes Hill .... Y 19	Timber Hill .... Z 43
Castle Meadow .... Z 6	London St .... YZ 26	Tombland .... Y 45
Cattle Market St. .... Z 7	Market Ave. .... Z 28	Upper King St .... Z 46
Chapel Field North .... Z 9	Rampant Horse St. .... Z 32	Wensum St .... Y 49
Charing Cross .... Y 10	Red Lion St. .... Z 33	Westlegate .... Z 50
Coslany St .... Y 14	St Andrew's St. .... Y 36	Whitefriars .... Y 51

Great Ryburgh · Guist · Foulsham · Aylsham · Swanton Abbott · Worstead · Stalham · Hickling Green · Sea Palling

Marsham · Scottow · Low Street

Brisley · Reepham · Cawston · Buxton · Neatishead · Catfield · Potter Heigham · Somerton

N. Elmham · Bawdeswell · Hevingham · Coltishall · Norfolk Broads · Martham

Norfolk Wildlife Park · Lenwade · Felthorpe · Horstead · Hoveton · Ludham · Bastwick · Wir

Swanton Morley · Elsing · Lyng · Wensum · Attlebridge · Hainford · Wroxham · Horning · Thurne · Ormesby

East Dereham · Hockering · Taverham · Horsford · Horsham St. Faith · Spixworth · Salhouse · S. Walsham · Billockby · Filby

Costessey · Drayton · Sprowston · New Rackheath · Acle · R. Bure

Mattishall · Catton · **NORWICH** · Blofield

Yaxham · Easton · Thorpe St. Andrew · Brundall · Freethorpe · Burgh Castl

Bradenham · Barford · Bawburgh · Cringleford · Surlingham · R. Yare · Cantley · Reedham · Belton

Shipdham · Garvestone · Barnham Broom · Hethersett · Caistor St. Edmund · Claxton · Thurton · Loddon · Thurlton · Fritton Lake · Blund

Cranworth · Kimberley · Hingham · Mulbarton · Stoke Holy Cross · East Poringland · Brooke · Hales · Haddiscoe · Burgh St. Peter

Wymondham · Ashwellthorpe · Newton Flotman · Shotesham · Seething · Ellingham · Gillingham

Great Ellingham · Spooner Row · Saxlingham Nethergate · Woodton · Ditchingham

Attleborough · Bunwell · Hempnall · Long Stratton

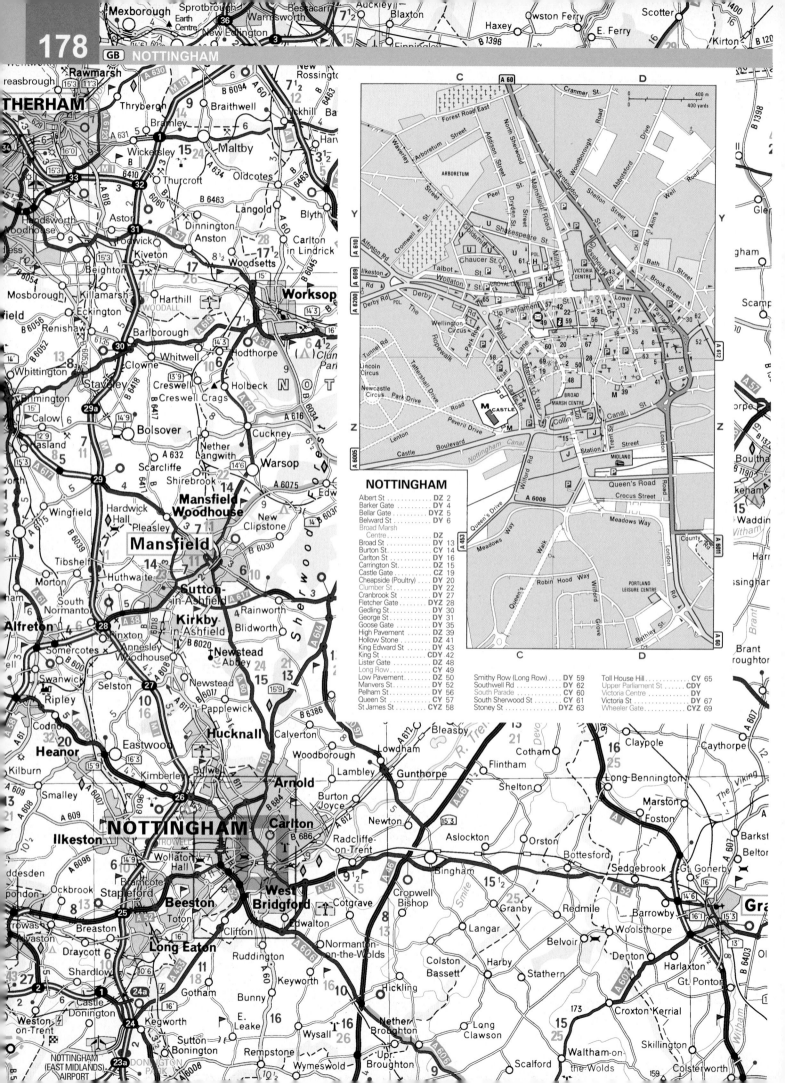

OXFORD

Blue Boar St	BY 2
Broad St	BZ 3
Castle St	BZ 5
Clarendon Shopping Centre	BZ
Cornmarket St	BZ 6
George St	BZ 9
High St	BZ
Hythe Bridge St	BZ 12

Little Clarendon St	BY 13
Logic Lane	BZ 14
Magdalen St	BYZ 16
Magpie Lane	BZ 17
New Inn Hall St	BZ 20
Norfolk St	BZ 21
Old Greyfriars St	BZ 23
Oriel Square	BZ 24
Park End St	BZ 30

Pembroke St	BZ 31
Queen St	BZ 34
Queen's Lane	BZ 33
Radcliffe Square	BZ 35
St Michael St	BZ 40
Turl St	BZ 41
Walton Crescent	BY 42
Westgate Shopping Centre	BZ
Worcester St	BZ 47

COLLEGES

All Souls	BZ A
Balliol	BY B
Brasenose	BZ B
Christ Church	BZ
Corpus Christi	BZ D
Exeter	BZ E
Hertford	BZ
Jesus	BZ

Keble	BY
Linacre	BZ N
Lincoln	BZ
Magdalen	BZ
Merton	BZ
New	BZ P
Nuffield	BZ F
Oriel	BZ Q
Pembroke	BZ
Queen's	BZ

St Catherine's	BY R
St Cross	BY V
St Edmund Hall	BZ K
St Hilda's	BZ W
St John's	BY
Sommerville	BY Y
Trinity	BZ
University	BZ L
Wadham	BY Z
Worcester	BY

Ashmolean Museum	BY M¹
Bodleian Library	BZ A¹
Pitt Rivers Museum	BY M³
Radcliffe Camera	BZ P¹

St Peter's	BZ X
Sheldonian Theatre	BYZ T
University Museum of Natural History	BY M⁴

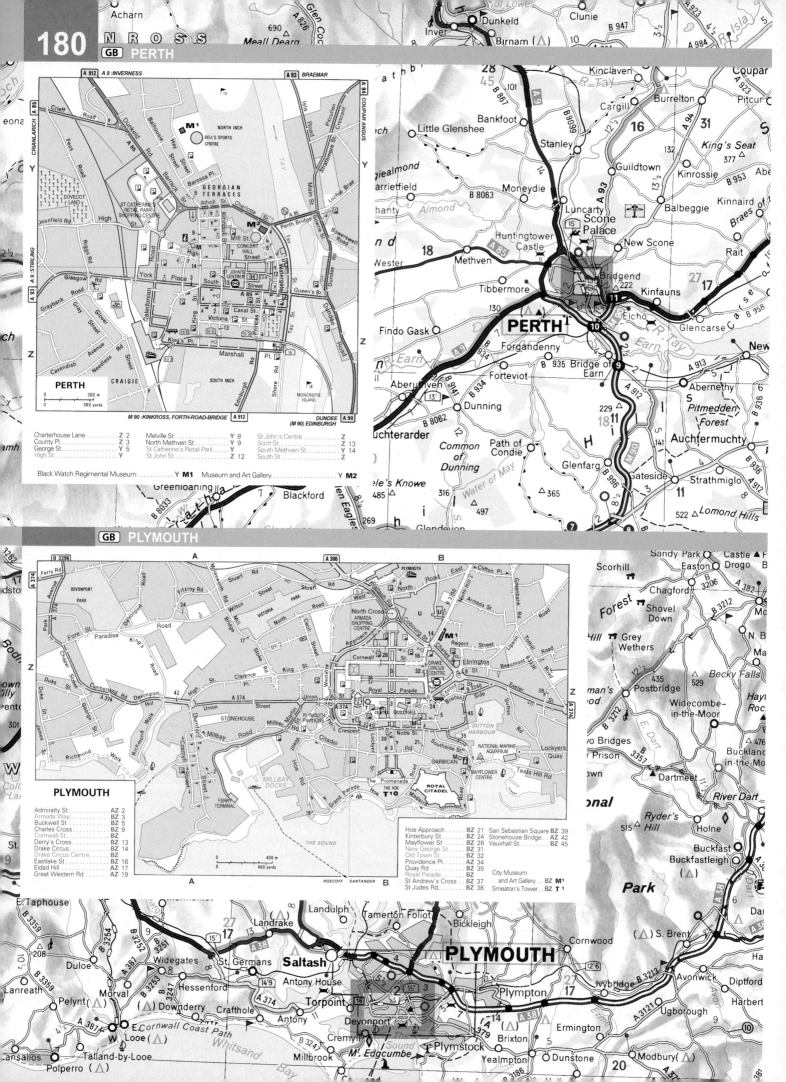

PERTH

Charterhouse Lane .... Z 2
County Pl. .... Z 3
George St. .... Y 5
High St. .... Y
Melville St .... Y 8
North Methven St. .... Y 9
St Catherine's Retail Park ... Y
St John St .... Z 12
St John's Centre .... Z
Scott St. .... Z 13
South Methven St. .... Y 14
South St .... Z

Black Watch Regimental Museum .... Y **M1**   Museum and Art Gallery .... Y **M2**

GB PLYMOUTH

PLYMOUTH

Admiralty St .... AZ 2
Armada Way .... BZ 3
Buckwell St .... BZ 5
Charles Cross .... BZ 9
Cornwall St .... BZ
Derry's Cross .... BZ 13
Drake Circus .... BZ 14
Drake Circus Centre .... BZ
Eastlake St .... BZ 16
Eldad Hill .... AZ 17
Great Western Rd .... AZ 19

Hoe Approach .... BZ 21
Kinterbury St .... BZ 24
Mayflower St .... BZ 28
New George St .... BZ 31
Old Town St .... BZ 32
Providence Pl. .... AZ 34
Quay Rd .... BZ 35
Royal Parade .... BZ
St Andrew's Cross ... BZ 37
St Judes Rd .... BZ 38

San Sebastian Square BZ 39
Stonehouse Bridge ... AZ 42
Vauxhall St. .... BZ 45

City Museum
and Art Gallery .. BZ **M1**
Smeaton's Tower .. BZ **T1**

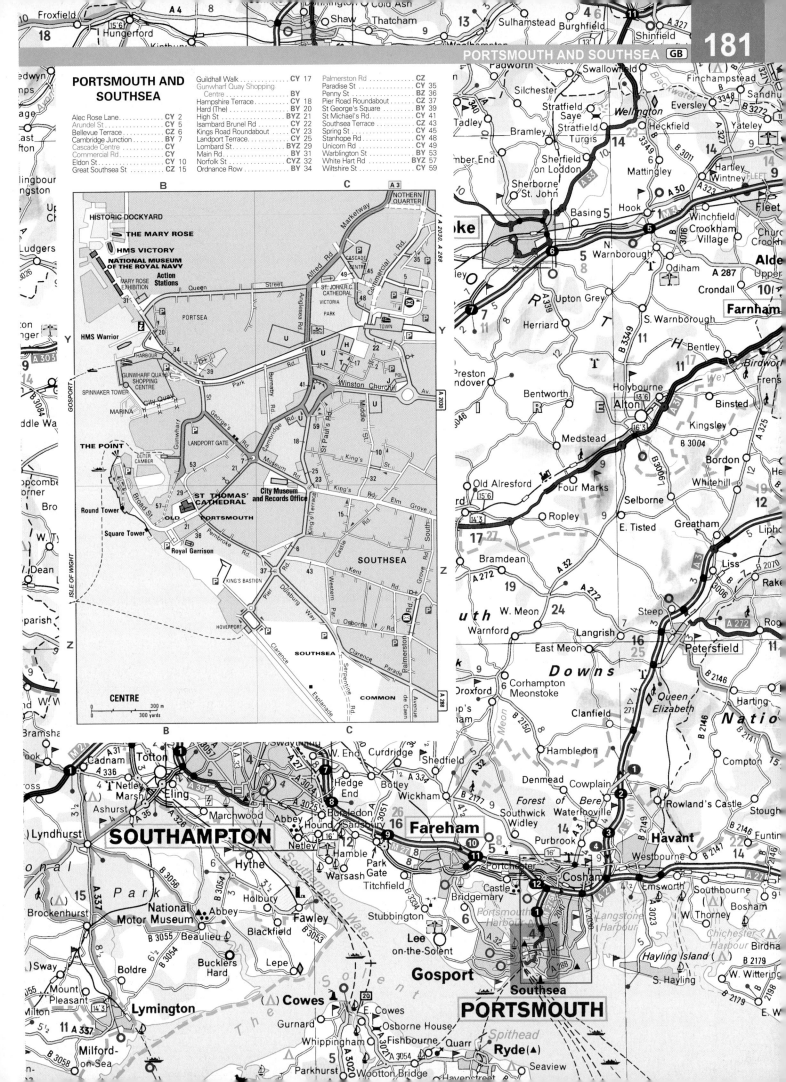

READING

Blagrave St	Y 3	Crown St	Z 13	Queen Victoria St ... Y 28
Bridge St	Y 4	Duke St	Z 15	St Mary's Butts ... Z 29
Broad St	Y	Greyfriars Rd	Y 17	Station Hill ... Y 30
Broad St Mall Shopping		Gun St	Z 18	Station Rd ... Y 31
Centre	Z	King St	Z 20	Tilehurst Rd ... Z 33
Castle St	Z 6	Mill Lane	Z 21	Tudor Rd ... Y 34
Chain St	Z 7	Minster St	Z 22	Valpy St ... Y 37
		Mount Pleasant	Z 23	Watlington St ... Y 40
		Oracle Shopping		West St ... Y 41
		Centre	Z	

CENTRE

SHEFFIELD

Angel St	DY 3	Furnival Gate	CZ 21	Snig Hill ... DY 42
Blonk St	DY 6	Furnival St	CZ 22	Waingate ... DY 44
Castle Gate	DY 13	Gibraltar St	CY 23	West Bar Green ... CY 45
Charter Row	CZ 14	Haymarket	DY 25	West St ... CZ
Church St	CZ 15	High St	DZ	
Commercial St	DZ 16	Leopold St	CY 31	
Corporation St	CY 18	Moorfields	CY 35	
Cumberland St	CZ 17	Pinstone St	CZ 37	Cathedral Church of St Peter
Fargate	CZ	Queen St	CY 38	and St Paul ... CZ B
Fitzwilliam Gate	CZ 19	St Mary's Gate	CZ 40	Cutler's Hall ... CZ A
Flat St	DZ 20	Shalesmoor	CY 41	

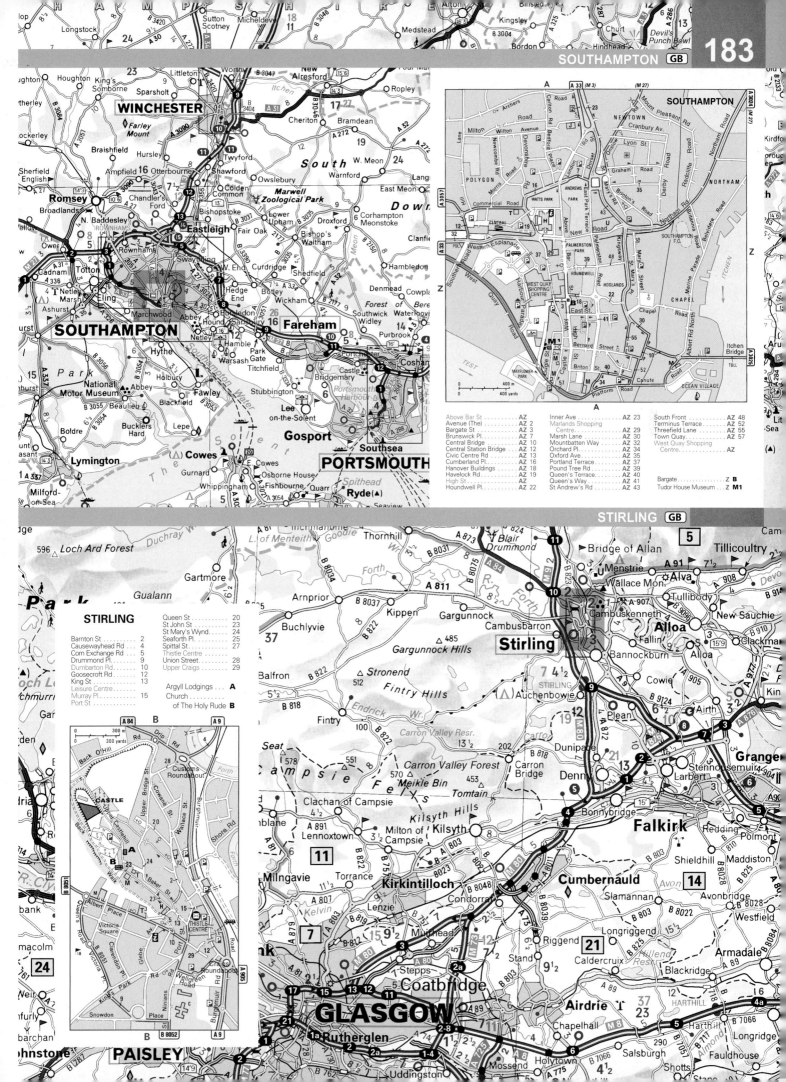

Above Bar St . . . . AZ
Avenue (The) . . . . AZ 2
Bargate St . . . . AZ 3
Brunswick Pl. . . . . AZ 7
Central Bridge . . . . AZ 10
Central Station Bridge . . . AZ 12
Civic Centre Rd . . . . AZ 13
Cumberland Pl. . . . . AZ 16
Hanover Buildings . . . . . AZ 18
Havelock Rd . . . . AZ 19
High St. . . . . AZ
Houndwell Pl. . . . . AZ 22

Inner Ave . . . . AZ 23
Marlands Shopping
  Centre . . . . AZ 29
Marsh Lane . . . . AZ 30
Mountbatten Way . . . . . . AZ 32
Orchard Pl. . . . . AZ 34
Oxford Ave. . . . . AZ 35
Portland Terrace . . . . . . AZ 37
Pound Tree Rd . . . . AZ 39
Queen's Terrace . . . . . . AZ 40
Queen's Way . . . . AZ 41
St Andrew's Rd . . . . AZ 43

South Front . . . . AZ 48
Terminus Terrace . . . . . . AZ 52
Threefield Lane . . . . AZ 55
Town Quay. . . . . AZ 57
West Quay Shopping
  Centre . . . . AZ

Bargate . . . . Z B
Tudor House Museum . . . Z M1

STIRLING

Barnton St 2
Causewayhead Rd 4
Corn Exchange Rd . . . 5
Drummond Pl. 9
Dumbarton Rd. 10
Goosecroft Rd 12
King St 13
Leisure Centre . . . .
Murray Pl. 15
Port St . . . .

Queen St 20
St John St 23
St Mary's Wynd 24
Seaforth Pl. 25
Spittal St 27
Thistle Centre . . . .
Union Street. 28
Upper Craigs 29

Argyll Lodgings . . . A
Church
  of The Holy Rude B

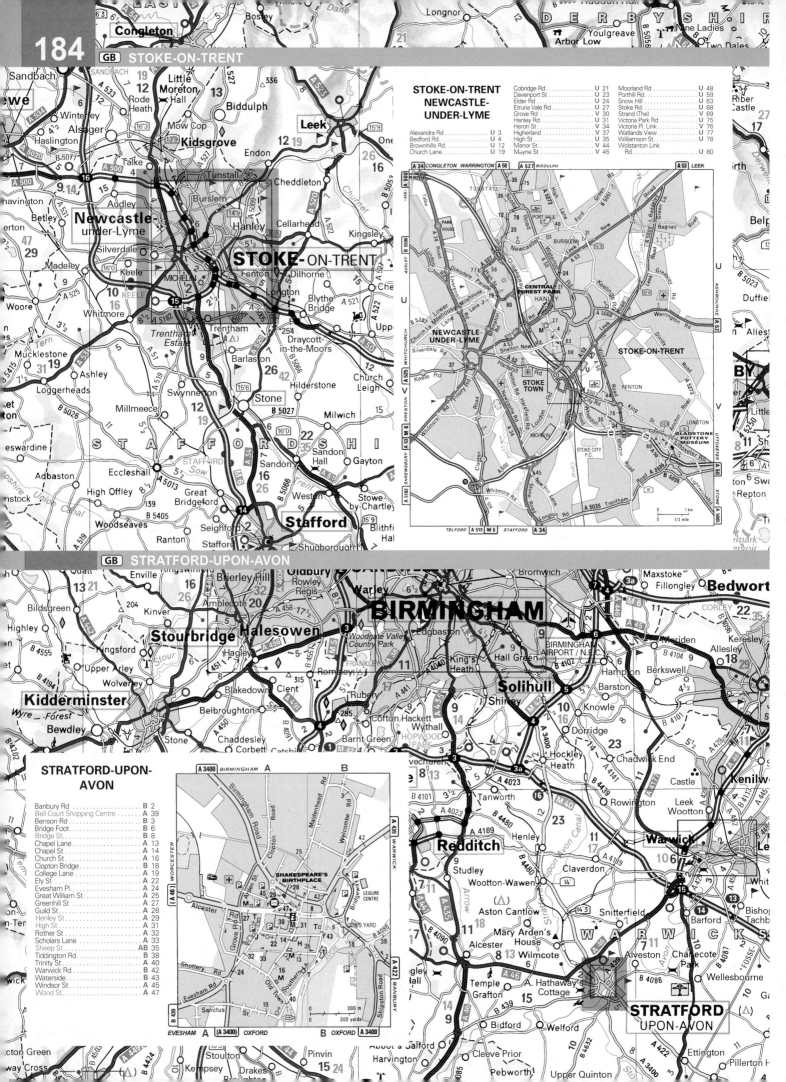

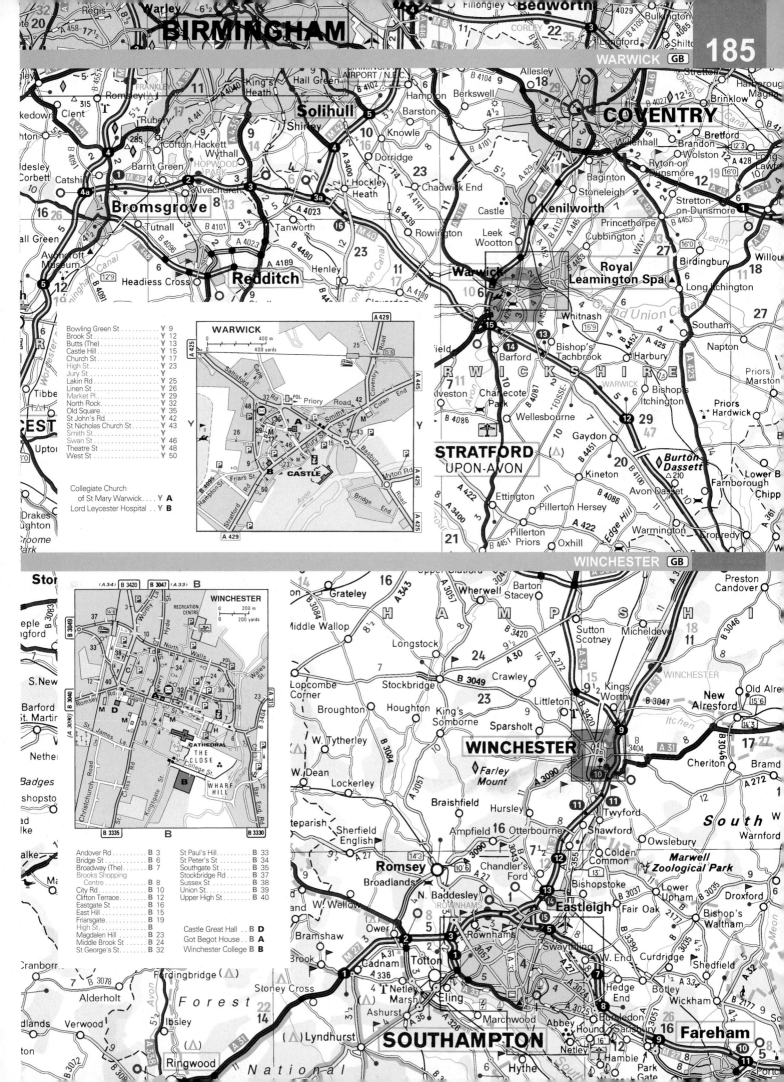

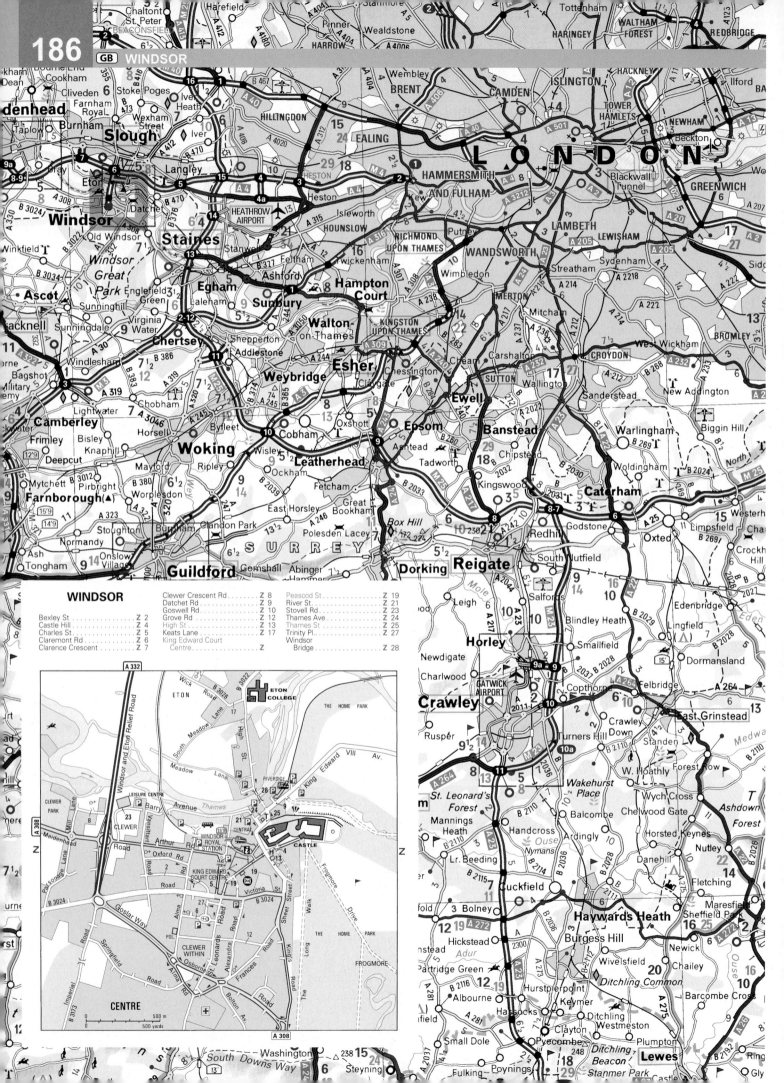

WINDSOR

Bexley St	Z 2	Clewer Crescent Rd	Z 8	Peascod St	Z 19
Castle Hill	Z 4	Datchet Rd	Z 9	River St	Z 21
Charles St	Z 5	Goswell Rd	Z 10	Stovell Rd	Z 23
Claremont Rd	Z 6	Grove Rd	Z 12	Thames Ave	Z 24
Clarence Crescent	Z 7	High St	Z 13	Thames St	Z 25
		Keats Lane	Z 17	Trinity Pl	Z 27
		King Edward Court		Windsor	
		Centre	Z	Bridge	Z 28

CENTRE

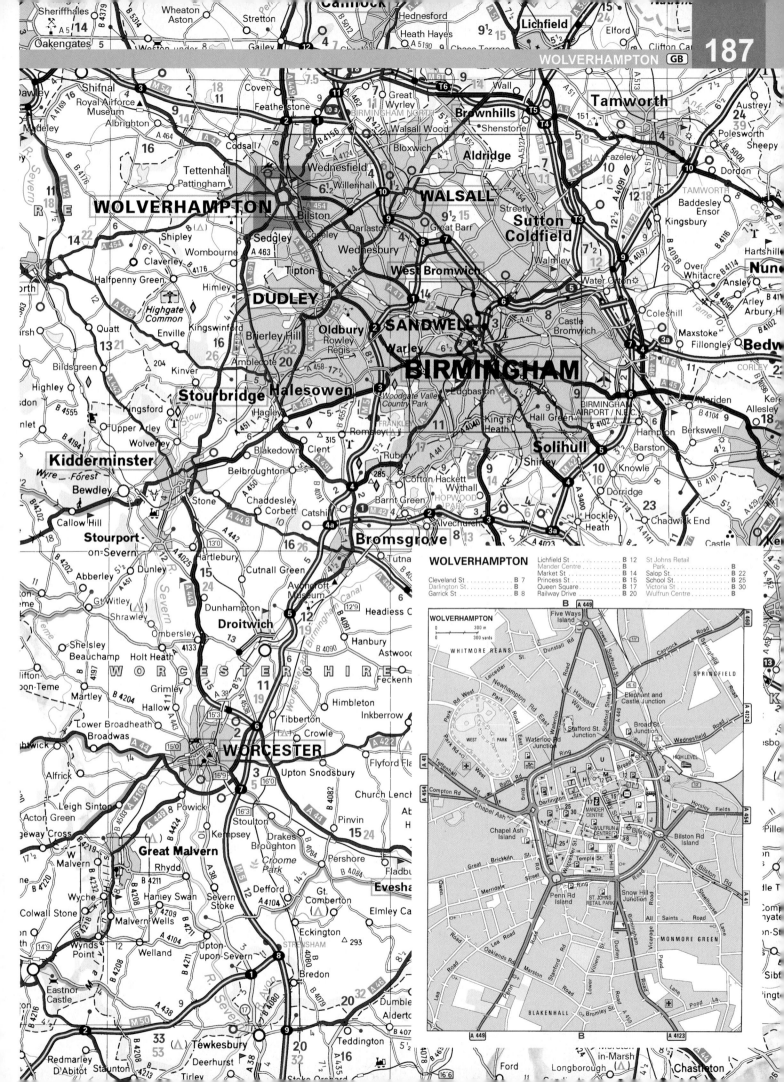

WOLVERHAMPTON

Cleveland St . . . . B 7	Lichfield St . . . . B 12
Darlington St . . . . B	Mander Centre . . . . B
Garrick St . . . . B 8	Market St . . . . B 14
	Princess St . . . . B 15
	Queen Square . . . . B 17
	Railway Drive . . . . B 20

St Johns Retail	
Park . . . . B	
Salop St . . . . B 22	
School St . . . . B 25	
Victoria St . . . . B 30	
Wulfrun Centre . . . . B	

YORK

Bishopgate St . . . CZ 3
Bishophill Senior . . CZ 4
Blake St . . . . CY 5
Church St . . . . . . DY 8
Clifford St . . . . . . DY 10
Colliergate . . . . . DY 12
Coney St . . . . . . CY 13
Cromwell Rd . . . . CY 15
Davygate . . . . . . CY 16
Deangate . . . . . . DY 18
Duncombe Pl. . . . CY 20
Fawcett St. . . . . . DZ 21

Fetter Lane . . . . . CY 22
Goodramgate . . . DY 25
High Ousegate . . . DY 26
High Petergate . . CY 28
Leeman Rd . . . . . CY 30
Lendal . . . . CY 32
Lord Mayor's
Walk . . . . DX 33
Low Petergate . . . DY 35
Museum St . . . . . CY 39
Parliament St. . . . DY 42
Pavement . . . . . . DY 43
Peasholme Green DY 45
Penley's Grove St DX 46
Queen St . . . . . . CZ 49

St Leonard's Pl. . . CY 52
St Maurice's Rd DXY 53
Shambles (The) . . DY 54
Station Rd . . . . . CY 55
Stonebow (The). . DY 56
Stonegate . . . . . DY 58
Tower St . . . . . . DZ 59

Castle Museum DZ **M2**
Fairfax House . . DY **A**
Jorvik Viking
Centre. . . . . . DY **M1**

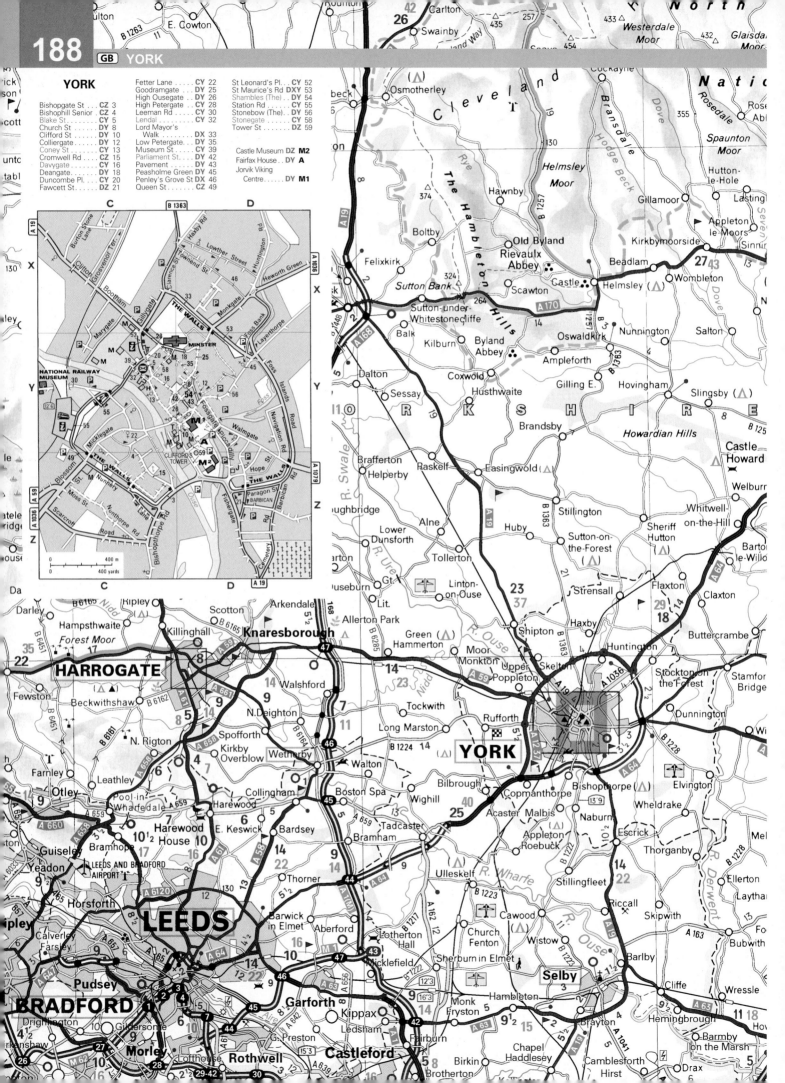

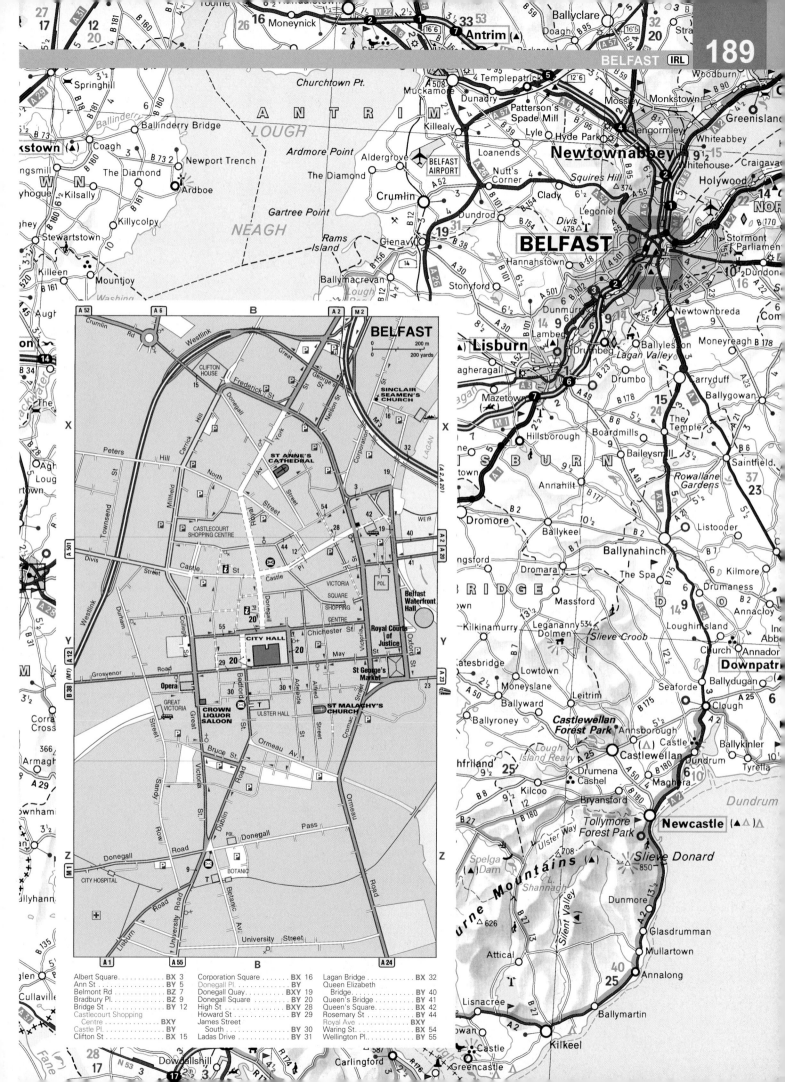

BELFAST

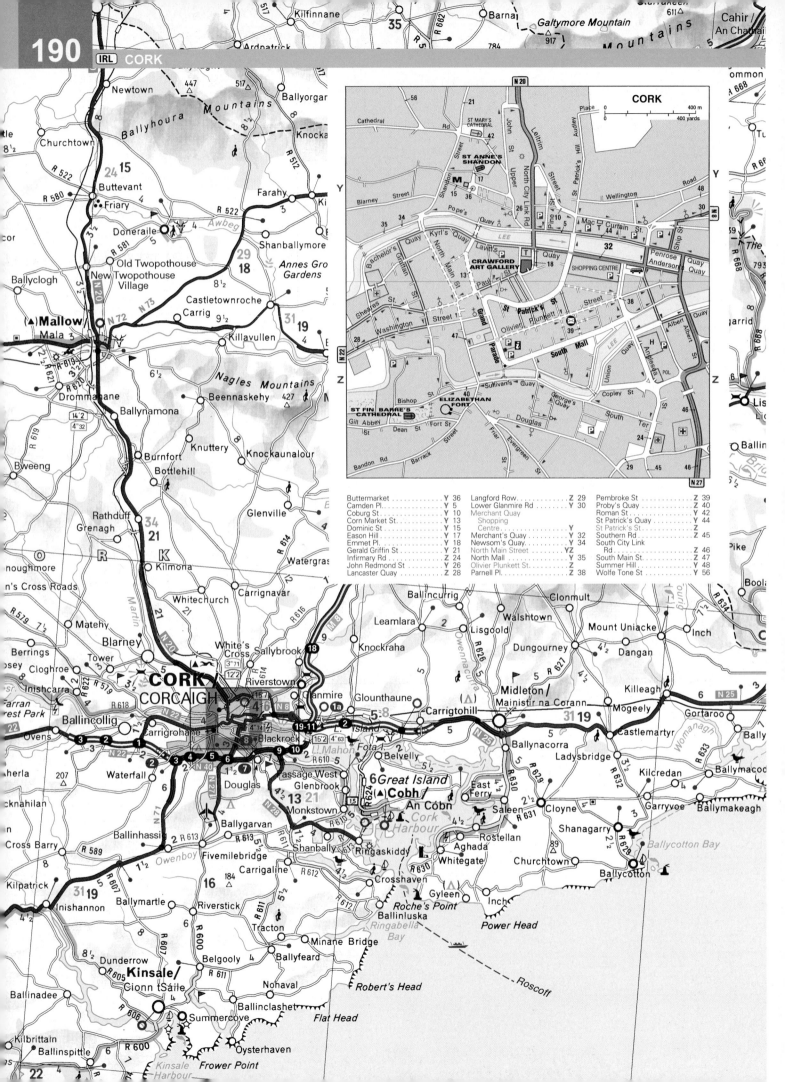

CORK

Buttermarket	Y 36	Langford Row	Z 29
Camden Pl.	Y 5	Lower Glanmire Rd	Y 30
Coburg St.	Y 10	Merchant Quay Shopping Centre	Y
Corn Market St.	Y 13		
Dominic St.	Y 15	Merchant's Quay	Y 32
Eason Hill	Y 17	Newsom's Quay	Y 34
Emmet Pl.	Y 18	North Main Street	YZ
Gerald Griffin St	Y 21	North Mall	Y 35
Infirmary Rd	Z 24	Olivier Plunkett St.	Z
John Redmond St	Y 26	Parnell Pl.	Z 38
Lancaster Quay	Z 28		

Pembroke St	Z 39
Proby's Quay	Z 40
Roman St.	Y 42
St Patrick's Quay	Y 44
St Patrick's St.	Z
Southern Rd	Y 45
South City Link Rd	Z 46
South Main St.	Z 47
Summer Hill	Y 48
Wolfe Tone St	Y 56

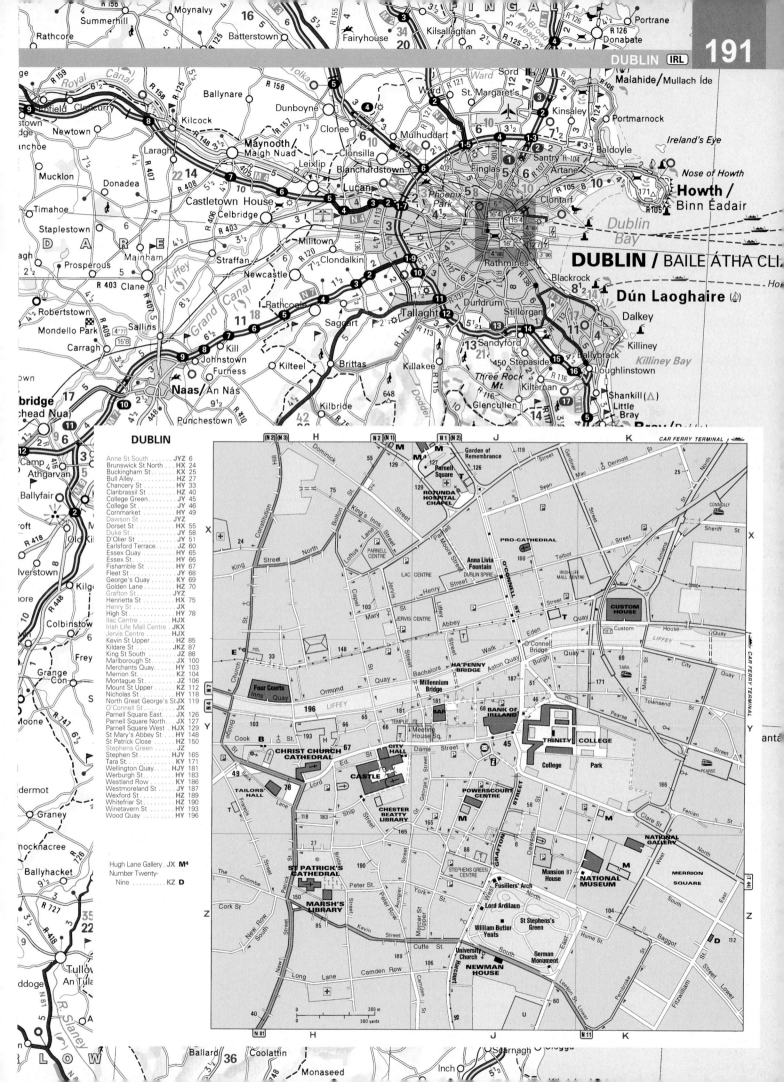

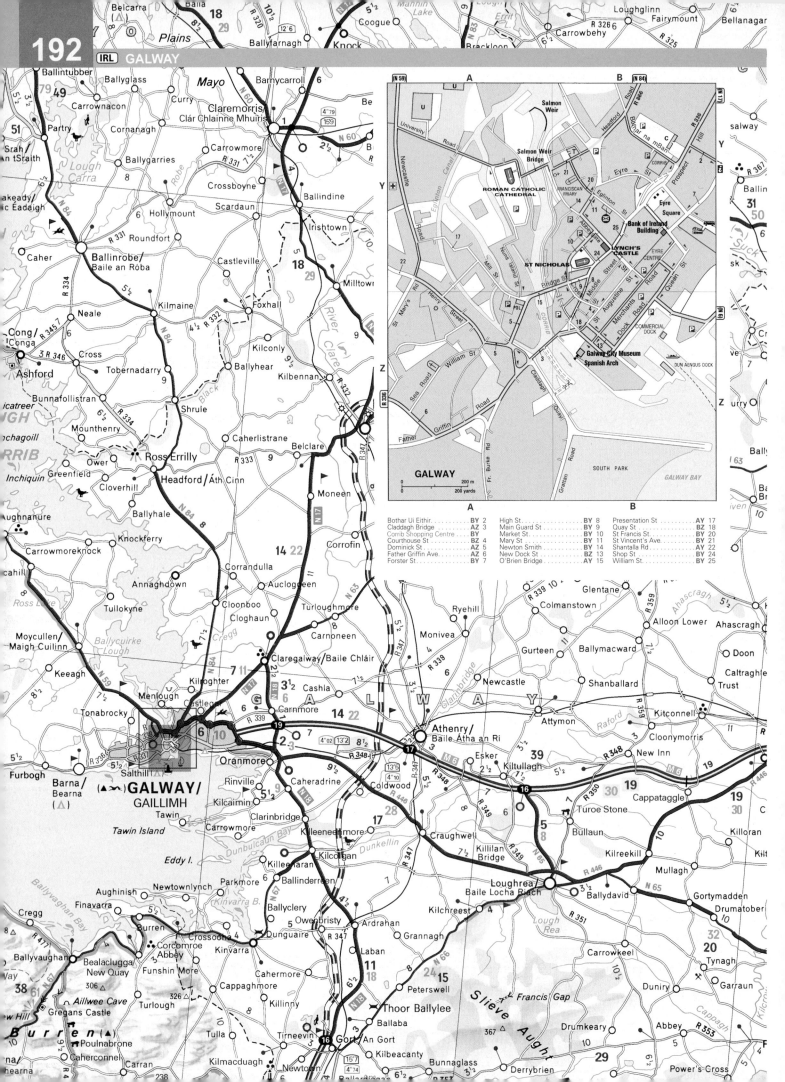

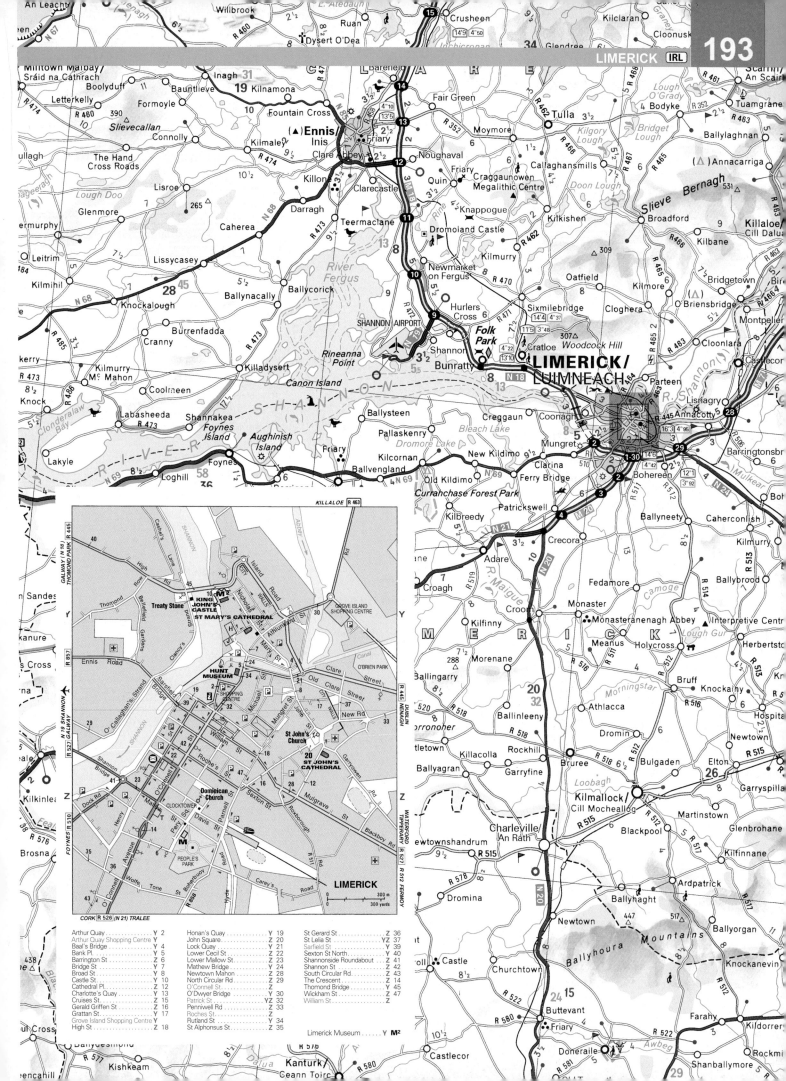

LIMERICK

Arthur Quay	Y	2
Arthur Quay Shopping Centre	Y	
Baal's Bridge	Y	4
Bank Pl.	Y	5
Barrington St	Z	6
Bridge St	Y	7
Broad St	Y	8
Castle St	Y	10
Cathedral Pl.	Z	12
Charlotte's Quay	Y	13
Cruises St	Y	15
Gerald Griffen St	Z	16
Grattan St	Y	17
Grove Island Shopping Centre	Y	
High St	Z	18
Honan's Quay	Y	19
John Square	Z	20
Lock Quay	Y	21
Lower Cecil St	Z	22
Lower Mallow St	Z	23
Mathew Bridge	Y	24
Newtown Mahon	Z	28
North Circular Rd	Y	29
O'Connell St	Z	
O'Dwyer Bridge	Y	30
Patrick St	YZ	32
Penniwell Rd	Z	33
Roches St	Z	
Rutland St	Y	34
St Alphonsus St	Z	35
St Gerard St	Z	36
St Lelia St	YZ	37
Sarfield St	Y	39
Sexton St North	Z	40
Shannonside Roundabout	Z	41
Shannon St	Z	42
South Circular Rd.	Z	43
The Crescent	Z	
Thomond Bridge	Y	45
Wickham St	Z	47
William St	Z	

Limerick Museum . . . . . . Y M²

Eochair

Allwedd

Comnarthai ar phleanna bailte

Bóithre

Mótarbhealach - Limistéar seirbhíse
Carrbhealach dúbailte le saintréithe mótarbhealaigh
Acomhail mótarbhealaigh: iomlán - teoranta
Vimhreacha ceangail
Líonra idirnáisiúnta agus náisiúnta bóithre
Bóthar idir-réigiúnach nach bhfuil chomh plódaithe
Bóthar nuadheisithe - gan réitiú
Cosán - Conair mharcáilte / Cosán marcaíochta
Mótarbhealach, bóthar á dhéanamh
(an dáta oscailte sceidealta, mas eol)

Leithead bóithre

Carrshlí dhéach
4 lána - 2 leathanlána
2 lána - 2 chunglána

Fad bóthar (iomlán agus meánfhad)

Bhóithre dola ar an mótarbhealach
Saor ó dhola ar an mótarbhealach
i mílte - i gciliméadair
ar an mbóthar

Aicmiú oifigiúil bóithre

Mótarshl - GB: Priomhbhealach
IRL: Bóithre eile ,
Priomhbhóithre agus fobhóithre náisiúnta
Ceann scríbe ar ghréasán bóithre priomha

Constaicí

Timpeall - Beamas agus a airde os cionn leibhéal na mara (i méadar)
Fána ghéar (suas treo an gha)
IRL: Bealach deacair nó baolach
Bóthar cúng le hionaid phasála (in Albain)
Crosaire comhréidh: iarnród ag dul, faoi bhóthar, os cionn bóthair
Bóthar toirmeasctha - Bóthar faoi theorannú
Bacainn dola - Bóthar aonslí
(Ar phríomhbhóithre agus ar bhóithre réigiúnacha)
Teorainneacha airde (faoi 15'6" IRL, faoi 16'6" GB)
Teorann Mheáchain (faoi 16t)

Iompar

Leithead caighdeánach - Staisiún paisinéirí
Aerfort - Aerpháirc
Longsheirbhísí : (Seirbhísí séasúracha: dearg)
Árthach foluaineach - Bád
Fartha (uas - ulach : tonnaí méadracha)
Coisithe agus lucht rothar

Lóistín - Riarachán

Plean baile san :
GUIDE MICHELIN EOLAÍ UAINE
Teorainneacha riaracháin
Teorainn na hAlban agus teorainn na Breataine Bige
Teorainn idirnáisiúnta - Custam

Áiseanna Spóirt agus Súgartha

Machaire Gailf - Ráschúrsa
Timpeall rásaíochta - Cuan bád aeraíochta
Láthair champa , láthair charbhán
Conair mharcáilte - Páirc thuaithe
Zú - Tearmannéan mara
IRL: Lascaireacht - Ráschúrsa con Lárnród thraein ghaile
Traein cábla
Carr cábla , cathaoir cábla

Amhairc

Príomhradharcanna: féach AN EOLAÍ UAINE
Bailte nó áiteanna inspéise, baill lóistín
Foirgneamh Eaglasta - Caisleán
Fothrach - Leacht meigiliteach - Pluais
Páirc, Gáirdíní - Ionaid eile spéisiúla
IRL: Dunfort - Cros Cheilteach - Cloigtheach
Lánléargas - Cothrom Radhairc - Bealach Aoibhinn

Comharthaí Eile

Cáblashlí thionsclaíoch
Crann teileachumarsáide - Teach solais
Stáisiún Giniúna - Cairéal
Mianach - Tionsclaíocht
Scaglann - Aill
Páirc Fhoraoise Naisiúnta - Páirc Naisiúnta

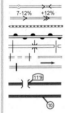

Ffyrdd

Traffordd - Mannau gwasanaeth
Ffordd ddeuol â nodweddion traffordd
Cyfnewidfeyd: wedi'i chwblhau - cyfyngedig
Rhifau'r cyffyrdd
Ffordd ar rwydwaith rhyngwladol a chenedlaethol
Ffordd rhyngranbarthol a llai prysur
Ffordd ac wyneb iddi - heb wyneb
Llwybr troed - Llwybr troed ag arwyddion / Llwybr ceffyl
Traffordd - ffordd yn cael ei hadeiladu
(Os cyfodi yr achos: dyddiad agor disgwyliedig)

Ffyrdd

ffordd ddeuol
4 lôn - 2 lôn lydan
2 lôn - 2 lôn gul

Pellter (cyfanswm a'r rhyng-bellter)

Tollffyrdd ar y draffordd
Rhan di-doll ar y draffordd
mewn miltiroedd - mewn kilometrau
ar y ffordd

Dosbarthiad ffyrdd swyddogol

Traffordd - GB : Prif ffordd
IRL: Prif ffordd genedlaethol a ffordd eilradd
Ffyrdd eraill
Cylchfan ar rwydwaith a'r prif ffyrdd

Rhwystrau

Cylchfan - Bwlch a'i uchder uwchlaw lefel y môr (mewn metrau)
Rhiw serth (esgyn gyda'r saeth)
IRL: Darn anodd neu beryglus o ffordd
Yn yr Alban : ffordd gul â mannau pasio
Croesfan rheilffordd: croesfan rheilffordd, o dan y ffordd, dros y ffordd
Ffordd waharddedig - Ffordd a chyfyngiadau arni
Rhwystr Toll - Unffordd
(Ar brif ffyrdd a ffyrdd rhanbarthol)
Terfyn uchder (llai na 15'6" IRL, 16'6" GB)
Terfyn pwysau (llai na 16t)

Cludiant

Lled safonol - Gorsaf deithwyr
Maes awyr - Maes glanio
Llongau ceir: (Gwasanaethau tymhorol: mewn coch)
Llong hofran - llong
Fferi (llwyth uchaf: mewn tunelli metrig)
Teithwyr ar droed neu feic yn unig

Llety - Gweinyddiaeth

Tref y dangosir ei chynllun yn :
THE MICHELIN GUIDE
THE GREEN GUIDE
Ffiniau gweinyddol
Ffin Cymru, ffin yr Alban
Ffin ryngwladol - Tollau

Cyfleusterau Chwaraeon a Hamdden

Cwrs golf - Rasio Ceffylau
Rasio Cerbydau - Harbwr cychod pleser
Leoedd i wersylla
Llwybr troed ag arwyddion - Parc gwlad
Parc saffari, sw - Gwarchodfa natur
IRL: Pysgota - Maes rasio milgwn
Trên twristiaid
Rhaffordd, car cêbl, cadair esgyn

Golygfeydd

Gweler Llyfr Michelin
Trefi new fannau o ddiddordeb, mannau i aros
Adeilag eglwysig - Castell
Adfeilion - Heneb fegalithig - Ogof
Gerddi, parc - Mannau eraill o ddiddordeb
IRL: Caer - Croes Geltaidd - twr crwn
Panorama - Golygfan - Ffordd dygfeydd

Symbolau eraill

Lein gêbl ddiwydiannol
Mast telathrebu - Goleudy
Gorsaf bwer - Chwarel
Mwyngloddio - Gweitharwch diwydiannol
Purfa - Clogwyn
Parc Coedwig Cenedlaethol - Parc Cenedlaethol

Comnarthai ar phleanna bailte

Ionaid inspéise

Ionad inspéise agus
Ionad inspéise adhartha

Bóithre

Mótarbhealach, carrbhealach dúbailte le saintréithe mótarbhealaigh
Priomh-thrébhealach
Bóthar aonslí - Sráid: neamhoiriúnach do thrácht, ach í stáit speisialta
Sráid: coisithe
Sráid siopadóireacha - Carrchlós
Droichead starrmhaidí - Bád fartha feithiclí

Comharthaí Éagsúla

Ionad eolais turasóireachta - Ospidéal
Gairdín, páirc, coill - Reilig
Staidiam
Galfchúrsa - Galfchúrsa (sainrialacha do chuairteoiri)
Stáisiún traenach faoi thalamh
Príomhoifig phoist le poste restante
Foirgneamh poiblí curtha in iúl le litir thagartha:
Oifigí rialtais áitiúil - Halla baile
Músaem - Amharclann - Ollscoil, Coláiste
Póitíní (ceanncheathrú)

Londain

Buirg
Limistéar
Teorainn bhuirge - Teorainn limistéir
Táille Ceantar Brú Tráchta i bhfeidhm Luan go haoine 07.00-18.00

Symbolau ar gynlluniau'r trefi

Golygfeydd

Man diddorol
Lle diddorol o addoliad

Ffyrdd

Traffordd, ffordd ddeuol
Prif ffordd drwodd
Unffordd - Stryd : Anaddas i draffig, cyfyngedig
Stryd: Cerddwr
Stryd siopa - Parc ceir
Pont liferi - Fferi geir

Arwyddion amrywiol

Canolfan croeso - Ysbyty
Gardd, parc, coedwig - Mynwent
Stadiwm
Cwrs golff - Cwrs golff (â chyfyngiadau i ymwelwyr)
Gorsaf danddaearol
Prif swyddfa bost gyda poste restante
Adeilad cyhoeddus a ddynodir gan lythyren:
Swyddfeydd llywodraeth leol - Neuadd y Dref
Amgueddfa - Theatr - Prifysgol, Coleg
Yr Heddlu (pencadlys)

Llundain

Bwrdeistref
Ardal
Ffin Bwrdeistref - Ffin yr Ardal
Parth Tagfeydd - Codir tâl Llun-Gwener 07.00-18.00